SONGS OF FELLOWSHIP

IMPORTANT NOTE ON THE ORDER OF SONGS

In this edition, the songs are numbered sequentially, and ordered alphabetically by first line in three sections: songs numbered 1–640 make up the first section, songs 641–1150 the second section, and songs 1151–1690 the third section.

An integrated index is included for reference at the back.

ALSO AVAILABLE . . .

The songs in this *Words* edition are also available in three *Large Print Words* editions. The contents are compatible with the three *Songs of Fellowship Music* editions.

songs of
fellowship

COMBINED WORDS EDITION

KINGSWAY MUSIC
EASTBOURNE

Compilation copyright © 2003 Kingsway Music
26–28 Lottbridge Drove, Eastbourne, East Sussex, BN23 6NT, UK.
First published 2003

For information about the above licences contact:
CCL (Europe), P.O. Box 1339, Eastbourne, East Sussex, BN21 1AD.
Website: www.ccli.co.uk / e-mail: info@ccli.co.uk
Tel: 01323 417711

ISBN 1 84291 132 5

Book design and production by Bookprint Creative Services
P.O. Box 827, BN21 3YJ, England for
KINGSWAY COMMUNICATIONS LTD
Lottbridge Drove, Eastbourne BN23 6NT, UK.
Printed in Great Britain.

1 Dave Bilbrough
Copyright © 1977 Thankyou Music

ABBA FATHER, let me be
Yours and Yours alone.
May my will for ever be
Ever more Your own.
Never let my heart grow cold,
Never let me go.
Abba Father, let me be
Yours and Yours alone.

2 Henry F. Lyte (1793–1847)

ABIDE WITH ME, fast falls the eventide;
The darkness deepens, Lord, with me abide;
When other helpers fail and comforts flee,
Help of the helpless, O abide with me.

Swift to its close ebbs out life's little day;
Earth's joys grow dim, its glories pass away;
Change and decay in all around I see;
O Thou who changest not, abide with me.

I need Thy presence every passing hour;
What but Thy grace can foil the tempter's
    power?
Who like Thyself my guide and stay can be?
Through cloud and sunshine, O abide with me.

I fear no foe, with Thee at hand to bless;
Ills have no weight, and tears no bitterness.
Where is death's sting? Where, grave, thy
    victory?
I triumph still, if Thou abide with me.

Reveal Thyself before my closing eyes;
Shine through the gloom, and point me to
    the skies,
Heaven's morning breaks, and earth's vain
    shadows flee;
In life, in death, O Lord, abide with me.

3 Kay Chance
Copyright © 1976 Kay Chance

AH LORD GOD, Thou hast made the heavens
And the earth by Thy great power.
Ah Lord God, Thou hast made the heavens
And the earth by Thine outstretched arm.

Nothing is too difficult for Thee,
Nothing is too difficult for Thee.
O great and mighty God,
Great in counsel and mighty in deed,
Nothing, nothing, absolutely nothing,
Nothing is too difficult for Thee.

4 Jerry Sinclair
Copyright © 1972 Manna Music Inc./
Kingsway Music

ALLELUIA, alleluia,
Alleluia, alleluia.
Alleluia, alleluia,
Alleluia, alleluia.

He's my Saviour…

He is worthy…

I will praise Him…

5 Sherrell Prebble & Howard Clark
Copyright © 1978 Celebration/
Kingsway Music

ALLELUIA! ALLELUIA!
Opening our hearts to Him,
Singing alleluia! alleluia!
Jesus is our King!

Create in us, O God
A humble heart that sets us free
To proclaim the wondrous majesty
Of our Father in heaven.

We bear the name of Christ,
Justified, we meet with Him.
His words and presence calm our fear,
Revealing God our Father here.

Let kindred voices join,
Honouring the Lamb of God
Who teaches us by bread and wine
The mystery of His body.

Pour out Your Spirit on us,
Empowering us to live as one,
To carry Your redeeming love
To a world enslaved by sin.

6 Donald Fishel
Copyright © 1973 The Word of God Music/
Adm. by CopyCare

ALLELUIA, ALLELUIA,
Give thanks to the risen Lord,
Alleluia, alleluia, give praise to His name.

Jesus is Lord of all the earth,
He is the King of creation.

Spread the good news o'er all the earth,
Jesus has died and has risen.

We have been crucified with Christ,
Now we shall live for ever.

God has proclaimed the just reward,
Life for all men, alleluia!

Come let us praise the living God,
Joyfully sing to our Saviour.

7 Dave Moody
Copyright © 1981 Dayspring Music Inc./
Adm. by CopyCare

ALL HAIL KING JESUS! All hail Emmanuel!
King of kings, Lord of lords,
Bright Morning Star.
And throughout eternity I'll sing Your praises,
And I'll reign with You throughout eternity.

8 Dave Bilbrough
Copyright © 1987 Thankyou Music

ALL HAIL THE LAMB, enthroned on high;
His praise shall be our battle cry.
He reigns victorious, for ever glorious,
His name is Jesus, He is the Lord.

9 Edward Perronet (1726–92)
Revised by John Rippon (1751–1836)

ALL HAIL THE POWER OF JESUS' NAME!
Let angels prostrate fall;
Bring forth the royal diadem,
And crown Him Lord of all.

Crown Him, ye martyrs of your God,
Who from His altar call;
Extol Him in whose path ye trod,
And crown Him Lord of all.

Ye seed of Israel's chosen race,
Ye ransomed of the fall,
Hail Him who saves you by His grace,
And crown Him Lord of all.

Sinners, whose love can ne'er forget
The wormwood and the gall,
Go, spread your trophies at His feet,
And crown Him Lord of all.

Let every kindred, every tribe
On this terrestrial ball,
To Him all majesty ascribe,
And crown Him Lord of all.

O that, with yonder sacred throng,
We at His feet may fall,
Join in the everlasting song,
And crown Him Lord of all!

10 Noel & Tricia Richards
Copyright © 1987 Thankyou Music

ALL HEAVEN DECLARES
The glory of the risen Lord.
Who can compare
With the beauty of the Lord?
Forever He will be
The Lamb upon the throne.
I gladly bow the knee
And worship Him alone.

I will proclaim
The glory of the risen Lord,
Who once was slain
To reconcile man to God.
Forever You will be
The Lamb upon the throne.
I gladly bow the knee
And worship You alone.

11 Graham Kendrick & Chris Rolinson
Copyright © 1986 Thankyou Music

ALL HEAVEN WAITS with bated breath,
For saints on earth to pray.
Majestic angels ready stand
With swords of fiery blade.
Astounding power awaits a word
From God's resplendent throne.
But God awaits our prayer of faith
That cries 'Your will be done.'

Awake, O church, arise and pray;
Complaining words discard.
The Spirit comes to fill your mouth
With truth, His mighty sword.
Go place your feet on Satan's ground
And there proclaim Christ's name,
In step with heaven's armies march
To conquer and to reign!

Now in our hearts and on our lips
The word of faith is near,
Let heaven's will on earth be done,
Let heaven flow from here.
Come blend your prayers with Jesus' own
Before the Father's throne,
And as the incense clouds ascend
God's holy fire rains down.

Soon comes the day when with a shout
King Jesus shall appear,
And with Him all the church,
From every age, shall fill the air.
The brightness of His coming shall
Consume the lawless one,
As with a word the breath of God
Tears down his rebel throne.

One body here, by heaven inspired,
We seek prophetic power;
In Christ agreed, one heart and voice,
To speak this day, this hour,
In every place where chaos rules
And evil forces brood;
Let Jesus' voice speak like the roar
Of a great multitude.

12 Roy Turner
Copyright © 1984 Thankyou Music

ALL OVER THE WORLD THE SPIRIT IS MOVING,

All over the world as the prophet said it
    would be;
All over the world there's a mighty revelation
Of the glory of the Lord, as the waters cover
    the sea.

All over His church God's Spirit is moving,
All over His church as the prophet said it
    would be;
All over His church there's a mighty
    revelation
Of the glory of the Lord, as the waters cover
    the sea.

Right here in this place the Spirit is moving,
Right here in this place as the prophet said it
    would be;
Right here in this place there's a mighty
    revelation
Of the glory of the Lord, as the waters cover
    the sea.

13 William Kethe (d. 1594)

ALL PEOPLE THAT ON EARTH DO DWELL,

Sing to the Lord with cheerful voice;
Him serve with mirth, His praise forthtell,
Come ye before Him and rejoice.

Know that the Lord is God indeed,
Without our aid He did us make:
We are His flock, He doth us feed,
And for His sheep He doth us take.

O enter then His gates with praise,
Approach with joy His courts unto:
Praise, laud, and bless His name always,
For it is seemly so to do.

For why, the Lord our God is good;
His mercy is for ever sure;
His truth at all times firmly stood,
And shall from age to age endure.

Praise God from whom all blessings flow,
Praise Him all creatures here below,
Praise Him above, ye heavenly hosts;
Praise Father, Son and Holy Ghost.

14 Cecil F. Alexander (1818–95)

ALL THINGS BRIGHT AND BEAUTIFUL,
All creatures great and small,
All things wise and wonderful,
The Lord God made them all.

Each little flower that opens,
Each little bird that sings,
He made their glowing colours,
He made their tiny wings.

The purple-headed mountain,
The river running by,
The sunset, and the morning
That brightens up the sky.

The cold wind in the winter,
The pleasant summer sun,
The ripe fruits in the garden,
He made them every one.

He gave us eyes to see them,
And lips that we might tell
How great is God Almighty,
Who has made all things well.

15 Marc Nelson
Copyright © 1989 Mercy/Vineyard Publishing/
Adm. by CopyCare

ALL YOU ANGELS ROUND HIS THRONE,
    praise Him!
All you people on earth below, praise Him!
Mountains high and oceans wide, praise
    Him!
Beasts of the field and birds of the sky, praise
    Him!

    Give Him praise, give Him praise,
    Give Him praise from your hearts.
    Give Him praise, give Him praise,
    Give Him praise for He is God.

All the angels round Your throne praise You!
All the people on earth below praise You!
Mountains high and oceans wide praise You!
Beasts of the field and birds of the sky praise
    You!

    We give You praise, we give You praise,
    We give You praise from our hearts.
    We give You praise, we give You praise,
    We give You praise for You are God.

16
Austin Martin
Copyright © 1983 Thankyou Music

ALMIGHTY GOD, we bring You praise
For Your Son, the Word of God,
By whose power the world was made,
By whose blood we are redeemed.
Morning Star, the Father's glory,
We now worship and adore You.
In our hearts Your light has risen;
Jesus, Lord, we worship You.

17
The Alternative Service Book 1980
Copyright © The Central Board of
Finance of the Church of England 1980;
The Archbishops' Council 1999

ALMIGHTY GOD, OUR HEAVENLY FATHER,
We have sinned against You,
And against our fellow men,
In thought and word and deed,
Through negligence, through weakness,
Through our own deliberate fault.
We are truly sorry
And repent of all our sins.
For the sake of Your Son Jesus Christ,
Who died for us,
Who died for us,
Who died for us,
Forgive us all that is past;
And grant that we may serve You
In newness of life.
To the glory of Your name, *(Men)*
To the glory of Your name, *(Women)*
To the glory of Your name, *(Men)*
To the glory of Your name, *(Women)*
To the glory of Your name. *(All)*
Amen, amen.

18
Phil Lawson Johnston
Copyright © 1988 Thankyou Music

ALMIGHTY SOVEREIGN LORD, Creator God,
You made the heavens and the earth.
You've spoken to the world,
Yourself the living Word,
You give us eyes to see Your kingdom.

So stretch out Your hand, O God,
In signs and wonders,
We rest our faith on Your almighty power.
Stretch out Your hand, O God,
To heal and deliver. We declare,
We declare Your kingdom is here.

Stir up Your people like a mighty wind,
Come shake us, wake us from our sleep.
Give us compassion, Lord,
Love for Your holy word,
Give us the courage of Your kingdom.

Why do so many stand against You now,
Bringing dishonour to Your name?
Consider how they mock,
But we will never stop
Speaking with boldness of Your kingdom.

19 John Newton (1725–1807)

AMAZING GRACE! how sweet the sound
That saved a wretch like me;
I once was lost, but now am found,
Was blind, but now I see.

'Twas grace that taught my heart to fear,
And grace my fears relieved;
How precious did that grace appear,
The hour I first believed!

Through many dangers, toils and snares
I have already come;
'Tis grace that brought me safe thus far,
And grace will lead me home.

The Lord has promised good to me,
His word my hope secures;
He will my shield and portion be
As long as life endures.

Yes, when this heart and flesh shall fail,
And mortal life shall cease,
I shall possess within the veil
A life of joy and peace.

When we've been there a thousand years,
Bright shining as the sun,
We've no less days to sing God's praise
Than when we first begun.

20
Dave Bilbrough
Copyright © 1983 Thankyou Music

AN ARMY OF ORDINARY PEOPLE,
A kingdom where love is the key,
A city, a light to the nations,
Heirs to the promise are we.
A people whose life is in Jesus,
A nation together we stand.
Only through grace are we worthy,
Inheritors of the land.

A new day is dawning,
A new age to come,
When the children of promise
Shall flow together as one.
A truth long neglected,
But the time has now come
When the children of promise
Shall flow together as one.

A people without recognition,
But with Him a destiny sealed,
Called to a heavenly vision,
His purpose shall be fulfilled.
Come, let us stand strong together,
Abandon ourselves to the King,
His love shall be ours for ever,
This victory song we shall sing.

21 Charles Wesley (1707–88)

AND CAN IT BE that I should gain
An interest in the Saviour's blood?
Died He for me, who caused His pain?
For me, who Him to death pursued?
Amazing love! how can it be
That Thou, my God, shouldst die for me?

'Tis mystery all! The Immortal dies:
Who can explore His strange design?
In vain the first-born seraph tries
To sound the depths of love divine!
'Tis mercy all! let earth adore,
Let angel minds inquire no more.

He left His Father's throne above,
So free, so infinite His grace;
Emptied Himself of all but love,
And bled for Adam's helpless race.
'Tis mercy all, immense and free;
For, O my God, it found out me.

Long my imprisoned spirit lay
Fast bound in sin and nature's night;
Thine eye diffused a quickening ray,
I woke, the dungeon flamed with light;
My chains fell off, my heart was free;
I rose, went forth, and followed Thee.

No condemnation now I dread;
Jesus, and all in Him, is mine!
Alive in Him, my living Head,
And clothed in righteousness divine,
Bold I approach the eternal throne,
And claim the crown, through Christ my own.

22 Author unknown
Copyright control

A NEW COMMANDMENT
I give unto you,
That you love one another
As I have loved you,
That you love one another
As I have loved you.
By this shall all men know
That you are My disciples,
If you have love one for another.
By this shall all men know
That you are My disciples,
If you have love one for another.

23 James Montgomery (1771–1854)

ANGELS, FROM THE REALMS OF GLORY,
Wing your flight o'er all the earth;
Ye who sang creation's story,
Now proclaim Messiah's birth:

Come and worship
Christ, the new-born King.
Come and worship
Worship Christ, the new-born King.

Shepherds, in the field abiding,
Watching o'er your flocks by night,
God with man is now residing,
Yonder shines the infant-light:

Sages, leave your contemplations,
Brighter visions beam afar;
Seek the great desire of nations,
Ye have seen His natal star:

Saints, before the altar bending,
Watching long in hope and fear,
Suddenly the Lord descending
In His temple shall appear:

24 Francis Pott (1832–1909)

ANGEL VOICES EVER SINGING
Round Thy throne of light,
Angel harps for ever ringing,
Rest not day nor night;
Thousands only live to bless Thee,
And confess Thee
Lord of might.

Thou who art beyond the farthest
Mortal eye can scan,
Can it be that Thou regardest
Songs of sinful man?
Can we know that Thou art near us
And wilt hear us?
Yes, we can.

Yes, we know that Thou rejoicest
O'er each work of Thine;
Thou didst ears and hands and voices
For Thy praise design;
Craftsman's art and music's measure
For Thy pleasure
All combine.

In Thy house, great God, we offer
Of Thine own to Thee,
And for Thine acceptance proffer,
All unworthily,
Hearts and minds and hands and voices
In our choicest
Psalmody.

Honour, glory, might, and merit
Thine shall ever be,
Father, Son, and Holy Spirit,
Blessèd Trinity.
Of the best that Thou hast given
Earth and heaven
Render Thee.

25 Martin Luther (1483–1546)
Tr. Thomas Carlyle (1795–1881)

A SAFE STRONGHOLD OUR GOD IS STILL,
A trusty shield and weapon;
He'll help us clear from all the ill
That hath us now o'ertaken.
The ancient prince of hell
Hath risen with purpose fell;
Strong mail of craft and power
He weareth in this hour;
On earth is not His fellow.

With force of arms we nothing can,
Full soon were we down-ridden;
But for us fights the proper Man,
Whom God Himself hath bidden.
Ask ye: Who is this same?
Christ Jesus is His name,
The Lord Sabaoth's Son;
He, and no other one,
Shall conquer in the battle.

And were this world all devils o'er,
And watching to devour us,
We lay it not to heart so sore;
Not they can overpower us.
And let the prince of ill
Look grim as e'er he will,
He harms us not a whit;
For why? his doom is writ;
A word shall quickly slay him.

God's word, for all their craft and force,
One moment will not linger,
But, spite of hell, shall have its course;
'Tis written by His finger.
And though they take our life,
Goods, honour, children, wife,
Yet is their profit small:
These things shall vanish all;
The city of God remaineth.

26 Mary R. Barthow & Mary Lou King
Copyright © 1979 Mary R. Barthow &
Mary Lou King

ASCRIBE GREATNESS to our God, the Rock,
His work is perfect and all His ways are just.
Ascribe greatness to our God, the Rock,
His work is perfect and all His ways are just.
A God of faithfulness and without injustice,
Good and upright is He;
A God of faithfulness and without injustice,
Good and upright is He.

27 Martin Nystrom
Copyright © 1983 Restoration Music Ltd/
Sovereign Music UK

AS THE DEER pants for the water,
So my soul longs after You.
You alone are my heart's desire
And I long to worship You.

You alone are my strength, my shield,
To You alone may my spirit yield.
You alone are my heart's desire
And I long to worship You.

I want You more than gold or silver,
Only You can satisfy.
You alone are the real joy-giver
And the apple of my eye.

You're my Friend and You are my Brother,
Even though You are a King.
I love You more than any other,
So much more than anything.

28 John Daniels
Copyright © 1979 Authentic Publishing/
Adm. by CopyCare

AS WE ARE GATHERED Jesus is here;
One with each other, Jesus is here.
Joined by the Spirit, washed in the blood,
Part of the body, the church of God.
As we are gathered Jesus is here,
One with each other, Jesus is here.

29 Dale Garratt
Copyright © 1985 Scripture in Song
(a div. of Integrity Music, Inc.)/
Sovereign Music UK

AS WE COME WITH PRAISE *before His*
majesty,
We will celebrate with joy and victory,
For the Lord has come and set His people
free,
We are marching on with Him,
He's our deliverer.
(Repeat)

The two-edgèd sword is sharpened in our
  hand.
We come with vengeance to possess our
  land.
We bind the kings because of God's right
  hand,
And carry out the sentence that our God has
  planned.

  (Last time)
  As we come with praise before His
    majesty,
  We will celebrate with joy and victory,
  For the Lord has come and set His people
    free,
  We are marching on with Him,
  He's our deliverer,
  He's our deliverer,
  He's our deliverer,
  He's our deliverer.

30 Dave Bilbrough
Copyright © 1990 Thankyou Music

AS WE SEEK YOUR FACE,
May we know Your heart,
Feel Your presence, acceptance,
As we seek Your face.

Move among us now,
Come reveal Your power,
Show Your presence, acceptance,
Move among us now.

At Your feet we fall,
Sovereign Lord,
We cry 'holy, holy',
At Your feet we fall.

31 William C. Dix (1837–98)

AS WITH GLADNESS men of old
Did the guiding star behold;
As with joy they hailed its light,
Leading onward, beaming bright,
So, most gracious God, may we
Evermore be led by Thee.

As with joyful steps they sped,
Saviour, to Thy lowly bed,
There to bend the knee before
Thee whom heaven and earth adore,
So may we with willing feet
Ever seek Thy mercy-seat.

As they offered gifts most rare
At Thy cradle rude and bare,
So may we with holy joy,
Pure, and free from sin's alloy,
All our costliest treasures bring,
Christ, to Thee, our heavenly King.

Holy Jesus, every day
Keep us in the narrow way;
And, when earthly things are past,
Bring our ransomed souls at last
Where they need no star to guide,
Where no clouds Thy glory hide.

In the heavenly country bright
Need they no created light;
Thou its light, its joy, its crown,
Thou its sun, which goes not down.
There for ever may we sing
Hallelujahs to our King.

32 Caroline M. Noel (1817–77)

AT THE NAME OF JESUS
Every knee shall bow,
Every tongue confess Him
King of glory now;
'Tis the Father's pleasure
We should call Him Lord,
Who from the beginning
Was the mighty Word.

Humbled for a season,
To receive a name
From the lips of sinners
Unto whom He came;
Faithfully He bore it
Spotless to the last,
Brought it back victorious,
When from death He passed.

Bore it up triumphant
With its human light,
Through all ranks of creatures
To the central height,
To the throne of Godhead,
To the Father's breast,
Filled it with the glory
Of that perfect rest.

In your hearts enthrone Him;
There let Him subdue
All that is not holy,
All that is not true;
Crown Him as your Captain
In temptation's hour,
Let His will enfold you
In its light and power.

Brothers, this Lord Jesus
Shall return again,
With His Father's glory,
With His angel-train;
For all wreaths of empire
Meet upon His brow,
And our hearts confess Him
King of glory now.

 33   Graham Kendrick
Copyright © 1988 Make Way Music

AT THIS TIME OF GIVING,
Gladly now we bring
Gifts of goodness and mercy
From a heavenly King.

Earth could not contain the treasures
Heaven holds for you,
Perfect joy and lasting pleasures,
Love so strong and true.

May His tender love surround you
At this Christmastime;
May you see His smiling face
That in the darkness shines.

But the many gifts He gives
Are all poured out from one;
Come receive the greatest gift,
The gift of God's own Son.

Lai, lai, lai … (*etc.*)

34   David Fellingham
Copyright © 1982 Thankyou Music

AT YOUR FEET WE FALL, mighty risen
Lord,
As we come before Your throne to worship
You.
By Your Spirit's power You now draw our
hearts,
And we hear Your voice in triumph ringing
clear.

I am He that liveth, that liveth and was
dead,
Behold I am alive for evermore.

There we see You stand, mighty risen Lord,
Clothed in garments pure and holy, shining
bright.
Eyes of flashing fire, feet like burnished
bronze,
And the sound of many waters is Your
voice.

Like the shining sun in its noonday strength,
We now see the glory of Your wondrous face.
Once that face was marred, but now You're
glorified,
And Your words like a two-edged sword have
mighty power.

 35   David J. Hadden
Copyright © 1982 Authentic Publishing/
Adm. by CopyCare

AWAKE, AWAKE, O ZION,
Come clothe yourself with strength.
Awake, awake, O Zion,
Come clothe yourself with strength.

Put on your garments of splendour,
O Jerusalem.
Come sing your songs of joy and triumph,
See that your God reigns.

Burst into songs of joy together,
O Jerusalem.
The Lord has comforted His people,
The redeemed Jerusalem.

36   Vv. 1–2 unknown,
v. 3 John T. McFarland (b. *circa* 1906)

AWAY IN A MANGER, no crib for a bed,
The little Lord Jesus laid down His sweet
head;
The stars in the bright sky looked down
where He lay;
The little Lord Jesus asleep on the hay.

The cattle are lowing, the Baby awakes,
But little Lord Jesus, no crying He makes:
I love You, Lord Jesus! Look down from the sky
And stay by my side until morning is nigh.

Be near me, Lord Jesus: I ask You to stay
Close by me for ever and love me, I pray;
Bless all the dear children in Your tender care,
And fit us for heaven to live with You there.

 37   Morris Chapman
Copyright © 1983 Word Music/Adm. by CopyCare

BE BOLD, BE STRONG,
For the Lord your God is with you.
Be bold, be strong,
For the Lord your God is with you.
I am not afraid,
I am not dismayed,
Because I'm walking in faith and victory,
Come on and walk in faith and victory,
For the Lord your God is with you.

BEHOLD THE DARKNESS shall cover the
  earth,
And gross darkness the people,
But the Lord shall arise upon thee
And His glory shall be seen upon thee.

So arise, shine, for thy light is come
And the glory of the Lord is risen;
So arise, shine, for thy light is come
And the glory of the Lord is upon thee.

The Gentiles shall come to thy light,
And kings to the brightness of thy rising,
And they shall call thee the city of the Lord,
The Zion of the Holy One of Israel.

Lift up thine eyes round about and see,
They gather themselves together;
And they shall come, thy sons from afar,
And thy daughters shall be nursed at thy
  side.

Then shalt thou see and flow together,
And thy heart shall be enlarged.
The abundance of the sea is converted unto
  thee,
And the nations shall come unto thee.

The sun shall no more go down,
Neither shall the moon withdraw itself;
But the Lord shall be thine everlasting light,
And the days of thy mourning shall be
  ended.

BENEATH THE CROSS OF JESUS
I fain would take my stand,
The shadow of a mighty rock
Within a weary land;
A home within the wilderness,
A rest upon the way,
From the burning of the noontide heat,
And the burden of the day.

O safe and happy shelter!
O refuge tried and sweet!
O trysting place where heaven's love
And heaven's justice meet!
As to the holy patriarch
That wondrous dream was given,
So seems my Saviour's cross to me
A ladder up to heaven.

There lies, beneath its shadow,
But on the farther side,
The darkness of an awful grave
That gapes both deep and wide;
And there between us stands the cross,
Two arms outstretched to save;
Like a watchman set to guard the way
From that eternal grave.

Upon that cross of Jesus
Mine eye at times can see
The very dying form of One
Who suffered there for me;
And from my smitten heart, with tears,
Two wonders I confess—
The wonders of His glorious love,
And my own worthlessness.

I take, O cross, thy shadow,
For my abiding place;
I ask no other sunshine than
The sunshine of His face;
Content to let the world go by,
To know no gain nor loss—
My sinful self my only shame,
My glory all the cross.

BE STILL, for the presence of the Lord, the
  Holy One is here;
Come bow before Him now with reverence
  and fear.
In Him no sin is found, we stand on holy
  ground;
Be still, for the presence of the Lord, the Holy
  One is here.

Be still, for the glory of the Lord is shining all
  around;
He burns with holy fire, with splendour He is
  crowned.
How awesome is the sight, our radiant King
  of light!
Be still, for the glory of the Lord is shining all
  around.

Be still, for the power of the Lord is moving in
  this place;
He comes to cleanse and heal, to minister His
  grace.
No work too hard for Him, in faith receive
  from Him;
Be still, for the power of the Lord is moving in
  this place.

41

BE STILL AND KNOW that I am God,
Be still and know that I am God,
Be still and know that I am God.

I am the Lord that healeth thee ... *(etc.)*

In Thee, O Lord, do I put my trust ... *(etc.)*

42

BE THOU MY VISION, O Lord of my heart,
Be all else but naught to me, save that Thou
    art;
Be Thou my best thought in the day and the
    night,
Both waking and sleeping, Thy presence my
    light.

Be Thou my wisdom, be Thou my true word,
Be Thou ever with me, and I with Thee, Lord;
Be Thou my great Father, and I Thy true son;
Be Thou in me dwelling, and I with Thee one.

Be Thou my breastplate, my sword for the
    fight;
Be Thou my whole armour, be Thou my true
    might;
Be Thou my soul's shelter, be Thou my
    strong tower:
O raise Thou me heavenward, great Power of
    my power.

Riches I need not, nor man's empty praise:
Be Thou mine inheritance now and always;
Be Thou and Thou only the first in my heart:
O Sovereign of heaven, my treasure Thou art.

High King of heaven, Thou heaven's bright
    Sun,
O grant me its joys after victory is won;
Great Heart of my own heart, whatever befall,
Still be Thou my vision, O Ruler of all.

43

BIND US TOGETHER, *Lord,*
Bind us together
With cords that cannot be broken.
Bind us together, Lord,
Bind us together,
Bind us together with love.

There is only one God,
There is only one King;
There is only one Body,
That is why we sing:

Made for the glory of God,
Purchased by His precious Son;
Born with the right to be clean,
For Jesus the victory has won.

You are the family of God,
You are the promise divine;
You are God's chosen desire,
You are the glorious new wine.

44

BLESSÈD ASSURANCE, Jesus is mine:
O what a foretaste of glory divine!
Heir of salvation, purchase of God;
Born of His Spirit, washed in His blood.

> *This is my story, this is my song,*
> *Praising my Saviour all the day long.*
> *This is my story, this is my song,*
> *Praising my Saviour all the day long.*

Perfect submission, perfect delight,
Visions of rapture burst on my sight;
Angels descending bring from above
Echoes of mercy, whispers of love.

Perfect submission, all is at rest,
I in my Saviour am happy and blessed;
Watching and waiting, looking above,
Filled with His goodness, lost in His love.

45

BLESSÈD BE the God and Father
Of our Lord Jesus Christ,
Who has blessed us with every spiritual
    blessing
In heavenly places in Christ.

And He has chosen us
Before the world was formed
To be holy and blameless before Him.
In His love He has predestined us
To be adopted as sons
Through Jesus Christ to Himself.

46
Danny Daniels & Kevin Prosch
Copyright © 1989 Mercy/Vineyard
Publishing/Adm. by CopyCare

BLESSED BE THE NAME OF THE LORD.
Blessed be the name of the Lord.
Blessed be the name of the Lord.
Blessed be the name of the Lord.
For He is our Rock, for He is our Rock,
He is the Lord.
For He is our Rock, for He is our Rock,
He is the Lord.

Jesus reigns on high in all the earth.
Jesus reigns on high in all the earth.
Jesus reigns on high in all the earth.
Jesus reigns on high in all the earth.
The universe is in the hands
Of the Lord.
The universe is in the hands
Of the Lord.

47
Phil Rogers
Copyright © 1989 Thankyou Music

BLESS THE LORD, O MY SOUL,
And let all that is within me bless His
  name.
O Lord my God, You are so great,
For You are clothed with splendour and
  with majesty.

How can I forget all Your benefits to me?
You forgive my sin in its entirety.
You heal me when I'm sick, from the pit
  You set me free!
You crown my life with Your love.

48
Author unknown
Copyright control

BLESS THE LORD, O MY SOUL,
Bless the Lord, O my soul,
And all that is within me
Bless His holy name.
Bless the Lord, O my soul,
Bless the Lord, O my soul,
And all that is within me
Bless His holy name.

King of kings, (for ever and ever,)
Lord of lords, (for ever and ever,)
King of kings, (for ever and ever,)
King of kings and Lord of lords.

49
John Fawcett (1740–1817) altd

BLEST BE THE TIE that binds
Our hearts in Christian love;
The fellowship of kindred minds
Is like to that above.

Before our Father's throne
We pour our ardent prayers;
Our fears, our hopes, our aims are one,
Our comforts and our cares.

We share our mutual woes,
Our mutual burdens bear,
And often for each other flows
The sympathising tear.

When for a while we part,
This thought will soothe our pain,
That we shall still be joined in heart,
And hope to meet again.

This glorious hope revives
Our courage by the way,
While each in expectation lives,
And longs to see the day.

From sorrow, toil and pain,
And sin we shall be free;
And perfect love and friendship reign
Through all eternity.

50
Mary A. Lathbury (1841–1913) &
Alexander Groves (1843–1909)

BREAK THOU THE BREAD OF LIFE,
Dear Lord, to me,
As Thou didst break the bread
Beside the sea;
Beyond the sacred page
I seek Thee, Lord;
My spirit longs for Thee,
Thou Living Word.

Thou art the Bread of Life,
O Lord, to me,
Thy holy Word the truth
That saveth me;
Give me to eat and live
With Thee above;
Teach me to love Thy truth,
For Thou art love.

O send Thy Spirit, Lord,
Now unto me,
That He may touch my eyes
And make me see;
Show me the truth concealed
Within Thy Word,
And in Thy Book revealed,
I see Thee, Lord.

Bless Thou the Bread of Life
To me, to me,
As Thou didst bless the loaves
By Galilee;
Then shall all bondage cease,
All fetters fall,
And I shall find my peace,
My all in all.

51 Edwin Hatch (1835–89)

BREATHE ON ME, BREATH OF GOD,
Fill me with life anew;
That I may love what Thou dost love
And do what Thou wouldst do.

Breathe on me, Breath of God,
Until my heart is pure;
Until my will is one with Thine
To do and to endure.

Breathe on me, Breath of God,
Till I am wholly Thine;
Until this earthly part of me
Glows with Thy fire divine.

Breathe on me, Breath of God,
So shall I never die,
But live with Thee the perfect life
Of Thine eternity.

52 Brent Chambers
Copyright © 1979 Scripture in Song
(a div. of Integrity Music, Inc.)/
Sovereign Music UK

BRING A PSALM to the Lord,
From the Spirit and from His word.
Lift your voice and rejoice,
For our God is a mighty King,
So come and clap your hands,
Raise a shout, as we stand before the Lord,
For the Lord is He who has the power to free,
Who by His mighty arm gives strength and
    victory.
So as we hail the King
Then let His praises ring,
And bring a psalm of joy before the Lord.

53 Janet Lunt
Copyright © 1978 Sovereign Music UK

   BROKEN FOR ME, *broken for you,*
   The body of Jesus, broken for you.

He offered His body, He poured out His soul;
Jesus was broken, that we might be whole:

Come to My table and with Me dine;
Eat of My bread and drink of My wine.

This is My body given for you;
Eat it remembering I died for you.

This is My blood I shed for you;
For your forgiveness, making you new.

54 Richard Gillard
Copyright © 1977 Scripture in Song
(a div. of Integrity Music, Inc.)/
Sovereign Music UK

BROTHER, SISTER, LET ME SERVE YOU,
Let me be as Christ to you;
Pray that I may have the grace
To let you be my servant, too.

We are pilgrims on a journey,
We're together on this road;
We are here to help each other
Walk the mile and bear the load.

I will hold the Christ-light for you
In the night-time of your fear;
I will hold my hand out to you,
Speak the peace you long to hear.

I will weep when you are weeping,
When you laugh I'll laugh with you;
I will share your joy and sorrow
Till we've seen this journey through.

When we sing to God in heaven
We shall find such harmony,
Born of all we've known together
Of Christ's love and agony.

Brother, sister, let me serve you,
Let me be as Christ to you;
Pray that I may have the grace
To let you be my servant, too.

55 Noel & Tricia Richards
Copyright © 1989 Thankyou Music

BY YOUR SIDE I would stay;
In Your arms I would lay.
Jesus, lover of my soul,
Nothing from You I withhold.

   Lord, I love You, and adore You;
   What more can I say?
   You cause my love to grow stronger
   With every passing day.
   (Repeat)

AUSE ME TO COME to Thy river, O Lord,
ause me to come to Thy river, O Lord,
ause me to come to Thy river, O Lord,
ause me to come,
ause me to drink,
ause me to live.

ause me to drink from Thy river, O Lord,
ause me to drink from Thy river, O Lord,
ause me to drink from Thy river, O Lord,
ause me to come,
ause me to drink,
ause me to live.

ause me to live by Thy river, O Lord,
ause me to live by Thy river, O Lord,
ause me to live by Thy river, O Lord,
ause me to come,
ause me to drink,
ause me to live.

ELEBRATE JESUS, celebrate!
elebrate Jesus, celebrate!
elebrate Jesus, celebrate!
elebrate Jesus, celebrate!

le is risen, He is risen,
nd He lives for evermore.
le is risen, He is risen,
ome on and celebrate
he resurrection of our Lord.

CHANGE MY HEART, O GOD,
Make it ever true;
Change my heart, O God,
May I be like You.

ou are the potter,
am the clay;
Mould me and make me,
his is what I pray.

CHRISTIANS AWAKE! Salute the happy
  morn,
Whereon the Saviour of mankind was born;
Rise to adore the mystery of love
Which hosts of angels chanted from above;
With them the joyful tidings first begun
Of God Incarnate and the Virgin's Son.

Then to the watchful shepherds it was told,
Who heard the angelic herald's voice 'Behold,
I bring good tidings of a Saviour's birth
To you and all the nations upon earth:
This day hath God fulfilled His promised
  word,
This day is born a Saviour, Christ the Lord.'

He spake; and straightway the celestial choir
In hymns of joy unknown before conspire;
High praise of God's redeeming love they
  sang,
And heaven's whole orb with hallelujahs
  rang;
God's highest glory was their anthem still,
'On earth be peace, and unto men goodwill.'

O may we keep and ponder in our mind
God's wondrous love in saving lost mankind;
Trace we the Babe who hath retrieved our
  loss,
From His poor manger to His bitter cross;
Tread in His steps, assisted by His grace,
Till man's first heavenly state again takes
  place.

Then may we hope, the angelic hosts among,
To sing, redeemed, a glad triumphant song:
He that was born upon this joyful day
Around us all His glory shall display;
Saved by His love, incessant we shall sing
Eternal praise to heaven's almighty King.

CHRIST IS RISEN!
Hallelujah, hallelujah!
Christ is risen!
Risen indeed, hallelujah!

Love's work is done,
The battle is won:
Where now, O death, is your sting?
He rose again
To rule and to reign,
Jesus our conquering King.

Lord over sin,
Lord over death,
At His feet Satan must fall!
Every knee bow,
All will confess
Jesus is Lord over all!

Tell it abroad
'Jesus is Lord!'
Shout it and let your praise ring!
Gladly we raise
Our songs of praise,
Worship is our offering.

61 Charles Wesley (1707–88)

CHRIST THE LORD IS RISEN TODAY:
   Hallelujah!
Sons of men and angels say: Hallelujah!
Raise your joys and triumphs high:
   Hallelujah!
Sing, ye heavens, and earth reply: Hallelujah!

Love's redeeming work is done: Hallelujah!
Fought the fight, the battle won: Hallelujah!
Vain the stone, the watch, the seal:
   Hallelujah!
Christ hath burst the gates of hell: Hallelujah!

Lives again our glorious King: Hallelujah!
Where, O death, is now thy sting? Hallelujah!
Once He died, our souls to save: Hallelujah!
Where thy victory, O grave? Hallelujah!

Soar we now where Christ hath led:
   Hallelujah!
Following our exalted Head: Hallelujah!
Made like Him, like Him we rise: Hallelujah!
Ours the cross, the grave, the skies:
   Hallelujah!

Hail the Lord of earth and heaven: Hallelujah!
Praise to Thee by both be given: Hallelujah!
Thee we greet, in triumph sing: Hallelujah!
Hail our resurrected King: Hallelujah!

62 Michael Saward
Copyright © Michael Saward/
Jubilate Hymns Ltd

CHRIST TRIUMPHANT, ever reigning,
Saviour, Master, King,
Lord of heaven, our lives sustaining,
Hear us as we sing:

   Yours the glory and the crown,
   The high renown, the eternal name.

Word incarnate, truth revealing,
Son of Man on earth!
Power and majesty concealing
By your humble birth:

Suffering Servant, scorned, ill-treated,
Victim crucified!
Death is through the cross defeated,
Sinners justified:

Priestly King, enthroned for ever
High in heaven above!
Sin and death and hell shall never
Stifle hymns of love:

So, our hearts and voices raising
Through the ages long,
Ceaselessly upon You gazing,
This shall be our song:

63 Graham Kendrick
Copyright © 1988 Make Way Music

CLEAR THE ROAD, make wide the way. *(echo)*
Welcome now the God who saves.   *(echo)*
Fill the streets with shouts of joy.   *(echo)*
(Cheers, etc.)

   Prepare the way of the Lord!   *(echo)*
   Prepare the way of the Lord!   *(echo)*

Raise your voice and join the song,   *(echo)*
God made flesh to us has come.   *(echo)*
Welcome Him, your banners wave.   *(echo)*
(Cheers, shouts, wave banners, etc.)

For all sin the price is paid,   *(echo)*
All our sins on Jesus laid.   *(echo)*
By His blood we are made clean.   *(echo)*
(Cheers, shouts of thanksgiving)

At His feet come humbly bow,   *(echo)*
In your lives enthrone Him now.   *(echo)*
See, your great Deliverer comes.   *(echo)*
(Cheers, shouts welcoming Jesus)

64 Sue McClellan, John Pac & Keith Ryecroft
Copyright © 1974 Thankyou Music

COLOURS OF DAY dawn into the mind,
The sun has come up, the night is behind.
Go down in the city, into the street,
And let's give the message to the people we
   meet.

   So light up the fire and let the flame burn
   Open the door, let Jesus return.
   Take seeds of His Spirit, let the fruit grow,
   Tell the people of Jesus, let His love show

o through the park, on into the town;
he sun still shines on, it never goes down.
he light of the world is risen again;
he people of darkness are needing a friend.

pen your eyes, look into the sky,
he darkness has come, the Son came to
  die.
he evening draws on, the sun disappears,
ut Jesus is living, His Spirit is near.

5 Andy Carter
Copyright © 1977 Thankyou Music

OME AND PRAISE HIM, ROYAL PRIESTHOOD,
ome and worship, holy nation.
Worship Jesus, our Redeemer,
e is precious, King of glory.

6 Mike Kerry
Copyright © 1982 Thankyou Music

COME AND PRAISE THE LIVING GOD,
Come and worship, come and worship.
He has made you priest and king,
Come and worship the living God.

Ve come not to a mountain of fire and
  smoke,
ot to gloom and darkness or trumpet
  sound;
Ve come to the new Jerusalem,
he holy city of God.

y His voice He shakes the earth,
is judgements known throughout the
  world.
ut we have a city that for ever stands,
he holy city of God.

7 Graham Kendrick
Copyright © 1989 Make Way Music

OME AND SEE, come and see,
ome and see the King of love;
ee the purple robe and crown of thorns He
  wears.
oldiers mock, rulers sneer,
s He lifts the cruel cross;
one and friendless now He climbs towards
  the hill.

We worship at Your feet,
Where wrath and mercy meet,
And a guilty world is washed
By love's pure stream.
For us He was made sin—
Oh, help me take it in.
Deep wounds of love cry out
'Father, forgive.'
I worship, I worship,
The Lamb who was slain.

Come and weep, come and mourn
For your sin that pierced Him there;
So much deeper than the wounds of thorn
  and nail.
All our pride, all our greed,
All our fallenness and shame;
And the Lord has laid the punishment on
  Him.

Man of heaven, born to earth
To restore us to Your heaven,
Here we bow in awe beneath Your searching
  eyes.
From Your tears comes our joy,
From Your death our life shall spring;
By Your resurrection power we shall rise.

68 Author unknown
Copyright control

COME BLESS THE LORD,
All ye servants of the Lord,
Who stand by night in the house of the Lord.
Lift up your hands in the holy place,
Come bless the Lord,
Come bless the Lord.

69 John Sellers
Copyright © 1984 Integrity's Hosanna! Music/
Sovereign Music UK

COME INTO THE HOLY OF HOLIES,
Enter by the blood of the Lamb;
Come into His presence with singing,
Worship at the throne of God.
(Repeat)

Lifting holy hands
To the King of kings,
Worship Jesus.

70 Isaac Watts (1674–1748)

COME, LET US JOIN OUR CHEERFUL SONGS
With angels round the throne;
Ten thousand thousand are their tongues,
But all their joys are one.

'Worthy the Lamb that died,' they cry,
'To be exalted thus.'
'Worthy the Lamb,' our lips reply,
'For He was slain for us.'

Jesus is worthy to receive
Honour and power divine:
And blessings, more than we can give,
Be, Lord, for ever Thine.

Let all that dwell above the sky,
And air, and earth, and seas,
Conspire to lift Thy glories high,
And speak Thine endless praise.

The whole creation join in one
To bless the sacred name
Of Him that sits upon the throne
And to adore the Lamb.

71 Brent Chambers
Copyright © 1985 Scripture in Song
(a div. of Integrity Music, Inc.)/
Sovereign Music UK

COME, LET US SING for joy to the Lord,
Come let us sing for joy to the Lord,
Come let us sing for joy to the Lord,
Come let us sing for joy to the Lord!

> *Come let us sing for joy to the Lord,*
> *Let us shout aloud to the Rock of our*
> *salvation!*
> (Repeat)

Let us come before Him with thanksgiving,
And extol Him with music and song;
For the Lord, our Lord, is a great God,
The great King above all gods.

Let us bow before Him in our worship,
Let us kneel before God, our great King;
For He is our God, and we are His people,
That's why we shout and sing!

72 Robert Walmsley (1831–1905)

COME, LET US SING OF A WONDERFUL LOVE,
Tender and true;
Out of the heart of the Father above,
Streaming to me and to you:
Wonderful love
Dwells in the heart of the Father above.

Jesus, the Saviour, this gospel to tell,
Joyfully came;
Came with the helpless and hopeless to
dwell,
Sharing their sorrow and shame;
Seeking the lost,
Saving, redeeming at measureless cost.

Jesus is seeking the wanderers yet;
Why do they roam?
Love only waits to forgive and forget;
Home, weary wanderer, home!
Wonderful love
Dwells in the heart of the Father above.

Come to my heart, O Thou wonderful love,
Come and abide,
Lifting my life, till it rises above
Envy and falsehood and pride,
Seeking to be
Lowly and humble, a learner of Thee.

73 Patricia Morgan & Dave Bankhead
Copyright © 1984 Thankyou Music

COME ON AND CELEBRATE
His gift of love, we will celebrate
The Son of God who loved us
And gave us life.
We'll shout Your praise, O King,
You give us joy nothing else can bring,
We'll give to You our offering
In celebration praise.

Come on and celebrate,
Celebrate,
Celebrate and sing,
Celebrate and sing to the King.
Come on and celebrate,
Celebrate,
Celebrate and sing,
Celebrate and sing to the King.

74 Graham Kendrick
Copyright © 1985 Thankyou Music

COME SEE THE BEAUTY OF THE LORD,
Come see the beauty of His face.
See the Lamb that once was slain,
See on His palms is carved your name.
See how our pain has pierced His heart,
And on His brow He bears our pride;
A crown of thorns.

But only love pours from His heart
As silently He takes the blame.
He has my name upon His lips,
My condemnation falls on Him.
This love is marvellous to me,
His sacrifice has set me free
And now I live.

Come see the beauty of the Lord,
Come see the beauty of His face.

75 Henry Alford (1810–71)

COME, YE THANKFUL PEOPLE, COME,
Raise the song of harvest home!
All is safely gathered in
Ere the winter storms begin;
God, our Maker, doth provide
For our needs to be supplied;
Come to God's own temple, come,
Raise the song of harvest-home.

All the world is God's own field,
Fruit unto His praise to yield;
Wheat and tares together sown,
Unto joy or sorrow grown;
First the blade, and then the ear,
Then the full corn shall appear:
Lord of harvest, grant that we
Wholesome grain and pure may be.

For the Lord our God shall come
And shall take His harvest home;
From His field shall in that day
All offences purge away,
Give His angels charge at last
In the fire the tares to cast,
But the fruitful ears to store
In His garner evermore.

Even so, Lord, quickly come,
Bring Thy final harvest home;
Gather Thou Thy people in,
Free from sorrow, free from sin;
There, for ever purified,
In Thy garner to abide;
Come, with all Thine angels, come,
Raise the glorious harvest-home.

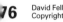

76 David Fellingham
Copyright © 1983 Thankyou Music

CREATE IN ME a clean heart, O God,
And renew a right spirit in me.
Create in me a clean heart, O God,
And renew a right spirit in me.
Wash me, cleanse me, purify me;
Make my heart as white as snow.
Create in me a clean heart, O God,
And renew a right spirit in me.

77 Matthew Bridges (1800–94) &
Godfrey Thring (1823–1903)

CROWN HIM WITH MANY CROWNS,
The Lamb upon His throne;
Hark, how the heavenly anthem drowns
All music but its own!
Awake, my soul, and sing
Of Him who died for thee,
And hail Him as thy matchless King
Through all eternity.

Crown Him the Lord of life,
Who triumphed o'er the grave
And rose victorious in the strife
For those He came to save:
His glories now we sing,
Who died and rose on high,
Who died eternal life to bring
And lives that death may die.

Crown Him the Lord of love;
Behold His hands and side,
Those wounds yet visible above
In beauty glorified:
No angel in the sky
Can fully bear that sight,
But downward bends His burning eye
At mysteries so bright.

Crown Him the Lord of peace,
Whose power a sceptre sways
From pole to pole, that wars may cease,
And all be prayer and praise:
His reign shall know no end,
And round His piercèd feet
Fair flowers of paradise extend
Their fragrance ever sweet.

Crown Him the Lord of years,
The Potentate of time,
Creator of the rolling spheres,
Ineffably sublime!
All hail, Redeemer, hail!
For Thou hast died for me;
Thy praise shall never, never fail
Throughout eternity.

78 Graham Kendrick
Copyright © 1985 Thankyou Music

DARKNESS LIKE A SHROUD covers the
earth;
Evil like a cloud covers the people.
But the Lord will rise upon you,
And His glory will appear on you—
Nations will come to your light.

Arise, shine, your light has come,
The glory of the Lord has risen on you!
Arise, shine, your light has come,
Jesus the Light of the world has come.

Children of the light, be clean and pure.
Rise, you sleepers, Christ will shine on
    you.
Take the Spirit's flashing two-edged s
    word
And with faith declare God's mighty
    word;
Stand up and in His strength be strong.

Here among us now, Christ the light
Kindles brighter flames in our trembling
    hearts.
Living Word, our lamp, come guide our
    feet
As we walk as one in light and peace,
Till justice and truth shine like the sun.

Like a city bright so let us blaze;
Lights in every street turning night to day.
And the darkness shall not overcome
Till the fulness of Christ's kingdom comes,
Dawning to God's eternal day.

79   John G. Whittier (1807–92)

DEAR LORD AND FATHER OF MANKIND,
Forgive our foolish ways;
Reclothe us in our rightful mind;
In purer lives Thy service find,
In deeper reverence, praise,
In deeper reverence, praise.

In simple trust like theirs who heard,
Beside the Syrian sea,
The gracious calling of the Lord,
Let us, like them, without a word
Rise up and follow Thee,
Rise up and follow Thee.

O sabbath rest by Galilee!
O calm of hills above,
Where Jesus knelt to share with Thee
The silence of eternity,
Interpreted by love,
Interpreted by love.

With that deep hush subduing all
Our words and works that drown
The tender whisper of Thy call,
As noiseless let Thy blessing fall
As fell Thy manna down,
As fell Thy manna down.

Drop Thy still dews of quietness,
Till all our strivings cease;
Take from our souls the strain and stress,
And let our ordered lives confess
The beauty of Thy peace,
The beauty of Thy peace.

Breathe through the heats of our desire
Thy coolness and Thy balm;
Let sense be dumb, let flesh retire;
Speak through the earthquake, wind and fire
O still small voice of calm,
O still small voice of calm!

80   Chris Bowater

DO SOMETHING NEW, LORD,
In my heart, make a start;
Do something new, Lord,
Do something new.

I open up my heart,
As much as can be known;
I open up my will
To conform to Yours alone.

I lay before Your feet
All my hopes and desires;
Unreservedly submit
To what Your Spirit may require.

I only want to live
For Your pleasure now;
I long to please You, Father—
Will You show me how?

81   Stuart Devane & Glen Gore

DRAW ME CLOSER, Lord,
Draw me closer, dear Lord,
So that I might touch You,
So that I might touch You,
Lord, I want to touch You.

Touch my eyes, Lord,
Touch my eyes, dear Lord,
So that I might see You,
So that I might see You,
Lord, I want to see You:

Your glory and Your love,
Your glory and Your love,
Your glory and Your love,
And Your majesty.

2
John Thompson & Michael Card
Copyright © 1981 Whole Armor &
Full Armor Publishing Companies/
Adm. by TKO Publishing Ltd

EL-SHADDAI, *El-Shaddai,*
El-Elyon na Adonai,
Age to age You're still the same
By the power of the Name.
El-Shaddai, El-Shaddai,
Erkamka na Adonai,
We will praise and lift You high.
El-Shaddai.

Through Your love and through the ram
You saved the son of Abraham;
Through the power of Your hand,
Turned the sea into dry land.
To the outcast on her knees
You were the God who really sees,
And by Your might You set Your children free.

Through the years You made it clear
That the time of Christ was near,
Though the people couldn't see
What Messiah ought to be.
Though Your word contained the plan,
They just could not understand
Your most awesome work was done
Through the frailty of Your Son.

3
Bob McGee
Copyright © 1976 C.A. Music/Music Services/
Adm. by CopyCare

EMMANUEL, Emmanuel,
We call Your name, Emmanuel.
God with us, revealed in us,
We call Your name, Emmanuel.

4
Carol Mundy
Copyright © 1988 Thankyou Music

ENTER IN to His great love,
Kneel before His throne;
For His blood has washed away your sin,
So enter in and worship Him.

5
David Fellingham
Copyright © 1983 Thankyou Music

ETERNAL GOD, we come to You,
We come before Your throne;
We enter by a new and living way,
With confidence we come.
We declare Your faithfulness,
Your promises are true;
We will now draw near to worship You.

(Men)
O holy God, we come to You,
O holy God, we see Your faithfulness and
    love;
Your mighty power, Your majesty,
Are now revealed to us in Jesus who has
    died,
Jesus who was raised,
Jesus now exalted on high.

(Women)
O holy God, full of justice,
Wisdom and righteousness, faithfulness and
    love;
Your mighty power and Your majesty
Are now revealed to us in Jesus who has
    died for our sin,
Jesus who was raised from the dead,
Jesus now exalted on high.

86
Dave Bilbrough
Copyright © 1990 Thankyou Music

EXALTED, YOU ARE EXALTED,
Lord of heaven and the earth.
Exalted, You are exalted,
Ruler of the universe.
For at the name of Jesus
Every knee shall bow,
Honour and praise to Jesus,
We give You glory now.
Lord, we come before You,
Worship and adore You.

87
Rick Ridings
Copyright © 1977 Scripture in Song
(a div. of Integrity Music, Inc.)/
Sovereign Music UK

EXALT THE LORD OUR GOD,
Exalt the Lord our God,
And worship at His footstool,
Worship at His footstool;
Holy is He, holy is He.

88
Frank Houghton
Copyright © 1930 OMF International

FACING A TASK UNFINISHED,
That drives us to our knees,
A need that, undiminished,
Rebukes our slothful ease:
We, who rejoice to know Thee,
Renew before Thy throne
The solemn pledge we owe Thee
To go and make Thee known.

Where other lords beside Thee
Hold their unhindered sway,
Where forces that defied Thee
Defy Thee still today;
With none to heed their crying
For life, and love, and light,
Unnumbered souls are dying,
And pass into the night.

We bear the torch that flaming
Fell from the hands of those
Who gave their lives proclaiming
That Jesus died and rose.
Ours is the same commission,
The same glad message ours;
Fired by the same ambition,
To Thee we yield our powers.

O Father who sustained them,
O Spirit who inspired,
Saviour, whose love constrained them
To toil with zeal untired,
From cowardice defend us,
From lethargy awake!
Forth on Thine errands send us
To labour for Thy sake.

89

FAITHFUL ONE, so unchanging,
Ageless One, You're my Rock of peace.
Lord of all, I depend on You,
I call out to You again and again.
I call out to You again and again.
You are my rock in times of trouble.
You lift me up when I fall down.
All through the storm Your love is the anchor,
My hope is in You alone.

90

FATHER, I can call You Father,
For I am Your child today,
Tomorrow and always,
You are my Father.

Father, how I love You, Father,
I will sing Your praise today,
Tomorrow and always,
For You're my Father.

Father, Father,
Father to me.
Father, holy Father,
Father to me.

Father, I will serve You, Father,
I will seek Your face today,
Tomorrow and always,
You are my Father.

91

FATHER GOD,
I give all thanks and praise to Thee,
Father God,
My hands I humbly raise to Thee;
For Your mighty power and love
Amazes me, amazes me,
And I stand in awe and worship, Father God

92

FATHER GOD, I WONDER how I managed to
exist
Without the knowledge of Your parenthood
and Your loving care.
But now I am Your son, I am adopted in Your
family,
And I can never be alone,
'Cause Father God, You're there beside me.

I will sing Your praises,
I will sing Your praises,
I will sing Your praises,
Forever more.
I will sing Your praises,
I will sing Your praises,
I will sing Your praises,
Forever more.

93

FATHER GOD, we worship You,
Make us part of all You do.
As You move among us now
We worship You.

Jesus King, we worship You,
Help us listen now to You.
As You move among us now
We worship You.

Spirit pure, we worship You,
With Your fire our zeal renew.
As You move among us now
We worship You.

94
Danny Daniels
Copyright © 1990 Mercy/Vineyard
Publishing/Adm. by CopyCare

FATHER HERE I AM again,
In need of mercy, hurt from sin,
So by the blood and Jesus' love,
Let forgiveness flow.

To me, from me,
So my heart will know;
Fully and sweetly,
Let forgiveness flow.

In my heart and in my mind,
In word and deed, I've been so blind,
So by the blood and Jesus' love,
Let forgiveness flow.

95
Dave Bilbrough
Copyright © 1985 Thankyou Music

FATHER IN HEAVEN,
Our voices we raise;
Receive our devotion,
Receive now our praise,
As we sing of the glory
Of all that You've done,
The greatest love story
That's ever been sung.

And we will crown You Lord of all,
Yes, we will crown You Lord of all,
For You have won the victory,
Yes, we will crown You Lord of all.

Father in heaven,
Our lives are Your own;
We've been caught by a vision
Of Jesus alone,
Who came as a servant
To free us from sin.
Father in heaven,
Our worship we bring:

We will sing 'Hallelujah,'
We will sing to the King,
To our Mighty Deliverer
Our hallelujahs will ring.
Yes, our praise is resounding
To the Lamb on the throne;
He alone is exalted
Through the love He has shown.

96
Bob Fitts
Copyright © 1984 Scripture in Song
(a div. of Integrity Music, Inc.)/
Sovereign Music UK

FATHER IN HEAVEN, HOW WE LOVE YOU,
We lift Your name in all the earth.
May Your kingdom be established in our
praises
As Your people declare Your mighty works.

Blessèd be the Lord God Almighty,
Who was and is and is to come;
Blessèd be the Lord God Almighty,
Who reigns for evermore.

97
Jenny Hewer
Copyright © 1975 Thankyou Music

FATHER, I PLACE INTO YOUR HANDS
The things I cannot do.
Father, I place into Your hands
The things that I've been through.
Father, I place into Your hands
The way that I should go,
For I know I always can trust You.

Father, I place into Your hands
My friends and family.
Father, I place into Your hands
The things that trouble me.
Father, I place into Your hands
The person I would be,
For I know I always can trust You.

Father, we love to see Your face,
We love to hear Your voice.
Father, we love to sing Your praise
And in Your name rejoice.
Father, we love to walk with You
And in Your presence rest,
For we know we always can trust You.

Father, I want to be with You
And do the things You do.
Father, I want to speak the words
That You are speaking too.
Father, I want to love the ones
That You will draw to You,
For I know that I am one with You.

98
Rick Ridings
Copyright © 1976 Scripture in Song
(a div. of Integrity Music, Inc.)/
Sovereign Music UK

FATHER, MAKE US ONE,
Father, make us one,
That the world may know
Thou hast sent the Son,
Father, make us one.

Behold how pleasant and how good it is
For brethren to dwell in unity,
For there the Lord commands the blessing,
Life for evermore.

99 Terry Coelho
Copyright © 1972 CCCM Music/
Maranatha! Music/Adm. by CopyCare

FATHER, WE ADORE YOU,
Lay our lives before You,
How we love You.

Jesus, we adore You … *(etc.)*

Spirit, we adore You … *(etc.)*

100 Phil Lawson Johnston
Copyright © 1989 Thankyou Music

FATHER, WE ADORE YOU,
We are Your children gathered here;
To be with You is our delight,
A feast beyond compare.

Father, in Your presence
There is such freedom to enjoy.
We find in You a lasting peace
That nothing can destroy.

> *You are the Fountain of life,*
> *You are the Fountain of life,*
> *And as we drink, we are more than*
> *satisfied*
> *By You, O Fountain of life.*

101 Carl Tuttle
Copyright © 1982 Mercy/Vineyard
Publishing/Adm. by CopyCare

FATHER, WE ADORE YOU,
You've drawn us to this place.
We bow down before You,
Humbly on our face.

> *All the earth shall worship*
> *At the throne of the King.*
> *Of His great and awesome power,*
> *We shall sing!*
> (Repeat)

Jesus, we love You,
Because You first loved us;
You reached out and healed us
With Your mighty touch.

Spirit, we need You
To lift us from this mire;
Consume and empower us
With Your holy fire.

Faithful is He;
Awesome is He;
Saviour is He;
Master is He;
Mighty is He;
Have mercy on me.

102 Donna Adkins
Copyright © 1976 CCCM Music/
Maranatha! Music/Adm. by CopyCare

FATHER, WE LOVE YOU,
We worship and adore You,
Glorify Your name in all the earth.
Glorify Your name,
Glorify Your name,
Glorify Your name in all the earth.

Jesus, we love You … *(etc.)*

Spirit, we love You … *(etc.)*

103 Andy Park
Copyright © 1990 Mercy/Vineyard
Publishing/Adm. by CopyCare

FATHER, YOU ARE MY PORTION in this life,
And You are my hope and my delight,
And I love You, yes, I love You,
Lord, I love You, my delight.

Jesus, You are my treasure in this life,
And You are so pure and so kind,
And I love You, yes, I love You,
Lord, I love You, my delight.

104 Everett Perry
Copyright © 1983 Thankyou Music

FATHER, YOUR LOVE IS PRECIOUS beyond
all loves,
Father, Your love overwhelms me.
Father, Your love is precious beyond all
loves,
Father, Your love overwhelms me.

So I lift up my hands, an expression of my
love,
And I give You my heart in joyful obedience.
Father, Your love is precious beyond all
loves,
Father, Your love overwhelms me.

:AR NOT, for I am with you,
›ar not, for I am with you,
›ar not, for I am with you,
ıys the Lord.
.epeat)

ıave redeemed you,
·e called you by name;
ıild, you are Mine.
•hen you walk through the waters,
✓ill be there,
ıd through the flame.
•u'll not be drowned,
•u'll not be burned,
•r I am with you.

FEAR NOT, REJOICE AND BE GLAD,
The Lord hath done a great thing;
Hath poured out His Spirit on all mankind,
On those who confess His name.

ıe fig tree is budding, the vine beareth fruit,
ıe wheat fields are golden with grain.
ırust in the sickle, the harvest is ripe,
ıe Lord has given us rain.

· shall eat in plenty and be satisfied,
ıe mountains will drip with sweet wine.
✓ children shall drink of the fountain of life,
✓ children will know they are Mine.

✓ people shall know that I am the Lord,
ıeir shame I have taken away.
✓ Spirit will lead them together again,
✓ Spirit will show them the way.

✓ children shall dwell in a Body of love,
light to the world they will be.
·e shall come forth from the Father above,
✓ Body will set mankind free.

07 John S. B. Monsell (1811–75)

ЗHT THE GOOD FIGHT with all thy might,
ırist is thy strength, and Christ thy right;
✓ hold on life, and it shall be
ıy joy and crown eternally.

ın the straight race through God's good grace,
·t up thine eyes and seek His face;
·e with its way before thee lies,
ırist is the path, and Christ the prize.

Cast care aside, lean on thy Guide;
His boundless mercy will provide;
Lean, and the trusting soul shall prove
Christ is its life, and Christ its love.

Faint not, nor fear, His arms are near,
He changeth not, and thou art dear;
Only believe, and thou shalt see
That Christ is all in all to thee.

108 Horatius Bonar (1808–89)

FILL THOU MY LIFE, O Lord my God,
In every part with praise,
That my whole being may proclaim
Thy being and Thy ways.

Not for the lip of praise alone,
Nor e'en the praising heart
I ask, but for a life made up
Of praise in every part:

Praise in the common things of life,
Its goings out and in;
Praise in each duty and each deed,
However small and mean.

Fill every part of me with praise;
Let all my being speak
Of Thee and of Thy love, O Lord,
Poor though I be and weak.

So shall Thou, gracious Lord, from me
Receive the glory due;
And so shall I begin on earth
The song for ever new.

So shall no part of day or night
From sacredness be free;
But all my life, in every step,
Be fellowship with Thee.

109 William W. How (1823–97)

FOR ALL THE SAINTS, who from their
labours rest,
Who Thee by faith before the world
confessed,
Thy name, O Jesus, be for ever blest.
Hallelujah! Hallelujah!

Thou wast their Rock, their fortress, and their
might;
Thou, Lord, their Captain in the well-fought
fight;
Thou in the darkness drear their one true
light.
Hallelujah! Hallelujah!

O may Thy soldiers, faithful, true and bold,
Fight as the saints who nobly fought of old,
And win, with them, the victor's crown of gold!
Hallelujah! Hallelujah!

O blest communion, fellowship divine!
We feebly struggle, they in glory shine;
Yet all are one in Thee, for all are Thine.
Hallelujah! Hallelujah!

And when the strife is fierce, the warfare
  long,
Steals on the ear the distant triumph song,
And hearts are brave again, and arms are
  strong.
Hallelujah! Hallelujah!

The golden evening brightens in the west;
Soon, soon to faithful warriors cometh rest;
Sweet is the calm of paradise the blest.
Hallelujah! Hallelujah!

But lo! there breaks a yet more glorious day;
The saints triumphant rise in bright array;
The King of glory passes on His way.
Hallelujah! Hallelujah!

From earth's wide bounds, from ocean's
  farthest coast,
Through gates of pearl streams in the
  countless host,
Singing to Father, Son and Holy Ghost.
Hallelujah! Hallelujah!

110 Dale Garratt
Copyright © 1972 Scripture in Song
(a div. of Integrity Music, Inc.)/
Sovereign Music UK

FOR HIS NAME IS EXALTED,
His glory above heaven and earth.
Holy is the Lord God Almighty,
Who was and who is and who is to come.
For His name is exalted,
His glory above heaven and earth.
Holy is the Lord God Almighty,
Who sitteth on the throne
And who lives for evermore.

111 Dave Richards
Copyright © 1977 Thankyou Music

FOR I'M BUILDING A PEOPLE OF POWER,
And I'm making a people of praise
That will move through this land by My Spirit,
And will glorify My precious name.

Build Your church, Lord,
Make us strong, Lord,
Join our hearts, Lord, through Your Son.
Make us one, Lord,
In Your Body,
In the kingdom of Your Son.

112 Folliott S. Pierpoint (1835–1917) altd

FOR THE BEAUTY OF THE EARTH,
For the beauty of the skies,
For the love which from our birth
Over and around us lies:
Father, unto Thee we raise
This our sacrifice of praise.

For the beauty of each hour
Of the day and of the night,
Hill and vale, and tree and flower,
Sun and moon, and stars of light:
Father, unto Thee we raise
This our sacrifice of praise.

For the joy of human love,
Brother, sister, parent, child,
Friends on earth, and friends above;
For all gentle thoughts and mild:
Father, unto Thee we raise
This our sacrifice of praise.

For each perfect gift of Thine
To our race so freely given,
Graces, human and divine,
Flowers of earth, and buds of heaven:
Father, unto Thee we raise
This our sacrifice of praise.

113 Bonnie Low
Copyright © 1976 Scripture in Song
(a div. of Integrity Music, Inc.)/
Sovereign Music UK

FOR THE LORD IS MARCHING ON,
And His army is ever strong;
And His glory shall be seen upon our land.
Raise the anthem, sing the victor's song;
Praise the Lord for the battle's won.
No weapon formed against us shall stand.

For the Captain of the host is Jesus;
We're following in His footsteps.
No foe can stand against us in the fray.
(Repeat)

We are marching in Messiah's band,
The keys of victory in His mighty hand;
Let us march on to take our promised land!
For the Lord is marching on,
And His army is ever strong;
And His glory shall be seen upon our land.

114

FOR THIS PURPOSE Christ was revealed,
To destroy all the works
Of the Evil One.
Christ in us has overcome,
So with gladness we sing
And welcome His kingdom in.

(Men)
Over sin He has conquered,
(Women)
Hallelujah, He has conquered.
(Men)
Over death victorious,
(Women)
Hallelujah, victorious.
(Men)
Over sickness He has triumphed,
(Women)
Hallelujah, He has triumphed.
(All)
Jesus reigns over all!

In the name of Jesus we stand,
By the power of His blood
We now claim this ground.
Satan has no authority here;
Powers of darkness must flee,
For Christ has the victory.

115

FOR THOU O LORD ART HIGH above all the
earth,
Thou art exalted far above all gods.
For Thou O Lord art high above all the earth,
Thou art exalted far above all gods.

I exalt Thee, I exalt Thee,
I exalt Thee, O Lord.
I exalt Thee, I exalt Thee,
I exalt Thee, O Lord.

116

FOR UNTO US A CHILD IS BORN,
Unto us a Son is given.
And the government shall be upon His
shoulder,
And His name shall be called
Wonderful Counsellor, the Mighty God,
The Everlasting Father,
And the Prince of Peace is He.

117

FOR WE SEE JESUS enthroned on high,
Clothed in His righteousness, we worship
Him.
Glory and honour we give unto You,
We see You in Your holiness
And bow before Your throne;
You are the Lord,
Your name endures for ever,
Jesus the Name high over all.

118

FOR YOUR WONDERFUL DEEDS we give You
thanks, Lord,
For Your marvellous acts on behalf of the
people You love.
We honour You, we honour You,
For Your wonderful deeds we honour You.

For Your bountiful grace we give You thanks,
Lord,
For the peace and the joy You bestow on the
people You love.
We honour You, we honour You,
For Your bountiful grace we honour You.

119

FROM ALL THAT DWELL BELOW THE
SKIES
Let the Creator's praise arise:
Alleluia! Alleluia!
Let the Redeemer's name be sung
Through every land, by every tongue.

Alleluia! Alleluia!
Alleluia! Alleluia!
Alleluia!

Eternal are Thy mercies, Lord;
Eternal truth attends Thy word:
Alleluia! Alleluia!
Thy praise shall sound from shore to
shore,
Till suns shall rise and set no more.

Your lofty themes, ye mortals, bring,
In songs of praise divinely sing:
Alleluia! Alleluia!
The great salvation loud proclaim,
And shout for joy the Saviour's name.

In every land begin the song;
To every land the strains belong.
Alleluia! Alleluia!
In cheerful sounds all voices raise,
And fill the world with loudest praise.

120 Graham Kendrick
Copyright © 1983 Thankyou Music

FROM HEAVEN YOU CAME,
Helpless babe,
Entered our world,
Your glory veiled;
Not to be served
But to serve,
And give Your life
That we might live.

This is our God,
The Servant King,
He calls us now
To follow Him,
To bring our lives
As a daily offering
Of worship to
The Servant King.

There in the garden
Of tears,
My heavy load
He chose to bear;
His heart with sorrow
Was torn,
'Yet not My will
But Yours,' He said.

Come see His hands
And His feet,
The scars that speak
Of sacrifice;
Hands that flung stars
Into space
To cruel nails
Surrendered.

So let us learn
How to serve,
And in our lives
Enthrone Him;
Each other's needs
To prefer,
For it is Christ
We're serving.

121 Paul S. Deming
Copyright © 1976 Integrity's Hosanna! Music/
Sovereign Music UK

FROM THE RISING OF THE SUN
To the going down of the same,
The Lord's name
Is to be praised.
From the rising of the sun
To the going down of the same
The Lord's name
Is to be praised.

Praise ye the Lord,
Praise Him all ye servants of the Lord,
Praise the name of the Lord.
Blessèd be the name of the Lord
From this time forth and for evermore.

122 Graham Kendrick
Copyright © 1988 Make Way Music

FROM THE SUN'S RISING
Unto the sun's setting,
Jesus our Lord
Shall be great in the earth;
And all earth's kingdoms
Shall be His dominion,
All of creation
Shall sing of His worth.

Let every heart, every voice,
Every tongue join with spirits ablaze;
One in His love, we will circle the world
With the song of His praise.
O, let all His people rejoice,
And let all the earth hear His voice!

To every tongue, tribe
And nation He sends us,
To make disciples,
To teach and baptise.
For all authority
To Him is given;
Now as His witnesses
We shall arise.

Come let us join with
The church from all nations,
Cross every border,
Throw wide every door;
Workers with Him
As He gathers His harvest,
Till earth's far corners
Our Saviour adore.

23 Danny Daniels
Copyright © 1987 Mercy/Vineyard
Publishing/Adm. by CopyCare

GIVE ME LIFE, HOLY SPIRIT,
Guide my steps in Your sight;
Help me always give You pleasure,
Keep me walking in Your light.
Give me life, Holy Spirit,
Fill me now, make us one;
I will dwell with You for ever,
In the Father and the Son.

I will dwell with You,
I will dwell with You.
I will dwell with You
In the Father and the Son.

24 Henry Smith
Copyright © 1978 Integrity's Hosanna! Music/
Sovereign Music UK

GIVE THANKS with a grateful heart.
Give thanks to the Holy One.
Give thanks because He's given
Jesus Christ, His Son.
(Repeat)

And now let the weak say 'I am strong,'
Let the poor say 'I am rich,'
Because of what the Lord has done for us.
(Repeat)

(Last time)
Give thanks.

25 Kevin Gould
Copyright © 1988 Coronation Music
Publishing/Kingsway Music

GIVE THANKS TO THE LORD,
Call upon His name,
Make known among the nations
That He has done.
(Repeat)

Sing to Him,
Sing praise to Him,
Tell of all His wonderful acts.
Glory in His holy name,
Let the hearts of those
Who seek the Lord rejoice.

26 Danny Reed
Copyright © 1987 Thankyou Music

GLORIOUS FATHER, we exalt You,
We worship, honour and adore You.
We delight to be in Your presence, O Lord,
We magnify Your holy name.

And we sing, 'Come, Lord Jesus,
Glorify Your name.'
And we sing, 'Come, Lord Jesus,
Glorify Your name.'

127 John Newton (1725–1807)

GLORIOUS THINGS OF THEE ARE SPOKEN,
Zion, city of our God!
He whose word cannot be broken
Formed thee for His own abode.
On the Rock of Ages founded,
What can shake thy sure repose?
With salvation's walls surrounded,
Thou mayest smile at all thy foes.

See! The streams of living waters,
Springing from eternal love,
Well supply thy sons and daughters,
And all fear of want remove;
Who can faint, whilst such a river
Ever flows their thirst to assuage?
Grace which, like the Lord, the Giver,
Never fails from age to age.

Round each habitation hovering,
See the cloud and fire appear!
For a glory and a covering,
Showing that the Lord is near.
He who gives them daily manna,
He who listens when they cry:
Let Him hear the loud hosanna
Rising to His throne on high.

Saviour, if of Zion's city
I, through grace, a member am,
Let the world deride or pity,
I will glory in Thy name.
Fading is the worldling's pleasure,
All his boasted pomp and show,
Solid joys and lasting treasure
None but Zion's children know.

128 Danny Daniels
Copyright © 1987 Mercy/Vineyard
Publishing/Adm. by CopyCare

GLORY, glory in the highest;
Glory, to the Almighty;
Glory to the Lamb of God,
And glory to the living Word;
Glory to the Lamb!

I give glory, (glory)
Glory, (glory)
Glory, glory to the Lamb!
I give glory, (glory)
Glory, (glory)
Glory, glory to the Lamb!
I give glory to the Lamb!

129 Carol Owens
Copyright © 1972 Bud John Songs/
EMI Christian Music Publishing/
Adm. by CopyCare

GOD FORGAVE MY SIN in Jesus' name,
I've been born again in Jesus' name;
And in Jesus' name I come to you
To share His love as He told me to.

He said: 'Freely, freely, you have received,
Freely, freely give;
Go in My name, and because you believe
Others will know that I live.'

All power is given in Jesus' name,
In earth and heaven in Jesus' name;
And in Jesus' name I come to you
To share His power as He told me to.

130 Austin Martin
Copyright © 1984 Thankyou Music

GOD HAS EXALTED HIM
To the highest place,
Given Him the name
That is above every name.

And every knee shall bow,
And every tongue confess
That Jesus Christ is Lord
To the glory of God the Father.

131 Stuart Baugh
Copyright © 1982 Restoration Music Ltd/
Sovereign Music UK

GOD HAS SPOKEN TO HIS PEOPLE,
Through His prophets long ago,
Of the days in which we're living,
And the things His church should know.
Listen then, you sons of Zion,
Lend your ears to what God says,
Then respond in full obedience,
Gladly walk in all His ways.

These are times of great refreshing
Coming from the throne in heaven,
Times of building and of shaking,
When God rids His church of leaven.
Not a patching up of wineskins
Or of garments that are old,
But a glorious restoration
Just exactly as foretold.

Reign on, O God victorious,
Fulfil Your promises.
Seed of Abraham, remember
You will see all nations blessed.

Powers of darkness, we remind you
Of Christ's victory on the cross.
Hear the truth we are declaring,
Jesus won and you have lost.

132 Graham Kendrick
Copyright © 1985 Thankyou Music

GOD IS GOOD, *we sing and shout it.*
God is good, we celebrate.
God is good, no more we doubt it.
God is good, we know it's true.

And when I think of His love for me,
My heart fills with praise
And I feel like dancing.
For in His heart there is room for me,
And I run with arms open wide.

(Last time)
We know it's true.
Hey!

133 Ian Smale
Copyright © 1987 Thankyou Music

GOD IS HERE, GOD IS PRESENT,
God is moving by His Spirit;
Can you hear what He is saying,
Are you willing to respond?
God is here, God is present,
God is moving by His Spirit;
Lord, I open up my life to You,
Please do just what You will.

Lord, I won't stop loving You,
You mean more to me than anything else.
Lord, I won't stop loving You,
You mean more to me than life itself.

134 Alex Simons & Freda Kimmey
Copyright © 1977 Celebration/
Kingsway Music

GOD IS OUR FATHER,
For He has made us His own,
Made Jesus our brother
And hand in hand we'll grow together as one.
Sing praise to the Lord with the tambourine,
Sing praise to the Lord with clapping hands,
Sing praise to the Lord with dancing feet,
Sing praise to the Lord with our voice.

La, la, la ... *(etc.)*

135 Arthur C. Ainger (1841–1919)

GOD IS WORKING HIS PURPOSE OUT,
As year succeeds to year;
God is working His purpose out,
And the time is drawing near;
Nearer and nearer draws the time,
The time that shall surely be,
When the earth shall be filled
With the glory of God,
As the waters cover the sea.

From utmost East to utmost West,
Where'er man's foot hath trod,
By the mouth of many messengers
Goes forth the voice of God;
Give ear to Me, ye continents,
Ye isles, give ear to Me,
That the earth may be filled
With the glory of God,
As the waters cover the sea.

March we forth in the strength of God
With the banner of Christ unfurled,
That the light of the glorious gospel of truth
May shine throughout the world:
Fight we the fight with sorrow and sin,
To set their captives free,
That the earth may be filled
With the glory of God,
As the waters cover the sea.

All we can do is nothing worth,
Unless God blesses the deed;
Vainly we hope for the harvest-tide
Till God gives life to the seed;
Yet nearer and nearer draws the time,
The time that shall surely be,
When the earth shall be filled
With the glory of God,
As the waters cover the sea.

136 John Wimber
Copyright © 1988 Mercy/Vineyard
Publishing/Adm. by CopyCare

GOD OF ALL COMFORT,
God of all grace,
Oh, we have come to seek You,
We have come to seek Your face.

Because You have called us,
We're gathered in this place.
Oh, we have come to seek You,
We have come to seek Your face.

137 David Fellingham
Copyright © 1982 Thankyou Music

GOD OF GLORY, we exalt Your name,
You who reign in majesty.
We lift our hearts to You
And we will worship, praise and magnify
Your holy name.

In power resplendent
You reign in glory,
Eternal King, You reign for ever.
Your word is mighty,
Releasing captives,
Your love is gracious,
You are my God.

138 Chris Bowater
Copyright © 1990 Sovereign
Lifestyle Music

GOD OF GRACE, I turn my face
To You, I cannot hide;
My nakedness, my shame, my guilt,
Are all before Your eyes.

Strivings and all anguished dreams
In rags lie at my feet,
And only grace provides the way
For me to stand complete.

And Your grace clothes me in
    righteousness,
And Your mercy covers me in love.
Your life adorns and beautifies,
I stand complete in You.

139 Harry E. Fosdick (1878–1969)
Copyright control

GOD OF GRACE AND GOD OF GLORY,
On Thy people pour Thy power;
Crown Thine ancient church's story;
Bring her bud to glorious flower.
Grant us wisdom,
Grant us courage,
For the facing of this hour.

Lo! the hosts of evil round us
Scorn Thy Christ, assail His ways!
Fears and doubts too long have bound us;
Free our hearts to work and praise.
Grant us wisdom,
Grant us courage,
For the living of these days.

Heal Thy children's warring madness;
Bend our pride to Thy control;
Shame our wanton, selfish gladness,
Rich in things and poor in soul.
Grant us wisdom,
Grant us courage,
Lest we miss Thy kingdom's goal.

Set our feet on lofty places;
Gird our lives that they may be
Armoured with all Christlike graces
In the fight to set men free.
Grant us wisdom,
Grant us courage,
That we fail not man nor Thee.

Save us from weak resignation
To the evils we deplore;
Let the search for Thy salvation
Be our glory ever more.
Grant us wisdom,
Grant us courage,
Serving Thee whom we adore.

140
John M. Neale (1818–66) altd

GOOD CHRISTIAN MEN, REJOICE
With heart and soul and voice;
Give ye heed to what we say,
Jesus Christ is born today;
Ox and ass before Him bow,
And He is in the manger now.
Christ is born today;
Christ is born today!

Good Christian men, rejoice
With heart and soul and voice;
Now ye hear of endless bliss,
Jesus Christ was born for this:
He hath opened heaven's door
And man is blessed for evermore.
Christ was born for this;
Christ was born for this!

Good Christian men, rejoice
With heart and soul and voice;
Now ye need not fear the grave,
Jesus Christ was born to save:
Calls you one and calls you all
To gain His everlasting hall.
Christ was born to save;
Christ was born to save!

141
Bob Pitcher
Copyright © 1980 Thankyou Music

GREAT AND MARVELLOUS are Thy works,
O Lord God the Almighty.
Righteous and true are Thy ways,
O Thou King of the nations.
Who will not fear, O Lord,
And glorify Thy name?
For Thou alone art holy,
And all the nations will come before Thee
And worship, worship, worship before Thee,
And worship, worship, worship before Thee.

142
Kevin Prosch
Copyright © 1989 Mercy/Vineyard
Publishing/Adm. by CopyCare

**GREAT AND MARVELLOUS ARE THY
    WORKS,**
Lord God Almighty;
Just and true are Thy ways, O Lord,
For You are the King of saints.

Who shall not fear Thee,
Who shall not glorify Thy name, O Lord?
For only Thou art holy.
All the nations shall come and worship
    before Thee,
For Thy judgements are made manifest.
For Thy judgements are made manifest.

Hallelujah, (hallelujah)
Hallelujah to the King of saints.
Glory hallelujah, (glory hallelujah)
Glory hallelujah to the King of saints.

143
Stuart Dauermann
Copyright © 1972 Lillenas Publishing Co./
Adm. by CopyCare

GREAT AND WONDERFUL are Thy wondrous
    deeds,
O Lord God the Almighty.
Just and true are all Thy ways, O Lord,
King of the ages art Thou.
Who shall not fear and glorify
Thy name, O Lord?
For Thou alone art holy,
Thou alone.
All the nations shall come and worship Thee,
For Thy glory shall be revealed.
Hallelujah, hallelujah, hallelujah, Amen.

Lai, lai, lai … *(etc.)*

144

GREAT IS THE LORD and greatly to be
    praised,
In the city of our God,
In the mountain of His holiness.
Beautiful for situation, the joy of the whole
    earth
Is Mount Zion on the sides of the north,
The city of the great King,
Is Mount Zion on the sides of the north,
The city of the great King.

One body, one Spirit, one faith, one Lord,
One people, one nation, praise ye the Lord.

145

GREAT IS THE LORD and most worthy of
    praise,
The city of our God, the holy place,
The joy of the whole earth.
Great is the Lord in whom we have the
    victory,
He aids us against the enemy,
We bow down on our knees.

    And Lord, we want to lift Your name on
        high,
    And Lord, we want to thank You,
    For the works You've done in our lives;
    And Lord, we trust in Your unfailing love,
    For You alone are God eternal,
    Throughout earth and heaven above.

146

GREAT IS THE LORD AND MIGHTY IN
    POWER,
His understanding has no limit;
The Lord delights in those who fear Him,
Who put their hope in His unfailing love.

He strengthens the bars of your gates,
He grants you peace in your borders,
He reveals His word to His people;
He has done this for no other nation.

Great is the Lord and mighty in power,
His understanding has no limit;
Extol the Lord, O Jerusalem,
Praise your God, O people of Zion.

147

GREAT IS THY FAITHFULNESS, O God my
    Father,
There is no shadow of turning with Thee;
Thou changest not, Thy compassions, they
    fail not;
As Thou hast been Thou for ever wilt be.

    Great is Thy faithfulness!
    Great is Thy faithfulness!
    Morning by morning new mercies I see;
    All I have needed Thy hand hath provided,
    Great is Thy faithfulness, Lord, unto me!

Summer and winter, and springtime and
    harvest,
Sun, moon and stars in their courses above,
Join with all nature in manifold witness
To Thy great faithfulness, mercy and love.

Pardon for sin and a peace that endureth,
Thine own dear presence to cheer and to
    guide;
Strength for today and bright hope for
    tomorrow,
Blessings all mine, with ten thousand beside!

148

GUIDE ME, O THOU GREAT JEHOVAH,
Pilgrim through this barren land;
I am weak, but Thou art mighty,
Hold me with Thy powerful hand:
Bread of heaven, Bread of heaven,
Feed me now and ever more,
Feed me now and ever more.

Open Thou the crystal fountain
Whence the healing stream doth flow;
Let the fiery, cloudy pillar
Lead me all my journey through:
Strong Deliverer, strong Deliverer,
Be Thou still my strength and shield,
Be Thou still my strength and shield.

When I tread the verge of Jordan
Bid my anxious fears subside;
Death of death, and hell's destruction,
Land me safe on Canaan's side:
Songs of praises, songs of praises,
I will ever give to Thee,
I will ever give to Thee.

149 John Bakewell (1721–1819)

HAIL, THOU ONCE DESPISÈD JESUS,
Hail, Thou Galilean King!
Thou didst suffer to release us,
Thou didst free salvation bring.
Hail, Thou agonising Saviour,
Bearer of our sin and shame;
By Thy merits we find favour,
Life is given through Thy name.

Paschal Lamb, by God appointed,
All our sins on Thee were laid.
With almighty love anointed
Thou hast full atonement made.
All Thy people are forgiven
Through the virtue of Thy blood:
Opened is the gate of heaven,
Man is reconciled to God.

Jesus, hail! enthroned in glory,
There for ever to abide;
All the heavenly hosts adore Thee,
Seated at Thy Father's side:
There for sinners Thou art pleading,
There Thou dost our place prepare,
Ever for us interceding,
Till in glory we appear.

Worship, honour, power, and blessing
Thou art worthy to receive:
Loudest praises, without ceasing,
Right it is for us to give:
Come, O mighty Holy Spirit,
As our hearts and hands we raise,
Help us sing our Saviour's merits,
Help us sing Immanuel's praise.

150 James Montgomery (1771–1854)

HAIL TO THE LORD'S ANOINTED,
Great David's greater Son!
Hail, in the time appointed,
His reign on earth begun!
He comes to break oppression,
To set the captive free,
To take away transgression,
And rule in equity.

He comes, with succour speedy,
To those who suffer wrong;
To help the poor and needy,
And bid the weak be strong;
To give them songs for sighing,
Their darkness turn to light,
Whose souls, condemned and dying,
Were precious in His sight.

He shall come down like showers
Upon the fruitful earth;
Love, joy and hope, like flowers,
Spring in His path to birth;
Before Him, on the mountains,
Shall peace, the herald, go;
And righteousness, in fountains,
From hill to valley flow.

Kings shall fall down before Him,
And gold and incense bring;
All nations shall adore Him,
His praise all people sing;
To Him shall prayer unceasing
And daily vows ascend,
His kingdom still increasing,
A kingdom without end.

O'er every foe victorious,
He on His throne shall rest;
From age to age more glorious,
All-blessing and all-blessed.
The tide of time shall never
His covenant remove;
His name shall stand for ever,
His changeless name of Love.

151 Dale Garrett
Copyright © 1972 Scripture in Song
(a div. of Integrity Music, Inc.)/
Sovereign Music UK

HALLELUJAH, FOR THE LORD OUR GOD
The Almighty reigns.
Hallelujah, for the Lord our God
The Almighty reigns.
Let us rejoice and be glad
And give the glory unto Him.
Hallelujah, for the Lord our God
The Almighty reigns.

152 Tim Cullen
Copyright © 1975 Celebration/
Kingsway Music

HALLELUJAH, MY FATHER,
For giving us Your Son;
Sending Him into the world,
To be given up for men.
Knowing we would bruise Him
And smite Him from the earth.
Hallelujah, my Father,
In His death is my birth;
Hallelujah, my Father,
In His life is my life.

153 William C. Dix (1837–98)

HALLELUJAH! SING TO JESUS;
His the sceptre, His the throne;
Hallelujah! His the triumph,
His the victory alone.
Hark, the songs of holy Zion
Thunder like a mighty flood:
'Jesus out of every nation
Hath redeemed us by His blood.'

Hallelujah! not as orphans
Are we left in sorrow now;
Hallelujah! He is near us,
Faith believes, nor questions how.
Though the clouds from sight received
    Him
When the forty days were o'er,
Shall our hearts forget His promise,
'I am with you ever more'?

Hallelujah! Bread of heaven,
Thou on earth our food, our stay;
Hallelujah! here the sinful
Flee to Thee from day to day.
Intercessor, Friend of sinners,
Earth's Redeemer, plead for me
Where the songs of all the sinless
Sweep across the crystal sea.

Hallelujah! sing to Jesus;
His the sceptre, His the throne;
Hallelujah! His the triumph,
His the victory alone.
Hark, the songs of holy Zion
Thunder like a mighty flood:
'Jesus out of every nation
Hath redeemed us by His blood.'

154 Philip Doddridge (1702–51) altd

HARK THE GLAD SOUND! The Saviour
    comes,
The Saviour promised long;
Let every heart prepare a throne,
And every voice a song.

He comes the prisoners to release,
In Satan's bondage held;
The gates of brass before Him burst,
The iron fetters yield.

He comes the broken heart to bind,
The bleeding soul to cure,
And with the treasures of His grace
To enrich the humble poor.

Our glad hosannas, Prince of Peace,
Thy welcome shall proclaim;
And heaven's eternal arches ring
With Thy belovèd name.

155 Charles Wesley (1707–88) altd

HARK! THE HERALD ANGELS SING:
'Glory to the new-born King!
Peace on earth, and mercy mild,
God and sinners reconciled!'
Joyful, all ye nations rise,
Join the triumph of the skies,
With the angelic host proclaim,
'Christ is born in Bethlehem.'
Hark! the herald angels sing:
'Glory to the new-born King!'

Christ, by highest heaven adored,
Christ, the everlasting Lord,
Late in time behold Him come,
Offspring of a virgin's womb.
Veiled in flesh the Godhead see!
Hail the incarnate Deity!
Pleased as man with man to dwell,
Jesus, our Immanuel.
Hark! the herald angels sing:
'Glory to the new-born King.'

Hail the heaven-born Prince of Peace!
Hail, the Sun of righteousness!
Light and life to all He brings,
Risen with healing in His wings,
Mild, He lays His glory by;
Born that men no more may die;
Born to raise the sons of earth;
Born to give them second birth.
Hark! the herald angels sing:
'Glory to the new-born King.'

156 A. A. Pollard (1862–1934)
Copyright control

HAVE THINE OWN WAY, LORD,
Have Thine own way;
Thou art the Potter,
I am the clay.
Mould me and make me,
After Thy will,
While I am waiting
Yielded and still.

Have Thine own way, Lord,
Have Thine own way;
Search me and try me,
Master today.
Whiter than snow, Lord,
Wash me just now,
As in Thy presence
Humbly I bow.

Have Thine own way, Lord,
Have Thine own way;
Wounded and weary,
Help me, I pray.
Power, all power,
Surely is Thine;
Touch me and heal me,
Saviour divine.

Have Thine own way, Lord,
Have Thine own way;
Hold o'er my being
Absolute sway.
Fill with Thy Spirit
Till all shall see
Christ only, always,
Living in me.

157 Dave Bilbrough
Copyright © 1990 Thankyou Music

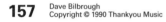

HEALING GRACE, healing grace,
Show me more of Your healing grace.
Fill my life anew as I worship You,
For Your healing grace to me.

My eyes have been opened,
And now I can see
The love of the Father
Given to me.

My Saviour, Deliverer,
The reason I sing,
To You I surrender,
For You are my King.

158 Graham Kendrick
Copyright © 1989 Make Way Music

HEAR, O LORD, OUR CRY,
Revive us, revive us again.
For the sake of Your glory,
Revive us, revive us again.
Lord, hear our cry.
Lord, hear our cry.

Hear, O Lord, our cry,
Revive us, revive us again.
For the sake of the children,
Revive us, revive us again.
Lord, hear our cry.
Lord, hear our cry.

159 David Fellingham
Copyright © 1988 Thankyou Music

HEAR, O SHEPHERD of Your people,
Let Your face shine and we will be saved.
Shine forth, O God, in this pagan darkness.
Awaken Your power, and come to restore.

O Lord of hosts, turn again now,
Make Your church strong to speak out
Your word.
We'll not turn back from our great
commission
To reach the lost and save this land.

Let Your power fall upon us,
Give strength unto the sons of Your right hand.
We now hear the call to seek You,
Awaken Your power, and come to restore.

160 Author unknown
Copyright control

HEAVENLY FATHER, I APPRECIATE YOU.
Heavenly Father, I appreciate You.
I love You, adore You,
I bow down before You.
Heavenly Father, I appreciate You.

Son of God, what a wonder You are.
Son of God, what a wonder You are.
You cleansed my soul from sin,
You set the Holy Ghost within.
Son of God, what a wonder You are.

Holy Ghost, what a comfort You are.
Holy Ghost, what a comfort You are.
You lead us, You guide us,
You live right inside us.
Holy Ghost, what a comfort You are.

161 John Pantry
Copyright © 1990 Thankyou Music

HE CAME TO EARTH, not to be served,
But gave His life to be a ransom for many;
The Son of God, the Son of man,
He shared our pain and bore our sins in His
body.

King of kings and Lord of lords,
I lift my voice in praise;
Such amazing love, but I do believe
This King has died for me.

And so I stand, a broken soul,
To see the pain that I have brought to Jesus;
And yet each heart will be consoled,
To be made new, the joy of all believers.

And from now on, through all my days,
I vow to live each moment here for Jesus;
Not looking back, but giving praise
For all my Lord has done for this believer.

162 Robert Whitney Manzano
Copyright © 1984 Thankyou Music

HE GAVE ME BEAUTY for ashes,
The oil of joy for mourning,
The garment of praise
For the spirit of heaviness.
That we might be trees of righteousness,
The planting of the Lord,
That He might be glorified.

163 Joan Parsons
Copyright © 1978 Thankyou Music

HE HOLDS THE KEY to salvation,
Jesus is over all.
He is the Lord of creation:

Allelu, alleluia.
Allelu, alleluia, Lord.

He is the Rock ever standing,
No man could break Him down.
He is the Truth everlasting:

He is a Light in the darkness,
All men shall see His face.
He breaks all chains to redeem us:

All power to Him who is mighty,
All praise to Him who is God.
All glory now and for ever:

164 Twila Paris
Copyright © 1985 Straightway Music/
Mountain Spring Music/EMI Christian Music
Publishing/Adm. by CopyCare

HE IS EXALTED,
The King is exalted on high,
I will praise Him.
He is exalted,
Forever exalted
And I will praise His name!

He is the Lord,
Forever His truth shall reign.
Heaven and earth
Rejoice in His holy name.
He is exalted,
The King is exalted on high!

165 Author unknown.
Copyright control

HE IS LORD, He is Lord,
He is risen from the dead
And He is Lord.
Every knee shall bow,
Every tongue confess
That Jesus Christ is Lord.

166 Kandela Groves
Copyright © 1975 CCCM Music/
Maranatha! Music/Adm. by CopyCare

HE IS OUR PEACE,
Who has broken down every wall;
He is our peace,
He is our peace.
He is our peace,
Who has broken down every wall;
He is our peace,
He is our peace.

Cast all your cares on Him,
For He cares for you;
He is our peace,
He is our peace.
Cast all your cares on Him,
For He cares for you;
He is our peace,
He is our peace.

167 Chris Bowater
Copyright © 1981 Sovereign Lifestyle Music

HERE I AM, *wholly available;*
As for me, I will serve the Lord.
Here I am, wholly available;
As for me, I will serve the Lord.

The fields are white unto harvest,
But O, the labourers are so few;
So Lord, I give myself to help the reaping,
To gather precious souls unto You.

The time is right in the nation
For works of power and authority;
God's looking for a people who are willing
To be counted in His glorious victory.

As salt are we ready to savour?
In darkness are we ready to be light?
God's seeking out a very special people
To manifest His truth and His might.

168 William Rees (1802–83)

HERE IS LOVE vast as the ocean,
Loving kindness as the flood,
When the Prince of life, our ransom
Shed for us His precious blood.
Who His love will not remember?
Who can cease to sing His praise?
He can never be forgotten
Throughout heaven's eternal days.

On the Mount of Crucifixion
Fountains opened deep and wide;
Through the floodgates of God's mercy
Flowed a vast and gracious tide.
Grace and love, like mighty rivers,
Poured incessant from above,
And heaven's peace and perfect justice
Kissed a guilty world in love.

169 Steve Hampton
Copyright © 1983 Scripture in Song
(a div. of Integrity Music, Inc.)/
Sovereign Music UK

HERE WE ARE,
Gathered together as a family;
Bound as one,
Lifting up our voices
To the King of kings.
We cry:

Abba, Father, worthy is Your name.
Abba, Father, worthy is Your name.

Here we are,
Singing together as a family;
Bound as one,
Lifting up our voices
To the King of kings.
We sing:

Abba, Father, holy is Your name.
Abba, Father, holy is Your name.

170 John Watson & Stuart Townend
Copyright © 1991 Ampelos Music/
Adm. by CopyCare & Thankyou Music

HE SHALL REIGN as King of kings,
He shall reign as Lord of lords;
Messiah God, the living Word,
Hallelujah, hallelujah,
Let earth declare Him King!

171 Graham Kendrick
Copyright © 1986 Thankyou Music

HE THAT IS IN US *is greater than he*
That is in the world.
He that is in us is greater than he
That is in the world.

Therefore I will sing and I will rejoice
For His Spirit lives in me.
Christ the Living One has overcome
And we share in His victory.

All the powers of death and hell and sin
Lie crushed beneath His feet;
Jesus owns the Name above all names,
Crowned with honour and majesty.

172 Graham Kendrick
Copyright © 1988 Make Way Music

HE WALKED WHERE I WALK,   *(echo*
He stood where I stand,   *(echo*
He felt what I feel,   *(echo*
He understands.   *(echo*
He knows my frailty,   *(echo*
Shared my humanity,   *(echo*
Tempted in every way,   *(echo*
Yet without sin.   *(echo*

God with us, so close to us.   *(all*
God with us, Immanuel!
(Repeat)

One of a hated race,   *(echo*
Stung by the prejudice,   *(echo*
Suffering injustice,   *(echo*
Yet He forgives.   *(echo*
Wept for my wasted years,   *(echo*
Paid for my wickedness,   *(echo*
He died in my place   *(echo*
That I might live.   *(echo*

173 Maggi Dawn
Copyright © 1987 Thankyou Music

HE WAS PIERCED for our transgressions,
And bruised for our iniquities;
And to bring us peace He was punished,
And by His stripes we are healed.

He was led like a lamb to the slaughter,
Although He was innocent of crime;
And cut off from the land of the living,
He paid for the guilt that was mine.

We like sheep have gone astray,
Turned each one to his own way,
And the Lord has laid on Him
The iniquity of us all.

(Descant)
Like a lamb, like a lamb
To the slaughter He came.
And the Lord laid on Him
The iniquity of us all.

174 John Bunyan (1628–88) and others

HE WHO WOULD VALIANT BE
'Gainst all disaster,
Let him in constancy
Follow the Master.
There's no discouragement
Shall make him once relent
His first avowed intent
To be a pilgrim.

Who so beset him round
With dismal stories,
Do but themselves confound—
His strength the more is.
No foes shall stay his might,
Though he with giants fight;
He will make good his right
To be a pilgrim.

Since, Lord, Thou dost defend
Us with Thy Spirit,
We know we at the end
Shall life inherit.
Then fancies flee away!
I'll fear not what men say,
I'll labour night and day
To be a pilgrim.

175 Isaac Belinda
Copyright © 1990 Integrity's Hosanna! Music/
Sovereign Music UK

HIGHER, HIGHER,
Higher, higher, higher,
Higher, higher, lift up Jesus higher.
Higher, higher,
Higher, higher, higher,
Higher, higher, lift up Jesus higher.

Lower, lower,
Lower, lower, lower,
Lower, lower, lower Satan lower.
Lower, lower,
Lower, lower, lower,
Lower, lower, lower Satan lower.

Cast your burdens onto Jesus,
He cares for you.
Cast your burdens onto Jesus,
He cares for you.

176 Author unknown
Copyright control

HIS NAME IS HIGHER than any other,
His name is Jesus, His name is Lord.
His name is Wonderful,
His name is Counsellor,
His name is Prince of Peace,
The mighty God.
His name is higher than any other,
His name is Jesus, His name is Lord.

177 Audrey Mieir
Copyright © 1959, Renewed 1987
Manna Music/Kingsway Music

HIS NAME IS WONDERFUL,
His name is Wonderful,
His name is Wonderful,
Jesus my Lord.
He is the mighty King,
Master of everything,
His name is Wonderful,
Jesus my Lord.

He's the great Shepherd,
The Rock of all ages,
Almighty God is He.
Bow down before Him,
Love and adore Him,
His name is Wonderful,
Jesus my Lord.

178 Bill Anderson
Copyright © 1985 Thankyou Music

HIS VOICE IS THE SEA
And the sounding of the trumpets;
And the calling of the Shepherd is so sweet.
His face is the sun,
Brighter than the morning;
And all creation bows down at His feet.

Jesus is Lord, and all the earth adores
Him.
Jesus is Lord, He sits upon the throne.
When all men stand before Him,
Then every knee shall bow,
And every tongue cry 'Jesus is Lord.'

His mouth is a sword
That rules o'er the nations,
And His sword will draw His children to His
side.
His eyes are a fire
That burns throughout the kingdom,
And the burning purifies the Master's bride.

179 Danny Daniels
Copyright © 1982 Mercy/Vineyard
Publishing/Adm. by CopyCare

(Men and women in canon)
HOLD ME LORD, in Your arms,
Fill me Lord, with Your Spirit.
Touch my heart with Your love,
Let my life
Glorify Your name. *(All)*

Singing, Alleluia,
Singing, Alleluia,
Singing, Alleluia,
Singing, Alleluia.

Alleluia, (Alleluia,)
Allelu, (Allelu,)
Alleluia, (Alleluia,)
Allelu, (Allelu.)

180 Danny Daniels
Copyright © 1989 Mercy/Vineyard
Publishing/Adm. by CopyCare

HOLINESS UNTO THE LORD,
Unto the King.
Holiness unto Your name
I will sing.

> *Holiness unto Jesus,*
> *Holiness unto You, Lord.*
> *Holiness unto Jesus,*
> *Holiness unto You, Lord.*

I love You, I love Your ways,
I love Your name.
I love You, and all my days
I'll proclaim:

181 Andy Park
Copyright © 1989 Mercy/Vineyard
Publishing/Adm. by CopyCare

HOLY, HOLY, HOLY is the Lord God
Almighty.
Holy, holy, holy is the Lord God Almighty.
All the angels cry out holy;
All the angels exalt Your name,
Crying holy, holy, holy,
Holy is the Lord.

Holy, holy, holy is the Lord God Almighty.
Holy, holy, holy is the Lord God Almighty.
All Your people cry out holy;
All Your people exalt Your name,
Crying holy, holy, holy,
Holy is the Lord.

Glory, glory, glory to the Lord God
Almighty.
Glory, glory, glory to the Lord God
Almighty.
The whole earth is filled with Your glory;
The whole earth will exalt Your name,
Crying holy, holy, holy,
Holy is the Lord.

182 Author unknown
Copyright control

HOLY, HOLY, HOLY IS THE LORD,
Holy is the Lord God Almighty.
Holy, holy, holy is the Lord,
Holy is the Lord God Almighty,
Who was and is and is to come,
Holy, holy, holy is the Lord.

Worthy, worthy, worthy is ... *(etc.)*

Jesus, Jesus, Jesus is ... *(etc.)*

Glory, glory, glory to ... *(etc.)*

183 Reginald Heber (1783–1826)

HOLY, HOLY, HOLY, LORD GOD ALMIGHTY!
Early in the morning
Our song shall rise to Thee:
Holy, holy, holy, merciful and mighty,
God in three Persons, blessèd Trinity!

Holy, holy, holy! all the saints adore Thee,
Casting down their golden crowns
Around the glassy sea;
Cherubim and seraphim falling down before
Thee,
Who were, and are, and ever more shall be.

Holy, holy, holy! though the darkness hide
Thee,
Though the eye of sinful man
Thy glory may not see;
Only Thou art holy, there is none beside
Thee,
Perfect in power, in love and purity.

Holy, holy, holy, Lord God Almighty!
All Thy works shall praise Thy name
In earth, and sky, and sea;
Holy, holy, holy, merciful and mighty,
God in three Persons, blessèd Trinity!

184 Peter Scholtes
Copyright © 1966 F.E.L. Publications/
Lorenz Corporation/Adm. by CopyCare

HOLY, HOLY, HOLY LORD,
God of power and might,
Heaven and earth are filled with Your glory.
Holy, holy, holy Lord,
God of power and might,
Heaven and earth are filled with Your glory.
Hosanna, hosanna in the highest!
Hosanna, hosanna in the highest!

185 Kelly Green
Copyright © 1982 Mercy/Vineyard
Publishing/Adm. by CopyCare

(Men and women in canon)
HOLY IS THE LORD,
Holy is the Lord.
Holy is the Lord.
Righteousness and mercy,
Judgement and grace.
Faithfulness and sovereignty;
Holy is the Lord,
Holy is the Lord.

186 Chris Bowater
Copyright © 1991 Sovereign Lifestyle Music

HOLY ONE, Holy One,
Blessèd be the Holy One,
Almighty ever-living God,
worship only You.

(Last time)
Holy One.

187 Alun Leppitt
Copyright © 1991 Thankyou Music

HOLY SPIRIT, LEAD ME TO MY FATHER,
To bow before Him, and worship at His throne,
For He's my refuge, my strength and
deliverer,
I will dwell in the shadow of Almighty God.

188 Chris Bowater
Copyright © 1986 Sovereign Lifestyle Music

HOLY SPIRIT, WE WELCOME YOU.
Holy Spirit, we welcome You.
Move among us with holy fire,
As we lay aside all earthly desires,
Hands reach out and our hearts aspire.
Holy Spirit, Holy Spirit,
Holy Spirit, we welcome You.

Holy Spirit, we welcome You.
Holy Spirit, we welcome You.
Let the breeze of Your presence blow,
That Your children here might truly know
How to move in the Spirit's flow.
Holy Spirit, Holy Spirit,
Holy Spirit, we welcome You.

Holy Spirit, we welcome You.
Holy Spirit, we welcome You.
Please accomplish in me today
Some new work of loving grace, I pray;
Unreservedly have Your way.
Holy Spirit, Holy Spirit,
Holy Spirit, we welcome You.

189 Carl Tuttle
Copyright © 1985 Mercy/Vineyard
Publishing/Adm. by CopyCare

HOSANNA, hosanna, hosanna in the
highest.
Hosanna, hosanna, hosanna in the highest.
Lord we lift up Your name, with hearts full of
praise,
Be exalted, O Lord, my God,
Hosanna in the highest.

Glory, glory, glory to the King of kings.
Glory, glory, glory to the King of kings.
Lord, we lift up Your name, with hearts full of
praise,
Be exalted, O Lord, my God,
Glory to the King of kings.

190 Keith Green & Melody Green
Copyright © 1982 BMG Songs Inc./Birdwing Music/
Ears to Hear/EMI Christian Music Publishing/
Adm. by CopyCare

HOW I LOVE YOU,
You are the One,
You are the One.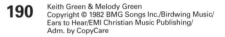
How I love You,
You are the One for me.

I was so lost,
But You showed the way,
'Cause You are the Way.
I was so lost,
But You showed the way to me!

I was lied to,
But You told the truth,
'Cause You are the Truth.
I was lied to,
But You showed the truth to me!

I was dying,
But You gave me life,
'Cause You are the Life.
I was dying,
And You gave Your life for me!

How I love You,
You are the One,
You are the One.
How I love You,
You are the One,
God's risen Son.
You are the One for me!

Hallelujah!
You are the One,
You are the One.
Hallelujah!
You are the One for me!

191 Author unknown
Copyright control

HOW LOVELY IS THY DWELLING PLACE,
O Lord of hosts,
My soul longs and yearns for Your courts,
And my heart and flesh sing for joy
To the living God.
One day in Your presence
Is far better to me than gold,
Or to live my whole life somewhere else;
And I would rather be
A doorkeeper in Your house
Than to take my fate upon myself.
You are my sun and my shield,
You are my lover from the start,
And the highway to Your city
Runs through my heart.

192 Leonard E. Smith Jr
Copyright © 1974 New Jerusalem Music/
Adm. by Kingsway Music

Popular version

HOW LOVELY ON THE MOUNTAINS are the
feet of Him
Who brings good news, good news,
Proclaiming peace, announcing news of
happiness,
Our God reigns, our God reigns.

Our God reigns, our God reigns,
Our God reigns, our God reigns.

You watchmen lift your voices joyfully as
one,
Shout for your King, your King.
See eye to eye the Lord restoring Zion:
Your God reigns, your God reigns!

Waste places of Jerusalem break forth with
joy,
We are redeemed, redeemed.
The Lord has saved and comforted His
people:
Your God reigns, your God reigns!

Ends of the earth, see the salvation of your
God,
Jesus is Lord, is Lord.
Before the nations He has bared His holy
arm:
Your God reigns, your God reigns!

Original version

HOW LOVELY ON THE MOUNTAINS are the
feet of Him
Who brings good news, good news,
Announcing peace, proclaiming news of
happiness,
Saying to Zion: Your God reigns.
Your God reigns, your God reigns,
Your God reigns, your God reigns.

He had no stately form, He had no majesty,
That we should be drawn to Him.
He was despised and we took no account of
Him,
Yet now He reigns with the Most High.
Now He reigns, now He reigns,
Now He reigns with the Most High!

It was our sin and guilt that bruised and
wounded Him,
It was our sin that brought Him down.
When we like sheep had gone astray, our
Shepherd came
And on His shoulders bore our shame.
On His shoulders, on His shoulders,
On His shoulders He bore our shame.

Meek as a lamb that's led out to the
slaughterhouse,
Dumb as a sheep before its shearer,
His life ran down upon the ground like
pouring rain,
That we might be born again.
That we might be, that we might be,
That we might be born again.

Out from the tomb He came with grace and
majesty,
He is alive, He is alive.
God loves us so, see here His hands, His feet
His side,
Yes, we know He is alive.
He is alive, He is alive,
He is alive, He is alive.

How lovely on the mountains are the feet of
Him
Who brings good news, good news,
Announcing peace, proclaiming news of
happiness:
Our God reigns, our God reigns.
Our God reigns, our God reigns,
Our God reigns, our God reigns.

193 Phil Rogers
Copyright © 1982 Thankyou Music

HOW PRECIOUS, O LORD,
Is Your unfailing love,
We find refuge in the shadow of Your wings.
We feast, Lord Jesus, on the abundance of
Your house
And drink from Your river of delights.
With You is the fountain of life,
In Your light we see light.
With You is the fountain of life,
In Your light we see light.

194 John Newton (1725–1807)

**HOW SWEET THE NAME OF JESUS
SOUNDS**
In a believer's ear!
It soothes his sorrows, heals his wounds,
And drives away his fear.

It makes the wounded spirit whole,
And calms the troubled breast;
'Tis manna to the hungry soul,
And to the weary, rest.

Dear name, the rock on which I build,
My shield and hiding place,
My never-failing treasury, filled
With boundless stores of grace!

Jesus! My Shepherd, Saviour, Friend,
My Prophet, Priest and King,
My Lord, my Life, my Way, my End,
Accept the praise I bring.

Weak is the effort of my heart,
And cold my warmest thought;
But when I see Thee as Thou art,
I'll praise Thee as I ought.

Till then I would Thy love proclaim
With every fleeting breath;
And may the music of Thy name
Refresh my soul in death.

195 Chris Welch
Copyright © 1987 Thankyou Music

HOW YOU BLESS OUR LIVES, Lord God!
How You fill our lives, Lord God!
I simply want to say I love You, Lord.
I simply want to say I bless You,
I simply want to say I adore You,
And I want to lift Your name even higher.

196 Graham Kendrick
Copyright © 1985 Thankyou Music

I AM A LIGHTHOUSE, a shining and bright
house,
Out in the waves of a stormy sea.
The oil of the Spirit keeps my lamp burning;
Jesus, my Lord, is the light in me.
And when people see the good things that I
do,
They'll give praises to God who has sent us
Jesus.
We'll send out a lifeboat of love and
forgiveness
And give them a hand to get in.
(Repeat)

While the storm is raging, whoosh, whoosh,
And the wind is blowing, ooo, ooo,
And the waves are crashing,
Crash! crash! crash! crash!

197 Dave Bilbrough
Copyright © 1983 Thankyou Music

I AM A NEW CREATION,
No more in condemnation,
Here in the grace of God I stand.
My heart is overflowing,
My love just keeps on growing,
Here in the grace of God I stand.

And I will praise You Lord,
Yes, I will praise You Lord,
And I will sing of all that You have done.

A joy that knows no limit,
A lightness in my spirit,
Here in the grace of God I stand.

198

I AM A WOUNDED SOLDIER but I will not
  leave the fight,
Because the Great Physician is healing me.
So I'm standing in the battle, in the armour of
  His light,
Because His mighty power is real in me.

  I am loved, I am accepted,
  By the Saviour of my soul.
  I am loved, I am accepted
  And my wounds will be made whole.

199

  I AM NOT ASHAMED *to belong to Jesus;*
  I am not afraid to stand my ground,
  For there is no higher cause
  Than working for the King.
  To Him I lift my praise,
  For I am not ashamed.

Whom then shall I fear?
What shall daunt my spirit?
Sure and steadfast, anchored firm to the
  cross,
Standing with my brothers,
Serving God and others.
Though the world may ridicule, I'll still say:

At the King's returning,
Every soul will know Him,
All creation shall bow down to His name;
Brothers all, together
Serving Him for ever,
He who gave His life for me, I will praise:

  (Last chorus)
  We are not ashamed to belong to Jesus,
  We are not afraid to stand our ground,
  For there is no higher cause
  Than working for the King.
  To Him we lift our praise,
  For we are not ashamed.

200

I AM THE BREAD OF LIFE,
He who comes to Me shall not hunger,
He who believes in Me shall not thirst.
No one can come to Me
Unless the Father draw him.

  And I will raise him up,
  And I will raise him up,
  And I will raise him up on the last day.

The bread that I will give
Is My flesh for the life of the world,
And he who eats of this bread,
He shall live for ever,
He shall live for ever.

Unless you eat
Of the flesh of the Son of Man
And drink of His blood,
And drink of His blood,
You shall not have life within you.

I am the resurrection,
I am the life,
He who believes in Me
Even if he die,
He shall live for ever.

Yes, Lord, we believe
That You are the Christ,
The Son of God
Who has come
Into the world.

201

I AM THE GOD THAT HEALETH THEE,
I am the Lord, your healer.
I sent My word and healed your disease,
I am the Lord, your healer.

You are the God that healeth me,
You are the Lord, my healer.
You sent Your word and healed my disease,
You are the Lord, my healer.

202

I AM TRUSTING THEE, LORD JESUS,
Trusting only Thee!
Trusting Thee for full salvation,
Great and free.

I am trusting Thee for pardon,
At Thy feet I bow;
For Thy grace and tender mercy,
Trusting now.

I am trusting Thee for cleansing
In the crimson flood;
Trusting Thee to make me holy,
By Thy blood.

am trusting Thee for power,
Thine can never fail;
Words which Thou Thyself shalt give me
Must prevail.

I am trusting Thee to guide me,
Thou alone shalt lead;
Every day and hour supplying
All my need.

I am trusting Thee, Lord Jesus;
Never let me fall;
I am trusting Thee for ever,
And for all.

203
Marc Nelson
Copyright © 1987 Mercy/Vineyard
Publishing/Adm. by CopyCare

I BELIEVE IN JESUS:
I believe He is the Son of God.
I believe He died and rose again,
I believe He paid for us all.

(Men)   And I believe He's here now,
(Women) I believe that He is here,
(All)   Standing in our midst.
(Men)   Here with the power to heal now,
(Women) With the power to heal,
(All)   And the grace to forgive.

I believe in You, Lord;
I believe You are the Son of God.
I believe You died and rose again,
I believe You paid for us all.

(Men)   And I believe You're here now,
(Women) I believe that You're here,
(All)   Standing in our midst.
(Men)   Here with the power to heal now,
(Women) With the power to heal,
(All)   And the grace to forgive.

204
Peter & Hanneke Jacobs
Copyright © 1985 Maranatha! Praise Inc./
Adm. by CopyCare

I CAN ALMOST SEE Your holiness,
As I look around this place;
With my hands stretched out,
To receive Your love,
I can see You on each face.

Spirit of God, lift me up,
Spirit of God, lift me up,
Fill me again with Your love,
Sweet Spirit of God.
(Repeat)

205   William Y. Fullerton (1857–1932)

I CANNOT TELL why He, whom angels
   worship,
Should set His love upon the sons of men,
Or why, as Shepherd, He should seek the
   wanderers,
To bring them back, they know not how or
   when.
But this I know, that He was born of Mary,
When Bethlehem's manger was His only
   home,
And that He lived at Nazareth and laboured,
And so the Saviour, Saviour of the world, is
   come.

I cannot tell how silently He suffered,
As with His peace He graced this place of
   tears,
Or how His heart upon the cross was
   broken,
The crown of pain to three-and-thirty years.
But this I know, He heals the broken-
   hearted,
And stays our sin, and calms our lurking
   fear,
And lifts the burden from the heavy-laden,
For yet the Saviour, Saviour of the world, is
   here.

I cannot tell how He will win the nations,
How He will claim His earthly heritage,
How satisfy the needs and aspirations
Of east and west, of sinner and of sage.
But this I know, all flesh shall see His glory,
And He shall reap the harvest He has sown,
And some glad day His sun shall shine in
   splendour,
When He the Saviour, Saviour of the world, is
   known.

I cannot tell how all the lands shall worship,
When, at his bidding, every storm is stilled,
Or who can say how great the jubilation
When all the hearts of men with love are
   filled.
But this I know, the skies will thrill with
   rapture,
And myriad, myriad human voices sing,
And earth to heaven, and heaven to earth,
   will answer:
'At last the Saviour, Saviour of the world, is
   King!'

206

Chris Bowater
Copyright © 1981 Sovereign Lifestyle Music

I DELIGHT GREATLY IN THE LORD,
My soul rejoices in my God.
I delight greatly in the Lord,
My soul rejoices in my God.
For He has clothed me with garments of
   salvation,
And arrayed me in a robe of righteousness.
He has clothed me with garments of
   salvation,
And arrayed me in a robe of righteousness.

207

Cecily Feldman
Copyright © 1989 Cecily Feldman/
Kingsway Music

I EXALT YOU,
Just and true are all Your ways.
I exalt You,
And glorify Your name.
(Repeat)

For You are resplendent in Your majesty,
There is no other god beside You;
Magnificent in power and in glory,
You are Jehovah God Almighty.
Holy is the Lord of hosts,
Holy is the Lord.
Holy is the Lord of hosts,
Holy is the Lord!

208

Brian Howard
Copyright © 1975 Mission Hills Music/
Adm. by CopyCare

IF I WERE A BUTTERFLY,
I'd thank You, Lord, for giving me wings.
And if I were a robin in a tree,
I'd thank You, Lord, that I could sing.
And if I were a fish in the sea,
I'd wiggle my tail and I'd giggle with glee;
But I just thank You, Father,
For making me 'me'.

For You gave me a heart
And You gave me a smile,
You gave me Jesus
And You made me Your child,
And I just thank You, Father,
For making me 'me'.

If I were an elephant,
I'd thank You, Lord, by raising my trunk.
And if I were a kangaroo,
You know I'd hop right up to You.
And if I were an octopus,
I'd thank You, Lord, for my fine looks;
But I just thank You, Father,
For making me 'me'.

If I were a wiggily worm,
I'd thank You, Lord, that I could squirm.
And if I were a billy goat,
I'd thank You, Lord, for my strong throat.
And if I were a fuzzy-wuzzy bear,
I'd thank You, Lord, for my fuzzy-wuzzy hair;
But I just thank You, Father,
For making me 'me'.

209

Mick Ray
Copyright © 1978 Thankyou Music

I GET SO EXCITED, LORD,
Every time I realise
I'm forgiven, I'm forgiven.
Jesus, Lord, You've done it all,
You've paid the price:
I'm forgiven, I'm forgiven.

Hallelujah, Lord,
My heart just fills with praise;
My feet start dancing, my hands rise up,
And my lips they bless Your name.
I'm forgiven, I'm forgiven, I'm forgiven.
I'm forgiven, I'm forgiven, I'm forgiven.

Living in Your presence, Lord,
Is life itself:
I'm forgiven, I'm forgiven.
With the past behind, grace for today
And a hope to come,
I'm forgiven, I'm forgiven.

210

Carl Tuttle
Copyright © 1982 Mercy/Vineyard
Publishing/Adm. by CopyCare

I GIVE YOU ALL THE HONOUR
And praise that's due Your name,
For You are the King of glory,
The Creator of all things.

And I worship You,
I give my life to You,
I fall down on my knees.
Yes, I worship You,
I give my life to You,
I fall down on my knees.

As Your Spirit moves upon me now
You meet my deepest need,
And I lift my hands up to Your throne,
Your mercy I've received.

You have broken chains that bound me,
You've set this captive free;
I will lift my voice to praise Your name
For all eternity.

211
Amy Rose
Copyright © 1988 Coronation Music
Publishing/Kingsway Music

GIVE YOU NOW all I have;
give to you My everything.
You have the power inside of you
To overcome all the hosts of darkness.

Go, go into the world,
Tell them I'm alive,
Go into the streets,
Tell them that I live,
Ooh, that I live in you.
Go, go into the world,
Claim it for your King,
Go into the streets,
Dry those people's tears,
Ooh, make the old things new.

212
Mark Altrogge
Copyright © 1986 People of Destiny International/
Word Music/Adm. by CopyCare

I HAVE A DESTINY *I know I shall fulfil,*
I have a destiny in that city on a hill.
I have a destiny and it's not an empty
wish,
For I know I was born for such a time as
this.

Long before the ages You predestined me
To walk in all the works You have prepared
for me.
You've given me a part to play in history
To help prepare a bride for eternity.

I did not choose You but You have chosen
me
And appointed me for bearing fruit
abundantly.
I know You will complete the work begun in
me,
By the power of Your Spirit working mightily.

213
Marc Nelson
Copyright © 1987 Mercy/Vineyard
Publishing/Adm. by CopyCare

I HAVE FOUND such joy in my salvation
Since I gave my heart to You,
I have found the reason I'm living,
So in love, so near to You.

I worship You, my Lord,
With all my life, praise Your name.
I worship You, worship You, my Lord.

Oh my Lord, my life I'm giving,
A living sacrifice to You.
Oh my Lord, the reason I'm living
Is to serve and worship You.

214
Karen Barrie
Copyright © 1973 Karen Barrie

I HAVE MADE A COVENANT with My chosen,
Given My servant My word.
I have made Your name to last for ever,
Built to outlast all time.

I will celebrate Your love for ever, Yahweh,
Age on age my words proclaim Your love.
For I claim that love is built to last for ever,
Founded firm Your faithfulness.

Yahweh, that assembly of those who love
You
Applaud Your marvellous word.
Who in the skies can compare with Yahweh?
Who can rival Him?

Happy the people who learn to acclaim You,
They rejoice in Your light.
You are our glory and You are our courage,
Our hope belongs to You.

I have revealed My chosen servant
And He can rely on Me,
Given Him My love to last for ever,
He shall rise in My name.

He will call to Me, 'My Father, My God!'
For I make Him My firstborn Son.
I cannot take back My given promise,
I've called Him to shine like the sun.

215
Horatius Bonar (1808–89)

I HEARD THE VOICE OF JESUS SAY:
'Come unto Me and rest;
Lay down, thou weary one, lay down
Thy head upon My breast.'
I came to Jesus as I was,
Weary and worn and sad;
I found in Him a resting place,
And He has made me glad.

I heard the voice of Jesus say:
'Behold I freely give
The living water, thirsty one,
Stoop down and drink and live.'
I came to Jesus, and I drank
Of that life-giving stream;
My thirst was quenched, my soul revived,
And now I live in Him.

I heard the voice of Jesus say:
'I am this dark world's light;
Look unto Me, thy morn shall rise,
And all thy day be bright.'
I looked to Jesus, and I found
In Him my Star, my Sun;
And in that light of life I'll walk,
Till travelling days are done.

216

Ronnie Wilson
Copyright © 1979 Thankyou Music

I HEAR THE SOUND OF RUSTLING in the
leaves of the trees,
The Spirit of the Lord has come down on the
earth.
The church that seemed in slumber has now
risen from its knees,
And dry bones are responding with the fruits
of new birth.
Oh, this is now a time for declaration,
The word will go to all men everywhere;
The church is here for healing of the nations,
Behold the day of Jesus drawing near.

*My tongue will be the pen of a ready
writer,
And what the Father gives to me I'll sing;
I only want to be His breath,
I only want to glorify the King.*

And all around the world the body waits
expectantly,
The promise of the Father is now ready to
fall.
The watchmen on the tower all exhort us to
prepare,
And the church responds—a people who will
answer the call.
And this is not a phase which is passing;
It's the start of an age that is to come.
And where is the wise man and the scoffer?
Before the face of Jesus they are dumb.

A body now prepared by God and ready for
war,
The prompting of the Spirit is our word of
command.
We rise, a mighty army, at the bidding of the
Lord,
The devils see and fear, for their time is at
hand.
And children of the Lord hear our
commission
That we should love and serve our God as
one.
The Spirit won't be hindered by division
In the perfect work that Jesus has begun.

217

Dave Moody
Copyright © 1984 C.A. Music/
Music Services/Adm. by CopyCare

**I HEAR THE SOUND OF THE ARMY OF THE
LORD,**
I hear the sound of the army of the Lord.
It's the sound of praise,
It's the sound of war,
The army of the Lord,
The army of the Lord,
The army of the Lord is marching on.

218

Arthur Tannous
Copyright © 1984 Thankyou Music

I JUST WANT TO PRAISE YOU,
Lift my hands and say: 'I love You.'
You are everything to me,
And I exalt Your holy name on high.
I just want to praise You,
Lift my hands and say: 'I love You.'
You are everything to me,
And I exalt Your holy name,
I exalt Your holy name,
I exalt Your holy name on high.

219

Dave Bilbrough
Copyright © 1988 Thankyou Music

I JUST WANT TO PRAISE YOU, I just want to
sing.
I just want to give You, Lord, my everything,
In every situation, in everything I do,
To give You my devotion, for my delight is
You.

*Lord, I lift You high.
Your love will never die.*

220

Daniel W. Whittle (1840–1901)

**I KNOW NOT WHY GOD'S WONDROUS
GRACE**
To me hath been made known;
Nor why, unworthy as I am,
He claimed me for His own.

*But I know whom I have believèd;
And am persuaded that He is able
To keep that which I've committed
Unto Him against that day.*

I know not how this saving faith
To me He did impart;
Or how believing in His word
Wrought peace within my heart.

know not how the Spirit moves,
onvincing men of sin;
evealing Jesus through the word,
reating faith in Him.

know not what of good or ill
ay be reserved for me,
f weary ways or golden days
efore His face I see.

know not when my Lord may come;
know not how, nor where;
I shall pass the vale of death,
r 'meet Him in the air'.

 21

I LIFT MY EYES UP *to the mountains,*
Where does my help come from?
My help comes from You, Maker of
heaven,
Creator of the earth.

, how I need You, Lord,
ou are my only hope;
ou're my only prayer.
o I will wait for You
o come and rescue me,
ome and give me life.

22

LIFT MY HANDS,
aise my voice,
give my heart to You, my Lord,
nd I rejoice.
here are many, many reasons why I do the
things I do,
, but most of all I praise You,
ost of all I praise You,
esus, most of all I praise You because You're
You.

ift my hands,
aise my voice,
give my life to You, my Lord,
nd I rejoice.
here are many, many reasons why I do the
things I do,
, but most of all I love You,
ost of all I love You,
esus, most of all I love You because You're
You.

I lift my hands,
I raise my voice,
I give my love to You, my Lord,
And I rejoice.
There are many, many reasons why I do the
things I do,
O, but most of all I love You,
Most of all I love You,
Jesus, most of all I love You because You're
You.

223

I LIFT MY HANDS *(echo)*
To the coming King, *(echo)*
To the great I AM, *(echo)*
To You I sing, *(echo)*
For You're the One *(echo)*
Who reigns within my heart. *(all)*

And I will serve no foreign god,
Or any other treasure;
You are my heart's desire,
Spirit without measure.
Unto Your name
I will bring my sacrifice.

224

I LIFT MY VOICE to praise Your name,
That through my life I might proclaim
The praises of the One who reigns:
Jesus, my Lord.

Like a mighty flame that burns so bright,
I am a bearer of His light.
No longer I, for He is my life:
Jesus, my Lord.

Jesus, Jesus, alive in me.
Jesus, Jesus, setting me free.

225

I LIVE, I live because He is risen,
I live, I live with power over sin;
I live, I live because He is risen,
I live, I live to worship Him.

Thank You Jesus, thank You Jesus,
Because You're alive,
Because You're alive,
Because You're alive I live.

226 Laurie Klein
Copyright © 1978 House of Mercy Music/
Maranatha! Music/Adm. by CopyCare

I LOVE YOU, LORD, and I lift my voice
To worship You, O my soul rejoice.
Take joy, my King, in what You hear,
May it be a sweet, sweet sound in Your ear.
(Let me)

227 David Fellingham
Copyright © 1984 Thankyou Music

I LOVE YOU, MY LORD,
For giving to me Your great salvation,
Setting me free from sin and death
And the kingdom of Satan's destruction.
There's power in the blood
To cleanse all my sin, I know I'm forgiven;
I'm reigning in life, I'm living by faith,
I'm now united with Christ.

(First part)
I confess with my mouth that Jesus is Lord,
Jesus is Lord, and believe in my heart
He's been raised from the dead.
I confess with my mouth that Jesus is Lord,
Jesus is Lord, and now I have life,
Now I have life by the Spirit of God.

(Second part)
I confess with my mouth that Jesus is Lord,
And believe in my heart
He's been raised from the dead.
I confess with my mouth that Jesus is my Lord,
And now I have life by the Spirit of God.

228 James Gilbert
Copyright © 1977 Bud John Songs/
EMI Christian Music Publishing/
Adm. by CopyCare

I LOVE YOU WITH THE LOVE OF THE LORD,
Yes, I love you with the love of the Lord.
I can see in you the glory of my King,
And I love you with the love of the Lord.

229 Rob Hayward
Copyright © 1985 Thankyou Music

I'M ACCEPTED, I'm forgiven,
I am fathered by the true and living God.
I'm accepted, no condemnation,
I am loved by the true and living God.
There's no guilt or fear as I draw near
To the Saviour and Creator of the world.
There is joy and peace
As I release my worship to You, O Lord.

230 Dave Bilbrough
Copyright © 1977 Thankyou Music

I'M GONNA THANK THE LORD, He set me
   free.
I'm gonna thank the Lord, He set me free,
For my Saviour He redeemed me,
For my Saviour rescued me.
Yes, I'm gonna thank the Lord, He set me
   free.

I'm gonna clap my hands and stamp my feet
   … *(etc.)*

I'm gonna sing and shout aloud for joy …
   (etc.)

I'm gonna raise my hands in victory … *(etc.)*

231 Danny Daniels
Copyright © 1987 Mercy/Vineyard
Publishing/Adm. by CopyCare

I'M IN LOVE WITH YOU,
For You have called me child.
I'm in love with You,
For You have called me child.
You reached out and touched me,
You heard my lonely cry;
I will praise Your name for ever,
And give You all my life.

232 Graham Kendrick
Copyright © 1979 Thankyou Music

IMMANUEL,
God is with us,
Immanuel,
He is here.
Immanuel,
He is among us,
Immanuel,
His kingdom is here.

Wonderful Counsellor, they laughed at His
   wisdom,
The Mighty God on a dusty road.
Everlasting Father, a friend of sinners,
The Prince of Peace in a cattle stall.

He was despised and rejected,
A man of sorrows acquainted with grief.
From Him we turned and hid our faces;
He was despised, Him we did not esteem.

But He was wounded for our transgressions,
He was bruised for our iniquities.
On Him was the punishment that made us
  whole,
And by His stripes we are healed.

He was oppressed, He was afflicted,
And yet He opened not His mouth.
Like a lamb that is led to the slaughter,
Like a sheep before his shearers He did not
  speak.

233 Graham Kendrick
Copyright © 1988 Make Way Music

IMMANUEL, O IMMANUEL,
Bowed in awe I worship at Your feet,
And sing Immanuel, God is with us;
Sharing my humanness, my shame,
Feeling my weaknesses, my pain,
Taking the punishment, the blame,
Immanuel.
And now my words cannot explain,
All that my heart cannot contain,
How great are the glories of Your name,
Immanuel.

234 Walter C. Smith (1824–1908)

IMMORTAL, INVISIBLE, God only wise,
In light inaccessible hid from our eyes,
Most blessèd, most glorious, the Ancient of
  Days,
Almighty, victorious, Thy great name we
  praise.

Unresting, unhasting, and silent as light,
Nor wanting, nor wasting, Thou rulest in
  might;
Thy justice like mountains high soaring
  above
Thy clouds which are fountains of goodness
  and love.

To all life Thou givest, to both great and
  small;
In all life Thou livest, the true life of all;
We blossom and flourish as leaves on the
  tree,
And wither and perish; but naught changeth
  Thee.

Great Father of glory, pure Father of light,
Thine angels adore Thee, all veiling their
  sight;
All laud we would render: O help us to see
'Tis only the splendour of light hideth Thee.

Immortal, invisible, God only wise,
In light inaccessible hid from our eyes,
Most blessèd, most glorious, the Ancient of
  Days,
Almighty, victorious, Thy great name we
  praise.

235 Diane Davis Andrew
Copyright © 1971 Celebration/
Kingsway Music

I'M NOT ALONE *for my Father is with me,*
With me wherever I go.
Speaking words of faith, of courage and of
  love,
He's with me, He loves me, wherever I go.

Waking in the morning,
Getting ready for school,
Walking down the road;
In class, at work, or at play,
He's with me, He loves me, wherever I go.

And when I find myself in a mess,
I can trust in Him;
Call on His name and watch Him move,
He's with me, He loves me, wherever I go.

All of my life, everywhere that I go,
I will walk with Him;
Praising Him and blessing His name,
He's with me, He loves me, wherever I go.

236 Graham Kendrick
Copyright © 1986 Thankyou Music

I'M SPECIAL because God has loved me,
For He gave the best thing that He had to
  save me;
His own Son Jesus, crucified to take the
  blame
For all the bad things I have done.
Thank You Jesus, thank You Lord,
For loving me so much.
I know I don't deserve anything.
Help me feel Your love right now,
To know deep in my heart
That I'm Your special friend.

237 Jamie Owens-Collins
Copyright © 1984 Fairhill Music/
Adm. by CopyCare

IN HEAVENLY ARMOUR we'll enter the land,
The battle belongs to the Lord.
No weapon that's fashioned against us will
  stand,
The battle belongs to the Lord.

And we sing glory, honour,
Power and strength to the Lord.
We sing glory, honour,
Power and strength to the Lord.

When the power of darkness comes in like a
   flood,
The battle belongs to the Lord.
He's raised up a standard, the power of His
   blood,
The battle belongs to the Lord.

When your enemy presses in hard, do not
   fear,
The battle belongs to the Lord.
Take courage, my friend, your redemption is
   near.
The battle belongs to the Lord.

238   Anna L. Waring (1820–1910)

IN HEAVENLY LOVE ABIDING,
No change my heart shall fear;
And safe is such confiding,
For nothing changes here:
The storm may roar without me,
My heart may low be laid;
But God is round about me,
And can I be dismayed?

Wherever He may guide me,
No want shall turn me back;
My Shepherd is beside me,
And nothing can I lack:
His wisdom ever waketh,
His sight is never dim;
He knows the way He taketh,
And I will walk with Him.

Green pastures are before me,
Which yet I have not seen;
Bright skies will soon be o'er me,
Where darkest clouds have been;
My hope I cannot measure,
My path to life is free;
My Saviour has my treasure,
And He will walk with me.

**239**   Randy Speir
Copyright © 1986 Integrity's Hosanna! Music/
Sovereign Music UK

IN HIM WE LIVE AND MOVE
And have our being,
In Him we live and move
And have our being.

Make a joyful noise,
Sing unto the Lord,
Tell Him of your love,
Dance before Him.
Make a joyful noise,
Sing unto the Lord,
Tell Him of your love:
Hallelujah!

240   David Fellingham
Copyright © 1990 Thankyou Music

IN MAJESTY HE COMES,
The Lamb who once was slain;
Riding in majesty, faithful and true,
Eyes ablaze, crowns on His head,
Robe dipped in blood from His suffering,
He is the Word of God,
Coming again, King of kings.

> *We shall rise,*
> *We shall meet Him in the air*
> *When He comes again,*
> *And we will worship Him, worship Him,*
> *Give Him praise for evermore,*
> *King of kings and Lord of lords.*

241   David Graham
Copyright © 1980 C.A. Music/
Music Services/Adm. by CopyCare

IN MOMENTS LIKE THESE I sing out a song,
I sing out a love song to Jesus.
In moments like these I lift up my hands,
I lift up my hands to the Lord.

> *Singing, I love You, Lord,*
> *Singing, I love You, Lord,*
> *Singing, I love You, Lord,*
> *I love You.*

242   Bob Kilpatrick
Copyright © 1978 Bob Kilpatrick Music/
Lorenz Publishing Co./Adm. by CopyCare

IN MY LIFE, LORD, be glorified, be glorified.
In my life, Lord, be glorified today.

In Your church, Lord, be glorified, be
   glorified.
In Your church, Lord, be glorified today.

IN THE BLEAK MIDWINTER,
Frosty wind made moan;
Earth stood hard as iron,
Water like a stone.
Snow had fallen, snow on snow,
Snow on snow;
In the bleak midwinter,
Long ago.

Our God, heaven cannot hold Him,
Nor earth sustain,
Heaven and earth shall flee away
When He comes to reign.
In the bleak midwinter
A stable-place sufficed
The Lord God Almighty,
Jesus Christ.

Angels and archangels
May have gathered there,
Cherubim and seraphim
Thronged the air.
But His mother only,
In her maiden bliss,
Worshipped the Belovèd
With a kiss.

What can I give Him,
Poor as I am?
If I were a shepherd,
I would bring a lamb.
If I were a wise man,
I would do my part;
Yet what can I give Him—
Give my heart.

244 Brent Chambers
Copyright © 1977 Scripture in Song
(a div. of Integrity Music, Inc.)/
Sovereign Music UK

IN THE PRESENCE OF YOUR PEOPLE
I will praise Your name,
For alone You are holy,
Enthroned in the praises of Israel.
Let us celebrate Your goodness
And Your steadfast love,
May Your name be exalted
Here on earth and in heaven above.

Lai, lai, lai-lai-lai-lai-lai-lai … *(etc.)*

245 Graham Kendrick
Copyright © 1986 Thankyou Music

IN THE TOMB SO COLD they laid Him,
Death its victim claimed.
Powers of hell, they could not hold Him;
Back to life He came!

> *Christ is risen! (Christ is risen!)*
> *Death has been conquered. (Death has*
> *been conquered.)*
> *Christ is risen! (Christ is risen!)*
> *He shall reign for ever.*

Hell had spent its fury on Him,
Left Him crucified.
Yet, by blood, He boldly conquered,
Sin and death defied.

Now the fear of death is broken,
Love has won the crown.
Prisoners of the darkness listen,
Walls are tumbling down.

Raised from death to heaven ascending,
Love's exalted King.
Let His song of joy, unending,
Through the nations ring!

246 Bruce Clewett
Copyright © 1983 Thankyou Music

IN THROUGH THE VEIL now we enter,
Boldly approaching Your throne,
Bearing a sacrifice of fragrance sweet;
The fruit of some seeds You have sown.
From our lips we offer these praises,
May You be blessed as we sing.
Lord, we adore You, like incense before You
Our worship ascends to the King.
Welling up within our hearts
Is a song of praise to You,
We lift up our hands with our voice.
Blessings and honour,
Glory and power be unto You,
Let us rejoice, rejoice.
Blessings and honour,
Glory and power be unto You,
Let us rejoice.

247 Mike Kerry
Copyright © 1982 Thankyou Music

IN THY PRESENCE there's fulness of joy,
Fulness of joy, fulness of joy.
At Thy right hand are pleasures for ever,
Pleasures for evermore.

I keep the Lord before me,
I shall not be moved.
My heart is glad and my soul rejoices;
I shall dwell in safety.

And in Thy presence there's fulness of joy,
Fulness of joy, fulness of joy.
At Thy right hand are pleasures for ever,
Pleasures for evermore.

 248   Paul Armstrong
Copyright © 1980 Authentic Publishing/
Adm. by CopyCare

I RECEIVE YOUR LOVE,
I receive Your love,
In my heart I receive Your love, O Lord.
I receive Your love
By Your Spirit within me,
I receive, I receive Your love.

I confess Your love,
I confess Your love,
From my heart I confess Your love, O Lord.
I confess Your love
By Your Spirit within me,
I confess, I confess Your love.

 249   Author unknown
Copyright control

I SEE THE LORD, I see the Lord,
He is high and lifted up
And His train fills the temple.
He is high and lifted up
And His train fills the temple.
The angels cry, Holy,
The angels cry, Holy,
The angels cry, Holy is the Lord.

 250   John Wimber
Copyright © 1980 Mercy/Vineyard
Publishing/Adm. by CopyCare

ISN'T HE BEAUTIFUL, beautiful isn't He?
Prince of Peace, Son of God, isn't He?
Isn't He wonderful, wonderful isn't He?
Counsellor, Almighty God, isn't He, isn't He,
   isn't He?

Yes, You are beautiful...

251   Edmund H. Sears (1810–76)

IT CAME UPON THE MIDNIGHT CLEAR,
That glorious song of old,
From angels bending near the earth
To touch their harps of gold:
'Peace on the earth, goodwill to men
From heaven's all gracious King!'
The world in solemn stillness lay
To hear the angels sing.

Still through the cloven skies they come,
With peaceful wings unfurled,
And still their heavenly music floats
O'er all the weary world:
Above its sad and lowly plains
They bend on hovering wing,
And ever o'er its Babel sounds
The blessèd angels sing.

Yet with woes of sin and strife
The world has suffered long,
Beneath the angel-strain have rolled
Two thousand years of wrong;
And man, at war with man, hears not
The love-song which they bring:
O hush the noise, ye men of strife,
And hear the angels sing.

For lo! the days are hastening on,
By prophet bards foretold,
When with the ever-circling years
Comes round the age of gold;
When peace shall over all the earth
Its ancient splendours fling,
And all the world send back the song
Which now the angels sing.

252    William W. How (1823–97)

IT IS A THING MOST WONDERFUL,
Almost too wonderful to be,
That God's own Son should come from
   heaven
And die to save a child like me.

And yet I know that it is true;
He came to this poor world below,
And wept, and toiled, and mourned, and
   died,
Only because He loved us so.

I cannot tell how He could love
A child so weak and full of sin;
His love must be most wonderful,
If He could die my love to win.

It is most wonderful to know
His love for me so free and sure;
But 'tis more wonderful to see
My love for Him so faint and poor.

And yet I want to love Thee, Lord;
O light the flame within my heart,
And I will love Thee more and more,
Until I see Thee as Thou art.

IT IS GOOD FOR ME to draw near unto God;
Lord, I put my trust in Thee,
That I may declare all Thy works, O my God,
Lord, I put my trust in Thee.
My flesh and my heart they fail me,
But God is the strength of my life;
You are my portion both now and ever more,
There is none that I desire but Thee.

IT IS NO LONGER I THAT LIVETH
But Christ that liveth in me,
It is no longer I that liveth
But Christ that liveth in me.
He lives, He lives,
Jesus is alive in me.
It is no longer I that liveth
But Christ that liveth in me.

The life that I live in the body
I live by faith in the Son.
The life that I live in the body
I live by faith in the Son.
He loves, He loves,
Jesus gave Himself for me.
The life that I live in the body
I live by faith in the Son.

IT'S A HAPPY DAY, and I thank God for the
weather.
It's a happy day, living it for my Lord.
It's a happy day, things are gonna get better,
Living each day by the promises in God's
word.

It's a grumpy day, and I can't stand the
weather.
It's a grumpy day, living it for myself.
It's a grumpy day, and things aren't gonna get
better
Living each day with my Bible up on my
shelf.

**IT'S THE PRESENCE OF YOUR SPIRIT, LORD,
WE NEED,**
It's the presence of Your Spirit, Lord, we
need,
So help us, Lord, to worship You,
It's the presence of Your Spirit, Lord, we
need.

It's the presence of Your Spirit, Lord, we love,
It's the presence of Your Spirit, Lord, we love,
So help us, Lord, to worship You,
It's the presence of Your Spirit, Lord, we love.

For the moving of Your Spirit, Lord,
we pray … *(etc.)*

IT'S YOUR BLOOD that cleanses me,
It's Your blood that gives me life.
It's Your blood that took my place
In redeeming sacrifice,
And washes me whiter than the snow, than
the snow.
My Jesus, God's precious sacrifice.

I WANNA SING, wanna sing.
I wanna sing, wanna sing
For Jesus, for Jesus, for Jesus.
Oh, I wanna sing for Him.

I wanna clap, wanna clap.
I wanna clap, wanna clap
For Jesus, for Jesus, for Jesus.
Oh, I wanna clap for Him.

I wanna dance, praise, work,
love, live … *(etc.)*

I WANT TO BE A HISTORY MAKER, *(echo)*
I want to be a world shaker, *(echo)*
To be a pen on history's pages, *(echo)*
Faithful to the end of the ages. *(echo)*

I want to see Your kingdom come,
I want to see Your will be done
On the earth.
I want to see Your kingdom come,
I want to see Your will be done
On the earth as it is in heaven.

I believe I was called and chosen *(echo)*
Long before the world's creation, *(echo)*
Called to be a holy person, *(echo)*
Called to bear good fruit for heaven. *(echo)*

We want to be the generation *(echo)*
Taking the news to every nation, *(echo)*
Filled with the Spirit without measure, *(echo)*
Working for a heavenly treasure. *(echo)*

260 Mark Altrogge
Copyright © 1982 People of Destiny International/
Word Music/Adm. by CopyCare

I WANT TO SERVE THE PURPOSE OF GOD
In my generation.
I want to serve the purpose of God
While I am alive.
I want to give my life
For something that will last for ever.
Oh, I delight, I delight to do Your will.

I want to build with silver and gold
In my generation.
I want to build with silver and gold
While I am alive.
I want to give my life
For something that will last for ever.
Oh, I delight, I delight to do Your will.

What is on Your heart?
Tell me what to do;
Let me know Your will
And I will follow You.
(Repeat)

I want to see the kingdom of God
In my generation.
I want to see the kingdom of God
While I am alive.
I want to live my life
For something that will last for ever.
Oh, I delight, I delight to do Your will.

I want to see the Lord come again
In my generation.
I want to see the Lord come again
While I am alive.
I want to give my life
For something that will last for ever.
Oh I delight, I delight to do Your will.

261 Clive Simmonds
Copyright © 1964 Clive Simmonds

I WANT TO WALK WITH JESUS CHRIST
All the days I live of this life on earth;
To give to Him complete control
Of body and of soul.

Follow Him, follow Him, yield your life to
Him,
He has conquered death, He is King of
kings;
Accept the joy which He gives to those
Who yield their lives to Him.

I want to learn to speak to Him,
To pray to Him, confess my sin;
To open my life and let Him in,
For joy will then be mine:

I want to learn to speak of Him,
My life must show that He lives in me;
My deeds, my thoughts, my words must
speak
All of His love for me:

I want to learn to read His word,
For this is how I know the way
To live my life as pleases Him,
In holiness and joy:

O Holy Spirit of the Lord,
Enter now into this heart of mine;
Take full control of my selfish will,
And make me wholly Thine:

262 Chris Christensen
Copyright © 1990 Integrity's Hosanna! Music/
Sovereign Music UK

I WAS MADE TO PRAISE YOU,
I was made to glorify Your name,
In every circumstance
To find a chance to thank You.
I was made to love You
I was made to worship at Your feet,
And to obey You, Lord.
I was made for You.

I will always praise You,
I will always glorify Your name.
In every circumstance
I'll find a chance to thank You.
I will always love You,
I will always worship at Your feet,
And I'll obey You, Lord.
I was made for You.

63 Joan Parsons
Copyright © 1978 Thankyou Music

WAS ONCE IN DARKNESS, now my eyes
can see,
was lost but Jesus sought and found me.
what love He offers, O what peace He
gives,
will sing for evermore, He lives.

allelujah Jesus! Hallelujah Lord!
allelujah Father, I am shielded by His
word.
will live for ever, I will never die,
will rise up to meet Him in the sky.

64 Graham Kendrick
Copyright © 1988 Make Way Music

WILL BUILD MY CHURCH, *(Men)*
will build My church, *(Women)*
nd the gates of hell *(Men)*
nd the gates of hell *(Women)*
hall not prevail *(Men)*
hall not prevail *(Women)*
gainst it. *(All)*
(Repeat)

o you powers in the heavens above, bow
down!
nd you powers on the earth below, bow
down!
nd acknowledge that Jesus,
esus, Jesus is Lord, is Lord.

65 Victor Rubbo
Copyright © 1989 Mercy/Vineyard
Publishing/Adm. by CopyCare

(Men and women in canon)
WILL CALL upon the Lord,
ho is worthy to be praised.
will call upon the Lord,
ho is worthy to be praised.

(Together)
o shall I be saved,
o shall I be saved from my enemies.

66 Michael O'Shields
Copyright © 1981 Sound III, Inc./
MCA Music Publishing

WILL CALL UPON THE LORD, *(echo)*
ho is worthy to be praised, *(echo)*
o shall I be saved from mine enemies. *(echo)*

The Lord liveth, and blessèd be my Rock,
And may the God of my salvation be
exalted.
The Lord liveth, and blessèd be my Rock,
And may the God of my salvation be
exalted.

267 D. J. Butler
Copyright © 1987 Mercy/Vineyard
Publishing/Adm. by CopyCare

I WILL CHANGE YOUR NAME,
You shall no longer be called
Wounded, outcast, lonely or afraid.
I will change your name,
Your new name shall be,
Confidence, joyfulness, overcoming one;
Faithfulness, friend of God,
One who seeks My face.

268 Leona von Brethorst
Copyright © 1976 Maranatha! Praise Inc./
Adm. by CopyCare

I WILL ENTER HIS GATES with thanksgiving
in my heart,
I will enter His courts with praise;
I will say this is the day that the Lord has
made,
I will rejoice for He has made me glad.

He has made me glad,
He has made me glad,
I will rejoice for He has made me glad.
He has made me glad,
He has made me glad,
I will rejoice for He has made me glad.

269 Brent Chambers
Copyright © 1977 Scripture in Song
(a div. of Integrity Music, Inc.)/
Sovereign Music UK

I WILL GIVE THANKS TO THEE,
O Lord, among the people,
I will sing praises to Thee
Among the nations.
For Thy steadfast love is great,
Is great to the heavens,
And Thy faithfulness,
Thy faithfulness to the clouds.

Be exalted, O God,
Above the heavens.
Let Thy glory be over all the earth.
Be exalted, O God,
Above the heavens.
Let Thy glory be over all the earth.

(Last time only)
Be exalted, O God,
Above the heavens.
Let Thy glory be over all the earth.
Be exalted, O God,
Above the heavens.
Let Thy glory, let Thy glory,
Let Thy glory be over all the earth.

270 Tommy Walker
Copyright © 1985 Thankyou Music

I WILL GIVE YOU PRAISE,
I will sing Your song,
I will bless Your holy name;
For there is no other god
Who is like unto You,
You're the only way.

Only You are the Author of life,
Only You can bring the blind their sight,
Only You are called Prince of Peace,
Only You promised You'd never leave.
Only You are God.

271 Scott Palazzo
Copyright © 1985 Mercy/Vineyard
Publishing/Adm. by CopyCare

I WILL MAGNIFY Thy name
Above all the earth.
I will magnify Thy name
Above all the earth.

I will sing unto Thee
The praises in my heart.
I will sing unto Thee
The praises in my heart.

272 Mark Altrogge
Copyright © 1988 People of Destiny International/
Word Music/Adm. by CopyCare

I WILL PRAISE YOU ALL MY LIFE;
I will sing to You with my whole heart.
I will trust in You, my hope and my help,
My Maker and my faithful God.

O faithful God, O faithful God,
You lift me up and You uphold my cause;
You give me life, You dry my eyes,
You're always near, You're a faithful God.

273 Author unknown
Copyright control

I WILL REJOICE IN YOU AND BE GLAD,
I will extol Your love more than wine.
Draw me after You and let us run together,
I will rejoice in You and be glad.

274 David Fellingham
Copyright © 1982 Thankyou Music

I WILL REJOICE, I WILL REJOICE,
I will rejoice in the Lord with my whole
   heart.
I will rejoice, I will rejoice,
I will rejoice in the Lord.
You anoint my head with oil,
And my cup surely overflows,
Goodness and love shall follow me
All the days that I dwell in Your house.

275 Diane Fung
Copyright © 1983 Thankyou Music

I WILL RISE AND BLESS YOU, LORD,
Lift my hands and shout Your praise,
I will tell of the marvellous things You have
   done
And declare Your faithfulness.
I will rise and bless You, Lord,
Lift You high and dance for joy.
Oh, nothing can separate me
From Your wonderful, wonderful love.

276 Noel & Tricia Richards
Copyright © 1990 Thankyou Music

I WILL SEEK YOUR FACE, *O Lord;*
I will seek Your face, O Lord.
I will seek Your face, O Lord;
I will seek Your face, O Lord.

Lord, how awesome is Your presence;
Who can stand in Your light?
Those who by Your grace and mercy
Are made holy in Your sight.

I will dwell in Your presence
All the days of my life;
There to gaze upon Your glory,
And to worship only You.

277 James H. Fillmore (1849–1936)
Copyright control

I WILL SING OF THE MERCIES of the Lord f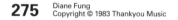
   ever,
I will sing, I will sing.
I will sing of the mercies of the Lord for eve
I will sing of the mercies of the Lord.

With my mouth will I make known
Thy faithfulness, Thy faithfulness.
With my mouth will I make known
Thy faithfulness to all generations.

278
Francis H. Rowley
Copyright © HarperCollins
Religious/Adm. by CopyCare

I WILL SING THE WONDROUS STORY
Of the Christ who died for me;
How He left His home in glory
For the cross on Calvary.
I was lost but Jesus found me,
Found the sheep that went astray;
Threw His loving arms around me,
Drew me back into His way.

I was bruised but Jesus healed me,
Faint was I from many a fall;
Sight was gone, and fears possessed me,
But He freed me from them all.
Days of darkness still come o'er me;
Sorrow's paths I often tread,
But the Saviour still is with me,
By His hand I'm safely led.

He will keep me till the river
Rolls its waters at my feet,
Then He'll bear me safely over,
All my joys in Him complete.
Yes, I'll sing the wondrous story
Of the Christ who died for me;
Sing it with the saints in glory,
Gathered by the crystal sea.

279
Donya Brockway
Copyright © 1972 His Eye Music/
Multisongs/EMI Christian Music Publishing/
Adm. by CopyCare

I WILL SING UNTO THE LORD as long as I
live,
I will sing praise to my God while I have my
being.
My meditation of Him shall be sweet,
I will be glad, I will be glad in the Lord.

Bless thou the Lord, O my soul,
Praise ye the Lord.
Bless thou the Lord, O my soul,
Praise ye the Lord.
Bless thou the Lord, O my soul,
Praise ye the Lord.
Bless thou the Lord, O my soul,
Praise ye the Lord.

280
Dave Bankhead, Ray Goudie, Steve Bassett &
Sue Rinaldi
Copyright © 1990 Authentic Publishing/
Adm. by CopyCare

I WILL SPEAK OUT for those who have no
voices,
I will stand up for the rights of all the
oppressed;
I will speak truth and justice,
I'll defend the poor and the needy,
I will lift up the weak in Jesus' name.

I will speak out for those who have no choices,
I will cry out for those who live without love;
I will show God's compassion
To the crushed and broken in spirit,
I will lift up the weak in Jesus' name.

281
Daniel Gardner
Copyright © 1981 Integrity's Hosanna! Music/
Sovereign Music UK

I WILL WORSHIP YOU, LORD, with all of my
might,
I will praise You with a psalm.
I will worship You, Lord, with all of my might,
I will praise You all day long.

For Thou, O Lord, art glorious,
And Thy name is greatly to be praised;
May my heart be pure and holy in Thy sight,
As I worship You with all of my might.

282
Sondra Corbett Wood
Copyright © 1983 Integrity's Hosanna! Music/
Sovereign Music UK

I WORSHIP YOU, ALMIGHTY GOD,
There is none like You.
I worship You, O Prince of Peace,
That is what I love to do.
I give You praise,
For You are my righteousness.
I worship You, Almighty God,
There is none like You.

283
Ian Smale
Copyright © 1987 Thankyou Music

JEHOVAH JIREH, God will provide,
Jehovah Rophe, God heals;
Jehovah M'keddesh, God who sanctifies,
Jehovah Nissi, God is my banner.

Jehovah Rohi, God my Shepherd,
Jehovah Shalom, God is peace;
Jehovah Tsidkenu, God our righteousness,
Jehovah Shammah, God who is there.

284

JEHOVAH JIREH, MY PROVIDER,
His grace is sufficient for me, for me, for me.
Jehovah Jireh, my Provider,
His grace is sufficient for me.

My God shall supply all my needs
According to His riches in glory;
He will give His angels charge over me,
Jehovah Jireh cares for me, for me, for me,
Jehovah Jireh cares for me.

285

JESUS CHRIST IS RISEN TODAY; Hallelujah!
Our triumphant holy day; Hallelujah!
Who did once upon the cross; Hallelujah!
Suffer to redeem our loss; Hallelujah!

Hymns of praise then let us sing; Hallelujah!
Unto Christ our heavenly King; Hallelujah!
Who endured the cross and grave; Hallelujah!
Sinners to redeem and save: Hallelujah!

But the pains which He endured; Hallelujah!
Our salvation have procured; Hallelujah!
Now in heaven above He's King; Hallelujah!
Where the angels ever sing: Hallelujah!

286

JESUS HAS SAT DOWN at God's right hand,
He is reigning now on David's throne.
God has placed all things beneath His feet,
His enemies will be His footstool.

*For the government is now upon His
    shoulder,*
*For the government is now upon His
    shoulder,*
*And of the increase of His government
    and peace*
There will be no end, there will be no end,
There will be no end.

God has now exalted Him on high,
Given Him a name above all names.
Every knee will bow and tongue confess
That Jesus Christ is Lord.

Jesus is now living in His church,
Men who have been purchased by His blood.
They will serve their God, a royal priesthood,
And they will reign on earth.

Sound the trumpets, good news to the poor,
Captives will go free, the blind will see;
The kingdom of this world will soon become
The kingdom of our God.

287

JESUS, HOW LOVELY YOU ARE,
You are so gentle, so pure and kind.
You shine as the morning star,
Jesus, how lovely You are.

Hallelujah, Jesus is my Lord and King;
Hallelujah, Jesus is my everything.

Hallelujah, Jesus died and rose again;
Hallelujah, Jesus forgave all my sin.

Hallelujah, Jesus is meek and lowly;
Hallelujah, Jesus is pure and holy.

Hallelujah, Jesus is the Bridegroom;
Hallelujah, Jesus will take His Bride soon.

288

JESUS, I LOVE YOU;
I bow down before You.
Praises and worship
To our King.

Alleluia, alleluia;
Alleluia, allelu.

289

JESUS IS KING and I will extol Him,
Give Him the glory, and honour His name.
He reigns on high, enthroned in the
    heavens,
Word of the Father, exalted for us.

We have a hope that is steadfast and certain,
Gone through the curtain and touching the
    throne.
We have a Priest who is there interceding,
Pouring His grace on our lives day by day.

We come to Him, our Priest and Apostle,
Clothed in His glory and bearing His name,
Laying our lives with gladness before Him;
Filled with His Spirit we worship the King.

Holy One, our hearts do adore You;
hrilled with Your goodness we give You our
    praise.
ngels in light with worship surround Him,
esus, our Saviour, for ever the same.

 90 David Mansell
Copyright © 1982 Authentic Publishing/
Adm. by CopyCare

ESUS IS LORD! Creation's voice proclaims it,
or by His power each tree and flower
Vas planned and made.
esus is Lord! The universe declares it,
un, moon and stars in heaven
ry, 'Jesus is Lord!'

Jesus is Lord! Jesus is Lord!
Praise Him with hallelujahs
For Jesus is Lord!

esus is Lord! Yet from His throne eternal
 flesh He came to die in pain
n Calvary's tree.
esus is Lord! From Him all life proceeding,
et gave His life a ransom
hus setting us free.

esus is Lord! O'er sin the mighty conqueror,
rom death He rose, and all His foes
hall own His name.
esus is Lord! God sent His Holy Spirit
o show by works of power
hat Jesus is Lord.

91 Marilyn Baker
Copyright © 1986 Authentic Publishing/
Adm. by CopyCare

ESUS IS LORD OF ALL,
atan is under His feet,
esus is reigning on high
nd all power is given to Him
 heaven and earth.

Ve are joined to Him,
atan is under our feet,
Ve are seated on high
nd all authority is given
o us through Him.

ne day we'll be like Him,
erfect in every way,
hosen to be His bride,
uling and reigning with Him
orever more.

292 Chris Bowater
Copyright © 1982 Sovereign Lifestyle Music

JESUS, I WORSHIP YOU,
Worship, honour and adore Your lovely
    name.
Jesus, I worship You,
Lord of lords and King of kings, I worship
    You,
From a thankful heart I sing;
I worship You.

293 John Barnett
Copyright © 1980 Mercy/Vineyard
Publishing/Adm. by CopyCare

JESUS, JESUS,
Holy and anointed One,
Jesus.
Jesus, Jesus,
Risen and exalted One,
Jesus.

Your name is like honey on my lips,
Your Spirit like water to my soul.
Your word is a lamp unto my feet;
Jesus I love You, I love You.

294 Chris Bowater
Copyright © 1979 Sovereign Lifestyle Music

JESUS, JESUS, JESUS,
Your love has melted my heart.
Jesus, Jesus, Jesus,
Your love has melted my heart.

295 Chris Rolinson
Copyright © 1988 Thankyou Music

JESUS, KING OF KINGS,
We worship and adore You.
Jesus, Lord of heaven and earth,
We bow down at Your feet.
Father, we bring to You our worship;
Your sovereign will be done,
On earth Your kingdom come,
Through Jesus Christ, Your only Son.

Jesus, Sovereign Lord,
We worship and adore You.
Jesus, Name above all names,
We bow down at Your feet.
Father, we offer You our worship;
Your sovereign will be done,
On earth Your kingdom come,
Through Jesus Christ, Your only Son.

Jesus, Light of the world,
We worship and adore You.
Jesus, Lord Emmanuel,
We bow down at Your feet.
Father, for Your delight we worship;
Your sovereign will be done,
On earth Your kingdom come,
Through Jesus Christ, Your only Son.

296 Christian F. Gellert (1715–69)
Tr. Frances E. Cox (1812–97)

JESUS LIVES! thy terrors now
Can, O death, no more appal us;
Jesus lives! by this we know,
Thou, O grave, canst not enthral us.
Hallelujah!

Jesus lives! henceforth is death
But the gate of life immortal;
This shall calm our trembling breath,
When we pass its gloomy portal.
Hallelujah!

Jesus lives! for us He died;
Then, alone to Jesus living,
Pure in heart may we abide,
Glory to our Saviour giving.
Hallelujah!

Jesus lives! our hearts know well,
Naught from us His love shall sever;
Life, nor death, nor powers of hell,
Tear us from His keeping ever.
Hallelujah!

Jesus lives! to Him the throne
Over all the world is given:
May we go where He is gone,
Rest and reign with Him in heaven.
Hallelujah!

297 Charles Wesley (1707–88)

JESUS, LOVER OF MY SOUL,
Let me to Thy bosom fly,
While the nearer waters roll,
While the tempest still is high;
Hide me, O my Saviour, hide,
Till the storm of life is past;
Safe into the haven guide,
O receive my soul at last.

Other refuge have I none,
Hangs my helpless soul on Thee;
Leave, ah, leave me not alone,
Still support and comfort me.
All my trust on Thee is stayed,
All my help from Thee I bring;
Cover my defenceless head
With the shadow of Thy wing.

Thou, O Christ, art all I want;
More than all in Thee I find;
Raise the fallen, cheer the faint,
Heal the sick, and lead the blind.
Just and holy is Thy name,
I am all unrighteousness;
False and full of sin I am,
Thou art full of truth and grace.

Plenteous grace with Thee is found,
Grace to cover all my sin;
Let the healing streams abound,
Make and keep me pure within.
Thou of life the fountain art;
Freely let me take of Thee;
Spring Thou up within my heart,
Rise to all eternity.

298 Naida Hearn
Copyright © 1974 Scripture in Song
(a div. of Integrity Music, Inc.)/
Sovereign Music UK

JESUS, NAME ABOVE ALL NAMES,
Beautiful Saviour, Glorious Lord;
Emmanuel, God is with us,
Blessèd Redeemer, Living Word.

299 Graham Kendrick
Copyright © 1986 Thankyou Music

**JESUS PUT THIS SONG INTO OUR
HEARTS,**
Jesus put this song into our hearts,
It's a song of joy no one can take away,
Jesus put this song into our hearts.

Jesus taught us how to live in harmony,
Jesus taught us how to live in harmony,
Different faces, different races, He made us
one,
Jesus taught us how to live in harmony.

Jesus taught us how to be a family,
Jesus taught us how to be a family,
Loving one another with the love that He
gives,
Jesus taught us how to be a family.

esus turned our sorrow into dancing,
esus turned our sorrow into dancing,
hanged our tears of sadness into rivers of joy,
esus turned our sorrow into a dance.

300 Chris Rolinson
Copyright © 1987 Thankyou Music

ESUS, SEND MORE LABOURERS,
or, Lord, we see the need;
he land is ready for harvest,
he fields are ripe indeed.

Oh Lord, but start with me,
Jesus, begin with me.
Who will go for You, Lord?
Who will go for You, Lord?
Here I am, Lord,
Send me,
Send me, Lord,
Send me.

ord, we love our country,
ountless lives to be won;
esus, bring revival,
hat through us Your will be done.

ord, we sense Your moving,
ouching our lives with power;
We are ready to serve You,
o go this day, this hour.

301 Isaac Watts (1674–1748)

ESUS SHALL REIGN where'er the sun
oth his successive journeys run;
his kingdom stretch from shore to shore,
ill moons shall wax and wane no more.

or Him shall endless prayer be made,
nd praises throng to crown His head;
his name like sweet perfume shall rise
With every morning sacrifice.

eople and realms of every tongue
well on His love with sweetest song,
nd infant voices shall proclaim
heir early blessings on His name.

lessings abound where'er He reigns;
he prisoner leaps to lose his chains;
he weary find eternal rest,
nd all the sons of want are blessed.

et every creature rise and bring
eculiar honours to our King;
ngels descend with songs again,
nd earth repeat the loud Amen!

302 Chris Bowater
Copyright © 1988 Sovereign Lifestyle Music

JESUS SHALL TAKE THE HIGHEST HONOUR,
Jesus shall take the highest praise.
Let all earth join heaven in exalting
The Name which is above all other names.
Let's bow the knee in humble adoration,
For at His name every knee must bow.
Let every tongue confess He is Christ, God's
    only Son;
Sovereign Lord, we give You glory now.

For all honour and blessing and power
Belongs to You, belongs to You.
All honour and blessing and power
Belongs to You, belongs to You,
Lord Jesus Christ, Son of the living God.

303 Graham Kendrick
Copyright © 1977 Thankyou Music

JESUS, STAND AMONG US
At the meeting of our lives;
Be our sweet agreement
At the meeting of our eyes.
O Jesus, we love You, so we gather here;
Join our hearts in unity and take away our
    fear.

So to You we're gathering
Out of each and every land;
Christ the love between us
At the joining of our hands.
O Jesus, we love You, so we gather here;
Join our hearts in unity and take away our
    fear.

(Optional verse for Communion:)
Jesus, stand among us
At the breaking of the bread;
Join us as one body
As we worship You, our Head.
O Jesus, we love You, so we gather here;
Join our hearts in unity and take away our
    fear.

304 William Pennefather (1816–73)

JESUS, STAND AMONG US,
IN THY RISEN POWER,
Let this time of worship
Be a hallowed hour.

Breathe Thy Holy Spirit
Into every heart,
Bid the fears and sorrows
From each soul depart.

Thus with quickened footsteps
We'll pursue our way,
Watching for the dawning
Of eternal day.

305 Dave Bryant
Copyright © 1978 Thankyou Music

JESUS TAKE ME AS I AM,
I can come no other way.
Take me deeper into You,
Make my flesh life melt away.
Make me like a precious stone,
Crystal clear and finely honed,
Life of Jesus shining through,
Giving glory back to You.

306 Hilary Davies
Copyright © 1988 Samsongs/
Coronation Music/Kingsway Music

JESUS, THE NAME ABOVE ALL NAMES,
Forever more the same,
And lifting up our hands we exalt You;
Come among us once again,
And glorify Your name,
So everyone will know
You are Emmanuel.

*Emmanuel, Emmanuel,
Emmanuel, God is with us.*

307 Charles Wesley (1707–88)

JESUS! THE NAME HIGH OVER ALL,
In hell, or earth, or sky;
Angels and men before it fall,
And devils fear and fly,
And devils fear and fly.

Jesus! the name to sinners dear,
The name to sinners given;
It scatters all their guilty fear,
It turns their hell to heaven,
It turns their hell to heaven.

Jesus! the prisoners' fetters breaks,
And bruises Satan's head;
Power into strengthless souls it speaks,
And life into the dead,
And life into the dead.

O that the world might taste and see
The riches of His grace!
The arms of love that compass me
Would all mankind embrace,
Would all mankind embrace.

His only righteousness I show,
His saving grace proclaim;
'Tis all my business here below
To cry: 'Behold the Lamb!'
To cry: 'Behold the Lamb!'

Happy if with my latest breath
I might but gasp His name;
Preach Him to all, and cry in death:
'Behold, behold the Lamb!'
'Behold, behold the Lamb!'

308 Bernard of Clairvaux (1091–1153)
Tr. Edward Caswall (1814–78)

JESUS, THE VERY THOUGHT OF THEE
With sweetness fills the breast;
But sweeter far Thy face to see,
And in Thy presence rest.

Nor voice can sing, nor heart can frame,
Nor can the memory find
A sweeter sound than Thy blessed name,
O Saviour of mankind!

O hope of every contrite heart,
O joy of all the meek,
To those who fall how kind Thou art,
How good to those who seek!

But what to those who find? Ah, this
Nor tongue nor pen can show:
The love of Jesus, what it is
None but His loved ones know.

Jesus, Thy mercies are untold
Through each returning day;
Thy love exceeds a thousandfold
Whatever we can say.

Jesus, our only joy be Thou,
As Thou our prize wilt be;
Jesus, be Thou our glory now,
And through eternity.

309 John Gibson
Copyright © 1987 Thankyou Music

JESUS, WE CELEBRATE YOUR VICTORY:
*Jesus, we revel in Your love.
Jesus, we rejoice, You've set us free;
Jesus, Your death has brought us life.*

It was for freedom that Christ has set us free
No longer to be subject to a yoke of slavery;
So we're rejoicing in God's victory,
Our hearts responding to His love.

is Spirit in us releases us from fear,
he way to Him is open, with boldness we
  draw near;
nd in His presence our problems
  disappear,
ur hearts responding to His love.

310 Paul Kyle
Copyright © 1980 Thankyou Music

JESUS, WE ENTHRONE YOU,
We proclaim You our King.
Standing here in the midst of us,
We raise You up with our praise.
And as we worship, build a throne,
And as we worship, build a throne,
And as we worship, build a throne:
Come, Lord Jesus, and take Your place.

311 Marilyn Baker
Copyright © 1981 Authentic Publishing/
Adm. by CopyCare

JESUS, YOU ARE CHANGING ME,
By Your Spirit You're making me like You.
Jesus, You're transforming me,
That Your loveliness may be seen in all I do.
You are the potter and I am the clay,
Help me to be willing to let You have Your
  way.
Jesus, You are changing me,
As I let You reign supreme within my heart.

312 David Fellingham
Copyright © 1985 Thankyou Music

JESUS, YOU ARE THE RADIANCE of the
  Father's glory,
You are the Son, the appointed heir,
Through whom all things are made.
You are the One who sustains all things by
  Your powerful word.
You have purified us from sin,
You are exalted, O Lord,
Exalted, O Lord,
To the right hand of God.

(Last time)
Crowned with glory,
Crowned with honour,
We worship You.

313 Isaac Watts (1674–1748)

JOIN ALL THE GLORIOUS NAMES
Of wisdom, love, and power,
That ever mortals knew,
That angels ever bore:
All are too mean to speak His worth,
Too mean to set my Saviour forth.

Great Prophet of my God,
My tongue would bless Thy name:
By Thee the joyful news
Of our salvation came:
The joyful news of sins forgiven,
Of hell subdued and peace with heaven.

Jesus, my great High Priest,
Offered His blood, and died;
My guilty conscience seeks
No sacrifice beside:
His powerful blood did once atone,
And now it pleads before the throne.

My Saviour and my Lord,
My Conqueror and my King,
Thy sceptre and Thy sword,
Thy reigning grace I sing:
Thine is the power; behold, I sit
In willing bonds beneath Thy feet.

Now let my soul arise,
And tread the tempter down:
My Captain leads me forth
To conquest and a crown.
March on, nor fear to win the day,
Though death and hell obstruct the way.

Should all the hosts of death,
And powers of hell unknown,
Put their most dreadful forms
Of rage and malice on,
I shall be safe; for Christ displays
Superior power and guardian grace.

314 Isaac Watts (1674–1748)

JOY TO THE WORLD! the Lord has come;
Let earth receive her King.
Let every heart prepare Him room,
And heaven and nature sing,
And heaven and nature sing,
And heaven, and heaven and nature sing!

Joy to the earth! the Saviour reigns;
Your sweetest songs employ.
While fields and streams and hills and plains
Repeat the sounding joy,
Repeat the sounding joy,
Repeat, repeat the sounding joy!

He rules the world with truth and grace,
And makes the nations prove
The glories of His righteousness,
The wonders of His love,
The wonders of His love,
The wonders, the wonders of His love.

315 Fred Dunn
Copyright © 1977 Thankyou Music

JUBILATE, EVERYBODY,
Serve the Lord in all your ways,
And come before His presence singing,
Enter now His courts with praise.
For the Lord our God is gracious,
And His mercy's everlasting.
Jubilate, Jubilate, Jubilate Deo.

316 Charlotte Elliott (1789–1871)

JUST AS I AM, without one plea
But that Thy blood was shed for me,
And that Thou bid'st me come to Thee,
O Lamb of God, I come.

Just as I am, and waiting not
To rid my soul of one dark blot,
To Thee, whose blood can cleanse each spot,
O Lamb of God, I come.

Just as I am, though tossed about
With many a conflict, many a doubt,
Fightings and fears within, without,
O Lamb of God, I come.

Just as I am, poor, wretched, blind;
Sight, riches, healing of the mind,
Yea, all I need in Thee to find,
O Lamb of God, I come.

Just as I am, Thou wilt receive,
Wilt welcome, pardon, cleanse, relieve,
Because Thy promise I believe,
O Lamb of God, I come.

Just as I am, Thy love unknown
Has broken every barrier down;
Now to be Thine, yea, Thine alone,
O Lamb of God, I come.

Just as I am, of that free love
The breadth, length, depth and height to
   prove,
Here for a season, then above,
O Lamb of God, I come.

317 Patty Kennedy
Copyright © 1989 Mercy/Vineyard
Publishing/Adm. by CopyCare

JUST LIKE YOU PROMISED, You've come;
Just like You told us, You're here,
And our desire is that You know
We love You, we worship You,
We welcome You here.

318 Jane Norton
Copyright © 1986 Thankyou Music

KING FOR EVER, Lord Messiah,
He who was, and is, and is to come;
Prince of glory, name of Jesus,
Be Your praise and worship ever sung.

   And we will sing hosanna to Jesus,
   We exalt and raise Your name above;
   And we proclaim the glory of Jesus,
   Prince of Peace, and worthy King of love.

Lord anointed, our salvation,
He whom angels call the Word of God;
True and faithful, Lamb of mercy,
Now receive our worship and our love.

319 Graham Kendrick
Copyright © 1988 Make Way Music

KING OF KINGS, Lord of lords,
Lion of Judah, Word of God.
King of kings, Lord of lords,
Lion of Judah, Word of God.

And here He comes, the King of glory comes
In righteousness He comes to judge the
   earth.
And here He comes, the King of glory comes
With justice He'll rule the earth.

320 Chris Bowater
Copyright © 1988 Sovereign Lifestyle Music

LAMB OF GOD, Holy One,
Jesus Christ, Son of God,
Lifted up willingly to die,
That I the guilty one may know
The blood once shed, still freely flowing,
Still cleansing, still healing.

   I exalt You, Jesus my sacrifice;
   I exalt You, my Redeemer and my Lord.
   I exalt You, worthy Lamb of God,
   And in honour I bow down before Your
   throne.

321 James Edmeston (1791–1867) altd

LEAD US, HEAVENLY FATHER, LEAD US
O'er the world's tempestuous sea;
Guard us, guide us, keep us, feed us,
For we have no help but Thee;
Yet possessing every blessing
If our God our Father be.

Saviour, breathe forgiveness o'er us;
All our weakness Thou dost know,
Thou didst tread this earth before us,
Thou didst feel its keenest woe;
Tempted, taunted, yet undaunted,
Through the desert Thou didst go.

Spirit of our God, descending,
Fill our hearts with heavenly joy,
Love with every passion blending,
Pleasure that can never cloy;
Thus provided, pardoned, guided,
Nothing can our peace destroy.

322 Graham Kendrick
Copyright © 1983 Thankyou Music

LED LIKE A LAMB to the slaughter
In silence and shame,
There on Your back You carried a world
Of violence and pain.
Bleeding, dying, bleeding, dying.

You're alive, You're alive,
You have risen, Alleluia!
And the power and the glory is given,
Alleluia, Jesus, to You.

At break of dawn, poor Mary,
Still weeping she came,
When through her grief she heard Your
voice
Now speaking her name.
Mary, Master, Mary, Master!

At the right hand of the Father
Now seated on high
You have begun Your eternal reign
Of justice and joy.
Glory, glory, glory, glory.

323 Graham Kendrick
Copyright © 1984 Thankyou Music

LET GOD ARISE
And let His enemies
Be scattered;
And let those who hate Him
Flee before Him.
Let God arise,
And let His enemies
Be scattered;
And let those who hate Him
Flee away.

(Men)
But let the righteous be glad,
Let them exult before God,
Let them rejoice with gladness,
Building up a highway for the King.
We go in the name of the Lord,
Let the shout go up
In the name of the Lord.

(Women)
The righteous be glad,
Let them exult before God,
O let them rejoice
For the King,
In the name of the Lord.

324 Ian Smale
Copyright © 1982 Thankyou Music

LET GOD SPEAK and I will listen,
Let God speak, there's things I'm needing
to put right.
Let God speak and I will obey what He
says,
Please God, I want to hear Your voice
tonight.

Lord I want to hear Your voice,
Lord I want to hear Your voice,
Lord I want to hear Your voice
Tonight, tonight.

325 Graham Kendrick
Copyright © 1977 Thankyou Music

LET ME HAVE MY WAY AMONG YOU,
Do not strive, do not strive.
Let Me have My way among you,
Do not strive, do not strive.
For Mine is the power and the glory
For ever and ever the same.
Let Me have My way among you,
Do not strive, do not strive.

We'll let You have Your way among us,
We'll not strive, we'll not strive.
We'll let You have Your way among us,
We'll not strive, we'll not strive.
For Yours is the power and the glory
For ever and ever the same.
We'll let You have Your way among us,
We'll not strive, we'll not strive.

Let My peace rule within your hearts,
Do not strive, do not strive.
Let My peace rule within your hearts,
Do not strive, do not strive.
For Mine is the power and the glory,
For ever and ever the same.
Let My peace rule within your hearts,
Do not strive, do not strive.

We'll let Your peace rule within our hearts,
We'll not strive, we'll not strive.
We'll let Your peace rule within our hearts,
We'll not strive, we'll not strive.
For Yours is the power and the glory,
For ever and ever the same.
We'll let Your peace rule within our hearts,
We'll not strive, we'll not strive.

326 Brent Chambers
Copyright © 1979 Scripture in Song
(a div. of Integrity Music, Inc.)/
Sovereign Music UK

LET OUR PRAISE TO YOU BE AS INCENSE,
Let our praise to You be as pillars of Your
throne.
Let our praise to You be as incense,
As we come before You and worship You
alone.
As we see You in Your splendour,
As we gaze upon Your majesty,
As we join the hosts of angels
And proclaim together Your holiness.

Holy, holy, holy,
Holy is the Lord.
Holy, holy, holy,
Holy is the Lord.

327 Mike McIntosh
Copyright © 1982 Mike & Claire McIntosh

LET PRAISES RING, let praises ring,
Lift voices up to love Him,
Lift hearts and hands to touch Him,
O let praises ring.
And fill the skies with anthems high
That tell His excellencies,
As priests and kings who rule with Him
Through all eternity;

Let praises ring, let praises ring
To our glorious King.

Let praises ring, let praises ring,
Bow down in adoration,
Cry out His exaltation,
O let praises ring.
And lift the Name above all names
Till every nation knows
The love of God has come to men,
His mercies overflow.

328 James & Elizabeth Greenelsh
Copyright © 1978 Integrity's Hosanna! Music/
Sovereign Music UK

(First part)
LET THERE BE GLORY AND HONOUR and
praises,
Glory and honour to Jesus,
Glory, honour, glory and honour to Him.

(Second part)
Glory, glory and honour to Jesus,
Glory, honour, glory and honour to Him.

(First and Second parts)
Keep your light shining brightly
As the darkness covers the earth;
For a people that walk in darkness,
They shall see, they shall see a great light.

329 Dave Bilbrough
Copyright © 1979 Thankyou Music

LET THERE BE LOVE shared among us,
Let there be love in our eyes;
May now Your love sweep this nation,
Cause us, O Lord, to arise.
Give us a fresh understanding
Of brotherly love that is real;
Let there be love shared among us,
Let there be love.

330 Anonymous African-American
Copyright control

**LET US BREAK BREAD TOGETHER, WE ARE
ONE.**
Let us break bread together, we are one.
We are one as we stand
With our face to the risen Son.
O Lord, have mercy on us.

Let us drink wine together, we are one …
(etc.)

Let us praise God together, we are one …
(etc.)

331 Ian White
Copyright © 1985 Little Misty Music/
Kingsway Music

LET US GO TO THE HOUSE OF THE LORD.

I rejoiced with those who said to me,
'Let us go to the house of the Lord.'
Our feet are standing in your gates,
    Jerusalem;
Like a city built together,
Where the people of God go up
To praise the name of the Lord.

For peace for all Jerusalem
And loved ones this we pray;
May all men be secure where they must
    live.
And to all my friends and brothers,
May the peace be within you
For the sake of the house of the Lord.

332 Pale Sauni
Copyright © 1983 Scripture in Song
(a div. of Integrity Music, Inc.)/
Sovereign Music UK

LET US PRAISE HIS NAME WITH DANCING
And with the tambourine.
Let us praise His name with dancing,
Make a joyful noise and sing.

Dance, dance, dance before the King.
Dance, dance, celebrate and sing.

Let us celebrate with dancing;
The King has set us free.
Let us celebrate with dancing,
Rejoice in victory.

333 John Milton (1608–74)

LET US WITH A GLADSOME MIND
Praise the Lord, for He is kind:

For His mercies shall endure,
Ever faithful, ever sure.

Let us blaze His name abroad,
For of gods He is the God:

He, with all-commanding might,
Filled the new-made world with light:

He the golden-tressèd sun
Caused all day his course to run:

And the silver moon by night,
'Mid her spangled sisters bright:

He His chosen race did bless
In the wasteful wilderness:

All things living He doth feed,
His full hand supplies their need:

Let us with a gladsome mind
Praise the Lord, for He is kind:

334 John Watson
Copyright © 1986 Ampelos Music/
Adm. by CopyCare

LET YOUR LIVING WATER FLOW over my soul.
Let Your Holy Spirit come and take control
Of every situation that has troubled my mind.
All my cares and burdens on to You I roll.

Jesus, Jesus, Jesus.
Father, Father, Father.
Spirit, Spirit, Spirit.

Come now, Holy Spirit, and take control.
Hold me in Your loving arms and make me
    whole.
Wipe away all doubt and fear and take my
    pride,
Draw me to Your love and keep me by Your
    side.

Give your life to Jesus, let Him fill your soul.
Let Him take you in His arms and make you
    whole.
As you give your life to Him He'll set you free.
You will live and reign with Him eternally.

335 Graham Kendrick
Copyright © 1989 Make Way Music

LIFT HIGH THE CROSS.
Lift high the cross.
In majesty,
In victory.

Here raged the fight, *(Women echo)*
Darkness and light. *(Women echo)*
All heaven and hell *(Women echo)*
Battled here. *(All)*

Here once for all *(Women echo)*
Was sacrificed *(Women echo)*
The Lamb of God, *(Women echo)*
Jesus Christ. *(All)*

Raise now your voices give glory and praise
    Him, *(Leader – All echo)*
For He has poured out His blood as a
    ransom. *(Leader – All echo)*
Hell's power is broken and heaven stands
    open, *(Leader – All echo)*
Lift high the cross. *(All)*

336

LIFT UP YOUR HEADS to the coming King;
Bow before Him and adore Him, sing
To His majesty, let your praises be
Pure and holy, giving glory
To the King of kings.

337

LIFT UP YOUR HEADS, O you gates,
Swing wide you everlasting doors.
Lift up your heads, O ye gates,
Swing wide you everlasting doors.

    That the King of glory may come in,
    That the King of glory may come in.
    That the King of glory may come in,
    That the King of glory may come in.

Up from the dead He ascends,
Through every rank of heavenly power.
Let heaven prepare the highest place,
Throw wide the everlasting doors:

With trumpet blast and shouts of joy,
All heaven greets the risen King.
With angel choirs come line the way,
Throw wide the gates and welcome Him.

338

    LIFT UP YOUR HEADS, O YE GATES,
    And be ye lifted up, ye everlasting doors.
    Lift up your heads, O ye gates,
    And be ye lifted up, ye everlasting doors;
    And the King of glory shall come in,
    The King of glory shall come in,
    The King of glory shall come in.

(Women)
Who is the King of glory?
What is His name?
(Men)
The Lord strong and mighty,
The Lord, mighty in battle, strong to save.

(Women)
Who shall ascend the hill,
The hill of the Lord?
(Men)
Even he that hath clean hands
And a pure heart with which to praise his
    God.

339

    LIGHT A FLAME *within my heart*
    That's burning bright;
    Fan the fire of joy in me
    To set the world alight.
    Let my flame begin to spread,
    My life to glow;
    God of light may I reflect
    Your love to all I know.

From heaven's splendour
He comes to earth,
While all the angels celebrate
The goodness of His birth.

We too exalt You,
Our glorious King;
Jesus our Saviour
Paid the price to take away our sin.

340

LIGHTEN OUR DARKNESS, Lord we
    pray; *(echo)*
And in Your mercy defend us *(echo)*
From all perils and dangers of this
    night, *(echo)*
For the love of Your only Son, *(all)*
Our Saviour Jesus Christ.
Amen, Amen.
Amen, Amen.

341

LIGHT HAS DAWNED that ever shall blaze;
Darkness flees away.
Christ the light has shone in our hearts,
Turning night to day.

We proclaim Him King of kings,
We lift high His name.
Heaven and earth shall bow at His feet
When He comes to reign.

Saviour of the world is He,
Heaven's King come down.
Judgement, love and mercy meet
At His thorny crown.

Life has sprung from hearts of stone,
By the Spirit's breath.
Hell shall let her captives go,
Life has conquered death.

Blood has flowed that cleanses from sin,
God His love has proved.
Men may mock and demons may rage,
We shall not be moved!

 342 Craig Musseau
Copyright © 1990 Mercy/Vineyard
Publishing/Adm. by CopyCare

LIGHT OF THE WORLD, shine Your light
Into my heart.
God of love, pierce my soul
With Your mercy.

So we might see Your glory,
So we might see Your face.
So we can feel Your heartbeat,
And hear You call our name.

Fire of God, burn away
What is not holy.
Jesus, take our hearts
And make them new.

343 Maggi Dawn
Copyright © 1990 Thankyou Music

LIKE A GENTLE BREEZE, like a mighty wind,
Like a roaring fire,
You will visit us, you will cleanse our souls,
And our hearts inspire,
Bringing peace to us, like a healing balm,
Or a gentle dove;
O come to us, O bring to us
God's gifts of love.

Come with holy fire,
Melt these hearts of clay.
Let them beat with love
That will never fade.
Holy Spirit come,
Holy Spirit come,
Holy Spirit come again.

344 Frances R. Havergal (1836–79)

LIKE A RIVER GLORIOUS is God's perfect
peace,
Over all victorious, in its bright increase:
Perfect, yet it floweth fuller every day;
Perfect, yet it groweth deeper all the way.

Stayed upon Jehovah, hearts are fully
blest;
Finding, as He promised, perfect peace
and rest.

Hidden in the hollow of His blessèd hand,
Never foe can follow, never traitor stand;
Not a surge of worry, not a shade of care,
Not a blast of hurry touched the Spirit there.

Every joy or trial falleth from above,
Traced upon our dial by the sun of love.
We may trust Him fully, all for us to do;
They who trust Him wholly find Him wholly
true.

 345 Ted Sandquist
Copyright © 1976 Lion of Judah Music,
USA/Adm. by Bucks Music Ltd

LION OF JUDAH on the throne,
I shout Your name, let it be known
That You are the King of kings,
You are the Prince of Peace,
May Your kingdom's reign never cease.
Hail to the King!
Hail to the King!

Lion of Judah come to earth,
I want to thank You for Your birth,
For the living Word,
For Your death on the tree,
For Your resurrection victory.
Hallelujah! Hallelujah!

Lion of Judah, come again,
Take up Your throne Jerusalem,
Bring release to this earth
And the consummation
Of Your kingdom's reign, let it come.
Maranatha! Maranatha!

Lion of Judah on the throne,
I shout Your name, let it be known
That You are the King of kings,
You are the Prince of Peace,
May Your kingdom's reign never cease.
Hail to the King!
Hail to the King!
You are my King!

346 David J. Hadden & Bob Silvester
Copyright © 1983 Restoration Music Ltd/
Sovereign Music UK

LIVING UNDER THE SHADOW OF HIS WING
We find security.
Standing in His presence we will bring
Our worship, worship, worship to the King.

Bowed in adoration at His feet
We dwell in harmony.
Voices joined together that repeat,
Worthy, worthy, worthy is the Lamb.

Heart to heart embracing in His love
Reveals His purity.
Soaring in my spirit like a dove,
Holy, holy, holy is the Lord.

347 Charles Wesley (1707–88)

LO, HE COMES WITH CLOUDS DESCENDING,
Once for favoured sinners slain;
Thousand thousand saints attending
Swell the triumph of His train:
Alleluia!
Alleluia!
Alleluia!
God appears on earth to reign.

Every eye shall now behold Him
Robed in glorious majesty;
Those who set at naught and sold Him,
Pierced and nailed Him to the tree,
Deeply wailing,
Deeply wailing,
Deeply wailing,
Shall their true Messiah see.

Those dear tokens of His passion
Still His dazzling body bears;
Cause of endless exultation
To His ransomed worshippers:
With what rapture,
With what rapture,
With what rapture,
Gaze we on those glorious scars.

Yea, Amen, let all adore Thee,
High on Thine eternal throne;
Saviour, take the power and glory,
Claim the kingdom for Thine own:
Come, Lord Jesus!
Come, Lord Jesus!
Come, Lord Jesus!
Everlasting God, come down!

348 Martin F. Ball
Copyright © 1982 Restoration Music Ltd/
Sovereign Music UK

LOOK AND SEE THE GLORY OF THE KING,
Sense the presence of the Lord amongst His people.
Feel Him fill the temple of our lives
As He sits upon the throne of our praise.

We are His church,
We are all God's own people.
We all proclaim that He is King, He is King.

At God's right hand
Jesus Christ is exalted.
His rule is now, and shall be for evermore.

349 Thomas Kelly (1769–1854)

LOOK, YE SAINTS, THE SIGHT IS GLORIOUS;
See the Man of Sorrows now,
From the fight returned victorious;
Every knee to Him shall bow:
Crown Him! Crown Him!
Crown Him! Crown Him!
Crowns become the Victor's brow.

Crown the Saviour, angels, crown Him;
Rich the trophies Jesus brings;
In the seat of power enthrone Him,
While the vault of heaven rings:
Crown Him! Crown Him!
Crown Him! Crown Him!
Crown the Saviour, King of kings!

Sinners in derision crowned Him,
Mocking thus the Saviour's claim;
Saints and angels throng around Him,
Own His title, praise His name:
Crown Him! Crown Him!
Crown Him! Crown Him!
Spread abroad the Victor's fame.

Hark, those bursts of acclamation!
Hark, those loud triumphant chords!
Jesus takes the highest station:
O what joy the sight affords!
Crown Him! Crown Him!
Crown Him! Crown Him!
King of kings, and Lord of lords!

350
Noel Richards
Copyright © 1982 Thankyou Music

LORD AND FATHER, KING FOR EVER,
Throned with majesty and power,
We adore You, we exalt You,
Worship we bring, our offering,
Worship we bring to You our King.

351
Chris Rolinson
Copyright © 1988 Thankyou Music

LORD, COME AND HEAL YOUR CHURCH,
Take our lives and cleanse with Your fire.
Let Your deliverance flow,
As we lift Your name up higher.

We will draw near,
And surrender our fear;
Lift our hands to proclaim
Holy Father, You are here.

Spirit of God, come in
And release our hearts to praise You.
Make us whole, for
Holy we'll become, and serve You.

Show us Your power, we pray,
That we might share in Your glory.
We shall arise and go
To proclaim Your works most holy.

352
George H. Bourne (1840–1925)

**LORD, ENTHRONED IN HEAVENLY
  SPLENDOUR,**
First-begotten from the dead,
Thou alone, our strong Defender,
Liftest up Thy people's head.
Alleluia! Alleluia!
Jesus, true and living Bread.

Here our humblest homage pay we,
Here in loving reverence bow;
Here for faith's discernment pray we,
Lest we fail to know Thee now.
Alleluia! Alleluia!
Thou art here, we ask not how.

Though the lowliest form doth veil Thee
As of old in Bethlehem,
Here as there Thine angels hail Thee
Branch and Flower of Jesse's stem.
Alleluia! Alleluia!
We in worship join with them.

Paschal Lamb, Thine offering, finished
Once for all when Thou wast slain,
In its fulness undiminished
Shall for evermore remain,
Alleluia! Alleluia!
Cleansing souls from every stain.

Life-imparting, heavenly Manna,
Stricken Rock with streaming side,
Heaven and earth with loud hosanna
Worship Thee, the Lamb who died,
Alleluia! Alleluia!
Risen, ascended, glorified!

353
Sue Hutchinson
Copyright © 1979 Authentic Publishing/
Adm. by CopyCare

LORD GOD, HEAVENLY KING,
You are our God, to You we sing;
Receive the worship of our hearts,
The adoration of our lips;
How we love You,
Lord God, heavenly King.

354
Graham Kendrick
Copyright © 1986 Thankyou Music

LORD HAVE MERCY on us,
Come and heal our land.
Cleanse with Your fire, heal with Your touch,
Humbly we bow and call upon You now.
O Lord, have mercy on us,
O Lord, have mercy on us.

355
Stuart Townend
Copyright © 1990 Thankyou Music

LORD HOW MAJESTIC YOU ARE,
My eyes meet Your gaze
And my burden is lifted.
Your word is a lamp to my feet,
Your hand swift to bless
And Your banner a shield.

You are my everything,
You who made earth and sky and sea,
All that You've placed inside of me
Calls out Your name.
To You I bow,
The King who commands my every breath,
The Man who has conquered sin and
*   death,*
My Lord and my King,
My everything!

Lord, how resplendent You are,
When I think of Your heavens,
The work of Your fingers—
What is man, that You are mindful of him?
Yet You've crowned him with glory
And caused him to reign!

356 Dave Bilbrough
Copyright © 1987 Thankyou Music

LORD, I WILL CELEBRATE YOUR LOVE,
From deep within my heart,
I celebrate Your love;
I celebrate Your love given to me.

You are the one that I adore;
Lord, in Your presence is life for evermore;
The one that I adore.
You are my Lord.

Healing me, releasing me,
More and more reveal Yourself in me,
My Lord, my Lord!

357 Patrick Appleford
Copyright © 1960 Josef Weinberger Ltd

LORD JESUS CHRIST,
You have come to us,
You are one with us,
Mary's son.
Cleansing our souls from all their sin,
Pouring Your love and goodness in;
Jesus, our love for You we sing,
Living Lord.

(Optional communion verse:)
Lord Jesus Christ,
Now and every day,
Teach us how to pray,
Son of God.
You have commanded us to do
This in remembrance, Lord, of You:
Into our lives Your power breaks through,
Living Lord.

Lord Jesus Christ,
You have come to us,
Born as one of us,
Mary's son.
Led out to die on Calvary,
Risen from death to set us free,
Living Lord Jesus, help us see
You are Lord.

Lord Jesus Christ,
We would come to You,
Live our lives for You,
Son of God.
All Your commands we know are true,
Your many gifts will make us new,
Into our lives Your power breaks through,
Living Lord.

358 Rae Ranford
Copyright © 1990 Thankyou Music

LORD JESUS, HERE I STAND before You,
To worship You, glorify Your name,
I humbly bow the knee before Your majesty,
Give You the glory, give You the praise.
I love You, lay my life before You,
I trust You for my every need;
I lift my hands to You, surrender everything,
You are my Saviour, My Lord and King.

359 Peter Mattacola
Copyright © 1990 Jesus Fellowship Songs/
Adm. by CopyCare

LORD, KEEP MY HEART TENDER,
Reaching with outstretched hands
To Jesus Christ;
Feeling my hardness melt,
Knowing how Jesus felt,
Possessed by love,
Warm Calvary love.

Lord, keep my heart tender,
Reaching with outstretched hands
For healing grace;
Believe the word revealed—
'By His stripes we are healed'—
Possessed by love,
Whole Calvary love.

Lord, keep my heart tender,
Reaching with outstretched hands
To those in need;
Finding, as tears I weep,
Compassion's well is deep,
Possessed by love,
Fresh Calvary love.

Lord, keep my heart tender,
Reaching with outstretched hands
To God most high;
Worshipping with desire,
My heart consumed by fire,
Possessed by love,
Strong Calvary love.

360
Robert Bicknell
Copyright © 1977 ZionSong Music/
Adm. by CopyCare

LORD MAKE ME AN INSTRUMENT,
An instrument of worship;
I lift up my hands in Your name.
Lord make me an instrument,
An instrument of worship;
I lift up my hands in Your name.

I'll sing You a love song,
A love song of worship,
I'll lift up my hands in Your name.
I'll sing You a love song,
A love song to Jesus,
I'll lift up my hands in Your name.

For we are a symphony,
A symphony of worship;
We lift up our hands in Your name.
For we are a symphony,
A symphony of worship;
We lift up our hands in Your name.

We'll sing You a love song,
A love song of worship,
We'll lift up our hands in Your name.
We'll sing you a love song,
A love song to Jesus,
We'll lift up our hands in Your name.

361
Jessy Dixon/Randy Scruggs/John W. Thompson
Copyright © 1983 Whole Armor & Full Armor
Publishing Companies & Dixon Music/
Adm. by TKO Publishing Ltd

LORD OF LORDS, King of kings,
Maker of heaven and earth and all good
  things,
We give You glory.
Lord Jehovah, Son of Man,
Precious Prince of Peace and the great I AM,
We give You glory.

  Glory to God!
  Glory to God!
  Glory to God Almighty,
  In the highest!

Lord, You're righteous in all Your ways.
We bless Your holy name and we will give
  You praise,
We give You glory.
You reign for ever in majesty,
We praise You and lift You up for eternity,
We give You glory.

362
Graham Kendrick
Copyright © 1987 Make Way Music

LORD, THE LIGHT OF YOUR LOVE is shining,
In the midst of the darkness, shining;
Jesus, Light of the world, shine upon us,
Set us free by the truth You now bring us,
Shine on me, shine on me.

  Shine, Jesus, shine,
  Fill this land with the Father's glory;
  Blaze, Spirit, blaze,
  Set our hearts on fire.
  Flow, river, flow,
  Flood the nations with grace and mercy;
  Send forth Your word,
  Lord, and let there be light.

Lord, I come to Your awesome presence,
From the shadows into Your radiance;
By the blood I may enter Your brightness,
Search me, try me, consume all my darkness.
Shine on me, shine on me.

As we gaze on Your kingly brightness
So our faces display Your likeness.
Ever changing from glory to glory,
Mirrored here may our lives tell Your story.
Shine on me, shine on me.

363
Graham Kendrick
Copyright © 1991 Make Way Music

LORD WE COME in Your name,
Gathered here to worship You.
Join us all in harmony,
Spirit, come.

  And join our hearts together in love,
    (men)
  Join our hearts together in love, *(women)*
  Join our hearts together in love, *(men)*
  Join our hearts, *(women)*
  And come like the dew on the mountains
    descending. *(all)*
  Join our hearts together in love, *(men)*
  Join our hearts together in love, *(women)*
  Join our hearts together in love, *(men)*
  Join our hearts, *(women)*
  For there the Lord has commanded the
    blessing. *(all)*

O how good, how beautiful
When we live in unity;   *(women)*
Flowing like anointing oil
On Jesus' head.   *(men)*

  So join our hearts ... (etc.)

So let us all agree
To make strong our bonds of peace.
Here is life for evermore,
Spirit, come.

And join our hearts ... (etc.)

364 Mick Ray
Copyright © 1987 Thankyou Music

LORD, WE GIVE YOU PRAISE;
Our prayer of thanks to You we bring.
We sing our songs to You,
For praise belongs to You;
Lord, we give You praise.

Your love goes on and on;
You never change, You never turn.
Our hands we raise to You,
And bring our praise to You;
Lord, we give You praise.

365 Trish Morgan, Ray Goudie,
Ian Townend & Dave Bankhead
Copyright © 1986 Thankyou Music

LORD, WE LONG FOR YOU to move in power;
There's a hunger deep within our hearts,
To see healing in our nation.
Send Your Spirit to revive us:

Heal our nation,
Heal our nation,
Heal our nation,
Pour out Your Spirit on this land.

Lord we hear Your Spirit, coming closer,
A mighty wave to break upon our land,
Bringing justice, and forgiveness.
God we cry to You, 'Revive us':

366 Dave Bilbrough
Copyright © 1984 Thankyou Music

LORD, WE WORSHIP YOU,
Lord, we worship You,
Lord, we worship You,
Lord, we worship You.

In humble adoration
We lift our voices to You,
And sing in acclamation
Our song of praise to You.

367 Simon & Lorraine Fenner
Copyright © 1989 Thankyou Music

LORD, YOU ARE CALLING the people of Your kingdom
To battle in Your name against the enemy;
To stand before You, a people who will serve You,
Till Your kingdom is released throughout the earth.

Let Your kingdom come,
Let Your will be done
On earth as it is in heaven.
(Repeat)

At the name of Jesus every knee must bow;
The darkness of this age must flee away.
Release Your power to flow throughout the land;
Let Your glory be revealed as we praise.

368 Lynn DeShazo
Copyright © 1982 Integrity's Hosanna! Music/
Sovereign Music UK

LORD, YOU ARE MORE PRECIOUS than silver,
Lord, You are more costly than gold.
Lord, You are more beautiful than diamonds,
And nothing I desire compares with You.

369 Graham Kendrick
Copyright © 1986 Thankyou Music

LORD, YOU ARE SO PRECIOUS TO ME,
Lord, You are so precious to me,
And I love You,
Yes, I love You,
Because You first loved me.

Lord, You are so gracious to me,
Lord, You are so gracious to me,
And I love You,
Yes, I love You,
Because You first loved me.

370 Ian Smale
Copyright © 1983 Thankyou Music

LORD, YOU PUT A TONGUE IN MY MOUTH
And I want to sing to You.
Lord, You put a tongue in my mouth
And I want to sing to You.
Lord, You put a tongue in my mouth
And I want to sing only to You.
Lord Jesus, free us in our praise;
Lord Jesus, free us in our praise.

ord, You put some hands on my arms
which I want to raise to You ... *(etc.)*

ord, You put some feet on my legs
and I want to dance to You ... *(etc.)*

71 Don Moen
Copyright © 1988 Integrity's Hosanna! Music/
Sovereign Music UK

ORD, YOU'RE FAITHFUL AND JUST,
You I put my trust, mighty God,
verlasting Father.
our word is faithful and true,
What You promised You will do, oh Lord.
our word endures for ever.

*You're faithful, faithful, and Your mercy
    never ends;
The world will pass away, but Your words
    are here to stay.
You're wonderful, Counsellor, Mighty
    God.
Lord Jehovah, You are the great I AM.*

72 Craig Musseau
Copyright © 1990 Mercy/Vineyard
Publishing/Adm. by CopyCare

ORD, YOUR GLORY FILLS MY HEART,
our presence deep within me stirs my
    soul.
Lord, how awesome are Your ways,
our majesty surrounding all the earth.

*All wisdom and honour and glory for ever,
All power and greatness and splendour,
They are Yours above all others, my Lord.*

ord, Your Spirit moves me now,
see a picture of Your holiness.
Lord, I look into Your eyes,
and feel a fire burn into my heart.

73 Tom Shirley
Copyright © 1987 Mercy/Vineyard
Publishing/Adm. by CopyCare

ORD, YOUR NAME IS HOLY,
ord, Your name is holy,
oly, Lord,
ou are holy,
ord, You are holy,
oly, Lord.

*I love You, Lord,
I glorify and praise Your holy name.
Lord, I love You, Lord,
I glorify and praise Your holy name.*

Lord, Your name is mighty,
Lord, Your name is mighty,
Mighty, Lord,
You are mighty,
Lord, You are mighty,
Mighty, Lord.

374 Barry Taylor
Copyright © 1992 Thankyou Music

LORD, YOUR NAME IS WONDERFUL,
*At Your name the captives shall go free.
We declare the mighty name of Jesus,
And proclaim Your holy victory.*

At Your name the kingdoms fall;
We declare You Lord of all.
At Your name the enemy shall flee,
You are mighty,
You are mighty Lord of all.
Mighty Lord of all.

(Last time)
Mighty Lord of all!

375 Dave Bilbrough
Copyright © 1984 Thankyou Music

LOVE BEYOND MEASURE, mercy so free,
Your endless resources given to me.
Strength to the weary, healing our lives,
Your love beyond measure has opened my
    eyes,
Opened my eyes.

376 Christina Rossetti (1830–94)

LOVE CAME DOWN AT CHRISTMAS,
Love all lovely, Love divine;
Love was born at Christmas,
Star and angels gave the sign.

Worship we the Godhead,
Love Incarnate, Love divine;
Worship we our Jesus:
But wherewith for sacred sign?

Love shall be our token,
Love be yours and love be mine,
Love to God and all men,
Love for plea and gift and sign.

377
Charles Wesley (1707–88)

LOVE DIVINE, all loves excelling,
Joy of heaven to earth come down!
Fix in us Thy humble dwelling,
All Thy faithful mercies crown.
Jesus, Thou art all compassion,
Pure unbounded love Thou art;
Visit us with Thy salvation,
Enter every trembling heart.

Breathe, O breathe Thy loving Spirit
Into every troubled breast!
Let us all in Thee inherit,
Let us find Thy promised rest.
Take away the love of sinning;
Alpha and Omega be;
End of faith, as its beginning,
Set our hearts at liberty.

Come, Almighty to deliver,
Let us all Thy grace receive;
Suddenly return, and never,
Never more Thy temples leave.
Thee we would be always blessing,
Serve Thee as Thy hosts above,
Pray, and praise Thee without ceasing,
Glory in Thy perfect love.

Finish then Thy new creation,
Pure and spotless let us be;
Let us see Thy great salvation
Perfectly restored in Thee!
Changed from glory into glory,
Till in heaven we take our place;
Till we cast our crowns before Thee,
Lost in wonder, love and praise.

378
Robert Lowry (1826–99)

LOW IN THE GRAVE HE LAY,
Jesus, my Saviour,
Waiting the coming day,
Jesus, my Lord:

> *Up from the grave He arose,*
> *With a mighty triumph o'er His foes;*
> *He arose a Victor from the dark domain,*
> *And He lives for ever with His saints to*
> * reign:*
> *He arose! He arose!*
> *Alleluia! Christ arose!*

Vainly they watch His bed,
Jesus, my Saviour;
Vainly they seal the dead,
Jesus, my Lord:

Death cannot keep his prey,
Jesus, my Saviour;
He tore the bars away,
Jesus, my Lord:

379

Jack W. Hayford
Copyright © 1981 Rocksmith Music,
USA/Adm. by Bucks Music Ltd

MAJESTY, worship His majesty,
Unto Jesus be glory, honour and praise.
Majesty, kingdom authority,
Flows from His throne unto His own,
His anthem raise.

So exalt, lift up on high the name of Jesus,
Magnify, come glorify Christ Jesus the King
Majesty, worship His majesty,
Jesus who died, now glorified,
King of all kings.

380
Dave Bilbrough
Copyright © 1988 Thankyou Music

MAKE A JOYFUL MELODY,
Join together in harmony,
We are a part of a family,
The family of God.

His Spirit is our guarantee
That He lives in you and me,
We are a part of a family,
The family of God.

> *Lord, we praise You, praise You,*
> *Your love is great!*
> *Lord, we praise You, praise You,*
> *We celebrate!*

381
Sebastian Temple. Dedicated to Mrs Frances Tracy
Copyright © 1967 OCP Publications

MAKE ME A CHANNEL OF YOUR PEACE.
Where there is hatred let me bring Your love
Where there is injury, Your pardon, Lord;
And where there's doubt, true faith in You.

> *Oh, Master, grant that I may never seek*
> *So much to be consoled as to console;*
> *To be understood as to understand;*
> *To be loved as to love with all my soul.*

Make me a channel of Your peace.
Where there's despair in life let me bring
  hope;
Where there is darkness, only light;
And where there's sadness, ever joy.

Make me a channel of Your peace.
is in pardoning that we are pardoned,
giving to all men that we receive,
nd in dying that we're born to eternal life.

382 Chris Bowater
Copyright © 1983 Sovereign Lifestyle Music

MAKE ME, LORD, A DREAMER for Your
    kingdom;
ant in my heart heavenly desires.
rant faith that can say, impossibilities shall
    be,
nd vision lest a world should perish not
    knowing Thee.

Make me, Lord, a dreamer for Your kingdom;
would aspire to greater goals in God.
o cause faith to rise, to motivate each word
    and deed,
faith that's well convinced that Jesus meets
    every need.

Make me, Lord, a dreamer for Your kingdom,
reams that will change a world that's lost its
    way.
ay dreams that first found their birth in
    Your omnipotence,
ome alive in me, becoming reality.

383 Maldwyn Pope
Copyright © 1988 Coronation Music
Publishing/Kingsway Music

MAKE US ONE, LORD, *make us one, Lord,*
By Your Spirit, make us one, Lord.
We are members of one body,
Make us one, Lord, we pray.

very tribe and nation
represented here,
Vatching with each other
s the day of Christ draws near;
Vorshipping the Saviour
Vho died to set us free,
Ve belong together;
Ve are family.

384 Graham Kendrick
Copyright © 1986 Thankyou Music

MAKE WAY, make way, for Christ the King
splendour arrives.
ling wide the gates and welcome Him
nto your lives.

Make way! (Make way!)
Make way! (Make way!)
For the King of kings.
(For the King of kings.)
Make way! (Make way!)
Make way! (Make way!)
And let His kingdom in.

He comes the broken hearts to heal,
The prisoners to free.
The deaf shall hear, the lame shall dance,
The blind shall see.

And those who mourn with heavy hearts,
Who weep and sigh;
With laughter, joy and royal crown
He'll beautify.

We call you now to worship Him
As Lord of all.
To have no gods before Him,
Their thrones must fall!

385 Philipp Bliss (1838–76)

MAN OF SORROWS! what a name
For the Son of God, who came
Ruined sinners to reclaim!
Hallelujah! what a Saviour!

Bearing shame and scoffing rude,
In my place condemned He stood;
Sealed my pardon with His blood:
Hallelujah! what a Saviour!

Guilty, vile, and helpless, we;
Spotless Lamb of God was He:
Full atonement—can it be?
Hallelujah! what a Saviour!

Lifted up was He to die,
'It is finished!' was His cry:
Now in heaven exalted high:
Hallelujah! what a Saviour!

When He comes, our glorious King,
All His ransomed home to bring,
Then anew this song we'll sing:
'Hallelujah! what a Saviour!'

386 Frances R. Havergal (1836–79)

MASTER, SPEAK! THY SERVANT HEARETH,
Longing for Thy gracious word,
Longing for Thy voice that cheereth;
Master, let it now be heard.
I am listening, Lord, for Thee;
What hast Thou to say to me?

Speak to me by name, O Master,
Let me know it is to me;
Speak, that I may follow faster,
With a step more firm and free,
Where the Shepherd leads the flock
In the shadow of the rock.

Master, speak! though least and lowest,
Let me not unheard depart;
Master, speak! for O Thou knowest
All the yearning of my heart,
Knowest all its truest need;
Speak and make me blessed indeed.

Master, speak! and make me ready,
When Thy voice is truly heard,
With obedience glad and steady
Still to follow every word.
I am listening, Lord, for Thee;
Master, speak! O speak to me!

387

MAY MY LIFE declare the honour of Your
   name,
Reveal the heart of Christ who came
To light the darkest place
With sacrificial love.
(Last time)
Sacrificial love.

Cause me, Lord, to reach out in the Father's
   name,
To glorify the Lamb once slain,
To light the darkest place
With sacrificial love.

   Teach me, Lord, to make my life as an
      offering,
   To tell the world that Jesus Christ is King,
   For the glory of God.

388

MAY THE FRAGRANCE of Jesus fill this
   place. *(Men)*
May the fragrance of Jesus fill this
   place. *(Women)*
May the fragrance of Jesus fill this
   place. *(Men)*
Lovely fragrance of Jesus, *(Women)*
Rising from the sacrifice *(All)*
Of lives laid down in adoration.

May the glory of Jesus fill His church. *(Men)*
May the glory of Jesus fill His
   church. *(Women)*
May the glory of Jesus fill His church. *(Men)*
Radiant glory of Jesus, *(Women)*
Shining from our faces *(All)*
As we gaze in adoration.

May the beauty of Jesus fill my life. *(Men)*
May the beauty of Jesus fill my life. *(Women)*
May the beauty of Jesus fill my life. *(Men)*
Perfect beauty of Jesus, *(Women)*
Fill my thoughts, my words, my deeds, *(All)*
My all I give in adoration.

389

MAY WE BE A SHINING LIGHT to the nations
A shining light to the peoples of the earth;
Till the whole world sees the glory of Your
   name,
May Your pure light shine through us.

May we bring a word of hope to the
   nations,
A word of life to the peoples of the earth;
Till the whole world knows there's salvation
   through Your name,
May Your mercy flow through us.

May we be a healing balm to the nations,
A healing balm to the peoples of the earth;
Till the whole world knows the power of Your
   name,
May Your healing flow through us.

May we sing a song of joy to the nations,
A song of praise to the peoples of the earth;
Till the whole world rings with the praises of
   Your name,
May Your song be sung through us.

May Your kingdom come to the nations,
Your will be done in the peoples of the
   earth;
Till the whole world knows that Jesus Christ
   is Lord,
May Your kingdom come in us,
May Your kingdom come in us,
May Your kingdom come on earth.

90 Graham Kendrick
Copyright © 1986 Thankyou Music

MEEKNESS AND MAJESTY,
Manhood and Deity,
In perfect harmony,
The Man who is God.
Lord of eternity
Dwells in humanity,
Kneels in humility
And washes our feet.

O what a mystery,
Meekness and majesty.
Bow down and worship
For this is your God,
This is your God.

Father's pure radiance,
Perfect in innocence,
Yet learns obedience
To death on a cross.
Suffering to give us life,
Conquering through sacrifice,
And as they crucify
Prays: 'Father forgive.'

Wisdom unsearchable,
God the invisible,
Love indestructible
In frailty appears.
Lord of infinity,
Stooping so tenderly,
Lifts our humanity
To the heights of His throne.

91 Maggi Dawn
Copyright © 1987 Thankyou Music

MIGHTY GOD, gracious King, strong
Deliverer;
You have heard all our prayers, and You've
answered;
So we give to You our deep appreciation,
You're the living God, You are Lord;
You're the living God, You are Lord.

92 Jude Del Hierro
Copyright © 1987 Mercy/Vineyard
Publishing/Adm. by CopyCare

MORE LOVE (more love),
MORE POWER (more power),
More of You in my life.
More love (more love),
More power (more power),
More of You in my life.

And I will worship You with all of my
heart,
And I will worship You with all of my
mind,
And I will worship You with all of my
strength,
For You are my Lord.

(Last time)
And I will seek Your face with all of my
heart,
And I will seek Your face with all of my
mind,
And I will seek Your face with all of my
strength,
For You are my Lord,
You are my Lord.

393 Eleanor Farjeon (1881–1965)
Copyright © David Higham Associates Ltd

MORNING HAS BROKEN
Like the first morning;
Blackbird has spoken
Like the first bird.
Praise for the singing!
Praise for the morning!
Praise for them, springing
Fresh from the Word!

Sweet the rain's new fall
Sunlit from heaven,
Like the first dewfall
On the first grass.
Praise for the sweetness
Of the wet garden,
Sprung in completeness
Where His feet pass.

Mine is the sunlight!
Mine is the morning
Born of the one light
Eden saw play!
Praise with elation,
Praise every morning,
God's re-creation
Of the new day!

394 Patricia Morgan
Copyright © 1984 Thankyou Music

MOVE HOLY SPIRIT,
We ask You to
Fill us afresh.
We receive You.

395

Frederick W. Faber (1814–63)

MY GOD, HOW WONDERFUL THOU ART,
Thy majesty how bright!
How beautiful Thy mercy-seat,
In depths of burning light!

How dread are Thine eternal years,
O everlasting Lord,
By prostrate spirits day and night
Incessantly adored!

How wonderful, how beautiful
The sight of Thee must be,
Thine endless wisdom, boundless power,
And awesome purity!

O how I fear Thee, living God,
With deepest, tenderest fears,
And worship Thee with trembling hope
And penitential tears!

Yet I may love Thee too, O Lord,
Almighty as Thou art,
For Thou hast stooped to ask of me
The love of my poor heart.

No earthly father loves like Thee;
No mother e'er so mild
Bears and forbears as Thou hast done
With me, Thy sinful child.

Father of Jesus, love's reward,
What rapture will it be
Prostrate before Thy throne to lie,
And gaze, and gaze on Thee.

396

Graham Kendrick
Copyright © 1991 Make Way Music

MY HEART IS FULL of admiration
For You, my Lord, my God and King.
Your excellence my inspiration,
Your words of grace have made my spirit
    sing.

> *All the glory, honour and power*
> *Belong to You, belong to You.*
> *Jesus, Saviour, Anointed One,*
> *I worship You, I worship You.*

You love what's right and hate what's evil,
Therefore Your God sets You on high,
And on Your head pours oil of gladness,
While fragrance fills Your royal palaces.

Your throne, O God, will last for ever,
Justice will be Your royal decree.
In majesty, ride out victorious,
For righteousness, truth and humility.

397

Joan Parsons
Copyright © 1978 Thankyou Music

MY LORD, HE IS THE FAIREST OF THE FAIR
He is the lily of the valley,
The bright and morning star.
His love is written deep within my heart,
He is the never-ending fountain
Of everlasting life.

And He lives, He lives,
He lives, He lives in me.

398

Graham Kendrick
Copyright © 1989 Make Way Music

MY LORD, WHAT LOVE IS THIS
That pays so dearly,
That I, the guilty one,
May go free!

> *Amazing love, O what sacrifice,*
> *The Son of God given for me.*
> *My debt He pays, and my death He*
> *   dies,*
> *That I might live, that I might live.*
> (Last time only)
> *That I might live!*

And so they watched Him die,
Despised, rejected;
But oh, the blood He shed
Flowed for me!

And now, this love of Christ
Shall flow like rivers;
Come wash your guilt away,
Live again!

399

Keith Routledge
Copyright © 1975 Sovereign Music UK

MY PEACE I give unto you,
It's a peace that the world cannot give,
It's a peace that the world cannot
    understand:
Peace to know, peace to live,
My peace I give unto you.

My joy…*(etc.)*
My love…*(etc)*

400 Samuel Crossman (1624–84)

MY SONG IS LOVE UNKNOWN,
My Saviour's love to me:
Love to the loveless shown,
That they might lovely be.
O who am I, that for my sake
My Lord should take frail flesh and die?

He came from His blessed throne,
Salvation to bestow;
But men made strange, and none
The longed-for Christ would know:
But O! my Friend, my Friend indeed,
Who at my need His life did spend.

Sometimes they strew His way,
And His sweet praises sing;
Resounding all the day
Hosannas to their King:
Then 'Crucify!' is all their breath,
And for His death they thirst and cry.

They rise and needs will have
My dear Lord made away;
A murderer they save,
The Prince of life they slay,
Yet cheerful He to suffering goes,
That He His foes from thence might free.

In life no house, no home
My Lord on earth might have;
In death, no friendly tomb,
But what a stranger gave.
What may I say? Heaven was His home;
And mine the tomb wherein He lay.

Here might I stay and sing,
No story so divine;
Never was love, dear King!
Never was grief like Thine.
This is my Friend, in whose sweet praise
I all my days could gladly spend.

 401 David Fellingham
Copyright © 1988 Thankyou Music

MY SOUL LONGS FOR YOU, O my God;
I seek You with all of my heart.
In this dry and thirsty land
My voice cries out to You;
Only Your presence can satisfy my need.

And so I enter into Your sanctuary,
To behold Your glory.
I'll give You my praise as long as I live,
Raise my hands, my life I'll give
To You, O I love You, Lord.

 402 Andy Park
Copyright © 1988 Mercy/Vineyard
Publishing/Adm. by CopyCare

NO ONE BUT YOU, LORD,
Can satisfy the longing in my heart.
Nothing I do, Lord,
Can take the place of drawing near to You.

Only You can fill my deepest longing,
Only You can breathe in me new life;
Only You can fill my heart with laughter,
Only You can answer my heart's cry.

Father, I love You,
Come satisfy the longing in my heart.
Fill me, overwhelm me,
Until I know Your love deep in my heart.

 403 Phil Lawson Johnston
Copyright © 1989 Thankyou Music

NOT UNTO US, *but unto Your name*
Be glory, honour and praise.
Not unto us, but unto Your name
Be glory, honour and praise.

Yours is the greatness and power.
You alone deserve all the fame.
Yours is the splendour and majesty.
From everlasting You're the same.

Yours is the glorious kingdom.
You alone are the King over all.
The earth is under Your dominion now.
You say when nations rise or fall.

404 Bill Anderson
Copyright © 1985 Thankyou Music

NOT WITHOUT A CAUSE do we go marching
forth to war,
Not without a cause that we'll see
righteousness restored.
Clean your weapons, stir your hearts, shed all
fears before we start,
When we stand to do our part we shall say:

'Not without a right do we unsheath our
silent swords,
Not without a fight but we will crown Him
Lord of lords.
Lift your banner, lift it high, Jesus is our
battle cry.
As we've lived, so we shall die, by His
side.'

Not without a foe do we prepare ourselves to
    fight,
Not without a shout will we scale hell's
    unconquered height.
Let the hosts of Satan pray, when we rise as
    one that day,
Let them run in disarray, when we say:

Not without a cheer will we hear bells and
    trumpets ring,
Not without a tear we'll set Him on the throne
    of kings.
Eyes on fire and faces grim, we will free
    Jerusalem,
Through the gates we'll follow Him, as we
    say:

405 Martin Rinkart (1586–1649)
Tr. Catherine Winkworth (1829–78)

NOW THANK WE ALL OUR GOD,
With hearts and hands and voices;
Who wondrous things has done,
In whom His world rejoices;
Who from our mother's arms
Has blessed us on our way
With countless gifts of love,
And still is ours today.

O may this bounteous God
Through all our life be near us,
With ever joyful hearts
And blessèd peace to cheer us;
And keep us in His grace,
And guide us when perplexed,
And free us from all ills
In this world and the next.

All praise and thanks to God
The Father now be given,
The Son, and Him who reigns
With them in highest heaven,
The one eternal God,
Whom earth and heaven adore;
For thus it was, is now,
And shall be ever more.

406 Joey Holder
Copyright © 1984 Far Lane Publishing/
Kingsway Music

NOW UNTO THE KING eternal,
Unto the King immortal,
Unto the King invisible,
The only wise God,
The only wise God.
(Repeat)

Unto the King be glory and honour,
Unto the King for ever,
Unto the King be glory and honour for ever
And ever, Amen, Amen.

407 Elizabeth P. Head (1850–1936)
Copyright control

O BREATH OF LIFE, COME SWEEPING
THROUGH US,
Revive Thy church with life and power.
O Breath of Life, come, cleanse, renew us,
And fit Thy church to meet this hour.

O Wind of God, come, bend us, break us,
Till humbly we confess our need;
Then in Thy tenderness remake us,
Revive, restore; for this we plead.

O Breath of Love, come, breathe within us,
Renewing thought and will and heart:
Come, love of Christ, afresh to win us,
Revive Thy church in every part.

Revive us, Lord! is zeal abating
While harvest fields are vast and white?
Revive us, Lord, the world is waiting,
Equip Thy church to spread the light.

408 Anonymous Latin,
Tr. Frederick Oakley (1802–80) altd

O COME, ALL YE FAITHFUL,
Joyful and triumphant,
O come ye, O come ye to Bethlehem;
Come and behold Him,
Born the King of angels;

>   *O come, let us adore Him,*
>   *O come, let us adore Him,*
>   *O come, let us adore Him,*
>   *Christ the Lord!*

God of God,
Light of light,
Lo, He abhors not the virgin's womb;
Very God,
Begotten, not created:

Sing, choirs of angels,
Sing in exultation,
Sing, all ye citizens of heaven above;
Glory to God
In the highest:

Yea, Lord, we greet Thee,
Born this happy morning,
Jesus, to Thee be glory given;
Word of the Father
Now in flesh appearing:

09   John F. Wade (1711–86)

COME LET US ADORE HIM,
come let us adore Him,
come let us adore Him,
rist the Lord.

r He alone is worthy… *(etc.)*

e'll give Him all the glory… *(etc.)*

10   Tr. John M. Neale (1818–66) altd

COME, O COME, IMMANUEL,
d ransom captive Israel,
at mourns in lonely exile here
ntil the Son of God appear.

Rejoice, rejoice! Immanuel
Shall come to thee, O Israel.

come, O come, Thou Lord of might
ho to Thy tribes on Sinai's height
ancient times didst give the law
cloud, and majesty, and awe.

come, Thou Rod of Jesse, free
ine own from Satan's tyranny;
om depths of hell Thy people save
nd give them victory o'er the grave.

come, Thou Dayspring, come and cheer
ur spirits by Thine advent here;
sperse the gloomy clouds of night,
nd death's dark shadows put to flight.

come, Thou Key of David, come
nd open wide our heavenly home;
ake safe the way that leads on high,
nd close the path to misery.

11   Charles Wesley (1707–88)

FOR A HEART TO PRAISE MY GOD,
heart from sin set free;
heart that always feels Thy blood
freely shed for me;

heart resigned, submissive, meek,
y great Redeemer's throne,
here only Christ is heard to speak,
here Jesus reigns alone;

humble, lowly, contrite heart,
elieving, true, and clean;
hich neither life nor death can part
om Him who dwells within;

A heart in every thought renewed,
And full of love divine;
Perfect and right, and pure, and good:
A copy, Lord, of Thine.

Thy nature, gracious Lord, impart;
Come quickly from above;
Write Thy new name upon my heart,
Thy new best name of love.

412   Charles Wesley (1707–88)

O FOR A THOUSAND TONGUES to sing
My great Redeemer's praise,
My great Redeemer's praise!
The glories of my God and King,
The triumphs of His grace!

Jesus! the name that charms our fears,
That bids our sorrows cease,
That bids our sorrows cease;
'Tis music in the sinner's ears,
'Tis life, and health, and peace.

See all your sins on Jesus laid;
The Lamb of God was slain,
The Lamb of God was slain;
His soul was once an offering made
For every soul of man.

He breaks the power of cancelled sin,
He sets the prisoner free,
He sets the prisoner free;
His blood can make the foulest clean,
His blood availed for me.

He speaks and, listening to His voice,
New life the dead receive,
New life the dead receive;
The mournful, broken hearts rejoice,
The humble poor believe.

Hear Him, ye deaf; His praise, ye dumb,
Your loosened tongues employ,
Your loosened tongues employ;
Ye blind, behold your Saviour come;
And leap, ye lame, for joy!

My gracious Master and my God,
Assist me to proclaim,
Assist me to proclaim,
To spread through all the earth abroad
The honours of Thy name.

413 Joanne Pond
Copyright © 1980 Thankyou Music

O GIVE THANKS to the Lord,
All you His people.
O give thanks to the Lord for He is good.
Let us praise, let us thank,
Let us celebrate and dance,
O give thanks to the Lord for He is good.

414 Graham Kendrick
Copyright © 1979 Thankyou Music

O GOD MY CREATOR, create in me
That river of water that flows full and free.
Let it bring life to the dead and stagnant sea;
Spring up, O well, and flow on out of me.

We come to the throne
Where flows the living stream,
And drink from the water,
And drink from the water,
And drink from the water that flows from
* Thee.*

O God my Creator, create in me
That new way of living that flows full and
  free.
Let it bring life to the wilderness of man;
Spring up, O well, and flood this thirsty land.

415 Isaac Watts (1674–1748)

O GOD, OUR HELP IN AGES PAST,
Our hope for years to come,
Our shelter from the stormy blast,
And our eternal home.

Under the shadow of Thy throne
Thy saints have dwelt secure;
Sufficient is Thine arm alone,
And our defence is sure.

Before the hills in order stood,
Or earth received her frame,
From everlasting Thou art God,
To endless years the same.

A thousand ages in Thy sight
Are like an evening gone,
Short as the watch that ends the night
Before the rising sun.

Time, like an ever-rolling stream,
Bears all its sons away;
They fly forgotten, as a dream
Dies at the opening day.

O God, our help in ages past,
Our hope for years to come,
Be Thou our guard while troubles last,
And our eternal home.

416 Graham Kendrick
Copyright © 1991 Make Way Music

O HEAVEN, IS IN MY HEART.
O, heaven is in my heart.

The kingdom of our God is here, *(Leader)*
Heaven is in my heart. *(All)*
The presence of His majesty, *(Leader)*
Heaven is in my heart. *(All)*
And in His presence joy abounds, *(Leader)*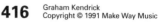
Heaven is in my heart. *(All)*
The light of holiness surrounds, *(Leader)*
Heaven is in my heart. *(All)*

His precious life on me He spent, *(All)*
Heaven is in my heart.
To give me life without an end,
Heaven is in my heart.
In Christ is all my confidence,
Heaven is in my heart.
The hope of my inheritance,
Heaven is in my heart.

We are a temple for His throne, *(Women)*
Heaven is in my heart. *(All)*
And Christ is the foundation stone, *(Wome*
Heaven is in my heart. *(All)*
He will return to take us home, *(Women)*
Heaven is in my heart. *(All)*
The Spirit and the Bride say 'Come!'
  (Women)
Heaven is in my heart.

417 Shona Pink-Martin
Copyright © 1981 Scripture in Song
(a div. of Integrity Music, Inc.)/
Sovereign Music UK

O I WILL SING UNTO YOU WITH JOY, O Lo
For You're the rock of my salvation,
Come before You with thanksgiving
And extol You with a song.
For You're the greatest King above all else,
You hold the depths of the earth in Your
  hand.
O I will sing unto You with joy, O Lord,
For You're the rock of my salvation.

418   John E. Bode (1816–74)

O JESUS, I HAVE PROMISED

To serve Thee to the end;
Be Thou for ever near me,
My Master and my Friend;
I shall not fear the battle
If Thou art by my side,
Nor wander from the pathway
If Thou wilt be my Guide.

O let me feel Thee near me;
The world is ever near;
I see the sights that dazzle,
The tempting sounds I hear;
My foes are ever near me,
Around me and within;
But Jesus, draw Thou nearer,
And shield my soul from sin.

O let me hear Thee speaking
In accents clear and still,
Above the storms of passion,
The murmurs of self-will;
O speak to reassure me,
To hasten, or control;
O speak, and make me listen,
Thou Guardian of my soul.

O Jesus, Thou hast promised
To all who follow Thee
That where Thou art in glory
There shall Thy servants be;
And, Jesus, I have promised
To serve Thee to the end;
O give me grace to follow
My Master and my Friend.

O let me see Thy footmarks,
And in them plant mine own;
My hope to follow duly
Is in Thy strength alone.
O guide me, call me, draw me,
Uphold me to the end;
And then in heaven receive me,
My Saviour and my Friend.

419   John Wimber
Copyright © 1979 Mercy/Vineyard
Publishing/Adm. by CopyCare

O LET THE SON OF GOD ENFOLD YOU

With His Spirit and His love,
Let Him fill your heart and satisfy your soul.
O let Him have the things that hold you,
And His Spirit like a dove
Will descend upon your life and make you
whole.

*Jesus, O Jesus,
Come and fill Your lambs.
Jesus, O Jesus,
Come and fill Your lambs.*

O come and sing this song with gladness
As your hearts are filled with joy,
Lift your hands in sweet surrender to His name.
O give Him all your tears and sadness,
Give Him all your years of pain,
And you'll enter into life in Jesus' name.

420   Phillips Brooks (1835–93)

O LITTLE TOWN OF BETHLEHEM,

How still we see thee lie!
Above thy deep and dreamless sleep
The silent stars go by.
Yet in thy dark streets shineth
The everlasting Light;
The hopes and fears of all the years
Are met in thee tonight.

O morning stars, together
Proclaim the holy birth,
And praises sing to God the King,
And peace to men on earth;
For Christ is born of Mary,
And gathered all above,
While mortals sleep, the angels keep
Their watch of wondering love.

How silently, how silently
The wondrous gift is given!
So God imparts to human hearts
The blessings of His heaven.
No ear may hear His coming;
But in this world of sin,
Where meek souls will receive Him, still
The dear Christ enters in.

O holy Child of Bethlehem,
Descend to us, we pray;
Cast out our sin, and enter in;
Be born in us today.
We hear the Christmas angels
The great glad tidings tell;
O come to us, abide with us,
Our Lord Immanuel!

421   Chris Roe & Dave Markee
Copyright © 1990 Thankyou Music

O LORD, GIVE ME AN UNDIVIDED HEART

To follow You.
O Lord, give me an undiminished love,
To see what You see, to do what You do,
O Lord, give me an undivided heart.

O Lord, give me an unrelenting mind
To seek Your face.
O Lord, give me an undefeated faith,
To see victory in all that I do,
To worship in spirit and truth.
To see less of me, and much more of You,
O Lord, give me an undivided heart.
O Lord, give me an undivided heart.

422 Carl Tuttle
Copyright © 1985 Mercy/Vineyard
Publishing/Adm. by CopyCare

O LORD, HAVE MERCY ON ME, and heal me;
O Lord, have mercy on me, and free me.
Place my feet upon a rock,
Put a new song in my heart, in my heart;
O Lord, have mercy on me.

O Lord, may Your love and Your grace protect
me;
O Lord, may Your ways and Your truth direct
me.
Place my feet upon a rock,
Put a new song in my heart, in my heart;
O Lord, have mercy on me.

423 Taizé, Music: Jacques Berthier (1923–94)
Copyright © Ateliers et Presses
de Taizé

O LORD, HEAR MY PRAYER,
O Lord, hear my prayer:
When I call answer me.
O Lord, hear my prayer,
O Lord, hear my prayer:
Come and listen to me.

424 Wendy Churchill
Copyright © 1980 Authentic Publishing/
Adm. by CopyCare

O LORD, MOST HOLY GOD,
Great are Your purposes,
Great is Your will for us,
Great is Your love.
And we rejoice in You,
And we will sing to You,
O Father, have Your way,
Your will be done.

For You are building
A temple without hands,
A city without walls
Enclosed by fire.
A place for You to dwell,
Built out of living stones,
Shaped by a Father's hand
And joined in love.

425 Stuart K. Hine
Copyright © 1953 Stuart K. Hine/The Stuart
Hine Trust/Published by Kingsway Music

O LORD MY GOD! When I in awesome
wonder
Consider all the works Thy hand hath made,
I see the stars, I hear the mighty thunder,
Thy power throughout the universe displayed

*Then sings my soul, my Saviour God, to
Thee,
How great Thou art! How great Thou art!
Then sings my soul, my Saviour God, to
Thee,
How great Thou art! How great Thou art!*

When through the woods and forest glades I
wander
And hear the birds sing sweetly in the trees;
When I look down from lofty mountain
grandeur,
And hear the brook, and feel the gentle
breeze:

And when I think that God, His Son not
sparing,
Sent Him to die—I scarce can take it in.
That on the cross, my burden gladly bearing,
He bled and died to take away my sin:

When Christ shall come with shout of
acclamation
And take me home—what joy shall fill my
heart!
Then shall I bow in humble adoration,
And there proclaim, my God, how great Thou
art!

426 Phil Lawson Johnston
Copyright © 1982 Thankyou Music

O LORD OUR GOD, how majestic is Your
name,
The earth is filled with Your glory.
O Lord our God, You are robed in majesty,
You've set Your glory above the heavens.

*We will magnify, we will magnify
The Lord enthroned in Zion.
We will magnify, we will magnify
The Lord enthroned in Zion.*

O Lord our God, You have established a
throne,
You reign in righteousness and splendour.
O Lord our God, the skies are ringing with
Your praise,
Soon those on earth will come to worship.

Lord our God, the world was made at Your
command,
You all things now hold together.
ow to Him who sits on the throne and to the
Lamb,
praise and glory and power for ever.

LORD OUR GOD, YOU ARE A GREAT GOD,
ur majesty beyond compare.
ho is a God like unto You,
nd who like me could know Your care?

good, dear Lord, to know Your
greatness,
good, dear Lord, to know Your care.
good just to be in Your presence,
good just to know that You are there.

O LORD, OUR LORD, *how excellent is*
Your name in all the earth.
O Lord, our Lord, how excellent is Your
name in all the earth.

u have set Your glory above the
heavens,
om children's lips You have ordained
praise;
u have set the moon and the stars in
place,
nd You still remember me.

hat is man that You are mindful of him;
e son of man that You take care of him?
u have put everything beneath his feet,
nd made him ruler of Your works.

LORD, THE CLOUDS ARE GATHERING,
e fire of judgement burns,
w we have fallen!
Lord, You stand appalled to see
ur laws of love so scorned,
d lives so broken.

Have mercy, Lord, (Men)
Have mercy, Lord, (Women)
Forgive us, Lord, (Men)
Forgive us, Lord, (Women)
Restore us, Lord, (All)
Revive Your church again.
Let justice flow (Men)
Let justice flow (Women)
Like rivers, (Men)
Like rivers, (Women)
And righteousness like a (All)
Never failing stream.

O Lord, over the nations now
Where is the dove of peace?
Her wings are broken.
O Lord, while precious children starve
The tools of war increase;
Their bread is stolen.

O Lord, dark powers are poised to flood
Our streets with hate and fear;
We must awaken!
O Lord, let love reclaim the lives
That sin would sweep away
And let Your kingdom come.

Yet, O Lord, Your glorious cross shall tower
Triumphant in this land,
Evil confounding.
Through the fire Your suffering church display
The glories of her Christ:
Praises resounding!

O LORD, YOU ARE MY GOD,
I will exalt You and praise Your name,
I will exalt You and praise Your name.
For in Your perfect faithfulness
You have done marvellous things.
O Lord, You are my God,
I will exalt You and praise Your name.

O LORD, YOU ARE MY LIGHT,
O Lord, You are my salvation.
You have delivered me from all my fear,
For You are the defence of my life.

For my life is hidden with Christ in God,
You have concealed me in Your love,
You've lifted me up, placed my feet on a rock;
I will shout for joy in the house of God.

432
Keith Green
Copyright © 1980 Birdwing Music/
BMG Songs Inc./EMI Christian Music Publishing/
Adm. by CopyCare

O LORD, YOU'RE BEAUTIFUL,
Your face is all I seek,
For when Your eyes are on this child,
Your grace abounds to me.

O Lord, please light the fire
That once burned bright and clear,
Replace the lamp of my first love
That burns with holy fear!

*I wanna take Your word
And shine it all around,
But first help me just to live it, Lord!
And when I'm doing well,
Help me to never seek a crown,
For my reward is giving glory to You.*

433
Graham Kendrick
Copyright © 1986 Thankyou Music

O LORD, YOUR TENDERNESS,
Melting all my bitterness,
O Lord, I receive Your love.
O Lord, Your loveliness,
Changing all my ugliness,
O Lord, I receive Your love.
O Lord, I receive Your love,
O Lord, I receive Your love.

434
George Matheson (1842–1906)

O LOVE THAT WILT NOT LET ME GO,
I rest my weary soul in thee:
I give thee back the life I owe,
That in thine ocean depths its flow
May richer, fuller be.

O light that followest all my way,
I yield my flickering torch to thee:
My heart restores its borrowed ray,
That in thy sunshine's blaze its day
May brighter, fairer be.

O joy that seekest me through pain,
I cannot close my heart to thee:
I trace the rainbow through the rain,
And feel the promise is not vain,
That morn shall tearless be.

O cross that liftest up my head,
I dare not ask to fly from thee:
I lay in dust life's glory dead,
And from the ground there blossoms red
Life that shall endless be.

435
Maggi Dawn
Copyright © 1986 Thankyou Music

O MAGNIFY THE LORD *with me,*
And let us exalt His name together.
O magnify the Lord with me,
And let us exalt His name together.

I called to the Lord and He answered,
Saved me from all of my trouble;
He delivered me from all my fear,
So I'll rejoice, I'll rejoice!

We will boast about the Lord,
Tell of the things He has done;
Let the whole world hear about it,
And they'll rejoice, they'll rejoice!

We will magnify Jesus together;
We will magnify You, O Lord.
We will magnify Jesus together;
We will magnify You, O Lord.

436
Geoff Roberts
Copyright © 1990 Thankyou Music

O MY LORD, YOU ARE MOST GLORIOUS,
King of kings and Prince of Peace.
By Your word this world was created;
By Your love I have been set free.
And I lift my hands in worship up to Your throne
I will declare how much You mean to me.
You are my Lord, it's You I worship;
Son of God, You reign in majesty.

437
William W. How (1823–97)

O MY SAVIOUR, LIFTED
From the earth for me,
Draw me, in Thy mercy,
Nearer unto Thee.

Lift my earthbound longings,
Fix them, Lord, above;
Draw me with the magnet
Of Thy mighty love.

And I come, Lord Jesus;
Dare I turn away?
No! Thy love hath conquered,
And I come today.

Bringing all my burdens,
Sorrow, sin, and care;
At Thy feet I lay them,
And I leave them there.

438 Cecil F. Alexander (1818–95)

ONCE, IN ROYAL DAVID'S CITY,
Stood a lowly cattle shed,
Where a mother laid her baby
In a manger for His bed.
Mary was that mother mild,
Jesus Christ, her little child.

He came down to earth from heaven,
Who is God and Lord of all,
And His shelter was a stable,
And His cradle was a stall:
With the poor and meek and lowly
Lived on earth our Saviour holy.

And through all His wondrous childhood
He would honour and obey,
Love and watch the lowly mother
In whose gentle arms He lay.
Christian children all should be
Mild, obedient, good as He.

For He is our childhood's pattern:
Day by day like us He grew;
He was little, weak and helpless;
Tears and smiles like us He knew:
And He feeleth for our sadness,
And He shareth in our gladness.

And our eyes at last shall see Him
Through His own redeeming love;
For that child, so dear and gentle,
Is our Lord in heaven above;
And He leads His children on
To the place where He is gone.

Not in that poor lowly stable,
With the oxen standing by,
We shall see Him, but in heaven,
Set at God's right hand on high;
When like stars His children crowned,
All in white shall wait around.

439 Graham Kendrick
Copyright © 1981 Thankyou Music

ONE SHALL TELL ANOTHER,
And he shall tell his friend,
Husbands, wives and children
Shall come following on.
From house to house in families
Shall more be gathered in,
And lights will shine in every street,
So warm and welcoming.

Come on in and taste the new wine,
The wine of the kingdom,
The wine of the kingdom of God.
Here is healing and forgiveness,
The wine of the kingdom,
The wine of the kingdom of God.

Compassion of the Father
Is ready now to flow,
Through acts of love and mercy
We must let it show.
He turns now from His anger
To show a smiling face,
And longs that men should stand beneath
The fountain of His grace.

He longs to do much more than
Our faith has yet allowed,
To thrill us and surprise us
With His sovereign power.
Where darkness has been darkest
The brightest light will shine,
His invitation comes to us,
It's yours and it is mine.

440 Andy Park
Copyright © 1989 Mercy/Vineyard
Publishing/Adm. by CopyCare

ONE THING I ASK, one thing I seek,
That I may dwell in Your house, O Lord.
All of my days, all of my life,
That I may see You, Lord.

Hear me, O Lord, hear me when I cry;
Lord, do not hide Your face from me.
You have been my strength,
You have been my shield,
And You will lift me up.

One thing I ask,
One thing I desire
Is to see You,
Is to see You.

441 Gerrit Gustafson
Copyright © 1990 Integrity's Hosanna! Music/
Sovereign Music UK

ONLY BY GRACE can we enter,
Only by grace can we stand;
Not by our human endeavour,
But by the blood of the Lamb.
Into Your presence You call us,
You call us to come.
Into Your presence You draw us,
And now by Your grace we come,
Now by Your grace we come.

Lord, if You mark our transgressions,
Who would stand?
Thanks to Your grace we are cleansed
By the blood of the Lamb.
(Repeat)

442 Sabine Baring-Gould (1834–1924)

ONWARD, CHRISTIAN SOLDIERS,
Marching as to war,
With the cross of Jesus
Going on before!
Christ, the royal Master,
Leads against the foe;
Forward into battle,
See, His banners go!

> *Onward, Christian soldiers,*
> *Marching as to war,*
> *With the cross of Jesus*
> *Going on before.*

At the name of Jesus
Satan's host doth flee;
On then, Christian soldiers,
On to victory!
Hell's foundations quiver
At the shout of praise;
Brothers, lift your voices;
Loud your anthems raise:

Like a mighty army
Moves the church of God:
Brothers we are treading
Where the saints have trod.
We are not divided,
All one body we,
One in hope and doctrine,
One in charity.

Crowns and thrones may perish,
Kingdoms rise and wane,
But the church of Jesus
Constant will remain;
Gates of hell can never
'Gainst that church prevail;
We have Christ's own promise,
And that cannot fail:

Onward, then, ye people!
Join our happy throng;
Blend with ours your voices
In the triumph-song:
Glory, laud, and honour
Unto Christ the King!
This through countless ages
Men and angels sing:

443 Robert Cull

OPEN OUR EYES, LORD,
We want to see Jesus,
To reach out and touch Him
And say that we love Him.
Open our ears, Lord,
And help us to listen.
Open our eyes, Lord,
We want to see Jesus.

444 Carl Tuttle

OPEN YOUR EYES, see the glory of the King.
Lift up your voice and His praises sing.
I love You, Lord, I will proclaim:
Hallelujah, I bless Your name.

445 Henry W. Baker (1821–77)

O PRAISE YE THE LORD!
Praise Him in the height;
Rejoice in His word,
Ye angels of light;
Ye heavens adore Him
By whom ye were made,
And worship before Him
In brightness arrayed.

O praise ye the Lord!
Praise Him upon earth,
In tuneful accord,
Ye sons of new birth;
Praise Him who hath brought you
His grace from above,
Praise Him who hath taught you
To sing of His love.

O praise ye the Lord,
All things that give sound;
Each jubilant chord,
Re-echo around:
Loud organs, His glory
Forthtell in deep tone,
And sweet harp, the story
Of what He hath done.

O praise ye the Lord!
Thanksgiving and song
To Him be outpoured
All ages along;
For love in creation,
For heaven restored,
For grace of salvation,
O praise ye the Lord!

446 Tr. James W. Alexander (1804–59)

O SACRED HEAD, ONCE WOUNDED,
With grief and pain weighed down,
How scornfully surrounded
With thorns, Thine only crown!
How pale art Thou with anguish,
With sore abuse and scorn!
How does that visage languish,
Which once was bright as morn!

O Lord of life and glory,
What bliss till now was Thine!
I read the wondrous story,
I joy to call Thee mine.
Thy grief and Thy compassion
Were all for sinners' gain;
Mine, mine was the transgression,
But Thine the deadly pain.

What language shall I borrow
To praise Thee, heavenly Friend,
For this, Thy dying sorrow,
Thy pity without end?
Lord, make me Thine for ever,
Nor let me faithless prove;
O let me never, never
Abuse such dying love!

Be near me, Lord, when dying;
O show Thyself to me;
And for my succour flying,
Come, Lord, to set me free:
These eyes, new faith receiving,
From Jesus shall not move;
For he who dies believing,
Dies safely through Thy love.

447 Phil Rogers
Copyright © 1984 Thankyou Music

O TASTE AND SEE that the Lord is good,
How blessèd is the man who hides himself in
 Him.
I sought the Lord and He answered me
And set me free from all my fears.

I will give thanks to Him, for He is good,
His steadfast love to me will never end.
I will give thanks to Him, for He is good,
His steadfast love to me will never end.

448 Phil Rogers
Copyright © 1988 Thankyou Music

O, THAT YOU WOULD BLESS ME,
And enlarge my borders,
That Your hand would be with me,
O Lord, O Lord.
O, that You would keep me,
Keep me from all evil,
So that I may not be ashamed,
O Lord, O Lord.

May Your kingdom come,
May Your will be done
On earth as it is in heaven;
May Your kingdom come,
May Your will be done
Through me, O Lord, O Lord.

O, that You would fill me,
Fill me with Your Spirit,
So that I may know Your power,
O Lord, O Lord.
O, that You would use me
To fulfil Your purposes,
That through me Your glory would shine,
O Lord, O Lord.

449 Dave Bilbrough
Copyright © 1988 Thankyou Music

O, THE JOY OF YOUR FORGIVENESS,
Slowly sweeping over me;
Now in heartfelt adoration
This praise I'll bring
To You, my King,
I'll worship You, my Lord.

450 Dave Bilbrough
Copyright © 1980 Thankyou Music

O THE VALLEYS SHALL RING
With the sound of praise,
And the lion shall lie with the lamb.
Of His government there shall be no end,
And His glory shall fill the earth.

May Your will be done,
May Your kingdom come,
Let it rule, let it reign in our lives.
There's a shout in the camp as we answer the
 call,
Hail the King, Hail the Lord of lords!

451 Charles Wesley (1707–88)

O THOU WHO CAMEST FROM ABOVE
The pure celestial fire to impart,
Kindle a flame of sacred love
On the mean altar of my heart.

There let it for Thy glory burn
With inextinguishable blaze,
And trembling to its source return,
In humble prayer and fervent praise.

Jesus, confirm my heart's desire
To work, and speak, and think for Thee;
Still let me guard the holy fire,
And still stir up Thy gift in me.

Ready for all Thy perfect will,
My acts of faith and love repeat,
Till death Thy endless mercies seal,
And make the sacrifice complete.

452 Noel & Tricia Richards
Copyright © 1989 Thankyou Music

OUR CONFIDENCE IS IN THE LORD,
The source of our salvation.
Rest is found in Him alone,
The Author of creation.
We will not fear the evil day,
Because we have a refuge;
In every circumstance we say,
Our hope is built on Jesus.

He is our fortress,
We will never be shaken.
He is our fortress,
We will never be shaken.
(Repeat)

We will put our trust in God.
We will put our trust in God.

453 Rich Mullins
Copyright © 1988 BMG Songs Inc./
Adm. by CopyCare

OUR GOD IS AN AWESOME GOD,
He reigns from heaven above,
With wisdom, power and love,
Our God is an awesome God!
Our God is an awesome God,
He reigns from heaven above,
With wisdom, power and love,
Our God is an awesome God!

454 Patricia Morgan
Copyright © 1986 Thankyou Music

OUT OF YOUR GREAT LOVE, You have
relented.
Out of Your great love, You have shown us
grace.
Though we've caused You pain, and we have
hurt You,
Out of Your great love, You've turned again.

455 Steven Fry
Copyright © 1986 Birdwing Music/
BMG Songs Inc./EMI Christian Music Publishing/
Adm. by CopyCare

O, WE ARE MORE THAN CONQUERORS.
O, we are more than conquerors,
And who can separate us from
The love, the love of God?
O yes, we are,
We are more than conquerors.
O, we are more than conquerors.

For He has promised to fulfil His will in us,
He said that He would guide us with His eye;
For He has blessed us with all gifts in Christ,
And we are His delight.

For He's within to finish what's begun in me,
He opens doors that no one can deny;
He makes a way where there's no other way,
And gives me wings to fly.

456 Robert Grant (1779–1838)

O WORSHIP THE KING,
All glorious above;
O gratefully sing
His power and His love:
Our Shield and Defender,
The Ancient of Days,
Pavilioned in splendour
And girded with praise.

O tell of His might,
O sing of His grace,
Whose robe is the light,
Whose canopy space;
His chariots of wrath
The deep thunder-clouds form,
And dark is His path
On the wings of the storm.

The earth, with its store
Of wonders untold,
Almighty, Thy power
Hath founded of old;
Hath 'stablished it fast,
By a changeless decree,
And round it hath cast,
Like a mantle, the sea.

Thy bountiful care
What tongue can recite?
It breathes in the air,
It shines in the light;
It streams from the hills,
It descends to the plain,
And sweetly distils
In the dew and the rain.

Frail children of dust,
And feeble as frail,
In Thee do we trust,
Nor find Thee to fail;
Thy mercies how tender,
How firm to the end,
Our Maker, Defender,
Redeemer, and Friend!

457 John S. B. Monsell (1811–75)

O WORSHIP THE LORD in the beauty of
    holiness,
Bow down before Him, His glory proclaim;
With gold of obedience and incense of
    lowliness,
Kneel and adore Him; the Lord is His name.

Low at His feet lay thy burden of carefulness,
High on His heart He will bear it for thee,
Comfort thy sorrows, and answer thy
    prayerfulness,
Guiding thy steps as may best for thee be.

Fear not to enter His courts in the
    slenderness
Of the poor wealth thou wouldst reckon as
    thine;
Truth in its beauty, and love in its tenderness,
These are the offerings to lay on His shrine.

These, though we bring them in trembling
    and fearfulness,
He will accept for the name that is dear;
Mornings of joy give for evenings of
    tearfulness,
Trust for our trembling, and hope for our fear.

O worship the Lord in the beauty of holiness,
Bow down before Him, His glory proclaim;
With gold of obedience and incense of
    lowliness,
Kneel and adore Him: the Lord is His name.

458 Author unknown
Copyright control

PEACE IS FLOWING LIKE A RIVER,
Flowing out through you and me,
Spreading out into the desert,
Setting all the captives free.

*Let it flow through me,
Let it flow through me,
Let the mighty peace of God
Flow out through me.
Let it flow through me,
Let it flow through me,
Let the mighty peace of God
Flow out through me.*

Love is flowing … *(etc.)*

Joy is flowing … *(etc.)*

Faith is flowing … *(etc.)*

Hope is flowing … *(etc.)*

459 John Watson
Copyright © 1986 Ampelos Music/
Adm. by CopyCare

PEACE LIKE A RIVER,
Love like a mountain,
The wind of Your Spirit
Is blowing everywhere.
Joy like a fountain,
Healing spring of life;
Come, Holy Spirit,
Let Your fire fall.

460 Graham Kendrick
Copyright © 1988 Make Way Music

PEACE TO YOU.
We bless you now in the name of the Lord.
Peace to you.
We bless you now in the name of the Prince
    of Peace.
Peace to you.

461 Anne Ortlund
Copyright © 1970 Singspiration
Music Corp., USA/
Adm. by Bucks Music Ltd

PRAISE GOD FOR THE BODY,
Praise God for the Son;
Praise God for the life
That binds our hearts in one.

*Joy is the food we share;
Love is our home, brothers.
Praise God for the body;
Shalom, Shalom.*

Guard your circle, brothers,
Clasp your hand in hand;
Satan cannot break
The bond in which we stand.

Shed your extra clothing,
Keep your baggage light;
Rough will be the battle,
Long will be the fight, but...

Praise God for the body,
Praise God for the Son;
Praise God for the life
That binds our hearts in one.

462
Thomas Ken (1637–1710)

PRAISE GOD FROM WHOM ALL BLESSINGS FLOW,
Praise Him, all creatures here below,
Praise Him above, ye heavenly host;
Praise Father, Son and Holy Ghost.

463
Twila Paris
Copyright © 1984 Singspiration Music
Corp., USA/Adm. by Bucks Music Ltd

PRAISE HIM, praise Him,
Praise Him with your song.
Praise Him, praise Him,
Praise Him all day long!

For the Lord is worthy,
Worthy to receive our praise.
For the Lord is worthy,
Worthy to receive our praise.

Praise Him, praise Him,
Praise Him with your heart.
Praise Him, praise Him,
Give Him all you are.

Praise Him, praise Him,
Praise Him with your life.
Praise Him, praise Him,
Lift His name up high.

464
John Kennett
Copyright © 1981 Thankyou Music

PRAISE HIM ON THE TRUMPET,
The psaltery and harp,
Praise Him on the timbrel and the dance,
Praise Him with stringed instruments, too.
Praise Him on the loud cymbals,
Praise Him on the loud cymbals,
Let everything that has breath praise the
Lord.

Hallelujah, praise the Lord,
Hallelujah, praise the Lord,
Let everything that has breath praise the
Lord.
Hallelujah, praise the Lord,
Hallelujah, praise the Lord,
Let everything that has breath praise the
Lord.

465
Fanny J. Crosby (1820–1915)

PRAISE HIM, PRAISE HIM! JESUS, OUR BLESSÈD REDEEMER;
Sing, O earth, His wonderful love proclaim!
Hail Him, hail Him! highest archangels in
glory,
Strength and honour give to His holy name.
Like a shepherd, Jesus will guard His
children,
In His arms He carries them all day long;
O ye saints that dwell in the mountains of
Zion,
Praise Him! praise Him! ever in joyful song.

Praise Him, praise Him! Jesus, our blessèd
Redeemer;
For our sins He suffered and bled and died.
He, our Rock, our hope of eternal salvation,
Hail Him, hail Him! Jesus the Crucified.
Loving Saviour, meekly enduring sorrow,
Crowned with thorns that cruelly pierced His
brow;
Once for us rejected, despised, and forsaken,
Prince of glory, ever triumphant now.

Praise Him, praise Him! Jesus, our blessèd
Redeemer;
Heavenly portals loud with hosannas ring!
Jesus, Saviour, reigneth for ever and ever,
Crown Him, crown Him! Prophet and Priest
and King!
Death is vanquished, tell it with joy, ye
faithful!
Where is now thy victory, boasting grave?
Jesus lives, no longer thy portals are
cheerless;
Jesus lives, the mighty and strong to save.

466
Henry F. Lyte (1793–1847)

PRAISE, MY SOUL, THE KING OF HEAVEN;
To His feet thy tribute bring.
Ransomed, healed, restored, forgiven,
Who like thee His praise should sing?
Praise Him! Praise Him!
Praise Him! Praise Him!
Praise the everlasting King!

raise Him for His grace and favour
o our fathers in distress;
raise Him, still the same for ever,
ow to chide, and swift to bless.
raise Him! Praise Him!
raise Him! Praise Him!
lorious in His faithfulness.

ather-like, He tends and spares us;
ell our feeble frame He knows;
His hands He gently bears us,
escues us from all our foes.
raise Him! Praise Him!
raise Him! Praise Him!
idely as His mercy flows.

ngels in the height, adore Him;
e behold Him face to face;
un and moon, bow down before Him,
wellers all in time and space.
raise Him! Praise Him!
raise Him! Praise Him!
raise with us the God of grace!

67 David Fellingham
Copyright © 1986 Thankyou Music

RAISE THE LORD, praise Him in His temple,
raise Him in the sanctuary of His power.
ft your voices with great rejoicing,
or God is great in all the earth.

raise Him for His excellence,
raise Him for His love;
raise Him for His mercy,
iving us new life.

68 Roy Hicks
Copyright © 1976 Latter Rain Music/
EMI Christian Music Publishing/
Adm. by CopyCare

RAISE THE NAME OF JESUS,
raise the name of Jesus,
e's my rock, He's my fortress,
e's my deliverer, in Him will I trust.
raise the name of Jesus.

69 John H. Newman (1801–90)

RAISE TO THE HOLIEST IN THE HEIGHT,
nd in the depth be praise;
all His words most wonderful,
ost sure in all His ways.

loving wisdom of our God!
hen all was sin and shame,
second Adam to the fight
nd to the rescue came.

O wisest love! that flesh and blood,
Which did in Adam fail,
Should strive afresh against the foe,
Should strive and should prevail;

And that a higher gift than grace
Should flesh and blood refine,
God's presence and His very self,
And essence all-divine.

O generous love! that He, who smote
In Man for man the foe,
The double agony in Man
For man should undergo;

And in the garden secretly,
And on the cross on high,
Should teach His brethren, and inspire
To suffer and to die.

Praise to the Holiest in the height,
And to the depth be praise;
In all His words most wonderful,
Most sure in all His ways.

470 Joachim Neander (1650–80)
Adpt. Percy Dearmer (1867–1936) after translation
by Catherine Winkworth (1829–78)
Copyright © Oxford University Press

PRAISE TO THE LORD, THE ALMIGHTY, the
King of creation!
O my soul, praise Him, for He is thy health
and salvation!
All ye who hear,
Brothers and sisters, draw near,
Praise Him in glad adoration.

Praise to the Lord, who doth prosper thy
work and defend thee;
Surely His goodness and mercy here daily
attend thee:
Ponder anew
What the Almighty can do,
Who with His love doth befriend thee.

Praise to the Lord, who doth nourish thy life
and restore thee,
Fitting thee well for the tasks that are ever
before thee,
Then to thy need
He like a mother doth speed,
Spreading the wings of grace o'er thee.

Praise to the Lord, who when tempests their
warfare are waging,
Who, when the elements madly around thee
are raging,
Biddeth them cease,
Turneth their fury to peace,
Whirlwinds and waters assuaging.

Praise to the Lord, who, when darkness of sin
is abounding,
Who, when the godless do triumph, all virtue
confounding,
Sheddeth His light,
Chaseth the horrors of night,
Saints with His mercy surrounding.

Praise to the Lord! O let all that is in me
adore Him!
All that hath life and breath, come now with
praises before Him!
Let the Amen
Sound from His people again:
Gladly for aye we adore Him.

471 Chris Bowater
Copyright © 1980 Sovereign Lifestyle Music

PRAISE YE THE LORD, praise ye the Lord,
For He has done marvellous things
Whereof we are glad,
We are glad,
Praise ye the Lord, praise ye the Lord.

472 Nettie Rose
Copyright © 1977 Thankyou Music

PRAISE YOU, LORD,
For the wonder of Your healing.
Praise You, Lord,
For Your love so freely given;
Outpouring, anointing,
Flowing in to heal our wounds:
Praise You, Lord, for Your love for me.

Praise You, Lord,
For Your gift of liberation.
Praise You, Lord,
You have set the captives free;
The chains that bind are broken
By the sharpness of Your sword:
Praise You, Lord, You gave Your life for me.

Praise You, Lord,
You have borne the depths of sorrow.
Praise You, Lord,
For Your anguish on the tree;
The nails that tore Your body
And the pain that tore Your soul:
Praise You, Lord, Your tears they fell for me.

Praise You, Lord,
You have turned our thorns to roses.
Glory, Lord,
As they bloom upon Your brow;
The path of pain is hallowed,
For Your love has made it sweet:
Praise You, Lord, and may I love You now.

473 Mary Smail
Copyright © Mary Smail

PREPARE THE WAY of the Lord,
Make His paths straight,
Open the gates,
That He may enter freely into our life.
'Hosanna!' we cry to the Lord.

*And we will fill the earth with the sound
of His praise.
Jesus is Lord!
Let Him be adored!
Yes, we will have this Man to reign over
us,
Hosanna! We follow the Lord!*

And He will come to us as He came before,
Clothed in His grace,
To stand in our place.
And we behold Him now our Priest and
King,
'Hosanna!' we sing to the Lord.

His kingdom shall increase,
To fill all the earth
And show forth His worth.
Then every knee shall bow and every tongue
confess
That Jesus Christ is Lord.

474 Robert Gay
Copyright © 1988 Integrity's Hosanna! Music/
Sovereign Music UK

PRINCE OF PEACE YOU ARE,
You're bright and morning star;
Wondrous royal King,
You have made my heart to sing.
I worship You in spirit and in truth;
Lifting my praise, Your name in song I
raise.
I give to You my life,
I offer up my sacrifice,
I pledge my love to You,
My God and King.

475 Brian Doerksen
Copyright © 1990 Mercy/Vineyard
Publishing/Adm. by CopyCare

PURIFY MY HEART,
Let me be as gold
And precious silver.
Purify my heart,
Let me be as gold,
Pure gold.

Refiner's fire,
My heart's one desire
Is to be holy,
Set apart for You, Lord.
I choose to be holy,
Set apart for You, my Master,
Ready to do Your will.

Purify my heart,
Cleanse me from within
And make me holy.
Purify my heart,
Cleanse me from my sin,
Deep within.

476 Steve & Vikki Cook
Copyright © 1987 PDI Music/
Adm. by CopyCare

RAISE UP AN ARMY, *O God,*
Awake Your people throughout the earth.
Raise up an army, O God,
To proclaim Your kingdom,
To declare Your word,
To declare Your glory, O God.

Our hope, our heart, our vision,
To see in every land
Your chosen people coming forth.
Fulfilling Your holy mission,
United as we stand,
Pledging our lives unto You, Lord.

O God, our glorious Maker,
We marvel at Your grace,
That You would use us in Your plan.
Rejoicing at Your favour,
Delighting in Your ways,
We'll gladly follow Your command!

477 Mike Kerry
Copyright © 1984 Thankyou Music

RECONCILED, I'm reconciled,
I'm reconciled to God for ever;
Know He took away my sin,
I know His love will leave me never.
Reconciled, I am His child,
I know it was on me He smiled,
I'm reconciled, I'm reconciled to God.

Hallelujah, I'm justified, I'm justified,
It's just as if I'd never sinned,
And once I knew such guilty fear,
But now I know His peace within me.
Justified, I'm justified,
It's all because my Jesus died,
I'm justified, I'm justified by God.

Hallelujah I'll magnify, I'll magnify,
I'll magnify His name for ever,
Wear the robe of righteousness
And bless the name of Jesus, Saviour.
Magnify the One who died,
The One who reigns for me on high,
I'll magnify, I'll magnify my God.

478 Chris Bowater
Copyright © 1985 Sovereign Lifestyle Music

REIGN IN ME, sovereign Lord,
Reign in me.
Reign in me, sovereign Lord,
Reign in me.

Captivate my heart,
Let Your kingdom come,
Establish there Your throne,
Let Your will be done.

479 Dave Bilbrough
Copyright © 1984 Thankyou Music

REIGNING IN ALL SPLENDOUR,
Victorious love,
Christ Jesus the Saviour,
Transcendent above.
All earthly dominions
And kingdoms shall fall,
For His name is Jesus
And He is the Lord.

He is Lord,
He is Lord,
He is Lord,
He is Lord.

480 Graham Kendrick
Copyright © 1983 Thankyou Music

REJOICE! *Rejoice!*
Christ is in you,
The hope of glory
In our hearts.
He lives! He lives!
His breath is in you,
Arise a mighty army,
We arise.

Now is the time for us
To march upon the land,
Into our hands
He will give the ground we claim.
He rides in majesty
To lead us into victory,
The world shall see
That Christ is Lord!

God is at work in us
His purpose to perform,
Building a kingdom
Of power not of words,
Where things impossible,
By faith shall be made possible;
Let's give the glory
To Him now.

Though we are weak, His grace
Is everything we need;
We're made of clay
But this treasure is within.
He turns our weaknesses
Into His opportunities,
So that the glory
Goes to Him.

 481 Chris Bowater
Copyright © 1986 Sovereign Lifestyle Music

REJOICE, REJOICE, REJOICE!
Rejoice, rejoice, rejoice!
My soul rejoices in the Lord.
(Repeat)

My soul magnifies the Lord,
And my spirit rejoices in God my
  Saviour;
My soul magnifies the Lord,
And my spirit rejoices in my God.

482 Charles Wesley (1707–88)

REJOICE, THE LORD IS KING!
Your Lord and King adore;
Mortals, give thanks, and sing,
And triumph ever more:

> *Lift up your heart, lift up your voice;*
> *Rejoice! Again I say: rejoice!*

Jesus the Saviour reigns,
The God of truth and love;
When He had purged our stains,
He took His seat above:

His kingdom cannot fail,
He rules o'er earth and heaven;
The keys of death and hell
Are to our Jesus given:

He sits at God's right hand
Till all His foes submit,
And bow to His command,
And fall beneath His feet:

Rejoice in glorious hope;
Jesus the Judge shall come,
And take His servants up
To their eternal home:

> *We soon shall hear the archangel's voice;*
> *The trump of God shall sound: rejoice!*

483 Graham Kendrick & Chris Rolinson
Copyright © 1981 Thankyou Music

RESTORE, O LORD,
The honour of Your name,
In works of sovereign power
Come shake the earth again;
That men may see
And come with reverent fear
To the living God,
Whose kingdom shall outlast the years.

Restore, O Lord,
In all the earth Your fame,
And in our time revive
The church that bears Your name.
And in Your anger,
Lord, remember mercy,
O living God,
Whose mercy shall outlast the years.

Bend us, O Lord,
Where we are hard and cold,
In Your refiner's fire
Come purify the gold.
Though suffering comes
And evil crouches near,
Still our living God
Is reigning, He is reigning here.

Restore, O Lord,
The honour of Your name,
In works of sovereign power
Come shake the earth again;
That men may see
And come with reverent fear
To the living God,
Whose kingdom shall outlast the years.

 484 Doug Horley
Copyright © 1991 Thankyou Music

REVIVAL! *We're praying for revival,*
That Your kingdom may come,
Your will may be done
Throughout this land.
(Repeat)

Send now Your Spirit, Lord, may He come;
Cause us to glorify Jesus Your Son,
That all in this nation might know
He is the Lord.
Send now Your Spirit, let truth arise;
Where darkness has blinded, open closed eyes,
Bring spiritual health to this nation
As we cry to You:
Come heal our land.
Come heal our land.
Come heal our land.
Come heal our land.

485 Henry H. Milman (1791–1868)

RIDE ON, RIDE ON IN MAJESTY!
In lowly pomp ride on to die!
O Christ, Thy triumphs now begin
O'er captive death and conquered sin.

Ride on, ride on in majesty!
Hark all the tribes 'hosanna' cry;
Thine humble beast pursues his road
With palms and scattered garments strowed.

Ride on, ride on in majesty!
Thy last and fiercest strife is nigh;
The Father on His sapphire throne
Expects His own anointed Son.

Ride on, ride on in majesty!
In lowly pomp ride on to die!
Bow Thy meek head to mortal pain,
Then take, O God, Thy power, and reign!

486 Mark Altrogge
Copyright © 1987 People of Destiny
International/Adm. by CopyCare

RISE UP, you champions of God,
Rise up, you royal nation;
Rise up, and bear His light abroad,
We'll reach this generation.
We've got our marching orders,
We've got our marching orders;
Now is the time to carry them forth.

Go forth! Jesus loves them.
Go forth! Take the gospel.
Go forth! The time is now.
The harvest is ripening:
Go forth!

Feel now the burden of the Lord,
Feel how He longs to save them;
Feel now for those who never heard
About the Son He gave them.
We've got our marching orders,
We've got our marching orders;
Now is the time to carry them forth.

487 Dougie Brown
Copyright © 1980 Thankyou Music

RIVER, WASH OVER ME,
Cleanse me and make me new.
Bathe me, refresh me and fill me anew,
River wash over me.

Spirit, watch over me,
Lead me to Jesus' feet.
Cause me to worship and fill me anew,
Spirit, watch over me.

Jesus, rule over me,
Reign over all my heart.
Teach me to praise You and fill me anew,
Jesus, rule over me.

488 Augustus M. Toplady (1740–78)

ROCK OF AGES, cleft for me,
Let me hide myself in Thee;
Let the water and the blood,
From Thy riven side which flowed,
Be of sin the double cure,
Cleanse me from its guilt and power.

Not the labour of my hands
Can fulfil Thy law's demands;
Could my zeal no respite know,
Could my tears for ever flow,
All for sin could not atone:
Thou must save, and Thou alone.

Nothing in my hand I bring,
Simply to Thy cross I cling;
Naked, come to Thee for dress;
Helpless, look to Thee for grace;
Foul, I to the fountain fly:
Wash me, Saviour, or I die.

While I draw this fleeting breath,
When mine eyes shall close in death,
When I soar to worlds unknown,
See Thee on Thy judgement throne,
Rock of ages, cleft for me,
Let me hide myself in Thee.

489 Edward Caswall (1814–78)

SEE, AMID THE WINTER'S SNOW,
Born for us on earth below,
See, the Lamb of God appears,
Promised from eternal years.

Hail, thou ever-blessèd morn!
Hail, redemption's happy dawn!
Sing through all Jerusalem:
Christ is born in Bethlehem!

Lo, within a manger lies
He who built the starry skies,
He who throned in height sublime
Sits amid the cherubim.

Say, ye holy shepherds, say,
What your joyful news today;
Wherefore have ye left your sheep
On the lonely mountain steep?

'As we watched at dead of night,
Lo, we saw a wondrous light:
Angels singing, "Peace on earth"
Told us of the Saviour's birth.'

Sacred Infant, all divine,
What a tender love was Thine,
Thus to come from highest bliss
Down to such a world as this!

Teach, O teach us, holy Child,
By Thy face so meek and mild,
Teach us to resemble Thee
In Thy sweet humility.

490 Hilary Davies
Copyright © 1988 Coronation Music
Publishing/Kingsway Music

SEE HIM COME, the King upon a donkey.
Where is all His majesty and power?
He who was glorious, yet for my sake
Put away glory to die upon the cross.
His body was broken,
His heart was torn apart for me upon the
  cross.

See the people line His path with palm
  leaves;
Hear the children shouting out His name.
He who was glorious, yet for my sake
Put away power to die upon the cross.
His body was broken,
His heart was torn apart for me upon the
  cross.

491 Michael Perry
Copyright © Mrs B. Perry/
Jubilate Hymns Ltd

SEE HIM LYING ON A BED OF STRAW,
A draughty stable with an open door;
Mary cradling the babe she bore;
The Prince of glory is His name.

O now carry me to Bethlehem,
To see the Lord appear to men;
Just as poor as was the stable then,
The Prince of glory when He came.

Star of silver, sweep across the skies,
Show where Jesus in the manger lies;
Shepherds, swiftly from your stupor rise
To see the Saviour of the world.

Angels, sing again the song you sang,
Bring God's glory to the heart of man;
Sing that Bethlehem's little baby can
Be salvation to the soul.

Mine are riches, from Thy poverty,
From Thine innocence, eternity;
Mine, forgiveness by Thy death for me,
Child of sorrow for my joy.

492 Chris Bowater
Copyright © 1986 Sovereign Lifestyle Music

SEE HIS GLORY, see His glory,
See His glory now appear.
See His glory, see His glory,
See His glory now appear.
God of light,
Holiness and truth, power and might,
See His glory, see it now appear.

Now we declare our God is good
And His mercies endure for ever.
Now we declare our God is good,
And His mercies endure for ever.

493 Karen Lafferty
Copyright © 1972 CCCM Music/
Maranatha! Music/Adm. by CopyCare

SEEK YE FIRST the kingdom of God
And His righteousness,
And all these things shall be added unto you
Hallelu, hallelujah!

Hallelujah! Hallelujah!
Hallelujah! Hallelu, hallelujah!

Man shall not live by bread alone,
But by every word
That proceeds from the mouth of God,
Hallelu, hallelujah!

Ask and it shall be given unto you,
Seek and ye shall find.
Knock and it shall be opened unto you,
Hallelu, hallelujah!

If the Son shall set you free,
Ye shall be free indeed.
Ye shall know the truth and the truth shall set
  you free,
Hallelu, hallelujah!

Let your light so shine before men
That they may see your good works
And glorify your Father in heaven,
Hallelu, hallelujah!

Trust in the Lord with all thine heart,
He shall direct thy paths,
In all thy ways acknowledge Him,
Hallelu, hallelujah!

494 Author unknown
Copyright control

SET MY SPIRIT FREE that I might worship
Thee,
Set my spirit free that I might praise Thy name.
Let all bondage go and let deliverance flow,
Set my spirit free to worship Thee.

495 Dave Bilbrough
Copyright © 1983 Thankyou Music

SHOUT FOR JOY and sing,
Let your praises ring;
See that God is building
A kingdom for a King.
His dwelling place with men,
The new Jerusalem;
Where Jesus is Lord over all.

And we will worship, worship,
We will worship Jesus the Lord.
We will worship, worship,
We will worship Jesus the Lord.

A work so long concealed,
In time will be revealed,
As the sons of God shall rise and take their
stand.
Clothed in His righteousness,
The church made manifest,
Where Jesus is Lord over all.

Sovereign over all,
Hail Him risen Lord.
He alone is worthy of our praise.
Reigning in majesty,
Ruling in victory,
Jesus is Lord over all.

496 David Fellingham
Copyright © 1988 Thankyou Music

SHOUT FOR JOY AND SING your praises to
the King,
Lift your voice and let your hallelujahs ring;
Come before His throne to worship and adore,
Enter joyfully now the presence of the Lord.

You are my Creator, You are my
Deliverer,
You are my Redeemer, You are Lord,
And You are my Healer.
You are my Provider,
You are now my Shepherd and my
Guide,
Jesus, Lord and King, I worship You.

497 Graham Kendrick
Copyright © 1988 Make Way Music

SHOW YOUR POWER, O LORD,
Demonstrate the justice of Your kingdom.
Prove Your mighty word.
Vindicate Your name
Before a watching world.
Awesome are Your deeds, O Lord;
Renew them for this hour.
Show Your power, O Lord,
Among the people now.

Show Your power, O Lord,
Cause Your church to rise and take action.
Let all fear be gone,
Powers of the age to come
Are breaking through.
We Your people are ready to serve,
To arise and to obey.
Show Your power, O Lord,
And set the people free.

498 Joseph Mohr (1792–1848)
Tr. S. A. Brooke (1832–1916)

SILENT NIGHT, holy night!
Sleeps the world; hid from sight,
Mary and Joseph in stable bare
Watch o'er the Child beloved and
fair,
Sleeping in heavenly rest,
Sleeping in heavenly rest.

Silent night, holy night!
Shepherds first saw the light,
Heard resounding clear and long,
Far and near, the angel-song:
'Christ the Redeemer is here,
Christ the Redeemer is here.'

Silent night, holy night!
Son of God, O how bright
Love is smiling from Thy face!
Strikes for us now the hour of
grace,
Saviour, since Thou art born,
Saviour, since Thou art born.

499
Linda Stassen
Copyright © 1974 Linda Stassen

(Men)
SING HALLELUJAH TO THE LORD,
Sing Hallelujah to the Lord,
Sing Hallelujah, sing Hallelujah,
Sing Hallelujah to the Lord.

(Women)
Sing Hallelujah to the Lord,
Sing Hallelujah,
Hallelujah,
Sing Hallelujah to the Lord.

Jesus is risen from the dead ... *(etc.)*

Jesus is Lord of heaven and earth ... *(etc.)*

Jesus is living in His church ... *(etc.)*

Jesus is coming for His own ... *(etc.)*

500
Melva Lea
Copyright © 1981 Melva Lea,
Larry Lea Ministries

SING PRAISES UNTO GOD, *sing praises,*
Sing praises unto God, sing praises,
Sing praises unto God, sing praises,
Hallelujah!
(Repeat)

For God is the King over all the earth,
Sing praises unto Him with understanding.
O clap your hands and shout, all ye people,
For He is to be greatly praised.

501
Noel & Tricia Richards
Copyright © 1990 Thankyou Music

SING TO THE LORD, be joyful in praise,
Exalt His magnificent ways.
Sing to the Lord again and again,
Forever His glory proclaim.
Let anthems of worship ascend to the King,
Giving all honour to Him.
Great is His name throughout all the earth,
With all of our strength let us sing,
Let us sing:

Glory to the Lord!
Glory to the Lord!
With our voices we shall give
Glory to the Lord!

502
Mick Ray
Copyright © 1977 Thankyou Music

SING UNTO THE LORD A NEW SONG,
Sing unto the Lord, all the earth.
Sing to the Lord, bless His name,
He is greatly to be praised,
Sing unto the Lord a new song.

Tell among the nations the Lord reigns,
The world shall never be moved.
Let the heavens be glad
And the earth rejoice,
Sing unto the Lord a new song.

Then shall all the trees sing for joy
Before the Lord, for He comes.
He will judge the world
With His righteousness,
Sing unto the Lord a new song.

503
Dave Bilbrough
Copyright © 1983 Thankyou Music

SO FREELY,
Flows the endless love You give to me;
So freely,
Not dependent on my part.
As I am reaching out
Reveal the love within Your heart,
As I am reaching out
Reveal the love within Your heart.

Completely,
That's the way You give Your love to me;
Completely,
Not dependent on my part.
As I am reaching out
Reveal the love within Your heart,
As I am reaching out
Reveal the love within Your heart.

So easy,
I receive the love You give to me;
So easy,
Not dependent on my part.
Flowing out to me
The love within Your heart,
Flowing out to me
The love within Your heart.

504 Cindy Gough
Copyright © 1989 Mercy/Vineyard
Publishing/Adm. by CopyCare

SOFTEN MY HEART Lord, I want to meet You here.
Soften my heart Lord, tender me with tears,
For Your presence is beyond anything I could desire;
Soften my heart Lord, consume me with Your holy fire.

Soften my heart Lord, I have made a choice.
Soften my heart Lord, I want to hear Your voice,
For Your presence is beyond anything I could desire;
Soften my heart Lord, consume me with Your holy fire.

505 Graham Kendrick
Copyright © 1988 Make Way Music

SOFTEN MY HEART, LORD,
Soften my heart.
From all indifference
Set me apart,
To feel Your compassion,
To weep with Your tears;
Come soften my heart, O Lord,
Soften my heart.

506 Charles Wesley (1707–88)

SOLDIERS OF CHRIST, ARISE,
And put your armour on;
Strong in the strength which God supplies,
Through His eternal Son;

Strong in the Lord of hosts,
And in His mighty power;
Who in the strength of Jesus trusts
Is more than conqueror.

Stand, then, in His great might,
With all His strength endued;
And take, to arm you for the fight,
The panoply of God.

Leave no unguarded place,
No weakness of the soul;
Take every virtue, every grace,
And fortify the whole.

From strength to strength go on,
Wrestle and fight and pray;
Tread all the powers of darkness down,
And win the well-fought day.

That having all things done,
And all your conflicts past,
Ye may o'ercome, through Christ alone,
And stand complete at last.

507 John Wimber
Copyright © 1979 Mercy/Vineyard
Publishing/Adm. by CopyCare

SON OF GOD, this is our praise song.
Jesus, my Lord, I sing to You.
Come now, Spirit of God,
Breathe life into these words of love;
Angels join from above
As we sing our praise song.

We praise You, we praise You,
We praise You, we worship You.
We praise You, we worship You.

Son of God, this is our love song.
Jesus, my Lord, I sing to You.
Come now, Spirit of God,
Breathe life into these words of love;
Angels join from above
As we sing our love song.

We love You, we love You,
We love You, we worship You.
We love You, we worship You.

508 Noel & Tricia Richards
Copyright © 1990 Thankyou Music

SOVEREIGN LORD, I am Yours,
Now and ever more.
You're my King, You're the One
I am living for.
I choose to do what pleases You,
Lord, may my life for ever be
A living sacrifice.

509 Dave Bilbrough & Graham Kendrick
Copyright © 1990 Thankyou Music

SPIRIT BREATHE ON US, fall afresh on us,
As we gather in Your name.
Bring Your healing touch, do Your work in us,
As we gather in Your holy name.
Join us together, one to another,
As we surrender to You,
To You, O Lord.

510 Daniel Iverson
Copyright © 1935 Birdwing Music/
EMI Christian Music Publishing/Adm. by CopyCare

SPIRIT OF THE LIVING GOD,
Fall afresh on me;
Spirit of the living God,
Fall afresh on me.
Break me, melt me, mould me, fill me.
Spirit of the living God,
Fall afresh on me.

511 Paul Armstrong
Copyright © 1984 Restoration Music Ltd/
Sovereign Music UK

SPIRIT OF THE LIVING GOD,
Fall afresh on me;
Spirit of the living God,
Fall afresh on me.
Fill me anew,
Fill me anew.
Spirit of the Lord
Fall afresh on me.

512 James Montgomery (1771–1854)

STAND UP, AND BLESS THE LORD,
Ye people of His choice;
Stand up, and bless the Lord your God
With heart, and soul, and voice.

Though high above all praise,
Above all blessing high,
Who would not fear His holy name,
And laud and magnify?

O for the living flame
From His own altar brought,
To touch our lips, our minds inspire,
And wing to heaven our thought!

God is our strength and song,
And His salvation ours;
Then be His love in Christ proclaimed
With all our ransomed powers.

Stand up, and bless the Lord,
The Lord your God adore;
Stand up, and bless His glorious name
Henceforth for evermore.

513 George Duffield (1818–88)

STAND UP! STAND UP FOR JESUS,
Ye soldiers of the cross!
Lift high His royal banner,
It must not suffer loss.
From victory unto victory
His army He shall lead,
Till every foe is vanquished,
And Christ is Lord indeed.

Stand up, stand up for Jesus!
The trumpet-call obey;
Forth to the mighty conflict
In this His glorious day!
Ye that are His, now serve Him
Against unnumbered foes;
Let courage rise with danger,
And strength to strength oppose.

Stand up, stand up for Jesus!
Stand in His strength alone;
The arm of flesh will fail you,
Ye dare not trust your own.
Put on the gospel armour,
Each piece put on with prayer;
Where duty calls, or danger,
Be never wanting there.

Stand up, stand up for Jesus!
The strife will not be long;
This day the noise of battle,
The next the victor's song.
To him that overcometh
A crown of life shall be;
He with the King of glory
Shall reign eternally.

514   Graham Kendrick
Copyright © 1988 Make Way Music

SUCH LOVE, pure as the whitest snow;
Such love, weeps for the shame I know;
Such love, paying the debt I owe;
O Jesus, such love.

Such love, stilling my restlessness;
Such love, filling my emptiness;
Such love, showing me holiness;
O Jesus, such love.

Such love, springs from eternity;
Such love, streaming through history;
Such love, fountain of life to me;
O Jesus, such love.

515 Dave Bryant
Copyright © 1982 Thankyou Music

SUCH LOVE! Such grace!
Makes the pieces come falling into place,
Breaks through the darkness,
Turns on the light,
Making blindness give way to sight.
Your love has conquered,
Has set us free
To become all You've called us to be,
Healing the wounded, making us stand,
Bringing peace and a sword in our hand.
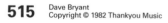

And no power in the universe
Can separate us from the love of God.
We're Yours for ever
With nothing to fear,
Willing slaves to the love that brought us here.

516 Ronnie Wilson
Copyright © 1978 Thankyou Music

SWEET FELLOWSHIP, Jesus in the midst,
Life blossoms in the church,
Men by men are blessed
When Jesus is in the midst.

Peace and harmony—Jesus reigning here;
The church moves at His command,
No room for doubt or fear,
For Jesus is reigning here.

I've never known a time like this,
Feel the spirit within me rise.
Come and see what God is doing.
Lord, we love You.

Sweet fellowship, Jesus in the midst,
Life blossoms in the church,
Men by men are blessed
When Jesus is in the midst.

517 Chris Bowater
Copyright © 1986 Sovereign Lifestyle Music

SWING WIDE THE GATES,
Let the King come in;
Swing wide the gates,
Make a way for Him.

Here He comes, the King of glory,
Here He comes, mighty in victory,
Here He comes, in splendour and majesty.
Swing wide the gates,
Swing wide the gates,
Let the King come in.

518 Paul Simmons
Copyright © 1985 Thankyou Music

TAKE, EAT, THIS IS MY BODY,
Broken for you,
For I am come that you might have life;
Eat of My flesh and live,
Eat of My flesh and live.

My blood was shed for many,
Taking away your sin,
And if I shall make you free
Then you shall be free indeed,
You shall be free indeed.

Though your sins be as scarlet
They shall be white as snow,
Though they be red like crimson
They shall be as wool,
They shall be as wool.

For God so loved the world
He gave His only Son,
That whosoever believeth on Him
Might have everlasting life,
Might have everlasting life.

519 Frances R. Havergal (1836–79)

TAKE MY LIFE, AND LET IT BE
Consecrated, Lord, to Thee;
Take my moments and my days,
Let them flow in ceaseless praise.

Take my hands, and let them move
At the impulse of Thy love;
Take my feet, and let them be
Swift and beautiful for Thee.

Take my voice, and let me sing
Always, only, for my King;
Take my lips, and let them be
Filled with messages from Thee.

Take my silver and my gold,
Not a mite would I withhold;
Take my intellect, and use
Every power as Thou shalt choose.

Take my will, and make it Thine;
It shall be no longer mine:
Take my heart, it is Thine own;
It shall be Thy royal throne.

Take my love; my Lord, I pour
At Thy feet its treasure store:
Take myself, and I will be
Ever, only, all for Thee.

520 Timothy Dudley-Smith
Copyright © 1961 Timothy Dudley-Smith

TELL OUT, MY SOUL, the greatness of the
    Lord!
Unnumbered blessings give my spirit voice;
Tender to me the promise of His word;
In God my Saviour shall my heart rejoice.

Tell out, my soul, the greatness of His name!
Make known His might, the deeds His arm
    has done;
His mercy sure, from age to age the same;
His holy name—the Lord, the mighty One.

Tell out, my soul, the greatness of His
  might!
Powers and dominions lay their glory by;
Proud hearts and stubborn wills are put to
  flight,
The hungry fed, the humble lifted high.

Tell out, my soul, the glories of His word!
Firm is His promise, and His mercy sure:
Tell out, my soul, the greatness of the Lord
To children's children and for evermore!

521 Robert Stoodley
       Copyright © 1978 Sovereign Music UK

THANKS BE TO GOD
Who gives us the victory,
Gives us the victory,
Through our Lord Jesus Christ.
Thanks be to God
Who gives us the victory,
Gives us the victory
Through our Lord Jesus Christ.

He is able to keep us from falling,
And to set us free from sin;
So let us each live up to our calling,
And commit our way to Him.

Jesus knows all about our temptations,
He has had to bear them too;
He will show us how to escape them,
If we trust Him He will lead us through.

He has led us from the power of darkness
To the kingdom of His blessed Son.
So let us join in praise together
And rejoice in what the Lord has done.

Praise the Lord for sending Jesus
To the cross of Calvary;
Now He's risen, reigns in power,
And death is swallowed up in victory.

522 Graham Kendrick
       Copyright © 1985 Thankyou Music

THANK YOU FOR THE CROSS,
The price You paid for us,
How You gave Yourself,
So completely,
Precious Lord (precious Lord).
Now our sins are gone,
All forgiven,
Covered by Your blood,
All forgotten,
Thank You, Lord (thank You, Lord).

Oh, I love You, Lord,
Really love You, Lord.
I will never understand
Why You love me.
You're my deepest joy,
You're my heart's desire,
And the greatest thing of all, O Lord, I see
You delight in me!

For our healing there,
Lord, You suffered,
And to take our fear
You poured out Your love,
Precious Lord (precious Lord).
Calvary's work is done,
You have conquered,
Able now to save
So completely,
Thank You, Lord (thank You, Lord).

523 Author unknown
       Copyright control

THANK YOU, JESUS, *thank You, Jesus,*
Thank You, Lord, for loving me.
Thank You, Jesus, thank You, Jesus,
Thank You, Lord, for loving me.

You went to Calvary,
And there You died for me,
Thank You, Lord, for loving me.
You went to Calvary,
And there You died for me,
Thank You, Lord, for loving me.

You rose up from the grave,
To me new life You gave,
Thank You, Lord, for loving me.
You rose up from the grave,
To me new life You gave,
Thank You, Lord, for loving me.

524 Diane Davis Andrew
       Copyright © 1971 Celebration/
       Kingsway Music

THANK YOU, LORD, FOR THIS FINE DAY,
Thank You, Lord, for this fine day,
Thank You, Lord, for this fine day,
Right where we are.

> *Alleluia, praise the Lord!*
> *Alleluia, praise the Lord!*
> *Alleluia, praise the Lord,*
> *Right where we are.*

Thank You, Lord, for loving us … *(etc.)*

Thank You, Lord, for giving us peace … *(etc.)*

Thank You, Lord, for setting us free … *(etc.)*

25 Samuel J. Stone (1839–1900)

HE CHURCH'S ONE FOUNDATION
Jesus Christ, her Lord;
He is His new creation
By water and the word;
From heaven He came and sought her
To be His holy bride,
With His own blood He bought her,
And for her life He died.

Elect from every nation,
Yet one o'er all the earth,
Her charter of salvation—
One Lord, one faith, one birth;
One holy name she blesses,
Partakes one holy food,
And to one hope she presses
With every grace endued.

Though with a scornful wonder
Men see her sore oppressed,
By schisms rent asunder,
By heresies distressed,
Yet saints their watch are keeping,
Their cry goes up, 'How long?'
And soon the night of weeping
Shall be the morn of song.

Mid toil, and tribulation,
And tumult of her war,
She waits the consummation
Of peace for evermore;
Till with the vision glorious
Her longing eyes are blessed,
And the great church victorious
Shall be the church at rest.

Yet she on earth hath union
With God the Three in One,
And mystic sweet communion
With those whose rest is won:
O happy ones and holy!
Lord, give us grace that we,
Like them, the meek and lowly,
On high may dwell with Thee.

26 Dave Bilbrough
Copyright © 1986 Thankyou Music

HE CHURCH'S ONE FOUNDATION
Jesus Christ the Lord,
And on that revelation
Each one of us is called
To taste His full salvation,
To know His life within;
A pure and holy nation
To glorify the King.

Hallelujah, how great You are,
Reigning in glory, enthroned in power;
Bright Morning Star, how great You are;
Reigning in glory, enthroned in power.

This time of preparation
Eventually will yield
The fruit of all His labours;
His heart will be fulfilled.
From every tribe and nation
His people shall be known;
Drawn to be His kingdom,
Made out of living stones.

See Him and be radiant,
Taste the Lord and know
He wants to take us deeper,
For what we are we sow;
With streams of living water
He longs to overflow,
That out to all creation
His glory He will show.

527 John Ellerton (1826–93)

THE DAY THOU GAVEST, LORD, IS ENDED,
The darkness falls at Thy behest;
To Thee our morning hymns ascended,
Thy praise shall sanctify our rest.

We thank Thee that Thy church unsleeping,
While earth rolls onward into light,
Through all the world her watch is keeping,
And rests not now by day or night.

As o'er each continent and island
The dawn leads on another day,
The voice of prayer is never silent,
Nor dies the strain of praise away.

The sun that bids us rest is waking
Our brethren 'neath the western sky,
And hour by hour fresh lips are making
Thy wondrous doings heard on high.

So be it, Lord! Thy throne shall never,
Like earth's proud empires, pass away;
Thy kingdom stands, and grows for ever,
Till all Thy creatures own Thy sway.

528 Graham Kendrick
Copyright © 1986 Thankyou Music

THE EARTH IS THE LORD'S (Men)
And everything in it, (Women)
The earth is the Lord's, (Men)
The work of His hands. (Women)
The earth is the Lord's (Men)
And everything in it; (Women)
And all things were made (All)
For His glory.

(Last time)
And all things were made,
Yes, all things were made,
And all things were made
For His glory.

The mountains are His,
The seas and the islands,
The cities and towns,
The houses and streets.
Let rebels bow down
And worship before Him,
For all things were made
For His glory.

529 Traditional

THE FIRST NOWELL the angel did say
Was to certain poor shepherds in fields as
    they lay;
In fields where they lay keeping their sheep,
On a cold winter's night that was so deep.

    Nowell, nowell, nowell, nowell,
    Born is the King of Israel!

They lookèd up and saw a star
Shining in the east, beyond them far,
And to the earth it gave great light,
And so it continued both day and night.

And by the light of that same star
Three wise men came from country far;
To seek for a King was their intent,
And to follow the star wherever it went.

This star drew nigh to the north-west;
Over Bethlehem it took its rest,
And there it did both stop and stay
Right over the place where Jesus lay.

Then entered in those wise men three
Full reverently upon their knee,
And offered there in His presence
Their gold, and myrrh, and frankincense.

Then let us all with one accord
Sing praises to our heavenly Lord,
That hath made heaven and earth of nought,
And with His blood mankind hath bought.

530 Thomas Olivers (1725–99)

THE GOD OF ABRAHAM PRAISE,
Who reigns enthroned above,
Ancient of everlasting days,
And God of love.
Jehovah! Great I AM!
By earth and heaven confessed;
I bow and bless the sacred name
Forever blessed.

The God of Abraham praise,
At whose supreme command
From earth I rise, and seek the joys
At His right hand.
I all on earth forsake—
Its wisdom, fame, and power—
And Him my only portion make,
My shield and tower.

The God of Abraham praise,
Whose all-sufficient grace
Shall guide me all my happy days
In all my ways.
He calls a worm His friend,
He calls Himself my God;
And He shall save me to the end
Through Jesu's blood.

He by Himself hath sworn,
I on His oath depend:
I shall, on eagles' wings upborne,
To heaven ascend;
I shall behold His face,
I shall His power adore,
And sing the wonders of His grace
Forever more.

There dwells the Lord our King,
The Lord our Righteousness,
Triumphant o'er the world and sin,
The Prince of Peace;
On Zion's sacred height
His kingdom still maintains,
And glorious with His saints in light
Forever reigns.

The God who reigns on high
The great archangels sing;
And, holy, holy, holy, cry,
Almighty King.
Who was and is the same,
And ever more shall be;
Jehovah, Father, Great I AM,
We worship Thee.

Before the Saviour's face
The ransomed nations bow;
O'erwhelmed at His almighty grace,
Forever new:
He shows His prints of love,
They kindle to a flame,
And sound through all the worlds above
The slaughtered Lamb.

The whole triumphant host
Give thanks to God on high;
Hail, Father, Son, and Holy Ghost!
They ever cry.
Hail, Abraham's God, and mine!
I join the heavenly lays;
All might and majesty are Thine,
And endless praise.

531

Thomas Kelly (1769–1854)

**THE HEAD THAT ONCE WAS CROWNED
        WITH THORNS**
Is crowned with glory now;
A royal diadem adorns
The mighty Victor's brow.

The highest place that heaven affords
Is His by sovereign right,
The King of kings, the Lord of lords,
And heaven's eternal light.

The joy of all who dwell above,
The joy of all below,
To whom He manifests His love,
And grants His name to know.

To them the cross, with all its shame,
With all its grace, is given;
Their name an everlasting name,
Their joy the joy of heaven.

They suffer with their Lord below,
They reign with Him above;
Their profit and their joy to know
The mystery of His love.

The cross He bore is life and health,
Though shame and death to Him;
His people's hope, His people's wealth,
Their everlasting theme.

532

Graham Kendrick
Copyright © 1981 Thankyou Music

THE KING IS AMONG US,
His Spirit is here,
Let's draw near and worship,
Let songs fill the air.

He looks down upon us,
Delight in His face,
Enjoying His children's love,
Enthralled by our praise.

For each child is special,
Accepted and loved,
A love gift from Jesus
To His Father above.

And now He is giving
His gifts to us all,
For no one is worthless
And each one is called.

The Spirit's anointing
On all flesh comes down,
And we shall be channels
For works like His own.

We come now believing
Your promise of power,
For we are Your people
And this is Your hour.

The King is among us,
His Spirit is here,
Let's draw near and worship,
Let songs fill the air.

533

Henry W. Baker (1821–77)

THE KING OF LOVE my Shepherd is,
Whose goodness faileth never;
I nothing lack if I am His
And He is mine for ever.

Where streams of living water flow
My ransomed soul He leadeth,
And where the verdant pastures grow
With food celestial feedeth.

Perverse and foolish oft I strayed,
But yet in love He sought me,
And on His shoulder gently laid,
And home rejoicing brought me.

In death's dark vale I fear no ill
With Thee, dear Lord, beside me;
Thy rod and staff my comfort still,
Thy cross before to guide me.

Thou spread'st a table in my sight;
Thy unction grace bestoweth:
And O what transport of delight
From Thy pure chalice floweth!

And so through all the length of days
Thy goodness faileth never;
Good Shepherd, may I sing Thy praise
Within Thy house for ever.

534

Author unknown
Copyright control

THE LORD HAS GIVEN a land of good things,
I will press in and make them mine.
I'll know His power, I'll know His glory,
And in His kingdom I will shine.

*With the high praises of God in our mouth
And a two-edged sword in our hand,
We'll march right on to the victory side,
Right into Canaan's land.*

Gird up your armour, ye sons of Zion,
Gird up your armour, let's go to war.
We'll win the battle with great rejoicing,
And so we'll praise Him more and more.

We'll bind their kings in chains and fetters,
We'll bind their nobles tight in iron,
To execute God's written judgement;
March on to glory, sons of Zion!

535 Chris Bowater
Copyright © 1982 Sovereign Lifestyle Music

THE LORD HAS LED FORTH *His people
with joy,
And His chosen ones with singing,
singing.
The Lord has led forth His people with joy,
And His chosen ones with singing.*

He has given to them the lands of the
nations,
To possess the fruit and keep His laws,
And praise, praise His name.

536 Graham Kendrick
Copyright © 1986 Thankyou Music

THE LORD IS MARCHING OUT in splendour,
In awesome majesty He rides,
For truth, humility and justice,
His mighty army fills the skies.

> *O give thanks to the Lord for His love
> endures,
> O give thanks to the Lord for His love
> endures,
> O give thanks to the Lord for His love
> endures,
> For ever, for ever.*

His army marches out with dancing
For He has filled our hearts with joy.
Be glad the kingdom is advancing,
The love of God our battle cry!

537 Scottish Psalter (1650)

THE LORD'S MY SHEPHERD, I'll not want;
He makes me down to lie
In pastures green; He leadeth me
The quiet waters by.

My soul He doth restore again;
And me to walk doth make
Within the paths of righteousness,
E'en for His own name's sake.

Yea, though I walk in death's dark vale,
Yet will I fear no ill;
For Thou art with me; and Thy rod
And staff me comfort still.

My table Thou hast furnishèd
In presence of my foes;
My head Thou dost with oil anoint,
And my cup overflows.

Goodness and mercy all my life
Shall surely follow me;
And in God's house for evermore
My dwelling place shall be.

538 Author unknown
Copyright control

THE LORD YOUR GOD IS IN YOUR MIDST,
The Lord of lords His name;
He will exult over you with joy,
He will renew you in His love,
He will rejoice over you
With shouts of joy, shouts of joy.
Shouts of joy, shouts of joy,
Shouts of joy.

539 Mark Altrogge
Copyright © 1986 People of Destiny
International/Adm. by CopyCare

THE NATIONS ARE WAITING for us,
They're dying to hear the song we sing.
The nations are waiting for us,
Waiting for the gospel we will bring,
That in each nation men might come to know
the King.

Jesus, You lead us,
Calling us onward,
A glorious army
With banners unfurled.
It's our decision
To follow Your vision,
We're on a mission,
A mission to the world.
And the nations are waiting,
The nations are waiting,
Waiting.

540 Graham Kendrick
Copyright © 1983 Thankyou Music

THE PRICE IS PAID,
Come let us enter in
To all that Jesus died
To make our own.
For every sin
More than enough He gave,
And bought our freedom
From each guilty stain.

The price is paid,
Alleluia,
Amazing grace,
So strong and sure;
And so with all my heart,
My life in every part,
I live to thank You for
The price You paid.

he price is paid,
ee Satan flee away;
or Jesus crucified
estroys his power.
o more to pay,
et accusation cease,
Christ there is
o condemnation now.

he price is paid,
nd by that scourging cruel
e took our sicknesses
s if His own.
nd by His wounds,
is body broken there,
is healing touch may now
y faith be known.

he price is paid,
Vorthy the Lamb' we cry,
ternity shall never
ease His praise.
he church of Christ
hall rule upon the earth,
Jesus' name we have
uthority.

41 Ruth Lake
Copyright © 1972 Scripture in Song
(a div. of Integrity Music, Inc.)/
Sovereign Music UK

HEREFORE THE REDEEMED of the Lord
shall return
nd come with singing unto Zion,
nd everlasting joy shall be upon their head.
Repeat)

hey shall obtain gladness and joy,
nd sorrow and mourning shall flee away.

herefore the redeemed of the Lord shall
return
nd come with singing unto Zion,
nd everlasting joy shall be upon their head.

542 Cecil F. Alexander (1818–95)

THERE IS A GREEN HILL FAR AWAY,
Outside a city wall,
Where the dear Lord was crucified,
Who died to save us all.

We may not know, we cannot tell,
What pains He had to bear;
But we believe it was for us
He hung and suffered there.

He died that we might be forgiven,
He died to make us good,
That we might go at last to heaven,
Saved by His precious blood.

There was no other good enough
To pay the price of sin;
He only could unlock the gate
Of heaven, and let us in.

O dearly, dearly has He loved!
And we must love Him too,
And trust in His redeeming blood,
And try His works to do.

543 Frederick Whitfield (1829–1904)

THERE IS A NAME I LOVE TO HEAR,
I love to speak its worth;
It sounds like music in my ear,
The sweetest name on earth.

O, how I love the Saviour's name,
O, how I love the Saviour's name,
O, how I love the Saviour's name,
The sweetest name on earth.

It tells me of a Saviour's love,
Who died to set me free;
It tells me of His precious blood,
The sinner's perfect plea.

It tells of One whose loving heart
Can feel my deepest woe;
Who in my sorrow bears a part
That none can bear below.

It bids my trembling heart rejoice,
It dries each rising tear;
It tells me in a still, small voice
To trust and never fear.

Jesus, the name I love so well,
The name I love to hear!
No saint on earth its worth can tell,
No heart conceive how dear!

544 Melody Green
Copyright © 1982 Ears to Hear Music/
Birdwing Music/EMI Christian Music Publishing/
BMG Songs, Inc./Adm. by CopyCare

THERE IS A REDEEMER,
Jesus, God's own Son,
Precious Lamb of God, Messiah,
Holy One.

Thank You, O my Father,
For giving us Your Son,
And leaving Your Spirit—
Till the work on earth is done.

Jesus my Redeemer,
Name above all names,
Precious Lamb of God, Messiah,
O for sinners slain.

When I stand in glory
I will see His face,
And there I'll serve my King for ever
In that holy place.

545 Noel Richards
Copyright © 1989 Thankyou Music

THERE IS POWER IN THE NAME OF JESUS;
We believe in His name.
We have called on the name of Jesus;
We are saved! We are saved!
At His name the demons flee.
At His name captives are freed.
For there is no other name that is higher
Than Jesus!

There is power in the name of Jesus,
Like a sword in our hands.
We declare in the name of Jesus,
We shall stand! We shall stand!
At His name God's enemies
Shall be crushed beneath our feet.
For there is no other name that is higher
Than Jesus!

546 Tedd Smith
Copyright © 1973 Hope Publishing Co./
Adm. by CopyCare

THERE'S A QUIET UNDERSTANDING
When we're gathered in the Spirit,
It's a promise that He gives us
When we gather in His name.
There's a love we feel in Jesus,
There's a manna that He feeds us,
It's a promise that He gives us
When we gather in His name.

And we know when we're together,
Sharing love and understanding,
That our brothers and our sisters
Feel the oneness that He brings.
Thank You, thank You, thank You, Jesus,
For the way You love and feed us,
For the many ways You lead us;
Thank You, thank You, Lord.

547 Graham Kendrick
Copyright © 1978 Thankyou Music

THERE'S A SOUND ON THE WIND like a
victory song,
Listen now, let it rest on your soul.
It's a song that I learned from a heavenly
King,
It's the song of a battle royal.

There's a loud shout of victory that leaps
from our hearts
As we wait for our conquering King.
There's a triumph resounding from dark ages
past
To the victory song we now sing.

Come on heaven's children,
The city is in sight.
There will be no sadness
On the other side.

There'll be crowns for the conquerors and
white robes to wear,
There will be no more sorrow or pain.
And the battles of earth shall be lost in the
sight
Of the glorious Lamb that was slain.

Now the King of the ages approaches the
earth,
He will burst through the gates of the sky,
And all men shall bow down to His beautiful
name,
We shall rise with a shout, we shall fly!

Come on, heaven's children,
The city is in sight.
There will be no sadness
On the other side.

Now the King of the ages approaches the
earth,
He will burst through the gates of the sky,
And all men shall bow down to His beautiful
name
We shall rise with a shout, we shall fly!

548 Chris Bowater
Copyright © 1985 Sovereign Lifestyle Music

THE SPIRIT OF THE LORD,
The sovereign Lord, is on me,
Because He has anointed me
To preach good news to the poor:

Proclaiming Jesus, only Jesus—
It is Jesus, Saviour, healer and baptiser,
And the mighty King,
The victor and deliverer—
He is Lord, He is Lord, He is Lord!

And He has called on me
To bind up all the broken hearts,
To minister release
To every captivated soul:

Let righteousness arise
And blossom as a garden;
Let praise begin to spring
In every tongue and nation:

549 Edith McNeil
Copyright © 1974 Celebration/
Kingsway Music

THE STEADFAST LOVE OF THE LORD never
ceases,
His mercies never come to an end;
They are new every morning,
New every morning,
Great is Thy faithfulness, O Lord,
Great is Thy faithfulness.

550 Graham Kendrick
Copyright © 1989 Make Way Music

THE TRUMPETS SOUND, the angels sing,
The feast is ready to begin;
The gates of heaven are open wide,
And Jesus welcomes you inside.

Tables are laden with good things,
O taste the peace and joy He brings;
He'll fill you up with love divine,
He'll turn your water into wine.

Sing with thankfulness songs of pure
delight.
Come and revel in heaven's love and light;
Take your place at the table of the King.
The feast is ready to begin.
The feast is ready to begin.

The hungry heart He satisfies,
Offers the poor His paradise;
Now hear all heaven and earth applaud
The amazing goodness of the Lord.

Ldr: Jesus,   *(All echo each line)*
We thank You
For Your love,
For Your joy.
Jesus,
We thank You
For the good things
You give to us.

551 Edmond L. Budry (1854–1932)
Tr. Richard B. Hoyle (1875–1939)
Copyright control

THINE BE THE GLORY,
Risen, conquering Son;
Endless is the victory
Thou o'er death hast won.
Angels in bright raiment
Rolled the stone away,
Kept the folded grave-clothes
Where Thy body lay.

Thine be the glory,
Risen, conquering Son;
Endless is the victory
Thou o'er death hast won!

Lo, Jesus meets us,
Risen from the tomb!
Lovingly He greets us,
Scatters fear and gloom.
Let the church with gladness
Hymns of triumph sing,
For her Lord now liveth,
Death hath lost its sting.

No more we doubt Thee,
Glorious Prince of life;
Life is naught without Thee:
Aid us in our strife;
Make us more than conquerors,
Through Thy deathless love;
Lead us in Thy triumph
To Thy home above.

552 Suella Behrns
Copyright © Gary Behrns

THINE, O LORD, IS THE GREATNESS,
And the power and the glory.
Thine, O Lord, is the victory,
And majesty, and majesty.

All that is in heaven and earth is Thine,
Thou art exalted as head over all!

In Thy hand is power and might to make
great,
In Thy hand is power to give strength to all!

Now is come salvation and power and might,
For the kingdom of our God has been given
   to His Christ!

553 Les Garrett
Copyright © 1967 Scripture in Song
(a div. of Integrity Music, Inc.)/
Sovereign Music UK

THIS IS THE DAY, this is the day
That the Lord has made, that the Lord has
   made;
We shall rejoice, we shall rejoice
And be glad in it, and be glad in it.
This is the day that the Lord has made,
We shall rejoice and be glad in it;
This is the day, this is the day
That the Lord has made.

554 Pauline Michael Mills
Copyright © 1963 Fred Bock Music
Company/Kingsway Music

THOU ART WORTHY, Thou art worthy,
Thou art worthy, O Lord.
To receive glory, glory and honour,
Glory and honour and power.
For Thou hast created, hast all things created,
Thou hast created all things;
And for Thy pleasure they are created,
Thou art worthy, O Lord.

555 Emily E. S. Elliott (1836–97)

THOU DIDST LEAVE THY THRONE and Thy
   kingly crown,
When Thou camest to earth for me;
But in Bethlehem's home there was found no
   room
For Thy holy nativity:
O come to my heart, Lord Jesus!
There is room in my heart for Thee.

Heaven's arches rang when the angels sang,
Proclaiming Thy royal degree;
But of lowly birth cam'st Thou, Lord, on earth,
And in great humility,
O come to my heart, Lord Jesus!
There is room in my heart for Thee.

The foxes found rest, and the birds had their
   nest,
In the shade of the cedar tree;
But Thy couch was the sod, O Thou Son of
   God,
In the deserts of Galilee.
O come to my heart, Lord Jesus!
There is room in my heart for Thee.

Thou camest, O Lord, with the living word
That should set Thy children free;
But with mocking scorn, and with crown of
   thorn,
They bore Thee to Calvary.
O come to my heart, Lord Jesus!
Thy cross is my only plea.

When heaven's arches shall ring, and her
   choirs shall sing,
At Thy coming to victory,
Let Thy voice call me home, saying, 'Yet there
   is room,
There is room at My side for thee.'
And my heart shall rejoice, Lord Jesus,
When Thou comest and callest for me.

556 Donn Thomas & Charles Williams
Copyright © 1980 Spoone Music/
Word Music/Adm. by CopyCare

THOU, O LORD, ART A SHIELD ABOUT ME,
You're my glory,
You're the lifter of my head.
Thou, O Lord, art a shield about me,
You're my glory,
You're the lifter of my head.

Hallelujah,
Hallelujah.
Hallelujah,
You're the lifter of my head.

557 John Marriott (1780–1825)

THOU, WHOSE ALMIGHTY WORD
Chaos and darkness heard,
And took their flight;
Hear us, we humbly pray,
And where the gospel-day
Sheds not its glorious ray,
Let there be light!

Thou who didst come to bring,
On Thy redeeming wing,
Healing and sight;
Health to the sick in mind,
Sight to the inly blind,
O now to all mankind
Let there be light!

Spirit of truth and love,
Life-giving, holy Dove,
Speed forth Thy flight;
Move on the waters' face,
Bearing the lamp of grace,
And in earth's darkest place
Let there be light!

essèd and holy Three,
lorious Trinity,
'isdom, love, might;
oundless as ocean's tide
olling in fullest pride,
arough the world far and wide
at there be light!

58 Dale Garratt
Copyright © 1979 Scripture in Song
(a div. of Integrity Music, Inc.)/
Sovereign Music UK

THROUGH OUR GOD *we shall do*
  valiantly,
  It is He who will tread down our enemies.
  We'll sing and shout His victory,
  Christ is King!
  (Last time only)
  Christ is King! Christ is King!

ar God has won the victory
ad set His people free;
s word has slain the enemy,
ae earth shall stand and see that—

59 Fanny J. Crosby (1820–1915)

) **GOD BE THE GLORY!** great things He
  hath done!
) loved He the world that He gave us His
  Son,
tho yielded His life an atonement for sin,
ad opened the life-gate that all may go in.

  Praise the Lord! Praise the Lord!
  Let the earth hear His voice!
  Praise the Lord! Praise the Lord!
  Let the people rejoice!
  O come to the Father through Jesus the
    Son;
  And give Him the glory, great things He
    hath done!

perfect redemption, the purchase of blood!
› every believer the promise of God;
ae vilest offender who truly believes,
aat moment from Jesus a pardon receives.

˜eat things He hath taught us, great things
 He hath done,
ad great our rejoicing through Jesus the
 Son:
at purer and higher and greater will be
 ur wonder, our worship, when Jesus we
 see!

560 Debbye C. Graafsma
Copyright © 1984 Integrity's Hosanna! Music/
Sovereign Music UK

TO HIM WHO SITS ON THE THRONE and
  unto the Lamb,
To Him who sits on the throne and unto the
  Lamb
Be blessing and glory and honour and power
  for ever,
Be blessing and glory and honour and power
  for ever.

561 Charles F. Munroe
Copyright © 1971 Charles Munroe Music/
CCCM Music/Maranatha! Music/Adm. by CopyCare

UNTO THEE, O LORD, do I lift up my soul,
Unto Thee, O Lord, do I lift up my soul.

  O my God, I trust in Thee,
  Let me not be ashamed,
  Let not mine enemies triumph over me.

Yea, let none that wait on Thee be ashamed,
Yea, let none that wait on Thee be ashamed.

Show me Thy ways, Thy ways, O Lord,
Teach me Thy paths, Thy paths, O Lord.

Remember not the sins of my youth,
Remember not the sins of my youth.

The secret of the Lord is with them that fear
  Him,
The secret of the Lord is with them that fear
  Him.

Unto Thee, O Lord, do I lift up my soul,
Unto Thee, O Lord, do I lift up my soul.

562 Phil Townend
Copyright © 1986 Thankyou Music

UNTO YOU, O LORD,
Do I open up my heart.
Unto You, O Lord,
Do I lift my voice.
Unto You, O Lord,
Do I raise my hands,
Unto You, O Lord of hosts.

563

WE ARE A CHOSEN PEOPLE, *a royal*
priesthood,
A holy nation, belonging to God.
We are a chosen people, a royal
priesthood,
A holy nation, belonging to God.

You have called us out of darkness
To declare Your praise.
We exalt You and enthrone You,
Glorify Your name.

You have placed us into Zion
In the new Jerusalem.
Thousand thousand are their voices,
Singing to the Lamb.

564

WE ARE ALL TOGETHER
To call upon Your name;
There is nothing we like better
Than to sing and give You praise.

Lord, we welcome You,
We welcome You,
We welcome You,
Come fill this place.

Bring healing and salvation,
Let Your kingdom come
Right here just like in heaven,
Lord, may Your will be done.

Father, come fill this place,
We welcome You;
Jesus, we seek Your face,
'Cause all we want to do
Is give our love to You.

565

WE ARE A PEOPLE OF POWER,
We are a people of praise;
We are a people of promise,
Jesus has risen, He's conquered the grave!
Risen, yes, born again,
We walk in the power of His name;
Power to be the sons of God,
The sons of God! The sons of God!
We are the sons, sons of God!

566

WE ARE BEING BUILT INTO A TEMPLE,
Fit for God's own dwelling place;
Into the house of God which is the church,
The pillar and the ground of truth,
As precious stones that Jesus owns,
Fashioned by His wondrous grace.
And as we love and trust each other
So the building grows and grows.

567

WE ARE HERE TO PRAISE YOU,
Lift our hearts and sing.
We are here to give You
The best that we can bring.
And it is our love
Rising from our hearts,
Everything within us cries:
'Abba Father.'
Help us now to give You
Pleasure and delight,
Heart and mind and will that say:
'I love You Lord.'

568

WE ARE IN GOD'S ARMY,
We are in the army of the Lord, yeah,
yeah, yeah.
We are in God's army,
Glorie, Glorie, Glorie,
The Glorie Company.

The enemy's attacking, convinced he's
gaining ground,
But the only voice that he can hear is the one
he shouts around;
But we're not fooled by his lies, we know that
he is wrong—
We may be weak as soldiers, but as an army
we are strong.

The enemy's regrouping, as he tries another
plan,
He can't pick off an army but he can pick out
a man;
So we'll stay close together, and sing this
battle-song—
We may be weak as soldiers, but as an army
we are strong.

the enemy's realising that his future's looking
poor,
though he loves single combat, he's already
lost the war;
United, not divided, together we belong—
We may be weak as soldiers, but as an army
we are strong.

569 Geron Davis
Copyright © 1983 Songchannel Music/
Meadowgreen Music/EMI Christian Music
Publishing/Adm. by CopyCare

WE ARE STANDING on holy ground,
And I know that there are angels all around.
Let us praise Jesus now.
We are standing in His presence on holy ground.

570 John Pantry
Copyright © 1990 Thankyou Music

WE ARE THE HANDS OF GOD,
Our task to do His will,
To lay our hands upon this world,
And by His Spirit see it healed.

We are the Church invincible,
The flesh and blood of Christ.
We are the Gospel visible,
Our lives the Saviour's light to the world.

We are the word of God,
And by the things we say
This world will judge the Prince of life
And be drawn in or turn away.

We are the feet of God,
Who walk the narrow way,
And every step we take is watched
By those for whom we fast and pray.

Though persecution comes,
And governments oppose,
Beneath the crushing weight of law
The church of Jesus grows and grows.

571 David Fellingham
Copyright © 1986 Thankyou Music

WE ARE YOUR PEOPLE who are called by
Your name.
We call upon You now to declare Your fame.
In this nation of darkness You've called us to
be light.
As we seek Your face, Lord, stir up Your might.

Build Your church and heal this land,
Let Your kingdom come.
Build Your church and heal this land,
Let Your will be done.

572 Graham Kendrick
Copyright © 1986 Thankyou Music

WE BELIEVE in God the Father,
Maker of the universe,
And in Christ His Son our Saviour,
Come to us by virgin birth.
We believe He died to save us,
Bore our sins, was crucified.
Then from death He rose victorious,
Ascended to the Father's side.

Jesus, Lord of all, Lord of all,
Jesus, Lord of all, Lord of all,
Jesus, Lord of all, Lord of all,
Jesus, Lord of all, Lord of all.
Name above all names,
Name above all names.
(Last time only)
Name above all names.

We believe He sends His Spirit,
On His church with gifts of power.
God His word of truth affirming,
Sends us to the nations now.
He will come again in glory,
Judge the living and the dead.
Every knee shall bow before Him,
Then must every tongue confess.

573 The Alternative Service Book 1980
Copyright © The Central Board of Finance
of the Church of England 1980;
The Archbishops' Council 1999

WE BREAK THIS BREAD to share in the body
of Christ: *(Men)*
We break this bread to share in the body of
Christ. *(Women)*

Though we are many, we are one body,
Because we all share, we all share in one
bread.
(Repeat)

We drink this cup to share in the body of
Christ: *(Men)*
We drink this cup to share in the body of
Christ. *(Women)*

574

WE BRING THE SACRIFICE OF PRAISE
Into the house of the Lord,
We bring the sacrifice of praise
Into the house of the Lord.
We bring the sacrifice of praise
Into the house of the Lord,
We bring the sacrifice of praise
Into the house of the Lord.
And we offer up to You
The sacrifices of thanksgiving,
And we offer up to You
The sacrifices of joy.

575

(Men and women in canon)
WE DECLARE THAT THE KINGDOM OF GOD IS HERE,
We declare that the kingdom of God is here,
Among you, among you.

(Last time)
We declare that the kingdom of God is here (Men)
We declare that the kingdom of God is here (Women)
We declare that the (Men)
Kingdom of God is here. (All)

The blind see, the deaf hear,
The lame men are walking;
Sicknesses flee at His voice.
The dead live again,
And the poor hear the good news:
Jesus is King, so rejoice!

576

WE DECLARE THERE'S ONLY ONE LORD,
And the earth belongs to Him,
We proclaim the day of salvation,
It's His kingdom and He's the King.

There is none like our mighty King,
He gave His life to free us.
There is none more worthy of
Our lives and our allegiance.

577

WE DECLARE YOUR MAJESTY,
We proclaim that Your name is exalted;
For You reign magnificently,
Rule victoriously,
And Your power is shown throughout the earth.
And we exclaim our God is mighty,
Lift up Your name, for You are holy.
Sing it again, all honour and glory,
In adoration we bow before Your throne.

578

WE EXTOL YOU, our God and King.
We bless Your name
For ever and for ever,
For You open up Your hand
And shower us with goodness.
Your mercy and Your grace
Are freely lavished on us.

So we sing Your praise, (Jesus is Lord)
We extol Your name, (Jesus is Lord)
Tell the glory of Your kingdom and Your mighty power;
Clothed in majesty, (Jesus is Lord)
Reigning sovereignly, (Jesus is Lord)
Your greatness is unsearchable, O God.

579

WE HAVE COME INTO THIS PLACE
And gathered in His name to worship Him,
We have come into this place
And gathered in His name to worship Him,
We have come into this place
And gathered in His name
To worship Christ the Lord,
Worship Him, Christ the Lord.

So forget about yourself
And concentrate on Him and worship Him,
So forget about yourself
And concentrate on Him and worship Him,
So forget about yourself
And concentrate on Him
And worship Christ the Lord,
Worship Him, Christ the Lord.

e is all my righteousness,
stand complete in Him and worship Him,
e is all my righteousness,
stand complete in Him and worship Him,
e is all my righteousness,
stand complete in Him
nd worship Christ the Lord,
Worship Him, Christ the Lord.

et us lift up holy hands
nd magnify His name and worship Him,
et us lift up holy hands
nd magnify His name and worship Him,
et us lift up holy hands
nd magnify His name
nd worship Christ the Lord,
Worship Him, Christ the Lord.

80 Robert Newey
Copyright © 1987 Thankyou Music

E HAVE COME TO MOUNT ZION,
o the city of the living God,
o Jesus our Redeemer,
nd the sprinkling of His blood.
e're part of a kingdom that cannot be shaken,
e've got a foundation that cannot be moved;
o let us praise Him,
allelujah,
et us praise the living God.

ow we draw near to Him by faith,
ome through the veil,
or Jesus brings us by His new and living
way into His holy place.
o let us come with boldness to the very
throne of God the Father,
nter in with confidence to meet Him face to
face.

81 David Hadden
Copyright © 1983 Restoration
Music Ltd/Sovereign Music UK

E KNOW THAT ALL THINGS work together
for our good
or good to those who love the Lord;
or God has called us to be just like His Son,
o live and walk according to His word.

We are more than conquerors,
We are more than conquerors,
Through Christ, through Christ.

m persuaded that neither death nor life,
or angels, principalities, nor powers,
or things that are now, nor things that are to
come,
n separate us from the love of Christ.

If God is for us, who against us can prevail?
No one can bring a charge against His
chosen ones;
And there will be no separation from our
Lord,
He has justified us through His precious
blood.

 582 Diane Fung
Copyright © 1979 Authentic Publishing/
Adm. by CopyCare

WE'LL SING A NEW SONG of glorious
triumph,
For we see the government of God in our
lives.
We'll sing a new song of glorious triumph,
For we see the government of God in our
lives.

He is crowned, God of the whole world
crowned,
King of creation crowned,
Ruling the nations now.
Yes, He is crowned, God of the whole world
crowned,
King of creation crowned,
Ruling the nations now.

583 Graham Kendrick
Copyright © 1989 Make Way Music

WE'LL WALK THE LAND
With hearts on fire,
And every step
Will be a prayer.
Hope is rising,
New day dawning,
Sound of singing
Fills the air.

Two thousand years,
And still the flame
Is burning bright
Across the land.
Hearts are waiting,
Longing, aching,
For awakening
Once again.

Let the flame burn brighter
In the heart of the darkness,
Turning night to glorious day.
Let the song grow louder
As our love grows stronger,
Let it shine, let it shine.

We'll walk for truth,
Speak out for love;
In Jesus' name
We shall be strong,
To lift the fallen,
To save the children,
To fill the nation
With Your song.

 584 Ramon Pink
Copyright © 1983 Scripture in Song
(a div. of Integrity Music, Inc.)/
Sovereign Music UK

WE PLACE YOU ON THE HIGHEST PLACE,
For You are the great High Priest,
We place You high above all else;
And we come to You and worship at Your
feet.

585 Matthias Claudius (1740–1815)
Tr. Jane M. Campbell (1817–78)

WE PLOUGH THE FIELDS and scatter
The good seed on the land,
But it is fed and watered
By God's almighty hand;
He sends the snow in winter,
The warmth to swell the grain,
The breezes and the sunshine,
And soft refreshing rain.

All good gifts around us
Are sent from heaven above;
Then thank the Lord, O thank the Lord,
For all His love.

He only is the Maker
Of all things near and far;
He paints the wayside flower,
He lights the evening star;
The winds and waves obey Him,
By Him the birds are fed;
Much more to us, His children,
He gives our daily bread.

We thank Thee, then, O Father,
For all things bright and good;
The seedtime and the harvest,
Our life, our health, our food.
No gifts have we to offer
For all Thy love imparts,
But that which Thou desirest,
Our humble, thankful hearts.

 586 Ed Baggett
Copyright © 1974 Celebration/
Kingsway Music

WE REALLY WANT TO THANK YOU, LORD,
We really want to bless Your name,
Hallelujah! Jesus is our King!
We really want to thank You, Lord,
We really want to bless Your name,
Hallelujah! Jesus is our King!

We thank You, Lord, for Your gift to us,
Your life so rich beyond compare,
The gift of Your body here on earth
Of which we sing and share.

We thank You, Lord, for our life together,
To live and move in the love of Christ,
Tenderness which sets us free
To serve You with our lives.

587 Edith Gilling Cherry (1872–97)

WE REST ON THEE, OUR SHIELD AND OUR DEFENDER!
We go not forth alone against the foe;
Strong in Thy strength, safe in Thy keeping
tender,
We rest on Thee and in Thy name we go.
Strong in Thy strength, safe in Thy keeping
tender,
We rest on Thee, and in Thy name we go.

Yes, in Thy name, O Captain of salvation!
In Thy dear name, all other names above,
Jesus our Righteousness, our sure Foundation,
Our Prince of glory and our King of love.
Jesus our Righteousness, our sure Foundation,
Our Prince of glory and our King of love.

We go in faith, our own great weakness
feeling,
And needing more each day Thy grace to
know:
Yet from our hearts a song of triumph pealing,
We rest on Thee, and in Thy name we go.
Yet from our hearts a song of triumph pealing,
We rest on Thee, and in Thy name we go.

We rest on Thee, our Shield and our Defender,
Thine is the battle, Thine shall be the praise;
When passing through the gates of pearly
splendour,
Victors, we rest with Thee, through endless
days.
When passing through the gates of pearly
splendour,
Victors, we rest with Thee, through endless
days.

WE SHALL BE AS ONE,
We shall be as one,
He the Father of us all,
We His chosen sons;
And by His command
Take each other's hand,
Live our lives in unity,
We shall be as one.

We shall be as one,
We shall be as one;
And by this shall all men know
Of the work He has done.
Love will take us on
Through His precious Son;
Love of Him who first loved us,
We shall be as one.

WE SHALL STAND
With our feet on the Rock.
Whatever men may say,
We'll lift Your name up high.
And we shall walk
Through the darkest night.
Setting our faces like flint;
We'll walk into the light.

Lord, You have chosen me
For fruitfulness,
To be transformed into
Your likeness.
I'm gonna fight on through
Till I see You face to face.

Lord, as Your witnesses
You've appointed us.
And with Your Holy Spirit
Anointed us.
And so I'll fight on through,
Till I see You face to face.

WE WILL GLORIFY the King of kings,
We will glorify the Lamb;
We will glorify the Lord of lords,
Who is the great 'I Am'.

Lord Jehovah reigns in majesty,
We will bow before His throne;
We will worship Him in righteousness,
We worship Him alone.

He is Lord of heaven, Lord of earth,
He is Lord of all who live;
He is Lord above the universe,
All praise to Him we give.

Hallelujah to the King of kings,
Hallelujah to the Lamb;
Hallelujah to the Lord of lords,
Who is the great 'I Am'.

WE WILL HONOUR YOU, *we will honour*
You,
We will exalt the Holy One of Israel.
We will honour You, yes, we will honour
You,
We will enthrone You in our praise.

You are the Alpha and Omega;
You are the beginning and the end.
There is no other we can turn to,
No other rock on which we can depend.

You will not share Your praise with idols;
All glory belongs to You alone.
Who in the skies can be compared with
The Lord Almighty Father God and King?

All of the earth will bow before You;
They will be left no place to hide.
No longer Satan's rule of darkness,
But the name of Jesus ever glorified.

WE WORSHIP AND ADORE YOU,
Christ our King. (Christ our King.)
We worship and adore You,
Christ our King. (Christ our King.)
And we follow You together,
We follow You together,
And we follow You together,
Christ our King. (Christ our King.)

WHAT A FRIEND WE HAVE IN JESUS,
All our sins and griefs to bear!
What a privilege to carry
Everything to God in prayer!
O what peace we often forfeit!
O what needless pain we bear!
All because we do not carry
Everything to God in prayer.

Have we trials and temptations?
Is there trouble anywhere?
We should never be discouraged;
Take it to the Lord in prayer.
Can we find a friend so faithful
Who will all our sorrows share?
Jesus knows our every weakness;
Take it to the Lord in prayer.

Are we weak and heavy-laden,
Cumbered with a load of care?
Precious Saviour, still our refuge,
Take it to the Lord in prayer.
Do thy friends despise, forsake thee?
Take it to the Lord in prayer;
In His arms He'll take and shield thee,
Thou wilt find a solace there.

594 Keri Jones & David Matthew
Copyright © 1978 Authentic Publishing/
Adm. by CopyCare

WHEN I FEEL THE TOUCH
Of Your hand upon my life,
It causes me to sing a song
That I love You, Lord.
So from deep within
My spirit singeth unto Thee,
You are my King, You are my God,
And I love You, Lord.

595 Wayne & Cathy Perrin
Copyright © 1981 Integrity's Hosanna! Music/
Sovereign Music UK

WHEN I LOOK INTO YOUR HOLINESS,
When I gaze into Your loveliness,
When all things that surround
Become shadows in the light of You;
When I've found the joy of reaching Your heart,
When my will becomes enthralled in Your love,
When all things that surround
Become shadows in the light of You:

I worship You, I worship You,
The reason I live is to worship You.
I worship You, I worship You,
The reason I live is to worship You.

596 Isaac Watts (1674–1748)

WHEN I SURVEY THE WONDROUS CROSS
On which the Prince of glory died,
My richest gain I count but loss,
And pour contempt on all my pride.

Forbid it, Lord, that I should boast,
Save in the death of Christ my God:
All the vain things that charm me most,
I sacrifice them to His blood.

See from His head, His hands, His feet,
Sorrow and love flow mingled down:
Did e'er such love and sorrow meet,
Or thorns compose so rich a crown?

Were the whole realm of Nature mine,
That were an offering far too small;
Love so amazing, so divine,
Demands my soul, my life, my all!

597 Author unknown
Tr. Edward Caswall (1814–78)

WHEN MORNING GILDS THE SKIES
My heart awaking cries:
'May Jesus Christ be praised!'
Alike at work and prayer
To Jesus I repair:
'May Jesus Christ be praised!'

Does sadness fill my mind?
A solace here I find:
'May Jesus Christ be praised!'
When evil thoughts molest,
With this I shield my breast:
'May Jesus Christ be praised!'

To God, the Word, on high
The hosts of angels cry:
'May Jesus Christ be praised!'
Let mortals, too, upraise
Their voice in hymns of praise:
'May Jesus Christ be praised!'

Let earth's wide circle round
In joyful notes resound:
'May Jesus Christ be praised!'
Let air, and sea, and sky,
From depth to height, reply:
'May Jesus Christ be praised!'

Be this while life is mine
My canticle divine:
'May Jesus Christ be praised!'
Be this the eternal song,
Through all the ages long:
'May Jesus Christ be praised!'

598 Author unknown
Copyright control

WHEN THE SPIRIT OF THE LORD is within my heart
I will sing as David sang.
When the Spirit of the Lord is within my heart
I will sing as David sang.
I will sing, I will sing,
I will sing as David sang.
I will sing, I will sing,
I will sing as David sang.

When the Spirit of the Lord is within my
  heart
will clap ... dance ... praise ... *(etc.)*

599 John H. Sammis (1846–1919)

WHEN WE WALK WITH THE LORD
In the light of His word,
What a glory He sheds on our way!
While we do His good will,
He abides with us still,
And with all who will trust and obey!

Trust and obey!
For there's no other way
To be happy in Jesus,
But to trust and obey.

Not a shadow can rise,
Not a cloud in the skies,
But His smile quickly drives it away;
Not a doubt nor a fear,
Not a sigh nor a tear,
Can abide while we trust and obey!

Not a burden we bear,
Not a sorrow we share,
But our toil He doth richly repay:
Not a grief nor a loss,
Not a frown nor a cross,
But is blessed if we trust and obey!

But we never can prove
The delights of His love
Until all on the altar we lay;
For the favour He shows,
And the joy He bestows,
Are for those who will trust and obey.

Then in fellowship sweet
We will sit at His feet,
Or we'll walk by His side in the way;
What He says we will do,
Where He sends we will go;
Never fear, only trust and obey!

600 Author unknown
Copyright control

WHERE YOU GO I WILL GO,
Where you lodge I will lodge,
Do not ask me to turn away,
For I will follow you.
We'll serve the Lord together
And praise Him day to day,
For He brought us together
To love Him and serve Him always.

601 Graham Kendrick
Copyright © 1986 Thankyou Music

WHETHER YOU'RE ONE or whether you're
  two
Or three or four or five,
Six or seven or eight or nine it's good to be
  alive.
It really doesn't matter how old you are,
Jesus loves you whoever you are.

La, la, la, la, la, la, la, la, la,
Jesus loves us all.
(Repeat)

Whether you're big or whether you're small
Or somewhere in between,
First in the class or middle or last,
We're all the same to Him.
It really doesn't matter how clever you are,
Jesus loves you whoever you are.

602 Nahum Tate (1652–1715)

WHILE SHEPHERDS WATCHED their flocks by
  night,
All seated on the ground,
The angel of the Lord came down
And glory shone around.

'Fear not' said he, for mighty dread
Had seized their troubled mind;
'Glad tidings of great joy I bring
To you and all mankind.

'To you in David's town this day
Is born of David's line
A Saviour, who is Christ the Lord,
And this shall be the sign.

'The heavenly babe you there shall find
To human view displayed,
All meanly wrapped in swaddling bands,
And in a manger laid.'

Thus spake the seraph; and forthwith
Appeared a shining throng
Of angels, praising God, who thus
Addressed their joyful song:

'All glory be to God on high
And on the earth be peace;
Goodwill henceforth from heaven to men
Begin and never cease.'

603 Dave Bilbrough
Copyright © 1989 Thankyou Music

WHO CAN EVER SAY THEY UNDERSTAND

All the wonders of His master plan?
Christ came down and gave Himself to
    man
Forevermore.

He was Lord before all time began,
Yet made Himself the sacrificial lamb,
Perfect love now reconciled to man
Forevermore.

> *Forevermore we'll sing the story*
> *Of love come down.*
> *Forevermore the King of glory*
> *We will crown.*

He is coming back to earth again,
Every knee shall bow before His name,
'Christ is Lord', let thankful hearts proclaim
Forevermore.

604 Graham Kendrick
Copyright © 1988 Make Way Music

WHO CAN SOUND THE DEPTHS OF SORROW

In the Father heart of God,
For the children we've rejected,
For the lives so deeply scarred?
And each light that we've extinguished
Has brought darkness to our land:
Upon our nation, upon our nation,
Have mercy, Lord.

We have scorned the truth You gave us,
We have bowed to other lords.
We have sacrificed the children
On the altars of our gods.
O let truth again shine on us,
Let Your holy fear descend:
Upon our nation, upon our nation,
Have mercy, Lord.

(Men only)
Who can stand before Your anger?
Who can face Your piercing eyes?
For You love the weak and helpless,
And You hear the victims' cries.
(All)
Yes, You are a God of justice,
And Your judgement surely comes:
Upon our nation, upon our nation,
Have mercy, Lord.

(Women only)
Who will stand against the violence?
Who will comfort those who mourn?
In an age of cruel rejection,
Who will build for love a home?
(All)
Come and shake us into action,
Come and melt our hearts of stone:
Upon Your people, upon Your people,
Have mercy, Lord.

Who can sound the depths of mercy
In the Father heart of God?
For there is a Man of sorrows
Who for sinners shed His blood.
He can heal the wounds of nations,
He can wash the guilty clean:
Because of Jesus, because of Jesus,
Have mercy, Lord.

605 Benjamin R. Hanby (1833–67)

WHO IS HE IN YONDER STALL,

At whose feet the shepherds fall?

> *'Tis the Lord!*
> *O wondrous story!*
> *'Tis the Lord, the King of glory!*
> *At His feet we humbly fall.*
> *Crown Him! Crown Him, Lord of all!*

Who is He to whom they bring
All the sick and sorrowing?

Who is He that stands and weeps
At the grave where Lazarus sleeps?

Who is He on yonder tree
Dies in pain and agony?

Who is He who from the grave
Comes to rescue, help, and save?

Who is He who from His throne
Sends the Spirit to His own?

Who is He who comes again,
Judge of angels and of men?

606 Judy Horner Montemayor
Copyright © 1975 Integrity's Hosanna! Music/
Sovereign Music UK

WHO IS LIKE UNTO THEE,

O Lord, amongst gods?
Who is like unto Thee, glorious in holiness,
Fearful in praises, doing wonders?
Who is like unto Thee?

607 Frances R. Havergal (1836–79)

WHO IS ON THE LORD'S SIDE?
Who will serve the King?
Who will be His helpers
other lives to bring?
Who will leave the world's side?
Who will face the foe?
Who is on the Lord's side?
Who for Him will go?
By Thy call of mercy,
By Thy grace divine,
We are on the Lord's side;
Saviour, we are Thine.

Jesus, Thou hast bought us
not with gold or gem,
but with Thine own life-blood,
for Thy diadem.
With Thy blessing filling
each who comes to Thee
Thou hast made us willing,
Thou hast made us free.
By Thy grand redemption,
By Thy grace divine,
We are on the Lord's side;
Saviour, we are Thine.

Fierce may be the conflict,
strong may be the foe,
but the King's own army
none can overthrow;
Round His standard ranging
victory is secure;
for His truth unchanging
makes the triumph sure.
Joyfully enlisting,
By Thy grace divine,
We are on the Lord's side;
Saviour, we are Thine.

Chosen to be soldiers
in an alien land,
chosen, called, and faithful,
for our Captain's band;
in the service royal
let us not grow cold,
let us be right loyal,
noble, true, and bold.
Master, Thou wilt keep us,
By Thy grace divine,
always on the Lord's side,
Saviour, always Thine.

608 Phil Rogers
Copyright © 1984 Thankyou Music

WHO IS THIS that grows like the dawn,
As bright as the sun, as fair as the moon?
Who is this that grows like the dawn,
As awesome as an army, as an army with
banners?

It is the church in the eyes of the Lord,
The bride of Christ preparing for her King.

Washed in His blood and clothed in
righteousness,
Anointed with the Spirit and waiting for her
Lord.
Who is this that grows like the dawn,
As awesome as an army, as an army with
banners?

609 Jane & Betsy Clowe
Copyright © 1974 Celebration/
Kingsway Music

WIND, WIND, BLOW ON ME,
Wind, wind, set me free,
Wind, wind, my Father sent
The blessèd Holy Spirit.

Jesus told us all about You,
How we could not live without You,
With His blood the power bought,
To help us live the life He taught.

When we're weary, You console us;
When we're lonely You enfold us;
When in danger You uphold us,
Blessèd Holy Spirit.

When unto the church You came
It was not in Your own but Jesus' name.
Jesus Christ is still the same,
He sends the Holy Spirit.

Set us free to love our brothers;
Set us free to live for others,
That the world the Son might see,
And Jesus' name exalted be.

610 Paul Field
Copyright © 1987 Thankyou Music

WITH ALL MY HEART I thank You, Lord.
With all my heart I thank You, Lord,
For this bread and wine we break,
For this sacrament we take,
For the forgiveness that You make,
I thank You, Lord.

With all my soul I thank You, Lord.
With all my soul I thank You, Lord,
For this victory that You've won,
For this taste of things to come,
For this love that makes us one,
I thank You, Lord.

With all my voice I thank You, Lord.
With all my voice I thank You, Lord,
For the sacrifice of pain,
For the Spirit and the flame,
For the power of Your name,
I thank You, Lord.

611 Graham Kendrick
Copyright © 1981 Thankyou Music

WITH MY WHOLE HEART I will praise You,
Holding nothing back, Hallelujah!
You have made me glad and now
I come with open arms to thank You,
With my heart embrace, Hallelujah!
I can see Your face is smiling.
With my whole life I will serve You,
Captured by Your love, Hallelujah!
O amazing love, O amazing love!

Lord, Your heart is overflowing
With a love divine, Hallelujah!
And this love is mine for ever.
Now Your joy has set You laughing
As You join the song, Hallelujah!
Heaven sings along, I hear the
Voices swell to great crescendos,
Praising Your great love, Hallelujah!
O amazing love, O amazing love!

Come, O Bridegroom, clothed in splendour,
My Belovèd One, Hallelujah!
How I long to run and meet You.
You're the fairest of ten thousand,
You're my life and breath, Hallelujah!
Love as strong as death has won me.
All the rivers, all the oceans
Cannot quench this love, Hallelujah!
O amazing love, O amazing love!

612 David Fellingham
Copyright © 1990 Thankyou Music

WONDERFUL LOVE coming to me,
Wonderful grace, freedom and mercy;
Bought with a price, death on a cross,
Wonderful love, Jesus, You've given to me.

You are Christ, Son of God,
Suffering Lamb, pouring out Your life;
You've conquered death,
And You're reigning supreme in my life.

613 John Watson
Copyright © 1986 Ampelos Music/
Adm. by CopyCare

WORSHIP THE LORD! In His presence we
    stand;
He cares for you and He understands.
Come Holy Spirit, reaching us now;
Grace, joy and peace, love abound.

Holy, holy, holy is the Lord.

(Additional choruses)
Worthy...
Faithful...
Mighty...

614 Dave Richards
Copyright © 1979 Thankyou Music

WORTHY ART THOU, O Lord our God,
Of honour and power,
For You are reigning now on high, hallelujah
Jesus is Lord of all the earth,
Hallelujah, hallelujah, hallelujah!

615 David Hadden
Copyright © 1983 Restoration
Music Ltd/Sovereign Music UK

WORTHY IS THE LAMB SEATED ON THE
    THRONE,
Worthy is the Lamb who was slain,
To receive power and riches
And wisdom and strength,
Honour and glory, glory and praise,
For ever and ever more.

616 Andy Park
Copyright © 1994 Mercy/Vineyard
Publishing/Adm. by CopyCare

WORTHY IS THE LAMB WHO WAS SLAIN.
Worthy is the Lamb who was slain,
Who was slain.
Worthy is the Lamb who was slain,
Who was slain.

To receive power and wealth,
To receive wisdom and strength.
To receive honour and glory.
To receive glory and praise.

Now to Him who sits on the throne
And to the Lamb who was slain,
Now be praise and honour and glory,
And power for ever,
And power for ever.

Worthy of power and wealth,
Worthy of wisdom and strength.
Worthy of honour and glory,
Worthy of glory and praise.

(Final chorus)
Unto the Lamb be power and wealth,
Unto the Lamb be wisdom and strength.
Unto the Lamb be honour and glory,
Unto the Lamb be glory and praise.

617 Mark S. Kinzer
Copyright © 1976 The Word of God Music/
Adm. by CopyCare

WORTHY, O WORTHY ARE YOU, LORD,
Worthy to be thanked and praised
And worshipped and adored.
Worthy, O worthy are You, Lord,
Worthy to be thanked and praised
And worshipped and adored.

Singing, Hallelujah, Lamb upon the throne,
We worship and adore You, make Your glory
known.
Hallelujah, glory to the King:
You're more than a conqueror,
You're Lord of everything.

618 Ian White
Copyright © 1986 Little Misty Music/
Kingsway Music

WORTHY, THE LORD IS WORTHY,
And no one understands the greatness of His
name.
Gracious, so kind and gracious,
And slow to anger, and rich, so rich in love.

My mouth will speak in praise of my Lord,
Let every creature praise His holy name.
For ever, and ever more.
For ever, and ever more.
For ever, and ever more.
For ever, and ever more.

Faithful, the Lord is faithful
To all His promises, and loves all He has made.
Righteous, in all ways righteous,
And He is near to all who call on Him in truth.

619 Richard Baxter (1615–91) altd by John H. Gurney
(1802–62) & Richard R. Chope (1830–1928)

YE HOLY ANGELS BRIGHT,
Who wait at God's right hand,
Or through the realms of light
Fly at your Lord's command,
Assist our song,
Or else the theme too high
Doth seem for mortal tongue.

Ye blessèd souls at rest,
Who see your Saviour's face,
Whose glory, e'en the least
Is far above our grace,
God's praises sound,
As in His sight
With sweet delight
Ye do abound.

Ye saints who toil below,
Adore your heavenly King,
And onward as ye go,
Some joyful anthem sing;
Take what He gives,
And praise Him still
Through good and ill,
Who ever lives.

My soul, bear thou thy part,
Triumph in God above,
And with a well-tuned heart
Sing thou the songs of love.
Let all thy days
Till life shall end,
Whate'er He send,
Be filled with praise.

620 Charles Wesley (1707–88)

YE SERVANTS OF GOD,
Your Master proclaim,
And publish abroad
His wonderful name;
The name all-victorious
Of Jesus extol;
His kingdom is glorious
And rules over all.

God ruleth on high,
Almighty to save;
And still He is nigh,
His presence we have;
The great congregation
His triumph shall sing,
Ascribing salvation
To Jesus our King.

Salvation to God,
Who sits on the throne!
Let all cry aloud,
And honour the Son;
The praises of Jesus
The angels proclaim,
Fall down on their faces,
And worship the Lamb.

Then let us adore,
And give Him His right,
All glory and power,
All wisdom and might,
All honour and blessing,
With angels above,
And thanks never ceasing,
And infinite love.

621 Mark Altrogge
Copyright © 1987 People of Destiny
International/Adm. by CopyCare

YOU ARE BEAUTIFUL beyond description,
Too marvellous for words,
Too wonderful for comprehension,
Like nothing ever seen or heard.
Who can grasp Your infinite wisdom?
Who can fathom the depth of Your love?
You are beautiful beyond description,
Majesty, enthroned above.

And I stand, I stand in awe of You.
I stand, I stand in awe of You.
Holy God, to whom all praise is due,
I stand in awe of You.

622 Mark Altrogge
Copyright © 1988 People of Destiny
International/Adm. by CopyCare

YOU ARE COMPASSIONATE and gracious,
Patient and abounding in love;
As far as the east is from the west
You took the sins we were guilty of.
And You deal tenderly with us,
And You deal tenderly with us.

And higher than the heavens,
So great is Your love;
Yes, higher than the heavens
Is Your love for us.

623 John Sellers
Copyright © 1984 Integrity's Hosanna! Music/
Sovereign Music UK

YOU ARE CROWNED WITH MANY CROWNS,
And rule all things in righteousness.
You are crowned with many crowns,
Upholding all things by Your word.
You rule in power and reign in glory!
You are Lord of heaven and earth!
You are Lord of all.
You are Lord of all.

624 Patty Kennedy
Copyright © 1985 Mercy/Vineyard Publishing/
Adm. by CopyCare

YOU ARE HERE and I behold Your beauty,
Your glory fills this place.
Calm my heart to hear You,
Cause my eyes to see You.
Your presence here is the answer
To the longing of my heart.

I lift my voice to worship and exalt You,
For You alone are worthy.
A captive now set free,
Your kingdom's come to me.
Glory in the highest,
My heart cries unto You.

625 Michael Ledner
Copyright © 1981 CCCM Music/
Maranatha! Music/Adm. by CopyCare

YOU ARE MY HIDING PLACE,
You always fill my heart with songs of
    deliverance,
Whenever I am afraid
I will trust in You.
I will trust in You;
Let the weak say 'I am strong
In the strength of my God.'

626 Andy Park
Copyright © 1988 Mercy/Vineyard
Publishing/Adm. by CopyCare

YOU ARE THE HOLY ONE,
The Lord Most High.
You reign in majesty,
You reign on high.

You are the Worthy One
Lamb that was slain.
You bought us with Your blood,
And with You we'll reign.

We exalt Your name,
High and mighty One of Israel,
We exalt Your name.
Lead us on to war,
In the power of Your name.
We exalt Your name,
The Name above all names,
Our victorious King,
We exalt Your name.

You are the King of kings,
The Lord of lords;
All men will bow to You,
Before Your throne.

627

YOU ARE THE KING OF GLORY,
You are the Prince of Peace;
You are the Lord of heaven and earth,
You're the Sun of righteousness.
Angels bow down before You,
Worship and adore, for
You have the words of eternal life,
You are Jesus Christ the Lord.

Hosanna to the Son of David!
Hosanna to the King of kings!
Glory in the highest heaven,
For Jesus the Messiah reigns.

628

YOU ARE THE MIGHTY KING,
The living Word;
Master of everything,
You are the Lord.

And I praise Your name,
And I praise Your name.

You are Almighty God,
Saviour and Lord;
Wonderful Counsellor,
You are the Lord.

And I praise Your name,
And I praise Your name.

You are the Prince of Peace,
Emmanuel;
Everlasting Father,
You are the Lord.

And I love Your name,
And I love Your name.

You are the Mighty King,
The living Word;
Master of everything,
You are the Lord.

629

YOU ARE THE VINE,
We are the branches,
Keep us abiding in You.
You are the Vine,
We are the branches,
Keep us abiding in You.

And we'll go in Your love,
And we'll go in Your name,
That the world will surely know
That You have power to heal and to save.

630

YOU ARE WORTHY,
Lord, You're worthy,
So I lift my heart, I lift my voice and cry
 'Holy'.
You have saved me, and I love You,
Jesus ever more I live to praise Your name.

631

YOU DID NOT WAIT FOR ME to draw near to
 You,
But You clothed Yourself in frail humanity.
You did not wait for me to cry out to You,
But You let me hear Your voice calling me.

And I'm for ever grateful to You,
I'm for ever grateful for the cross;
I'm for ever grateful to You,
That You came to seek and save the lost.

632

YOU HAVE BEEN GIVEN the Name above all
 names,
And we worship You, yes we worship You.
You have been given the Name above all
 names,
And we worship You,
Yes we worship You.

We are Your people, made for Your glory,
And we worship You, yes we worship You.
We are Your people, made for Your glory,
And we worship You,
And we worship You.

You have redeemed us from every nation,
And we worship You, yes we worship You.
You have redeemed us from every nation,
And we worship You,
And we worship You.

633 Noel Richards
Copyright © 1985 Thankyou Music

YOU LAID ASIDE YOUR MAJESTY,
Gave up everything for me,
Suffered at the hands of those You had
 created.
You took all my guilt and shame,
When You died and rose again;
Now today You reign,
In heaven and earth exalted.

I really want to worship You, my Lord,
You have won my heart
And I am Yours for ever and ever;
I will love You.
You are the only one who died for me,
Gave Your life to set me free,
So I lift my voice to You in adoration.

634 Trish Morgan & Sue Rinaldi
Copyright © 1990 Thankyou Music

YOU MAKE MY HEART FEEL GLAD.
You make my heart feel glad.
Jesus, You bring me joy;
You make my heart feel glad.

Lord, Your love brings healing and a peace
 into my heart,
I want to give myself in praise to You.
Though I've been through heartache
You have understood my tears,
O Lord, I will give thanks to You.

When I look around me, and I see the life You
 made,
All creation shouts aloud in praise;
I realise Your greatness, how majestic is Your
 name,
O Lord, I love You more each day.

635 Mark Veary & Paul Oakley
Copyright © 1986 Thankyou Music

YOU, O LORD, rich in mercy,
Because of Your great love.
You, O Lord, so loved us,
Even when we were dead in our sins.

(Men)
You made us alive together with Christ,
And raised us up together with Him,
And seated us with Him in heavenly places,
And raised us up together with Him,
And seated us with Him in heavenly places in
 Christ.

(Women)
You made us alive together with Christ,
And raised us up,
And seated us,
And raised us up,
And seated us in Christ.

636   John G. Elliott
Copyright © 1987 Lorenz Creative Services/
BMG Gospel Music Inc./Adm. by CopyCare

YOU PURCHASED MEN with precious blood,
From every nation, tribe and tongue;
Brought from slavery, freed from prison
 chains;
Brought through death so they might rise
 again,
Born to serve and to reign:

 Worthy is the Lamb that was slain, to
 * receive*
 Highest honour, and glory, and power,
 * and praise!*
 Worthy is the Lamb that was slain, to
 * receive*
 Highest honour, and glory, and praise!

Holy, holy to our God,
Who was, and is, and is to come;
Let us join the throng who see His face,
Bowing down to Him both night and day,
Lost in wonder and praise.

637 Wes Sutton
Copyright © 1987 Sovereign Lifestyle Music

YOUR MERCY FLOWS upon us like a river.
Your mercy stands unshakeable and true.
Most holy God, of all good things the Giver,
We turn and lift our fervent prayer to You.

 Hear our cry, (echo)
 O Lord, (echo)
 Be merciful (echo)
 Once more; (echo)
 Let Your love (echo)
 Your anger stem, (echo)
 Remember mercy, O Lord, again.

Your church once great, though standing
 clothed in sorrow,
Is even still the bride that You adore;
Revive Your church, that we again may honour
Our God and King, our Master and our Lord.

As we have slept, this nation has been taken
By every sin ever known to man;
So at its gates, though burnt by fire and broken,
In Jesus' name we come to take our stand.

638 Andy Park
Copyright © 1987 Mercy/Vineyard
Publishing/Adm. by CopyCare

YOUR WORKS, LORD, (Your works Lord)
Are awesome, (are awesome)
Your power (Your power)
Is great.
(Repeat)

> *Great are Your works Lord,*
> *Great are Your deeds,*
> *Awesome in power,*
> *So awesome to me.*

You will reign (You will reign)
For ever, (for ever)
In power (in power)
You will reign.
(Repeat)

Because of (because of)
Your greatness, (Your greatness)
All the earth (all the earth)
Will sing.
(Repeat)

639 Mark Altrogge
Copyright © 1987 Integrity's Praise! Music/
People of Destiny International/
Sovereign Music UK

YOU SAT DOWN at the right hand of the
Father in majesty.
You sat down at the right hand of the Father
in majesty.
You are crowned Lord of all,
You are faithful and righteous and true;
You're my Master, You're my Owner,
And I love serving You.

640 Steffi Geiser Rubin & Stuart Dauermann
Copyright © 1975 Lillenas Publishing Co./
Adm. by CopyCare

YOU SHALL GO OUT WITH JOY
And be led forth with peace,
And the mountains and the hills
Shall break forth before you.
There'll be shouts of joy,
And the trees of the field
Shall clap, shall clap their hands.
And the trees of the field shall clap their
hands,
And the trees of the field shall clap their
hands,
And the trees of the field shall clap their
hands,
And you'll go out with joy.

641 Bob Baker
Copyright © 1994 Mercy/Vineyard
Publishing/Adm. by CopyCare

ABRAHAM'S SON, Chosen One,
Zion's cornerstone;
Passover Lamb, Son of Man,
Seated upon Your throne.

> *Hail to the King,*
> *Hail to the King,*
> *Hail to the King of kings.*
> (Repeat)

O promised Seed, beneath Your feet
Sin and death shall fall.
Now through us tread the serpent's head
Till You are all in all.

The world's yet to see Your glory,
But You'll be revealed in power,
And You will reign with the Bride ordained
For Your consummating hour.

642 Paul Oakley
Copyright © 1997 Thankyou Music

ALL AROUND THE WORLD *there's a new*
> *day dawning,*
> *There's a sound coming round,*
> *There's a new song rising up,*
> *Ah, it's a new day!*
> *Everywhere you go you can hear this*
> *story,*
> *There's a power coming down,*
> *There's a glimpse of glory now,*
> *Ah, it's a new day!*

There's a sound of praise,
There's a sound of war;
Lift the banner high, let the Lion roar.
Can you hear the sound in the tops of the
trees?
Heaven's armies come! Crush the enemy!

Let the lame run, let the blind see!
Let Your power come, set the captives free!
Let the lost return to the Lover of our souls,
Let the prodigal find the way back home.

Lift your hands before the King,
The sovereign Ruler of the earth;
Let the nations come to Him,
Let the cry of hearts be heard:

Revive us! Revive us! Revive us again!
(Repeat)

643

ALL CONSUMING FIRE,
You're my heart's desire,
And I love You dearly, dearly Lord.
You're my meditation,
And my consolation,
And I love You dearly, dearly Lord.

Glory to the Lamb,
I exalt the great I AM;
Reigning on Your glorious throne,
You are my eternal home.

644

ALL CREATION BOWS at the name of Jesus,
Every star is in His hands.
Yet the glorious mystery of ages,
He delights in fragile man.

There is mercy in the name of Jesus,
Mercy to forgive our sin.
The mighty King of heaven became the
    humble servant,
To bring His children back to Him.
And this is why I will sing:

Hallelujah, Christ is risen,
Hallelujah, we are saved.
He has purchased our salvation,
Hallelujah, praise His name.

There is shelter in the name of Jesus,
He accepts the refugee;
And His mighty strength will never fail us,
His arm is always close to me.
And all my life I will sing:

645

ALL CREATURES OF OUR GOD AND KING,
Lift up your voice and with us sing:
Hallelujah, hallelujah!
Thou burning sun with golden beam,
Thou silver moon with softer gleam:

O praise Him, O praise Him,
Hallelujah, hallelujah, hallelujah!

Thou rushing wind that art so strong,
Ye clouds that sail in heaven along,
O praise Him, hallelujah!
Thou rising morn, in praise rejoice,
Ye lights of evening, find a voice:

Thou flowing water, pure and clear,
Make music for thy Lord to hear,
Hallelujah, hallelujah!
Thou fire so masterful and bright,
That givest man both warmth and light:

And all ye men of tender heart,
Forgiving others, take your part,
O sing ye, hallelujah!
Ye who long pain and sorrow bear,
Praise God and on Him cast your care:

Let all things their Creator bless,
And worship Him in humbleness,
O praise Him, hallelujah!
Praise, praise the Father, praise the Son,
And praise the Spirit, Three-in-One:

646

ALL I ONCE HELD DEAR, built my life upon,
All this world reveres, and wars to own,
All I once thought gain I have counted loss;
Spent and worthless now, compared to
    this.

Knowing You, Jesus,
Knowing You, there is no greater thing.
You're my all, You're the best,
You're my joy, my righteousness,
And I love You, Lord.

Now my heart's desire is to know You
    more,
To be found in You and known as Yours.
To possess by faith what I could not earn,
All-surpassing gift of righteousness.

Oh, to know the power of Your risen life,
And to know You in Your sufferings.
To become like You in Your death, my Lord,
So with You to live and never die.

647

ALL THAT I AM *I lay before You;*
All I possess, Lord, I confess
Is nothing without You.
Saviour and King, I now enthrone You;
Take my life, my living sacrifice to You.

Lord, be the strength within my weakness;
Be the supply in every need,
That I may prove Your promises to me,
Faithful and true in word and deed.

Into Your hands I place the future;
The past is nailed to Calvary,
That I may live in resurrection power,
No longer I but Christ in me.

648

David Fellingham
Copyright © 1992 Thankyou Music

ALL THE ENDS OF THE EARTH will
  remember,
And turn to the Lord of glory;
All the families of the nations will bow down
  to the Lord,
As His righteous acts of power are displayed.

And we will awaken the nations,
To bring their worship to Jesus.
And righteousness and praise shall spring
  forth
In all the earth.
And we will awaken the nations,
To bring their worship to Jesus,
And the kingdom shall be revealed in
  power,
With signs, wonders and miracles,
And righteousness and praise shall spring
  forth
In all the earth.

Who will not fear the Lord of glory,
Or bring honour to His holy name?
For God has spoken with integrity and truth,
A word which cannot be revoked.

649

Jan Harrington
Copyright © 1975 Celebration/Kingsway Music

ALL THE RICHES OF HIS GRACE,
All the fulness of His blessings,
All the sweetness of His love
He gives to you,
He gives to me.

Oh, the blood of Jesus,
Oh, the blood of Jesus,
Oh, the blood of Jesus,
It washes white as snow.

Oh, the word of Jesus,
Oh, the word of Jesus,
Oh, the word of Jesus,
It cleanses white as snow.

Oh, the love of Jesus,
Oh, the love of Jesus,
Oh, the love of Jesus,
It makes His Body whole.

650

John Gibson
Copyright © 1996 Thankyou Music

(Leader) **ALL YOU PEOPLE,**
(All) *Sing unto the Lord.*
(Leader) *All you nations,*
(All) *Sing unto the Lord.*
Come with dancing,
Come and raise Your voice to the King,
Come and sing unto the Lord.

From the sun's rising
To the sun's setting,
In every place, every land,
He will be glorified;
Offerings of worship from every nation,
Let every tribe, every tongue,
Join in one song of praise.

(Leader) People of Africa,...
(All) Sing unto the Lord. *(After each line)*
Europe and Asia,...
All of Australasia,...
And all across America,...
The rich and poor will ...
The weak and strong can ...
Every generation, ...
Every tribe and nation, ...

651

Nathan Fellingham & Adrian Watts
Copyright © 1997 Thankyou Music

ALMIGHTY GOD, I have heard of Your fame;
I stand in awe of Your wondrous deeds.
The heavens declare Your glorious name;
I worship You above all my needs.

The skies display the work of Your hands,
I will praise You for the rest of my days.
Who can You ask to approve Your plans?
For You are sovereign in all of Your ways.

I will only worship You,
There is nothing I want more
Than to be with You,
More and more I love You, Lord.
The only One I bow before,
I worship You with all that You've put in me;
This is what You made me for.

652

Darlene Zschech
Copyright © 1996 Darlene Zschech/
Hillsong Publishing/Kingsway Music

ALMIGHTY GOD, MY REDEEMER,
My hiding place, my safe refuge;
No other name like Jesus,
No power can stand against You.

My feet are planted on this rock,
And I will not be shaken;
My hope it comes from You alone,
My Lord and my salvation.

Your praise is always on my lips,
Your word is living in my heart,
And I will praise You with a new song:
My soul will bless You, Lord.
You fill my life with greater joy;
Yes, I delight myself in You,
And I will praise You with a new song:
My soul will bless You, Lord.

When I am weak, You make me strong;
When I'm poor, I know I'm rich,
For in the power of Your name
All things are possible. (×4)

653 Carol Owen
Copyright © 1993 Thankyou Music

AMONG THE GODS there is none like You,
O Lord, O Lord.
There are no deeds to compare with Yours, O
Lord.
All the nations You have made will come;
They'll worship before You, O Lord,
O Lord.

For You are great and do marvellous
deeds.
Yes, You are great and do marvellous
deeds.
You alone are God, You alone are God.

You are so good and forgiving,
O Lord, O Lord.
You're rich in love to all who call to You.
All the nations You have made will come;
They'll glorify Your name, O Lord,
O Lord.

Teach me Your ways, O Lord,
And I'll walk in Your truth.
Give me an undivided heart,
That I may fear Your name.

654 Mark Altrogge
Copyright © 1992 People of Destiny
International/Word Music Inc./Adm. by CopyCare

AND FROM YOUR FULNESS *we have all*
received
Grace upon grace,
Kindness on kindness.
And from Your fulness we have all received
Grace upon grace,
Like wave upon wave
From the ocean of Your love.

Lord, You stand willing
And ready to bless,
You bid us bring You
Great requests;
Though many are saying
'Who will show us good?'
Day after day we see Your mercies.

Lord, You're the Author
Of every good gift;
You give us all
We need to live.
Lord, You became poor
To make us rich,
You crown our lives with Your compassion.

655 Graham Kendrick
Copyright © 1993 Make Way Music

AND HE SHALL REIGN *for ever,*
His throne and crown shall ever endure.
And He shall reign for ever,
And we shall reign with Him.

What a vision filled my eyes,
One like a Son of man,
Coming with the clouds of heaven
He approached an awesome throne.

He was given sovereign power,
Glory and authority.
Every nation, tribe and tongue
Worshipped Him on bended knee.

On the throne for ever,
See the Lamb who once was slain.
Wounds of sacrificial love
Forever shall remain.

656 Donn Thomas
Copyright © 1992 Paragon Music Corp., USA/
Adm. by Bucks Music Ltd

ANOINTING, FALL ON ME,
Anointing, fall on me;
Let the power of the Holy Ghost
Fall on me,
Anointing, fall on me.

Touch my hands, my mouth and my heart;
Fill my life, Lord, every part.
Let the power of the Holy Ghost
Fall on me,
Anointing, fall on me.

657
Noel & Tricia Richards
Copyright © 1996 Thankyou Music

ARE WE THE PEOPLE
Who will see God's kingdom come,
When He is known in every nation?
One thing is certain,
We are closer than before;
Keep moving on, last generation.

These are the days for harvest,
To gather in the lost;
Let those who live in darkness
Hear the message of the cross.

We'll go where God is sending,
We'll do what He commands;
These years that He has waited
Could be coming to an end.

658
Richard Lewis
Copyright © 1997 Thankyou Music

AS THE DEER PANTS for the water,
So my soul, it thirsts for You,
For You, O God,
For You, O God.
(Repeat)

When can I come before You
And see Your face?
My heart and my flesh cry out
For the living God,
For the living God.

Deep calls to deep
At the thunder of Your waterfalls.
Your heart of love is calling out to me.
By this I know that I am Yours
And You are mine.
Your waves of love are breaking over me.
Your waves of love are breaking over me.
Your waves of love are breaking over me.

659
Timothy Dudley-Smith
Copyright © Timothy Dudley-Smith

AS WATER TO THE THIRSTY,
As beauty to the eyes,
As strength that follows weakness,
As truth instead of lies;
As songtime and springtime
And summertime to be,
So is my Lord,
My living Lord,
So is my Lord to me.

Like calm in place of clamour,
Like peace that follows pain,
Like meeting after parting,
Like sunshine after rain;
Like moonlight and starlight
And sunlight on the sea,
So is my Lord,
My living Lord,
So is my Lord to me.

As sleep that follows fever,
As gold instead of grey,
As freedom after bondage,
As sunrise to the day;
As home to the traveller
And all he longs to see,
So is my Lord,
My living Lord,
So is my Lord to me.

660
David Baroni
Copyright © 1992 Pleasant Hill
Music, USA/Adm. by Bucks Music Ltd

AS WE BEHOLD YOU, as we behold You,
We are changing into Your image.
As we behold You, as we behold You,
We are changing from glory to glory.

As we behold You in all of Your glory,
Lord, by Your Spirit we are changing
Into Your image from glory to glory,
As we behold You, living God.

661
Lex Loizides
Copyright © 1996 Thankyou Music

AS WE SEE THE WORLD in tatters,
As we watch their dreams break down,
We can hear their quiet anguish:
'Come and help us!'
Brought to life by God's own Spirit,
Joined together in His Son,
Now the church with strength arises
Like an army.

Every place, every place
Where our feet shall tread,
Every tribe, every race
God has given us.

In the midst of boastful darkness
Shines a Light that cannot fail,
And the blind behold His glory,
Jesus! Jesus!
Not content with restoration
Of the remnant in the land,
He has filled us with His power
For the nations.

662 Derek Bond
Copyright © 1992 Sovereign Music UK

AT THE FOOT OF THE CROSS,
I can hardly take it in,
That the King of all creation
Was dying for my sin.
And the pain and agony,
And the thorns that pierced Your head,
And the hardness of my sinful heart
That left You there for dead.

And O what mercy I have found
At the cross of Calvary;
I will never know Your loneliness,
All on account of me.
And I will bow my knee before Your throne,
'cause Your love has set me free;
And I will give my life to You, dear Lord,
And praise Your majesty,
And praise Your majesty,
And praise Your majesty.

663 Gill Broomhall
Copyright © 1992 Thankyou Music &
Sovereign Lifestyle Music

BABY JESUS IN THE MANGER,
To the world He's still a stranger.
Wise men bring their gifts
Of gold and myrrh,
Baby Jesus in the manger.

Noel, Noel, Noel,
Hail the Immanuel.

Gentle Jesus, meek and lowly,
Full of love so pure and holy.
He will teach and pray,
Show mankind the way,
Gentle Jesus, meek and lowly.

Loving Jesus, mocked and beaten,
He the sin of man has taken.
He has paid the price,
He has given His life,
Loving Jesus, mocked and beaten.

Mighty Jesus, He is risen,
He has broken out of prison.
He has conquered sin,
Brought new life to men,
Mighty Jesus, He is risen.

664 Graham Kendrick
Copyright © 1993 Make Way Music

BEAUTY FOR BROKENNESS,
Hope for despair,
Lord, in Your suffering world
This is our prayer:
Bread for the children,
Justice, joy, peace;
Sunrise to sunset,
Your kingdom increase!

Shelter for fragile lives,
Cures for their ills,
Work for the craftsman,
Trade for their skills;
Land for the dispossessed,
Rights for the weak,
Voices to plead the cause
Of those who can't speak.

God of the poor,
Friend of the weak,
Give us compassion we pray:
Melt our cold hearts,
Let tears fall like rain;
Come, change our love
From a spark to a flame.

Refuge from cruel wars,
Havens from fear,
Cities for sanctuary,
Freedoms to share;
Peace to the killing-fields,
Scorched earth to green,
Christ for the bitterness,
His cross for the pain.

Rest for the ravaged earth,
Oceans and streams
Plundered and poisoned—
Our future, our dreams.
Lord, end our madness,
Carelessness, greed;
Make us content with
The things that we need.

Lighten our darkness,
Breathe on this flame
Until Your justice
Burns brightly again;
Until the nations
Learn of Your ways,
Seek Your salvation
And bring You their praise.

665
Dave Bilbrough
Copyright © 1991 Thankyou Music

BE FREE *in the love of God,*
Let His Spirit flow within you.
Be free in the love of God,
Let it fill your soul.
Be free in the love of God,
Celebrate His name with dancing.
Be free in the love of God,
He has made us whole.

For His purpose He has called us,
In His hands He will uphold us.
He will keep us and sustain us
In the Father's love.

God is gracious, He will lead us
Through His power at work within us.
Spirit, guide us, and unite us
In the Father's love.

666
Billy Funk
Copyright © 1991 Integrity's Praise! Music/
Sovereign Music UK

BE GLORIFIED, be glorified.
Be glorified, be glorified.
Be glorified in the heavens,
Be glorified in the earth;
Be glorified in the temple,
Jesus, Jesus,
Be Thou glorified.
Jesus, Jesus,
Be Thou glorified.

Worship the Lord, worship the Lord.
Worship the Lord, worship the Lord.
Worship the Lord in the heavens,
Worship the Lord in the earth;
Worship the Lord in the temple,
Jesus, Jesus,
Be Thou glorified.
Jesus, Jesus,
Be Thou glorified.

667
Gerald Coates & Noel Richards
Copyright © 1991 Thankyou Music

BEHOLD THE LORD upon His throne;
His face is shining like the sun.
With eyes blazing fire, and feet glowing
    bronze,
His voice like mighty water roars.
Holy, holy, Lord God Almighty.
Holy, holy, we stand in awe of You.

The First, the Last, the living One
Laid down His life for all the world;
Behold He now lives for evermore,
And holds the keys of death and hell.
Holy, holy, Lord God Almighty;
Holy, holy, we bow before Your throne.

So let our praises ever ring
To Jesus Christ, our glorious King.
All heaven and earth resound as we cry:
'Worthy is the Son of God!'
Holy, holy, Lord God Almighty;
Holy, holy, we fall down at Your feet.

668   Charles Wesley (1707–88)

BEHOLD THE SERVANT OF THE LORD:
I wait Thy guiding eye to feel,
To hear and keep Thy every word,
To prove and do Thy perfect will;
Joyful from my own works to cease,
Glad to fulfil all righteousness.

Me if Thy grace vouchsafe to use,
Meanest of all Thy creatures, me.
The deed, the time, the manner choose:
Let all my fruit be found of Thee.
Let all my works in Thee be wrought,
By Thee to full perfection brought.

My every weak though good design
O'errule or change, as seems Thee meet:
Jesus, let all my work be Thine –
Thy work, O Lord, is all complete,
And pleasing in Thy Father's sight;
Thou only hast done all things right.

Here then to Thee Thine own I leave;
Mould as Thou wilt Thy passive clay;
But let me all Thy stamp receive,
But let me all Thy words obey,
Serve with a single heart and eye,
And in Thy glory live and die.

669   James Montgomery (1771–1854)

BE KNOWN TO US IN BREAKING BREAD,
But do not then depart;
Saviour, abide with us, and spread
Thy table in our heart.

There sup with us in love divine;
Thy body and Thy blood,
That living bread, that heavenly wine,
Be our immortal food.

We would not live by bread alone,
But by Thy word of grace,
In strength of which we travel on
To our abiding place.

670 Jim Bailey
Copyright © 1996 Thankyou Music

BELLS THEY ARE RINGING,
Children are singing,
And we are exalting the Name over all.
Flags they are dancing,
The church is advancing,
As we are romancing the Name over all.

Jesus' kingdom can't be shaken,
Jesus' promise can't be broken,
Jesus, Lord of all creation,
Name over all.
Jesus, Truth of liberation,
Jesus, Light of our salvation,
Jesus, only way to heaven,
The Name over all.

671 Lex Loizides
Copyright © 1995 Thankyou Music

BE STILL AND KNOW that I am God:
I will be glorified and praised in all the earth.
For My great name I will be found,
And I can never be resisted,
Never be undone;
I'm never lacking power
To glorify My Son.
The gates of hell are falling
And the church is coming forth,
My name will be exalted in the earth.

Be still and know that I am God;
I have poured out My Holy Spirit like a flood.
The land that cries for holy rain
Shall be inheriting her promises
And dancing like a child;
A holy monsoon deluge
Shall bless the barren heights,
And those who sat in silence
Shall speak up and shall be heard:
My name will be exalted in the earth.

Be still and know that I am God;
My Son has asked me for
The nations of the world.
His sprinkled blood has made a way
For all the multitudes of India and
    Africa to come;
The Middle East will find its peace
Through Jesus Christ My Son.
From London down to Cape Town,
From L.A. to Beijing,
My Son shall reign the undisputed King!

672 Psalm 46

BE STILL AND KNOW THAT I AM GOD.
Be still and know that I am God.

673 Clinton Utterbach
Copyright © 1989 Utterbach Music Inc./
Polygram International Publishing Corp.,
USA/Polygram Music Publishing Ltd

BLESSÈD BE THE NAME OF THE LORD,
Blessed be the name of the Lord,
Blessed be the name of the Lord Most High!
(Repeat)

> *The Name of the Lord is a strong tower,*
> *The righteous run into it,*
> *And they are saved.*
> (Repeat)

Glory to the name of the Lord...

Holy is the name of the Lord...

674 Joey Holder
Copyright © 1987 Far Lane Publishing/
Kingsway Music

BLESSÈD JESUS, come to me,
Soothe my soul with songs of peace.
As I look to You alone,
Fill me with Your love.

> *Glorious, marvellous*
> *Grace that rescued me;*
> *Holy, worthy*
> *Is the Lamb who died for me.*

Mountains high and valleys low,
You will never let me go;
By Your fountain let me drink,
Fill my thirsty soul.

675 Jamie Harvill & Gary Sadler
Copyright © 1992 Integrity's Hosanna! Music/
Integrity's Praise! Music/Sovereign Music UK

BLESSING AND HONOUR, glory and power
Be unto the Ancient of Days;
From every nation, all of creation
Bow before the Ancient of Days.

> *Every tongue in heaven and earth*
> *Shall declare Your glory,*
> *Every knee shall bow at Your throne*
> *In worship;*
> *You will be exalted, O God,*
> *And Your kingdom shall not pass away,*
> *O Ancient of Days.*

our kingdom shall reign over all the earth:
ng unto the Ancient of Days.
or none shall compare to Your matchless
worth:
ng unto the Ancient of Days.

76 Taizé, Music: Jacques Berthier (1923–94)
Copyright © 1987 Ateliers et Presses de Taizé

BLESS THE LORD, MY SOUL,
And bless God's holy name.
Bless the Lord, my soul,
Who leads me into life.

is God who forgives all your guilt,
'ho heals every one of your ills,
'ho redeems your life from the grave,
'ho crowns you with love and compassion.

ue Lord is compassion and love,
ue Lord is patient and rich in mercy.
od does not treat us according to our sins,
or repay us according to our faults.

s a father has compassion on his children,
ue Lord has mercy on those who revere Him;
or God knows of what we are made,
nd remembers that we are dust.

77 Tina Pownall
Copyright © 1987 Sovereign Music UK

REATHE ON ME, Spirit of Jesus.
reathe on me, Holy Spirit of God.

ll me again, Spirit of Jesus.
ll me again, Holy Spirit of God.

nange my heart, Spirit of Jesus.
nange my heart, Holy Spirit of God.

ing peace to the world, Spirit of Jesus.
ing peace to the world, Holy Spirit of God.

78 Edwin Hatch (1835–89) adpt. David Fellingham
Copyright © 1995 Thankyou Music

REATHE ON ME, BREATH OF GOD,
nd fill my life anew;
nat I may love as You love,
nd do the works that You do.
oly Spirit, breathe on me.

eathe on me, breath of God,
ntil my heart is pure;
ntil my will is one with Yours
et holiness and love endure.
oly Spirit, breathe on me.

And let every part of me
Glow with fire divine;
With passion in my life,
Jesus, let Your glory shine.
(Repeat)

679 Kent & Carla Henry
Copyright © 1989 Kent Henry Ministries/
Kingsway Music

BURN IT DEEP within my soul,
New strength and fire, O Lord.
Burn it deep within my soul,
New zeal and fire, O Lord.
Burn it deep within my soul,
New strength and fire,
It makes me whole.
Burn it deep,
Deep within my soul.

And You came
With the Holy Spirit's desire.
You came
With a zeal for Your Father's house.
Consume me, Lord,
With Your purifying fire,
And strengthen me
By Your mighty hand.

680 David Fellingham
Copyright © 1997 Thankyou Music

BY YOUR BLOOD I can enter the holiest
place,
To the throne of my Father and King.
There I find Your acceptance, mercy and
grace,
And my life is renewed again.

Far away from the stress and the turmoil of
life,
I now come to seek Your face.
In the house of the Lord where Your presence
is found,
I now come to worship You.

I see the King upon the throne,
Jesus, full of majesty.
I will fall down at Your feet,
I will worship You alone.

In the light of Your presence I find deepest joy,
There is no other place I would be.
To behold Your beauty is all my desire,
You're the one my heart longs for,
You're the one my heart longs for.

681 Noel & Tricia Richards
Copyright © 1992 Thankyou Music

CALLED TO A BATTLE, heavenly war;
Though we may struggle, victory is sure.
Death will not triumph, though we may die;
Jesus has promised our eternal life.

*By the blood of the Lamb we shall
    overcome,
See the accuser thrown down.
By the word of the Lord we shall
    overcome,
Raise a victory cry,
Like thunder in the skies,
Thunder in the skies.*

Standing together, moving as one;
We are God's army, called to overcome.
We are commissioned, Jesus says go;
In every nation, let His love be known.

682 Matt Redman
Copyright © 1996 Thankyou Music

CAN A NATION BE CHANGED?
Can a nation be saved?
Can a nation be turned back to You?
(Repeat)

*We're on our knees,
We're on our knees again.
We're on our knees,
We're on our knees again.*

Let this nation be changed,
Let this nation be saved,
Let this nation be turned back to You.
(Repeat)

683 Matt Redman
Copyright © 1995 Thankyou Music

CAN I ASCEND the hill of the Lord?
Can I stand in that holy place?
There to approach the glory of my God;
Come towards to seek Your face.
Purify my heart,
And purify my hands,
For I know it is on holy ground I'll stand.

I'm coming up the mountain, Lord;
I'm seeking You and You alone.
I know that I will be transformed,
My heart unveiled before You.
I'm longing for Your presence, Lord;
Envelop me within the cloud.
I'm coming up the mountain, Lord,
My heart unveiled before You,
I will come.

I'm coming to worship,
I'm coming to bow down,
I'm coming to meet with You.
(Repeat)

684 Chris Bowater
Copyright © 1996 Sovereign Lifestyle Music

CATCH THE FIRE,
Swim through the waters,
Fly on the wings of the Spirit.
(Repeat)

*Hear the sound that fills heaven,
Hear the beat of my heart.*
(Repeat)

As a Lover, gazing on His bride;
As a Father looking for His child;
As the Shepherd,
Searching for the one that's lost;
As the Saviour, weeping for the world.

685 John L. Bell & Graham Maule
Copyright © 1989 WGRG Iona Community

CHRIST'S IS THE WORLD in which we move,
Christ's are the folk we're summoned to love,
Christ's is the voice which calls us to care,
And Christ is the One who calls us here.

*To the lost Christ shows His face;
To the unloved He gives His embrace:
To those who cry in pain or disgrace,
Christ makes with His friends
A touching place.*

Feel for the people we most avoid,
Strange or bereaved or never employed;
Feel for the women, and feel for the men
Who fear that their living is all in vain.

Feel for the parents who've lost their child,
Feel for the women whom men have defiled,
Feel for the baby for whom there's no breast,
And feel for the weary who find no rest.

Feel for the lives by life confused,
Riddled with doubt, in loving abused;
Feel for the lonely heart, conscious of sin,
Which longs to be pure but fears to begin.

686 Ian White
Copyright © 1987 Little Misty Music/
Kingsway Music

CLAP YOUR HANDS, ALL YOU NATIONS,
Shout to God with cries of joy,
O how awesome is the Lord most high,
The King over all the earth!

e subdued nations under us,
he peoples under our feet,
nd He chose our inheritance for us,
he pride of Jacob, whom He loved.

ow our God has ascended
 the midst of shouts of joy,
nd the Lord is in among the trumpet sound,
mong the trumpet sound.

Sing praise to God,
Sing praises to the King,
Sing praises to the King.
(Repeat)

or our God is King of all the earth,
ing Him a psalm of praise,
or He rules above the nations on His throne,
n His holy throne.

ll the people are gathered
f the God of Abraham.
or the kings of all the earth belong to God,
nd He is lifted high!

87 Trish Morgan
Copyright © 1991 Thankyou Music

LOSER TO YOU, Lord, and closer still,
ll I am wholly in Your will.
loser to hear Your beating heart,
nd understand what You impart.
 Breath of Life, come purify
his heart of mine and satisfy.
ly deep desire is to worship You,
ord of my life, come closer still.

88 Valerie Collison
Copyright © 1972 High-Fye Music

COME AND JOIN THE CELEBRATION,
It's a very special day;
Come and share our jubilation,
There's a new King born today!

ee the shepherds
urry down to Bethlehem;
aze in wonder
t the Son of God who lay before them.

ise men journey,
ed to worship by a star,
neel in homage,
ringing precious gifts from lands afar, so

od is with us,'
ound the world the message bring;
e is with us,
Velcome!' all the bells on earth are pealing.

689   Loralee Thiessen
Copyright © 1993 Mercy/Vineyard Publishing/
Adm. by CopyCare

COME, HOLY SPIRIT,
Come, Holy Spirit,
Come to this place,
We will embrace Your presence.

Come, soften our hearts,
Come, soften our hearts,
That we may obey,
Teach us Your way, come lead us.

Come, Holy Spirit.
Come, Holy Spirit.

690 Billy Funk
Copyright © 1992 Integrity's Praise! Music/
Sovereign Music UK

COME INTO THE HEAVENLIES
And sing the song the angels sing,
Worthy, worthy.
Come into the heavenlies,
And sing the song the angels sing,
Worthy, worthy.

Worthy is the Lamb.
Worthy is the Lamb.
Worthy is the Lamb.
Worthy is the Lamb.

Worthy of blessing and honour,
Worthy of glory and power,
Worthy is the Lamb.
(Repeat)

691 K. Prosch
Copyright © 1993 Liber Media &
Publishing, LLC/Kingsway Music

COME LET US RETURN unto the Lord.
(Men – Women echo)
Come let us return unto the Lord.
(Men – Women echo)
(Repeat)

For He has torn us,
But He will heal us.
For He has wounded us,
But He will bandage us.

And He will come,
He'll come to us
Like rain, spring rain.
He will come to us
Like rain, spring rain.

692 Graham Kendrick
Copyright © 1992 Make Way Music

COME, LET US WORSHIP JESUS,
King of nations, Lord of all.
Magnificent and glorious,
Just and merciful.

Jesus, King of the nations,
Jesus, Lord of all.
Jesus, King of the nations,
Lord of all.

Lavish our hearts' affection,
Deepest love and highest praise.
Voice, race and language blending,
All the world amazed.

Bring tributes from the nations,
Come in joyful cavalcades,
One thunderous acclamation,
One banner raised.

Come, Lord, and fill Your temple,
Glorify Your dwelling place,
Till nations see Your splendour
And seek Your face.

Fear God and give Him glory,
For His hour of judgement comes.
Creator, Lord Almighty,
Worship Him alone.

693 John Pantry
Copyright © 1992 Thankyou Music

COME, MY SOUL, AND PRAISE THE LORD.
(Men – Women echo)
Sing to Christ, the living Word,
(Men – Women echo)
Who heals my broken heart,
(Men – Women echo)
And binds my wounds. *(Men – Women echo)*

Holy, holy is the Lord, *(Men – Women echo)*
Who may stand before His word?
(Men – Women echo)
He knows my life so well,
(Men – Women echo)
Yet loves me still. *(Men – Women echo)*

As His eye is on the sparrow,
So His thoughts are for my life.
Not a moment passes by
But He thinks of me,
And He hears me when I cry.
So come my soul...

694 Noel Richards & Doug Horley
Copyright © 1996 Thankyou Music

COME OUT OF DARKNESS *into the lig*
Come out of darkness into the light.
Come out of darkness into the arms of
love,
Into the arms of love.

To a world in darkness,
To a world in pain,
At this time You've called us,
Your love to proclaim;
Through Your willing people
To the nations say,
To the nations say:

Do not be discouraged,
See what God has done;
He is working through us,
This world shall be won.
There will be a harvest
When the nations hear.
What are they going to hear?

By the blood of Jesus sin is washed away,
All who call upon Him, He will surely save
This will be the promise that the nations h
When we sing it loud and clear.

695 Richard Lewis
Copyright © 1996 Thankyou Music

COME TO THE POWER,
The power of the living God;
His name is higher,
Higher than any other name.
Mighty Jehovah, awesome Deliverer;
His power is greater,
Greater than any principality.

A mighty fortress is our God,
He sits enthroned in the heavens,
The Lord of Hosts is He.
A mighty fortress is our God,
He sits enthroned in the heavens,
He reigns in majesty.
(Repeat)
In majesty.

696 Chris Bowater
Copyright © 1994 Sovereign Lifestyle Music

CONFIDENCE, WE HAVE CONFIDENCE
To come, to ask for mercy.
Confidence, we have confidence,
To come, to ask for mercy.

erciful God, we cry: 'Don't pass us by.'
erciful God, we pray: 'Don't turn away;'
Your love remember mercy.
Your love remember mercy.

97 Geoff Bullock
Copyright © 1997 Watershed Productions/
Kingsway Music

AY BY DAY and hour by hour,
our love for me from heaven flows;
ke streams of water in the desert,
ving waters flow.
ou walk beside me, gently guiding,
eading me through every storm.
verlasting, never changing
race and love divine.

ercy's healing grace, relieving
very spot and every stain.
orgiven freely, no more guilty,
ove has conquered shame.
he broken mended, night has ended,
ost and lonely lost no more;
or I am carried in the arms of
race and love divine.

*I am carried in the arms
Of grace and love divine;
I am held by hands of healing,
Washed by water pure;
Lifting up my heavy heart,
Held in grace scarred hands,
I am carried in the arms
Of grace and love divine.*

ever worthy, never earning,
ll my works now left behind.
ver onwards, ever upwards,
ou've called me on to rise
bove my darkness, all my failure,
very fear and every pain.
lways carried, always covered by
race and love divine.

98 David Fellingham
Copyright © 1995 Thankyou Music

AY OF FAVOUR, day of grace;
his is the day of jubilee.
he Spirit of the sovereign Lord
falling now on me.
et the oil from heaven flow
rom the presence of the King.
esus, let Your power flow
s we worship, as we sing.
et us free to make You known
o a world that's full of shame.
esus, let Your glory fall,
ive us power to speak Your name.

Day of favour, day of grace;
This is the day of jubilee.
The Spirit of the sovereign Lord
Is falling now on me.
Open wide the prison doors,
Where satan's held the key.
Bring deliverance to the bound,
And set the captives free.
Bring the good news to the poor,
And cause the blind to see.
The Spirit of the Lord
Is falling now on me.

699 David Fellingham
Copyright © 1994 Thankyou Music

DAYS OF HEAVEN here on the earth;
Touched by power, touched by love.
By Your word, and by Your Spirit
You send Your blessing here on us.

*Lord, send the rain,
Let Your Spirit come and glorify Jesus.
Lord, send the rain,
Let Your Spirit come like a pent up flood,
Driven by the breath of God.*

We bring our worship, we see Your face;
We stand in wonder of Your grace.
Your kingdom presence, Your majesty;
Jesus, You're here now, hear our plea.

700 Martin Smith
Copyright © 1994 Curious? Music UK/
Adm. by Bucks Music Ltd

DID YOU FEEL THE MOUNTAINS TREMBLE?
Did you hear the oceans roar,
When the people rose to sing of
Jesus Christ, the risen One?

Did you feel the people tremble?
Did you hear the singers roar,
When the lost began to sing of
Jesus Christ, the saving One?

And we can see that God, You're moving,
A mighty river through the nations.
And young and old will turn to Jesus.
Fling wide you heavenly gates,
Prepare the way of the risen Lord.

*Open up the doors
And let the music play,
Let the streets resound with singing.
Songs that bring Your hope,
Songs that bring Your joy,
Dancers who dance upon injustice.*

Do you feel the darkness tremble,
When all the saints join in one song,
And all the streams flow as one river,
To wash away our brokenness?

And we can see that God, You're moving,
A time of jubilee is coming,
When young and old will turn to Jesus.
Fling wide you heavenly gates,
Prepare the way of the risen Lord.

 701 Ian Smale
Copyright © 1987 Thankyou Music

DON'T BE LAZY,
Lazy, lazy, lazy,
But copy those who through faith and
patience
Receive what God has promised.

 702 Brian Doerksen
Copyright © 1994 Mercy/Vineyard Publishing/
Adm. by CopyCare

DON'T LET MY LOVE GROW COLD;
I'm calling out, 'Light the fire again.'
Don't let my vision die;
I'm calling out, 'Light the fire again.'

You know my heart, my deeds;
I'm calling out, 'Light the fire again.'
I need Your discipline;
I'm calling out, 'Light the fire again.'

I am here to buy gold,
Refined in the fire:
Naked and poor,
Wretched and blind, I come.
Clothe me in white,
So I won't be ashamed:
Lord, light the fire again!

 703 Andy Park
Copyright © 1994 Mercy/Vineyard Publishing/
Adm. by CopyCare

DOWN THE MOUNTAIN THE RIVER FLOWS,
And it brings refreshing wherever it goes.
Through the valleys and over the fields,
The river is rushing and the river is here.

The river of God sets our feet a-dancing,
The river of God fills our hearts with
cheer;
The river of God fills our mouths with
laughter,
And we rejoice for the river is here.

The river God is teeming with life,
And all who touch it can be revived.
And those who linger on this river's shore
Will come back thirsting for more of the L

Up to the mountain we love to go
To find the presence of the Lord.
Along the banks of the river we run,
We dance with laughter, giving praise to t
Son.

 704 Geoff & Judith Roberts
Copyright © 1996 Thankyou Music

DRAW ME CLOSE TO THE CROSS,
To the place of Your love,
To the place where You poured out Your
mercy;
Where the river of life
That flows from Your wounded side
Brings refreshing to those who draw near.
Draw me close to Your throne
Where Your majesty is shown,
Where the crown of my life I lay down.
Draw me close to Your side,
Where my heart is satisfied,
Draw me close to You, Lord,
Draw me close.

705 David Fellingham
Copyright © 1992 Thankyou Music

ETERNAL COVENANT of God
Down through time has been declared;
Drawing the heart of man
Into redemption's plan,
Mercy and grace revealed,
By the blood and Spirit sealed.
All our sins have been forgiven,
Raised from death to heights of heaven.

And we're living to the praise of His glory,
Eternally secure in His love;
The eyes of our hearts have been opened
To receive the blessing of God.
(Repeat)

 706 Dave Bilbrough
Copyright © 1995 Thankyou Music

FAITHFUL AND TRUE
Are all Your ways;
Your love for me will never fade away.
Always the same,
You never change;
Your love for me will never fade away.

ven in my hour of deepest need,
ou are always there to walk with me.
ou know my words before I speak;
ord, I know that You will never forsake me.

07   Chris Bowater
Copyright © 1990 Sovereign Lifestyle Music

AITHFUL GOD, faithful God,
ll sufficient One, I worship You.
halom my peace,
ly strong Deliverer,
lift You up, faithful God.

08   David Fellingham
Copyright © 1997 Thankyou Music

AR ABOVE ALL OTHER LOVES,
ar beyond all other joys,
eaven's blessings poured on me,
y the Holy Spirit's power.

Love's compelling power
Draws my heart into Yours;
Jesus, how I love You,
You're my Friend and my Lord.
You have died and risen
So what else can I say?
How I love You, Lord,
Love You, Lord.

ll ambition now has gone,
leasing You my only goal;
lotivated by Your grace,
iving for eternity.

ooking with the eye of faith
or the day of Your return;
 that day I want to stand
nashamed before Your throne.

 09   Graham Kendrick
Copyright © 1996 Make Way Music

AR AND NEAR hear the call,
/orship Him, Lord of all;
amilies of nations come,
elebrate what God has done.

eep and wide is the love
eaven sent from above;
od's own Son for sinners died,
ose again, He is alive.

Say it loud, say it strong,
Tell the world what God has done;
Say it loud, praise His name,
Let the earth rejoice
For the Lord reigns.

At His name let praise begin,
Oceans roar, nature sing.
For He comes to judge the earth
In righteousness and in His truth.

710   Dave Bilbrough
Copyright © 1995 Thankyou Music

FATHER GOD, fill this place
With Your love, with Your grace.
As we call on Your name,
Visit us in power again.

Lord, we worship You.
Lord, we worship You.
(Repeat)

Spirit come with Your peace;
Heal our wounds, bring release.
Lord we long for Your touch,
Fill our hearts with Your love.

711   John Barnett
Copyright © 1989 Mercy/Vineyard Publishing/
Adm. by CopyCare

FATHER, I COME TO YOU, lifting up my
  hands
In the name of Jesus, by Your grace I stand.
Just because You love me and I love Your
  Son,
I know Your favour, unending love.

I receive Your favour, Your unending love,
Not because I've earned it, not for what I've
  done;
Just because You love me and I love Your
  Son,
I know Your favour, unending love.

Unending love,
Your unending love.

It's the presence of Your kingdom as Your
  glory fills this place,
And I see how much You love me as I look
  into Your face.
Nothing could be better, there's nothing I
  would trade
For Your favour, unending love.

712 Jim Bailey
Copyright © 1996 Thankyou Music

FATHER IN HEAVEN, holy is Your name.
Your kingdom come, Your will be done,
Let it be the same.
(Repeat)
On earth as it is in heaven,
On earth as it is in heaven.
(Repeat)

Give us today all our daily bread,
As we forgive our debtors,
So You forgive our debts.
(Repeat)
And lead us not into temptation;
Deliver us from evil.
(Repeat)

For Yours is the kingdom,
The power and the glory,
Forever and ever and ever, amen.
(Repeat)

713 Paul McWilliams & William Thompson
Copyright © 1993 Thankyou Music

FATHER, LIKE RAIN FROM THE SKIES,
Send Your word into our lives.
We cry out: 'Show us Your way,
Come to us, Father, we pray.'

  Come and satisfy,
  Come and satisfy my soul.
  Come and satisfy,
  Come and satisfy my soul
  And make me whole.

When will our hearts understand,
You have our lives in Your hand?
We cry out: 'Come to us, Lord,
Guide us we pray with Your word.'

714 David Ruis
Copyright © 1992 Mercy/Vineyard Publishing/
Adm. by CopyCare

FATHER OF CREATION,
Unfold Your sovereign plan.
Raise up a chosen generation
That will march through the land.
All of creation is longing
For Your unveiling of power.
Would You release Your anointing;
O God, let this be the hour.

  Let Your glory fall in this room,
  Let it go forth from here to the nations.
  Let Your fragrance rest in this place,
  As we gather to seek Your face.

Ruler of the nations,
The world has yet to see
The full release of Your promise,
The church in victory.
Turn to us, Lord, and touch us,
Make us strong in Your might.
Overcome our weakness,
That we could stand up and fight.

(Men) Let Your kingdom come.
(Women) Let Your kingdom come.
(Men) Let Your will be done.
(Women) Let Your will be done.
(Men) Let us see on earth
(Women) Let us see on earth
(All) The glory of Your Son.

715 Robert Critchley
Copyright © 1996 Thankyou Music

FATHER, YOU HAVE GIVEN
Precious gifts from heaven,
Equipping us to serve You
As You move upon the earth.
You've prepared us for this hour,
And anointed us with power
For humble acts of righteousness,
We freely volunteer to do Your work.

Ambassadors of reconciliation,
Preaching the good news of Jesus Christ;
Praying for the increase of Your kingdom,
Piercing the darkness with Your light.

  Not to us, but to You be all the praises,
  Not to us, but to the glory of Your grace
  We will lift up a standard to this world,
  Not for us, but for the honour of Your
    name.
  Oh, Father, not for us,
  But for the honour of Your name.

  For the honour of Your name.
  Oh, Your name.
  (Repeat)

Father, You have chosen
The weak and the broken,
These ones are the vessels
Through whom You command Your
  strength.
We offer up our lives as living sacrifices,
Fill us with Your Spirit now,
And send us out to bring the harvest in.

Ambassadors of reconciliation...

16 Noel & Tricia Richards
Copyright © 1994 Thankyou Music

ILLED WITH COMPASSION for all creation,
esus came into a world that was lost.
here was but one way that He could save us,
nly through suffering death on a cross.

God, You are waiting,
Your heart is breaking
For all the people who live on the earth.
Stir us to action,
Filled with Your passion
For all the people who live on the earth.

reat is Your passion for all the people
iving and dying without knowing You.
aving no Saviour, they're lost for ever,
we don't speak out and lead them to You.

rom every nation we shall be gathered,
Iillions redeemed shall be Jesus' reward.
hen He will turn and say to His Father:
'ruly my suffering was worth it all.'

17 Timothy Dudley-Smith
Copyright © 1970 Timothy Dudley-Smith

ILL YOUR HEARTS WITH JOY and
gladness,
ing and praise your God and mine!
reat the Lord in love and wisdom,
light and majesty divine!
e who framed the starry heavens
nows and names them as they shine.

raise the Lord, His people, praise Him!
Vounded souls His comfort know;
hose who fear Him find His mercies,
eace for pain and joy for woe;
umble hearts are high exalted,
uman pride and power laid low.

raise the Lord for times and seasons,
loud and sunshine, wind and rain;
pring to melt the snows of winter
Il the waters flow again;
rass upon the mountain pastures,
olden valleys thick with grain.

Il your hearts with joy and gladness,
eace and plenty crown your days;
ove His laws, declare His judgements,
Valk in all His words and ways;
e the Lord and we His children –
raise the Lord, all people, praise!

718 Paul Oakley
Copyright © 1995 Thankyou Music

FIRE, *there's a fire,*
Sweet fire burning in my heart.
(Repeat)

And I will run with all of the passion
You've put in me.
I will spread the seed of the gospel
everywhere.

And I can feel the power of Your hand upon
me.
Now I know I'll never be the same again.
For as long as You will give me breath,
My heart is so resolved,
Oh, to lay my life before You, Lord,
Let everything I do be to Your praise.

Let me feel Your tongues of fire resting upon
me;
Let me hear the sound of
Your mighty rushing wind.
Let my life be like an offering of worship;
Let me be a living sacrifice of praise.

719 Ian Smale
Copyright © 1985 Thankyou Music

5000+ HUNGRY FOLK,
5000+ hungry folk,
5000+ hungry folk
Came 4 2 listen 2 Jesus.

The 6 x 2 said 0 0 0,
The 6 x 2 said 0 0 0,
The 6 x 2 said 0 0 0,
Where can I get some food from?

Just 1 had 1 2 3 4 5,
Just 1 had 1 2 3 4 5,
Just 1 had 1 2 3 4 5,
Loaves and 1 2 fishes.

When Jesus blessed the 5 + 2,
When Jesus blessed the 5 + 2,
When Jesus blessed the 5 + 2,
They were increased many x over.

5000 + 8 it up,
5000 + 8 it up,
5000 + 8 it up,
With 1 2 3 4 5 6 7 8 9 10 11 12 basketfuls left
over.

720

FOCUS MY EYES on You, O Lord,
Focus my eyes on You;
To worship in spirit and in truth,
Focus my eyes on You.

Turn round my life to You, O Lord,
Turn round my life to You;
To know from this night You've made me
    new,
Turn round my life to You.

Fill up my heart with praise, O Lord,
Fill up my heart with praise;
To speak of Your love in every place,
Fill up my heart with praise.

721

FOR THE JOYS AND FOR THE SORROWS,
The best and worst of times,
For this moment, for tomorrow,
For all that lies behind;
Fears that crowd around me,
For the failure of my plans,
For the dreams of all I hope to be,
The truth of what I am:

For this I have Jesus,
For this I have Jesus,
For this I have Jesus,
I have Jesus.
(Repeat)

For the tears that flow in secret,
In the broken times,
For the moments of elation,
Or the troubled mind;
For all the disappointments,
Or the sting of old regrets,
All my prayers and longings
That seem unanswered yet:

For the weakness of my body,
The burdens of each day,
For the nights of doubt and worry,
When sleep has fled away;
Needing reassurance,
And the will to start again,
A steely-eyed endurance,
The strength to fight and win:

722

FRIEND OF SINNERS, Lord of truth,
I am falling in love with You.
Friend of sinners, Lord of truth,
I have fallen in love with You.

Jesus, I love Your name,
The name by which we're saved.
Jesus, I love Your name,
The name by which we're saved.

Friend of sinners, Lord of truth,
I am giving my life to You.
Friend of sinners, Lord of truth,
I have given my life to You.

723

FROM EVERY TONGUE, tribe and nation,
Shouted out from all creation,
All the earth sings forth Your praise.
Even the trees clap their hands,
As the people of God take their stand,
Jesus Christ our banner we raise.

You're our God, our heart's desire,
Breathe on our lives, release Your power
Deep in our hearts we already know
That we'll be set free when we give up
*   control.*
Yeah, we'll be set free when we give up
*   control.*

In every circumstance or situation
We give thanks and adoration,
Jesus Christ is worthy of praise.
Whenever our minds give in to fear and
    doubting,
Feeling alone or left out,
We lift our hands and we start to sing.

724

La la la la la la. (×4)

FROM THE SLEEP OF AGES,
I am stirred by the kiss of love,
By the fragrant perfume
When His name is mentioned.
I have learned to wait for Him,
To receive His presence
With the sound of laughter,
And the joy of resting.
But listen, my Lover
Is coming from heaven's throne!

Over the mountains, leaping the hills,
He runs like a deer through the open plain;
Gazing through windows,
Peering through doors,
My Lover is calling and calling again:
'Rise up, my lovely, beautiful one,
The winter is past and the rains are gone;
Flowers appear all over the earth,
These are the promised days.'
This is the season of singing. (×4)

ere is no preferring
the Lover's loving;
e are all His treasure,
s desired inheritance.
 has come with blessings
om the Father's throne-room;
fts of power and healing,
r a needy people.
e wonder, the pleasure
knowing, of being known!

25 Chris Cartwright
Copyright © 1991 Thankyou Music

OM YOUR THRONE, O LORD,
t Your fire fall upon us;
t us feel the touch of the Spirit in our hearts,
 equip us and empower us,
nd us out to heal the land,
Your name to shine the light of Christ.

om the Father's heart
nd us waves of Your compassion;
ve us, Lord, to pray for
ur will to come on earth.
erceding for a nation
at is dying, lost and blind,
t us see them with the eyes of Christ.

rd, we lift one voice
a song of joy and triumph;
t Your word rise up from our lips, that in
 our lives
e will let the world know Jesus
he Victor and the King,
t our anthem ring throughout the land.

26 Jim Bailey
Copyright © 1997 Thankyou Music

VE ME A HEART OF COMPASSION,
ve me a hope for the lost.
ve me a passion for those
ho are broken and down.
rd, I am ready and willing
 serve the weak and the young;
lp me to put into action
e words of this song.

And enable Your servants,
Enable Your servants
To preach good news,
To preach good news.
(Repeat)

I'll sing the songs of salvation,
Boldly I'll speak out Your word.
I'll let them know by my life,
I will show You are Lord.
I'll tell them all about Jesus,
I'll tell them all about You;
I'm not ashamed of the gospel
Or what it can do.

We're moving forward together,
As one voice boldly proclaim
The old and the young will be strong,
And we'll lift up Your name
On to the streets to the people,
Every man, woman and child,
And as we go You are with us,
You've given Your power.

You've enabled Your servants...

727 Dave Bilbrough
Copyright © 1994 Thankyou Music

GIVE ME, LORD, A DREAM FROM HEAVEN,
Let me see the things You see;
Give me purpose and direction,
Holy Spirit, move on me.
I would set my face to serve You,
To do the things You'd have me do;
Stir within my heart a vision,
Lord, I will follow You.

By Your Spirit and Your word,
We would hasten Your return.
(Repeat)

Give to me a holy passion,
With every breath I will proclaim
The message of Your kingdom,
The glory of Your name.
Lead me into action,
Let me do the things You say;
Send me to the nations,
When You speak I will obey.

I believe that faith is rising,
I can see a tidal wave
Of Your Spirit that is moving
To end this final age.
There'll be shouts of acclamation
When You come back for Your Bride;
History's consummation
Is here before our eyes.

GIVE ME OIL IN MY LAMP, keep me burning.
Give me oil in my lamp, I pray.
Give me oil in my lamp, keep me burning,
Keep me burning till the break of day.

Sing hosanna, sing hosanna,
Sing hosanna to the King of kings.
Sing hosanna, sing hosanna,
Sing hosanna to the King.

Give me joy in my heart, keep me praising…

Give me peace in my heart, keep me
resting…

Give me love in my heart, keep me serving…

GIVE YOUR THANKS TO THE RISEN SON.
(Leader – all echo)
To the holy and anointed one. *(echo)*
Who fills our hearts with a joyful song. *(echo)*
Jesus. *(echo)*

Turn to Him, don't be afraid,
Give Him honour, give Him praise.
Lift Him up to the highest place.
Jesus.

Worship Him, crown Him King,
And give Him all your heart.
(Repeat)

GOD IS GREAT, *amazing!*
Come, let His praises ring.
God is great, astounding!
The whole creation sings.

His clothing is splendour and majesty bright,
For He wraps Himself in a garment of light.
He spreads out the heavens – His palace of
stars,
And rides on the wings of the wind.

What marvellous wisdom the Maker displays,
The sea vast and spacious, the dolphins and
whales,
The earth full of creatures, the great and the
small,
He watches and cares for them all.

The rain forest canopies darken the skies,
Cathedrals of mist that resound with the
choirs,
Of creatures discordant, outrageous, abla
In colourful pageants of praise.

Above His creation the Father presides:
The pulse of the planets, the rhythm of ti
The moon makes the seasons, the day
follows night,
Yet He knows every beat of my heart.

Let cannons of thunder salute their acclai
The sunsets fly glorious banners of flame
The angels shout 'holy' again and again
As they soar in the arch of the heavens.

 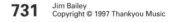
GOD IS RAISING UP AN ARMY
Made of those who are still young.
God is lifting up their voices,
Through the weak He'll shame the strong
It's been prophesied they will prophesy,
God's salvation they will show;
For the promise is to the children,
To our daughters and our sons.

Children of the cross,
A shining example,
Children of the cross
Are singing His praise.
Children of the cross
Are silencing the enemy,
Children of the cross
Are saying the Lord saves.

GOD IS SO GOOD,
God is so good,
God is so good,
He's so good to me.

He took my sin,
He took my sin,
He took my sin,
He's so good to me.

Now I am free,
Now I am free,
Now I am free,
He's so good to me.

God is so good,
He took my sin,
Now I am free,
He's so good to me.

(And) **GOD IS SO GOOD.**
(And) God is so good.

rides upon the wings of the wind,
is exalted by His name Jah.
walks in the midst of the stones of fire,
be His sons is our desire.
r the natural things speak of the invisible.
ok around and see,
o could deny the wonders of His love?

u reign on high in majesty,
d the widow's heart causes to sing.
u hear the cry of the fatherless,
d the depths of Your love who can
comprehend?
r the natural things speak of the invisible.
ok around and see,
o could deny the wonders of His love?

D OF HEAVEN, with the heart of a lover;
nquering King, with compassion in His
voice.
vereign Lord, with the care of a mother;
You we bring our lives, knowing You will
ake us in.

sus Christ, You're the Alpha and Omega:
g of kings, who laid aside His crown.
n of woes, but a Friend to the friendless:
You we bring our fears, knowing You will
et us free.

So let's be pure and holy, set apart for
Jesus;
A covenant people, who reflect the heart
of God.
With outstretched hands of mercy to the
broken-hearted,
A covenant people who reveal the love of
God.

D, OUR GOD, BLESSES US,
d blesses us,
at all the ends of the earth may fear Him.
peat)

all the peoples praise Thee, O God,
all the peoples praise Him.

GOD SENT HIS SON, they called Him Jesus;
He came to love, heal, and forgive;
He lived and died to buy my pardon,
An empty grave is there to prove my Saviour
lives.

> *Because He lives I can face tomorrow;*
> *Because He lives all fear is gone;*
> *Because I know He holds the future,*
> *And life is worth the living*
> *Just because He lives.*

How sweet to hold a new-born baby,
And feel the pride and joy he gives;
But greater still the calm assurance,
This child can face uncertain days because
He lives.

And then one day I'll cross the river;
I'll fight life's final war with pain;
And then as death gives way to victory,
I'll see the lights of glory and I'll know He
lives.

GOD, YOU ARE AN AWESOME GOD,
And Your dominion reaches to the heavens,
And all nations sing Your praise;
As Your people, we declare Your holiness.

> *Holy, holy, holy is the Lord.*
> *Holy, holy, holy is the Lord.*

GO FORTH AND TELL! O Church of God,
awake!
God's saving news to all the nations take:
Proclaim Christ Jesus, Saviour, Lord and
King,
That all the world His worthy praise may sing.

Go forth and tell! God's love embraces all;
He will in grace respond to all who call:
How shall they call if they have never heard
The gracious invitation of His word?

Go forth and tell where still the darkness lies,
In wealth or want, the sinner surely dies;
Give us, O Lord, concern of heart and mind,
A love like Yours, compassionate and kind.

Go forth and tell! The doors are open wide:
Share God's good gifts – let no one be
  denied;
Live out your life as Christ your Lord shall
  choose,
Your ransomed powers for His sole glory use.

Go forth and tell! O church of God, arise!
Go in the strength which Christ your Lord
  supplies;
Go till all nations His great name adore
And serve Him, Lord and King for evermore.

739 Graham Kendrick
Copyright © 1988 Make Way Music

**GOOD NEWS, GOOD NEWS TO YOU WE
  BRING,**
Alleluia!
News of great joy that angels sing,
Alleluia!

> *Tender mercy He has shown us,*
> *Joy to all the world;*
> *For us God sends His only Son,*
> *Alleluia!*

Let earth's dark shadows fly away,
Alleluia!
In Christ has dawned an endless day,
Alleluia!

Now God with us on earth resides,
Alleluia!
And heaven's door is open wide,
Alleluia!

740 Bryn Haworth
Copyright © 1991 Thankyou Music

GO TO ALL NATIONS, making disciples,
Baptising them in My name.
Go to all nations, making disciples,
Baptising them in My name.

> *I am coming soon.*
> *I am coming soon.*
> *I'm waiting at the gates*
> *For the Father's call.*
> *I am coming soon.*
> *Yes, I am coming soon.*

Teach them to do all I told you to do,
Teach them to walk in My ways.
I have authority in heaven and earth,
I will be with you always.

741 Doug Horley
Copyright © 1993 Thankyou Music

Oh, it's **GREAT, GREAT, BRILL, BRILL,**
Wicked, wicked, skill, skill,
To have a friend like Jesus.
Great, great, brill, brill,
Wicked, wicked, skill, skill,
To have a friend like Him.
(Repeat)

He's always there,
He always listens,
He always hears me when I talk to Him.
He loves me now
And will for ever,
I'll choose Him every day, day, day.

742 Gerald Coates & Noel Richards
Copyright © 1992 Thankyou Music

GREAT IS THE DARKNESS that covers the
  earth,
Oppression, injustice and pain.
Nations are slipping in hopeless despair,
Though many have come in Your name.
Watching while sanity dies,
Touched by the madness and lies.

> *Come, Lord Jesus, come, Lord Jesus,*
> *Pour out Your Spirit we pray.*
> *Come, Lord Jesus, come, Lord Jesus,*
> *Pour out Your Spirit on us today.*

May now Your church rise with power and
  love,
This glorious gospel proclaim.
In every nation salvation will come
To those who believe in Your name.
Help us bring light to this world
That we might speed Your return.

Great celebrations on that final day
When out of the heavens You come.
Darkness will vanish, all sorrow will end,
And rulers will bow at Your throne.
Our great commission complete,
Then face to face we shall meet.

743 David & Nathan Fellingham
Copyright © 1994 Thankyou Music

GREAT IS THE LORD;
Sovereign King,
We give You praise.

ou spoke Your word and You rescued me,
ou poured out Your grace and You set me
  free.
ow You've filled my life with the Spirit's
  power,
nd You've set my heart on fire.

nd by the power of Jesus' name
ou have raised me up from my sin and
  shame.
ou've anointed me with the Spirit's power,
nd You've set my heart on fire.

y grace I'm saved through faith in God,
ot by works alone but by Jesus' blood.
ow I'm filled with strength by the Spirit's
  power,
nd You've set my heart on fire.

reat is the Lord.
Repeat)

'44 Ron Kenoly
Copyright © 1987 Integrity's Hosanna! Music/
Sovereign Music UK

ALLELUJAH! JESUS IS ALIVE,
eath has lost its victory
nd the grave has been denied;
esus lives for ever,
e's alive, He's alive!
Last time)
allelujah! Jesus is alive!

e's the Alpha and Omega,
he First and Last is He;
he curse of sin is broken
nd we have perfect liberty.
he Lamb of God has risen,
e's alive, He's alive!

'45 Doug Horley
Copyright © 1996 Thankyou Music

HANDS, HANDS, FINGERS, THUMBS,
We can lift to praise You.
Hands, hands, fingers, thumbs,
We can lift to praise.
Hands, hands, fingers, thumbs,
We can lift to praise You.
Jump front, jump back, yeah!
We were made to praise.

e've got some hands that we can raise.
e've got a voice to shout Your praise,
  Jesus!
ot some feet a-made to dance;
et's use them now we've got the chance.
Repeat)

We were made to praise You,
We were made to praise.
We were made to praise You,
We were made to praise.
(Repeat)

746 Mick Gisbey
Copyright © 1985 Thankyou Music

HAVE YOU GOT AN APPETITE?
Do you eat what is right?
Are you feeding on the word of God?
Are you fat or are you thin?
Are you really full within?
Do you find your strength in Him or are you
  starving?

  You and me all should be
  Exercising regularly,
  Standing strong all day long,
  Giving God the glory.
  Feeding on the living Bread,
  Not eating crumbs but loaves instead;
  Standing stronger, living longer,
  Giving God the glory.

If it's milk or meat you need,
Why not have a slap-up feed,
And stop looking like a weed and start to
  grow?
Take the full of fitness food,
Taste and see that God is good,
Come on, feed on what you should and be
  healthy.

747 Stuart Garrard
Copyright © 1995 Curious? Music UK/
Adm. by Bucks Music Ltd

HAVE YOU HEARD THE GOOD NEWS?
Have you heard the good news?
We can live in hope
Because of what the Lord has done.
(Repeat)

There is a way
When there seems to be no way,
There is a light in the darkness:
There is a hope,
An everlasting hope,
There is a God who can help us.

A hope for justice
And a hope for peace,
A hope for those in desperation:
We have a future,
If only we believe
He works in every situation.

HAVE YOU NOT SAID as we pass through
water,
You will be with us?
And You have said as we walk through fire,
We will not be burned.
We are not afraid, for You are with us;
We will testify to the honour of Your name.
We are witnesses, You have shown us
You are the One who can save.

Fill us up and send us out
In the power of Your name.
Fill us up and send us out
In the power of Your name.

Bring them from the west, sons and
daughters,
Call them for Your praise.
Gather from the east all Your children,
Coming home again.
Bring them from afar, all the nations,
From the north and south,
Drawing all the peoples in.
Corners of the earth, come to see there's
Only one Saviour and King.

**HEAR THESE PRAISES FROM A GRATEFUL
HEART,**
Each time I think of You the praises start:
Love You so much, Jesus,
Love You so much.

Lord I love You, my soul sings,
In Your presence, carried on Your wings:
Love You so much, Jesus,
Love You so much.

How my soul longs for You,
Longs to worship You for ever
In Your power and majesty.
Lift my hands, lift my heart,
Lift my voice towards the heavens,
For You are my sun and shield.

**HE BROUGHT ME TO HIS BANQUETING
TABLE,** *(Men-Women echo)*
He brought me to His banqueting table,
(Men-Women echo)
And His banner over me is love. *(All)*

I am my Belovèd's and He is mine, *(Men-
Women echo)*
I am my Belovèd's and He is mine, *(Men-
Women echo)*
And His banner over me is love. *(All)*
Yes, His banner over me is love.

And we can feel the love of God in this pla
We believe Your goodness, we receive You
grace.
We delight ourselves at Your table, O God,
You do all things well, just look at our lives

HE HAS BEEN GIVEN a Name above all
names,
In earth and heaven, let all creation claim
That Jesus Christ is King, and Lord of all.
He is the Victor over satan's reign,
His blood has triumphed over sin and sha
Jesus Christ is King and Lord of all.

He is the likeness of Jehovah,
Through whom the world was made.
By His word the universe is sustained,
Every power is subject to His name.

The name of Jesus in victory will resound,
In every nation let the good news sound:
Jesus Christ is King, and Lord of all.

**HE HAS CLOTHED US WITH HIS
RIGHTEOUSNESS,**
Covered us with His great love.
He has showered us with mercy,
And we delight to know the glorious favou
Wondrous favour of God.

We rejoice in the grace of God
Poured upon our lives.
Loving kindness has come to us
Because of Jesus Christ.
We rejoice in the grace of God,
Our hearts overflow.
What a joy to know the grace of God!

He's brought us into His family,
Made us heirs with His own Son.
All good things He freely gives us,
And we cannot conceive what God's
preparing
God's preparing for us.

53 Gerald Coates, Noel & Tricia Richards
Copyright © 1993 Thankyou Music

HE HAS RISEN,
He has risen,
He has risen,
Jesus is alive.

hen the life flowed from His body,
eemed like Jesus' mission failed.
ut His sacrifice accomplished,
ctory over sin and hell.

 the grave God did not leave Him,
r His body to decay;
aised to life, the great awakening,
atan's power He overcame.

 there were no resurrection,
'e ourselves could not be raised;
ut the Son of God is living,
o our hope is not in vain.

hen the Lord rides out of heaven,
ighty angels at His side,
ney will sound the final trumpet,
om the grave we shall arise.

e has given life immortal,
'e shall see Him face to face;
rough eternity we'll praise Him,
hrist, the Champion of our faith.

54 Bob Fitts
Copyright © 1986 CA Music/Music Services/
Adm. by CopyCare

HE IS LOVELY, *He is holy,*
Gave supremely, that all men may see.
He is gentle, tender-hearted,
Risen Saviour, He is God.

aster, Maker, Life Creator,
ome and dwell in me,
nat my heart may know
ur tender mercy.
hine through me that all may see
ur love so full and free;
nd I'll declare Your praise
nrough endless ages.

755 Kevin Prosch
Copyright © 1991 Mercy/Vineyard Publishing/
Adm. by CopyCare

HE IS THE LORD, and He reigns on high:
He is the Lord.
Spoke into the darkness, created the light:
He is the Lord.
Who is like unto Him, never ending in days?
He is the Lord.
And He comes in power when we call on His
    name:
He is the Lord.

Show Your power, O Lord our God.
Show Your power, O Lord our God,
Our God.

Your gospel, O Lord, is the hope for our nation:
You are the Lord.
It's the power of God for our salvation:
You are the Lord.
We ask not for riches, but look to the cross:
You are the Lord.
And for our inheritance give us the lost:
You are the Lord.

Send Your power . . .

756 Gill Broomhall
Copyright © 1988 Coronation Music
Publishing/Kingsway Music

HE MADE THE EARTH, He made the sky,
He made the moon and the stars,
Jupiter and Mars.
He made the sun for everyone,
Our God made them all.
Our God is powerful, powerful,
Our God is great.
Our God is powerful, powerful,
Our God is great.

He made the fish, He made the birds,
Elephants and worms,
Creeping things that squirm.
Mice so small, giraffes so tall;
Our God made them all.
Our God is wonderful, wonderful,
Our God is great.
Our God is wonderful, wonderful,
Our God is great.

He made the boys, he made the girls,
He made our mums and dads,
To teach us good from bad.
He cares for me, He cares for You;
Our God loves us all.
Our God is beautiful, beautiful,
Our God is great.
Our God is beautiful, beautiful,
Our God is great.

757 Dave Bilbrough
Copyright © 1996 Thankyou Music

HE PICKED ME UP
And He dusted me down,
Put my feet back on solid ground.
He welcomed me home
And He caused me to sing,
I'm in love, I'm in love with the King.

For all my days I'll sing His praise,
I'm so grateful.
Yes, I will give my everything
To the One who sets me free.

Once I was lost, but now I'm found,
Yes, He saved me.
He called my name and my life was changed
By the power of His love.

758 Paul Oakley
Copyright © 1997 Thankyou Music

HERE I AM, and I have come
To thank You, Lord, for all You've done;
Thank You, Lord.
You paid the price at Calvary,
You shed Your blood, You set me free;
Thank You, Lord.
No greater love was ever shown,
No better life ever was laid down.

> *And I will always love Your name;*
> *And I will always sing Your praise.*
> (Repeat)

You took my sin, You took my shame,
You drank my cup, You bore my pain;
Thank You, Lord.
You broke the curse, You broke the chains,
In victory from death You rose again;
Thank You, Lord.
And not by works, but by Your grace
You clothe me now in Your righteousness.

You bid me come, You make me whole,
You give me peace, You restore my soul;
Thank You, Lord.
You fill me up, and when I'm full,
You give me more till I overflow;
Thank You, Lord.
You're making me to be like You,
To do the works of the Father, too.

759 Craig Musseau
Copyright © 1994 Mercy/Vineyard Publishing/
Adm. by CopyCare

HERE I AM ONCE AGAIN,
I pour out my heart for I know that You hear
Every cry; You are listening,
No matter what state my heart is in.

You are faithful to answer
With words that are true
And a hope that is real.
As I feel Your touch,
You bring a freedom to all that's within.

In the safety of this place
I'm longing to…

> *Pour out my heart, to say that I love You,*
> *Pour out my heart, to say that I need You*
> *Pour out my heart, to say that I'm thankful*
> *Pour out my heart, to say that You're*
> *wonderful.*

760 Rick Ridings
Copyright © 1990 Ariose Music/EMI Christian
Music Publishing/Adm. by CopyCare

HE REIGNS, *He reigns, Jesus reigns,*
He reigns enthroned in majesty.
Shout your praise, His banners raise,
For Jesus reigns.
Shout hosanna, Jesus reigns.

Our highest praise we bring
To our great eternal King.
His glory fills the skies,
Now from earth let praise arise.

He spoiled the hosts of hell,
And like blazing stars, they fell.
He led them forth in chains—
Now our mighty Victor reigns!

761 Chris Bowater
Copyright © 1996 Sovereign Lifestyle Music

HERE IN THE PRESENCE of the
Great and awesome God.
Here in the presence of the Holy One,
The only One.
Knowing not how best to bring adoring love
To bow, to weep, to fall, and yet
You whisper, 'Child, draw near:

> *And stand in the presence of the Lord,*
> *Stand in the presence of the Lord,*
> *Stand in the presence of the Holy One,*
> *Stand in the presence of the Lord.'*

re in the presence of the
eat and awesome God,
ajestic in His power yet full of grace:
eek His face.
e passion in His eyes
arches deep inside:
ich shining love intensifies,
t melts away my fears.

And I stand...

62   Graham Kendrick
Copyright © 1992 Make Way Music

RE IS BREAD, here is wine,
rist is with us – He is with us;
eak the bread, drink the wine –
rist is with us here.

re is grace, here is peace,
rist is with us – He is with us;
ow His grace, find His peace –
ast on Jesus here.

In this bread there is healing,
In this cup there's life for ever;
In this moment, by the Spirit
Christ is with us here.

re we are, joined in one,
rist is with us – He is with us;
e'll proclaim, till He comes –
sus crucified.

63   Michael Sandeman
Copyright © 1997 Thankyou Music

RE IS THE RISEN SON,
ding out in glory,
diating light all around.
re is the Holy Spirit,
ured out for the nations,
orifying Jesus the Lamb.

e will stand as a people
ho are upright and holy,
e will worship the Lord of hosts.
e will watch, we will wait
n the walls of the city,
e will look and see what He will say to us.

ery knee shall bow before Him,
ery tongue confess
at He is King of kings, Lord of lords,
d Ruler of the earth.

764   Gerald Coates, Noel & Tricia Richards
Copyright © 1996 Thankyou Music

HERE WE ARE, LORD,
More weak than strong;
Still believing, still pressing on.
Make us ready
With hearts that are brave.
We will silence the lies of this age.

For such a moment we have been born.
We're gonna rise up,
Take this world by storm.
Let evil tremble,
We come in His name.
Our God is with us,
We're dangerous people.

All God's heroes failed as we do,
Sometimes doubting all that is true.
Yet He calls us great people of faith,
Working through us as history is made.

765   Charlie Groves & Andy Piercy
Copyright © 1997 IQ Music Limited

HERE WE STAND IN TOTAL SURRENDER,
Lifting our voices, abandoned to Your cause.
Here we stand, praying in the glory
Of the one and only Jesus Christ, the Lord.

This time revival!
Lord, come and heal our land;
Bring to completion
The work that You've begun.
This time revival!
Stir up Your church again,
Pour out Your Spirit
On Your daughters and Your sons.

Here we stand in need of Your mercy;
Father, forgive us for the time that we have
    lost.
Once again make us an army
To conquer this nation with the message of
    the cross.

766   David Ruis
Copyright © 1992 Mercy/Vineyard Publishing/
Adm. by CopyCare

HIS LOVE is higher than the highest of
    mountains.
His love goes deeper that the deepest of
    seas.
His love, it stretches to the farthest horizon,
And His love, it reaches to me.

His love is stronger than the angels and
demons.
His love, it keeps me in my life's darkest hour.
His love secures me on the pathway to
heaven,
And His love is my strength and power.

His love is sweeter than the sweetest of
honey.
His love is better than the choicest of wine.
His love, it satisfies the deepest of hunger,
And His love, in Jesus it's mine.

Your love is higher...

 767

HOLD ME CLOSER TO YOU EACH DAY;
May my love for You never fade.
Keep my focus on all that's true;
May I never lose sight of You.

In my failure, in my success,
If in sadness or happiness,
Be the hope I am clinging to,
For my heart belongs to You.

You are only a breath away,
Watching over me every day;
In my heart I am filled with peace
When I hear You speak to me.

No one loves me the way You do,
No one cares for me like You do.
Feels like heaven has broken through;
God, You know how I love You.

768

HOLINESS IS YOUR LIFE IN ME,
Making me clean through Your blood.
Holiness is Your fire in me,
Purging my heart like a flood.
I know You are perfect in holiness.
Your life in me, setting me free,
Making me holy.

Only the blood of Jesus covers all of my sin.
Only the life of Jesus renews me from within.
Your blood is enough, Your mercy complete.
Your work of atonement, paid for my debts,
Making me holy.
Only the blood of Jesus.

769

HOLY CHILD, how still You lie!
Safe the manger, soft the hay;
Faint upon the eastern sky
Breaks the dawn of Christmas Day.

Holy Child, whose birthday brings
Shepherds from their field and fold,
Angel choirs and eastern kings,
Myrrh and frankincense and gold:

Holy Child, what gift of grace
From the Father freely willed!
In Your infant form we trace
All God's promises fulfilled.

Holy Child, whose human years
Span like ours delight and pain;
One in human joys and tears,
One in all but sin and stain:

Holy Child, so far from home,
All the lost to seek and save:
To what dreadful death You come,
To what dark and silent grave!

Holy Child, before whose name
Powers of darkness faint and fall;
Conquered death and sin and shame –
Jesus Christ is Lord of all!

Holy Child, how still You lie!
Safe the manger, soft the hay;
Clear upon the eastern sky
Breaks the dawn of Christmas Day.

770

HOLY GHOST,
You wonderful Holy Ghost,
A wind blowing strong,
Blowing from heaven.
(Repeat)

We have decided to go
All the way with our God.
Revival in the land, that's our goal;
As soldiers in His army
We'll fight with heart and soul.

(Final chorus)
Blood and fire,
We call upon blood and fire,
A wind blowing strong,
Blowing from heaven.
(Repeat)

71 Nathan Fellingham
Copyright © 1995 Thankyou Music

OLY, HOLY,
oly is the Lord God Almighty.
epeat)
ho was and is and is to come,
ho was and is and is to come.

ft up His name with the sound of singing,
ft up His name in all the earth.
ft up your voice and give Him glory,
or He is worthy to be praised.

72 Jimmy Collins-Owens
Copyright © 1972 Bud John Songs/EMI
Christian Music Publishing/Adm. by CopyCare

OLY, HOLY, HOLY, HOLY,
oly, holy, Lord God Almighty!
nd we lift our hearts before You
s a token of our love:
oly, holy, holy, holy.

racious Father, gracious Father,
e're so glad to be Your children, gracious
 Father;
nd we lift our heads before You
s a token of our love,
racious Father, gracious Father.

recious Jesus, precious Jesus,
e're so glad that You've redeemed us,
 precious Jesus;
nd we lift our hands before You
s a token of our love,
recious Jesus, precious Jesus,

oly Spirit, Holy Spirit,
ome and fill our hearts anew, Holy Spirit.
nd we lift our voice before You
s a token of our love,
oly Spirit, Holy Spirit.

allelujah, hallelujah,
allelujah, hallelujah –
nd we lift our hearts before You
s a token of our love,
allelujah, hallelujah.

73 Bryn Haworth
Copyright © 1991 Thankyou Music

OLY, HOLY, HOLY IS THE LORD.
oly, holy, holy is the Lord.

And He is precious in God's sight,
So precious in His eyes.

Worthy, worthy, worthy is the Lamb.
Worthy, worthy, worthy is the Lamb.

Glory, I give glory to the Lamb of God.
Glory, I give glory to the Lamb of God.

774 Richard Lewis
Copyright © 1997 Thankyou Music

HOLY, HOLY, LORD GOD ALMIGHTY,
Who was and who is
And is to come.
(Repeat)

All the angels cry 'holy,'
All the angels cry 'holy,'
All the angels cry 'holy is Your name.
Holy is Your name.
Holy is Your name.
Holy is Your name.
Holy is Your name.'

775 John Paculabo
Copyright © 1993 Thankyou Music

HOLY IS YOUR NAME,
Yeshua, my Deliverer.
Worthy of all praise,
You everliving God.

Perfect are Your ways,
Jehovah, my Father.
Faithful is Your love,
You gave Yourself for me.

In You I have security;
In You I put my trust.
In You I have confidence,
You meet my every need.

776 Mick Gisbey
Copyright © 1993 Thankyou Music

HOLY ONE, my life is in Your hand;
My song an offering of my heart,
Redeemed, washed clean,
By faith I stand secure.
In You, Jesus, I live.

To You the glory, to You the power,
To You the honour for evermore.
Your love brings healing,
Your love's eternal,
Your love's the answer,
The hope of the world,
The hope of the world.

777 Charlotte Exon
Copyright © 1991 Thankyou Music

HOLY SPIRIT, MOVE WITHIN ME,
Holy Spirit, come upon me now.
Holy Spirit, lead me to
The secret place of prayer,
Manifest the glory of God.
Holy Spirit, You are welcome,
Holy Spirit, we desire You.
Holy Spirit, worship through us,
Let us see the glory of God.

778 Robert Newey
Copyright © 1994 Thankyou Music

HOPE OF THE WORLD,
You stepped into our time,
And yet they spurned You and then turned
    away.
To a dying world You reached out,
But they didn't want to hear
The words You had to say.

> *But may the light*
> *You came to bring now shine*
> *In a world that finally lost its way.*
> *Holy love, now come,*
> *Come flow though me,*
> *Be my theme until my dying day.*

Mercy, love, truth,
You shared all these
And then to bring them life
Became a dying seed.
Now to all who will receive
A new way has been opened,
And Your children are the light they need.

> *And may the light...*

779 Graham Kendrick & Steve Thompson
Copyright © 1991 Make Way Music

HOW CAN I BE FREE FROM SIN?
Lead me to the cross of Jesus.
From the guilt, the power, the pain?
Lead me to the cross of Jesus.
There's no other way,
No price that I could pay;
Simply to the cross I cling.
This is all I need,
This is all I plead,
That His blood was shed for me.

How can I know peace within?
Lead me to the cross of Jesus.
Sing a song of joy again!
Lead me to the cross of Jesus.
Flowing from above,
All-forgiving love
From the Father's heart to me!
What a gift of grace –
His own righteousness
Clothing me in purity!

How can I live day by day?
Lead me to the cross of Jesus.
Following His narrow way?
Lead me to the cross of Jesus.

780   Stuart Townend
Copyright © 1995 Thankyou Music

HOW DEEP THE FATHER'S LOVE FOR US,
How vast beyond all measure,
That He should give His only Son
To make a wretch His treasure.
How great the pain of searing loss –
The Father turns His face away,
As wounds which mar the Chosen One
Bring many sons to glory.

Behold the man upon a cross,
My sin upon His shoulders;
Ashamed, I hear my mocking voice
Call out among the scoffers.
It was my sin that held Him there
Until it was accomplished;
His dying breath has brought me life –
I know that it is finished.

I will not boast in anything,
No gifts, no power, no wisdom;
But I will boast in Jesus Christ,
His death and resurrection.
Why should I gain from His reward?
I cannot give an answer;
But this I know with all my heart –
His wounds have paid my ransom.

781 Matt Redman
Copyright © 1995 Thankyou Music

HOW LOVELY IS YOUR DWELLING PLACE,
O Lord Almighty.
My soul longs and even faints for You.
For here my heart is satisfied,
Within Your presence.
I sing beneath the shadow of Your wings.

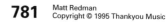

Better is one day in Your courts,
Better is one day in Your house,
Better is one day in Your courts
Than thousands elsewhere.
(Repeat)

One thing I ask and I would seek;
To see Your beauty,
To find You in the place Your glory dwells.

My heart and flesh cry out
For You, the living God;
Your Spirit's water for my soul.
I've tasted and I've seen,
Come once again to me;
I will draw near to You,
I will draw near to You.

782 John Newton (1725–1807),
adpt. Chris Bowater
Copyright © 1976 Sovereign Lifestyle Music

HOW SWEET THE NAME OF JESUS SOUNDS
In a believer's ear;
It soothes his sorrows, heals his wounds,
And drives away his fear.
It makes the wounded spirit whole,
And calms the troubled breast;
'Tis manna to the hungry soul
And to the weary, rest,
And to the weary, rest.

Dear name, the Rock on which I build,
My shield, and hiding place;
My never failing treasury, filled
With boundless stores of grace.
Jesus, my Shepherd, Saviour, Friend,
My Prophet, Priest, and King;
My Lord, my Life, my Way, my End,
Accept the praise I bring,
Accept the praise I bring.

Weak is the effort of my heart,
And cold my warmest thought;
But when I see You as You are,
I'll praise You as I ought.
I would Your boundless love proclaim
With every fleeting breath;
So shall the music of Your name
Refresh my soul in death,
Refresh my soul in death.

783 Dave Bilbrough
Copyright © 1994 Thankyou Music

HOW WONDERFUL, *how glorious*
Is the love of God,
Bringing healing, forgiveness,
Wonderful love.

Let celebration echo through this land;
We bring reconciliation,
We bring hope to every man:

We proclaim the kingdom
Of our God is here;
Come and join the heavenly anthem,
Ringing loud and ringing clear:

Listen to the music
As His praises fill the air;
With joy and with gladness
Tell the people everywhere:

784 Dave Bilbrough
Copyright © 1997 Thankyou Music

HUMBLE YOURSELVES
Under God's mighty hand,
So that He will lift you up.
(Repeat)

Cast all anxiety
On Him,
Because He cares for You.

Open your hearts
To the Lord your God,
And know His love for you.
(Repeat)

Cast all anxiety
On Him,
Because He cares for You.

I bow down
Before You, my Lord.
(Repeat)

785 Jim Bailey
Copyright © 1996 Thankyou Music

I AM THE APPLE OF GOD'S EYE,
His BANANA over me is love.
He ORANGES His angels to look after me,
As His blessings PLUM-met from above.

Never have to play the GOOSEBERRY,
Feel like a LEMON, no not me.
For wherever this MAN-GOES,
A RASPBERRY it never blows.

The GREAT FRUIT of God,
The GREAT FRUIT of God,
The GREAT FRUIT of God it overflows.
(Repeat)

I will praise Him on the TANGERINE,
Praise Him on the MANDARIN;
SATSUMA or later you will see
There is always a CLEMENTINE
   for praising Him.

 786 David Gate
Copyright © 1997 Thankyou Music

I AM YOURS
And You are mine,
Friend to me
For all of time.

   And all I have now
   I give to You.
   And all I want now
   Is to be pure, pure like You.

I'm not afraid
Of earthly things,
For I am safe
With You, my King.

787 Wayne Drain
Copyright © 1996 Thankyou Music

   I BELIEVE IN GOD THE FATHER,
   I believe in Jesus the Son:
   I believe in God the Holy Spirit,
   I believe in the Three in One.

I believe He was born of a virgin,
Was crucified and buried in the ground.
Descended into hell and won the battle,
But the devil, death and hell
Couldn't hold Him down.

O Lord, we're drowning in confusion,
So many of us going separate ways;
Wanting to be God is our delusion,
But some of us are standing up,
Not ashamed to say, I believe, I believe!

I believe He ascended into heaven,
Where He sits at God's right hand;
And I believe our King will be returning
To judge the living and the dead,
From every tribe and land.

788 Dave Bilbrough
Copyright © 1991 Thankyou Music

I BELIEVE THERE IS A GOD IN HEAVEN
Who paid the price for all my sin;
Shed His blood to open up the way
For me to walk with Him.

Gave His life upon a cross,
Took the punishment for us,
Offered up Himself in love,
Jesus, Jesus.

'It is finished' was His cry;
Not even death could now deny
The Son of God exalted high,
Jesus, Jesus,
Jesus.

789 David Fellingham
Copyright © 1992 Thankyou Music

I BOW DOWN in humble adoration,
Speak Your name with love and devotion,
Jesus, the Lamb sacrificed for me.
I see Your face, Your tender hands
Scarred for me.
I fall at Your feet with songs of praises
   singing;
My joy is complete, You fulfil my longing.
Prophet of God, my Priest and my King,
I worship and adore.

Before the Father's throne You ever interced
You always hear my prayer, whatever I may
   plead.
You wipe away my tears, You give me
   victory;
By Your blood I am cleansed, I am free.

 790 Martin Smith
Copyright © 1994 Curious? Music UK/
Adm. by Bucks Music Ltd

   (Oh) **I COULD SING UNENDING SONGS**
   Of how You saved my soul.
   Well, I could dance a thousand miles
   Because of Your great love.

My heart is bursting, Lord,
To tell of all You've done,
Of how You changed my life
And wiped away the past.
I wanna shout it out,
From every rooftop sing,
For now I know that God is for me,
Not against me.

Everybody's singing now,
'Cause we're so happy!
Everybody's dancing now,
'Cause we're so happy!
If only we could see Your face,
And see You smiling over us,
And unseen angels celebrate,
For joy is in this place!

791
Craig Musseau
Copyright © 1990 Mercy/Vineyard Publishing/
Adm. by CopyCare

CRY OUT
For your hand of mercy to heal me.
I am weak,
I need Your love to free me.
O Lord, my Rock,
My strength in weakness,
Come rescue me, O Lord.

You are my hope,
Your promise never fails me.
And my desire
Is to follow You for ever.
For You are good,
For You are good,
For You are good to me.
For You are good,
For You are good,
For You are good to me.

792
Ian Smale
Copyright © 1996 Thankyou Music

DON'T WANT TO BE A PHARISEE
Or anyone like that.
It's stupid swallowing camels
Whilst straining out a gnat.
To keep the letter of the law,
They forgot the people it was for.
So I don't want to be a Pharisee,
I don't want to be a Pharisee,
I don't want to be a Pharisee
Or anyone like that.

793
Matt Redman
Copyright © 1996 Thankyou Music

I **DREAM** of tongues of fire
Resting on Your people,
I dream of all the miracles to come.
I hope to see the coming
Healing of the nations,
I long to see the prodigals return.
So many hopes and longings in You;
When will all the dreams come true?

I'm a believer in Your kingdom,
I am a seeker of the new things,
I am a dreamer with some old dreams,
Let them now come.

I hope to see You come down,
Rend the mighty heavens,
And let Your glory cover all the earth;
To see Your sons and daughters
Come to know and love You,
And find a purer passion in the church.
These are the things my heart will pursue:
When will all the dreams come true?

May Your church now reach out,
Sowing truth and justice,
Learn to love the poor and help the weak.
When Your kingdom's coming
It will touch the broken,
Place the lonely in a family.
So many hopes and longings in You:
When will all the dreams come true?

794
Graham Kendrick
Copyright © 1987 Make Way Music

IF MY PEOPLE, who bear My name,
Will humble themselves and pray;
If they seek My presence
And turn their backs on their wicked ways:
Then I will hear from heaven,
I'll hear from heaven and will forgive;
I will forgive their sins
And will heal their land,
Yes, I will heal their land.

795
Tommy Walker
Copyright © Doulos Publishing/
Adm. by CopyCare

I HAVE A MAKER,
He formed my heart;
Before even time began
My life was in His hand.

I have a Father,
He calls me His own;
He'll never leave me,
No matter where I go.

He knows my name,
He knows my every thought;
He sees each tear that falls,
And hears me when I call.

796
Matt Redman
Copyright © 1995 Thankyou Music

I HAVE COME TO LOVE YOU,
I have come to love You today.
(Repeat)

*And today and for evermore
I'll love Your name.
And today and for evermore
I'll love Your name.*

I have come to worship,
I have come to worship today.
(Repeat)

I have come to thank You,
I have come to thank You today.
(Repeat)

797 Stuart Townend
Copyright © 1997 Thankyou Music

I HAVE HEARD that You are swift to bless the
seeker,
And I believe that You will hear the constant
cry;
So I will call until I know I've had an
answer,
I need Your power, Lord!
As Jacob wrestled, so I'll wrestle with Your
angel,
And though I'm weary, I will not be
overcome;
For You have given me a passion for Your
kingdom,
O let Your glory fall!

*I won't let go,
I won't let go until You bless me.
I won't take no for an answer;
Jesus, I won't let go!*

I have heard that You show mercy to a
nation,
And I believe that You give power to Your
church;
So now I'm asking You to open up the
heavens,
Pour out Your mercy, Lord!
For Your gospel to be lived among Your
people,
For Your miracle of healing on the streets;
For the government to fear the Lord
Almighty,
We need Your power, Lord!

I'm not ungrateful for the blessings You have
given,
But I can see the need around me;
I'm not ashamed to say I need all that You
have,
So Father, hear me knocking,
See me holding out my hands to You.

For a hunger that will overcome my
weakness,
For a love that will not seek its own reward;
For my life to make a difference in this natio
I need Your power, Lord!

798 Kent Henry
Copyright © 1993 Integrity's Hosanna! Music/
Sovereign Music UK

(And) **I HAVE LOVED YOU** *with an
everlasting love,
And I have drawn you with My loving
kindness.
And I have loved you with an everlasting
love,
And I have drawn you with My loving
kindness.*

Because God loved you and to keep His own
He brought you out with a mighty hand,
He redeemed you from the devil's yoke.
Oh, the Lord, He is the God
And faithful is He.
He'll keep His word and His covenant,
Giving mercy and prosperity.

And casting all of Your cares on Him
For He cares for you,
There's a love dimension
In the kingdom of God,
It's sure to take you through.
God commanded His love toward us,
Christ died on a tree,
Then He rose again, the living God,
More than conquerors now are we.

 Lynn DeShazo
Copyright © 1992 Integrity's Hosanna! Music/
Sovereign Music UK

**I HAVE MADE YOU TOO SMALL IN MY
EYES;**
O Lord, forgive me.
And I have believed in a lie
That You were unable to heal me.
But now, O Lord, I see my wrong;
Heal my heart, and show Yourself strong.
And in my eyes and with my song,
O Lord, be magnified,
O Lord, be magnified.

*Be magnified, O Lord;
You are highly exalted.
And there is nothing You can't do,
O Lord, my eyes are on You,
Be magnified,
O Lord, be magnified.*

have leaned on the wisdom of men;
God, forgive me.
nd I have responded to them
stead of Your light and Your mercy.
ut now, O Lord, I see my wrong;
eal my heart and show Yourself strong.
nd in my eyes and with my song,
Lord, be magnified,
Lord, be magnified.

00 Don Moen
Copyright © 1989 Integrity's Hosanna! Music/
Sovereign Music UK

JUST WANT TO BE WHERE YOU ARE,
welling daily in Your presence.
don't want to worship from afar,
raw me near to where You are.
just want to be where You are,
Your dwelling place for ever.
ake me to the place where You are,
just want to be with You.

I want to be where You are,
Dwelling in You presence,
Feasting at Your table,
Surrounded by Your glory.
In Your presence,
That's where I always want to be,
I just want to be,
I just want to be with You.

my God, You are my strength and my
song,
nd when I'm in Your presence,
hough I'm weak, You're always strong.

01 Nathan Fellingham
Copyright © 1997 Thankyou Music

KNOW A PLACE
Vhere blessings from heaven are poured,
Mercy and grace abounding.
hrough Jesus' blood
Ve have now been set free
nto the Father's loving.

know a place
Vhere there is no guilt or fear,
s I come into His presence.
can now know
peace which surpasses all,
lothing shall separate us.

And I will trust in You alone,
My refuge and strength.
For all the trials that come my way,
Your grace is sufficient for me.

I know a place
Where a wonderful river flows,
That fills me with His glory;
Bringing us life,
We're stirred to adore Him,
A perfect joy everlasting.

802 Randy & Terry Butler
Copyright © 1993 Mercy/Vineyard Publishing/
Adm. by CopyCare

I KNOW A PLACE, A WONDERFUL PLACE,
Where accused and condemned
Find mercy and grace.
Where the wrongs we have done,
And the wrongs done to us
Were nailed there with Him (You)
There on the cross.

(Men)	At the cross,
(Women)	At the cross,
(All)	He (You) died for my sin.
(Men)	At the cross,
(Women)	At the cross,
(All)	He (You) gave us life again.

803 Matt Redman
Copyright © 1996 Thankyou Music

**I KNOW YOU LOVE TO CROWN THE
  HUMBLE,**
Pouring out grace for the broken heart.
You bless the meek, You meet the lowly;
Lord, as I bow, lift me to You.

I keep on bowing down, bowing down,
Keep on bowing down,
What else can I do?
Keep on bowing down, bowing down.
What else can I do,
To give it all to You?

I'd like to be one such believer,
Keeping my knees firmly on the ground.
I'd like to tread humbly before You;
Lord, as I bow, lift me to You.

Do You smile when You see
A humble believer on their knees?
And my Lord, will You be pleased
To look upon me, to look upon me?

804

I LIFT MY EYES TO THE QUIET HILLS,
In the press of a busy day;
As green hills stand in a dusty land,
So God is my strength and stay.

I lift my eyes to the quiet hills,
To a calm that is mine to share;
Secure and still in the Father's will,
And kept by the Father's care.

I lift my eyes to the quiet hills,
With a prayer as I turn to sleep;
By day, by night,
Through the dark and light,
My Shepherd will guard His sheep.

I lift my eyes to the quiet hills,
And my heart to the Father's throne;
In all my ways to the end of days,
The Lord will preserve His own.

805

I LONG FOR YOU, O LORD.
I long to know You more;
I long to have Your heart placed in me every
day.
I long for, I long for You, O Lord.

I hunger to eat the bread
Only You can give.
I'm thirsting to drink Your water
That I might live,
To grow in You,
To know in You
My every desire is found.

806

I LOVE THE LORD for He has heard me,
He has heard my mercy plea.
From deep within my troubled heart,
I cried 'O Lord, save me!'
I love the Lord for His compassion
And His gracious, righteous ways.
He protects the simple-hearted ones,
And in my need,
The Lord saw me, and saved.

For as long, for as long as I live,
I will call, I will call on His name.
Be at rest once more, my soul,
For the Lord is good,
And He has been good to you.

I love the Lord for all the goodness
That I never can repay,
But I lift the cup of salvation,
And call upon His name.
I will fulfil my vows before the Lord,
In the presence of His saints;
O, make me now Your servant, Lord,
You have freed me from,
You have freed me from these chains.

807

I LOVE YOU, LORD, MY STRENGTH,
For You heard my cry.
You have been my help in trouble.
I've put my trust in You,
My refuge and my hope,
You're the Rock on which I stand.

You're my stronghold,
You're my stronghold,
You're the stronghold of my life.
You're my stronghold,
You're my stronghold,
You're the stronghold of my life.

I love You, Lord, my strength,
You reached down from on high,
And You rescued me from trouble.
You've taken hold of me,
And set me on a rock,
And now this is where I stand.

I love You, Lord, my strength,
There is no other rock,
And now I will not be shaken.
The sea may roar and crash,
The mountains quake and fall,
Ah, but on this Rock I stand.

808

I'M A FRIEND OF JESUS CHRIST, *(echo)*
He's God's Son and He's alive, *(echo)*
I will trust in Him it's true, *(echo)*
He's always there to see me through. *(echo)*

Sound off, *Jesus!*
Sound off, is *Lord!*
Sound off, *Jesus!*
Sound off, is *Lord!*

The gift of God is eternal life through Jesus
Christ,
(Repeat ×3)
Through Jesus, Jesus Christ.

Jesus is the Boss of my life,
He's the only one can make it come right.
Jesus is the Boss of my life,
Jesus is the Boss.

Rap)
said, come on everybody and move your
    feet;
he rhythm is hot, it's a powerful beat.
he time is right to do some business,
et on your feet and be a witness
o the Holy One,
he King of kings, God's only Son;
esus Christ, that's His name,
le died to take our sin and shame.

809   Ian Smale
           Copyright © 1982 Thankyou Music

M LOOKING UP TO JESUS,
lis face is shining beauty.
m feeling so unworthy,
et His Spirit leads me on.
m looking up to Jesus,
lis radiance surrounds me.
feel so pure and clean,
 taste of heaven on earth.

Last time)
m looking up to Jesus.

810   K. Prosch
           Copyright © 1992 Liber Media &
           Publishing, LLC/Kingsway Music

M STANDING HERE TO TESTIFY, *(Leader)*
, the Lord is good. *(All)*
o sing of how He changed my heart.
    (Leader)
), the Lord is good. *(All)*
was bound by hate and pride, *(Leader)*
), the Lord is good. *(All)*
lever knowing of His light. *(Leader)*
), the Lord is good. *(All)*

did not think I could have peace, *(Leader)*
), the Lord is good. *(All)*
rapped inside by fear and shame. *(Leader)*
, the Lord is good. *(All)*
le wiped away all of my grief, *(Leader)*
), the Lord is good. *(All)*
Vhen I believed upon His name. *(Leader)*

    Come to the light, come as you are;
    You can be the friend of God.
    Humble yourself, give Him your heart,
    He will meet you where you are.

(Last chorus)
Come to the light, just as you are;
Fall on the Rock for the wasted years.
He will restore all that was lost,
Surrender now, His power is here.

Clap Your hands, O God.
Clap Your hands, O God.
(Repeat)

811   Chris Bowater
           Copyright © 1995 Sovereign Lifestyle Music

I NEED YOU like dew in the desert,
Like refreshing summer rain,
Come and pour Your love again on me.
I'm finding that every time I come
And ask for something more,
You never fail to pour Your love on me.

And peace like a river flows,
Waves of mercy ever roll;
Take me deeper,
I want to know You more.
Pour Your love, pour Your love,
Pour Your love on me.

812   David Fellingham
           Copyright © 1994 Thankyou Music

IN EVERY CIRCUMSTANCE of life
You are with me, glorious Father.
And I have put my trust in You,
That I may know the glorious hope
To which I'm called.
And by the power that works in me,
You've raised me up and set me free;
And now in every circumstance
I'll prove Your love without a doubt,
Your joy shall be my strength,
Your joy shall be my strength.

813   Taizé, Music: Jacques Berthier (1923–94)
           Copyright © Ateliers et Presses de Taizé

IN GOD ALONE my soul can find rest and
    peace,
In God my peace and joy.
Only in God my soul can find its rest,
Find its rest and peace.

Mon âme se repose en paix sur Dieu seul:
De lui vient mon salut.
Oui, sur Dieu seul mon âme se repose,
Se repose en paix.

814
Geoff Bullock
Copyright © 1997 Watershed Productions/
Kingsway Music

IN MY LIFE PROCLAIM YOUR GLORY,

In my heart reveal Your majesty;
Then my soul shall speak the wonders of
  Your grace,
And this heart of mine shall sing Your praise.
In my words proclaim Your mercy,
In my life reveal Your power;
Then my soul shall be a mirror of Your love,
And this heart of mine shall sing Your praise.

> Lord of all mercy, God of all grace,
> Lord of all righteousness;
> Lord of the heavens, Lord of the earth
> Enthroned in majesty.
> Worthy of honour, worthy of praise,
> All glory and majesty;
> I give You the honour, I give You the praise,
> And proclaim Your glorious power.

In my soul unveil Your love, Lord,
Deep within my heart renewing me.
Day by day your life transforming all I am,
As this heart of mine reflects Your praise.
Lord of all, enthroned in glory,
Grace and mercy, truth and righteousness,
Every knee shall bow before this Christ, our Lord,
As all creation sings Your praise.

815
John Pantry
Copyright © 1990 Thankyou Music

IN MYSTERY REIGNING, King over all,

Hear angels proclaiming, Jesus is Lord.
To each generation Your love is the same;
Wonderful Saviour, we worship Your name.

A beauty that's timeless, who can compare?
All earth stands in silence, when You appear.
Your kingdom is boundless, Your love
  without end;
Wonder of wonders, this King is my friend!

All power has been given into Your hands;
Through blood and by suffering You now
  command.
And no opposition can stand in Your light;
Crowned King of heaven, we kneel at the sight.

816
Wayne Drain
Copyright © 1996 Thankyou Music

IN MY WEAKNESS You are strong,

When I fall short You carry me along.
Into my darkness You shine Your light,
When I feel blinded, You restore my sight.

> You are the Lord, You never change,
> You still the storm when I call Your name
> You're all I want, You're always there,
> No matter when, no matter where.
> You're the Lord, You never change.
> You're the Lord, You never change.

I'm inconsistent, but You are true;
I don't trust myself, but I depend on You.
Look through my selfishness, and see my
  heart;
Bring out the precious from the worthless
  parts.

I need courage, Lord, to make a change;
It's time my independence got rearranged.
I'm tired of chasing after my own ways;
So I'll serve You, Lord,
Serve You, Lord, serve You, Lord,
For the rest, rest of my days.

817
Taizé, Music: Jacques Berthier (1923–94)
Copyright © 1987 Ateliers et Presses de Taizé

IN THE LORD I'll be ever thankful,

In the Lord I will rejoice!
Look to God, do not be afraid;
Lift up your voices, the Lord is near,
Lift up your voices, the Lord is near.

> El Senyor és la meva força,
> El Senyor el meu cant.
> Ell m'haestat la salvació
> En ell confio, i no tinc por.
> En ell confio, i no tinc por.

818
Author unknown
Copyright control

IN THE NAME OF JESUS,

In the name of Jesus,
We have the victory.
In the name of Jesus,
In the name of Jesus,
Demons will have to flee.
Who can tell what God can do?
Who can tell of His love for you?
In the name of Jesus, Jesus,
We have the victory.

819
Sue Rinaldi & Steve Bassett
Copyright © 1994 Thankyou Music

IN THESE DAYS OF DARKNESS,

Who will bear the light?
In all of this confusion,
Who will rage against the night?
And who will light a beacon
In the face of this dark, dark sky?

Where there is oppression,
Who will raise the flame?
For the sake of all the children,
Who will touch the fields of shame?
And who will light a beacon
In the face of this dark, dark sky,
With a hope that is eternal,
With a love that will never die?

Oh I, I will carry the fire.
Oh I, I will carry the fire.

Who will burn with passion,
Blazing from the heart,
To forge a new tomorrow?
We must tell the world
Of a hope that is eternal,
Of a love that will never die.
And we will light a beacon
In the face of this dark, dark sky.

Oh I, I will carry the fire.
Oh I, I will carry the fire.
I will not rest, I will not tire,
With all my strength I'll carry the fire.
I will not rest, I will not tire,
With all my strength I'll carry the fire.

820 David Fellingham
Copyright © 1996 Thankyou Music

IN THESE DAYS OF REFRESHING,
In these days of visitation,
There is a reason why You've come.
We have tasted of Your fulness,
One blessing after another,
And that is the reason we say 'come'.

It's not just to make us laugh or cry,
To shake or fall, but to glorify
Jesus, Jesus, Jesus,
And that is the reason we say 'come'.

And let me know the power to speak
And witness for the gospel,
Let me know the power to pray for the sick
And see them healed.
Let me know the faith that can
Move the mighty mountain,
Let me know the love that joins me
To Your people.

And we say more, Lord,
More of Your power.
We say more, Lord,
More of Your power.
We say more, Lord,
More of Your power,
More of Your power in me.

821 Maggi Dawn
Copyright © 1993 Thankyou Music

INTO THE DARKNESS of this world,
Into the shadows of the night;
Into this loveless place You came,
Lightened our burdens, eased our pain,
And made these hearts Your home.
Into the darkness once again –
Oh come, Lord Jesus, come.

Come with Your love
To make us whole,
Come with Your light
To lead us on,
Driving the darkness
Far from our souls:
O come, Lord Jesus, come.

Into the longing of our souls,
Into these heavy hearts of stone,
Shine on us now Your piercing light,
Order our lives and souls aright,
By grace and love unknown,
Until in You our hearts unite –
Oh come, Lord Jesus, come.

O Holy Child, Emmanuel,
Hope of the ages, God with us,
Visit again this broken place,
Till all the earth declares Your praise
And Your great mercies own.
Now let Your love be born in us,
O come, Lord Jesus, come.

(Last chorus)
Come in Your glory,
Take Your place,
Jesus, the Name above all names,
We long to see You face to face,
O come, Lord Jesus, come.

822 Ian Smale
Copyright © 1994 Thankyou Music

I ONCE WAS FRIGHTENED OF SPIDERS,
I once was frightened of the dark;
I once was frightened of many, many
   things,
Especially things that barked.
But now I'm asking Jesus
To help these fears to go,
'Cause I don't want them to be part of me,
No, no, no, no, no.

I once was frightened by thunder,
And frightened by lightning too;
I once was frightened by many, many things
That crashed and banged and blew.
But now I'm asking Jesus
To help these fears to go,
'Cause I don't want them to be part of me,
No, no, no, no, no.

 823 Graham Kendrick
Copyright © 1994 Make Way Music

IS ANYONE THIRSTY, anyone?
Is anyone thirsty?
Is anyone thirsty, anyone?
Is anyone thirsty? Jesus said:
'Let them come to me and drink,
Let them come to me.'

> *O, let the living waters flow,*
> *O, let the living waters flow,*
> *Let the river of Your Spirit*
> *Flow through me.*
> *(Repeat)*
> *Flow through me.*

Let the living waters flow.
Let the living waters flow.
Let the living waters flow.
Let the living waters flow.

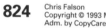 **824** Chris Falson
Copyright © 1993 Maranatha! Praise Inc./
Adm. by CopyCare

I SEE THE LORD
Seated on the throne, exalted:
And the train of His robe
Fills the temple with glory:
The whole earth is filled,
The whole earth is filled,
The whole earth is filled
With Your glory.

Holy, holy,
Holy, holy,
Yes, holy is the Lord.
Holy, holy,
Holy, holy,
Yes, holy is the Lord of lords.

825 Craig Musseau
Copyright © 1991 Mercy/Vineyard Publishing/
Adm. by CopyCare

I SING A SIMPLE SONG OF LOVE
To my Saviour, to my Jesus.
I'm grateful for the things You've done,
My loving Saviour, oh precious Jesus.
My heart is glad that You've called me Your own;
There's no place I'd rather be,

(Than) in Your arms of love,
In Your arms of love,
Holding me still,
Holding me near
In Your arms of love.

 826 Terry MacAlmon
Copyright © 1989 Integrity's Hosanna! Music/
Sovereign Music UK

I SING PRAISES TO YOUR NAME, O Lord,
Praises to Your name, O Lord,
For Your name is great and greatly to be
    praised.
I sing praises to Your name, O Lord,
Praises to Your name, O Lord,
For Your name is great and greatly to be
    praised.

I give glory to Your name...

827 Martin Smith
Copyright © 1996 Curious? Music UK/
Adm. by Bucks Music Ltd

IS IT TRUE TODAY that when people pray,
Cloudless skies will break,
Kings and queens will shake?
Yes it's true, and I believe it,
I'm living for You.

Well it's true today that when people pray
We'll see dead men rise,
And the blind set free?
Yes it's true and I believe it,
I'm living for You.

> *I'm gonna be a history maker in this land*
> *I'm gonna be a speaker of truth*
> *To all mankind.*
> *I'm gonna stand,*
> *I'm gonna run into Your arms,*
> *Into Your arms again,*
> *Into Your arms, into Your arms again.*

Well it's true today that when people stand
With the fire of God and the truth in hand,
We'll see miracles, we'll see angels sing,
We'll see broken hearts making history?
Yes it's true, and I believe it,
I'm living for You.

28 Paul Oakley
Copyright © 1990 Thankyou Music

STAND AMAZED when I realise
Your love for me is beyond all measure.
Lord, I can't deny
Your love for me is great.

It's as high, high as the heavens above,
Such is the depth of Your love
Toward those who fear You.
O Lord, far as the east is from west,
You have removed my transgressions.
You make my life brand new:
Father, I love You.

Your love is higher,
Higher as the heavens.
Your love is deeper,
Deeper than the deepest ocean.
Your love is stronger,
Stronger than the powers of darkness.
Your love is sweeter,
Sweeter than wine.

829 Charles H. Gabriel (1856–1932)

I STAND AMAZED IN THE PRESENCE
Of Jesus the Nazarene,
And wonder how He could love me,
A sinner, condemned, unclean.

How marvellous! How wonderful!
And my song shall ever be:
How marvellous! How wonderful!
Is my Saviour's love for me!

For me it was in the garden He prayed,
'Not My will, but Thine':
He had no tears for His own griefs,
But sweat drops of blood for mine.

In pity angels beheld Him,
And came from the world of light
To comfort Him in the sorrows
He bore for my soul that night.

He took my sins and my sorrows,
He made them His very own;
He bore the burden of Calvary,
And suffered and died alone.

When with the ransomed in glory
His face I at last shall see,
'Twill be my joy through the ages
To sing of His love for me.

830 Daniel L. Schutte
Copyright © 1981 Daniel L. Schutte &
New Dawn Music

I, THE LORD OF SEA AND SKY,
I have heard My people cry;
All who dwell in dark and sin
My hand will save.
I, who made the stars of night,
I will make their darkness bright.
I will speak My word to them.
Whom shall I send?

Here I am, Lord.
Is it I, Lord?
I have heard You calling in the night.
I will go, Lord,
If You lead me;
I will hold Your people in my heart.

I, the Lord of snow and rain,
I have borne my people's pain;
I have wept for love of them –
They turn away.
I will break their hearts of stone,
Give them hearts for love alone;
I will speak My word to them.
Whom shall I send?

I, the Lord of wind and flame,
I will tend the poor and lame,
I will set a feast for them –
My hand will save.
Finest bread I will provide
Till their hearts are satisfied;
I will give My life to them.
Whom shall I send?

831 Psalm 106, paraphrase by John L. Bell &
Graham Maule
Copyright © 1988 WGRG, Iona Community

IT IS GOOD TO GIVE THANKS TO THE LORD,
To remember all He has done;
Then God will remember our praises
When He looks with love on His people.

O give thanks to the Lord,
For His love endures for ever.
O give thanks to the Lord,
For the Lord alone is good.

Our sin is the sin of our fathers,
We have done wrong, we all have been evil;
Like those who once lived in bondage,
We paid no heed to all You had done.

Our fathers forsook Your love,
At the Red Sea they questioned their God;
They fell from their faith in the desert,
And put God to the test in the wilderness.

Time after time He would rescue them,
Yet in malice they dared to defy Him;
Despite this He came to their aid
When He heard their cries of distress.

Save us, O Lord, in Your love;
Bring us back from all that offends You.
Look not alone at our sins,
But remember your promise of mercy.

Blessed be the Lord God of Israel
Both now and through all eternity;
Let nations and people cry out
And sing Amen! Alleluia!

 832 Terry Butler
Copyright © 1991 Mercy/Vineyard Publishing/
Adm. by CopyCare

IT IS THE CRY OF MY HEART *to follow*
You.
It is the cry of my heart to be close to
You.
It is the cry of my heart to follow
All of the days of my life.

Teach me Your holy ways, O Lord,
So I can walk in Your truth.
Teach me Your holy ways, O Lord,
And make me wholly devoted to You.

Open my eyes so I can see
The wonderful things that You do.
Open my heart up more and more
And make it wholly devoted to You.

833 Ian Smale
Copyright © 1993 Thankyou Music

IT'S A WONDERFUL, WONDERFUL,
WONDERFUL FEELING,
It's a wonderful feeling to
Know you're saved.
It's a wonderful, wonderful,
Wonderful WONDERFUL!
Wonderful feeling to
Know you're saved.

My life is built on rock, not sand;
It's a wonderful feeling to know you're saved.
And none can steal me from God's hand;
It's a wonderful feeling to know you're saved.

I once was lost but now I'm found:
It's a wonderful feeling to know you're saved.
In Father's arms I'm safe and sound:
It's a wonderful feeling to know you're saved.

My old life's gone, I'm now brand new:
It's a wonderful feeling to know you're saved
Much less of me, much more of You:
It's a wonderful feeling to know you're saved

 834 Dave Bilbrough
Copyright © 1995 Thankyou Music

IT'S GETTING CLEARER, the light is dawning
I'm pressing on to a higher place.
The past behind me, I'm moving forward,
And I will follow after You.

You are my strength, You are my shield,
You are the Rock on which I want to build
my life,
O Lord, O Lord.
I won't compromise, I won't be denied,
I want to keep my eyes on the prize
Of knowing You, knowing You.

There is a passion that burns within me,
I long to see Your kingdom come.
To know Your presence, to seek no other;
I hunger, Lord, for more of You.

 835 Matt Redman & Martin Smith
Copyright © 1995 Thankyou Music

IT'S RISING UP from coast to coast,
From north to south, and east to west;
The cry of hearts that love Your name,
Which with one voice we will proclaim.

The former things have taken place,
Can this be the new day of praise?
A heavenly song that comes to birth,
And reaches out to all the earth.
Oh, let the cry to nations ring,
That all may come and all may sing:

'Holy is the Lord.' (Every heart sing:)
'Holy is the Lord.' (With one voice sing:)
'Holy is the Lord.' (Every heart sing:)
'Holy is the Lord.'

And we have heard the Lion's roar,
That speaks of heaven's love and power.
Is this the time, is this the call
That ushers in Your kingdom rule?
Oh, let the cry to nations ring,
That all may come and all may sing:

'Jesus is alive!' (Every heart sing:)...

336

'VE FALLEN IN LOVE (I've fallen in love)
Since the first time we met,
Since the first time we met)
There at the cross where You paid for my sin,
You opened the way to my heart and came
   in,
Oh, I've fallen in love, (I've fallen in love)
Yes, I've fallen in love. (I've fallen in love)

've fallen in love (I've fallen in love)
Since the first time we met,
Since the first time we met)
When I finally looked unto You,
You broke my hardened heart in two,
Oh, I've fallen in love, (I've fallen in love)
Yes, I've fallen in love. (I've fallen in love.)

Jesus my Lord, only You have my heart,
Only You can know;
Words don't express what my heart tries to
   say,
That I have fallen in love.

've fallen in love (I've fallen in love)
Since the first time we met,
Since the first time we met)
When You stole my love of the world
And placed my heart's affection on You,
Oh, I've fallen in love, (I've fallen in love)
Yes, I've fallen in love. (I've fallen in love.)

337

'VE GOT A LOVE SONG IN MY HEART,
It is for You, Lord my God.
've got a love song in my heart,
It is for You, Lord my God.

   La la la la la la la,
   La la la la la la la,
   La la la la la la la.
   (Repeat)

've got a passion in my heart...

've got rejoicing in my heart...

And there is dancing in my heart...

've never known a love like this...

838

I WAITED PATIENTLY for the Lord,
He turned and heard my cry.
He lifted me from the pit,
Out from the mud and mire.
He put my feet on a rock,
And gave me a firm place to stand.
He put a new song in my mouth,
A hymn of praise to God,
A hymn of praise to God.

   Many will see, many will fear,
   And many will put their trust in the Lord.
   Many will see, many will fear,
   And many will put their trust in the Lord.

Blessed is the man who trusts the Lord,
And turns from all the proud,
From all those who have turned aside,
To follow what is false.
Many are the wonders that You have done,
All the things You have planned;
Were I to count they still would be
Too many to declare,
Too many to declare.

839

I WALK BY FAITH,
Each step by faith,
To live by faith,
I put my trust in You.
(Repeat)

Every step I take is a step of faith;
No weapon formed against me shall prosper.
And every prayer I make is a prayer of faith;
And if my God is for me,
Then who can be against me?

840

I WANT TO BE HOLY,
I want to be righteous,
I want to live my life the way You want me to.
I want to be blameless,
Not walking in darkness,
I want to be a living sacrifice to You.

I'm gonna run the race,
I'm gonna run to win,
Throw off everything that hinders me.
I'm gonna fix my eyes upon the King,
And leave my sin behind.

I want to be so much better,
I want to be more like You.
Keep taking me further and deeper,
I want to right the wrong,
I want to live this song,
Now I'm pressing on,
I'm gonna leave my sin behind.

Singing, 'goodbye rage, goodbye hate,
Goodbye anger, goodbye malice,
Goodbye bitterness and slander,
Goodbye fear of man!'
(Repeat)

841 Penny Webb, Hayley Roberts,
Doug & Belinda Horley
Copyright © 1995 Thankyou Music

I WANT TO BE OUT OF MY DEPTH IN YOUR LOVE,
Feeling Your arms so strong around me.
Out of my depth in Your love,
Out of my depth in You.
(Repeat)

Learning to let You lead,
Putting all trust in You;
Deeper into Your arms,
Surrounded by You.
Things I have held so tight,
Made my security;
Give me the strength I need
To simply let go.

842 Evan Rogers
Copyright © 1997 Thankyou Music

I WANT TO KNOW
The glorious inheritance
That You have given to me.
And I want to know
The hope that You have called me to,
O Lord, I want to know Your truth.

> *I want to know You better,*
> *The Spirit without measure,*
> *To know the fulness that's in You.*
> *I want to know Your mystery,*
> *The grace You've given freely,*
> *I know my life is hidden in You.*

I want to know
Your wisdom and Your revelation,
Drawing me to You.
I want to know
The power of Your mighty strength
Which raised
Jesus from the dead.

843 Paul Oakley
Copyright © 1995 Thankyou Music

I WAS LOST without a trace,
All except for the eyes of heaven.
Now my Saviour's love has found me,
And His love has brought me home.

I can sleep in peace tonight,
I won't worry about tomorrow,
Now I know my Daddy loves me,
And His perfect love will conquer all.

> *I'm like a child in His eyes,*
> *And He will meet my needs*
> *With all the riches of heaven;*
> *And He loves me much too much*
> *To let me go,*
> *He will keep me in His love.*

Heaven and earth may pass away,
And mountains fall into the ocean;
But His word is everlasting,
And His love goes on and on.

844 Brian Doerksen
Copyright © 1994 Mercy/Vineyard Publishing/
Adm. by CopyCare

I WILL BE YOURS,
You will be mine
Together in eternity.
Our hearts of love
Will be entwined,
Together in eternity,
Forever in eternity.

No more tears of pain in our eyes;
No more fear or shame,
For we will be with You,
For we will be with You.

845 Martin J. Nystrom
Copyright © 1984 Integrity's Hosanna! Music/
Sovereign Music UK

I WILL COME AND BOW DOWN
At Your feet, Lord Jesus.
In Your presence is fulness of joy.
There is nothing, there is no one
Who compares with You;
I take pleasure in worshipping You, Lord.

846

I WILL CRY MERCY,
I will cry mercy for this land, O God.
I will cry justice,
I will cry justice for this land, O God,
For this land, O God.
Let Your tears flow from my eyes;
Let Your passion melt my heart of stone.
Let Your beauty be seen in my life;
Let Your heartbeat be my own.
So I'll cry mercy for this nation,
Let us see healing for the people,
And I'll cry justice for this nation, O God.

847

I WILL DANCE, I will sing,
To be mad for my King.
Nothing, Lord, is hindering
The passion in my soul.
(Repeat)

And I'll become
Even more undignified than this.
(Some would say it's foolishness but)
I'll become
Even more undignified than this.

Na, na, na, na, na, na! Hey!
Na, na, na, na, na, na! Hey!

848

I WILL EXTOL THE LORD with all my
heart.
I will extol the Lord with all my heart,
For holy and awesome,
For holy and awesome,
For holy and awesome is His name.

Holy and awesome is His name.
Holy and awesome is His name.
And the fear of the Lord
Is the start of wisdom.
Holy and awesome is His name.

Holy and awesome is His name.
Holy and awesome is His name.
Those who follow His ways
Have a good understanding.
Holy and awesome is His name.

Holy and awesome is His name.
Holy and awesome is His name.
And to Him belong eternal praise.
Holy and awesome is His name.
Holy and awesome is His name.
Holy and awesome is His name.

849

I WILL FOLLOW YOU TO THE CROSS
And lay myself down, lay myself down.
I will follow You to the cross,
And lay myself down, lay myself down.

Rid me of these dirty clothes,
Cleanse me from all this pollution.
I choose to walk in purity,
Oh, purify me, purify me.

Kiss me with Your healing touch,
Take me to the heat of the fire;
Bathe me in Your liquid love,
Oh, saturate me, saturate me.

Humbly I stand, humbly I kneel,
Humbly I fall at Your throne.
With a craving for You
That no words can describe:
Saturate me, saturate me;
Saturate me, saturate me;
Purify me, purify me;
Purify me, purify me;
Purify me, purify me.

850

I WILL GIVE THANKS TO THE LORD with all
my heart,
I will sing glorious praises to Your name;
I will be glad and exalt in You, my Lord,
Yesterday, today, for ever, You're the same.

O Most High,
You who are my stronghold,
When troubles come,
You're my hiding place;
O Most High,
Those who know You trust You,
You will not forsake the ones
Who seek Your face.

I WILL OFFER UP MY LIFE
In spirit and truth,
Pouring out the oil of love
As my worship to You.
In surrender I must give my every part;
Lord, receive the sacrifice
Of a broken heart.

*Jesus, what can I give, what can I bring
To so faithful a friend, to so loving a King?
Saviour, what can be said, what can be
sung
As a praise of Your name
For the things You have done?
Oh, my words could not tell, not even in
part,
Of the debt of love that is owed by this
thankful heart.*

You deserve my every breath
For You've paid the great cost;
Giving up Your life to death,
Even death on a cross.
You took all my shame away,
There defeated my sin,
Opened up the gates of heaven,
And have beckoned me in.

I WILL PRAISE YOU,
O Lord, with all of my heart.
I will praise You,
O Lord, with all of my heart.
Before the gods I will sing Your praise.
Before the gods I will praise Your name.

*The Lord will fulfil His purpose for me.
The Lord will fulfil His purpose for me.
Do not forsake the work of Your hands,
Revive me, Lord.*

You have exalted above all things
Your name and Your word.
You have exalted above all things
Your name and Your word.
I called to You, and You answered me.
When I called to You, You made me strong.

For Your love, O Lord, endures for ever,
And Your faithfulness is to the clouds.
Do not forsake the work of Your hands,
Revive me, Lord.

I WILL PRAISE YOU WITH THE HARP
For Your faithfulness, O my God.
I will sing my praise to You
With the lyre, with the lyre.

O Holy One of Israel, (×3)
*My lips will shout for joy,
My lips will shout for joy.*

When I sing my praise to You, (×3)
*For I have been redeemed,
I have been redeemed!*

I'll speak of all Your righteous acts, (×3)
*And tell them all day long,
And tell them all day long.*

Those who want to harm me
Are put to shame and confused.
I will sing my praise to You
With the lyre, with the lyre.

I've been redeemed, I've been redeemed!
I've been redeemed, I've been redeemed!

I WILL REST IN CHRIST
Like the calm within the storm;
I can find security in Him who leads me on.
I will put my faith, my trust and every hope,
For the peace of God will touch my soul,
In Him I will be whole.

I am not dismayed, I am not cast down;
I will never be alone, I need never fear.
I can always hope, I can always love;
For the love of God has touched my heart,
In Him I am secure.

*I will rest in Christ;
I will hope in Him.
I will find a place of comfort,
I can find a place of rest,
Held in love, loved in Him,
Safe, I am secure,
As I rest in Christ,
As I hope in Him.*

I will trust in Christ
Like a rock in stormy seas;
I have found a shelter in His life and peace in
me.
I have found the way,
The truth, this perfect life;
And the hope in me is found in Him,
The lover of my soul.

855 Max Dyer
Copyright © 1974 Celebration/
Kingsway Music

I WILL SING, I WILL SING a song unto the
    Lord, *(x3)*
Alleluia, glory to the Lord.

Allelu, alleluia, glory to the Lord,
Allelu, alleluia, glory to the Lord,
Allelu, alleluia, glory to the Lord,
Alleluia, glory to the Lord.

We will come, we will come as one before
    the Lord, *(x3)*
Alleluia, glory to the Lord.

If the Son, if the Son shall make you free,
    (x3)
You shall be free indeed.

They that sow in tears shall reap in joy, *(x3)*
Alleluia, glory to the Lord!

Every knee shall bow and every tongue
    confess, *(x3)*
That Jesus Christ is Lord.

In His name, in His name we have the
    victory, *(x3)*
Alleluia, glory to the Lord.

856 Stuart Townend
Copyright © 1997 Thankyou Music

I WILL SING OF THE LAMB,
Of the price that was paid for me,
Purchased by God,
Giving all He could give!
Here now I stand
In the garments of righteousness;
Death has no hold, for in Jesus I live.

I will sing of His blood
That flows for my wretchedness,
Wounds that are bared,
That I may be healed;
Power and compassion,
The marks of His ministry:
May they be mine as I harvest His field.

Oh, I will sing of the Lamb.
Oh, I will sing of the Lamb.
My heart fills with wonder,
My mouth fills with praise!
Hallelujah, hallelujah.

Once I was blind,
Yet believed I saw everything,
Proud in my ways,
Yet a fool in my part;
Lost and alone
In the company of multitudes,
Life in my body, yet death in my heart.

Oh, I will sing of the Lamb.
Oh, I will sing of the Lamb.
Oh, why should the King
Save a sinner like me?
Hallelujah, hallelujah.

What shall I give
To the Man who gave everything,
Humbling Himself
Before all He had made?
Dare I withold
My own life from His sovereignty?
I shall give all for the sake of His name!

Oh, I will sing of the Lamb.
Oh, I will sing of the Lamb.
I'll sing of His love
For the rest of my days!
Hallelujah, hallelujah.

857 Maggi Dawn
Copyright © 1993 Thankyou Music

I WILL WAIT for Your peace to come to me.
I will wait for Your peace to come to me,
And I'll sing in the darkness,
And I'll wait without fear,
And I'll sing in the darkness,
And I'll wait without fear.

858 Ian Smale
Copyright © 1985 Thankyou Music

I WILL WAVE MY HANDS in praise and
    adoration,
I will wave my hands in praise and adoration,
I will wave my hands in praise and adoration,
Praise and adoration to the living God.

For He's given me hands that just love clapping:
One, two, one two, three,
And He's given me a voice
That just loves shouting:
'Hallelujah!'
He's given me feet that just love dancing:
One, two, one, two, three,
And He's put me in a being
That has no trouble seeing
That whatever I am feeling
He is worthy to be praised.

859 David Ruis
Copyright © 1991 Shade Tree Music/
Maranatha! Music/Adm. by CopyCare

I WILL WORSHIP (I will worship)
WITH ALL OF MY HEART. (with all of my
heart)
I will praise You (I will praise You)
With all of my strength. (all my strength)
I will seek You (I will seek You)
All of my days. (all of my days)
I will follow (I will follow)
All of Your ways. (all Your ways)

I will give You all my worship,
I will give You all my praise.
You alone I long to worship,
You alone are worthy of my praise.

I will bow down, (I will bow down)
Hail You as King. (hail You as King)
I will serve You, (I will serve You)
Give You everything. (give You everything)
I will lift up (I will lift up)
My eyes to Your throne, (my eyes to Your throne)
I will trust You, (I will trust You)
I will trust You alone. (trust You alone)

860 Louise & Nathan Fellingham & Luke Fellingham
Copyright © 1997 Thankyou Music

I WORSHIP YOU, ALMIGHTY KING, the Holy
One,
For You alone have filled me with new life.
My greatest Friend, You've redeemed my soul;
You've won my heart with Your great love.

I have tasted of Your goodness
And I've heard of Your fame,
So we enter into Your presence
To praise Your holy name.

We lift our voice and sing,
There's an extravagant praise
That fills our hearts,
For You are Lord and King
And we bless Your name.
We dance for joy and bring
Our adoration to our faithful God,
To You our everything,
We bring extravagant praise.
Sing hallelujah, sing hallelujah.
Sing hallelujah, sing hallelujah.

You've called me, Lord, to live for You in
holiness,
I've been made clean and chosen as Your son.
Through Jesus Christ You've made me whole,
My heart is filled with love for You.

861 Callie Gerbrandt
Copyright © 1993 Mercy/Vineyard Publishing/
Adm. by CopyCare

I WORSHIP YOU, O LORD,
In spirit and truth;
I bow my face before Your throne,
I praise You, Lord.

I glorify Your name,
I magnify Your name;
And I exalt You Lord over all,
I praise You, Lord.

862 Evan Rogers
Copyright © 1996 Thankyou Music

I WOULD RATHER BE a doorkeeper in Your
house,
Than have the many things this world could
offer.
All that I have gained I now count as loss,
There's nothing that compares to knowing
You.

In Your presence is where I want to be,
The place where You reveal Your grace
and glory.
Your presence brings me to my knees,
I bow down and declare that You are holy.

I would rather have one day in Your courts, O
Lord,
Than have a thousand days somewhere else.
You are my sun and shield,
No good thing will you withhold,
For blessed are the ones who trust in You.

863 Andy Thorpe
Copyright © 1993 Thankyou Music

JESUS, (Jesus)
Jesus, (Jesus)
It's the Name above all names.
(Repeat)

And at the name of Jesus
Every knee shall bow,
And every tongue confess He is Lord.

864 Chris Bowater
Copyright © 1982 Sovereign Lifestyle Music

JESUS, AT YOUR NAME we bow the knee.
Jesus, at Your name we bow the knee.
Jesus at Your name we bow the knee,
And acknowledge You as Lord.

You are Christ,
You are the Lord;
Through Your Spirit in our lives
We know who You are.

 865 Matt Redman
Copyright © 1995 Thankyou Music

JESUS CHRIST, I think upon Your sacrifice,
You became nothing, poured out to death.
Many times I've wondered at Your gift of life,
And I'm in that place once again.
And I'm in that place once again.

> *And once again I look upon*
> *The cross where You died,*
> *I'm humbled by Your mercy*
> *And I'm broken inside.*
> *Once again I thank You,*
> *Once again I pour out my life.*

Now You are exalted to the highest place,
King of the heavens, where one day I'll bow.
But for now, I marvel at this saving grace,
And I'm full of praise once again.
I'm full of praise once again.

Thank You for the cross,
Thank You for the cross,
Thank You for the cross, my Friend.
(Repeat)

866 Steve Israel & Gerrit Gustafson
Copyright © 1988 Integrity's Hosanna! Music/
Sovereign Music UK

JESUS CHRIST IS THE LORD OF ALL,
Lord of all the earth.
Jesus Christ is the Lord of all,
Lord of all the earth.
Jesus Christ is the Lord of all,
Lord of all the earth.
Jesus Christ is the Lord of all,
Lord of all the earth.

Only one God over the nations,
Only one Lord of all.
In no other name is there salvation,
Jesus is Lord of all.

Jesus Christ is Lord of all.
Jesus Christ is Lord of all.
Jesus Christ is Lord of all.
Jesus Christ is Lord of all.

867 Martin Lore
Copyright © 1993 Thankyou Music

JESUS, FORGIVE ME.
Jesus, free me.
Jesus, touch me.
Jesus, fill me.

> *I lift my head, lift my heart,*
> *Lift my soul to You.*
> *I give my life, give myself,*
> *Give it all to You.*

Jesus, teach me.
Jesus, lead me.
Jesus, guide me.
Jesus, use me.

868 Don Harris & Martin J. Nystrom
Copyright © 1993 Integrity's Hosanna! Music/
Sovereign Music UK

JESUS, I AM THIRSTY,
Won't You come and fill me?
Earthly things have left me dry,
Only You can satisfy,
All I want is more of You.

All I want is more of You,
All I want is more of You;
Nothing I desire, Lord,
But more of You.
(Repeat)
More of You.

869 Judith Butler & Paul Hemingway
Copyright © 1996 Kingdom Faith Church

JESUS, I LOVE YOU,
I worship and adore You.
Jesus, I love You,
Lord, I glorify Your name.

You are mighty, O Lord,
The Ancient of Days.
Your love stands for ever,
Unfailing Your ways.

You are reigning on high,
Exalted King.
Your throne is eternal,
You are Lord over all.

870 Phil Lawson Johnston
Copyright © 1991 Thankyou Music

JESUS IS THE NAME WE HONOUR;
Jesus is the name we praise.
Majestic Name above all other names,
The highest heaven and earth proclaim
That Jesus is our God.

We will glorify,
We will lift Him high,
We will give Him honour and praise.
We will glorify,
We will lift Him high,
We will give Him honour and praise.

Jesus is the name we worship;
Jesus is the name we trust.
He is the King above all other kings,
Let all creation stand and sing
That Jesus is our God.

Jesus is the Father's splendour;
Jesus is the Father's joy.
He will return to reign in majesty,
And every eye at last shall see
That Jesus is our God.

871 Bryn Haworth
Copyright © 1993 Thankyou Music

JESUS, JESUS,
Son of God, Son of man,
Friend of sinners, gift of God.
Jesus, Jesus,
Light of life, Lord of all,
Full of grace and truth.

You have come to us,
Your presence has filled this place.
We will draw near to You,
We come, Lord, to seek Your face.

Jesus, Jesus,
My heart aches, my soul waits,
For Your healing, Lord, I pray.
Jesus, Jesus,
Mighty God, holy Child,
Name above all names.

Jesus, Jesus,
Son of God, Son of Man,
My soul thirsts for You.

872 Alan Rose
Copyright © 1997 Thankyou Music

JESUS, LAMB OF GOD,
I stand redeemed,
Washed in Your blood.
And in the holy place I'll bow
To worship and adore.

Jesus, conquering King,
You died for me,
You bore my sins.
Your love has brought me to my knees
To worship and adore,
To worship and adore.

How I love You,
How I love You,
How I love You,
How I love You,
How I love You.

873 Paul Oakley
Copyright © 1995 Thankyou Music

JESUS, LOVER OF MY SOUL,
All consuming fire is in Your gaze.
Jesus, I want You to know
I will follow You all my days.
For no one else in history is like You,
And history itself belongs to You.
Alpha and Omega, You have loved me,
And I will share eternity with You.

It's all about You, Jesus,
And all this is for You,
For Your glory and Your fame.
It's not about me,
As if You should do things my way;
You alone are God,
And I surrender to Your ways.

874 John Ezzy, Daniel Grul & Steve McPherson
Copyright © 1992 John Ezzy, Daniel Grul &
Steve McPherson/Hillsong Publishing/
Kingsway Music

JESUS, LOVER OF MY SOUL,
Jesus, I will never let You go:
You've taken me from the miry clay,
You've set my feet upon the rock and now I
  know:

I love You, I need You,
Though my world will fall,
I'll never let You go;
My Saviour, my closest Friend,
I will worship You until the very end.

375 Taizé, Music: Jacques Berthier (1923–94)
Copyright © Ateliers et Presses de Taizé

JESUS, REMEMBER ME
When You come into Your kingdom.
Jesus, remember me
When You come into Your kingdom.

376 Graham Kendrick
Copyright © 1992 Make Way Music

JESUS, RESTORE TO US AGAIN
The gospel of Your holy name,
That comes with power, not words alone,
Owned, signed and sealed from heaven's
    throne.
Spirit and word in one agreed;
The promise to the power wed.

The word is near, here in our mouths
And in our hearts, the word of faith;
Proclaim it on the Spirit's breath: Jesus!

Your word, O Lord, eternal stands,
Fixed and unchanging in the heavens;
The Word made flesh, to earth come down
To heal our world with nail-pierced hands.
Among us here You lived and breathed,
You are the Message we received.

Spirit of truth, lead us, we pray
Into all truth as we obey,
And as God's will we gladly choose,
Our ancient powers again will prove
Christ's teaching truly comes from God,
He is indeed the living Word.

Upon the heights of this great land
With Moses and Elijah stand.
Reveal Your glory once again,
Show us Your face, declare Your name.
Prophets and law, in You complete
Where promises and power meet.

Grant us in this decisive hour
To know the Scriptures and the power;
The knowledge in experience proved,
The power that moves and works by love.
May word and works join hands as one,
The word go forth, the Spirit come.

377 Tanya Riches
Copyright © 1995 Tanya Riches/
Hillsong Publishing/Kingsway Music

JESUS, WHAT A BEAUTIFUL NAME.
Son of God, Son of Man,
Lamb that was slain.
Joy and peace, strength and hope,
Grace that blows all fear away.
Jesus, what a beautiful name.

Jesus, what a beautiful name.
Truth revealed, my future sealed,
Healed my pain.
Love and freedom, life and warmth,
Grace that blows all fear away.
Jesus, what a beautiful name.

Jesus, what a beautiful name.
Rescued my soul, my stronghold,
Lifts me from shame.
Forgiveness, security, power and love,
Grace that blows all fear away.
Jesus, what a beautiful name.

878 Chris Bowater
Copyright © 1991 Sovereign Lifestyle Music

JUST THE MENTION OF YOUR NAME
Causes me to fall before You,
Tears flow as I adore You,
At the mention of Your name,
Just the mention of Your name.

Just the mention of Your name
Reaffirms the love that holds me,
Speaks once more of love that knows me,
At the mention of Your name,
Just the mention of Your name.

Jesus, Jesus,
Jesus, Jesus.
At the mention of Your name,
I worship.

879 George Herbert (1593–1633)

LET ALL THE WORLD in every corner sing:
'My God and King!'
The heavens are not too high;
His praise may thither fly:
The earth is not too low;
His praises there may grow.
Let all the world in every corner sing:
'My God and King!'

Let all the world in every corner sing:
'My God and King!'
The Church with psalms must shout,
No door can keep them out:
But, above all, the heart
Must bear the longest part.
Let all the world in every corner sing:
'My God and King!'

880
Matt Redman
Copyright © 1997 Thankyou Music

LET EVERYTHING THAT,
Everything that,
Everything that has breath
Praise the Lord.
(Repeat)

Praise You in the morning,
Praise You in the evening,
Praise You when I'm young
And when I'm old.
Praise You when I'm laughing,
Praise You when I'm grieving,
Praise You every season of the soul.

If we could see how much You're worth,
Your power, Your might, Your endless love,
Then surely we would never cease to
    praise :

Praise You in the heavens,
Joining with the angels,
Praising You for ever and a day.
Praise You on the earth now,
Joining with creation,
Calling all the nations to Your praise.

If they could see how much You're worth,
Your power, Your might, Your endless love,
Then surely they would never cease to
    praise:

881
Debbye C. Graafsma
Copyright © 1992 WordPsalm
Ministries Inc./Kingsway Music

LET EVERY TRIBE AND EVERY TONGUE
Bring praise to the Lamb,
For He has triumphed over all,
He has triumphed.
With His blood He has redeemed us
Forever to reign with Him in glory, amen.

We sing glory, glory to the Lamb;
Son of God, the Great I AM.
Awesome in splendour, triumphant King,
We give You praise and dominion over all.

Worthy, worthy is the Lamb;
Holy, resurrected Lamb.
Jesus, King Jesus, pre-eminent God,
We give You praise,
We give You praise over all.

882
Dave Bilbrough
Copyright © 1997 Thankyou Music

LET THE CHIMES OF FREEDOM RING
All across this earth;
Lift your voice in praise to Him
And sing of all His worth,
And sing of all His worth.

Open wide your prison doors
To greet the Lord of life;
Songs of triumph fill the air,
Christ Jesus is alive,
Christ Jesus is alive.

Let all the people hear the news
Of the One who comes to save:
He's the Lord of all the universe,
And for ever He shall reign.

And for evermore, yes for evermore,
And for evermore He will reign.
(Repeat)

In every corner of this earth,
To every tribe and tongue,
Make known that God so loved this
    world
That He gave His only Son,
He gave His only Son.

Spread the news and make it plain,
He breaks the power of sin;
Jesus died and He rose again,
His love will never end,
His love will never end.

He will return in majesty
To take His rightful place
As the King of all eternity,
The Name above all names,
The Name above all names.

883
Phil Wilthew
Copyright © 1996 Thankyou Music

LET THE CHURCH ARISE,
And let the darkness fall.
Say to those chains,
'You are now set free!'
Sickness has died its death
Through the blood of Christ.
To all the oppressed
He now promises life.

Jesus, Lord of all,
Come to us in a time of drought;
Send Your showers,
Let us know the riches of Your mercy.
Jesus, Lord of all,
Come to us in a time of need;
Send revival,
Let our nation see Your awesome glory.

Awake, O church,
Sing with all Your might;
The Lord of all the earth
Is in Your midst.
He is mending lives,
He is winning hearts;
In these coming days
Let revival start.

Come, let us go to the house of God,
With His praises in our hearts;
For the Lord has done great things for us,
And His glory's coming again.
(Repeat)

384 Bryn Haworth
Copyright © 1991 Thankyou Music

LET THE RIGHTEOUS SING,
Come let the righteous dance,
Rejoice before your God,
Be happy and joyful,
Give Him your praise.
We give You our praise.
Shout for joy to God
Who rides upon the clouds,
How awesome are His deeds,
So great is His power.
Give Him your praise.
We give You our praise.

He gives the desolate a home,
He leads the prisoners out with singing.
Father to the fatherless,
Defender of the widow
Is God in His holy place.

385 David Fellingham
Copyright © 1992 Thankyou Music

LET US DRAW NEAR to God
In full assurance of faith,
Knowing that as we draw near to Him,
He will draw near to us.
In the holy place
We stand in confidence,
Knowing our lives are cleansed in the blood
of the Lamb,
We will worship and adore.

886 Mark Altrogge
Copyright © 1991 People of Destiny
International/Adm. by CopyCare

LET US DRAW NEAR WITH CONFIDENCE,
We have a Great High Priest.
There's mercy enough for all our sins,
We have a Great High Priest.
He was made weak and He was tried,
We have a Great High Priest.
He's able to feel and sympathise,
We have a Great High Priest.

He's the Lamb of God,
Slain before the ages,
The only Son,
The Servant crowned as King.
The One who came
To crush the works of darkness,
And He will fill all things, all things.

Let us each come with conscience cleansed,
We have a Great High Priest.
It's by His shed blood we enter in,
We have a Great High Priest.
We trust in no merits of our own,
We have a Great High Priest.
But look to the power of the cross alone,
We have a Great High Priest.

887 Paul Oakley
Copyright © 1994 Thankyou Music

LET US GO up to the house of God
With a shout of praise,
With a song of celebration.
We'll ascend the hill of the Lord,
We can stand in the holy place.

We can have clean hands and a pure heart;
His blood can cleanse us from all our
    unrighteousness.
He has made a way though the cross;
Jesus' blood was shed for us.
We can draw near to our God.

Now His body has been broken,
And the curtain torn in two.
We can enter by a new and living way
Before His throne.
Yes, we can fellowship with Him,
The King of glory, King of kings.

888 Noel & Tricia Richards
Copyright © 1996 Thankyou Music

Oh . . .
Oh . . .
Oh . . .
LET YOUR LOVE COME DOWN.
(Repeat)

There is violence in the air.
Fear touches all our lives.
How much pain can people bear?
Are we reaping what we've sown,
Voices silent for too long?
We are calling,
Let Your love come down.

There is power in Your love,
Bringing laughter out of tears.
It can heal the wounded soul.
In the streets where anger reigns
Love will wash away the pain.
We are calling,
Heaven's love come down.

889 David & Nathan Fellingham
Copyright © 1992 Thankyou Music

LET YOUR WORD run freely through this
    nation,
Strong Deliverer, break the grip of satan's
    power.
Let the cross of Jesus stand above the idols
    of this land,
Let anointed lives rise up and take their
    stand.

And we will glorify the Lamb,
Slain from eternity.
Jesus is Lord, we declare His name,
And stand in His victory,
And stand in His victory.

With prophetic words of power, expose the
    darkness;
With apostolic wisdom build the church.
With zeal for the lost let the story be told,
Let the shepherds feed the lambs within their
    folds.

Let the Holy Spirit's fire burn within us,
Cleansed from sin and pure within we stand
    upright.
Not yielding to wrong, we will live in
    holiness,
Bringing glory to the Saviour, we will shine.

890 Dave Bilbrough
Copyright © 1994 Thankyou Music

LIFT HIM UP, *lift Him high,*
Let His praises fill the sky.
Oh, heaven's gates are open wide
To those who hear the call.
(Repeat)

Through every generation
This truth will always shine,
That Christ came down among us,
Now He is glorified.

The message of the kingdom
Stands unshakeable through time:
That man can be forgiven,
If you seek then you will find.

891 Graham Kendrick
Copyright © 1988 Make Way Music

LIKE A CANDLE FLAME,
Flickering small in our darkness.
Uncreated light
Shines through infant eyes.

God is with us, alleluia. (Men)
God is with us, alleluia. (Women)
Come to save us, alleluia. (Men)
Come to save us, (Women)
Alleluia! (All)

Stars and angels sing,
Yet the earth sleeps in shadows;
Can this tiny spark
Set a world on fire?

Yet His light shall shine
From our lives, Spirit blazing,
As we touch the flame
Of His holy fire.

892 Timothy Dudley-Smith
Copyright © 1967 Timothy Dudley-Smith

LORD, FOR THE YEARS Your love has kept
    and guided,
Urged and inspired us, cheered us on our way,
Sought us and saved us, pardoned and
    provided:
Lord of the years, we bring our thanks today.

Lord, for that word, the word of life which
    fires us,
Speaks to our hearts and sets our souls ablaze,
Teaches and trains, rebukes us and inspires us,
Lord of the word, receive Your people's praise.

Lord, for our land in this our generation,
Spirits oppressed by pleasure, wealth and
   care:
For young and old, for commonwealth and
   nation,
Lord of our land, be pleased to hear our
   prayer.

Lord, for our world where men disown and
   doubt You,
Loveless in strength, and comfortless in pain,
Hungry and helpless, lost indeed without
   You:
Lord of the world, we pray that Christ may
   reign.

Lord for ourselves; in living power remake
   us –
Self on the cross and Christ upon the throne,
Past put behind us, for the future take us:
Lord of our lives, to live for Christ alone.

 893

Dave Bilbrough
Copyright © 1995 Thankyou Music

LORD, HAVE MERCY,
Lord, have mercy:
Move in power on this land.
(Repeat)

Hear our prayer,
Hear our prayer,
O Lord, O Lord.
(Repeat)

 894

Robert & Dawn Critchley
Copyright © 1989 Thankyou Music

LORD, I COME BEFORE YOUR THRONE OF
GRACE;
I find rest in Your presence
And fulness of joy.
In worship and wonder
I behold Your face,
Singing what a faithful God have I.

> *What a faithful God have I,*
> *What a faithful God.*
> *What a faithful God have I,*
> *Faithful in every way.*

Lord of mercy, You have heard my cry;
Through the storm You're the beacon,
My song in the night.
In the shelter of Your wings,
Hear my heart's reply,
Singing what a faithful God have I.

Lord all sovereign, granting peace from heaven,
Let me comfort those who suffer
With the comfort You have given.
I will tell of Your great love for as long as I live,
Singing what a faithful God have I.

895

Geoff Bullock
Copyright © 1992 Word Music/
Maranatha! Music/Adm. by CopyCare

LORD, I COME TO YOU,
Let my heart be changed, renewed,
Flowing from the grace
That I found in You.
And Lord, I've come to know
The weaknesses I see in me
Will be stripped away
By the power of Your love.

> *Hold me close,*
> *Let Your love surround me.*
> *Bring me near, draw me to Your side.*
> *And as I wait*
> *I'll rise up like the eagle,*
> *And I will soar with You,*
> *Your Spirit leads me on*
> *In the power of Your love.*

Lord, unveil my eyes,
Let me see You face to face,
The knowledge of Your love
As You live in me.
Lord, renew my mind
As Your will unfolds in my life,
In living every day
By the power of Your love.

 896

Brian Doerksen
Copyright © 1990 Mercy/Vineyard Publishing/
Adm. by CopyCare

LORD, I HAVE HEARD OF YOUR FAME,
I stand in awe of Your deeds. O Lord,
I have heard of Your fame,
I stand in awe of Your deeds, O Lord.

Renew them, renew them,
In our day, and in our time
Make them known.
(Repeat)
In wrath remember mercy.

 897

Rick Founds
Copyright © 1989 Maranatha! Praise Inc./
Adm. by CopyCare

LORD, I LIFT YOUR NAME ON HIGH;
Lord, I love to sing Your praises.
I'm so glad You're in my life;
I'm so glad You came to save us.

*You came from heaven to earth to show
the way,
From the earth to the cross,
My debt to pay.
From the cross to the grave,
From the grave to the sky,
Lord, I lift Your name on high.*

 Steve McPherson
Copyright © 1996 Steve McPherson/
Hillsong Publishing/Kingsway Music

LORD, I LONG TO SEE YOU GLORIFIED
In everything I do;
All my heartfelt dreams I put aside,
To see Your Spirit move with power in my
life.

Jesus, Lord of all eternity,
Your children rise in faith;
All the earth displays Your glory,
And each word You speak
Brings life to all who hear.

*Lord of all,
All of creation sings Your praise
In heaven and earth.
Lord, we stand,
Hearts open wide,
Be exalted.*

899 Rick Founds
Copyright © 1989 Maranatha! Music/
Adm. by CopyCare

LORD, LOOK UPON MY NEED,
I need You, I need You.
Lord, have mercy now on me,
Forgive me, O Lord, forgive me,
And I will be clean.

*O Lord, You are familiar with my ways,
There is nothing hid from You.
O Lord, You know the number of my
days,
I want to live my life for You.*

900 Darlene Zschech
Copyright © 1997 Darlene Zschech/
Hillsong Publishing/Kingsway Music

LORD, MY HEART CRIES OUT,
'Glory to the King';
My greatest love in life,
I hand You everything:
'Glory, glory',
I hear the angels sing.

Open my ears,
Let me hear Your voice,
To know that sweet sound,
Oh, my soul rejoice:
'Glory, glory',
I hear the angels sing.

*You're the Father to the fatherless,
The answer to my dreams.
I see You crowned in righteousness,
We cry, 'Glory to the King'.
Comforter to the lonely,
The lifter of my head.
I see You veiled in majesty;
We cry, 'Glory, glory',
We cry, 'Glory to the King'.*

901 Joe King
Copyright © 1990 Thankyou Music

LORD OF ALL CREATION,
Let this generation
See a visitation of Your power;
Put to flight all the powers of darkness,
O come, Lord Jesus, come.

*Lord of all creation,
Let this generation
See a visitation of Your power.
Lord of all creation,
There's an expectation
Rising in this nation every hour.*

Father God, forgive us,
Send Your cleansing rivers,
Wash us now and give us holy power;
Fill this land with Your awesome presence,
O come, Lord Jesus, come.

902 Jan Struther (1901–53)
Copyright © Oxford University Press

LORD OF ALL HOPEFULNESS,
Lord of all joy,
Whose trust, ever child-like,
No cares could destroy;
Be there at our waking,
And give us, we pray,
Your bliss in our hearts, Lord,
At the break of the day.

Lord of all eagerness, Lord of all faith,
Whose strong hands were skilled
At the plane and the lathe;
Be there at our labours,
And give us, we pray,
Your strength in our hearts, Lord,
At the noon of the day.

Lord of all kindliness, Lord of all grace,
Your hands swift to welcome,
Your arms to embrace;
Be there at our homing,
And give us, we pray,
Your love in our hearts, Lord,
At the eve of the day.

Lord of all gentleness, Lord of all calm,
Whose voice is contentment,
Whose presence is balm;
Be there at our sleeping,
And give us, we pray,
Your peace in our hearts, Lord,
At the end of the day.

903 K. Prosch
Copyright © 1995 Liber Media &
Publishing, LLC/Kingsway Music

LORD OF THE DANCE,
You're the dancing Lord.
(Repeat ×4)
Everybody dance, yeah!

Well everybody dance, now,
Get in the Holy Ghost.
Everybody praise the One, love the One,
You want the One, yeah,
The One you want the most, now.
Can't nobody stop me now,
I'm gonna give it everything I've got.
I come to You, run to You,
Run to You, yeah,
Just like a child.

It's just this love I have inside,
Yeah, I want it.
I feel You pleasure in my heart,
Yeah, I need it.
I want Your love
More and more each day.
And when I dance before You, Lord,
I'm gonna dance with all my might.

904 Ray Goudie, Dave Bankhead & Steve Bassett
Copyright © 1993 Integrity's Hosanna! Music/
New Generation Music/Sovereign Music UK

LORD, POUR OUT YOUR SPIRIT
On all the peoples of the earth;
Let Your sons and daughters
Speak Your words of prophecy.
Send us dreams and visions,
Reveal the secrets of Your heart;
Lord, our faith is rising,
Let all heaven sound the coming of Your
   day.

There's gonna be a great awakening,
There's gonna be a great revival in our land.
There's gonna be a great awakening,
And everyone who calls on Jesus,
They will be saved.

Lord, pour out Your Spirit
On all the nations of the world;
Let them see Your glory,
Let them fall in reverent awe.
Show Your mighty power,
Shake the heavens and the earth;
Lord, the world is waiting,
Let creation see the coming of Your day.

905 Dave Bilbrough
Copyright © 1993 Thankyou Music

LORD, WE COME IN ADORATION,
Lay our lives before You now.
We are here to reach the nations,
To tell the world of Jesus' power.
We would seek Your awesome glory,
All the gifts that You endow;
Called to reach this generation,
And now is the appointed hour.

We will go in Your name;
Go and proclaim Your kingdom.
Go in Your name,
For we have been chosen to tell all
   creation
That Jesus is King of all kings.

We believe that You have spoken
Through Your Son to all the earth;
Given us this great commission
To spread the news of all Your worth.
Set apart to serve You only,
Let our lives display Your love;
Hearts infused that tell the story
Of God come down from heaven above.

Grant to us a fresh anointing,
Holy Spirit, be our guide;
Satisfy our deepest longing—
Jesus Christ be glorified.
Every tribe and every people,
Hear the message that we bring;
Christ has triumphed over evil,
Bow the knee and worship Him.

906 David Fellingham
Copyright © 1994 Thankyou Music

LORD, WE CRY TO YOU: God, break through!
Let Your presence come in revival.
Like the gentle dew, our lives renew;
Let Your presence come in revival.

(Men) *O God, break through!*
(Women) *Send Your Spirit, Lord.*
(Men) *O God, break through!*
(Women) *Send Your Spirit.*
(All) *Let the name of Jesus be*
   proclaimed.
(Repeat)
(All) *O God, break through.*

Lord, we cry to You: God break through!
Move upon Your church in revival.
Like a mighty wind and tongues of fire,
Let Your Spirit come in revival.

Lord, we cry to You: God, break through!
Sweep across this land in revival.
Like the mighty rain, flood this land again;
Let Your power come in revival.

907 Richard Lewis
Copyright © 1997 Thankyou Music

LORD, WE LONG TO SEE YOUR GLORY,
Gaze upon Your lovely face.
Holy Spirit, come among us,
Lead us to that secret place.

   Holy God,
   We long to see Your glory,
   To touch Your holy majesty, O Lord.
   Holy God,
   Let us stay in Your presence,
   And worship at Your feet for evermore.
   Holy God.
   Holy God.

908 Nathan Fellingham
Copyright © 1996 Thankyou Music

LORD, WE LONG TO SEE YOUR GLORY,
Lord, we long to feel Your power.
In these times of refreshing,
We long to know You more.
To behold You in Your majesty,
Our hearts are filled with joy;
As we look towards the coming King,
We cry 'Lord, let Your glory fall.'

There'll be a day when we will reign with
   Him,
The Bride of Christ born for perfect unity with
   Him.
We shall see Him face to face,
But until that day we shall pray,
'Show us Your glory.'

Help us to sing like the angels sing.
Help us to praise in the courts of our King
Help us to dance like David danced,
Stirred by the love of Your Son,
Stirred by the love of Your Son.

909 Ian Smale
Copyright © 1981 Thankyou Music

LORD, WE'VE COME TO WORSHIP YOU,
Lord, we've come to praise:
Lord, we've come to worship You
In oh, so many ways.
Some of us shout,
And some of us sing,
And some of us whisper the praise we bring,
But Lord, we all are gathering
To give to You our praise.

910 Judy Pruett
Copyright © 1985 Judy Pruett/
Kingsway Music

LORD, YOU ARE THE AUTHOR OF MY LIFE,
You have begun a work in me,
You have predestined me
To do Your perfect will.
And Lord, You are the Lord of all my days,
You are the Lord of all my nights,
You have chosen me
To carry forth Your word.

So Lord, finish in me what You've begun,
Guide me by Your mighty hand, Lord:
Let me trust in You.
And Lord, let me seek Your holy face,
May I always walk with You, Lord,
And let Your will be done.

911 David Baroni
Copyright © 1992 Pleasant Hill Music, USA/
Adm. by Bucks Music Ltd

LORD, YOU ARE WORTHY,
Lord, You are worthy,
Lord, You are worthy,
We give You praise.

Lord, You are worthy…

Lord, You are holy…

Lord, we adore You…

Lord, You are worthy…

912 Martin Smith
Copyright © 1992 Thankyou Music

ORD, YOU HAVE MY HEART,
And I will search for Yours;
esus, take my life and lead me on.
ord, You have my heart,
And I will search for Yours;
et me be to You a sacrifice.

And I will praise you, Lord. *(Men)*
will praise You, Lord. *(Women)*
And I will sing of love come down. *(Men)*
will sing of love come down. *(Women)*
And as You show Your face, *(Men)*
how Your face, *(Women)*
We'll see Your glory here. *(All)*

913 Wayne Drain
Copyright © 1996 Thankyou Music

LOST IN THE SHUFFLE,
was lost as a goose,
The devil had a rope out,
And it looked just like a noose.
But just before I went off of that deep end,
My Father threw me out a line,
orgave me of my sin.

Now we're dancin', me and the Father,
He's throwing me up in the air.
We're dancin', me and the Father,
He's swinging me,
I like it up there with my Father,
I like it up there with my Father.

He took me to the water,
And He cleaned me real good,
Then He raised me up to be with Him,
feel just like I should.
He filled me with His Spirit,
drank the whole cup,
Now when He calls I hear it,
Hey, turn that volume up!

'Cause we're dancin'…

God's got a big family, more than anyone can
count;
There's always room for one more,
No need to be left out.
So come on, come on, come on,

And you could be dancin', you and the
Father,
He'll throw you up in the air.
You'll be dancin', you and the Father,
He'll swing you up,
You'll like it up there with the Father,
You'll like it up there with the Father.

914 Noel & Tricia Richards
Copyright © 1996 Thankyou Music

LOVE SONGS FROM HEAVEN are filling the
earth,
Bringing great hope to all nations.
Evil has prospered, but truth is alive;
In this dark world the light still shines.

Nothing has silenced this gospel of Christ;
It echoes down through the ages.
Blood of the martyrs has made Your church
strong;
In this dark world the light still shines.

For You we live,
And for You we may die;
Through us may Jesus be seen.
For You alone we will offer our lives;
In this dark world our light will shine.

Let every nation be filled with Your song:
This is the cry of Your people.
We will not settle for anything less,
In this dark world our light must shine.

915 Graham Kendrick
Copyright © 1985 Thankyou Music

MAGNIFICENT WARRIOR, arrayed for
battle,
We see You ready to slay Your enemies.
O Mighty Captain of heaven's armies,
We bow before You, we worship You.

So take Your sword upon Your side
O Mighty One, clothe Yourself
With splendour and with majesty,
And in Your majesty ride forth.
Ride forth victoriously for truth.
Humility and righteousness.
Let Your strong right hand
Display Your awesome deeds.

Magnificent Warrior, we hear Your strong
command
To join the ranks of light and march into the
fight;
By faith to overthrow ten thousand
Jerichos,
To make Your judgements known in all the
earth.

916
Russell Fragar
Copyright © 1993 Russell Fragar/
Hillsong Publishing/Kingsway Music

MAKES YOU WANNA DANCE, *(echo)*
Makes you wanna sing, *(echo)*
Makes you wanna shout all about it,
Shout all about it,
Shout it that Jesus is King.
(Repeat)

Every nation, power and tongue
Will bow down to Your name;
Every eye will see,
Every ear will hear Your name proclaimed,
This is gonna be our cry
Until You come again:
'Jesus is the only name
By which man can be saved.'

> *All over the world people just like us
> Are calling Your name, living in Your love.
> All over the world people just like us
> Are following Jesus.*
> (Repeat)

> (Last time)
> *We're worshipping Jesus,
> We're following Jesus,
> We're worshipping Jesus,
> We're calling on Jesus.*

917
Daniel Brymer
Copyright © 1990 Grace! Music, USA

MAKE US A HOUSE OF PRAYER,
That we might meet You there,
On behalf of the nation,
To a dying generation,
Make us a house of prayer.

And Lord, teach us to pray
Unceasingly night and day.
Make our intercession
For You a mighty weapon.
O Lord, teach us to pray.

918
Adpt. Ian White from NIV (© 1973, 1978,
1984 International Bible Society)
Copyright © 1987 Little Misty Music/
Kingsway Music

MAY GOD BE GRACIOUS TO US and bless us,
Make His face to shine upon us.
May Your ways be known over the earth
And Your salvation among all nations.

> *May the peoples praise You;
> O God, may all the peoples praise You.
> May the peoples praise You;
> O God, may all the peoples praise You.*

May the nations be glad and sing for joy,
For with justice You rule the people You
guide.
May Your ways be known over all the earth,
And Your salvation among all nations.

Then the harvest will come to the land,
And God, our God, will bless us.
God will bless us, and all the ends
Of earth will fear Him.

919
David Gate
Copyright © 1997 Thankyou Music

MAY I SING A SONG OF LOVE
To the One who saved my soul?
May I bow my head today
In the presence of the King?

You have called and I will come,
Lift my hands up to Your throne;
Worship You on holy ground –
That's what I long to do.

> *Draw me near into Your heart.
> All I have is broken love,
> And a thirst that cries for more.
> Draw me near to You.*

920
Chris Bowater
Copyright © 1992 Sovereign Lifestyle Music

MAY OUR WORSHIP BE AS FRAGRANCE,
May our worship be as incense poured forth
May our worship be acceptable
As a living sacrifice,
As a living sacrifice.

We are willing to pay the price,
We are willing to lay down our lives
As an offering of obedience,
As a living sacrifice,
As a living sacrifice.

921
Martin Smith
Copyright © 1995 Curious? Music UK/
Adm. by Bucks Music Ltd

MEN OF FAITH, rise up and sing
Of the great and glorious King;
You are strong when you feel weak,
In your brokenness complete.

> *Shout to the north and the south,
> Sing to the east and the west:
> Jesus is Saviour to all,
> Lord of heaven and earth.*

(Last time)
Lord of heaven and earth,
Lord of heaven and earth,
Lord of heaven and earth.

Rise up women of the truth,
Stand and sing to broken hearts,
Who can know the healing power
Of our glorious King of love.

We've been through fire,
We've been through rain;
We've been refined
By the power of His name.
We've fallen deeper in love with You,
You've burned the truth on our lips.

Rise up church with broken wings;
Fill this place with songs again,
Of our God who reigns on high:
By His grace again we'll fly.

 922

John Chisum & Gary Sadler
Copyright © 1994 Integrity's Hosanna! Music/
Sovereign Music UK

MERCIFUL GOD AND FATHER,
Loving us like no other,
Hear our prayer, the cry of our hearts,
As we come to You.
We acknowledge our transgressions,
We confess to You our sins;
Show us mercy and compassion,
Touch our lives
With Your healing grace again.

Release us from the past,
As we seek Your face.
Wash us free at last,
We receive Your love,
We receive Your healing grace.
We receive Your love,
We receive Your healing grace.

923

Chris Bowater, Mark & Helen Johnson
Copyright © 1991 Sovereign Lifestyle Music

MIGHTY GOD,
Everlasting Father,
Wonderful Counsellor,
You're the Prince of Peace.
(Repeat)

You are Lord of heaven,
You are called Emmanuel;
God is now with us,
Ever present to deliver.
You are God eternal,
You are Lord of all the earth;
Love has come to us,
Bringing us new birth.

A light to those in darkness,
And a guide to paths of peace;
Love and mercy dawns,
Grace, forgiveness and salvation.
Light for revelation,
Glory to Your people;
Son of the Most High,
God's love gift to all.

924

Eugene Greco, Gerrit Gustafson & Don Moen
Copyright © 1989 Integrity's Hosanna! Music/
Sovereign Music UK

MIGHTY IS OUR GOD,
Mighty is our King;
Mighty is our Lord,
Ruler of everything.
Glory to our God,
Glory to our King;
Glory to our Lord,
Ruler of everything.

His name is higher,
Higher than any other name;
His power is greater,
For He has created everything.

925

A. P. Douglas
Copyright © 1997 Thankyou Music

MIGHTY IS THE LORD and most worthy of
    praise,
Praise Him all you people.
Look upon Him, God alone who saves:
Praise the Lord of all.
Nations will rise and nations will fall,
Praise Him all you people.
But there is One who is Lord of all:
Praise the Lord of all.

    He is Wonderful, Counsellor,
    Glorious Prince of Peace.
    He is Lord and King of everything,
    His praises never cease.
    (Repeat)

Awesome and great, like the strongest tower,
Praise Him all you people.
He is the one with limitless power,
Praise the Lord of all.
Leaders may come and presidents fall,
Praise Him all you people.
But there is One who is Lord of all:
Praise the Lord of all.

MIGHTY, MIGHTY LORD.
Precious is Your name.
Wonderful Your ways,
Worthy of all praise, Jehovah.

Mighty, mighty Lord.
Holy is Your name.
Glorious and true,
Great in all You do, Jehovah,
Jehovah.

Hallowed be Your name,
Lord God Almighty,
For Yours is the kingdom,
The power and the glory,
Forever more.

MORE THAN OXYGEN, I need Your love;
More than life-giving food
The hungry dream of.
More than an eloquent word
Depends on the tongue;
More than a passionate song
Needs to be sung.

More than a word could ever say,
More than a song could ever convey;
I need You more than all of these things.
Father, I need You more.

More than magnet and steel
Are drawn to unite;
More that poets love words
To rhyme as they write.
More than comforting warmth
Of sun in spring;
More than the eagle loves wind
Under its wings.

More than a blazing fire
On a winter's night;
More than tall evergreens
Reach for the light.
More than the pounding waves
Long for the shore;
More than these gifts You give,
I love You more.

MOST HOLY JUDGE,
I stood before You guilty,
When you sent Jesus to the cross for my si
There Your love was revealed,
Your justice vindicated,
One sacrifice has paid the cost
For all who trust in Jesus.

Now I'm justified,
You declare me righteous,
Justified by the blood of the Lamb.
Justified freely by Your mercy,
By faith I stand and I'm justified.

I come to You,
And I can call you 'Father',
There is no fear
There is no shame before You.
For by Your gift of grace
Now I am one of Your children,
An heir with those who bear Your name,
And share the hope of glory.

MUKTI DILAYE *Yesu naam,*
Shanti dilaye Yesu naam.
(Repeat)
(Peace comes to you in Jesus' name,
Salvation in no other name.)

Yesu daya ka behta sagar
Yesu daya ka behta sagar
Yesu hai data mahan
Yesu hai data mahan
(Jesus is the Ocean of Grace:
You are majestic, Lord.)

Charni main tooney janamliya Yesu
Charni main tooney janamliya Yesu
Sooley pay kiya vishram
Sooley pay kiya vishram
(Jesus, You were born in a manger (Made o
wood:)
You were crucified on the cross (Made of wood

Peace comes to you in Jesus' name,
Salvation in no other name.

Ham sab key papon ko mitane
Ham sab key papon ko mitane
Yesu hua hai balidan
Yesu hua hai balidan
(For the remission of our sins,
Jesus has been sacrificed on the cross.)

Krus par apna khoon bahaa kar
Krus par apna khoon bahaa kar
Sara chukaya daam
Sara chukaya daam
*(By shedding Your blood on the cross,
You paid the full price for our sins.)*

930 Stuart Townend
Copyright © 1996 Thankyou Music

MY FIRST LOVE is a blazing fire,
  feel His powerful love in me.
For He has kindled a flame of passion,
And I will let it grow in me.
And in the night I will sing Your praise, my
  love.
And in the morning I'll seek Your face, my
  love.

> *And like a child I will dance in Your
>   presence,
> Oh, let the joy of heaven pour down on
>   me.
> I still remember the first day I met You,
> And I don't ever want to lose that fire,
> My first love.*

My first love is a rushing river,
A waterfall that will never cease;
And in the torrent of tears and laughter,
  I feel a healing power released.
And I will draw from Your well of life, my
  love,
And in Your grace I'll be satisfied, my love.

Restore the years of the church's slumber,
Revive the fire that has grown so dim;
Renew the love of those first encounters,
That we may come alive again.
And we will rise like the dawn throughout the
  earth,
Until the trumpet announces Your return.

931 Ian Smale
Copyright © 1993 Thankyou Music

MY GOD SHALL SUPPLY ALL MY NEEDS,
My God shall supply all my needs,
My God shall supply all my needs
'Cause it says so in the Bible,
  Cause it says so (where?)
In the book that came from heaven,
  'Cause it says so (where?)
Isaiah fifty-eight eleven.
My God shall supply all my needs
'Cause it says so in the Bible.

932 Chris Williams
Copyright © 1993 Thankyou Music

MY HEART,
I want to give You my heart,
In service to the Lord, the One who cares
To ask for my life.
Take me,
Mould my life and make me
Into a child who longs to stay by Your side
And learn of Your ways.

For when I sought You, Lord, You heard me,
You delivered me from fear;
And by Your grace and mercy
You have brought us both so near.
I want to kneel before Your feet, Lord,
And to gaze upon Your face;
For the God who asks for my life
Loves me completely and always.

933 Maggi Dawn
Copyright © 1996 Thankyou Music

MY HEART IS NOT RAISED UP TOO HIGH,
My eyes don't search beyond the sky.
I do not seek what can't be known,
Nor fret myself over mysteries.

But I have calmed and soothed my soul,
Like a child at rest in its mother's arms;
Like this child sleeping by my side,
My soul, in God, knows peace and calm.

All you who love and trust your God,
In this God shall you put your hope,
For there you'll find unfailing love,
From this time forth, and for evermore.

934 Tim Hughes
Copyright © 1997 Thankyou Music

MY JESUS, MY LIFELINE,
I need You more than I've ever known.
There's no one quite like You,
I'm crying out for Your loving.

> *Oh Jesus, oh Jesus,
> I've never known a love like this before.
> Oh Jesus, oh Jesus,
> Accept this love I give to You,
> It's all I can do.*

I'm searching, I'm longing,
Please meet me just as You want to.
I'll stand here to offer,
Offer up this song of love to You.

935

MY JESUS, MY SAVIOUR,
Lord, there is none like You.
All of my days I want to praise
The wonders of Your mighty love.
My comfort, my shelter,
Tower of refuge and strength,
Let every breath, all that I am,
Never cease to worship You.

Shout to the Lord all the earth, let us sing
Power and majesty, praise to the King.
Mountains bow down
And the seas will roar
At the sound of Your name.
I sing for joy at the work of Your hands.
Forever I'll love You, forever I'll stand.
Nothing compares to the
Promise I have in You.

936

MY LIFE IS IN YOU, LORD,
My strength is in You, Lord,
My hope is in You, Lord,
In You, it's in You.
(Repeat)

(Last time)
In You.

I will praise You with all of my life;
I will praise You with all of my strength.
With all of my life,
With all of my strength;
All of my hope is in You.

937

MY LIPS SHALL PRAISE YOU,
My great Redeemer;
My heart will worship
Almighty Saviour.

You take all my guilt away,
Turn the darkest night to brightest day,
You are the restorer of my soul.

Love that conquers every fear,
In the midst of trouble You draw near,
You are the restorer of my soul.

You're the source of happiness,
Bringing peace when I am in distress,
You are the restorer of my soul.

938

MY TRUST IS IN THE NAME OF THE LORD
Who made heaven and earth;
My trust is in the name of the Lord
Who made heaven and earth.

Sing hallelujah, hallelujah.
Hallelujah, hallelu, hallelujah.

My hope is in the name of the Lord ...

My joy is in the name of the Lord ...

939

NAME OF ALL MAJESTY,
Fathomless mystery,
King of the ages
By angels adored;
Power and authority,
Splendour and dignity,
Bow to His mastery –
Jesus is Lord!

Child of our destiny,
God from eternity,
Love of the Father
On sinners outpoured;
See now what God has done,
Sending His only Son,
Christ the belovèd One –
Jesus is Lord!

Saviour of Calvary,
Costliest victory,
Darkness defeated
And Eden restored;
Born as a man to die,
Nailed to a cross on high,
Cold in the grave to lie –
Jesus is Lord!

Source of all sovereignty,
Light, immortality,
Life everlasting
And heaven assured;
So with the ransomed, we
Praise Him eternally,
Christ in His majesty –
Jesus is Lord!

940

Sarah F. Adams (1805–48)

NEARER, MY GOD, TO THEE,
Nearer to Thee:
E'en though it be a cross
That raiseth me,
Still all my song would be,
Nearer, my God, to Thee,
Nearer to Thee, nearer to Thee.

Though, like the wanderer,
The sun gone down,
Darkness be over me,
My rest a stone,
Yet in my dreams I'd be
Nearer, my God, to Thee,
Nearer to Thee, nearer to Thee.

There let the way appear,
Steps up to heaven;
All that Thou sendest me,
In mercy given;
Angels to beckon me
Nearer, my God, to Thee,
Nearer to Thee, nearer to Thee.

Then, with my waking thoughts
Bright with Thy praise,
Out of my stony griefs
Bethel I'll raise;
So by my woes to be
Nearer, my God, to Thee,
Nearer to Thee, nearer to Thee.

Or, if on joyful wing
Cleaving the sky,
Sun, moon, and stars forgot,
Upwards I fly,
Still all my song shall be,
Nearer, my God, to Thee,
Nearer to Thee, nearer to Thee.

941

Chris Roe
Copyright © Chris Roe, courtesy of
Ambushed Ltd

NEVER LET MY HEART GROW COLD.
Lord, help my to love You
With a love that never dies.
Set my heart ablaze with burning desire
To see Jesus glorified,
To see Jesus glorified.

942

David Fellingham
Copyright © 1992 Thankyou Music

NEW COVENANT PEOPLE rejoice,
Lift up your eyes and see your King.
Reigning in power on His heavenly throne,
Angels are joyfully singing:

To the Father, our Creator,
To our Judge and Lord.
And to Jesus, Mediator,
Who has cleansed us in His blood.

Let us through Jesus draw near to God,
Offering up our sacrifice,
Confessing that Jesus is Lord over all,
Joining with heavenly praises:

We give thanks to You with fear,
Holy God, consuming fire,
Confessing that Jesus is Lord over all,
We bring our love and devotion:

943

Mark Altrogge
Copyright © 1990 Integrity's Hosanna! Music/
People of Destiny International/
Sovereign Music UK

NO EYE HAS SEEN,
And no ear has heard,
And no mind has ever conceived
The glorious things
That You have prepared
For everyone who has believed;
You brought us near and You called us Your own,
And made us joint heirs with Your Son.

How high and how wide,
How deep and how long,
How sweet and how strong is Your love;
How lavish Your grace,
How faithful Your ways,
How great is Your love, O Lord.

Objects of mercy,
Who should have known wrath,
We're filled with unspeakable joy;
Riches of wisdom
Unsearchable wealth,
And the wonder of knowing Your voice.
You are our treasure and our great reward,
Our hope and our glorious King.

944

Paul Baloche & Ed Kerr
Copyright © 1992 Integrity's Hosanna! Music/
PDI Music/BMI/Adm. by Integrity's Praise! Music/
Sovereign Music UK

NO EYE HAS SEEN, NO EAR HAS HEARD,
No mind has conceived what the Lord has
  prepared;
But by His Spirit, He has revealed
His plan to those who love Him.
(Repeat)

We've been held by His everlasting love,
Led with loving kindness by His hand;
We have hope for the future yet to come,
In time we'll understand the mystery of His plan.

945 Carol Owen
Copyright © 1994 Thankyou Music

NO ONE IS LIKE YOU, O LORD;
You are great and Your name is mighty.
No one is like You, O Lord;
You are great and Your name is mighty.
Who should not revere You,
O King of the nations?
Who should not revere You,
For this is Your due?
Among all wise men
In all of their kingdoms,
There is none like You.

No one is like You, O Lord;
You're enthroned over all the nations.
No one is like You, O Lord;
You're enthroned over all the nations.
Who should not revere You,
O King of the nations?
Who should not revere You,
For this is Your due?
Among all the wise men
In all of their kingdoms,
There is none like You.

None like You, O Lord,
The King and the Creator.
None like You, O Lord,
Our Father and our Maker.
None like You, O Lord,
Your faithfulness surrounds You.
How majestic is Your name,
As Your people we proclaim:

946 Robert Gay
Copyright © 1988 Integrity's Hosanna! Music/
Sovereign Music UK

NO OTHER NAME but the name of Jesus,
No other name but the name of the Lord;
No other name but the name of Jesus
Is worthy of glory, and worthy of honour,
And worthy of power and all praise.

His name is exalted far above the earth,
His name is high above the heavens;
His name is exalted far above the earth,
Give glory and honour and praise unto His
name.

947 Noel & Tricia Richards
Copyright © 1989 Thankyou Music

NOTHING SHALL SEPARATE US
From the love of God.
Nothing shall separate us
From the love of God.

God did not spare His only Son,
Gave Him to save us all.
Sin's price was met by Jesus' death
And heaven's mercy falls.

Up from the grave Jesus was raised
To sit at God's right hand;
Pleading our cause in heaven's courts,
Forgiven we can stand.

Now by God's grace we have embraced
A life set free from sin;
We shall deny all that destroys
Our union with Him.

948 Tom Dowell
Copyright © Tom Dowell/
Copyright control

NO WEAPON FORMED, or army or king,
Shall be able to stand
Against the Lord and His anointed.
(Repeat)

All principalities and powers
Shall crumble before the Lord;
And men's hearts shall be released,
And they shall come unto the Lord.

No weapon formed, or army or king,
Shall be able to stand
Against the Lord and His anointed.

949 Alfred H. Vine (1845–1917)

O BREATH OF GOD, BREATHE ON US NOW,
And move within us while we pray;
The Spring of our new life art Thou,
The very light of our new day.

O strangely art Thou with us, Lord,
Neither in height nor depth to seek:
In nearness shall Thy voice be heard;
Spirit to spirit Thou dost speak.

Christ is our Advocate on high;
Thou art our Advocate within.
O plead the truth, and make reply
To every argument of sin.

But ah, this faithless heart of mine,
The way I know, I know my Guide;
Forgive me, O my Friend divine,
That I so often turn aside.

Be with me when no other friend
The mystery of my heart can share;
And be Thou known, when fears transcend,
By Thy best name of Comforter.

O FATHER OF THE FATHERLESS,
In whom all families are blessed,
I love the way You father me.
You gave me life, forgave the past,
Now in Your arms I'm safe at last,
I love the way You father me.

Father me, for ever You'll father me,
And in Your embrace I'll be for ever
secure.
I love the way You father me.
I love the way You father me.

When bruised and broken I draw near
You hold me close and dry my tears,
I love the way You father me.
At last my fearful heart is still,
Surrendered to Your perfect will,
I love the way You father me.

If in my foolishness I stray,
Returning empty and ashamed,
I love the way You father me.
Exchanging for my wretchedness
Your radiant robes of righteousness,
I love the way You father me.

And when I look into Your eyes
From deep within my spirit cries,
I love the way You father me.
Before such love I stand amazed
And ever will through endless days,
I love the way You father me.

O FOR A CLOSER WALK WITH GOD,
A calm and heavenly frame,
A light to shine upon the road
That leads me to the Lamb.

Where is the blessèdness I knew
When I first saw the Lord?
Where is that soul-refreshing view
Of Jesus and His word?

What peaceful hours I once enjoyed!
How sweet their memory still!
But they have left an aching void
The world can never fill.

Return, O holy Dove! return,
Sweet messenger of rest!
I hate the sins that made Thee mourn,
And drove Thee from my breast.

The dearest idol I have known,
Whate'er that idol be,
Help me to tear if from Thy throne,
And worship only Thee.

So shall my walk be close with God,
Calm and serene my frame;
So purer light shall mark the road
That leads me to the Lamb.

O GOD, BE MY STRENGTH
Through my doubt and my fear.
O God, be my comfort
When darkness is near.
O Lord of all hope,
You're my Saviour and Guide.
O Lord, have mercy on me.

O God of all mercy
And God of all grace,
Whose infinite gift
Was to die in my place,
Eternal Creator,
Redeemer and Friend,
O Lord, have mercy on me.

O God of all power,
Invisible King,
Restorer of man,
My life I bring,
O Lord of my heart,
Grant Your peace now I pray:
O Lord, have mercy on me.

O GOD BEYOND ALL PRAISING,
We worship You today,
And sing the love amazing
That songs cannot repay;
For we can only wonder
At every gift you send,
At blessings without number
And mercies without end:
We lift our hearts before You
And wait upon Your word,
We honour and adore You,
Our great and mighty Lord.

Then hear, O gracious Saviour,
Accept the love we bring,
That we who know Your favour
May serve You as our King;
And whether our tomorrows
Be filled with good or ill,
We'll triumph through our sorrows
And rise to bless You still:
To marvel at Your beauty
And glory in Your ways,
And make a joyful duty
Our sacrifice of praise!

954 Jamie Owens-Collins
Copyright © 1992 Fairhill Music/
Adm. by CopyCare

O GOD, MOST HIGH, Almighty King,
The Champion of heaven, Lord of everything;
You've fought, You've won, death's lost its
    sting,
And standing in Your victory we sing.

*You have broken the chains
That held our captive souls.
You have broken the chains
And used them on Your foes.
All Your enemies are bound,
They tremble at the sound of Your name;
Jesus, You have broken the chains.*

The power of hell has been undone,
Captivity held captive by the risen One,
And in the name of God's great Son,
We claim the mighty victory You've won.

955 William Booth (1829–1912)
Adpt. Lex Loizides
Copyright © 1994 Thankyou Music

O GOD OF BURNING, CLEANSING FLAME:
Send the fire!
Your blood-bought gift today we claim:
Send the fire today!
Look down and see this waiting host,
And send the promised Holy Ghost;
We need another Pentecost!
Send the fire today!
Send the fire today!

God of Elijah, hear our cry:
Send the fire!
And make us fit to live or die:
Send the fire today!
To burn up every trace of sin,
To bring the light and glory in,
The revolution now begin!
Send the fire today!
Send the fire today!

It's fire we want, for fire we plead:
Send the fire!
The fire will meet our every need:
Send the fire today!
For strength to always do what's right,
For grace to conquer in the fight,
For power to walk the world in white:
Send the fire today!
Send the fire today!

To make our weak hearts strong and brave:
Send the fire!
To live, a dying world to save:
Send the fire today!
Oh, see us on Your altar lay,
We give our lives to you today,
So crown the offering now we pray:
Send the fire today!
Send the fire today!
Send the fire today!

956 Martin Smith
Copyright © 1994 Curious? Music UK/
Adm. by Bucks Music Ltd

OH, LEAD ME
To the place where I can find You.
Oh, lead me
To the place where You'll be.

Lead me to the cross
Where we first met;
Draw me to my knees,
So we can talk.
Let me feel Your breath,
Let me know You're here with me.

957 Alan Rose
Copyright © 1997 Thankyou Music

OH, OUR LORD AND KING,
*Our praise to You we bring,
There is no other Rock but You.
Seated high above,
You are the One we love,
This is our song of praise to You.*

King for ever!
You are the First and You're the Last.
You are sovereign;
All Your commands will always
Come to pass, to give You glory!

Who is like You?
Who else is worthy of pur praise?
We exalt You;
You reign in majesty and
Awesome splendour,
King for ever!

bba Father,
our steadfast love will never fail.
ou are faithful,
ou are God and I will
worship in Your
ourts for ever.

 958
Geoff Bullock
Copyright © 1997 Watershed Productions/
Kingsway Music

H, THE MERCY OF GOD, the glory of grace,
hat You chose to redeem us, to forgive and
  restore,
nd You call us Your children, chosen in Him
o be holy and blameless to the glory of God.

To the praise of His glorious grace,
To the praise of His glory and power;
To Him be all glory, honour and praise
Forever and ever and ever, amen.

h, the richness of grace, the depths of His
  love,
 Him is redemption, the forgiveness of sin.
ou called us as righteous, predestined in
  Him
or the praise of His glory, included in Christ.

h, the glory of God expressed in His Son,
lis image and likeness revealed to us all;
he plea of the ages completed in Christ,
hat we be presented perfected in Him.

959
Craig Musseau
Copyright © 1992 Mercy/Vineyard Publishing/
Adm. by CopyCare

LORD, ARISE, release Your power,
catter Your foes this very hour.
May we hold on to Your holy commands.
ou are the Lord of every man.

ou hold our lives, You give us breath,
ou freed us from the power of death.
ou're our salvation, our only hope,
ou are the Lord of every man.

Your voice, it is like thunder
Over the waters.
Your voice echoes throughout the earth,
We will bow to the sound,
We will bow to the sound
Of Your voice.

960

Chris DuPré
Copyright © Heart of David Music

O LORD, HOW I LOVE TO SING YOUR PRAISES.
O Lord, how I love to dance for You.
O Lord, You have captured my affection,
Forever I will sing of Your love,
Forever I will bring to You my life,
Forever I will worship You.

And when I think of what You've done,
It makes me shout for joy.
And when I think of what's to come,
Living for ever in Your presence,
Face to face with my magnificent obsession,
Forever, for ever I will be with You.

Oh, la, la, la …
Oh, la, la, la …
Oh, la, la, la …
Forever, forever I will be with You.

961
Andy Park
Copyright © 1991 Andy Park/
Kingsway Music

O LORD I WANT TO SING YOUR PRAISES,
I want to praise Your name every day.
O Lord I want to sing Your praises,
I want to praise Your name every day.

Alleluia, allelu.
Alleluia, allelu.
(Alleluia.)

God, You are my God, and I will seek You;
I am satisfied when I find Your love.
God, You are my God, and I will seek You;
I am satisfied when I find Your love.

And I will praise You as long as I live,
For Your love is better than life.
In Your name I will lift up my hands,
For Your love is better than life.

962

Michael W. Smith
Copyright © Meadowgreen Music/EMI
Christian Music Publishing/Adm. by CopyCare

O LORD OUR LORD,
How majestic is Your name in all the earth.
O Lord our Lord,
How majestic is Your name in all the earth.
O Lord, we praise Your name;
O Lord, we magnify Your name.
Prince of Peace,
Mighty God,
O Lord God Almighty.

963 Jon Soper, Mark Robinson & John Peters

O LORD, YOU ARE MY ROCK AND MY REDEEMER;
My song, You are the Strength of my life.
O Lord, You are the Shepherd of Your people;
You keep us always walking in Your light.

You brought me out of darkness,
You took away my shame;
You broke the chains that bound me,
I praise Your name!

You carry all my sorrows,
You carry all my pain;
You fill me with Your Spirit,
I praise Your name!

964 Ian Smale

O LORD, YOU'RE GREAT, You are fabulous,
We love You more than any words can sing,
sing, sing.
O Lord, You're great, You are so generous,
You lavish us with gifts when we don't
deserve a thing.

Allelu, alleluia, praise You, Lord.
Alleluia, praise You, Lord.
Alleluia, praise You, Lord.
(Repeat)

O Lord, You're great, You are so powerful,
You hold the mighty universe in Your hand,
hand, hand.
O Lord, You're great, You are so beautiful,
You've poured out Your love on this
undeserving land.

965 Maggi Dawn

ONLY ONE THING I ask of the Lord:
Only one thing do I desire:
That I may dwell, may dwell in God's house
All of the days of my life,
All of the days of my life.

Even when days of trouble may come,
I will be safe if God is my home,
For I will hide in the shelter of love
All of the days of my life,
All of the days of my life.

I'll gaze on His beauty,
And sing of His glory;
While I have life within me,
What more could I need?

(Descant)
I'll sing to His holy name,
Forever He is the same,
His faithfulness never change,
Let all of the earth proclaim,
All of the days of my life.

966 Ian White

OPEN THE DOORS OF PRAISE.
Open the doors of praise.
Open the doors of praise
And let the Lord come in.
(Repeat)

In the spirit world
There's a battle going on,
And it rages endlessly.
But in the name of the Lord,
We can stand on His word,
For in Him we have the victory.

For He lives in the praises of His people, *(ech*
Here among us to empower us!

And the demons will flee,
As He said it would be,
And the skies will ring with shouts of praise
And the Lord Jesus Christ
Will be lifted high,
The Holy One who truly saves!

For He lives . . .

967 Mal Pope

O RIGHTEOUS GOD who searches minds a
hearts,
Bring to an end the violence of my foes,
And make the righteous more secure,
O righteous God.

Sing praise to the name of the Lord mos
high.
Sing praise to the name of the Lord mos
high.
Give thanks to the Lord who rescues me,
O righteous God.

O Lord my God, I take refuge in You;
Save and deliver me from all my foes.
My shield is God the Lord most high,
O Lord my God.

968 Samuel T. Francis (1834–1925)

O THE DEEP, DEEP LOVE OF JESUS!
Vast, unmeasured, boundless, free;
Rolling as a mighty ocean
In its fulness over me.
Underneath me, all around me,
Is the current of Thy love;
Leading onward, leading homeward,
To my glorious rest above.

O the deep, deep love of Jesus!
Spread His praise from shore to shore,
How He loveth, ever loveth,
Changeth never, nevermore;
How He watches o'er His loved ones,
Died to call them all His own;
How for them He intercedeth,
Watches over them from the throne.

O the deep, deep love of Jesus!
Love of every love the best:
'Tis an ocean vast of blessing,
'Tis a haven sweet of rest.
O the deep, deep love of Jesus!
'Tis a heaven of heavens to me;
And it lifts me up to glory,
For it lifts me up to Thee.

969 Brian Doerksen & Michael Hansen
Copyright © 1990 Mercy/Vineyard Publishing/
Adm. by CopyCare

OUR FATHER IN HEAVEN,
Holy is Your name.
Forgive us our sins, Lord,
As we forgive.
Our Father in heaven,
Give us our bread.
Lead us not into temptation,
But deliver us from the evil one.

Your kingdom come, Your will be done.
Your kingdom come, Your will be done

On the earth as it is in heaven.
Let it be done on the earth.
Amen. Amen.

970 Keith Routledge
Copyright © 1992 Thankyou Music &
Sovereign Music

OUR FATHER IN HEAVEN,
Hallowed be Your name,
Your kingdom come,
Your will be done on earth as in heaven.
Give us today our daily bread,
And forgive us our sins
As we forgive those who sin against us,
And lead us not into temptation,
But deliver us from evil;

For the kingdom, the power,
And the glory are Yours,
Now and for ever, Amen.

(Last time)
For the kingdom, the power
And the glory are Yours,
Now and for ever,
Now and for ever,
Now and for ever, Amen.

971 Noel & Tricia Richards
Copyright © 1992 Thankyou Music

OUR GOD IS AWESOME IN POWER,
Scatters His enemies;
Our God is mighty in bringing
The powerful to their knees.
He has put on His armour,
He is prepared for war;
Mercy and justice triumph
When the Lion of Judah roars.

The Lord is a warrior,
We will march with Him.
The Lord is a warrior,
Leading us to win.
(Repeat)

Waken the warrior spirit,
Army of God, arise;
Challenge the powers of darkness,
There must be no compromise.
We shall attack their strongholds,
Our hands are trained for war;
We shall advance the kingdom,
For the victory belongs to God.

972 Dave Bilbrough
Copyright © 1996 Thankyou Music

OUR GOD IS GREAT.
(Repeat ×4)

He gave us the wind,
The sun and the snow,
The sand on the sea shore,
The flowers that grow.
Morning and evening,
Winter and spring;
Come join all creation and sing.

The gifts that He brings
Are new every day,
From glorious sunset
To soft falling rain.
The mist on the hills,
The light and the shade;
Come join all creation in praise.

For music and dancing,
The sounds that we hear;
For colours and words,
The life that we share, we say:

973 John Gibson
Copyright © 1994 Thankyou Music

OUR PASSION IS FOR YOU, Lord Jesus;
Your grace has fuelled a fire
That burns within our hearts.
There's nowhere that compares
With Your presence;
We've tasted of Your Spirit,
So there's just one thing we ask:

More, more, more, more, more.
More, more, more, more, more.
Pour out, pour out,
Pour out Your Spirit, O Lord.
Pour out, pour out,
Pour out Your Spirit, O Lord

974 Nigel Leppitt
Copyright © 1992 Thankyou Music

OVER THE HEAVENS ABOVE,
Under the earth below,
Deeper than any sea
Shines the presence of Your glory.
A river with many streams
Flows to the heart of the holy King;
Full of such wonder and mystery,
Living in power and in glory.

Great are You Lord, and mighty,
Your splendour is reigning in the earth.
Your glory is revealed
In the hearts of those who You've redeemed.
Great are You, Lord, and mighty,
Great are You, Lord, and mighty.

975 Martin Smith
Copyright © 1994 Curious? Music UK/
Adm. by Bucks Music Ltd

OVER THE MOUNTAINS AND THE SEA
Your river runs with love for me,
And I will open up my heart,
And let the Healer set me free.
I'm happy to be in the truth,
And I will daily lift my hands,
For I will always sing of
When Your love came down, yeah.

I could sing of Your love for ever,
I could sing of Your love for ever.
I could sing of Your love for ever,
I could sing of Your love for ever.

Oh, I feel like dancing,
It's foolishness I know;
But when the world has seen the light,
They will dance with joy
Like we're dancing now.

976 Noel Richards
Copyright © 1994 Thankyou Music

OVERWHELMED BY LOVE,
Deeper than oceans,
High as the heavens.
Ever living God
Your love has rescued me.

All my sin was laid
On Your dear Son,
Your precious One.
All my debt He paid,
Great is Your love for me.

No-one could ever earn Your love,
Your grace and mercy is free.
Lord, these words are true,
So is my love for You.

977 Edward H. Bickersteth (1825–1906)

PEACE, PERFECT PEACE, in this dark world
sin?
The blood of Jesus whispers peace within.

Peace, perfect peace, by thronging duties
pressed?
To do the will of Jesus, this is rest.

Peace, perfect peace, with sorrows surging
round?
In Jesus' presence nought but calm is found

Peace, perfect peace, with loved ones far
away?
In Jesus' keeping we are safe, and they.

Peace, perfect peace, our future all unknown
Jesus we know, and He is on the throne.

Peace, perfect peace, death shadowing us
and ours?
Jesus has vanquished death and all its
powers.

It is enough: earth's struggles soon shall
cease,
And Jesus calls us to heaven's perfect peace

POWER FROM ON HIGH,
Power from on high,
Lord, we are waiting
For power from on high.
Power from on high,
Power from on high,
Lord, we are waiting
For power from on high.

May we taste Your heaven
Here on the earth,
May Your Spirit bring us new birth.

May we take Your heaven
To those on the earth,
May Your Spirit bring them new birth.

May the truth and power
Of life that You give
Very soon be ours to live.

PRAISE AND GLORY,
Wisdom and honour,
Power and strength and thanksgiving
Be to our God for ever and ever,
Amen.
(Repeat)

PRAISE GOD FROM WHOM ALL
BLESSINGS FLOW,
Praise Him all creatures here below.
Praise Him above, you heavenly host,
Praise Father, Son and Holy Ghost.
(Repeat)

Give glory to the Father,
Give glory to the Son,
Give glory to the Spirit
While endless ages run.
'Worthy the Lamb'
All heaven cries,
To be exalted thus:'
'Worthy the Lamb'
Our hearts reply,
'For He was slain for us.'

Praise God from whom all blessings flow,
Praise God from whom all blessings flow.
(×4)

PRAISE THE LORD,
ALL YOU SERVANTS OF THE LORD,
Who minister by night within His house.
Lift up your hands
Within the sanctuary,
And praise the Lord.

May the Lord,
The Maker of heaven and earth,
May this Lord bless you from Zion;
Lift up your hands
Within the sanctuary
And praise the Lord.

We praise You, Lord,
We praise You, Lord;
Hallelujah, we praise You, Lord.

PROMISE OF THE FATHER,
Given through the Son,
Of power for His children,
The Holy Spirit's come.
Young men will see visions,
Old men will dream dreams;
Sons and daughters prophesy.
Father, send Your Spirit and I'll...

Catch the fire,
As You let the power from heaven fall.
I'll catch the fire,
As Your glory falls on me.
I'll catch the fire
As I open up my life to You.
Your power will set me free.
Let Your power fall on me.

Jesus in His glory
Sends His Spirit now,
That we might be proclaimers
Of the gospel's power.
In worship and in witness
We declare God's love,
Speaking to a dying world,
Jesus has the power to save, I'll...

QUIET MY MIND, Lord,
Make me still before You;
Calm my restless heart, Lord,
Make me more like You.
(Repeat)

Raise up my hands that are hanging down;
Strengthen my feeble knees.
May Your love and joy abound,
And fill me with Your peace.

984 Luke & Nathan Fellingham
Copyright © 1997 Thankyou Music

RELEASE YOUR POWER *among us, Lord,*
That all may see Your glory.
(Repeat)

Lord, I give my life to You,
And trust Your holy name;
Help me grow in holiness,
And follow You in all Your ways.
Send Your Holy Spirit,
That I may truly be
Cleansed within my heart
And free from all impurity.

O Lord, as we come trusting our way to You,
Make our righteousness shine like the dawn.

Teach me, Lord, to listen
To the calling of Your Spirit,
Helping me and guiding me
To live my life as Jesus did.
I long to know Your power
And see the sick get healed;
Come and move among us, Lord,
That truth will be revealed.

985 Stuart Garrard
Copyright © 1994 Thankyou Music

RELEASE YOUR POWER, O GOD.
Release Your power, O God,
The visions and dreams in our hearts.
(Repeat)

> *Come, Holy God.*
> *Come, Holy God.*

Release Your fire, O God.
Release Your fire, O God,
A passion that burns in our hearts.
(Repeat)

986 Jim Bailey
Copyright © 1994 Thankyou Music

REMEMBER YOUR CREATOR
In the days of your youth.
(Repeat ×4)

See people old and grey,
Hear them say:
'Wish I had been that way
When I was young.
I wasn't like you, you see,
Missed the opportunity,
And now I am old
And wish I was told.'

While you are young and strong
You can sing this song,
You can serve the Lord
With all you have.
And you will have no regrets,
You have done what's best;
You have not forgot, to...

987 Helena Barrington
Copyright © 1988 Integrity's Praise! Music/
Sovereign Music UK

RIGHTEOUSNESS, PEACE, JOY IN THE HOL
GHOST;
Righteousness, peace and joy in the Holy
Ghost,
That's the kingdom of God.
(Repeat)

Don't you want to be a part of the kingdom
Don't you want to be a part of the kingdom,
Don't you want to be a part of the kingdom
Come on, everybody!
(Repeat)

There's love in the kingdom,
So much love in the kingdom;
There's love in the kingdom.
Come on, everybody!

There's peace in the kingdom...

There's joy in the kingdom...

I'm an heir of the kingdom...

988 Peter Arajs
Copyright © 1989 Thankyou Music

RISE UP, *let Your kingdom arise in us;*
We lift our eyes to the skies, and rise up
To the brightness of His rising.
(Repeat)

All creation awaits
The revealing of the sons of God,
And all the angels of heaven
Are listening for the prayers of us:
Hearing the sound of a powerful flood,
Saints of our God who've been bought by H
blood.

The redemption of God
Has given us a kingdom view,
And His promise to us,
The hope of glory, Christ in you.
Darkness shall run from the strength of His
   hand,
Our testimony, the blood of the Lamb.

989

Paul Oakley
Copyright © 1996 Thankyou Music

RIVER OF GOD, *flood over me,*
And lift my feet up off the ground.
Carry me out into Your sea,
And in Your presence I'll be found.

I've felt Your fire and I've felt Your rain;
And I've heard Your voice whisper my
   name.
I've been wading in Your river,
I've ridden on Your waves;
I've tasted of Your goodness,
Still I'm longing to be changed.

There's something inside me that just won't
   let go;
Why am I afraid of losing control?
Oh, I know Your love is for me,
And You'll never do me harm;
So melt away my fears,
And Holy Spirit come!

I've had enough of holding back,
I see Your goodness all around,
This time I'm opening up my heart,
So come and fill me now.
(Chorus)

Please help me, Lord, to be more like You,
To do all the things You've called me to do.
Let me help bring in Your harvest,
Oh, I want it for Your Son;
To fill me with Your power,
Holy Spirit come!

Come like a mighty rushing wind,
A tidal wave or a monsoon rain,
Like a stream in the desert,
Or a warm summer breeze;
Gentle Dove of heaven,
Bring me to my knees!

I've had enough of holding back,
I see Your goodness all around,
This time I'm opening up my heart,
So come and fill me now.
(Chorus)

990

David Fellingham
Copyright © 1994 Thankyou Music

RUACH, Ruach,
Holy wind of God, blow on me.
Touch the fading embers, breathe on me.
Fan into a flame all that You've placed in me.
Let the fire burn more powerfully.
Ruach, Ruach,
Holy wind of God,
Holy wind of God, breathe on me.

991

Timothy Dudley-Smith
Copyright © 1970 Timothy Dudley-Smith

SAFE IN THE SHADOW OF THE LORD,
Beneath His hand and power,
I trust in Him,
I trust in Him,
My fortress and my tower.

My hope is set on God alone,
Though Satan spreads his snare,
I trust in Him,
I trust in Him,
To keep me in His care.

From fears and phantoms of the night,
From foes about my way,
I trust in Him,
I trust in Him,
By darkness as by day.

His holy angels keep my feet
Secure from every stone;
I trust in Him,
I trust in Him,
And unafraid go on.

Strong in the everlasting Name,
And in my Father's care,
I trust in Him,
I trust in Him,
Who hears and answers prayer.

Safe in the shadow of the Lord,
Possessed by love divine,
I trust in Him,
I trust in Him,
And meet His love with mine.

992

Adrian Howard & Pat Turner
Copyright © 1985 Restoration Music Ltd/
Sovereign Music UK

SALVATION BELONGS TO OUR GOD,
Who sits on the throne,
And to the Lamb.
Praise and glory, wisdom and thanks,
Honour and power and strength:

Be to our God forever and ever,
Be to our God forever and ever,
Be to our God forever and ever, amen.

And we, the redeemed shall be strong
In purpose and unity,
Declaring aloud,
Praise and glory, wisdom and thanks,
Honour and power and strength:

993 Stuart Townend
Copyright © 1994 Thankyou Music

SAY THE WORD, I will be healed;
You are the great Physician,
You meet every need.
Say the word, I will be free;
Where chains have held me captive,
Come sing Your songs to me,
Say the word.

Say the word, I will be filled;
My hands reach out to heaven,
Where striving is stilled.
Say the word, I will be changed;
Where I am dry and thirsty,
Send cool, refreshing rain,
Say the word.

> *His tears have fallen like rain on my life;*
> *Each drop a fresh revelation.*
> *I will return to the place of the cross,*
> *Where grace and mercy*
> *Pour from heaven's throne.*

Say the word, I will be poor,
That I might know the riches
That You have in store.
Say the word, I will be weak;
Your strength will be the power
That satisfies the meek.
Say the word.

> *The Lord will see the travail of His soul,*
> *And He and I will be satisfied.*
> *Complete the work You have started in me:*
> *O, come Lord Jesus, shake my life again.*

994 Paul Oakley
Copyright © 1997 Thankyou Music

SEARCH ME, O GOD,
And know my heart;
Know all my thoughts and my ways.
Cleanse me, O God,
Give me a pure heart,
That I may see Your face.

For You are an all consuming fire!
For You are an all consuming fire!

Teach me, O God,
Show me Your ways,
And I will walk in Your truth.
Keep me, O God,
Keep me from falling,
That I may stand before You.

Fill me, O God,
And send me out,
And I will make You known.
Give me Your heart
And Your compassion,
And let Your mercy flow.

995 Geoff Twigg
Copyright © 1994 Thankyou Music

SEND FORTH YOUR LIGHT
AND YOUR TRUTH,
Let them guide me,
Let them bring me to Your holy mountain
To the place where You dwell.
(Repeat)
(Last time)
O Lord.

Then I will come to the altar of God,
My joy and my delight;
Then I will offer the whole of my life,
A living sacrifice.

Jesus, the Way and the Truth and the Life,
My Saviour and my Lord;
Knowing Your presence will be my delight,
Your glory my reward.

996 John Pantry
Copyright © 1986 HarperCollins Religious/
Adm. by CopyCare

SEND ME OUT FROM HERE, Lord,
To serve a world in need.
May I know no man by the coat he wears
But the heart that Jesus sees.
And may the light of Your face
Shine upon me, Lord.
You have filled my heart with the greatest
joy,
And my cup is overflowing.

'Go now, and carry the news
To all creation, every race and tongue.
Take no purse with you,
Take nothing to eat
For He will supply your needs.'

Go now, bearing the light,
Living for others,
Fearlessly walking into the night;
Take no thought for your lives,
Like lambs among wolves,
Full of the Spirit, ready to die.'

997   Dave Wellington
       Copyright © 1995 Thankyou Music

SEND US THE RAIN, LORD,
Rain of Your Spirit,
Rain on this dry barren land.
Send us the rain, Lord,
Rain to revive us;
Cleanse us and fill us again.
Here we are, of one accord,
Calling to You, singing:
Send Your Spirit,
Send Your Spirit,
Send the rain on us again.

Pour out Your wine, Lord,
Wine of Your Spirit,
Wine that would teach us to love.
Pour out Your wine, Lord,
Oh, how we need You
To quench the thirst of our hearts.
Here we are, of one accord,
Calling to You, singing:
Send Your Spirit,
Send Your Spirit,
Pour Your wine on us again.

Breathe now upon us,
Breath of Your Spirit,
Breath to bring life to these bones.
Breathe now upon us,
Life of abundance,
Holiness, wisdom, love, truth.
Here we are, of one accord,
Calling to You, singing:
Send Your Spirit,
Send Your Spirit,
Breathe Your life on us again.

Send down the fire,
Fire of Your Spirit,
Refiner's fire to fulfil.
Send down the fire,
Fire to consume us,
Reveal Your power once more.
Here we are, of one accord,
Calling to You, singing:
Send Your Spirit,
Send Your Spirit,
Send the fire on us again.

998   Dave Bilbrough
       Copyright © 1995 Thankyou Music

SEND YOUR RAIN down from the heavens;
Send Your rain to this earth.
Let there be a great outpouring;
Holy Spirit, come to us.

Send Your fire down from the heavens;
The fire of revival to Your church.
We can see the world is waiting;
Holy Spirit, come to us.

Fill this land with Your grace and mercy;
Cause our hearts to worship You.

999   Andy Park
       Copyright © 1989 Mercy/Vineyard Publishing/
       Adm. by CopyCare

SHOW ME, DEAR LORD, how You see me in
    Your eyes,
So that I can realise Your great love for me.
Teach me, O Lord, that I am precious in Your
    sight,
That as a father loves his child, so You love me.

    I am Yours because You have chosen me.
    I'm Your child because You've called my
       name,
    And Your steadfast love will never change;
    I will always be Your precious child.

Show me, dear Lord, that I can never earn
    Your love,
That a gift cannot be earned, only given.
Teach me, O Lord, that Your love will never
    fade,
That I can never drive away Your great mercy.

1000   Matt Redman
       Copyright © 1996 Thankyou Music

SHOW ME THE WAY OF THE CROSS once
    again,
Denying myself for the love that I've gained.
Everything's You now, everything's changed;
It's time You had my whole life,
You can have it all.

    Yes, I resolve to give it all;
    Some things must die, some things must
       live,
    Not 'what can I gain', but 'what can I give'.
    If much is required when much is
       received,
    Then You can have my whole life,
    Jesus, have it all.

I've given like a beggar but lived like the rich,
And crafted myself a more comfortable cross.
Yet what I am called to is deeper than this;
It's time You had my whole life,
You can have it all.

 1001

SING A SONG OF CELEBRATION,
Lift up a shout of praise,
For the Bridegroom will come,
The glorious One.
And oh, we will look on His face;
We'll go to a much better place.

Dance with all your might,
Lift up your hands and clap for joy:
The time's drawing near
When He will appear.
And oh, we will stand by His side;
A strong, pure, spotless Bride.

> *Oh, we will dance on the streets that are*
>   *golden,*
> *The glorious Bride and the great Son of*
>   *Man,*
> *From every tongue and tribe and nation*
> *Will join in the song of the Lamb.*

(Men-Women echo)
Sing aloud for the time of rejoicing is near.
The risen King, our Groom is soon to appear.
The wedding feast to come is now near at
  hand.
Lift up your voice, proclaim the coming
  Lamb.

 1002

SING TO GOD NEW SONGS of worship:
All His deeds are marvellous;
He has brought salvation to us
With His hand and holy arm:
He has shown to all the nations
Righteousness and saving power;
He recalled His truth and mercy
To His people Israel.

Sing to God new songs of worship:
Earth has seen His victory;
Let the lands of earth be joyful
Praising Him with thankfulness:
Sound upon the harp His praises,
Play to Him with melody;
Let the trumpets sound His triumph,
Show your joy to God the King!

Sing to God new songs of worship:
Let the sea now make a noise;
All on earth and in the waters
Sound your praises to the Lord:
Let the hills be joyful together,
Let the rivers clap their hands,
For with righteousness and justice
He will come to judge the earth.

1003

SING TO THE LORD with all of your heart;
Sing of the glory that's due to His name.
Sing to the Lord with all of your soul,
Join all of heaven and earth to proclaim:

> *You are the Lord, the Saviour of all,*
> *God of creation, we praise You.*
> *We sing the songs that awaken the*
>   *dawn,*
> *God of creation, we praise You.*

Sing to the Lord with all of your mind,
With understanding give thanks to the King.
Sing to the Lord with all of your strength,
Living our lives as a praise offering.

1004

SOFTEN MY HEART,
That I may know
The love You have for me,
More than words or well-worn phrases.

Soften my heart,
For love to grow,
The love I have for You,
That keeps my motives pure and
  blameless.

Enter in,
Come and have free reign
As I walk with You today.
Risen Lamb,
Holy One,
Overshadow me today.

SOMETIMES WHEN I FEEL YOUR LOVE

As I walk along the busy street,
I whisper Your name under my breath.
And sometimes when I feel Your touch
In the quiet place of my room,
I sing Your name in adoration.
And there are times when I feel like I'm
  bursting
With Your love so strong and so true;
And in my heart I feel such a yearning,
And I want all the world
To know You love them, too.

I love Your love,
Gonna shout it out aloud.
I love Your love,
Wanna tell the world about it.
I love Your love,
'Cause I've found it to be true,
And I live to love You, too.

SON OF MAN and Man of heaven,

Full of grace and truth;
Sinner's friend yet without sin,
I want to be like You:
Perfect in holiness,
Full of faithfulness and love.

I want to be like Jesus,
I want to be like Jesus,
I want to be like You,
O Lord, our God.
(Repeat)

You began a work in me,
I know You'll see it through.
There's a new song in my heart,
And I want to sing to You.
You lifted me from mire,
From sin and from shame You set me free,
And I know Your tenderness,
I know Your power at work in me.

You're making me like Jesus ...

SOON, AND VERY SOON,

We are going to see the King;
Soon, and very soon,
We are going to see the King;
Soon, and very soon,
We are going to see the King;
Alleluia, alleluia,
We're going to see the King!

No more crying there ...

No more dying there ...

Alleluia, alleluia,
Alleluia, alleluia.

Soon, and very soon ...

Alleluia ...

SOUND THE TRUMPET, strike the drum,

See the King of glory come,
Join the praises rising from
The people of the Lord.
Let your voices now be heard,
Unrestrained and unreserved,
Prepare the way for His return,
You people of the Lord.

Sing Jesus is Lord;
Jesus is Lord.

Bow down to His authority,
For He has slain the enemy.
Of heaven and hell He holds the key.
Jesus is Lord;
Jesus is Lord.

SPIRIT OF GOD, SHOW ME JESUS,

Remove the darkness,
Let truth shine through!
Spirit of God, show me Jesus,
Reveal the fulness of His love to me.

SPIRIT OF HOLINESS,

Wisdom and faithfulness,
Wind of the Lord,
Blowing strongly and free:
Strength of our serving
And joy of our worshipping;
Spirit of God,
Bring Your fulness to me!

You came to interpret
And teach us effectively
All that the Saviour
Has spoken and done;
To glorify Jesus is all Your activity;
Promise and Gift
Of the Father and Son:

You came with Your gifts
To supply all our poverty,
Pouring Your love
On the church in her need;
You came with Your fruit
For our growth to maturity,
Richly refreshing
The souls that You feed:

STANDING IN YOUR PRESENCE,

Lord, my heart and life are changed;
Just to love You and to live to
See Your beauty and Your grace.

Heaven and earth cry out Your name,
Nations rise up and see Your face;
And Your kingdom is established
As I live to know You more.
Now I will never be the same;
Spirit of God, my life You've changed,
And I'll for ever sing Your praise.
I live to know You, Lord.
I live to know You, Lord.

You've called me, I will follow;
Your will for me I'm sure.
Let Your heartbeat be my heart's cry,
Let me live to serve Your call.

TAKE ME PAST THE OUTER COURTS,

And through the holy place,
Past the brazen altar,
Lord, I want to see Your face.
Pass me by the crowds of people,
And the priests who sing their praise;
I hunger and thirst for Your righteousness,
But it's only found one place,

So take me into the Holy of holies,
Take me in by the blood of the Lamb;
So take me into the Holy of holies,
Take the coal, cleanse my lips, here I am.

TEACH ME TO DANCE *to the beat of You*
    heart,
Teach me to move in the power of Your
    Spirit,
Teach me to walk in the light of Your
    presence,
Teach me to dance to the beat of Your
    heart.
Teach me to love with Your heart of
    compassion,
Teach me to trust in the word of Your
    promise,
Teach me to hope in the day of Your
    coming,
Teach me to dance to the beat of Your
    heart.

You wrote the rhythm of life,
Created heaven and earth;
In You is joy without measure.
So, like a child in Your sight,
I dance to see Your delight,
For I was made for Your pleasure,
Pleasure.

Let all my movements express
A heart that loves to say 'yes',
A will that leaps to obey You.
Let all my energy blaze
To see the joy in Your face;
Let my whole being praise You,
Praise You.

1014 Kevin Prosch
Copyright © 1991 Mercy/Vineyard Publishing/
Adm. by CopyCare

EACH US, O LORD, what it really means
o rend our hearts instead of outer things.
and teach us, O God, what we do not see
about our hearts and of Your ways.
and Father deal with our carnal desires,
o move in Your power, but not live the life,
and to love our neighbour with all that we
   have,
and keep our tongues from saying things we
   have not seen.

   O, break our hearts with the things that
      break Yours,
   If we sow in tears, we will reap in joy,
   That we might pass through Your refining
      fire,
   Where brokenness awaits on the other
      side.

aise up an army like Joel saw,
'our church that is stronger than ever
   before.
hey do not break ranks when they plunge
   through defences,
ut the fear of the Lord will be their wisdom.
'hat they might weep as Jesus wept,
a fountain of tears for the wounded and lost;
Vhoever heard of an army, O God,
hat conquered the earth by weeping,
and mourning, and brokenness?

   But there will be a day when the nations
      will bow
   And our Lord will be King over all the
      earth;
   And He will be the only One,
   And also His name will be the only One.

1015 Martin Smith
Copyright © 1993 Curious? Music UK/
Adm. by Bucks Music Ltd

HANK YOU FOR SAVING ME;
Vhat can I say?
ou are my everything,
will sing Your praise.
ou shed Your blood for me;
Vhat can I say?
ou took my sin and shame,
a sinner called by name.

   Great is the Lord.
   Great is the Lord.
   For we know Your truth has set us free;
   You've set Your hope in me.

Mercy and grace are mine,
Forgiven is my sin;
Jesus, my only hope,
The Saviour of the world.
'Great is the Lord,' we cry;
God, let Your kingdom come.
Your word has let me see,
Thank You for saving me.

1016 Richard Lewis
Copyright © 1996 Thankyou Music

THE ANGELS AROUND YOUR THRONE,
They cry, 'Holy is the Lamb.'
The angels around Your throne,
They cry, 'Holy is the Lamb.'
So we sing holy, holy, holy,
Holy is the Lamb.
So we sing holy, holy, holy,
Holy is the Lamb.

The angels around Your throne,
They cry, 'Worthy is the Lamb.'
The angels around Your throne,
They cry, 'Worthy is the Lamb.'
So we sing worthy, worthy, worthy,
Worthy is the Lamb.
So we sing worthy, worthy, worthy,
Worthy is the Lamb.

1017 Matt Redman
Copyright © 1993 Thankyou Music

THE ANGELS, LORD, THEY SING
Around Your throne;
And we will join their song:
Praise You alone.
(Repeat)

   Holy, holy, holy,
   Lord our God,
   Who was and is and is to come.
   (Repeat)

The living creatures, Lord,
Speak endless praise;
And joining at Your throne,
We'll sing their sweet refrain.
(Repeat)

The elders, Lord, they fall
Before Your throne;
Our hearts we humbly bow
To You alone.
(Repeat)

1018 Doug Horley
Copyright © 1994 Thankyou Music

THE BATTLE IS THE LORD'S,
The battle is the Lord's,
The battle is the Lord's
That is our victory cry.
(Repeat)

We refuse to bow to satan's schemes,
Set our wills for righteousness;
We declare we'll choose for truth
In every situation.
We could battle in the heavenlies,
Yet in our lives neglect to fight:
Saying no to self and no to sin
Is where our warfare must begin.

As we're taking ground in daily war,
Living lives of righteousness,
We will grow in strength to face
The bigger situations.
And the more of us that battle through,
The purer then this church will be;
Who will stop us then as we proclaim:
'Strongholds, you have had your day!'

1019 Matt Redman & Martin Smith
Copyright © 1995 Thankyou Music

THE CROSS HAS SAID IT ALL,
The cross has said it all.
I can't deny what You have shown,
The cross speaks of a God of love;
There displayed for all to see,
Jesus Christ, our only hope,
A message of the Father's heart:
'Come, my children, come on home.'

As high as the heavens are above the
earth,
So high is the measure of Your great love;
As far as the east is from the west,
So far have You taken our sins from us.
(Repeat)

The cross has said it all,
The cross has said it all.
I never recognised Your touch
Until I met You at the cross;
We are fallen, dust to dust,
How could You do this for us?
Son of God shed precious blood:
Who can comprehend this love?

How high, how wide, how deep;
(Repeat ×4)
How high!

1020 Martin Smith
Copyright © 1993 Thankyou Music

THE CRUCIBLE FOR SILVER
And the furnace for gold,
But the Lord tests the heart of this child.
Standing in all purity,
God, our passion is for holiness,
Lead us to the secret place of praise.

Jesus, Holy One,
You are my heart's desire.
King of kings, my everything,
You've set this heart on fire.
(Repeat)

Father, take our offering, with our song we
humbly praise You.
You have brought Your holy fire to our lips.
Standing in Your beauty, Lord,
Your gift to us is holiness;
Lead us to the place where we can sing:

1021 Dave Bilbrough & Andy Piercy
Copyright © 1995 IQ Music Limited &
Thankyou Music

THE DAY OF THE STREAMS *is over,*
The time of the river is here.
(Repeat ×4)

I hear the sound of a mighty river,
Of rushing water running free
To every land, through every border,
Flowing now across this earth.

There is a time I know is coming,
When all God's people join as one;
They will become a great awakening,
Bringing life to all the world.

And the river is flowing,
Getting wider and wider,
Deeper and deeper
As it flows from the throne;
And the leaves on the trees
Are for the healing of the nations,
It's as clear as crystal,
It's the water of life.

1022 Geoff Bullock
Copyright © 1997 Watershed
Productions/Kingsway Music

THE EARTH RESOUNDS IN SONGS OF PRAISE
Creation shouts Your glorious name,
And the skies speak forth Your majesty,
And the heavens declare Your glory.
Your kingdom rules from age to age;
Every tribe and tongue shall bring You praise
And we come to bow before the throne
Of the Lord of the heavens and earth.

Jesus, King of kings,
Jesus, Lord of lords,
We proclaim Your kingdom come,
Jesus, Son of God.
Lord, enthroned on high
Above the heavens and the earth,
We proclaim Your kingdom come!

023 Judy Pruett
Copyright © 1990 Judy Pruett/
Kingsway Music

HE GRACE OF GOD upon my life
 not dependent upon me,
 n what I have done
 r deserved,
 ut a gift of mercy from God
 Vhich has been given unto me
 ecause of His love,
 is love for me.

 is unending, unfailing,
 nlimited, unmerited,
 he grace of God given unto me.
 is unending, unfailing,
 nlimited, unmerited,
 he grace of God given unto me.

024 Lex Loizides
Copyright © 1997 Thankyou Music

HE HEAVENS THEY PREACH, they preach,
 hey preach the glorious splendour of God.
 he stars in the sky seem so out of reach,
 et they whisper His wonderful love.
 ay after day in a sermon of nature
 he works of His hands lift their voice:
 Vake up, you nations, and serve Your Creator,
 here's mercy in Him, so rejoice!'

 And I'll lift my heart and my hands to Him,
 And I'll let my life shine with love
 To God's wonderful Son.
 He wears the crown, He's the King.
 Come and behold Him now,
 Come and delight in His excellent virtues;
 Seek Him while He can be found,
 For He is the help and the hope
 For all the world.

 he prophets, they preached, they preached,
 hey preached that one day a Saviour would
  come;
 nd suddenly men heard a heavenly speech,
 he voice of God's only Son.
 ay after day in the streets and the temple
 e taught them and met their needs,
 nd now through His death and His great
  resurrection
 is glorious purpose succeeds.

Your people will preach, we'll preach,
We'll preach the unfailing riches of Christ;
There's no one who's fallen too far from His
  reach,
Who can't come from death into life.
Day after day at the dawn of revival
The multitudes seek His face,
As we work to speed on His final arrival
And crown Him with glory and praise!

1025 Stuart Townend & J. K. Jamieson
Copyright © 1997 Thankyou Music

THE KING OF LOVE is my delight,
His eyes are fire, His face is light,
The First and Last, the Living One,
His name is Jesus.
And from His mouth there comes a sound
That shakes the earth and splits the ground,
And yet this voice is life to me,
The voice of Jesus.

 And I will sing my songs of love,
 Calling out across the earth;
 The King has come,
 The King of love has come.
 And troubled minds can know His peace,
 Captive hearts can be released;
 The King has come,
 The King of love has come.

My Lover's breath is sweetest wine,
I am His prize, and He is mine;
How can a sinner know such joy?
Because of Jesus.
The wounds of love are in His hands,
The price is paid for sinful man;
Accepted child, forgiven son,
Because of Jesus.

And my desire is to have You near;
Lord, You know that You are welcome here.
Before such love, before such grace
I will let the walls come down.

1026 Donald Fishel
Copyright © 1974 The Word of God Music/
Adm. by CopyCare

THE LIGHT OF CHRIST
Has come into the world;
The light of Christ
Has come into the world.

All men must be born again
To see the kingdom of God;
The water and the Spirit
Bring new life in God's love.

God gave up His only Son
Out of love for the world,
So that all men who believe in Him
Will live for ever.

The light of God has come to us
So that we might have salvation;
From the darkness of our sins we walk
Into glory with Christ Jesus.

1027 Merrilyn Billing
Copyright © 1989 Arise Ministries/
Kingsway Music

THE LORD FILLS ME WITH HIS STRENGTH,
And protects me wherever I go.
The Lord fills me with His strength,
And protects me wherever I go.

Wherever I go, wherever I go,
The Lord protects me wherever I go.
Wherever I go, wherever I go,
The Lord protects me wherever I go.

1028 Paul Oakley
Copyright © 1991 Thankyou Music

THE LORD HAS SPOKEN. *(Men/Women echo)*
His purpose stands. *(Men/Women echo)*
The Lord has spoken. *(Men/Women echo)*
His purpose stands. *(Men/Women echo)*

Does God speak and then not act?
Make a vow and not fulfil?
I will choose to serve the Lord
Wholeheartedly, wholeheartedly.

(Ch 1.)
Oh, raise up a church
With a different spirit,
Like Caleb's spirit, believing Your word.
Oh, raise up a church who will not sin,
They press on in to possess the land.

You began with just one man,
A covenant with Abraham,
Promising that through his seed
The nations would be blessed,
And now Your plan is manifest.

(Repeat Ch1.)

(Ch 2.)
Oh, raise up a church who walk by faith,
In the fear of God they overcome.
Oh, raise up a church
Whose God is with them,
They walk in wisdom, they fear no harm.

Deliver us from the fear of man,
And by Your grace we shall stand.
We'll call to mind Your mighty works
And Your acts of sovereign power;
We'll gather strength as we agree
The battle belongs to the Lord.

(Repeat Ch1. & Ch2.)

(Ch 3.)
Oh, raise up a church
Who revere Your judgements,
They lift up a banner of mercy and love.
Oh, raise up a church
Who'll not keep silent,
They speak of the glory of Your dear Son

1029 Daniel C. Stradwick
Copyright © 1980 Scripture in Song
(a div. of Integrity Music, Inc.)/
Sovereign Music UK

THE LORD REIGNS, *the Lord reigns,*
The Lord reigns,
Let the earth rejoice, let the earth rejoice
Let the earth rejoice.
Let the people be glad
That our God reigns.

A fire goes before Him
And burns up all His enemies;
The hills melt like wax
At the presence of the Lord,
At the presence of the Lord.

The heavens declare His righteousness,
The peoples see His glory;
For You, O Lord, are exalted
Over all the earth,
Over all the earth.

1030 Stuart Townend
Copyright © 1996 Thankyou Music

THE LORD'S MY SHEPHERD, I'll not want.
He makes me lie in pastures green.
He leads me by the still, still waters,
His goodness restores my soul.

And I will trust in You alone.
And I will trust in You alone,
For Your endless mercy follows me,
Your goodness will lead me home.

(Descant)
I will trust, I will trust in You.
I will trust, I will trust in You.
Endless mercy follows me,
Goodness will lead me home.

guides my ways in righteousness,
nd He anoints my head with oil,
nd my cup, it overflows with joy,
east on His pure delights.

nd though I walk the darkest path,
will not fear the evil one,
r You are with me, and Your rod and staff
e the comfort I need to know.

031 Geoff Bullock
Copyright © 1997 Watershed Productions/
Kingsway Music

HE LOVE OF GOD, heaven's hope;
his perfect peace, this rest for my soul.
his love divine, portrayed in pain,
he cross stands alone,
nfailing love.

his love of God, creation's cry;
erfection portrayed, broken for me.
he Author of life has suffered our pain.
he cross stands alone,
nfailing love.

The love of God was found in the nails;
The love of God was seen in the scars.
The light and the life was darkened by
*   death,*
My hope and salvation carried to life,
Unfailing love.

he love of God, written in blood;
his empty grave, the stone rolled away!
he mercy of God has triumphed in Christ.
he cross stands alone,
nfailing love.

032 Louise & Nathan Fellingham
Copyright © 1997 Thankyou Music

HE NAME OF THE LORD is a strong tower;
he name of the Lord brings refuge and
strength.
he name of the Lord gives hope to the
hopeless;
he name of the Lord breathes life to the
dead.

he name of the Lord give strength to the
weary,
he name of the Lord brings freedom from
fear;
he name of the Lord gives peace to the
restless,
he name of the Lord will heal the oppressed.

O Lord, You never change,
Holy God, You remain the same,
For Your love, it never fades,
Your faithfulness surrounds me.

For You alone are God, and I bow before
*   You.*
You alone are God, I worship, adore You.
You alone are God, none other before You,
And I offer up my life again.

The name of the Lord covers me with mercy,
The name of the Lord brings everlasting joy;
The name of the Lord will lift all my
    burdens,
The name of the Lord, it makes me
    complete.

I call, and You answer me,
For You know my every need.
In Your love I put my trust,
Your faithfulness surrounds me.

O taste and see
That the Lord is good.
How blessèd is the man
Who hides himself in Him.

1033 Stuart Townend
Copyright © 1994 Thankyou Music

THERE IS A HOME that wanderers seek,
There is a strength that lifts the weak;
There is hope for those that know despair.
There is a cup that satisfies,
There is a Friend who dries my eyes;
There is peace for those with heavy hearts.

Tender mercy,
The tender mercy of our God,
From lips of sinners
He has heard the faintest cry.
Tender mercy,
The tender mercy of our God,
He has relented and His grace is my
*   delight.*

I have resolved to know Him more,
He whom the hosts of heaven adore,
Mighty King, whose reign will never end.
Yet as I gaze at the Holy One,
He beckons me to closer come,
Bares the scars that show to me my worth.

1034 Matt Redman
Copyright © 1996 Thankyou Music

THERE IS A LOUDER SHOUT TO COME,
There is a sweeter song to hear;
All the nations with one voice,
All the people with one fear.
Bowing down before Your throne,
Every tribe and tongue will be;
All the nations with one voice,
All the people with one King.
And what a song we'll sing upon that day.

O what a song we'll sing and
O what a tune we'll bear;
You deserve an anthem of the highest
*   praise.*
O what a joy will rise and
O what a sound we'll make;
You deserve an anthem of the highest
*   praise.*

Now we see a part of this,
One day we shall see in full;
All the nations with one voice,
All the people with one love.
No one else will share Your praise,
Nothing else can take Your place;
All the nations with one voice,
All the people with one Lord.
And what a song we'll sing upon that day.

Even now upon the earth
There's a glimpse of all to come;
Many people with one voice,
Harmony of many tongues.
We will all confess Your name,
You will be our only praise;
All the nations with one voice,
All the people with one God.
And what a song we'll sing upon that day.

1035 Lenny LeBlanc
Copyright © 1991 Integrity's Hosanna! Music/
Sovereign Music UK

THERE IS NONE LIKE YOU,
No one else can touch my heart like You do.
I could search for all eternity long and find
There is none like You.

Your mercy flows like a river wide,
And healing comes from Your hands.
Suffering children are safe in Your arms;
There is none like You.

1036 Noel & Tricia Richards
Copyright © 1996 Thankyou Music

THERE IS NO ONE LIKE OUR GOD *in all*
*   the earth.*
There is no one like our God in all the
*   earth.*
No one like our God,
No one like our God.

Our God has made the heavens,
Our God has made the earth;
And everything that lives,
His word has brought to birth.

He numbers every star,
And calls each one by name;
He fills the skies with clouds,
Supplies the earth with rain.

Sing praises to our God,
Sing praises to His name;
His love will never end,
His word will never fail.

God is with us.
God is with us.
God is with us.

1037 David Ruis
Copyright © 1996 Mercy/Vineyard Publishing/
Adm. by CopyCare

THERE IS NO OTHER FRIEND,
There is no other friend like You, O Lord;
No other brother, no other sister like You.
There is no other love,
There is no other love like You, O Lord;
No other sweeter, no other fountain but Yo

How long until I'm satisfied?
I must have more of You.
For I was born in Zion,
Awakened love is crying out for You.
Lord, it must be You!

If I am healed by just one touch of Your
   garment, Lord,
Then how much more of Your love is for m
Than I'm tasting, Lord?
Draw me, take me, I will run
Over the mountains and down
Into the valley, I will run with You.

Ah, all my fountains are in You.
(Repeat)

1038 Robert Critchley
Copyright © 1993 Thankyou Music

HERE IS ONE NAME under heaven
By which men can be saved,
Jesus alone.
Only one name under heaven,
Jesus, and Jesus alone.

One sacrifice,
One holy Lamb
Shed His own blood,
Paid for my sin;
And this righteous One,
God's only Son,
I sing my praises to Him,
I sing my praises to Him.

1039 Geoff Bullock
Copyright © 1997 Watershed Productions/
Kingsway Music

HERE'S A LIGHT THAT SHINES, a lamp that
burns,
The hope, the peace of righteousness.
And You who hear the prayers of all,
You call us near to You.

There's a path that leads, a way that's true,
The life, the light, the perfect truth.
We come to You forgiven, free,
You call us near to You.

And the light shines so we can see,
And the truth came so we could know.
And the light of God is the light of men,
And His life gives life to all.

No other way, no other life,
No other truth, no other light.
The way ahead is found in Christ,
You call us near to You.

We will dance and sing, for freedom comes
To heal our hearts and dry our tears.
Forever more in glorious light
You call us near to You.

1040 Richard Lewis
Copyright © 1997 Thankyou Music

HERE'S AN AWESOME SOUND
On the winds of heaven,
Mighty thunder clouds
In the skies above.
The immortal King,
Who will reign for ever,
Is reaching out with His arms of love,
His arms of love,
His arms of love.

All creation sings
Of the Lamb of glory,
Who laid down His life
For all the world.
What amazing love,
That the King of heaven
Should be crucified,
Stretching out His arms,
His arms of love,
His arms of love.

Send revival to this land,
Fill this nation with Your love.
(Repeat)

1041 Paul Oakley
Copyright © 1995 Thankyou Music

**THERE'S A PLACE WHERE THE STREETS
SHINE**
With the glory of the Lamb.
There's a way, we can go there,
We can live there beyond time.

Because of You, because of You,
Because of Your love,
Because of Your blood.

No more pain, no more sadness,
No more suffering, no more tears.
No more sin, no more sickness,
No injustice, no more death.

Because of You, because of You,
Because of Your love,
Because of Your blood.

All our sins are washed away,
And we can live for ever,
Now we have this hope,
Because of You.
Oh, we'll see You face to face,
And we will dance together
In the city of our God,
Because of You.

There is joy everlasting,
There is gladness, there is peace.
There is wine ever flowing,
There's a wedding, there's a feast.

THERE'S A RIVER flowing from the throne,
Not a gentle stream but powerful flow.
It brings the city of our God such joy,
And springs up fountains in her midst.
On the banks the trees are full of life,
The fruit just grows and grows all the year
   round.
The leaves are green and never seem to die,
They're for the healing of this world.

    There's a river, there's a river,
    There's a river flowing from the throne.
    There's a river, there's a river
    And it flows through out the world.
    There's a river, there's a river,
    There's a river flowing from the throne.
    There's a river, there's a river
    And it's flooding over me.

You invited me to come for free,
Enjoy the feast You had prepared for me;
Draw with laughter from Your sparkling wells,
Bathe in Your river of delights.
First You led me to the edge of the stream,
Cautiously I put my ankles in;
The thrill was just too much to describe,
And I heard You call me deeper still!

THERE'S A RIVER OF JOY that flows from
   Your throne,
O river of joy flow through me.
There's a river of joy that flows from Your throne:
Come, Holy Spirit, with joy,
Come, Holy Spirit, with joy.

I will rise up on the wings of an eagle;
With joy I receive Your love.
I will praise You with a song everlasting.
Thank You, Lord, for Your love.
Thank You, Lord, for Your love.

THERE'S A WIND A-BLOWING
All across the land;
Fragrant breeze of heaven
Blowing once again.
Don't know where it comes from,
Don't know where it goes,
But let it blow over me.
Oh, sweet wind,
Come and blow over me.

There's a rain a-pouring,
Showers from above;
Mercy drops are coming,
Mercy drops of love.
Turn your face to heaven,
Let the water pour,
Well, let it pour over me.
Oh, sweet rain,
Come and pour over me.

There's a fire burning,
Falling from the sky;
Awesome tongues of fire,
Consuming you and I.
Can you feel it burning,
Burn the sacrifice?
Well, let it burn over me.
Oh, sweet fire,
Come and burn over me.

THERE'S NO ONE LIKE YOU, my Lord,
No one could take Your place;
My heart beats to worship You,
I live just to seek Your face.
There's no one like You, my Lord,
No one could take Your place;
There's no one like You, my Lord,
No one like You.

    You are my God,
    You're everything to me;
    There's no one like You, my Lord,
    No one like You.
    You are my God.
    You're everything to me;
    There's no one like You, my Lord,
    No one like You.

There's no one like You, my Lord,
No one could take Your place;
I long for Your presence, Lord,
To serve You is my reward.
There's no one like You, my Lord,
No one could take Your place;
There's no one like You, my Lord,
No one like You.

HERE'S NOTHING I LIKE BETTER HAN TO PRAISE.

here's nothing I like better
han to praise.
'ause Lord, I love You,
nd there's nothing I would rather do
han whisper about it,
lk all about it.
hout all about it all my days.

HESE ARE THE DAYS OF ELIJAH,

eclaring the word of the Lord:
nd these are the days of Your servant
  Moses,
ghteousness being restored.
nd though these are days of great trial,
f famine and darkness and sword,
ill, we are a voice in the desert crying
repare ye the way of the Lord.'

Behold He comes riding on the clouds,
Shining like the sun at the trumpet call;
Lift your voice, it's the year of jubilee,
Out of Zion's hill salvation comes.

nese are the days of Ezekiel,
ne dry bones becoming as flesh;
nd these are the days of Your servant David,
ebuilding the temple of praise.
nese are the days of the harvest,
ne fields are as white in the world,
nd we are the labourers in the vineyard,
eclaring the word of the Lord.

HE SKY IS FILLED with the glory of God.

iumphantly the angels sing:
ejoice, good news, a Saviour is born,
nd life will never be the same.'

Emmanuel.
Emmanuel.
Emmanuel.

aise and adoration spring from our hearts,
'e lift our voices unto You;
ou are the One, God's only Son,
ng of kings for evermore!

THE SPIRIT OF THE SOVEREIGN LORD is

upon you,
Because He has anointed you
To preach good news.
(Repeat)

He has sent you to the poor, *(Men)*
This is the year: *(Women)*
To bind up the brokenhearted, *(Men)*
This is the day: *(Women)*
To bring freedom to the captives, *(Men)*
This is the year: *(Women)*
And to release the ones in darkness. *(All)*

> *This is the year of the favour of the Lord.*
> *This is the day of the vengeance of our*
>   *God.*
> *This is the year of the favour of the Lord.*
> *This is the day of the vengeance of our*
>   *God.*

The Spirit of the Sovereign Lord is upon us,
Because He has anointed us
To preach good news.
(Repeat)

He will comfort all who mourn *(Men)*
This is the year: *(Women)*
He will provide for those who grieve; *(Men)*
This is the day: *(Women)*
He will pour out the oil of gladness, *(Men)*
This is the year: *(Women)*
Instead of mourning you will praise. *(All)*

THE VIRGIN MARY HAD A BABY BOY,

The Virgin Mary had a baby boy,
The Virgin Mary had a baby boy,
And they said that His name was Jesus.

> *He come from the glory,*
> *He come from the glorious kingdom.*
> *He come from the glory,*
> *He come from the glorious kingdom.*
> *Oh, yes! believer.*
> *Oh, yes! believer.*
> *He come from the glory,*
> *He come from the glorious kingdom.*

The angels sang when the baby was born,
The angels sang when the baby was born,
The angels sang when the baby was born,
And proclaiming Him the Saviour Jesus.

The wise men saw where the baby was born,
The wise men saw where the baby was born,
The wise men saw where the baby was born,
And they saw that His name was Jesus.

1051 Dave Bilbrough
Copyright © 1996 Thankyou Music

THE WAVES ARE BREAKING, the tide is
    turning,
God's Spirit is coming to this earth;
The harvest is waiting,
And we have been called
To go to the nations of this world.

> *To the ends of the earth,*
> *To the ends of the earth,*
> *To the ends of the earth we will go;*
> *Bearing the message*
> *That our God can be known,*
> *To the ends of the earth we will go.*

The fire is falling, the wind is blowing,
The flame is spreading across our land;
Revival is coming, let the world hear,
Tell every woman, child and man.

The drums are beating,
The trumpet is sounding,
A warrior spirit He's put in our hearts;
In the name of the Father, Spirit and Son,
We'll take this word to everyone.

1052 Noel & Tricia Richards
Copyright © 1994 Thankyou Music

THE WORLD IS LOOKING FOR A HERO;
We know the greatest One of all:
The mighty Ruler of the nations,
King of kings and Lord of lords;
Who took the nature of a servant,
And gave His life to save us all.

> *We will raise a shout,*
> *We will shout it out,*
> *He is the Champion of the world.*
> (Repeat)

The Lord Almighty is our hero,
He breaks the stranglehold of sin.
Through Jesus' love we fear no evil;
Powers of darkness flee from Him.
His light will shine in every nation,
A sword of justice He will bring.

1053 K. Prosch
Copyright © 1995 Liber Media &
Publishing, LLC/Kingsway Music

THEY THAT WAIT ON THE LORD
Will renew their strength,
Run and not get weary,
Walk and not faint.
(Repeat)

Do you not know?
Have you not heard?
My Father does not get weary.
He'll give passion to a willing heart:
Even the youths get tired and faint,
But strength will come for those who wait.

If you wait on the Lord
You'll renew your strength,
Run and not get weary,
Walk and not faint.
(Repeat)

I will wait, I will wait, I will wait on You;
I will run, I will run, I will run with You;
My love, my love, my love for You.

1054 Christopher Idle
Copyright © Christopher Idle/
Jubilate Hymns Ltd

THIS EARTH BELONGS TO GOD,
The world, its wealth, and all its people;
He formed the waters wide
And fashioned every sea and shore.
Who may go up the hill of the Lord
And stand in the place of holiness?
Only the one whose heart is pure,
Whose hands and lips are clean.

Lift high your heads, you gates,
Rise up, you everlasting doors,
As here now the King of glory
Enters into full command.
Who is the King, this King of glory?
Where is the throne He comes to claim?
Christ is the King, the Lord of glory,
Fresh from His victory.

Lift high your heads, you gates,
And fling wide open the ancient doors,
For here comes the King of glory
Taking universal power.
Who is the king, this King of glory,
What is the power by which He reigns?
Christ is the King, His cross His glory,
And by love He rules.

All glory be to God
The Father, Son and Holy Spirit;
From ages past it was,
Is now, and ever more shall be.

1055 Kent Henry & David Ortinau
Copyright © 1995 Kent Henry Ministries/
Kingsway Music

THIS GOD IS OUR GOD,
God of power, God of might.
This God is our God,
God of wisdom and light.
(Repeat)

And we meditate on Your great love,
Your praises fill the earth.
The villages of Judah shout
That you will be, for ever be
Our guide unto the end.

As we have heard, so we have seen
The safety of our God,
That we might tell all generations
You will be, for ever be
Our guide unto the end.

1056 Mark Altrogge
Copyright © 1992 People of Destiny
International/Word Music/
Adm. by CopyCare

THIS I KNOW, *my God is for me,*
This I know.
This I know, my God is on my side;
My God is for me, this I know.

If God did not spare His only Son,
But delivered Him up for us all,
Will He not give us every good thing
When we come in His name and call?

Let us draw near the throne of grace
For mercy and help in our need;
For Jesus is ever praying for us,
He is living to intercede.

1057 Christopher Beatty
Copyright © 1979 Birdwing Music/
BMG Songs Inc./EMI Christian Music Publishing/
Adm. by CopyCare

THIS IS HOLY GROUND,
We're standing on holy ground,
For the Lord is here
And where He is holy.
This is holy ground,
We're standing on holy ground,
For the Lord is here
And where He is holy.

These are holy hands,
He's given us holy hands,
He works through these hands
And so these hands are holy.
These are holy hands,
He's given us holy hands,
He works through these hands
And so these hands are holy.

1058 Graham Kendrick
Copyright © 1985 Thankyou Music

THIS IS MY BELOVÈD SON
Who tasted death
That you, my child, might live.
See the blood He shed for you,
What suffering!
Say what more could He give?
Clothed in His perfection,
Bring praise, a fragrance sweet,
Garlanded with joy,
Come worship at His feet:

> *That the Lamb who was slain*
> *Might receive the reward,*
> *Might receive the reward of His*
> *suffering.*

Look, the world's great harvest fields
Are ready now,
And Christ commands us: 'Go!'
Countless souls are dying
So hopelessly,
His wondrous love unknown.
Lord, give us the nations
For the glory of the King.
Father, send more labourers,
The lost to gather in.

Come the day when we will stand
There face to face,
What joy will fill His eyes.
For at last His Bride appears,
So beautiful,
Her glory fills the skies.
Drawn from every nation,
People, tribe and tongue;
All creation sings,
The wedding has begun.

> *And the Lamb who was slain*
> *Shall receive the reward,*
> *Shall receive the reward of His*
> *suffering.*

1059 Sue Rinaldi
Copyright © 1996 Thankyou Music

THIS IS MY PILGRIMAGE,
To climb into You.
This is my pilgrimage,
To be absorbed by You.

I'm so restless for more of You, O God.
I'm so restless, hear these words, O God.

Give me the eyes of a prophet,
Help me to see the unseen,
I long to hear the music of heaven,
As the angels play in my ears.
Sometimes I'm war torn and weary,
Sometimes I'm willing and strong,
But at this moment I'm standing before You
As Your restless pilgrim.

I'll fix my eyes on You,
I'll tread the path with You,
I'll be a warrior of love for You.

But I'm so restless . . .

1060 Phil Lawson Johnston & Chris Bowater
Copyright © 1992 Sovereign Lifestyle Music

THIS IS THE MYSTERY,
That Christ has chosen you and me
To be the revelation of His glory;
A chosen, royal, holy people,
Set apart and loved,
A Bride preparing for her King.

Let the Bride say 'come',
Let the Bride say 'come',
Let the Bride of the Lamb
Say 'come, Lord Jesus!'
Let the Bride say 'come',
Let the Bride say 'come',
Let the Bride of the Lamb
Say 'come, Lord Jesus, come!'

She's crowned in splendour
And a royal diadem,
The King is enthralled by her beauty.
Adorned in righteousness,
Arrayed in glorious light,
The Bride in waiting for her King.

Now hear the Bridegroom call,
'Beloved, come aside;
The time of betrothal is at hand.
Lift up your eyes and see
The dawning of the day,
When as King, I'll return to claim My Bride.'

1061 Dave Bilbrough
Copyright © 1997 Thankyou Music

THIS IS THE PLACE
Where dreams are found,
Where vision comes,
Called holy ground.

Holy ground,
I'm standing on holy ground,
For the Lord my God
Is here with me.

Your fire burns
But never dies;
I realise
This is holy ground.

The Great I AM,
Revealed to man;
Take off your shoes,
This is holy ground.

1062 Geoff Bullock
Copyright © 1994 Maranatha! Music/
Word Music/Adm. by CopyCare

THIS LOVE, this hope,
This peace of God, this righteousness,
This faith, this joy,
This life complete in me.

Now healed and whole,
And risen in His righteousness,
I live in Him,
He lives in me,
And filled with this hope in God,
Reflecting His glory.

Now is the time to worship You,
Now is the time to offer You
All of my thoughts, my dreams and plans;
I lay it down.
Now is the time to live for You,
Now is the time I'm found in You.
Now is the time Your kingdom comes.

1063 Ian White
Copyright © 1996 Thankyou Music

THOUGH I FEEL AFRAID
Of territory unknown,
I know that I can say
That I do not stand alone.
For Jesus, You have promised
Your presence in my heart;
I cannot see the ending,
But it's here that I must start.

And all I know is You have called me,
And that I will follow as I can say.
I will go where You will send me,
And Your fire lights my way.

What lies across the waves
May cause my heart to fear;
Will I survive the day,
Must I leave what's known and dear?
A ship that's in the harbour
Is still and safe from harm,
But it was not built to be there,
It was made for wind and storm.

1064 James Wright
Copyright © 1996 James Wright

**THROUGHOUT THE EARTH YOUR GLORY
WILL COME,**
A day of power, of salvation.
To thirsty hearts Your rivers will run,
Changing lives for the glory of God.
From Satan's hold this land will be free,
The deaf will hear, the blind will see;
To walk in truth, in victory,
To live for the glory of God.

Lord, come and reign by the power of
Your Spirit,
Shower this land with Your rivers of
life,
That Jesus the Son would be glorified
Within the heart of Your Bride,
Lord, come and reign.

Upon the earth may Your kingdom come,
Within our lives may Your will be done;
Under the reign of Jesus the Son
We will live for the glory of God.
The gates of heaven are open wide,
To bless this land, to turn back the tide,
To welcome in Your glorious Bride,
To live for the glory of God.

1065 Edward H. Plumptre (1821–91)

THY HAND, O GOD HAS GUIDED
Thy flock, from age to age;
The wondrous tale is written,
Full clear on every page.
Our fathers owned Thy goodness,
And we their deeds record;
And both of this bear witness:
One Church, one Faith, one Lord.

Thy heralds brought glad tidings
To greatest as to least;
They bade them rise and hasten
To share the great King's feast.
And this was all their teaching
In every deed and word;
To all alike proclaiming:
One Church, one Faith, one Lord.

Through many a day of darkness,
Through many a scene of strife,
The faithful few fought bravely
To guard the nation's life.
Their gospel of redemption,
Sin pardoned, man restored,
Was all in this enfolded:
One Church, one Faith, one Lord.

Thy mercy will not fail us,
Nor leave Thy work undone;
With Thy right hand to help us,
The victory shall be won.
And then, by men and angels,
Thy name shall be adored,
And this shall be their anthem:
One Church, one Faith, one Lord.

1066 Amy Grant & Michael W. Smith
Copyright © Bug & Bear Music/
LCS Music Group Inc./Meadowgreen Music/
EMI Christian Music Publishing/
Adm. by CopyCare

THY WORD *is a lamp unto my feet*
And a light unto my path.
(Repeat)

When I feel afraid,
Think I've lost my way,
Still You're there right beside me.
And nothing will I fear
As long as You are near;
Please be near me to the end.

I will not forget
Your love for me, and yet
My heart for ever is wandering.
Jesus, be my guide
And hold me to Your side,
And I will love You to the end.

1067 Noel Richards
Copyright © 1991 Thankyou Music

TO BE IN YOUR PRESENCE,
To sit at Your feet,
Where Your love surrounds me,
And makes me complete.

This is my desire, O Lord,
This is my desire.
This is my desire, O Lord,
This is my desire.

To rest in Your presence,
Not rushing away;
To cherish each moment,
Here I would stay.

1068
Bryn Haworth
Copyright © 1996 Thankyou Music

TO HIM WHO LOVES US,
And has freed us from our sins
By His blood,
And has made us to be a kingdom
And priests to serve His God.
(Repeat)
And Father.

> (Men-Women echo each line)
> *To Him be glory*
> *And power*
> *Forever*
> *And ever.*
> *To Him be glory*
> *And power*
> *Forever,*
> *Amen.* (Together)

1069
Sue Rinaldi & Steve Bassett
Copyright © 1988 Authentic Publishing/
Adm. by CopyCare

TO YOUR MAJESTY,
And Your beauty I surrender.
To Your holiness,
And Your love I surrender.
For You are an awesome God who is mighty,
You deserve my deepest praise;
With all of my heart,
With all of my life I surrender.

1070
Kirk & Debbye Dearman
Copyright © Ariose Music/EMI Christian
Music Publishing/Adm. by CopyCare

VISIT US, O LORD, with Your awesome
  presence.
Dwell in our midst in Your glory and power,
In Your strength and in Your love.

This is our cry, O Lord,
Let Your presence fill this place,
Fill this place.
(Repeat)

1071
Mick Gisbey
Copyright © 1995 Thankyou Music

WAITING FOR YOUR SPIRIT,
Thirsty for Your Spirit;
Touching us, Lord, as we pray,
Filling our lives with You again.
Fall on us, Lord,
As we call on You.

1072
Matt Redman
Copyright © 1994 Thankyou Music

WAKE UP, MY SOUL,
Worship the Lord of truth and life.
Have strength, my heart,
Press on as one who seeks the prize.
I'll run for You, my God and King,
I'll run as one who runs to win.
I'm pressing on, not giving in.
I will run, I will run for You, my King.

And Spirit come, give life to us,
Come breathe the Father's love in us.
Won't You fill us once again?
And we will run and run with Him.
We'll run with strength,
With all our might,
We'll fix our eyes on Jesus Christ;
He has conquered death and sin,
And we will run and run and run
With Him.

1073
Nathan Fellingham
Copyright © 1996 Thankyou Music

WAKE UP, WAKE UP O SLEEPER,
And rise from the dead.
(Repeat)

We are His people drawn by grace,
Chosen by His glorious name,
Called to give Him all our praise,
Set apart to worship Him.
We must be humble now and pray,
And turn from all our careless ways,
And in our hearts wait for the hour
For Christ to come in awesome power.

We are called to righteousness,
To be like God in holiness;
So let all slander now subside,
And flee from bitterness and rage.
And soon the night will fade away,
And in its place will come the day;
So we must clothe ourselves in light,
The armour that will help us fight.

Revere the name of the Lord,
And He will shine on you;
He will arise with healing
And set you free.

1074 Maggi Dawn
Copyright © 1994 Thankyou Music

WASH ME CLEAN in that cool river;
Wash my soul in the pure water.
Wash me clean in that cool river;
Lord, make me new.

1075 Kevin Prosch
Copyright © 1991 Mercy/Vineyard
Publishing/Adm. by CopyCare

WE ARE HIS PEOPLE,
He gives us music to sing.
There is a sound now,
Like the sound of the Lord when His enemies
 flee.
But there is a cry in our hearts,
Like when deep calls unto the deep,
For Your breath of deliverance,
To breathe on the music we so desperately
 need.

But without Your power
All we have are these simple songs.
If You'd step down from heaven,
Then the gates of hell would surely fall.

Shout to the Lord, shout to the Lord,
Shout to the Lord of Hosts.
Shout to the Lord, shout to the Lord,
Shout to the Lord of Hosts.
And it breaks the heavy yoke, breaks the
 heavy yoke
When you shout, you shout to the Lord.
It breaks the heavy yoke, breaks the heavy
 yoke,
When you shout, you shout to the Lord.

1076 Tr. Anders Nyberg (v.1) & Andrew Maries (vv.2–3)
Copyright © 1987 Wild Goose Publications &
Sovereign Music UK

WE ARE MARCHING IN THE LIGHT OF GOD,
We are marching in the light of God.
(Repeat)

We are marching, marching,
We are marching, marching,
We are marching in the light of God.
(Repeat)

Siyahamb' ekukhanyen' kwenkhos',
Siyahamb' ekukhanyen' kwenkhos'.
(Repeat)

Siyahamba, hamba, siyahamba, hamba,
Siyahamb' ekukhanyen' kwenkhos'.
(Repeat)

We are living in the love of God...

We are moving in the power of God...

1077 Lex Loizides
Copyright © 1997 Thankyou Music

**WE ARE MARCHING TO A DIFFERENT
 ANTHEM,**
We are dancing to a different song;
And our hearts have come alive with freedom,
Mercy has come, the God of mercy has come.
He is moving through the towns and cities,
He is binding up the broken ones;
And His healing hand is working wonders,
See how they come, He sets them free when
 they come.
And I sing:

I love the God of heaven,
I love His precious Son;
And in the Holy Spirit,
He's making us strong,
And giving us the victory.
I love the God of heaven,
I love His precious Son;
And in the Holy Spirit,
He's making us strong,
And giving us a victory song.

He is training up our hands for battle,
And equipping us to take the land;
For the promises to us are mighty,
We will be strong, and move together as
 one.
We are heading for our finest hour,
When our Saviour will be magnified,
And His glory will outshine all others:
Jesus is Lord, let Him be praised and
 adored.
And I sing:

1078 Bob Fitts
Copyright © 1992 Integrity's Hosanna! Music/
Sovereign Music UK

WE ARE SALT and we are the light;
We've come to break the powers of night,
And by the love of God proclaim His liberty.
We're ambassadors of grace,
In His name we take this place;
Lord, let Your will be done,
Let Your kingdom come,
Lord, let it rain, let it rain.

Let Your blessings pour
On the nations, Lord, let it rain.
Let Your blessings pour
On the nations, Lord, let it rain.
As we sing Your praises,
Break the curses, let it rain.
Hear Your people praying,
Send Your blessing, let it rain.
Oh, let it rain.

You have won the fight, O Lord;
By Your death our life's been restored,
And You have risen now
To vanquish all our foes.
Come, abolish every curse
O'er the nations of the earth;
In Your name we'll go,
To proclaim You rose to live and reign.
Lord, come and reign.

1079

WE ARE THE ARMY OF GOD,
Sons of Abraham,
We are a chosen generation.
Under a covenant,
Washed by His precious blood,
Filled with the mighty Holy Ghost.

And I hear the sound of the coming rain,
As we sing the praise to the great I AM.
And the sick are healed,
And the dead shall rise,
And Your church is the army that was
   prophesied.

1080

WE ARE YOUR INHERITANCE,
We are Your reward.
(Repeat)
And You're our glory
And the lifter of our heads;
You're our glory
And the lifter of our heads.

Listen, can you hear it?
The Spirit and the Bride.
(Repeat)
Whisper 'Jesus!
Maranatha! Come!'
Whisper 'Jesus!
Maranatha! Come!'

O come, O come to us!
O come, O come to us!
Jesus, Jesus, Jesus!
O come, O come to us!

1081

WE ASK YOU, O LORD,
For the rain of Your Spirit.
We ask You, O Lord,
For the rain of Your Spirit.
For now is the time,
For now is the time
Of the latter rain,
Of the latter rain.

Send Your rain, cleanse us by Your word;
Let us be Your pure and radiant Bride.
Make us strong, prepare us for revival;
Let us see the nations turn their hearts,
Let us see the nations turn their hearts,
Let us see the nations turn their hearts
To You, to You.

Send Your rain, mercy from heaven.
Send Your rain, the grace of Your Son.
Send Your rain, Word of Your power,
Send Your rain, come fill everyone.
(Repeat)

1082

WE BEHOLD YOUR GLORY,
Fountain of life, the Lord Jesus Christ.
Lord of the universe,
You die in weakness;
Strong Deliverer,
How You were wounded.
Sustainer of life,
Disfigured and shamed,
This is the medicine
That saves and heals us.
A crown of thorns
Was placed on Your brow;
Though You were scourged,
Blow after blow,
By Your stripes we are healed.

We behold Your glory,
Fountain of life, the Lord Jesus Christ.
Though You were fettered,
We are delivered;
Though You were condemned,
We are absolved.
Though You were exposed
To mocking and shame,
We are established
And raised up in honour.
Though You were laid
In the dust of death,
Though You went down
To hell's darkest depths,
The kingdom of heaven is ours.

1083 Ian Smale
Copyright © 1996 Thankyou Music

WE BELIEVE IN HEBREWS THIRTEEN, EIGHT,
Jesus Christ is never out of date.
If it's yesterday or today, or for evermore,
Jesus stays the same and that is great.

1084 Viola Grafstrom
Copyright © 1996 Thankyou Music

WE BOW DOWN and confess
You are Lord in this place.
We bow down and confess
You are Lord in this place.
You are all I need;
It's Your face I seek.
In the presence of Your light
We bow down, we bow down.

1085 Kevin Prosch
Copyright © 1991 Mercy/Vineyard
Publishing/Adm. by CopyCare

WE CONFESS THE SINS OF OUR NATION,
And, Lord, we are guilty
Of a prayerless life.
We've turned away our hearts from Your laws,
And have taken for granted Your unchanging
grace.
Turn away this curse from our country;
We say that we've robbed You,
And our storehouses are bare.
Open wide the floodgates of heaven,
Rebuke the devourer so we may not be
destroyed.

You said that if we'd humble ourselves
And begin to pray,
You would heal our barren land,
And cleanse us with Your rain.

Don't pass us by,
Let this be the generation, Lord,
That lifts up Your name to all the world.
Save us, O God,
Save a people for Yourself, O Lord,
Let the fear of the Lord be a standard.
Save us, O God,
Cleanse us from our unfaithfulness,
Let the place where we live
Be called a house of prayer.

 1086 Mark Altrogge
Copyright © 1988 Integrity's Praise! Music/
PDI Music/BMI/Adm. by Integrity's Praise! Music/
Sovereign Music UK

WE GIVE THANKS TO YOU, O Lord,
Almighty God,
The One who is, who was
And is to come.
You've taken up Your power
And begun to reign,
The nations bow before the Holy One.

Now Your salvation,
And Your power and Your kingdom
Have all come,
And You are Lord of all.
The accuser of the brothers
Has been hurled down for ever,
Overcome by the blood,
Overcome by the blood,
Overcome by the blood of the Lamb.

1087 Chris Falson
Copyright © 1990 Chris Falson Music/The
Copyright Company/Adm. by CopyCare

WE HAVE A VISION for this nation;
We share a dream for this land.
We join with angels in celebration,
By faith we speak revival to this land.

Where every knee shall bow and worship You,
And every tongue confess that You are Lord;
Give us an open heaven, anoint our prayers
this day,
And move Your sovereign hand across this
nation.

 1088 Stuart Garrard
Copyright © 1992 Thankyou Music

WE HAVE CALLED ON YOU, LORD,
And You have heard us.
We have called on Your name,
And You have answered.
Mercy has triumphed over judgement.
Mercy has triumphed over judgement.

You have stretched out Your hand,
And You have touched us,
Sent us Your holy fire,
And You have purged us.
Light has triumphed over darkness.
Light has triumphed over darkness.

We love You, and sing to You,
God of our salvation.
You've rescued us and we declare
Your glory to the nations.
We give our lives, a living sacrifice,
Empty and ready to be filled
With Your power.

1089 Robert Newey
Copyright © 1997 Thankyou Music

WE HAVE COME TO SEEK YOUR FACE,

Filled with wonder at Your grace,
Amazed at how You've come
And touched our lives.
But even as we've felt Your touch,
Desire for You has grown so much,
It only serves to make us realise
That the way ahead is in Your strength alone.
So we stand before You now and we cry,
'Lord, lead us on!'

'Cause after all You've brought us through,
We find we're even more dependent on You,
Not in power, not in might,
But through Your Spirit's guiding light.
We're driven by the things He says,
And glory in our weaknesses,
And knowing how we need You now, we
   come:
Here we stand before You.

And we will wait for You, wait for You;
Show us, Lord, what You would have us do.
We will wait for You, wait for You;
Show us, Lord, what You would have us do.

1090 Martin Smith
Copyright © 1994 Curious? Music UK/
Adm. by Bucks Music Ltd

WE HAVE FLOODED THE ALTAR with our
   tears;

We have wearied You, Lord, with our words.
Great God, our promises we've broken,
O Lord, forgive me.

You are breaking the pride in our hearts;
You have given us tears for the lost.
You crown the humble with salvation;
O Lord, humble me.

So lead me, oh lead me into Your arms;
I will be safe in the shadow of Your wing.
Lead me, oh lead me into Your arms;
I will be safe in Almighty.

You have paid back our sin with Your love;
Lover's arms You have offered us.
Faithful One, raise up a faithful people
Who find their treasure here.

1091 Paul Oakley
Copyright © 1994 Thankyou Music

WE HAVE PRAYED THAT YOU WOULD HAVE
   MERCY;

We believe from heaven You've heard.
Heal our land, so dry and so thirsty;
We have strayed so far from You, Lord.
Your cloud appeared on the horizon,
Small as a man's hand.
But now You're near,
Filling our vision,
Pour out Your Spirit again.

I felt the touch of Your wind on my face:
I feel the first drops of rain.

Let it rain, let it rain.
I will not be the same.
Let it rain, rain on me.
Let it pour down on me,
Let it rain.

Let it rain, let it rain,
Let it rain, let it rain on me.
Let it rain, let it rain,
Let it rain.

1092 Stuart Townend
Copyright © 1997 Thankyou Music

WE HAVE SUNG OUR SONGS OF VICTORY,

We have prayed to You for rain;
We have cried for Your compassion
To renew the land again.
Now we're standing in Your presence,
More hungry than before;
Now we're on Your steps of mercy,
And we're knocking at Your door.

How long before You drench the barren
*   land?*
How long before we see Your righteous
*   hand?*
How long before Your name is lifted high?
How long before the weeping turns to
*   songs of joy?*

Lord, we know Your heart is broken
By the evil that You see,
And You've stayed Your hand of judgement
For You plan to set men free.
But the land is still in darkness,
And we've fled from what is right;
We have failed the silent children
Who will never see the light.

But I know a day is coming
When the deaf will hear His voice,
When the blind will see their Saviour,
And the lame will leap for joy.
When the widow finds a Husband
Who will always love His bride,
And the orphan finds a Father
Who will never leave her side.

*How long before Your glory lights the
    skies?*
*How long before Your radiance lifts our
    eyes?*
How long before Your fragrance fills the air?
*How long before the earth resounds with
    songs of joy?*

 1093   Noel Richards
            Copyright © 1991 Thankyou Music

WELCOME, KING OF KINGS!
How great is Your name.
You come in majesty
Forever to reign.

You rule the nations,
They shake at the sound of Your name.
To You is given all power,
And You shall reign.

Let all creation bow down
At the sound of Your name.
Let every tongue now confess,
The Lord God reigns.

 1094   David Fellingham
            Copyright © 1997 Thankyou Music

WE LIFT UP OUR HEADS,
And we will sing our praise
To Him who sits on the throne.
We lift up our heads
To the King of kings,
Who reigns in heaven and earth.

Holy and mighty,
Awesome in power,
Full of compassion
And love.

Glorious in holiness,
Fearful in praises,
Working His wonders
In us.

1095   Martin Smith
            Copyright © 1994 Curious? Music UK/
            Adm. by Bucks Music Ltd

WELL, I HEAR THEY'RE SINGING in the
    streets
That Jesus is alive,
And all creation shouts aloud
That Jesus is alive.
Now surely we can all be changed
'cause Jesus is alive;
And everybody here can know
That Jesus is alive.

And I will live for all my days
To raise a banner of truth and light,
To sing about my Saviour's love—
And the best thing that happened,
It was the day I met You.

I've found Jesus.
I've found Jesus.
I've found Jesus.
I've found Jesus.

Well, I feel like dancing in the streets
'Cause Jesus is alive,
To join with all who celebrate
That Jesus is alive.
The joy of God is in this town
'Cause Jesus is alive;
For everybody's seen the truth
That Jesus is alive.

And I will live for all my days…

Well, You lifted me from where I was,
Set my feet upon a rock,
Humbled that You even know about me.
Now I have chosen to believe,
Believing that You've chosen me;
I was lost but now I've found…

 1096   Bob Baker
            Copyright © 1994 Mercy/Vineyard
            Publishing/Adm. by CopyCare

WELL, I THANK YOU, LORD,
That You are my Saviour;
You're my strength
And You're the Rock on which I stand.
You give me life,
And a grace that's greater,
When I humble myself
Beneath Your mighty hand.

You bring times of refreshing,
You bring times of refreshing,
You bring times of refreshing to my soul.
When I'm weary from the fight,
And trying to do what's right,
You bring times of refreshing to my soul.

For the day will come
When we'll all be gathered,
And the sun will rise with healing in its wings;
And all the years of pain
Won't seem to matter,
When our eyes behold
Our Teacher and our King.

1097 Chris Bowater
Copyright © 1996 Sovereign Lifestyle Music

WE'RE HERE FOR THE HARVEST,
Get ready to reap,
The call is for action,
It's not time to sleep.
We're here for the harvest,
The yield will be great;
The fields are now ripened,
So don't hesitate.

There's need for more labourers,
For many, not few,
The challenge set before us
Is who? And we cry:
Lord of the harvest,
In this day of Your power,
Hear the anthem of voices: 'send me!'

Send me, send me,
Lord of the harvest, send me!
Send me, send me,
Lord of the harvest, send me!

The Spirit is upon us,
To cause the blind to see;
The Spirit of the Sovereign Lord
To set the captive free.
The homeless and the needy
Can no longer be ignored,
And all oppressed will celebrate
The favour of the Lord.

There's need for more labourers…

1098 Carol Owen
Copyright © 1994 Thankyou Music

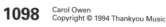

WE REJOICE IN THE GOODNESS OF OUR GOD,
We rejoice in the wonders of Your favour.
You've set the captives free,
You've caused the blind to see,
Hallelujah,
You give us liberty, hallelujah.

Always the same, You never change,
And Your mercies are new every day.
Compassionate and gracious,
Our faithful loving God,
Slow to anger, rich in love.

You give us hope, You give us joy,
You give us fulness of life to enjoy.
Our Shepherd and Provider,
Our God who's always there,
Never failing, always true.

1099 Matt Redman
Copyright © 1996 Thankyou Music

WE'RE LOOKING TO YOUR PROMISE of old,
That if we pray and humble ourselves,
You will come and heal our land,
You will come,
You will come.

We're looking to the promise You made,
That if we turn and look to Your face,
You will come and heal our land,
You will come,
You will come to us.

Lord, send revival, start with me.
For I am one of unclean lips,
And my eyes have seen the King;
Your glory I have glimpsed.
Send revival, start with me.

1100 Ian White
Copyright © 1997 Thankyou Music

WE'RE REACHING OUT TO YOU AGAIN.
We're in the upper room again.
We feel the Spirit's wave,
We're in pre-revival days.
We're kneeling on the floor again.
We're crying out for more again.
We're seeking for Your face
We're in pre-revival days.

You say where our treasure is,
There is our heart.
You say where our treasure is,
There is our heart.

We're looking at our lives again.
Your love has filled our eyes again.
We cherish Your embrace,
We're in pre-revival days.
We're praying for the lost again.
The hardened heart is soft again.
No one is turned away,
We're in pre-revival days.

We're talking in the streets again.
You're showing us what to speak again.
The demons scream with rage,
We're in pre-revival days.

But a single song
Can never change our ways,
So we cry to You, Lord,
You are mighty to save.

Jesus out in front again.
Jesus on our tongues again.
We're rising up in faith
To see revival days.
We're praying for our land again.
You've stayed Your patient hand again.
This nation needs Your grace
To see revival days.

1101 Chris Cartwright & Richard Lewis
Copyright © 1994 Thankyou Music

WE'RE SO THANKFUL TO YOU,
We're so grateful for the things You've done,
That You died for us on the cross—
Such a painful death,
That You paid the price for us,
You paid the price for us.

And we say thank You, Lord.
We say thank You, Lord.
We say thank You for what You have
*   done.*
And we say thank You, Lord.
We say thank You, Lord.
We say thank You
For the things You have done.

It's so wonderful that you rose,
Victorious over death and hell.
All authority is now Yours,
And the Comforter
You have sent in fulness to us,
You have come to us.

1102 Stuart Garrard
Copyright © 1993 Thankyou Music

WE'RE STANDING HERE with open hearts,
Our voices joined in unity.
We know we don't lead perfect lives,
And we cry to You for mercy.
Father in heaven, we honour Your name,
That we might bring You glory and fame;
Pour out Your Spirit upon us we pray,
To heal and deliver and save.

This is our heart cry;
This is our heart cry.
(Repeat)

We stand before the throne of grace,
A people for Your possession;
We hunger and thirst, we seek Your face,
Come touch us with Your presence.
Father in heaven, holy and true,
Stretch out Your hand, let power break
    through;
Pour out Your Spirit upon us today,
To heal and deliver and save.

1103 Lex Loizides
Copyright © 1996 Thankyou Music

WE STAND TOGETHER before our Saviour,
We stand together in the cause of our God.
We have a vision, we've been commissioned
To raise a banner in the name of our God.

Once, when we were dead in our sin,
Our hearts were turned away,
But then the light of Christ broke in
And made us live again.
And if You could heal our blindness,
You can save our nation too,
So we give ourselves this day to follow You.

We'll preach the gospel, we'll tell the people.
About a Saviour who has died on a cross.
With true compassion, without distraction,
While we have time we will deliver the lost.

Someday soon the King will come
With glory, power and might,
And all the hosts of heaven and hell
Will bow before the light.
And the nations will be gathered
For the righteous Judge will come,
And the blood-bought church
Will join the Risen One.

1104 Sue Rinaldi
Copyright © 1996 Thankyou Music

WE WANNA CHANGE THIS WORLD,
We wanna change this world.
(Repeat)

So wave those flags of justice
Over the nations,
And hit those drums of peace
Among the peoples.
We hear the sound of history in the making,
Let God's love run around the earth
And bring freedom!

So hold each other's hands
Across the oceans,
And play those chords of peace
Among the peoples.
We hear the sound of reconciliation:
Let God's love dance around the earth
And bring freedom!

And we wanna change this world
As we live out holy lives.
And we wanna change this world
As You wash our motives clean.
(Repeat)
Oh, wash us clean!

1105 Doug Horley
Copyright © 1993 Thankyou Music

WE WANT TO SEE JESUS LIFTED HIGH,
A banner that flies across this land,
That all men might see the truth and know
He is the way to heaven.
(Repeat)

> *We want to see, We want to see,*
> *We want to see Jesus lifted high.*
> *We want to see, we want to see,*
> *We want to see Jesus lifted high.*

Step by step we're moving forward,
Little by little taking ground,
Every prayer a powerful weapon,
Strongholds come tumbling down,
And down, and down, and down.

> *We're gonna see, we're gonna see,*
> *We're gonna see Jesus lifted high.*
> *We're gonna see, we're gonna see,*
> *We're gonna see Jesus lifted high.*

1106 Matt Redman & Steve Cantellow
Copyright © 1996 Thankyou Music

WE WILL GIVE OURSELVES NO REST
Till Your kingdom comes on earth;
You've positioned watchmen on the walls.
Now our prayers will flow like tears,
For You've shared Your heart with us;
God of heaven, on our knees we fall.
Come down in power,
Reveal Your heart again;
Come hear our cries,
The tears that plead for rain.

> *We're knocking,*
> *Knocking on the door of heaven,*
> *We're crying,*
> *Crying for this generation;*
> *We're praying for Your name to be known*
> *In all of the earth.*
> *We're watching,*
> *Watching on the walls to see You,*
> *We're looking,*
> *Looking for a time of breakthrough;*
> *We're praying for Your word to bear fruit*
> *In all of the earth, in all of the earth.*

1107 Dave Bilbrough
Copyright © 1991 Thankyou Music

WE WILL TEAR DOWN EVERY STRONGHOLD
Through the power of His word.
We will seek to bring His kingdom in,
Make a way for His return.

We will tell of His salvation,
For the church of Christ is called
To bring healing to the nations,
See His righteousness restored.

> *Satan is defeated,*
> *Christ has overcome,*
> *Seated at the Father's hand,*
> *Lord, on earth may Your will now be don*

1108 Dennis Jernigan
Copyright © 1988 Shepherd's Heart Music/
Sovereign Lifestyle Music

WE WILL WORSHIP THE LAMB OF GLORY,
We will worship the King of kings;
We will worship the Lamb of Glory,
We will worship the King.

> *And with our hands lifted high*
> *We will worship and sing,*
> *And with our hands lifted high*
> *We come before You rejoicing.*
> *With our hands lifted high to the sky,*
> *When the world wonders why,*
> *We'll just tell them we're loving our King.*
> *Oh, we'll just tell them we're loving our*
>   *King.*
> *Yes, we'll just tell them loving our King.*

Bless the name of the Lamb of Glory,
I bless the name of the King of kings;
Bless the name of the Lamb of Glory,
Bless the name of the King.

1109
Martin Smith
Copyright © 1996 Curious? Music UK/
Adm. by Bucks Music Ltd

WHAT A FRIEND I'VE FOUND,
Closer than a brother;
I have felt Your touch,
More intimate than lovers.

Jesus, Jesus,
Jesus, Friend forever.
(Repeat)

What a hope I've found,
More faithful than a mother;
It would break my heart
To ever lose each other.

1110
Geoff Bullock
Copyright © 1997 Watershed Productions/
Kingsway Music

WHATEVER I HAVE GAINED,
Whatever I have done,
I leave it all behind to follow You.
The things that I attained,
The goals I may have gained,
A prize or any glory of my own.

For I am lost without Your love,
All things are loss without Your love;
For I am lost without Your love,
All things are loss without Your love.

The wonder of Your love,
The wonder of Your grace;
To gain You and to know You as my Lord.
That I am found in You,
Your righteousness alone,
Is more than I could dream or ever ask.

1111
Bryn & Sally Haworth
Copyright © 1983 Bella Music Ltd

WHAT KIND OF LOVE IS THIS
That gave itself for me?
I am the guilty one,
Yet I go free.
What kind of love is this,
A love I've never known;
I didn't even know His name—
What kind of love is this?

What kind of man is this,
That died in agony?
He who had done no wrong
Was crucified for me.
What kind of man is this,
Who laid aside His throne
That I may know the love of God—
What kind of man is this?

By grace I have been saved;
It is the gift of God.
He destined me to be His son,
Such is His love.
No eye has ever seen,
No ear has ever heard,
Nor has the heart of man conceived
What kind of love is this.

1112
Matt Redman
Copyright © 1996 Thankyou Music

WHEN CAN I GO AND MEET WITH GOD?
My soul is weak, my body tired.
Can it be here, can it be now?
I need to find that place again.

When can I come and meet You, God?
I thirst inside for heaven's touch.
Let it be here, let it be now;
I need to find that place again...

Where deep calls to deep
In the roar of Your waterfalls,
You're calling me
With the force of Your love.
Let Your waves sweep
Over all the dry places, Lord;
Usher me in to the depths of Your
heart,
Where deep calls to deep,
Where deep calls to deep,
Where deep calls to deep,
Where deep calls to deep.

I want to know Your risen power.
I need to share Your sufferings;
And as I die to my own will,
Lord, raise me to that place again.

1113
Matt Redman
Copyright © 1997 Thankyou Music

WHEN THE MUSIC FADES, all is stripped
away,
And I simply come;
Longing just to bring something that's of
worth
That will bless Your heart.

I'll bring You more than a song,
For a song in itself
Is not what You have required.
You search much deeper within
Through the way things appear;
You're looking into my heart.

I'm coming back to the heart of worship,
And it's all about You,
All about You, Jesus.
I'm sorry, Lord, for the thing I've made it,
When it's all about You,
All about You, Jesus.

King of endless worth, no one could express
How much You deserve.
Though I'm weak and poor, all I have is Yours,
Every single breath.

1114 Noel Richards
Copyright © 1996 Thankyou Music

WHEN WE'RE IN TROUBLE,
When there are cares;
When faith is shaken up,
When we despair,
We call on Jesus,
Give Him our thanks;
We let His peace and joy
Come to our hearts.

> *We're gonna keep on praying,*
> *Keep on praying.*
> *We're gonna keep on praying,*
> *Keep on praying.*

When there is sickness,
When there is pain,
There is a healing touch,
Each time we pray.
God always listens,
Cares for our needs;
Prayers of the righteous one
Have power indeed.

Prayers for the nation,
Prayers for the world.
Prayers for the government,
Prayers for the church.
Prayers for the seekers,
Prayers for the saints,
Praying that people will come to faith.

1115 K. Prosch
Copyright © 1995 Liber Media &
Publishing, LLC/Kingsway Music

WHEN YOU'VE BEEN BROKEN, broken to
   pieces,
And your heart begins to faint,
'Cause you don't understand.
And when there is nothing
To rake from the ashes,
And you can't even walk
Onto the fields of praise.
But I bow down and kiss the Son.
Oh, I bow down and kiss the Son.

When the rock falls, falls upon you,
And you get ground to dust,
No music for your pain.
You open the windows,
The windows of heaven,
And then You opened me,
And You crushed me like a rose.
But I bow down and kiss the Son.
Oh, I bow down and kiss the Son.
Oh, I bow down and kiss the Son.

> *Let the praise of the Lord be in my mouth,*
> *Let the praise of the Lord be in my mouth.*

> *Though You slay me, I will trust You, Lord.*
> (Repeat ×4)

1116 Tommy Walker
Copyright © 1992 Integrity's Praise! Music/
Sovereign Music UK

WHERE THERE ONCE WAS ONLY HURT,
He gave His healing hand;
Where there once was only pain,
He brought comfort like a friend.
I feel the sweetness of His love
Piercing my darkness.
I see the bright and morning sun
As it ushers in His joyful gladness.

> *He's turned my mourning into dancing*
>   *again,*
> *He's lifted my sorrow.*
> *I can't stay silent, I must sing*
> *For His joy has come.*

His anger lasts for a moment in time;
But His favour is here
And will be on me for all my lifetime.

1117 Paul Oakley
Copyright © 1995 Thankyou Music

WHO IS THERE LIKE YOU,
And who else would give their life for me,
Even suffering in my place?
And who could repay You?
All of creation looks to You,
And You provide for all You have made.

o I'm lifting up my hands,
fting up my voice,
fting up Your name,
nd in Your grace I rest,
or Your love has come to me
nd set me free.
nd I'm trusting in Your word,
rusting in Your cross,
rusting in Your blood
nd all Your faithfulness,
or Your power at work in me
  changing me.

118 Stuart Townend
Copyright © 1995 Thankyou Music

WHO PAINTS THE SKIES into glorious day?
  nly the splendour of Jesus.
Who breathes His life into fists of clay?
  nly the splendour of Jesus.
Who shapes the valleys and brings the rain?
  nly the splendour of Jesus.
Who makes the desert to live again?
  nly the splendour of Jesus.

each every nation His marvellous ways;
ach generation shall sing His praise.

  He is wonderful, He is glorious,
  Clothed in righteousness,
  Full of tenderness.
  Come and worship Him,
  He's the Prince of life,
  He will cleanse our hearts
  In His river of fire.

Who hears the cry of the barren one?
  nly the mercy of Jesus.
Who breaks the curse of the heart of stone?
  nly the mercy of Jesus.
Who storms the prison and sets men free,
  nly the mercy of Jesus.
urchasing souls for eternity?
  nly the mercy of Jesus.

119 Alex Muir
Copyright © 1993 Thankyou Music

WHOSE LIPS WILL PLEAD
or the people of this land?
Who'll stand in the gap,
nd who'll build up the wall,
efore the long day of God's patience is
  over,
efore the night comes
When His judgement will fall?

And whose eyes will weep
For the people of this land?
And whose hearts will break
For the hearts made of stone,
For those who are walking out into
  darkness,
Away from God's love,
Without Christ, so alone?

And whose ears can hear
What the Spirit is saying
To those who are willing
To watch and to pray?
Pray on till God's light
Fills the skies over this land,
The light of revival that brings a new day.

1120 Graham Maule & John L. Bell
Copyright © 1987 WGRG, Iona Community

WILL YOU COME AND FOLLOW ME
If I but call your name?
Will you go where you don't know
And never be the same?
Will you let My love be shown,
Will you let My name be known,
Will you let My life be grown in you,
And you in Me?

Will you leave yourself behind
If I but call your name?
Will you care for cruel and kind
And never be the same?
Will you risk the hostile stare,
Should your life attract or scare?
Will you let Me answer prayer
In you and you in Me?

Will you let the blinded see
If I but call your name?
Will you set the prisoners free
And never be the same?
Will you kiss the leper clean,
And do such as this unseen,
And admit to what I mean
In you and you in Me?

Will you love the 'you' you hide
If I but call your name?
Will you quell the fear inside
And never be the same?
Will you use the faith you've found
To reshape the world around,
Through My sight and touch and
  sound
In you and you in Me?

Lord, Your summons echoes true
When You but call my name.
Let me turn and follow You
And never be the same.
In Your company I'll go
Where Your love and footsteps show;
Thus I'll move and live and grow
In You and You in me.

1121 Ruth Dryden
Copyright © 1978 Genesis Music/
Kingsway Music

WITHIN THE VEIL I now would come,
Into the holy place, to look upon Thy face.
I see such beauty there, no other can
   compare;
I worship Thee, my Lord, within the veil.

1122 Carol Owen
Copyright © 1995 Thankyou Music

WORTHY IS THE LAMB,
Worthy is the Lamb,
Worthy is the Lamb who was slain.
(Repeat)

> *My Lord and Saviour,*
> *My great Redeemer,*
> *Your blood has purchased me for God.*
> *My Lord and Saviour,*
> *My great Redeemer,*
> *You came to set the captives free.*

Holy is the Lamb . . .

Jesus, You're the Lamb . . .

Glory to the Lamb . . .

1123 Carl Tuttle
Copyright © 1992 Mercy/Vineyard Publishing/
Adm. by CopyCare

YET THIS WILL I CALL TO MIND,
And therefore I will hope,
Because of the Lord's great love
I've been redeemed.
The Lord is gracious and kind
To all who call on His name,
Because of the Lord's great love
I've been redeemed.

> *Because of the Lord's great love,*
> *Because of the Lord's great love,*
> *Because of the Lord's great love*
> *I've been redeemed.*

I know of His steadfast love,
His mercy renewed each day,
Because of the Lord's great love
I've been redeemed.
Washed in the blood of the Lamb,
Guiltless for ever I stand,
Because of the Lord's great love
I've been redeemed.

1124 Ian White
Copyright © 1997 Thankyou Music

YOU ARE MERCIFUL TO ME,
You are merciful to me,
You are merciful to me, my Lord.
(Repeat)

Every day my disobedience
Grieves Your loving heart;
But then redeeming love breaks through,
And causes me to worship You.

(Men – Women echo))
Redeemer,
Saviour,
Healer
And Friend.
Every day
Renew my ways,
Fill me with love
That never ends.

1125 Craig Musseau
Copyright © 1989 Mercy/Vineyard Publishing/
Adm. by CopyCare

YOU ARE MIGHTY,
You are holy,
You are awesome in Your power.
You have risen, You have conquered,
You have beaten the power of death.

> *Hallelujah, we will rejoice.*
> *Hallelujah, we will rejoice.*

1126 Brian Doerksen
Copyright © 1996 Mercy/Vineyard Publishing/
Adm. by CopyCare

YOU ARE MY KING, (You are my King)
And I love You.
You are my King, (You are my King)
And I worship You.

Kneeling before You now,
All of my life I gladly give to You.
Placing my hopes and dreams
In Your hands,
I give my heart to You.

I love You, love You, Jesus.
Yes, I love You, love You, Jesus,
My King.

1127 Noel & Tricia Richards
Copyright © 1995 Thankyou Music

YOU ARE MY PASSION,
Love of my life,
Friend and companion, my Lover.
All of my being
Longs for Your touch;
With all my heart I love You.

Now You will draw me close to You,
Gather me in Your arms;
Let me hear the beating of Your heart,
O my Jesus,
O my Jesus.

1128 Wynne Goss
Copyright © 1992 Thankyou Music

YOU ARE RIGHTEOUS in all Your ways,
You are good, You are good.
You are truthful in all You say,
You are good, You are good.

And I bow my knee before You,
In honour of Your name,
For You alone are worthy,
Worthy of my praise,
Worthy of my praise.

You are holy, faithful and true,
You are good, You are good.
You are gracious in all You do,
You are good, You are good.

1129 Tommy Walker
Copyright © 1991 Doulos Publishing/
Adm. by CopyCare

YOU ARE THE GREAT I AM,
Forever You will be.
Let every angel sing
Of Your perfect authority.
Every knee will bow
And every tongue confess;
You are the great I AM,
The First and Last

Mighty, (Mighty)
Eternal, (Eternal)
Immortal, (Immortal)
Awesome One. (Awesome One)
Mysterious, (Mysterious)
The Wonderful, (the Wonderful)
The Holy One, (the Holy One)
The Beginning and the End.

1130 Steve & Vikki Cook
Copyright © 1994 People of Destiny/
Word Music/Adm. by CopyCare

YOU ARE THE PERFECT AND RIGHTEOUS GOD
Whose presence bears no sin;
You bid me come to Your holy place:
How can I enter in
When Your presence bears no sin?
Through Him who poured out His life for me,
The atoning Lamb of God,
Through Him and His work alone I boldly come.

I come by the blood, I come by the cross,
Where Your mercy flows
From hands pierced for me.
For I dare not stand on my righteousness,
My every hope rests on what Christ has
done,
And I come by the blood.

You are the high and exalted King,
The One the angels fear;
So far above me in every way,
Lord, how can I draw near
To the One the angels fear?
Through Him who laid down His life for me
And ascended to Your side,
Through Him, through Jesus alone I boldly
come.

1131 Per Soetorp
Copyright © 1992 His Music/
Kingsway Music

YOU ARE WONDERFUL,
Counsellor, Mighty God.
You are Prince of Peace,
Our Father for evermore.
You're the Alpha and Omega,
Lord of all lords.
You are Wonderful,
Counsellor, Mighty God.

1132 John Pantry
Copyright © 1990 Thankyou Music

YOU ARE WORTHY TO RECEIVE
All the honour and praise.
Lamb of God, Prince of Peace,
We lift high Your name.

For Yours is the greatness,
The power and the glory;
Lord of the nations,
Have mercy on us.
Though heaven be shaken,
And earth's kingdoms fall,
We will still worship You.

In the footsteps of our King,
We walk unafraid;
Though the battle may rage,
Our praises will ring.

1133 Terry Butler
Copyright © 1992 Mercy/Vineyard Publishing/
Adm. by CopyCare

YOU BLESS MY LIFE, and heal me inside,
Over and over again.
You touched my heart and brought peace of
mind,
Over and over again.

> *All I can say is I love You.*
> *All I can say is I need You.*
> *All I can say is I thank You, Lord,*
> *For all that You've done in my life.*

You've been so kind and patient with me,
Over and over again.
When I have strayed You showed me the
way,
Over and over again.

1134 Robert Newey
Copyright © 1990 Thankyou Music

YOU CAME to heal the brokenhearted;
You came to make the blind eyes see.
Your light is burning now within us,
As Your word of truth sets us free.

> *And we will fill the earth with the love of*
> *   God*
> *That's been shed abroad in our hearts,*
> *Share with every nation and every land*
> *The grace that He imparts.*
> *And we will sing a new song of joy and*
> *   peace,*
> *A resounding trumpet call,*
> *Causing hearts to rise, opening eyes to*
> *   see*
> *That Jesus, Jesus is Lord of all.*

You come in all Your mighty power,
You come to bring the latter rain;
We know You've filled us with Your Spirit
And a love we cannot contain.

You'll come in glory and splendour,
You'll come to reign upon the earth;
We know we'll live with You for ever
And declare Your mighty worth.

1135 Mark Altrogge
Copyright © 1991 People of Destiny/
Word Music/Adm. by CopyCare

YOU HAVE BECOME FOR US WISDOM;
You have become for us righteousness.
You have become our salvation;
You have become all our holiness.

> *All that we need is found in You;*
> *Oh, all that we need is in You.*
> *All that we need is found in You;*
> *You are our all in all.*
> *You have become our all in all.*

You have become our provision;
In union with You we have victory.
In You we have died and have risen;
You are our great hope of glory.

1136 Andy Park
Copyright © 1991 Mercy/Vineyard Publishing/
Adm. by CopyCare

YOU HAVE CALLED US CHOSEN,
A royal priesthood,
A holy nation,
We belong to You.
(Repeat)

> *Take our lives as a sacrifice;*
> *Shine in us Your holy light.*
> *Purify our hearts' desire;*
> *Be to us a consuming fire.*

You have shown us mercy,
You have redeemed us;
Our hearts cry 'Father,
We belong to You.'
(Repeat)

1137 Alun Leppitt
Copyright © 1994 Thankyou Music

YOU HAVE LIFTED UP THE HUMBLE,
Filled the hungry with good things;
Shown Your mercy to the fearful,
You have healing in Your wings.
The rich will leave with nothing,
But the poor will have it all,
And the pure in heart will see their holy God

You will light the road from darkness,
As You lead us to Your throne;
You give strength to the weary,
And shelter from the storm.
You pour out living waters
So we will never thirst,
And You wipe away the tears from our eyes.

Holy is Your name,
Holy is Your name;
Perfect grace and rich in love,
Your mercy never ends.
Holy is Your name,
Holy is Your name;
Precious Lamb of sacrifice,
Forever You will reign.

You bring justice to the nations,
Salvation's at Your hand;
With your blood You made the purchase
From every tribe and land,
To be priests within Your kingdom,
Your Spirit's on us all
To show the love and favour of the Lord.

138 Kevin Prosch & Tom Davis
Copyright © 1991 Mercy/Vineyard Publishing/
Adm. by CopyCare

YOU HAVE TAKEN THE PRECIOUS
From the worthless and given us
Beauty for ashes, love for hate.
You have chosen the weak things
Of the world to shame that which is strong,
And the foolish things to shame the wise.

You are help to the helpless,
Strength to the stranger,
And a father to the child that's left alone.
And the thirsty You've invited
To come to the waters,
And those who have no money, come and
  buy.

So come, so come.
So come, so come.

Behold the days are coming
For the Lord has promised,
That the ploughman will overtake the
  reaper.
And our hearts will be the threshing floor,
And the move of God we've cried out for
Will come, it will surely come.

For You will shake the heavens,
And fill Your house with glory,
And turn the shame of the outcast into
  praise.
And all creation groans and waits
For the Spirit and the Bride to say
The word that Your heart has longed to
  hear.

1139 Darlene Zschech & Russell Fragar
Copyright © 1996 Darlene Zschech &
Russell Fragar/Hillsong Publishing/
Kingsway Music

YOU MAKE YOUR FACE TO SHINE ON ME,
And that my soul knows very well;
You lift me up, I'm cleansed and free,
And that my soul knows very well.

When mountains fall I'll stand
By the power of Your hand,
And in Your heart of hearts I'll dwell,
And that my soul knows very well.
(Repeat)

Joy and strength each day I'll find,
And that my soul knows very well;
Forgiveness, hope I know is mine,
And that my soul knows very well.

1140 Ian Smale
Copyright © 1994 Thankyou Music

**YOU NEVER PUT A LIGHT UNDER A DIRTY
OLD BUCKET.**
You never put a light under a dirty old
  bucket.
You never put a light under a dirty old
  bucket
If you want light to shine around, round,
  round.

Shine, shine around, round round.
Shine, shine around, round, round.
Shine a light that everyone can see.
Lord, help me let my little light shine,
Not just Sundays, all the time,
So friends give praise to You
When they see me.

1141 Carol Mundy
Copyright © 1998 Rhema Publishing/
Adm. by Worldwide Worship Ltd

YOU'RE AMAZING,
An amazing mighty God,
Full of compassion and true.
You're a loving heavenly Father
To whom all praise is due.
You're so amazing,
Father, I love You.

1142
Geoff Bullock
Copyright © 1992 Word Music/
Maranatha! Music/Adm. by CopyCare

YOU RESCUED ME, and picked me up,
A living hope of grace revealed,
A life transformed in righteousness,
O Lord You have rescued me.
Forgiving me, You healed my heart,
And set me free from sin and death.
You brought me life, You made me whole,
O Lord, You have rescued me.

And You loved me before I knew You,
And You knew me for all time.
I've been created in Your image,
O Lord.
And You bought me, and You sought me,
Your blood poured out for me;
A new creation in Your image,
O Lord.
You rescued me, You rescued me.

1143
Robin Mark
Copyright © 1996 Daybreak Music Ltd

YOU'RE THE LION OF JUDAH,
The Lamb that was slain,
You ascended to heaven
And ever more will reign;
At the end of the age
When the earth You reclaim,
You will gather the nations before You.
And the eyes of all men will be
Fixed on the Lamb who was crucified,
For with wisdom and mercy and justice
You'll reign at Your Father's side.

And the angels will cry:
'Hail the Lamb
Who was slain for the world,
Rule in power.'
And the earth will reply:
'You shall reign
As the King of all kings
And the Lord of all lords.'

There's a shield in our hand
And a sword at our side,
There's a fire in our spirit
That cannot be denied;
As the Father has told us,
For these You have died,
For the nations that gather before You.
And the ears of all men need to hear
Of the Lamb who was crucified,
Who descended to hell yet was raised up
To reign at the Father's side.

1144
Darlene Zschech
Copyright © 1996 Darlene Zschech/
Hillsong Publishing/Kingsway Music

YOUR EYE IS ON THE SPARROW,
And Your hand, it comforts me.
From the ends of the earth
To the depths of my heart,
Let Your mercy and strength be seen.
You call me to Your purpose,
As angels understand.
For Your glory may You draw all men,
As Your love and grace demands.

And I will run to You,
To Your words of truth;
Not by might, not by power
But by the Spirit of God.
Yes, I will run the race,
Till I see Your face.
Oh, let me live in the glory of Your grace.

1145
Chris Falson
Copyright © 1991 Maranatha! Music/
Adm. by CopyCare

YOUR LOVE LOOKS AFTER ME,
It never fails.
Your word takes care of me,
And keeps my mind on You.
(Repeat)

You are majestic
Through all the earth;
I am Your servant
For the rest of my days.

You are magnificent,
The God of glory;
I'm going to worship You
For the rest of my days,
For the rest of my days,
For the rest of my days.

1146
Peggy Caswell
Copyright © 1990 Sound Truth Publishing/
Kingsway Music

YOUR LOVE, O LORD,
It reaches to the heavens;
Your faithfulness,
It reaches to the skies.
Your righteousness is like
The mighty mountains;
How priceless is Your faithful love.

I will exalt You, O Lord,
I will exalt You, O Lord.
Praise Your holy name,
That my heart may sing to You;
I will exalt You, O Lord.

Your name, O Lord,
it is a mighty tower;
Your glory
it covers all the earth.
In Your hands alone
Are strength and power,
All praise be to Your glorious name.

1147 Dave Wellington
Copyright © 1994 Thankyou Music

YOUR NAME IS PEACE
Saviour so holy;
King of righteousness
Merciful and mighty.
God with us,
Revealed to us,
Awesome and eternal God,
Your name is peace.
Wonderful Counsellor,
Everlasting Father,
Lord, Your name is peace,
Your name is peace.

1148 Paul Oakley
Copyright © 1997 Thankyou Music

YOUR VOICE IS LIKE THUNDER,
Your eyes like fire;
Your throne is for ever,
In unapproachable light.
Your grace is so tender,
Your love like wine;
To You I surrender,
I lay down my life.

And all I want to do . . .

Is to build a house of gold,
Purest silver and costly stones;
Let it stand when the fire comes,
When the day brings Your light.
Be my wisdom and be my strength,
Fill me up with Your faithfulness;
Keep me loving until the end.
Let the fire in Your eyes
See a living sacrifice,
Pleasing in Your sight.

Let me build a house of gold . . .

1149 Dougie Brown
Copyright © 1990 Sovereign Lifestyle Music

YOUR WILL, NOT MINE, that is what I desire
to see,
Walking in righteousness, and holy liberty.
Your life, not mine, that is what I desire to
live,
Forgiving others, as always You forgive.

I bow before Your majesty,
I fall before Your throne;
I cannot understand Your love,
But I claim it as my own.
I rise and stand before You
As a living sacrifice;
I seek to do Your will, O God,
For the rest of my life.

Your voice, not mine, that is what I desire to
hear;
Speak in the stillness and whisper in my ear.
Your mind, not mine, that is what I desire to
have;
To prophesy Your word, release the captive
heart.

Your race, not mine, that is what I desire to
run;
To finish off the work that others have begun.
Your work, not mine, that is what I desire to
do;
To serve Your purposes, and worship only
You.

1150 Dave Dickerson
Copyright © 1988 Coronation Music
Publishing/Kingsway Music

YOU SHALL BE HOLY
And in everything be true,
For I, the Lord, am holy,
And My word belongs to you.

Stay in my presence,
Grow strong in My love,
With all the gifts I give you
From My kingdom here above.

We are Your children,
Abba Father, mighty God,
And growing in Your likeness,
Through grace of Jesus' blood.

Inspired by Your Spirit,
Our eternal source of power,
Release us to worship,
And to praise You every hour.

1151 Lenny LeBlanc & Paul Baloche
Copyright © 1999 Lensongs Publishing/
Integrity's Hosanna! Music/Sovereign Music UK

ABOVE ALL powers, above all kings,
Above all nature and all created things;
Above all wisdom and all the ways of man,
You were here before the world began.

Above all kingdoms, above all thrones,
Above all wonders the world has ever known;
Above all wealth and treasures of the earth,
There's no way to measure what You're
   worth.

Crucified, laid behind the stone;
You lived to die, rejected and alone;
Like a rose trampled on the ground,
You took the fall and thought of me,
Above all.

1152 Dave Bilbrough
Copyright © 2002 Thankyou Music

AGAIN AND AGAIN,
You have revealed Your love to me.
Again and again grace has shone through.
You've always been there for me
When I have come to You:
You are the Rock on which I stand.

You're wonderful, You're marvellous,
You're everything to me.
Your steadfast and unchanging love
Are all I'll ever need.
What peace and what security
Can be found in knowing You,
My Healer, Deliverer.

There is no limit to this never-ending stream
That's entered the castle of my soul.
You give me a hope and future
Beyond my wildest dreams.
Your love is greater than I know.

You've been my fortress
Through the shifting sands of time;
In change and adversity
You have answered my prayer to guide me.

1153 Brian Houston
Copyright © 2000 Thankyou Music

A HUMBLE HEART You have yet to despise,
And so I humble myself in this place.
If they that sow in tears shall reap in joy,
Let a million tears or more roll down my face
If You don't answer me today, Lord,
I'm gonna be right here tomorrow.
If You don't answer when I pray
From the morning to the evening,
'Cause it's You I do believe in,
I will say, every day, I'm gonna say that…

I won't let go till You bless me, Lord,
No, I won't let go till You bless me, Lord.
And I will cry out to You
Till I can't cry no more.
And I won't let go till You bless me, Lord.

Where can I go if You don't bid me go?
And I have no hope if You are not my hope.
And I have no peace if You don't give me
   peace,
And I have no faith if You don't help me to
   believe.
If You don't answer me today
Will the heathen nations mock Your name
And say You're made of wood or clay?
Ah, but I've seen You provide for me,
I've kissed Your lips and felt You heal my
   pain.
Hey, can You do it once again? 'Cause…

1154 Paul Oakley
Copyright © 1999 Thankyou Music

ALL AROUND YOUR THRONE,
Rainbow colours fly through light,
And heavy thunder rolls,
And the lightning blinds, so bright.
Living creatures cry "Holy is the Lord,"
As they try to hide their eyes.

Rulers of this world
Only join in vain as one.
There's no other power
Could ever overthrow Your Son.
Principalities and powers
Know that You are Lord,
And they try to hide their eyes.

'Cause You shine brighter than the sun,
Only Holy One,
And You shine on me,
Oh, Jesus, only risen Son,
Seated on Your throne,
Would You shine on me today?

here will be a day
When the stars will leave the sky,
Heaven and earth will shake,
And the moon will give no light;
While every tongue will cry
"Jesus Christ is Lord,"
Some will try to hide their eyes.

 155 Marty Sampson
Copyright © 2001 Marty Sampson/
Hillsong Publishing/Kingsway Music

ALL CREATION CRIES TO YOU,
Worshipping in spirit and in truth.
Glory to the Faithful One,
Jesus Christ, God's Son.

All creation gives You praise,
You alone are truly great;
You alone are God who reigns
For eternity.

    God is great and His praise
    Fills the earth, fills the heavens,
    And Your name will be praised
    Through all the world.
    God is great, sing His praise
    All the earth, all the heavens,
    'Cause we're living for the glory of Your
      name,
    The glory of Your name.

All to You, O God, we bring.
Jesus, teach us how to live.
Let Your fire burn in us
That all may hear and all may see.

"Holy is the Lord,"
The whole earth sings,
The whole earth sings.
(Repeat)

 156 Tony Ryce-Kelly & Rónán Johnston
Copyright © 1997 Emmausongs/
Adm. by Daybreak Music Ltd

ALLELUIA, ALLELUIA, Jesus is the Lord,
He's the Lord of all my heart.
Alleluia, alleluia, Jesus is the Lord,
He's the Lord of all my heart.

He's the way, He's the truth, He's the life. *(×3)*
(Last time)
You're the way, You're the truth, You're the
    light.

1157 Theodulph of Orleans (c.750–821)
Tr. John Mason Neale (1818–66)

ALL GLORY, LAUD AND HONOUR
To Thee, Redeemer, King,
To whom the lips of children
Made sweet hosannas ring.
Thou art the King of Israel,
Thou David's royal Son,
Who in the Lord's name comest,
The King and blessèd One.

The company of angels
Are praising Thee on high,
And mortal men and all things
Created make reply.
The people of the Hebrews
With psalms before Thee went;
Our praise and prayer and anthems
Before Thee we present.

To Thee before Thy passion
They sang their hymns of praise;
To Thee now high exalted
Our melody we raise.
Thou didst accept their praises;
Accept the prayers we bring,
Who in all good delightest,
Thou good and gracious King.

All glory, laud and honour
To Thee, Redeemer, King,
To whom the lips of children
Made sweet hosannas ring.

1158 Stuart Townend
Copyright © 1998 Thankyou Music

ALL MY DAYS I will sing this song of
    gladness,
Give my praise to the Fountain of delights;
For in my helplessness You heard my cry,
And waves of mercy poured down on my life.

I will trust in the cross of my Redeemer,
I will sing of the blood that never fails;
Of sins forgiven, of conscience cleansed,
Of death defeated and life without end.

    Beautiful Saviour, Wonderful Counsellor,
    Clothed in majesty, Lord of history,
    You're the Way, the Truth, the Life.
    Star of the Morning, glorious in holiness,
    You're the Risen One, heaven's Champion,
    And You reign, You reign over all!

I long to be where the praise is never-ending,
Yearn to dwell where the glory never fades;
Where countless worshippers will share one
    song,
And cries of 'worthy' will honour the Lamb!

1159 Liz Holland
Copyright © 1999 Thankyou Music

ALL MY LIFE, all my will, every day,
I lay it all before You.
All my life, all my will, every day,
I lay it all before You now.

*And Jesus takes us to the place of true
surrender,
Where we become less and You become
greater;
And Your holy ways into our lives will
enter,
And all that we are, and all that we have
become Yours.*

All my pain, all the fears, every tear,
I lay them all before You.
All my pain, all the fears, every tear,
I lay them all before You now.

1160 Gareth Robinson
Copyright © 2001 Thankyou Music

ALL OF ME,
All of me I give to You,
Only You, Jesus.
More of You,
More of You I long for,
Only You, Jesus.

For this life I live for You;
I truly worship You.
All of my days, in every way,
I will praise You.
In thought and word and deed,
Powered by Your life in me,
All of my days, in every way,
I will praise You, Lord.

1161 Chris Tomlin & Louie Giglio
Copyright © 2002 worshiptogether.com songs/
Six Steps Music/Adm. by Kingsway Music

*ALL OF YOU is more than enough for
All of me, for every thirst and every need,
You satisfy me with Your love,
And all I have in You
Is more than enough.*

You're my supply,
My breath of life;
Still more awesome than I know.
You're my reward,
Worth living for;
Still more awesome than I know.

You're my sacrifice
Of greatest price;
Still more awesome than I know.
You're my coming King,
You are everything;
Still more awesome than I know.

More than all I want,
More than all I need,
You are more than enough for me.
More than all I know,
More than all I can,
You are more than enough.

1162 Fanny Crosby (1820–1915)

ALL THE WAY MY SAVIOUR LEADS ME,
What have I to ask beside?
Can I doubt His tender mercy,
Who through life has been my guide?
Heavenly peace, divinest comfort,
Here by faith in Him to dwell,
For I know whate'er befall me,
Jesus doeth all things well.

All the way my Saviour leads me,
Cheers each winding path I tread.
Gives me grace for every trial,
Feeds me with the Living Bread.
Though my weary steps may falter
And my soul athirst may be,
Gushing from a Rock before me,
Lo! a spring of joy I see.

*And all the way my Saviour leads me,
Oh, the fullness of His love.
Perfect rest to me is promised
In my Father's house above.
And when my spirit clothed immortal
Wings its flight to realms of day,
This my song through endless ages,
Jesus led me all the way.*

1163 J.W. van de Venter (1855–1939)
Copyright © HarperCollins Religious/
Adm. by CopyCare

ALL TO JESUS I SURRENDER,
All to Him I freely give;
I will ever love and trust Him,
In His presence daily live.

*I surrender all,
I surrender all,
All to Thee, my blessèd Saviour,
I surrender all.*

All to Jesus I surrender,
Humbly at His feet I bow;
Worldly pleasures all forsaken,
Take me, Jesus, take me now.

All to Jesus I surrender,
Make me, Saviour, wholly Thine;
Let me feel the Holy Spirit,
Truly know that Thou art mine.

All to Jesus I surrender,
Lord, I give myself to Thee;
Fill me with Thy love and power,
Let Thy blessing fall on me.

All to Jesus I surrender,
Now I feel the sacred flame;
O the joy of full salvation!
Glory, glory to His name!

164 Brenton Brown & Glenn Robertson
Copyright © 1998 Vineyard Songs (UK/Eire)/
Adm. by CopyCare

ALL WHO ARE THIRSTY,
All who are weak,
Come to the fountain,
Dip your heart in the stream of life.
Let the pain and the sorrow
Be washed away
In the waves of His mercy,
As deep cries out to deep.
(We sing)

Come, Lord Jesus, come. *(x4)*

Holy Spirit come. *(x3)*

165 Mark Vargeson
Copyright © 2001 Thankyou Music

ALMIGHTY GOD, faithful and true,
In my worship I want to meet with You.
Unchanging God, for ever the same,
It's You I worship,
To know Your heart again.

And I fall down on my knees again,
As You show me what grace means;
And You love with such amazing love,
O my God, how can this be?

166 Rhys Scott
Copyright © 2001 Thankyou Music

ALMIGHTY GOD, HOLY ONE,
Who can stand before You,
Who can come?
Perfect Lamb, who bore our sin,
Who deserves such mercy,
Gracious King?

I come to Your throne of grace,
I'm standing in Christ,
I'm clothed in His righteousness.
To know Your presence,
To seek Your face.
Father, I delight in Your embrace.

1167 The Alternative Service Book (1980)
Copyright © The Central Board of Finance of the
Church of England, 1980; The Archbishops'
Council, 1999

ALMIGHTY GOD,
TO WHOM ALL HEARTS ARE OPEN,
All desires known,
And from whom no secrets are hidden:
Cleanse the thoughts of our hearts
By the inspiration of Your Holy Spirit,
That we may perfectly love You,
And worthily magnify,
That we may perfectly love You,
And worthily magnify
Your holy name;
Through Christ our Lord,
Amen.
Through Christ our Lord,
Amen.

1168 John Newton (1725–1807),
adapt. Nathan Fellingham
Copyright © 2000 Thankyou Music

AMAZING GRACE, how sweet the sound
That saved a wretch like me;
I once was lost, but now am found,
Was blind, but now I see.

Amazing love has come to me.
I lift up my voice to the heavens,
Lift up my hands to the King,
And I cry 'hosanna, hosanna in the
*   highest.'*
Jesus my Lord is exalted
Far above every name,
And I cry 'hosanna, hosanna in the
*   highest.'*

'Twas grace that taught my heart to fear,
And grace my fears relieved;
How precious did that grace appear,
The hour I first believed!

The Lord has promised good to me,
His word my hope secures;
He will my shield and portion be
As long as life endures.

1169
Paul Oakley
Copyright © 2001 Thankyou Music

AND AFTER ALL,
Everything I once held dear
Just proved to be so vain.
To lose it all,
And find a Friend who's always near
Could only be my gain.
And when I think of what You've done for me,
To bring me to the Father's side:

Unashamed and unafraid,
I will choose to wear Your name,
In a world so full of hate,
I will always live Your way.

Could it be
That You should put on human flesh,
Your glory laid aside?
Bruised for me,
Majesty upon the cross,
Forsaken and despised.
When I think of what it cost for You,
To bring me to the Father's side:

Unashamed and unafraid,
I will choose to wear Your name,
In a world so full of hate,
I will always live Your way.
Unashamed and unafraid,
I will love You all my days,
I don't care what people say,
I'm unashamed and unafraid.

I know some will say it's foolishness:
You can't make a blind man see.
But I know that there is power in the cross
To save those who believe.

1170
Billy James Foote
Copyright © 1999 worshiptogether.com songs/
Adm. by Kingsway Music

AND I'M FORGIVEN, because You were
   forsaken.
And I'm accepted: You were condemned.
And I'm alive and well,
Your Spirit is within me,
Because You died and rose again.

Amazing love, how can it be
That You, my King, would die for me?
Amazing love, I know it's true;
Now it's my joy to honour You.
In all I do, I honour You.

You are my King, You are my King,
Jesus, You are my King,
You are my King.

1171
Keith Getty
Copyright © 2002 Thankyou Music

ANGELS BOW before You,
Kings fall at Your command.
And yet Your love comes down to earth
To fallen man.
How can I know Your workings,
Eternal mystery?
I must bow down and give my life,
Must follow You.

And I love You, Lord,
Everything belongs to You,
Is known by You,
And made for Your eternal glory.
You, my Lord, receive the praise
Of my thankful heart.

1172
Chris Tomlin & Jesse Reeves
Copyright © 2000 worshiptogether.com songs/
Six Steps Music/Adm. by Kingsway Music

A REFUGE FOR THE POOR,
A shelter from the storm:
This is our God.
He will wipe away your tears
And return your wasted years:
This is our God.

Oh, mmm, this is our God.
Oh, mmm, this is our God.

A Father to the orphan,
A healer to the broken:
This is our God.
He brings peace to our madness
And comfort in our sadness:
This is our God.

A fountain for the thirsty,
A lover for the lonely:
This is our God.
He brings glory to the humble
And crowns for the faithful:
This is our God.

This is the One we have waited for,
This is the One we have waited for,
This is the One we have waited for.

1173
Matt Redman
Copyright © 1998 Thankyou Music

ARE THE PRAYERS OF THE SAINTS
Like sweet smelling incense,
Are the prayers of the saints
Like sweet smelling incense to Your heart,
To Your heart?
(Repeat)

t these prayers of the saints
e sweet smelling incense,
t these prayers of the saints
e sweet smelling incense to Your heart.

e the songs of the saints
ke sweet smelling incense,
e the songs of the saints
ke sweet smelling incense to Your heart,
your heart?
epeat)

t these songs of the saints
e sweet smelling incense,
t these songs of the saints
e sweet smelling incense to Your heart.

174 Steve & Vikki Cook
Copyright © 1999 PDI Worship/
Adm. by CopyCare

ROUND YOU SUCH BEAUTY,
ur majesty could fill an endless sky:
ply are You, Lord.
anscendent, exalted,
he heavens cannot contain Your presence:
ply are You, Lord.
nd as I behold Your glory
n undone.

I bow down at Your feet,
I bow down at Your feet,
I bow down at Your feet
For You are my God, my God.

ou saved me, the sinner,
ith crimson red You washed me white as
snow:
ow I love You, Lord.
ou loved me, the mocker,
ith kindness You won my heart for ever:
ow I love You, Lord.
nd as I behold this mercy
n undone.

175 Jim Bailey
Copyright © 1997 Thankyou Music

S FOR ME AND MY HOUSE,
s for me and my family,
s for me and my children,
e will serve the Lord.
epeat)

this family,
e're gonna do things properly,
ead God's word every day
nd then we'll try to pray;
though we get it wrong,
e will still carry on,
ake Jesus number one in this place.
this place we're gonna say grace.

1176 Robin Mark
Copyright © 1998 Daybreak Music Ltd

AS SURE AS GOLD IS PRECIOUS and the
honey sweet,
So You love this city and You love these
streets.
Every child out playing by their own front
door;
Every baby lying on the bedroom floor.

Every dreamer dreaming in her dead-end job;
Every driver driving through the rush hour
mob.
I feel it in my spirit, feel it in my bones,
You're going to send revival,
Bring them all back home.

I can hear that thunder in the distance,
Like a train on the edge of the town;
I can feel the brooding of Your Spirit:
'Lay your burdens down, lay your burdens
down.'

From the preacher preaching when the well
is dry,
To the lost soul reaching for a higher high.
From the young man working through his
hopes and fears,
To the widow walking through the vale of
tears.

Every man and woman, every old and young;
Every father's daughter, every mother's son.
I feel it in my spirit, feel it in my bones,
You're going to send revival,
Bring them all back home.

I can hear...

Revive us, revive us,
Revive us with Your fire!
(Repeat)

1177 Graham Kendrick
Copyright © 2002 Make Way Music

AS WE BRING OUR SONGS of love today,
Do you hear a sound more glorious?
Like the mighty roar of ocean waves,
Many witnesses surround us.
It's a harmony of costly praise
From the lips of those who suffer,
Of sighs and tears and martyrs' prayers
Until this age is over.

How long, Lord, till You come?
How long till the earth
Is filled with Your song?
How long until Your justice
Shines like the sun?
How long, Lord, till You come?
How long till the earth
Is filled with Your song?
How long? How long?

Lord, help us to live worthy of
Our sisters and our brothers
Who love You more than their own lives,
Who worship as they suffer:
To embrace the scandal of the cross.
Not ashamed to tell Your story,
To count all earthly gain as loss,
To know You and Your glory.

How long, Lord, till You come?
How long till the earth
Is filled with Your song?
How long until Your justice
Shines like the sun?
How long, Lord, till You come?
How long till the whole world hears
And the work is done,
Until at last we see You return?
How long, Lord, till You come?
How long till the earth
Is filled with Your song?
How long? How long?

1178 Matt Redman
Copyright © 2000 Thankyou Music

AS WE COME TODAY,
We remind ourselves of what we do;
That these songs are not just songs,
But signs of love for You.
This is a holy moment now,
Something of heaven touches earth,
Voices of angels all resound,
We join their song.

Come, come, come, let us worship God
With our hands held high,
And our hearts bowed down.
We will run, run, run
Through Your gates, O God,
With a shout of love,
With a shout of love.

Lord, with confidence
We come before Your throne of grace.
Not that we deserve to come
But You have paid the way.
You are the holy King of all,
Heaven and earth are in Your hands,
All of the angels sing Your song,
We join them now.

Let this be a holy moment now. *(Repeat)*

1179 Paul Baloche
Copyright © 1996 Integrity's Hosanna! Music/
Sovereign Music UK

AS WE LIFT UP YOUR NAME, *(Leader – ec*
Let Your fire fall.
Send Your wind and rain,
On Your wings of love.
Pour out from heaven *(All)*
Your passion and presence,
Bring down Your burning desire.

Revival fire, fall!
Revival fire, fall!
Fall on us here
In the power of Your Spirit;
Father, let revival fire fall.
Revival fire, fall!
Revival fire, fall!
Let the flame consume us
With hearts ablaze for Jesus;
Father, let revival fire fall!

As we lift up Your name, *(Leader – echo)*
Let Your kingdom come,
Have Your way in this place,
Let Your will be done.
Pour out from heaven *(All)*
Your passion and presence,
Bring down Your burning desire.

1180 Tré Sheppard
Copyright © 2002 Thankyou Music

AT THE FOOT OF THE CROSS
Where I kneel in adoration,
And I lay my burdens down
I exchange all my sin
For the promise of salvation,
And Your name across my brow.

At the foot of the cross
I give up my vain ambition,
And I leave my selfish pride.
In the peace that is there
Will You restore my vision
In all the places I am blind?

I will wait here at the cross. (×4)

At the foot of the cross
There is healing for this nation,
There is rest for those who wait;
And the love that we find
Is the hope of all creation,
We are stunned by what You gave.

We will wait here at the cross. (×4)

We will wait at the cross,
  hungry generation,
With our broken hearts and lives.
Will You hear, will You come,
Will You fill our desperation?
O God, let this be the time.

We will wait here at the cross. (×4)

181 Martin E. Leckebusch
Copyright © 2000 Kevin Mayhew Ltd

AT THIS TABLE WE REMEMBER
How and where our faith began:
In the pain of crucifixion
Suffered by the Son of Man.

Looking up in adoration
Faith is conscious – He is here!
Christ is present with His people,
This is the call that draws us near.

Heart and mind we each examine:
With honesty we face
All our doubt, our fear and failure,
Then we can receive His grace.

Peace we share with one another:
As from face to face we turn
In our brothers and our sisters
Jesus' body we discern.

Bread and wine are set before us;
As we eat, we look ahead:
We shall dine with Christ in heaven
Where the kingdom feast is spread.

Nourished by the bread of heaven,
Faith and strength and courage grow –
So to witness, serve and suffer,
Out into the world we go.

182 Nathan Fellingham
Copyright © 1999 Thankyou Music

AWAKE, AWAKE, O ZION,
And clothe yourself with strength,
Shake off your dust
And fix your eyes on Him.
For you have been redeemed by
The precious blood of Jesus,
And now you sit enthroned with Him.

*Our God reigns,
He is King of all the earth.
Our God reigns,
And He's seated on the throne.
Lift your voice,
And sing a song of praise.
Our God reigns,
The awesome Lord most high.*

How beautiful the feet are
Of those who bring good news,
For they proclaim the peace that comes from
  God.
Rise up, you holy nation,
Proclaim the great salvation,
And say to Zion 'Your God reigns.'

Emmanuel, Emmanuel,
Our God is with us now.

The watchmen lift their voices,
And raise a shout of joy,
For He will come again.
Then all eyes will see the
Salvation of our God,
For He has redeemed Jerusalem.

1183 Owen Hurter
Copyright © 2001 Thankyou Music

AWAKE, MY SOUL, rise up from your
  sleeping;
Do not slumber or sleep any more.
Raise your weary head to a new day;
Lift your shout, let your voice be heard.

Rocks will cry out if we are silent,
Trees will clap their hands and rejoice;
The mighty ocean roars with a new song,
Mountains bow down to honour Your name.

*Rise up, my soul, and sing.
Rise up, my soul, and sing.
Rise up, my soul, and give glory to the
  Lord.*
(Repeat)

Let the song of a bride in blooming
Thunder clap through the heavens above.
Rising up in true adoration,
Arise and shine for Your light has come.

I don't want to sleep any more,
But I'll awake the dawn with singing.
Hear this crying heart of mine,
As I lift up my song.
(Repeat)

Lift it up, lift it up, lift it up.

1184 Darlene Zschech
Copyright © 1997 Darlene Zschech/
Hillsong Publishing/Kingsway Music

BEAUTIFUL LORD, wonderful Saviour,
I know for sure, all of my days are
Held in Your hand,
Crafted into Your perfect plan.
You gently call me into Your presence,
Guiding me by Your Holy Spirit.
Teach me, dear Lord, to live all of my life
Through Your eyes.

I'm captured by Your holy calling,
Set me apart.
I know You're drawing me to Yourself;
Lead me, Lord, I pray.

Take me, mould me, use me, fill me;
I give my life to the Potter's hand.
Call me, guide me, lead me, walk beside me;
I give my life to the Potter's hand.

1185 Dave Bilbrough
Copyright © 1999 Thankyou Music

BECAUSE OF YOU, *I can be free;*
Because of You, I can be me.
Since that day when love broke through,
My life was changed because of You.

You fill my heart with melody,
Salvation is my song.
The way was opened up for me
To know You as my God.

So I will sing for joy, sing for joy,
Sing for joy to You.
Yes, I will sing for joy, sing for joy,
Sing for joy to You.
(Repeat)

1186 Lara Martin (Abundant Life Ministries,
Bradford, England)
Copyright © 2002 Thankyou Music

BEFORE ONE EVER CAME TO BE,
All the days ordained for me
Were written in Your book of days.
You are the One who fashioned me,
The One I praise continually,
So perfect are Your ways.
I will rejoice and be glad.
And in all things I give thanks.

This is the day You have made,
I will rejoice, I will rejoice:
In You I boast. (in my God)
This is the day You have made,
I will rejoice, I will rejoice:
In You I boast.

1187 Charitie L. Bancroft (1841–92)

BEFORE THE THRONE OF GOD ABOVE,
I have a strong, a perfect plea,
A great High Priest whose name is Love,
Who ever lives and pleads for me.
My name is graven on His hands,
My name is written on His heart;
I know that while in heaven He stands
No tongue can bid me thence depart,
No tongue can bid me thence depart.

When Satan tempts me to despair,
And tells me of the guilt within,
Upward I look and see Him there
Who made an end to all my sin.
Because the sinless Saviour died,
My sinful soul is counted free;
For God the Just is satisfied
To look on Him and pardon me,
To look on Him and pardon me.

Behold Him there! The risen Lamb,
My perfect, spotless righteousness;
The great unchangeable I AM,
The King of glory and of grace!
One with Himself I cannot die,
My soul is purchased with His blood;
My life is hid with Christ on high,
With Christ, my Saviour and my God,
With Christ my Saviour and my God.

1188 Matt Redman
Copyright © 2002 Thankyou Music

BEFRIENDED,
Befriended by the King above all kings.
Surrendered,
Surrendered to the Friend above all friends.

Invited,
Invited deep into this mystery.
Delighted,
Delighted by the wonders I have seen.

> *This will be my story,*
> *This will be my song:*
> *You'll always be my Saviour,*
> *Jesus, You will always have my heart.*

Astounded,
Astounded that Your gospel beckoned me.
Surrounded,
Surrounded, but I've never been so free.

Determined,
Determined now to live this life for You.
You're so worthy,
My greatest gift would be the least You're
due.

BEHOLD THE LAMB OF GLORY COMES,
In majesty He rides.
Behold the Lion of Judah comes,
In majesty He rides.

He rides in majesty, majesty He rides.
He rides in majesty, majesty He rides.

Behold the Sun of Righteousness,
On a white horse He rides.
His cavalry is following Him,
An army from on high.

And when the Lord goes to battle,
Who can stand against His awesome might?

Let God arise
And His enemies be scattered.
Whoa, whoa.
(Repeat)

The watchmen on the tower
Are interceding for the land.
The saints proclaim God's victory,
He stretches forth His hand.

BE LIFTED UP, be lifted up.
As we bow down,
Be lifted up.
(Repeat)

Let the heavens rejoice,
Let the nations be glad.
Let the whole earth tremble,
For You are God.
Come and worship the Lord
In the beauty of holiness.

As we bow down,
Be lifted up.
(Repeat)

BELOVÈD AND BLESSÈD,
The Father's pure delight.
Redeemer, Sustainer,
You're my passion and my prize.

My Brother, my Comforter,
My Shepherd and my Friend.
My Ransom, my Righteousness,
You're the Stream that never ends.

You're unchanging, You're magnificent,
You are all I could desire.
You're my Breath of life,
Sun of righteousness,
You're the Love that satisfies.

There's kindness, compassion
For those who will draw near;
Acceptance, forgiveness,
And a love that conquers fear.

You're the Word of life,
You're the Bread of heaven,
You're the Lion and the Lamb.
All within me cries,
'Lord be glorified
By everything I am.'

Belovèd, my Belovèd.

BLESSÈD ARE THE POOR in spirit,
For theirs is the kingdom of heaven.
Blessèd are the mourning hearts,
Comfort to them will be given.
Blessèd are the humble and meek,
They will inherit the earth.
Blessèd are those who hunger and thirst
For righteousness,
For they will be filled.

Rejoice and be glad,
For great your reward in heaven.
(Repeat)

Blessèd are the merciful,
For mercy to them will be shown.
Blessèd are the pure in heart,
For they will see their God.
Blessèd are the makers of peace,
They will be called sons of God.
Blessèd are those who suffer for Christ
And righteousness,
Theirs is the kingdom of heaven.

Give glory to God,
For He's our reward in heaven.
(Repeat)

Rejoice and be glad,
Give glory to God in heaven.
(Repeat)

1193 Matt & Beth Redman
Copyright © 2002 Thankyou Music

BLESSÈD BE YOUR NAME
In the land that is plentiful,
Where Your streams of abundance flow,
Blessèd be Your name.
And blessèd be Your name
When I'm found in the desert place,
Though I walk through the wilderness,
Blessèd be Your name.

Every blessing You pour out I'll
Turn back to praise.
When the darkness closes in, Lord,
Still I will say:

Blessèd be the name of the Lord,
Blessèd be Your name.
Blessèd be the name of the Lord,
Blessèd be Your glorious name.

Blessèd be Your name
When the sun's shining down on me,
When the world's 'all as it should be',
Blessèd be Your name.
And blessèd be Your name
On the road marked with suffering,
Though there's pain in the offering,
Blessèd be Your name.

You give and take away,
You give and take away.
My heart will choose to say:
Lord, blessèd be Your name.

1194 Geoffrey Ainger
Copyright © 1964 Stainer & Bell Ltd

BORN IN THE NIGHT, Mary's child,
A long way from Your home;
Coming in need, Mary's child,
Born in a borrowed room.

Clear shining light, Mary's child,
Your face lights up our way:
Light of the world, Mary's child,
Dawn on our darkened day.

Truth of our life, Mary's child,
You tell us God is good:
Prove it is true, Mary's child,
Go to Your cross of wood.

Hope of the world, Mary's child,
You're coming soon to reign:
King of the earth, Mary's child,
Walk in our streets again.

1195 Andrea Lawrence & Noel Robinson
Copyright © 2000 Thankyou Music

BREATHE ON ME, O wind of change,
Anoint me with fresh oil from Your throne.
Lord, restore me with new life,
So I'm ready to serve
And I'm ready to go,
Ready to do Your will.
So I'm ready to serve
And I'm ready to go,
Ready to do Your will.

Lord, help me to run this race
And to live by Your grace,
All I want to do is Your will.
(Repeat)

Ready to serve, ready to go,
Ready to do, ready to be,
Ready to do Your will.
(Repeat)

1196 John L. Bell
Copyright © 1998 WGRG, Iona Community

BRING YOUR BEST TO THEIR WORST, *(All*
Bring Your peace to their pain,
God of love, heal Your people.

That none who cry aloud may cry in vain:
(Lead

That those who fear may never walk alone:

That those near death may see the light of
day:

That guilty folk may find themselves forgive

That those who doubt may find a deeper
faith:

That broken folk may know they will be
whole:

1197 Noel Richards & Wayne Drain
Copyright © 1998 Thankyou Music

CALLING ALL NATIONS, *hear the story*
Of God's amazing grace.
Calling all nations, come and worship,
Fill the earth with praise.

Every woman, every man,
Rich and poor, old and young,
Heaven's love is coming down
To wipe all your tears away.

There's a bell to be rung,
There's a song to be sung.
Sweeter music yet to play
When we gather on that day.

1198 Evan Rogers
Copyright © 2000 Thankyou Music

CELEBRATE IN THE LORD,
He is the reason we rejoice;
For He has cast our sins away,
Forgotten now, for ever and always,
Always, always, yes, always,
Always, always.

This is our jubilee,
No debt, no bondage, we are free.
We're free to give Him everything
For we have nothing, now it is all His,
All His, all His, it's all His,
All His, all His.

This is where the party is,
This is where the joy of heaven abounds.
In His presence we are free
To praise, to shout aloud.
This is where the party is,
Singing with the angels, hear the sound.
This is where the party is,
We are dancing on holy ground,
Holy ground, holy ground, holy ground,
Holy ground, holy ground.

For freedom You have set us free,
No longer bound to slavery,
You've broken every chain that binds;
You've conquered sin for ever and all time.
All time, all time, yes, all time,
All time, all time.

Siyavuya, siyavuya, siyavuya. (Repeat)
Jabulani, jabulani, jabulani. (Repeat)

1199 From the Latin, J.M. Neale (1818–66)
Copyright © in this version Jubilate Hymns

CHRIST IS MADE THE SURE FOUNDATION,
Christ the Head and Cornerstone,
Chosen of the Lord and precious,
Binding all the church in one;
Holy Zion's help for ever,
And her confidence alone.

All within that holy city
Dearly loved of God on high,
In exultant jubilation
Sing, in perfect harmony;
God the One-in-Three adoring
In glad hymns eternally.

We as living stones invoke You:
Come among us, Lord, today!
With Your gracious loving-kindness
Hear Your children as we pray;
And the fullness of Your blessing
In our fellowship display.

Here entrust to all Your servants
What we long from You to gain –
That on earth and in the heavens
We one people shall remain,
Till united in Your glory
Evermore with You we reign.

Praise and honour to the Father,
Praise and honour to the Son,
Praise and honour to the Spirit,
Ever Three and ever One:
One in power and one in glory
While eternal ages run.

1200 Charles Wesley (1707–88)

CHRIST, WHOSE GLORY FILLS THE SKIES,
Christ, the true, the only light,
Sun of righteousness, arise,
Triumph o'er the shades of night:
Day-spring from on high, be near;
Day-star in my heart appear.

Dark and cheerless is the morn
Unaccompanied by Thee;
Joyless is the day's return,
Till Thy mercy's beams I see;
Till they inward light impart,
Glad my eyes, and warm my heart.

Visit then this soul of mine;
Pierce the gloom of sin and grief;
Fill me, radiancy divine;
Scatter all my unbelief;
More and more Thyself display,
Shining to the perfect day.

1201 Alexander Gondo
Copyright © World Council of Churches

COME ALL YOU PEOPLE, } (×3)
Come and praise your Maker.
Come now and worship the Lord.

Uyai mose, tinamate Mwari, (×3)
Uyai mose zvino.

1202 after Bianco da Siena (1367–1434)
Richard F. Littledale (1833–90)

COME DOWN, O LOVE DIVINE,
Seek Thou this soul of mine
And visit it with Thine own ardour glowing;
O Comforter, draw near,
Within my heart appear,
And kindle it, Thy holy flame bestowing.

O let it freely burn,
Till earthly passions turn
To dust and ashes, in its heat consuming;
And let Thy glorious light
Shine ever on my sight,
And clothe me round, the while my path
    illuming.

Let holy charity
Mine outward vesture be,
And lowliness become mine inner clothing;
True lowliness of heart,
Which takes the humbler part,
And o'er its own shortcomings weeps with
    loathing.

And so the yearning strong,
With which the soul will long,
Shall far outpass the power of human telling;
For none can guess its grace,
Till he become the place
Wherein the Holy Spirit makes His dwelling.

1203 Nathan Fellingham
Copyright © 2001 Thankyou Music

COME, LET US WORSHIP the King of kings,
The Creator of all things.
Let your soul arise to Him,
Come and bless the Lord our King.

Lord, my heart and voice I raise,
To praise Your wondrous ways,
And with confidence I come
To approach Your heavenly throne.

Come and fill this place with Your glory,
Come and captivate our gaze;
Come and fill us with Your fire,
That the world might know Your name.

(For) You are God,
And You're worthy to be praised,
And You are good,
For Your love will never end:
The great I Am,
You are faithful in all of Your ways.
(Repeat)

1204 Alan Rose
Copyright © 1998 Thankyou Music

COME NEAR TO ME, as I come near to You;
Pour out Your mercy and Your grace.
I need Your love, I need Your tenderness;
I'm longing for Your sweet embrace.

My heart cries out for more of You, Lord;
I'm so hungry for Your presence.
Your love is water to my soul.
I will be satisfied with You, Lord;
You fulfil my deepest longing.
Pour out Your Spirit once again.

Draw close to me, as I draw close to You.
Release Your power from above.
I'm dry and thirsty, Lord, come and fill me up
I'm waiting for Your touch of love.

I've felt Your presence, Lord,
I've tasted of Your love.
Now all I am cries out for more of You,
I want more of You;
More of Your Spirit poured from above,
More of Your power, more of Your love.

1205 Brian Doerksen
Copyright © 1998 Vineyard Songs (UK/Eire)/
Adm. by CopyCare

COME, NOW IS THE TIME to worship,
Come, now is the time to give your heart.
Come, just as you are to worship,
Come, just as you are before your God.
Come.

One day every tongue will confess You are
    God.
One day every knee will bow.
Still, the greatest treasure remains for those
Who gladly choose You now.

1206 Keith Getty & Kristyn Lennox
Copyright © 2002 Thankyou Music

COME, PRAISE THE LORD,
He is life in all its fullness;
Will you lift your voice?
Come, praise the Lord,
He is light that shatters darkness;
We have come to rejoice.
All around the world He is calling
People who would take up His call
And follow Him.

Every breath be praise,
Every heart be raised
To the King of all creation.
Every breath be praise,
Every heart be raised
To the Lord of all.

Come, praise the Lord,
He is love that welcomes sinners;
Will you give your life?
Come praise the Lord,
He is great above all others;
All His ways are right.
All around the world He is calling
People who would take up His call
And follow Him.

1207
Martin E. Leckebusch
Copyright © 2000 Kevin Mayhew Ltd

COME, SEE THE LORD in His breathtaking
  splendour:
Gaze at His majesty – bow and adore!
Enter His presence with wonder and
  worship –
He is the King and enthroned evermore.

He is the Word who was sent by the Father,
Born as a baby, a child of our race:
God here among us, revealed as a servant,
Walking the pathway of truth and of grace.

He is the Lamb who was slain to redeem us –
There at the cross His appearance was
  marred;
Though He emerged from the grave as the
  victor,
Still from the nails and the spear He is
  scarred.

He is the Lord who ascended in triumph –
Ever the sound of His praises shall ring!
Hail Him the First and the Last, the Almighty:
Jesus, our Prophet, our Priest and our King.

Come, see the Lord in His breathtaking
  splendour:
Gaze at His majesty – bow and adore!
Come and acknowledge Him Saviour and
  Sovereign:
Jesus our King is enthroned evermore.

1208
Stuart Townend
Copyright © 1999 Thankyou Music

COME, SEE THIS GLORIOUS LIGHT
As it shines on you,
Bringing grace and peace
To the depths of your soul.
Come, see the wounds of love,
Scars that make you whole,
Blood that paid the price
For the sins of the world.
He is the Light everlasting,
He is the First and the Last.

Blessing and honour and glory and power,
Blessing and honour and glory and power,
Blessing and honour and glory and power
To You, Lord,
You're the King of the Ages.
Justice and truth are the marks of Your
  reign,
Angels adore You, the Lamb who was
  slain,
They're crying 'holy' again and again,
Lord Jesus,
You're the King of the Ages.

Come, all you thirsty and poor,
Come and feast on Him,
That your souls may live
And be satisfied.
Come from the ends of the earth,
Every tribe and tongue,
Lift your voice and praise
Your eternal Reward.
He's the Desire of the nations,
He is the Faithful and True.

1209
Dave Bilbrough
Copyright © 1999 Thankyou Music

COME TO THE TABLE,
Drink from His cup;
Come to the table,
You can never get enough
Of His love for you,
Of His love for you.
Oh, such precious love.
Oh, such precious love.

Turn your face to Him.
Let the feast begin.
With the angels sing:
Hallelujah, hallelujah,
Hallelujah to the Lord.

We will come to the table,
Drink from Your cup;
Come to the table,
We can never get enough
Of the love You give,
Of the love You give.
Oh, such precious love.
Oh, such precious love.

1210
Martin E. Leckebusch
Copyright © 2000 Kevin Mayhew Ltd

COME, WOUNDED HEALER, Your sufferings
  reveal –
The scars You accepted, our anguish to heal.
Your wounds bring such comfort in body and
  soul
To all who bear torment and yearn to be
  whole.

Come, hated Lover, and gather us near,
Your welcome, Your teaching, Your challenge
    to hear:
Where scorn and abuse cause rejection and
    pain,
Your loving acceptance makes hope live
    again!

Come, broken Victor, condemned to a cross –
How great are the treasures we gain from
    Your loss!
Your willing agreement to share in our strife
Transforms our despair into fullness of life.

1211 Matt Redman
Copyright © 1996 Thankyou Music

CREATE IN ME the purest of hearts,
According to Your unfailing love.
Renew a steadfast spirit within
And wash away my sin.
And make me like the snow,
But even whiter still.

> *I just want to have a pure heart,*
> *I just want to have a pure, pure heart.*
> *I just want to have a pure heart,*
> *I just want to have a pure, pure heart.*

I'm clay within the Potter's hand
Where tenderness meets discipline.
I need it all, Lord, come and form
Your holiness in me.
And make me like the snow,
But even whiter still.

1212 Tim Hughes
Copyright © 2001 Thankyou Music

DAY AFTER DAY, I'll search to find You;
Day after day, I'll wait for You.
The deeper I go, the more I love Your name.

> *So keep my heart pure,*
> *And my ways true,*
> *As I follow You.*
> *Keep me humble,*
> *I'll stay mindful*
> *Of Your mercies, Lord.*

I'll cherish Your word,
I'll seek Your presence,
I'll chase after You with all I have.
As one day I know
I'll see You face to face.

1213 Gerard Markland
Copyright © 1978 Kevin Mayhew Ltd

DO NOT BE AFRAID,
For I have redeemed you.
I have called you by your name;
You are Mine.

When you walk through the waters I'll be
    with you;
You will never sink beneath the waves.

When the fire is burning all around you,
You will never be consumed by the flames.

When the fear of loneliness is looming,
Then remember I am at your side.

When you dwell in the exile of the stranger,
Remember you are precious in My eyes.

You are Mine, O My child; I am your Father,
And I love you with a perfect love.

1214 Karen Lafferty
Copyright © 1981 Maranatha! Praise Inc./
Adm. by CopyCare

DON'T BUILD YOUR HOUSE on the sandy
    land,
Don't build it too near the shore.
Well, it may look kind of nice,
But you'll have to build it twice,
Oh, you'll have to build your house once
    more.

You better build your house upon a rock,
Make a good foundation on a solid spot.
Oh, the storms may come and go,
But the peace of God you will know.

(Descant)
Rock of ages, cleft for me,
Let me hide myself in Thee.

1215 Wayne Drain, Noel Richards, Wayne Freeman,
Neil Costello & Bradley Mason
Copyright © 2001 Thankyou Music

DO YOU LOVE TO PRAISE THE LORD? *(echo)*
Do you love to praise the Lord? *(echo)*
Lift your voices high,
Raise your hands to the sky.
(First time)
Make a joyful noise!

(Second time)
Everybody dance!

Praise Him in the dance,
Everybody dance!
Praise Him in the dance,
Everybody dance!

We have come to praise the Lord. *(echo)*
We have come to praise the Lord. *(echo)*
Lift our voices high,
Raise our hands to the sky,
(First time)
Make a joyful noise!

(Second time)
Then we're gonna dance!

We love to praise the Lord;
It's what we're made for.
We love to praise the Lord;
It's in our nature.
We love to praise the Lord,
It's deep within us.
We love to praise the Lord
With everything that's in us *(x3)*
We will dance!

1216 Ian Hannah
Copyright © 2001 Thankyou Music

DRAW ME CLOSER, precious Saviour,
Nearer to Your holy throne;
Let me know Your cleansing power,
As I wait on You alone.
I am nothing without You, Lord,
I am naked, weak and poor;
But in You I find a fullness,
Nothing else can give me more.

When the waters of destruction
Try to sweep me far away,
Jesus, You are still my anchor;
I need never be afraid.
I will cling to You, my Master,
Holding on with surety.
Pressing onward, looking upward,
Until Jesus, You I see.

Help me listen to Your whisper,
Help me live obediently.
Give me courage in the battles,
Strength to face uncertainty.
Help me never to deny You,
But to cross that finish line.
Moving forward, never backward,
To claim the prize as mine.

1217 Kelly Carpenter
Copyright © 1994 Mercy/Vineyard Publishing/
Adm. by CopyCare

DRAW ME CLOSE TO YOU,
Never let me go.
I lay it all down again,
To hear You say that I'm Your friend.
You are my desire,
No one else will do,
'Cause nothing else could take Your place,
To feel the warmth of Your embrace.
Help me find the way,
Bring me back to You.

You're all I want,
You're all I've ever needed.
You're all I want,
Help me know You are near.

1218 Dave Doran
Copyright © 2001 Thankyou Music

DRAW ME NEAR TO YOU;
Can I come so close
That I can hear Your song of love
That heals my broken heart?

> *And I will walk with You,*
> *Another footstep now.*
> *Can we walk on again,*
> *Another footstep now?*
> *I've walked in fields of pain,*
> *I've sheltered in Your love;*
> *In the valley of death's shadow,*
> *I will fear no evil,*
> *For You are here with me.*
> *My comfort be, my comfort be.*

Draw me near to You,
Even closer still,
So I can see Your scars of love
That saved my wounded soul.

1219 Brian Houston & Tom Brock
Copyright © 2002 Thankyou Music

DRAW ME TO YOUR SIDE, Lord,
Let me feel Your breath,
The very breath of life, Lord,
Rest my head upon Your chest.
And hold me in Your arms, Lord,
Wrap me in Your embrace,
Close enough that I can feel
Your breath upon my face.

> *When I cry out in passion,*
> *To love You more than this,*
> *Renew me in Your presence*
> *And refresh me with Your kiss.*

Far too long I've begged You
For Your sweet release,
To be lost in Your presence
And to know the taste of Your lips.
And for a heart like Yours, God,
And for the mind of Christ
To know no shame and no restraint
In my worship sacrifice.

Well, the curse has been broken,
I know the curtain is torn in two,
No child, no man or woman
Need be separated from You.
The lonely and the broken,
Rejected and despised
Run through the gates of grace by faith,
Into the arms of Christ.

1220 David Lyle Morris & Faith Forster
Copyright © 2000 Thankyou Music

DRAWN FROM EVERY TRIBE,
Every tongue and nation,
Gathered before the throne.
Casting down their crowns,
They fall at His feet
And worship the Lord alone.
What a glorious sight,
Dressed in robes of white,
Washed by the blood of the Lamb.

Singing praise and glory,
Wisdom and thanks,
Honour, power and strength
Be to our God, for ever
And ever, amen.

We are those who follow,
Through scenes of fiery trial,
Drawing from wells of grace.
Through the darkest valley
From the depths of pain,
We'll come to that holy place.
We will overcome
By looking to the Lamb
And worshipping face to face.

Never will we hunger,
We'll no longer thirst,
There's shade from the heat of day.
Led to springs of life,
Jesus, our Shepherd,
Will wipe every tear away.
Our God upon the throne
Will shelter all His own
Who worship Him night and day.

All glory and honour and power to Jesus,
All glory and honour and power to Jesus,
Forever and ever and ever and ever,
Forever and ever and ever and ever,
Amen, amen, amen.

1221 Taizé, music: Jacques Berthier (1923–94)
Copyright © Ateliers et Presses de Taizé

EAT THIS BREAD, drink this cup,
Come to Him and never be hungry.
Eat this bread, drink this cup,
Trust in Him and you will not thirst.

(Alternative words)
Jesus Christ, Bread of Life,
Those who come to You will not hunger.
Jesus Christ, risen Lord,
Those who trust in You will not thirst.

1222 William Whiting (1825–78)

ETERNAL FATHER, STRONG TO SAVE,
Whose arm hath bound the restless wave,
Who bidd'st the mighty ocean deep
Its own appointed limits keep:
O hear us when we cry to Thee
For those in peril on the sea.

O Christ, whose voice the waters heard,
And hushed their raging at Thy word,
Who walkedst on the foaming deep,
And calm amid the storm didst sleep:
O hear us when we cry to Thee
For those in peril on the sea.

O Holy Spirit, who didst brood
Upon the waters dark and rude,
And bid their angry tumult cease,
And give, for wild confusion, peace:
O hear us when we cry to Thee
For those in peril on the sea.

O Trinity of love and power,
Our brethren shield in danger's hour;
From rock and tempest, fire and foe,
Protect them wheresoe'er they go:
Thus evermore shall rise to Thee
Glad hymns of praise from land and sea.

1223 Sue Rinaldi & Caroline Bonnett
Copyright © 2001 Thankyou Music

EVERLASTING, ever true,
All creation sings to You.
Ever faithful, living Lord,
Let the sound of praise be heard.

Jesus, You are
All that I am living for
And all that I believe is in You, Jesus,
All that I am living for
And all that I believe is in You.

Never changing, awesome God,
Sing the glory of the Lord.
Ever loving, holy One,
I will praise what You have done.

 1224 Lara Martin (Abundant Life Ministries, Bradford, England)
Copyright © 2002 Thankyou Music

EVERY BREATH I BREATHE comes from You,
I'll never take it for granted.
All that I have, all I've ever needed,
You have provided.

You know when I sit, You know when I rise,
You know my thoughts completely.
You hem me in before and behind:
Such love is hard to describe.

You are my God, You are my God.
As long as I have breath I will sing of Your
*   greatness.*
You are my source, my all in all,
My first love, the One I love,
You are my God.

Precious to me are Your thoughts, O God;
No wisdom or knowledge is greater.
Praise be to You, Name above all names:
Who reigns forever, ever and ever, *(×3)*
Who reigns forevermore.
You reign forever, ever and ever, *(×3)*
You reign forevermore.

1225 Matt Redman
Copyright © 1998 Thankyou Music

EVERY DAY, I see more of Your beauty.
Every day, I know more of my frailty, Lord.
And I can only hope that I'll be changed,
Even as I look upon Your face.

For the eyes of my heart,
They are on You forever,
They are on You forever.
Yes, the eyes of my heart,
They are on You forever,
They are on You forever.

Every day, I see more of Your greatness.
Every day, I know more of my weakness,
    Lord.
And I can only hope that I'll be changed,
Even as I look upon Your face.

1226 Robin Mark
Copyright © 2001 Thankyou Music

EVERY DAY HE IS WATCHING
From the heavens and the skies.
And He scans the horizon,
Looking for the sign
Of a son or a daughter
With a prodigal heart,
Coming back to the Father of life.

And the Shepherd is searching
For the sheep who's gone astray,
Though there's ninety and nine safe,
At the closing of the day.
His pursuit is relentless,
His obsession divine;
It's the heart of the Father of life.

Oh, His compassion is for everyone.
Yes, for the lost and the afraid.
And if you listen you can hear His voice,
Hear Him calling,
Hear Him calling your name.

Have you seen my belovèd?
He is radiant and most fair.
In the evening He calls me,
I can see His shadow there.
I will rise up to meet Him,
I will run to His side;
To the Son of the Father of life.

Oh, Your compassion is for everyone.
Yes, for the lost and the afraid.
And if I listen I can hear Your voice,
Hear You calling,
Hear You calling my name.

1227 Noel Richards & Wayne Drain
Copyright © 2001 Thankyou Music

EVERY MORNING I will praise You,
Every moment I am Yours.
Every evening I will worship,
Every day I love You more.

I revel in Your mercy,
I marvel at Your grace.
I need a thousand lifetimes
To give You all my praise.

At night, when I am sleeping,
In every waking hour,
I know You will protect me,
My God, my strong high tower.

1228 Dave Wellington

FALLING, moving closer,
Deep into You.
Feasting, drinking my fill,
Tasting of You.

Waiting, listening, hoping
Here's where You are.
Craving, calling Your name,
I need You more.

I will hold on,
Hold through the fire,
Cling through the rain,
I long to hear You.
I need You here,
All that You are,
Only Your touch
Will satisfy me.

1229 Love Maria Willis (1824–1908)

FATHER, HEAR THE PRAYER WE OFFER:
Not for ease that prayer shall be,
But for strength, that we may ever
Live our lives courageously.

Not for ever in green pastures
Do we ask our way to be:
But by steep and rugged pathways
Would we strive to climb to Thee.

Not for ever by still waters
Would we idly quiet stay;
But would smite the living fountains
From the rocks along our way.

Be our strength in hours of weakness,
In our wanderings be our Guide;
Through endeavour, failure, danger,
Father, be Thou at our side.

Let our path be bright or dreary,
Storm or sunshine be our share;
May our souls, in hope unweary,
Make Thy work our ceaseless prayer.

1230 Andrew Ulugia & Wayne Huirua

FATHER, INTO YOUR COURTS I WILL ENTER,
Maker of heaven and earth,
I tremble in Your holy presence.
Glory, glory in Your sanctuary,
Splendour and majesty, Lord, before You;
All life adores You.

All the earth will declare
That Your love is everywhere.
The fields will exalt, seas resound.
Hear the trees' joyful cry,
Praising You and so will I.
A new song I'll sing,
Lord, I will glorify and bless Your holy
  name.

1231 Darlene Zschech

FATHER OF LIFE, DRAW ME CLOSER,
Lord, my heart is set on You:
Let me run the race of time
With Your life enfolding mine,
And let the peace of God,
Let it reign.

O Holy Spirit, Lord, my comfort;
Strengthen me, hold my head up high:
And I stand upon Your truth,
Bringing glory unto You,
And let the peace of God,
Let it reign.

O Lord, I hunger for more of You;
Rise up within me, let me know Your truth
O Holy Spirit, saturate my soul,
And let the life of God fill me now,
Let Your healing power
Breathe life and make me whole,
And the peace of God,
Let it reign.

1232 Geoff Twigg

FATHER, WE HAVE SINNED AGAINST YOU,
Failed to do what's right;
We have walked alone in darkness,
Hiding from the light.
Father, we have run away
From what we know is true;
Now we turn around and we are
Coming home to You.

We have sinned, (we have sinned)
We have broken Your law,
We're returning once more home to You;
We have sinned, (we have sinned)
We are seeking Your face,
We return by Your grace home to You.

FIND REST, ALL THE EARTH, in God alone.
We find our only hope from heaven's throne.
Our Rock, our Salvation,
No, we shall not be shaken.
Find rest all the earth in God alone.

His peace holds you firm in the storm.
His love brings new life forevermore.
Our Rock, our Salvation,
No, we shall not be shaken.
His peace holds you firm in the storm.

Tell of the One who lifted your soul,
Share all His goodness.
Children of light declaring the truth,
That all may know.

FOR THE FRUITS OF HIS CREATION,
Thanks be to God!
For His gifts to every nation,
Thanks be to God!
For the ploughing, sowing, reaping,
Silent growth while we are sleeping;
Future needs in earth's safe keeping,
Thanks be to God!

In the just reward of labour,
God's will is done;
In the help we give our neighbour,
God's will is done;
In our worldwide task of caring
For the hungry and despairing,
In the harvests we are sharing,
God's will is done.

For the harvests of His Spirit,
Thanks be to God!
For the good we all inherit,
Thanks be to God!
For the wonders that astound us,
For the truths that still confound us;
Most of all, that love has found us,
Thanks be to God!

FOR THE HEALING OF THE NATIONS,
Lord, we pray with one accord;
For a just and equal sharing
Of the things that earth affords.
To a life of love in action
Help us rise and pledge our word.

Lead us forward into freedom;
From despair Your world release,
That, redeemed from war and hatred,
All may come and go in peace.
Show us how through care and goodness
Fear will die and hope increase.

All that kills abundant living,
Let it from the earth be banned;
Pride of status, race or schooling,
Dogmas that obscure Your plan.
In our common quest for justice
May we hallow life's brief span.

You, Creator-God, have written
Your great name on humankind;
For our growing in Your likeness
Bring the life of Christ to mind;
That by our response and service
Earth its destiny may find.

FOR THE LORD IS GOOD,
And His love endures forever;
He's a faithful God
To all generations.
For the Lord is good,
And His mercies will not fail us;
They are new each day,
O, lift your voice and say,
'The Lord is good!'

Great is Your faithfulness, O Lord. *(Leader)*
Great is Your faithfulness, O Lord. *(Echo)*
Your loving kindness fills our *(Leader)*
Hearts to overflowing. *(All)*
Songs of rejoicing and sweet praise, *(Leader)*
Songs of praise! *(Echo)*
They fill our hearts, *(Leader)*
They fill our hearts, *(Echo)*
They fill our days. *(All)*

FORTH IN THY NAME, O LORD, I GO,
My daily labour to pursue,
Thee, only Thee, resolved to know
In all I think, or speak, or do.

The task Thy wisdom hath assigned
O let me cheerfully fulfil;
In all my works Thy presence find,
And prove Thy acceptable will.

Thee may I set at my right hand,
Whose eyes my inmost substance see;
And labour on at Thy command,
And offer all my works to Thee.

Give me to bear Thy easy yoke,
And every moment watch and pray,
And still to things eternal look,
And hasten to Thy glorious day.

For Thee delightfully employ
Whate'er Thy bounteous grace hath given,
And run my course with even joy,
And closely walk with Thee to heaven.

1238   Viola Grafstrom
Copyright © 2002 Thankyou Music

FROM THE RISING OF THE SUN,
Even to its going down,
Shall Your name be great.
Through all the earth,
Among the nations, we give You praise;
Your name is high above
All other gods.

Jesus, Lover of my soul,
You alone are King, worthy of my praise.
My worship I'll give to only one;
O Lord, my heart I'll bring
When to You I come.

Holiness, Majesty and King,
Let Your will be done
When we worship bring.
Eternal, Your love will remain;
Before Your throne we bow,
With our voices sing.

1239   Stuart Townend
Copyright © 1999 Thankyou Music

FROM THE SQUALOR OF A BORROWED STABLE,
By the Spirit and a virgin's faith;
To the anguish and the shame of scandal
Came the Saviour of the human race!
But the skies were filled with the praise of heaven,
Shepherds listen as the angels tell
Of the Gift of God come down to man
At the dawning of Immanuel.

King of heaven now the Friend of sinners,
Humble servant in the Father's hands,
Filled with power and the Holy Spirit,
Filled with mercy for the broken man.
Yes, He walked my road and He felt my pain,
Joys and sorrows that I know so well;
Yet His righteous steps give me hope again –
I will follow my Immanuel!

Through the kisses of a friend's betrayal,
He was lifted on a cruel cross;
He was punished for a world's transgressions,
He was suffering to save the lost.
He fights for breath, He fights for me,
Loosing sinners from the claims of hell;
And with a shout our souls are free –
Death defeated by Immanuel!

Now He's standing in the place of honour,
Crowned with glory on the highest throne,
Interceding for His own belovèd
Till His Father calls to bring them home!
Then the skies will part as the trumpet sounds
Hope of heaven or the fear of hell;
But the Bride will run to her Lover's arms,
Giving glory to Immanuel!

1240   Stuart Townend
Copyright © 1998 Thankyou Music

GIVER OF GRACE,
How priceless Your love for me,
Purer than silver, more costly than gold.
Giver of life, all that I'll ever need,
Strength for my body and food for my soul.

Oh, You are good, so good to me.
Yes, You are good, so good to me.
Oh, You are good, so good to me.
Yes, You are good, so good to me

Giver of hope, Rock of salvation,
Tower of refuge, yet there in my pain.
Now I'm secure, loved for eternity,
Showered with blessings
And lavished with grace.

I've never known a love
So perfect in its faithfulness;
It lifts me up to the highest place.
A glimpse of heaven
And a taste of my inheritance,
I know that one day I'll be with You.

1241   Chris Tomlin
Copyright © 2000 worshiptogether.com songs/
Six Steps Music/Adm. by Kingsway Music

GIVE THANKS TO THE LORD,
Our God and King:
His love endures forever.
For He is good, He is above all things.
His love endures forever.
Sing praise, sing praise.

ith a mighty hand
nd an outstretched arm
is love endures forever.
or the life that's been reborn.
is love endures forever.
ing praise, sing praise.
ing praise, sing praise.

Forever God is faithful,
Forever God is strong.
Forever God is with us,
Forever.
(Repeat)
Forever.

om the rising to the setting sun,
is love endures forever.
y the grace of God, we will carry on.
is love endures forever.
ing praise, sing praise.
ing praise, sing praise.

242 Geraldine Latty
Copyright © 2000 Thankyou Music

IVING IT ALL TO YOU,
iving it all to You,
o more hidden agenda,
iving it all to You.
aying my burdens down,
owing in full surrender,
neeling before Your cross,
iving it all to You.

243 Kate & Miles Simmonds
Copyright © 2002 Thankyou Music

OD GAVE US HIS SON,
he sinless One to be sin for us,
hat we might be the righteousness of God.
our kingdom has come,
e're being changed into Your likeness;
hildren of light, it's our time to arise.

I am not ashamed,
I know whom I've believed,
For God Himself has come to me,
Now Jesus is my destiny.
I know I am changed,
And all You've given me,
This hope, this love, this life,
I can't deny Your power within me.
So here I am, send me.

ow we are in You,
nd You have given us Your message
o tell the world: be reconciled to God.
our favour is here
 this day of salvation.
ow is the time, let Your glory arise!

Purify us, Lord,
So we're spotless and pure
As we hold out Your word
To this generation.
How can they hear,
And how can they believe,
How can they call on Your name
Unless we tell them?
(Repeat)

1244 Don Moen & Paul Overstreet
Copyright © 1995 Integrity's Hosanna! Music/
Sovereign Music UK/Scarlet Moon Music/
Adm. by Copyright Management Services

GOD IS GOOD ALL THE TIME!
He put a song of praise in this heart of
mine.
God is good all the time!
Through the darkest night
His light will shine:
God is good, God is good all the time.

If you're walking through the valley
And there are shadows all around,
Do not fear, He will guide you,
He will keep you safe and sound;
'Cause He has promised to never leave you
Nor forsake you, and His word is true.

We were sinners, so unworthy,
Still for us He chose to die:
Filled us with His Holy Spirit,
Now we can stand and testify
That His love is everlasting
And His mercies, they will never end.

Though I may not understand
All the plans You have for me,
My life is in Your hands,
And through the eyes of faith
I can clearly see:

1245 David Lyle Morris & Nick Wynne-Jones
Copyright © 2001 Thankyou Music

GOD IS OUR FATHER in heaven above,
And He cares for His children with infinite
 love.
Our worries are needless; look up in the sky
Where carefree and singing the birds freely
 fly.
Their Maker who knows them,
Supplies all their food;
How much more is our Father
Concerned for our good?

For our Father in heaven
Knows all of our needs;
He will care for us always.
We surrender our all,
And make the kingdom of heaven our
    goal.

Look at the lilies and see how they grow:
They are clothed by God's goodness in
    beautiful show.
Our Father in heaven who cares for each
    flower,
Provides for us always, so great is His power.
The kingdom of heaven
And His righteousness
We will seek with a passion
So all may be blessed.

1246 Louise Fellingham
Copyright © 2002 Thankyou Music

GOD OF MERCY, hear our cry,
Turn Your hand today.
Bring relief from their pain,
Be their comfort.
And every day they're given breath,
Give them strength to live.
And as their weary bodies fail,
Fighting is over, flesh gives way,
Be their light to guide them home.

God of mercy, hear our cry,
Heal their souls today.
Give them peace from their fears,
Be their hope, Lord.
And every day they're given breath,
Give them strength to live.
And as their weary bodies fail,
Fighting is over, flesh gives way,
Be their star to guide them home.

Sometimes I don't know what to ask for,
Sometimes I don't know what to say,
But I know that You are watching over them.
Sometimes I don't know how to pray for,
Sometimes I don't know how to give,
But I know that You are watching over them,
And their life is not in vain.

1247 Matt Redman
Copyright © 1998 Thankyou Music

GOD OF RESTORATION,
My hope is in the life You bring to me.
Healer of my wounds,
I thank You, oh I thank You.
God of my salvation,
With saving love You came to rescue me.
Healer of my soul,
I thank You, oh I thank You,
Today and every day.

I am Yours, I am Yours,
Every breath that I breathe,
Every moment that's lived.
I am Yours, I am Yours,
You're the reason to breathe,
You're the reason to live.
And now everyone that You have saved
Will come to be Your praise,
I am Yours.

Singing of a love now,
You taught this broken heart to sing again.
Every day I'll come
To thank You, oh, to thank You.
Singing of a life now,
You taught this wounded soul to live again.
Every day I'll live
To thank You, oh, to thank You,
Today and every day.

And if my food is to do Your will,
Then I'm hungry, still hungry;
There's so much more that I need to give
To thank You, to thank You.
Yes, if my food is to do Your will,
Then I'm hungry, still hungry;
There's so much more that I need to give
Today and every day.

1248 Sue Rinaldi, Caroline Bonnett & Steve Bassett
Copyright © 2001 Thankyou Music

GOD OF THE MOUNTAINS,
God of the sea;
God of the heavens
Of eternity.
God of the future,
God of the past;
God of the present,
God of all history.

Creation praise will thunder to You,
Thunder to You, thunder to You.
Creation praise will thunder to You.
I'm lost in the wonder,
Lost in the wonder of You.

Wisdom of ages,
Light in the dark;
Home for the outcast,
Peace for the heart.
Friend of the lonely,
Strength for oppressed;
Voice of the voiceless,
God of all liberty.

1249 Brian Houston
Copyright © 2002 Thankyou Music

GOD, YOU ARE GOOD, God, You are kind.
God, You are sun, God, You are shine.
God, You are truth, God, You are pure.
You've melted my heart,
And now I am Yours.

I'm happy to be a friend of God.
I'm happy that God's a friend to me.

You're bursting with love
For the ones that You made.
You're happy to bless
Every one of their days.
You humble the proud
But You raise up the low.
You cry for the lost
But You eat with the poor.

And You love me so much
That You weep for my pain,
And You guide with Your touch.
For it is not Your heart to see me fall,
Or let my sin remain.

1250 Gareth Robinson
Copyright © 2001 Thankyou Music

GOOD AND GRACIOUS,
Attributes of a loving Father,
You're high and mighty,
But humble all the same.
You have made the heavens and the earth,
And You made us in Your image, Lord.

Holy, holy, holy is the Lord Almighty,
And we rejoice in You alone,
For You are worthy.
And You have given life to me,
And I love to worship at Your feet,
And I love to love You just for who You are.

Death and hell are
Now no longer things I fear because
You have saved me
And I'm grateful to the core.
I'm Your child because of Jesus' blood,
And Your Spirit leads me,
Guides me, fills me.

I'm so grateful for the things
You have given me:
Your love, Your grace, Your joy,
Your peace and more.
Holy, holy.
Holy, holy.

1251 Dave Bilbrough
Copyright © 2000 Thankyou Music

GRACE AND MERCY wash over me,
Cleanse my soul with Your healing stream.
Here I stand with this prayer within my heart.
Take me deeper in the river that flows with
    Your love.

Thank You, thank You,
Oh what riches are mine in Christ Jesus.
Thank You, thank You,
Your forgiveness is so undeserved.

1252 Ian Hannah
Copyright © 2001 Thankyou Music

GREAT AND MARVELLOUS are Your deeds,
    Lord;
Just and true are all of Your ways.
Who would dare to never fear You,
Or bring glory to Your name.
For nothing compares to You.

You are worthy to receive all
Of the glory, honour and power.
By You all things were created
And by You all things are sustained.
For nothing compares to You.
No, nothing compares to You.

Every nation rise and sing
Praises to our glorious King.
Every tongue in one accord
Cry out and confess:
'Jesus is Lord!'

'Hallelujah' cry Your servants,
'We will worship' both great and small.
King of all kings, Lord of all lords,
You will reign for evermore.
For nothing compares to You.
No, nothing compares to You.

1253 Geraldine Latty & Carey Luce
Copyright © 2002 Thankyou Music

GREAT AND MARVELLOUS are Your deeds,
O God, sovereign over all,
Just and righteous in every way.
Great King for all time eternal.
Who shall not fear You, Lord?
Who shall not honour Your name?
Who shall not fear You, Lord?
There is none the same.

All the nations, every race,
Coming now to seek Your face.
Singing to the Holy One,
Jesus Christ, God's only Son.
All the people in this place,
Thanking You for saving grace,
Burdens rolled to Calvary,
Once in chains but now set free.

Great and marvellous are Your deeds,
O Lord, how we long to see Your
Plan in our time revealed:
Hearts longing to worship Jesus.
And we will fear You, Lord;
And we will honour Your name.
Yes, we will fear You, Lord:
There is none the same.

1254 Author unknown
Copyright control

GREAT IS HE who's the King of kings
And the Lord of lords,
He is wonderful!

Alleluia, alleluia,
Alleluia, He is wonderful!

Alleluia, salvation and glory,
Honour and power, He is wonderful!

1255 Malcolm du Plessis & Victor S. Masondo
Copyright © 1993 Maranatha! Music/
Adm. by CopyCare/& Isondo Music

HALLELUJAH, HOSANNA,
Hallelujah, hosanna,
Hallelujah, hosanna,
Hallelujah, hosanna!
(Repeat)

God has exalted Jesus to the highest place,
And given Him the name that is above every
    name,
That at the name of Jesus every knee shall
    bow
And every tongue confess that He is Lord.

Hallalango Jesu, hallalango Jesu,
Hallalango Jesu, hallala O hallala.
Hallalango Jesu, hallalango Jesu,
Hallalango Jesu, Nkosi!

1256 Brian Houston
Copyright © 2002 Thankyou Music

HAVE I NOT BEEN FAITHFUL to You, Lord?
Have I not offered up my prayers
And tried to follow Your word?
Lord, will You search me,
Show me where I'm wrong?

I've been waiting for the blessing
For far too long,
I've been waiting for the blessing
For far too long.

Now Lord, forgive me,
For speaking this right out.
But I see the wicked prosper
While the godly go without.
No, I can't read human hearts,
But do You know where I'm coming from?

Do not be angry with me, O my God,
Please don't hide Your face away.
I'm like a child, and I'm down on my knees
And I'm begging for You
Just to bless me today.

Lord, up ahead You know
I see a lonely road.
Got this burden on my back,
It's such a heavy load.
These days I've questions,
But there's no answers in my songs.

1257 Andy Ferrett
Copyright © 1999 Thankyou Music

HAVE WE FORGOTTEN the price that's been
    paid?
Have we remembered the wage of our ways?
Can we dismiss what He's done on the cross
As foolishness?
Oh, thank You, oh, thank You.

O Saviour and Friend,
Redeemer of many,
You poured out Your blood to me,
And gave up Your life for me.
(Oh, thank You.)

It was my life He paid with His pain,
Suffered at the hands of those He had made.
Can we consider what He once went through
To be with us?
Oh, thank You, oh, thank You.

Oh, how can I repay such a love?
Oh, how can I repay such a love?
How can I repay such a love?
Oh, thank You.

258
Margaret Becker & Keith Getty
Copyright © 2001 Modern M. Music/
Music Services/Adm. by CopyCare/
& Thankyou Music

HEAR ALL CREATION lift its voice,
The mountains sing and the rivers rejoice
For the name of Jesus,
For His name.
And we His people saved by grace,
We bow our hearts and we bring our praise
To the sweet Redeemer,
For His name.

So with everything we are,
And everything we have
We pour out our offerings.
And if ever we should fail,
The rocks will rise up
And crown Him the King of kings.

He mends our hearts, He keeps our ways:
He lights our nights and He leads our days,
All for His glory, for His name.
There's nothing greater than to be His,
To bring Him glory and to fully live
For the name of Jesus,
For His name.

259
Brian Houston
Copyright © 2002 Thankyou Music

HEAR MY CONFESSION in Your compassion;
Would You lead me in the way that I should
go?
If I lose my life for You, I know I'll find it;
Could Your will become incarnate in my soul?

For I would rather learn to open doors in Your
house,
Than spend the rest of my days wasted
somewhere else.
For I could never be free or feel Your peace
Till I surrender to Your love.

Take my whole heart;
I won't hold back the least part.
I wanna fall face forward
Into the arms of grace.
Oh, may my passion become so
undivided
That I won't be satisfied with nothing less,
Nothing less than You.

Would You give me a hunger for Your
kingdom,
That my own desires would all take second
place?

1260
Gareth Robinson
Copyright © 2002 Thankyou Music

HEAR MY MOUTH SPEAK, see my mind
think,
Know my spirit tries to pray.
Lord, we're longing to see You moving,
Help us as we pray today.
Words don't seem enough to tell You our
desire,
To see Your kingdom come and Your light
shine.

Light of the world, would You shine on
me?
Light of the world, would You shine on
me?

Now I trust You, and I ask You,
Let Your will be done in me.
May Your light shine in all the earth and
Let it draw us all to You.
Now Your glory shines throughout Your holy
church,
'Cause You're our only hope, Saviour of the
world.

Shine on me so I reflect Your glory,
Live in me so people see Your beauty,
Pour on me, so out of me flow streams of
living water.
(Repeat)

1261
Debbie Owens
Copyright © 1993 Maranatha! Praise Inc./
Adm. by CopyCare

HEAR MY PRAYER, O LORD,
From the ends of the earth I cry.
Your peace will lead me to
The Rock that is higher than I.
(Repeat)

For You have been my strength in times of
trouble,
A tower above my enemies.
And Lord, I will abide with you forever
In the shelter of Your wings.
(Repeat)

1262
Dave Bilbrough
Copyright © 1999 Thankyou Music

HEAR OUR CRY for the nations,
O Lord of the heavens.
Hear our prayer for this fallen world.
Come by Your Spirit,
Pour out Your mercy
On this earth.

Hear our cry for this nation,
O Lord of the heavens.
Hear our prayer as we gather here.
Come by Your Spirit,
Pour out Your mercy,
Heal this land.

1263 Don Moen
Copyright © 2000 Integrity's Hosanna! Music/
Sovereign Music UK

HEAR OUR PRAYER, we are Your children,
And we've gathered here today.
We've gathered here to pray.
Hear our cry, Lord, we need Your mercy
And we need Your grace today,
Hear us as we pray.

Our Father, who art in heaven,
Hallowed be Thy name.
Our Father, hear us from heaven,
Forgive our sins, we pray.

Hear our song as it rises to heaven,
May Your glory fill the earth
As the waters cover the sea.
See our hearts and remove anything
That is standing in the way
Of coming to You today.

And though we are few, we're surrounded by
  many
Who have crossed that river before,
And this is the song we'll be singing forever:
Holy is the Lord, holy is the Lord,
Holy is the Lord, holy is the Lord.

1264 Gareth Robinson & Joannah Oyeniran
Copyright © 2002 Thankyou Music

HEAR OUR PRAYERS and hear our longing,
Hear our cry, O Lord.
Save the people, broken, hurting,
Lost without Your love.

How long will it be, O Lord,
How long will it be?
How long will it be, O Lord,
How long will it be?

1265 Ken Riley
Copyright © 2001 Thankyou Music

HEAVEN OPENED and You came to save me.
You were broken and became sin for me.
No death, no hate, no shame,
No slave again to fear;
New life, new hope, new love,
Your kingdom's coming near.

And I give You praise
And I lift my hands to You,
All of my days
I will bring my love to You.
I will give my life as an offering,
As a sacrifice to the coming King of grace,
Jesus.

You have risen from the grave forever.
Through eternity I'll praise my Saviour.
No death, no hate, no shame,
No slave again to fear;
New life, new hope, new love,
Your kingdom's coming near.

I love and adore You,
And live for Your praise.
In truth and in spirit
I long for You, my King.

1266 Dave Bilbrough
Copyright © 2002 Thankyou Music

HE DIED FOR MY SAKE,
Though I was a sinner;
Redeemed me by His grace,
To know His love forever.

With every breath that I take,
And every beat of my heart
I live to give Him worship,
And to make His glory known.
(Repeat)

1267 Ken Riley
Copyright © 1999 Thankyou Music

HE IS HOLY, HOLY, HOLY,
My Lord is holy, holy, holy, Jesus.
Give glory, glory, glory to the Son,
Glory, glory, glory to Jesus!

We're gonna give Him praise,
And His name we'll raise
As we celebrate with Jesus.
Let our voices sing to the King of kings,
Who was and is to come.

He's the Prince of Peace
And He will release
All the chains that keep you down.
He's the Son of Man,
He's the Great I Am,
He's the mighty Lamb of heaven!

He's the God of grace,
And if we seek His face
He'll demonstrate His power.
On the final day unto the bride He'll say:
'At My side you'll stay forever and ever.'

268

David Lyle Morris & Nick Wynne-Jones
Copyright © 2001 Thankyou Music

E ONCE WAS DEAD, BUT NOW HE LIVES:
he First, the Last, the Living One.
e holds the keys of death and hell:
he First, the Last, the Living One.

1ore love, our hearts on fire.
1ore power, so faith stands strong.
1ore life, both real and pure.
1ore faith that holds the truth.
1ore, Lord, of You within Your church.
ou, Lord, are King most glorious.

/e hear Your voice, we come to You:
he First, the Last, the Living One.
/e will obey and follow You:
he First, the Last, the Living One.

The First, the Last, the Living One.
Lord, by Your word we overcome.
We live our lives to You alone:
The First, the Last, the Living One.

ou, Lord, the One who knows us.
ou, Lord, the love that calls us.
ou, Lord, have power to keep us.
ou, Lord, speak words of promise.
ou, Lord, the life victorious.
ou, Lord, are King most glorious.

ou once were dead, but now You live:
he First, the Last, the Living One.
ou hold the keys of death and hell:
he First, the Last, the Living One.

269

Matt Redman
Copyright © 1993 Thankyou Music

ERE AM I, A SINNER FREE,
ardoned by Your majesty,
our love has led me into liberty.
oly King, upon the throne,
ou've made this heart Your very own.
feel like the leper who's been healed.

Lost and dirty, yet You found me.
Stained by sin, but You have cleansed me.
Can it be I'm precious in Your sight?
What is man, and who am I?
A child of God, my Father's pride,
What a joy to be the Lord's delight.

have known a love so sweet,
saving love that brings relief,
healing love that makes the blind eye see.
ing of Love and Prince of Peace,
our Shepherd's love is tending me –
love that satisfies my deepest needs.

1270

Andrew Ulugia
Copyright © 2001 Parachute Music New Zealand/
Adm. by Kingsway Music

HERE I AM, O GOD,
I bring this sacrifice,
My open heart, I offer up my life.
I look to You, Lord,
Your love that never ends
Restores me again.

So I lift my eyes to You, Lord,
In Your strength I will break through, Lord.
Touch me now, let Your love fall down on me.
I know Your love dispels all my fears.
Through the storm I will hold on, Lord,
And by faith I will walk on, Lord,
Then I'll see beyond my Calvary one day,
And I will be complete in You.

1271

Reuben Morgan
Copyright © 1998 Reuben Morgan/
Hillsong Publishing/Kingsway Music

HERE I AM WAITING,
Abide in me I pray.
Here I am longing for You.
Hide me in Your love,
Bring me to my knees.
May I know Jesus more and more.

Come, live in me all my life,
Take over.
Come, breathe in me and I will rise
On eagles' wings.
(Repeat)

1272

Ken Riley
Copyright © 1999 Thankyou Music

HERE IN YOUR ARMS,
I am lost in Your love.
Holding me close,
Never let me fall.

I will worship You,
I will worship You,
Oh I, I will worship You, Lord.

Here, face to face,
I am lost in praise.
Love's hunger grows,
Burning stronger still.

1273 Words: Revelation 3:20 / Paraphrase John L. Bell
Copyright © 1995 WGRG, Iona Community

(First part)
HERE I STAND at the door and knock, and
knock.
I will come and dine with those who ask me in.

(Second part)
Here I stand at the door and knock, and
knock.
I will dine with those who ask me in.

1274 James Gregory
Copyright © 2000 Thankyou Music

HERE I STAND, longing to meet with God;
I have come, bringing a grateful heart.
And I will sing of this amazing love again.
Here I am, falling before Your throne,
For my King laying down any crown,
And I'll sing of this amazing love again.

Here I am before Your throne of grace;
I can come, for You have made a way,
And I'll sing of this amazing love again.
Here I am, so overwhelmed by You;
I come near, for I belong to You,
And I'll sing of this amazing love again.

*I am in love with God,
I am in love with God,
I hear You call my name,
I give my heart again.
I am in love with God,
I am in love with God,
I hear You call my name,
I'm on my knees again.*

You have won my heart and I can say
That I could find no other way.
Now I am Yours, and here I'll stay
To offer up this praise.

I'm in love with You,
I'm in love with You.

1275 Tim Sherrington
Copyright © 2000 Thankyou Music

HERE I WAIT BENEATH THE CROSS,
Resting in the presence of Your love.
Here I wait to know Your heart,
As I worship You in spirit and in truth.

For You are my God,
You are my King,
You reveal deep within to my very soul.
For You alone are

Jesus, there's no other name,
Jesus, eternally the same,
Jesus, the King of kings.
Jesus, Redeemer, Saviour, Friend,
Jesus, faithful till the end,
Jesus, the King of kings.

Here I come to give my all,
My hands reach up in holy praise to You.
Here I cast all chains aside
To worship You in spirit and in truth.

1276 Kevin Prosch
Copyright © 1996 Kevin Prosch/
Adm. by Kingsway Music

HEY LORD, (Hey Lord),
O LORD, (O Lord),
Hey Lord, (Hey Lord),
You know what we need.
(Repeat)

Na na na na na na na,
Na na na na na na na,
Na na na na na na na na.

Jesus, (Jesus),
You're the One (You're the One),
You set my heart (You set my heart)
On fire (on fire).
(Repeat)

1277 Robin Mark
Copyright © 2000 Thankyou Music

HOLY, HOLY, holy, holy
Is the Lord God Almighty.
Holy, holy, holy, holy
Is the song around the throne.
Where the angels and the elders gather
There in sweet assembly,
Singing holy, singing holy
Is the Lord our God.

Worthy, worthy, worthy, worthy
Is the Lamb who was slain for me.
Worthy, worthy, worthy, worthy
Is the song within my heart.
I could choose to spend eternity
With this my sole refrain:
Singing worthy, singing worthy
Is the Lord our God.

*The Way, the Truth, the Life, the Light,
The King, the Great I Am.
My life, my all, my every breath,
The Rock on which I stand.*

h Jesus, oh Jesus,
ow You suffered and died for us.
h Jesus, oh Jesus,
ut that tomb is empty now.
nd I long to gaze upon Your throne
nd all Your risen glory:
inging Jesus, singing Jesus
the Lord of all.

278

OLY, HOLY is the Lord our God;
ho was and is and is to come,
nd evermore shall be.

ith a grateful heart I will give my praise
o the Lamb upon the throne;
ing of ages, Lord of life,
xalted over all.

279

OLY, HOLY ARE YOU, LORD,
he whole earth is filled with Your glory.
et the nations rise to give
onour and praise to Your name.
et Your face shine on us
nd the world will know You live.

ll the heavens shout Your praise,
eautiful is our God,
he universe will sing
allelujah to You, our King.

280

OLY, HOLY, GOD ALMIGHTY,
ho was and is to come.
od of glory, You're so worthy,
ll the saints bow down.

Holy is Your name in all the earth.
Righteous are Your ways, so merciful.
Everything You've done is just and true.
Holy, holy God are You.
Holy, holy God are You.

ll blessing, all honour belongs to You.
ll power, all wisdom is Yours.

1281

HOLY, HOLY, HOLY,
My heart, my heart adores You!
My heart is glad to say the words:
You are holy, Lord.

Santo, santo, santo,
Mí corazón te adora!
Mí corazón te sabe decir:
Santo eres Señor.

1282

HOLY, HOLY, HOLY LORD,
God of power and might.
Earth and heaven worship You,
Your majesty so bright.
Yet we, Your fallen children know
Your love beyond compare.
We lift our hands, surrender
To grace so undeserved.

Before You, Lord, forgiven,
We bow before Your throne.
At Your cross, we find in You
Our righteousness restored.
Before You, Lord, forgiven,
We stand in Your great love,
And live our lives in honour
To Your forgiving blood.

Living in Your presence, Lord,
Sin and guilt atoned;
Citizens of heaven,
Heirs unto Your throne.
To be with You in glory,
To see You face to face,
At last home with the Father,
Our holy dwelling place.

1283

HOLY ONE, righteous King,
Merciful You are:
Merciful I'll be.
Broken One, bruised for me,
In Your death, O Lord,
You have set me free.

Because Your Father loved me so,
You came to me, Lord Jesus,
So that I would know
Love unconditional and life eternal,
O my Lord, my God, my all.

Risen One, Majesty,
Restoration, come
Breathe new life in me.
(Repeat)

1284 Peter Brooks, Stuart Townend & Kate Simmonds
Copyright © 2002 Thankyou Music

HOLY SPIRIT, HOW I LOVE YOU;
Holy Spirit, flood my soul.
Holy Spirit, take me over;
Holy Spirit, lead me on.

You're the Strength that helps me in my
    weakness,
You're the Friend who comes to walk beside;
You're the peace that passes understanding,
As You reign in my life.

1285 Russell Fragar
Copyright © 1997 Russell Fragar/
Hillsong Publishing/Kingsway Music

HOLY SPIRIT, RAIN DOWN, rain down.
O Comforter and Friend,
How we need Your touch again.
Holy Spirit, rain down, rain down.
Let Your power fall,
Let Your voice be heard,
Come and change our hearts,
As we stand on Your word.
Holy Spirit, rain down.

No eye has seen, no ear has heard,
No mind can know what God has in store.
So open up heaven, open it wide
Over Your church, and over our lives.
(Repeat)

1286 Joel Houston
Copyright © 2000 Joel Houston/
Hillsong Publishing/Kingsway Music

HOPE HAS FOUND ITS HOME WITHIN ME,
Now that I've been found in You.
Let all I am be all You want me to be,
'Cause all I want is more of You,
All I want is more of You.

Let Your presence fall upon us,
I want to see You face to face;
Let me live forever lost in Your love,
'Cause all I want is more of You,
All I want is more of You.

*I'm living for this cause,
I lay down my life
Into Your hands.
I'm living for the truth,
The hope of the world,
In You I'll stand.
All I want is You.*

All I want is,
All I want is You, Jesus.

1287 Elwood H. Stokes (1815–95)

HOVER O'ER ME, Holy Spirit,
Bathe my trembling heart and brow;
Fill me with Thy hallowed presence,
Come, O come and fill me now.

*Fill me now, fill me now,
Jesus, come and fill me now.
Fill me with Thy hallowed presence,
Jesus, come and fill me now.*

Thou can fill me, gracious Spirit,
Though I cannot tell Thee how;
But I need Thee, greatly need Thee,
Come, O come and fill me now.

I am weakness, full of weakness,
At Thy sacred feet I bow;
Blest, divine, eternal Spirit,
Come with power, and fill me now.

1288 Lara Martin (Abundant Life Ministries,
Bradford, England)
Copyright © 2002 Thankyou Music

HOW CAN I NOT PRAISE YOU,
When I consider all You've done?
God of creation, all sufficient One.
How can I not worship
When I consider who You are?
You are my Master,
The One who has my heart.

*Hallelujah, praise the Lord, O my soul.
Hallelujah, it is You I adore.
Hallelujah, hallelujah, hallelujah.
Hallelujah, I am saved! I am saved!
Hallelujah, free to praise Your name.
Hallelujah, hallelujah, hallelujah.*

How can I not love You,
When Your love reached deep down to me?
Love so amazing, what a mystery.
How can I not give my all,
When You gave heaven's best to me?
Jesus, my treasure for all eternity.

Geraldine Latty
Copyright © 2000 Thankyou Music

HOW CAN I REPAY YOU, Lord,
For all You've done for me?
Nothing I can say or do
Will ever be enough.

I will live for You,
Walking in Your way,
Lifting high Your name,
Holding close the cross.
Not in words alone,
But in what I do,
I will live my life for You.

Dear Lord, Your heart is drawing me,
A calling from Your throne.
And in my brokenness I come
And whisper to You, Lord.

It's not by works, but by Your grace,
I'll never earn Your love.
You loved me first, You'll love me last,
Your cross, my only hope.

1290 Lara Martin (Abundant Life Ministries,
Bradford, England)
Copyright © 2002 Thankyou Music

HOW GOOD YOU HAVE BEEN TO ME,
Forever faithful.
How true are Your promises,
Never shaken.
You are the Light of my life,
You are the reason I live.

I live for You,
I place no one above You.
I'll walk with You always, always.
To talk with You,
And feel Your breath on my face,
How amazing,
How amazing You are!

How rich is Your word, O Lord,
At work within me.
How soft is Your voice I hear,
That gently calls me.
Each day I wake to Your love;
I know that I am blessed of God!

1291 Lynn DeShazo
Copyright © 1999 Integrity's Hosanna! Music/
Sovereign Music UK

HOW GREAT ARE YOU, LORD,
How great is Your mercy,
How great are the things
That You have done for me.
How great are You, Lord,
Your loving kindness
Is filling my heart as I sing,
How great are You, Lord.

How great is Your love,
It reaches to the heavens;
How great is the heart
That sought and rescued me.

1292 Neil Bennetts
Copyright © 2002 Thankyou Music

HOW SHALL I FIND my place of rest,
True wisdom and the hand of God?
Not by my own understanding,
But by Your Spirit in me.

How shall I know the kind of love
That cannot fade, that cannot fail?
Not from this world's empty treasure,
But by the promise of God.

For You are the strength in my heart,
So faithful when other loves fail me.
Forever the strength in my heart:
Jesus, Jesus.

Your river flows, it covers me,
Its blessing fills my life always,
And sets my eyes on Your beauty
And fills my heart with a song.

1293 Kathryn Scott
Copyright © 1999 Vineyard Songs (UK/Eire)/
Adm. by CopyCare

HUNGRY, I COME TO YOU,
For I know You satisfy.
I am empty, but I know
Your love does not run dry.
So I wait for You,
So I wait for You.

I'm falling on my knees,
Offering all of me.
Jesus, You're all this heart is living for.

Broken, I run to You,
For Your arms are open wide;
I am weary, but I know
Your touch restores my life.
So I wait for You,
So I wait for You.

1294

Lara Martin (Abundant Life Ministries, Bradford, England)
Copyright © 2000 Lara Martin/Abundant Life Ministries/Adm. by Kingsway Music

I AM AMAZED

By the power of Your grace,
I am amazed
That You took my sin and shame;
Restoring hope, restoring dignity:
Your grace covers me,
Your grace covers me, oh.

> *Saving grace, washing over me;*
> *Saving grace, that made a way for me:*
> *I was lost until You rescued me,*
> *Your grace covers me.*

I'm overwhelmed
By Your love and goodness,
I'm overwhelmed
That You took my brokenness:
Amazing love, how can this be?
Your grace covers me,
Your grace covers me.

1295

Sue Rinaldi, Caroline Bonnett & Steve Bassett
Copyright © 2001 Thankyou Music

I AM HELPLESSLY IN LOVE WITH YOU.

I am lost in something precious.
I am drowning in the sea of You.
I am found amongst Your treasures.

And I don't know why You give Yourself,
And I can't explain why You should care.
When all heaven sings Your glory,
I'm humbled that You hear my prayer.

> *I can only give my heart to You,*
> *I can only give my heart.*
> (Repeat)

I am helplessly devoted to You;
I am scorched by strange new fire.
I am running deeper into You.
I am high upon the wire.

It's like breathing some strange new air,
Walking on some distant moon.
I'll sing a song from the depths of my soul:
Seeking, finding, coming home.
Seeking, finding, coming home.

1296

Brian Houston
Copyright © 2002 Thankyou Music

I AM THE ONE WITH THE UNCLEAN LIPS,

I am the one whose mind is jaded.
I am the one with the impure heart,
And all my innocence has faded.

Wash me clean in Your river of mercy.
Restore my soul by a clear blue stream.
Wash me clean in Your river of mercy,
Restore my soul, renew me again.

I am the one whose walk is faithless,
I am the one who walks away.
I am the one whose debts are many
And I am the one who cannot pay.

You are the Lord who is my fortress;
You are the Lord who is my hope.
You are the Lord who is my refuge,
The only safe place for my soul.

1297

Darlene Zschech
Copyright © 2001 Darlene Zschech/
Hillsong Publishing/Kingsway Music

I BEHOLD YOUR POWER AND GLORY,

Bring an offering, come before You;
Worship You, Lord,
In the beauty of Your holiness.
(Repeat)

Whenever I call, You're there,
Redeemer and Friend;
Cherished beyond all words,
This love never ends.
Morning by morning
Your mercy awakens my soul.

I lift up my eyes to see
The wonders of heaven
Opening over me,
Your goodness abounds;
You've taken my breath away
With Your irresistible love.

1298

James Taylor
Copyright © 1999 Thankyou Music

I BELIEVE in everything You do,

All You have to say.
I've come to realise You're the only way,
Oh, I believe in You.

I've received something in my life
Greater than before:
Your truth has set me free and I love You,
Lord,
Oh, I believe in You.

> *Let the angels sing of the Lord's great*
> *love,*
> *Well, it's shining down like the heavens*
> *above.*
> *Let the nations bow to the living God*
> *And know Your truth,*
> *I believe in You.*

believe, I believe,
believe, I believe in You.
Repeat)

299 Stuart Townend & Keith Getty
Copyright © 2003 Thankyou Music

BELIEVE IN GOD THE FATHER,
Maker of heaven and earth.
believe in Christ the Saviour,
ord of all, Son of God.
orn to Mary, lived and suffered
t the hands of those He'd made.
rucified, was dead and buried,
nd descended to the grave.

believe that Jesus rose again,
nd ascended into heaven
Where He sits with God the Father,
nd will come to judge all men.
believe in God the Spirit,
His church that stands forgiven;
esurrection of the body,
nd eternal life to come.

300 Johnny Parks
Copyright © 2001 Thankyou Music

I CALL ON YOU, ALMIGHTY LORD;
I call on You, Almighty Lord.
I call on You, Almighty Lord;
I call on You, Almighty Lord.

come to You and stand before Your throne.
lift my voice in worship here once more.
ou turned the darkness in me into light.
ou took my blinded soul and gave me sight.
s I sank down to the depths You heard my
  cry,
ou lifted me and taught me how to fly.
ou promised me You're always here to stay,
o as I stand before You, Lord, I want to
  say…

he heavenly host are captured by the love
f the One who laid His life down at the
  cross.
We lift the name of Jesus to the skies,
o all might see and know that there is life.
nd where there's hatred let me bring Your
  love.
nd where there's sorrow let me bring Your
  joy.
s I stand before You, will You lift Your face
nd bring resurrection power to this place?

1301 Jim Bailey
Copyright © 1994 Thankyou Music

I CAN DO ALL (ALL!), ALL (ALL!), ALL THINGS
Through Christ who strengthens me.
I can do all (all!), all (all!), all things
Through Christ who strengthens me.

Go to school: all things.
Obey the rules: all things.
Keep my cool: all things
Through Christ who strengthens me.

Make new friends: all things.
Give and lend: all things.
Make amends: all things
Through Christ who strengthens me.

Pray and sing: all things.
Love our King: all things.
Everything: all things
Through Christ who strengthens me.

1302 Ken Riley
Copyright © 1995 McKenzie Music/
Adm. by Kingsway Music

I CAN FEEL YOUR ARMS surrounding,
Treasuring my soul.
Draw me ever closer into Your love,
Into Your love.
Lead me to Your place of wonder,
Shower me with grace.
Holy God, forgive my unrighteous ways,
Unrighteous ways.

Oh I love You, Lord,
All I am is Yours,
As Your mercy pours into my heart.
You're my faithful King,
Over everything,
Hear my spirit sing that Jesus is Lord.

1303 Ken Riley
Copyright © 1999 Thankyou Music

I COME AS I AM,
Baring all of my shame.
Surround me with love
And acceptance again.

> *Come closer, Lord,*
> *Come and restore;*
> *Come closer, Lord.*

Nothing I bring
Is too great to forgive,
Though each time Your grace
Is betrayed by my sin.

1304 Paul Oakley
Copyright © 2000 Thankyou Music

I COME RUNNING to You, Father,
Trying to find a secret place with You.
My soul crying out, just to hear Your voice,
Oh, I must have You.

I come running to You, Jesus,
I'm so hungry for Your truth.
I've found many treasures
Hidden in Your word,
But I must have You.

Only You, Lord, will I worship,
Only You will I serve.
And my hope lies in You, Lord,
Only You can make me whole.
And I will say 'I love You.'
Yes, I will sing to You, to You.

I come longing for You, Spirit,
So dry I need to know Your touch.
I know living waters deep within me,
But I must have more of You.

1305 Kate Simmonds
Copyright © 2002 Thankyou Music

I COME TO BOW DOWN,
I come to hear You speak.
I wait before You
Where deep can call to deep.

Be my life, be my all;
Heart and soul I seek You, Lord.

My heart will praise You;
In praises You dwell.
I long to be with You
And come away with You.

Wonder of heaven, joy of my heart;
Strength of my being, I love You.
Rock of salvation, love of my life;
God of all comfort, draw near.

Heart and soul I seek You, Lord;
Heart and soul I seek You, Lord.

1306 Matt Parker & Paul Oakley
Copyright © 1999 Thankyou Music

I COME TO YOU, Lord of all hope,
Giver of life, revive my soul.
I wait for You, Prince of all peace,
King of all love, draw near to me.
It feels sometimes like You're far away,
Yet I know You are with me.

And I know I cannot go from Your
   presence, O Lord,
But I need to feel You here with me.
What can I do just to draw near to You?
Oh, I need to know You here with me no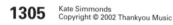

Come to me now, Lord of my heart,
I need to know unfailing love.
Consuming flame, passion and power,
Come let Your fire burn in me now.
It feels sometimes like You're far away,
Yet I know You are with me.

And I know...

Where can I go just to find You, O God?
Oh, I long to feel You holding me.
Know that I seek You with all of my hear
Oh, I need to find You here with me now

1307 Louise & Nathan Fellingham
Copyright © 2001 Thankyou Music

I COME TO YOU, to sit at Your feet,
I hear You call, I'm longing to meet You.
I lift my face to You, and catch Your eye,
Oh how You satisfy.

Jesus, Your love surrounds me.
Jesus, Your love completes me.

Now looking closer, I see the scars,
Stories of love, You paid the greatest price,
So that I may have life.
Thank You, my Friend,
You're showing me once again.

There's nothing like it,
There's nothing like it,
There's nothing like the love of God.
(Repeat)

No longer searching, I've found the One,
Just touched the surface, only begun;
This love goes deeper
Than any I've known.

1308 Paul Booth
Copyright © 1998 Thankyou Music

I COME, WANTING JUST TO BE WITH YOU
Today let me hear Your voice.
I come, wanting just to give to You,
To say, You are everything.

Don't ever let my heart grow cold,
Don't ever let me lose sight of Your truth.
Draw near that I may drink from eternal
   water.

u are the Fountain of all life,
u are the peace unto my soul.
u are the Way, the Truth, the Light;
sus, into Your arms I run.
u are the holy Son of God,
u gave up Your life to save my soul.
u have redeemed me through the cross;
sus, with thankfulness I come.

309 Neil Bennetts
Copyright © 2001 Thankyou Music

**COUNT AS NOTHING
VERY EARTHLY TREASURE**, Jesus;
hat You have shown me is that
u are the source of my life.
 what else can I do
t stay here?

hy would I look for
ny worldly pleasure, Jesus,
hen I have all things in You?
nd just a heartbeat away.
 what else can I do
t stay here with You?

*You're all that I need,
You're all that I need,
So here I'll stay
And give my praise to You.*

310 Sydney Carter
Copyright © 1963 Stainer & Bell Ltd

DANCED IN THE MORNING when the world
was begun,
nd I danced in the moon and the stars and
the sun,
nd I came down from heaven and I danced
on the earth:
 Bethlehem I had My birth.

*'Dance, then, wherever you may be,
I am the Lord of the dance,' said He,
'And I'll lead you all, wherever you may
 be,
And I'll lead you all in the dance,' said He.*

 danced for the scribe and the pharisee,
ut they would not dance and they wouldn't
follow Me.
 danced for the fishermen, for James and
John –
ney came with Me and the dance went on.

 danced on the Sabbath and I cured the
 lame;
ne holy people said it was a shame.
ney whipped and they stripped and they
 hung Me on high,
nd they left Me there on a cross to die.

'I danced on a Friday when the sky turned
 black;
It's hard to dance with the devil on your back.
They buried My body and they thought I'd
 gone,
But I am the dance, and I still go on.

'They cut Me down and I leapt up high;
I am the life that'll never, never die.
I'll live in you if you'll live in Me;
I am the Lord of the dance', said He.

1311 Noel & Tricia Richards & Wayne Drain
Copyright © 1998 Thankyou Music

I DON'T KNOW WHY, I can't see how
Your precious blood could cleanse me now;
When all this time I've lived a lie,
With no excuse, no alibi.

*All I know is I find mercy;
All my shame You take from me.
All I know, Your cross has power,
And the blood You shed cleanses me.*

It's way beyond what I can see,
How anyone could die for me.
So undeserved, this precious grace;
You've won my heart, I'll seek Your face.

1312 Bethan Stevens (Abundant Life Ministries,
Bradford, England)
Copyright © 2002 Thankyou Music

I ENTER IN before You now,
I come to You with an open heart.
I lift my voice to worship You,
I love You, Lord,
And I could stay in Your presence forever.

Lord God, I come before You
With my sacrifice of praise.
I am humbled in Your presence,
Jesus, Name above all names.

1313 Noel Richards & Wayne Drain
Copyright © 2001 Thankyou Music

IF I SEEK YOU, I will find You,
But I need to take the time.
If I call You, You will answer,
But I need to take the time.

*Give me a pure heart,
Give me a pure heart,
I'm calling to You.
Give me a pure heart,
Give me a pure heart,
I'm longing for You.*

If I listen, I will hear You,
But I need to take the time.
If I follow, You will lead me,
But I need to take the time.

1314 Matt Redman & Tom Lane
Copyright © 2002 Thankyou Music/
worshiptogether.com songs/The Bridge Worx/
Adm. by Kingsway Music

IF IT WASN'T FOR YOUR MERCY,
If it wasn't for Your love,
If it wasn't for Your kindness,
How could I stand?

If it wasn't for Your cleansing,
If it wasn't for Your blood,
If it wasn't for Your goodness,
How could I stand?

> *And yet I find myself again*
> *Where even angels fear to tread,*
> *Where I would never dare to come,*
> *But for the cleansing of Your blood.*

With You there is forgiveness,
And therefore You are feared.
Jesus, it's Your loving kindness
That brings me to my knees.

In the beauty of Your holiness. *(x4)*

1315 Ken Riley
Copyright © 1999 Thankyou Music

IF MY PEOPLE, who are called by My name,
Will humble themselves and pray,
And will seek My face,
And turn from their wicked ways.
(Repeat)

Then I will hear from heaven and forgive their
  sin.
Yes, I will hear from heaven and forgive their
  sin.
Yes, I will hear from heaven and forgive their
  sin,
And will heal their land,
Yes, I will heal their land.

Will You hear from heaven and forgive my
  sin?
Oh, will You hear from heaven and forgive
  my sin?
Will You hear from heaven and forgive my
  sin?
Oh, will You hear from heaven and forgive
  my sin?

1316 David Lyle Morris & Faith Forster
Copyright © 2001 Thankyou Music

IF WE DIED WITH CHRIST,
We'll also live with Him,
And if we endure,
We'll also reign with Christ.
If we deny Him, He will disown us,
But if we're faithless,
Faithful He remains.

> *A faithful Saviour and unending in merc*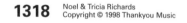
> *Is our God, the only true God.*
> *The suffering Servant,*
> *And our conquering Hero*
> *Are You, God, forever true God.*
> *You are worthy to receive our lives.*
> (Last time)
> *Cleansed from sin and alive to Christ.*

If we please the Lord
In this present world,
We will inherit eternal life to come.
For He has promised
To raise us from the dead
If we walk worthily of Christ the risen One.

1317 Noel Richards & Wayne Drain
Copyright © 2001 Thankyou Music

I GIVE MY HEART TO WHAT I TREASURE;
My devotion, everything I am.
Like a diamond, You treat me like I'm
  precious;
To be Yours is more than I deserve.

> *Jesus, You are my treasure;*
> *Jesus, nothing less will do.*
> *Jesus, I am Yours forever;*
> *Jesus, I want to live for You.*

We are a people holy to our Saviour;
For this moment He has gathered us
To bring hope and healing to the nations,
Till His name is known in all the earth.

1318 Noel & Tricia Richards
Copyright © 1998 Thankyou Music

I HAVE COME HOME,
I'm here again,
Worn feet and ragged heart.
Wasted my time,
Wandered from ways that are best.
I don't deserve from You
Mercy that falls anew every day:
All I want is You.

u know my name,
ll me Your friend,
u draw me to Your side.
ough I have failed,
llen so far, still You care.
ace covers all my shame.
sus, You took the blame, this is love:
I want is You.

m restored,
ere I belong,
one with You again.
th all my heart
hoose to walk in Your ways.
ld in Your strong embrace,
one will take Your place in my heart:
I want is You.

319 Martin Cooper & Paul Oakley
Copyright © 1999 Thankyou Music

AVE COME TO LOVE YOU,
r You have won my heart
hen You revealed Your love to me.
r life will be a witness
such love and such forgiveness,
r You have given me Your peace,
d You're everything I need.

I love to sing Your name,
To speak about Your fame,
You're worthy of my praise.
I long to worship You
In spirit and in truth,
It's all I want to do.

u have come to love me
d heal my broken heart,
w I am reaching out to You.
ur strength is in my weakness,
clinging to Your promise,
let Your work in me shine through
everything I do.

I come before You now,
Your Spirit touch me;
ill make this gospel known.
me with Your love and power
d Your compassion,
rough me let Your kingdom come.

 1320 Andrew Rogers
Copyright © 2001 Thankyou Music

I HAVE COME TO REALISE
The glory of the Lord resides
In this jar of clay.
And if my world is going to see
The glory of the Lord revealed,
Then my pride must break.
Then the fragrance of Jesus
Will be released,
And the glory of God will be revealed
In all my world.

Jesus, let Your name
Be fragrant in me,
Like perfume that's poured
From this vessel of clay.
(Repeat)

And I will live all my days
To be the praise,
And I will live all my days
To be the praise of Your glory.

 1321 Matt Redman
Copyright © 2000 Thankyou Music

I HAVE HEARD SO MANY SONGS,
Listened to a thousand tongues,
But there is one that sounds above them all.
The Father's song, the Father's love,
You sung it over me and for eternity
It's written on my heart.

Heaven's perfect melody,
The Creator's symphony,
You are singing over me
The Father's song.
Heaven's perfect mystery,
The King of love has sent for me,
And now You're singing over me
The Father's song.

1322 Lex Loizides
Copyright © 2000 Thankyou Music

I HAVE HIS WORD,
His great and precious promises.
He took my sin, His righteousness is mine.
I am in Christ,
Secure for all eternity:
No power can sever me, nor cast me off
From His abundant, free
And sovereign love.

I have His word,
The Master Builder will succeed.
The gates of hell, they never will prevail.
Throughout the earth
The joy of Jesus is His church;
She is the mystery that stirred His heart,
Drawing Him out of heaven
To shed His blood.

I have His word,
A day is fixed when all the world
In sudden awe the Son of God shall see.
And in that day
Our eyes shall see His majesty;
What then of sufferings? What then of tears?
We shall see perfectly
When He appears!

I have His word
That every race shall reign with Him,
We'll reach our home, the new Jerusalem.
The Triune God
Shall dwell with man eternally,
More joys than eye has seen or ear has heard
Wait for us certainly,
I have His word.

 1323 Tim Hughes
Copyright © 1998 Thankyou Music

I JUST WANT TO LOVE,
I just want to sing
To the One above
Who has touched this thirsty soul.
(Repeat)
And now I'll never be the same.

I'll always love You,
I'll always sing to You, Jesus.
I long to worship You in spirit and in truth.
(Repeat)

Every day I'll come,
Spend my life with You,
Learning of Your heart,
And what You're calling me to do.
(Repeat)
My every breath belongs to You.

And with this song
We'll lift the name of Jesus higher.
And with a shout
We'll raise up one voice.

 1324 Reuben Morgan
Copyright © 1998 Reuben Morgan/
Hillsong Publishing/Kingsway Music

I KNOW HE RESCUED MY SOUL,
His blood has covered my sin,
I believe, I believe.
My shame He's taken away,
My pain is healed in His name,
I believe, I believe.
I'll raise a banner;
My Lord has conquered the grave.

My Redeemer lives, my Redeemer lives
My Redeemer lives, my Redeemer lives

You lift my burden, I'll rise with You:
I'm dancing on this mountain-top
To see Your kingdom come.

1325 D.W. Whittle (1840–1901) adapt. Stuart Towne
Copyright © 1999 Thankyou Music

I KNOW NOT WHY GOD'S WONDROUS GRACE
To me hath been made known;
Nor why, unworthy as I am,
He claimed me for His own.

I know not how this saving faith
To me He did impart;
Or how believing in His word
Wrought peace within my heart.

But I know whom I've believèd;
He's able now to save
What I've committed unto Him
Until that final day.

I know not how the Spirit moves,
Convincing men of sin;
Revealing Jesus through the word,
Creating faith in Him.

I know not what of good or ill
May be reserved for me,
Of weary ways or golden days
Before His face I see.

I know not when my Lord may come;
I know not how or where,
If I shall pass the vale of death,
Or meet Him in the air.

KNOW YOU LOVE AN OFFERING
hat's costly, outreaching,
ouching Your heart for the poor.
he songs we sing as our offerings
re more fragrant in Your presence,
 we live a life of love.

And as we follow Your heart,
We are led to the lost,
Finding there a place of praise,
No matter what the cost.
So we will stand with the weak,
Give our most to the least,
Serving You with all we have,
Your kingdom, God, we seek.

ow I see what You command:
e faithful and humble,
utting selfish hopes aside,
o change my heart that I may love
ly neighbour as my brother,
nd to live a life of love.

LIFT YOU HIGH, and bow down low,
ow high can You be?
ow low can I go?
ift You high, and bow down low,
ow high can You be?
ow low can I go?
irst time only)
 Lord?

ou must increase,
must decrease, Lord.
 I bow down,
nd You will be adored.

LIVE MY LIFE TO WORSHIP YOU,
spend my days serving You,
nd now I come, I come.
want to spend some time with You,
 steal away and be with You,
o now I come, I come.

Just to be with You,
Just to know more of Your love;
Just to be with You,
And to love You.

And here You know me,
And here You know me,
And here You know me,
And here I love You.

I LOVE YOU, LORD, I worship You,
I love You, Lord, always.
So thankful, Lord, You saved my life,
You saved my life, today.

Let me be a shining light for You,
Let me be a joy to You always.
Let me be a shining light for You,
Let me be a joy to You always.

And Lord, I love to bring to You
The honour due Your name;
Just look at what You've done for me,
I'll never be the same.

I LOVE YOU MORE EACH DAY,
With all my heart can give;
Worship at Your feet,
Lost within Your gaze.
Just to know that You're near,
My treasure is here,
That You gave Your life
To save me;
How my heart sings with praise
And calls on Your name,
My Saviour, my Lover, my King,
Come to me again!

IMAGE OF INVISIBLE GOD,
Creator and Sustainer of all;
The King who came to ransom my soul,
Thank You for Your perfect love.

Holy One whom angels attend,
Righteous King who calls me His friend;
The Prince who offers peace without end,
Thank You for Your perfect love.

And it's You, O Lord,
You're all that I could ask for,
And in You, O Lord, I find the deepest joy:
Fountain of life, ocean of mercy and peace.
And it's You, O Lord,
Who gives me strength to follow,
And in You, O Lord, is grace for every day:
Boundless in love,
Fullness of heaven on earth.

Therefore I will not be afraid,
Though mountains fall and rivers may rage;
I'm safe within the city You've made,
Thank You for Your perfect love.

1332 Brian Houston
Copyright © 2000 Thankyou Music

I'M CALLING OUT TO YOU,
There must be something more,
Some deeper place to find,
Some secret place to hide
Where I have not gone before.
Where my soul is satisfied,
And my sin is put to death,
And I can hear Your voice,
Your purpose is my choice,
As natural as a breath.

The love I knew before,
When You first touched my life,
I need You to restore,
I want You to revive.

Oh, place in my heart a passion for Jesus,
A hunger that seizes my passion for You.
My one desire, my greatest possession,
My only confession, my passion for You.

1333 Dave Bilbrough
Copyright © 2002 Thankyou Music

I'M CRADLED,
Cradled in the arms of love.
Yes, I'm cradled,
Cradled in the arms of love.

My struggles for approval
Were never meant to be.
To know that I'm accepted
Is Your desire for me.
Because…

My fears about the future,
All my anxieties,
Are calmed when I surrender
To the One who's holding me.

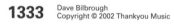

1334 Wayne Drain & Noel Richards
Copyright © 1998 Thankyou Music

I'M CRYING OUT, let everybody hear
This message loud and clear.
I'm crying out, I want the world to know
That Jesus is my hope.

I've chosen to believe
That God has chosen me
Now at this time.
He turned my life around,
I make a different sound,
Now I want to be a sign.
Harvest fields are white,
Wanna do what's right,
Can't keep it to myself,
Gotta go, gotta tell everyone, yeah.

1335 Geraldine Latty & Noel Robinson
Copyright © 2000 Thankyou Music

I'M DRAWN A LITTLE BIT CLOSER to You,
Hearing You whisper to me;
A little bit nearer to You,
Hearing the beat of Your heart.
Sensing Your power at work,
Seeing the need in Your world:
A little bit closer to You.

As I see Your faithfulness,
As I fix my eyes on You, O Lord;
As I run the race You've run,
Every day, every day.

1336 Ken Riley
Copyright © 2001 Thankyou Music

I MET YOU when You called my name,
Love surrounded and forgave,
And then You filled my heart with praise.
You are the Light that seeks to save:
A burning fire of purest grace,
Showering the world with love.

I will give glory unto You,
I will give glory unto You,
I give myself wholly, only to You.

You stand beside me when I fail,
And carry me through times of pain,
For You are with me all the way.
And when my life begins to fade
You'll be the lamp to guide my way,
Shining to eternity.

1337 Doug Horley
Copyright © 1999 Thankyou Music

I'M FOREVER IN YOUR LOVE,
I'm forever saved by grace.
You have chosen me
And crowned me with Your love.
I'll forever trust in You,
I'll forever say You're good.
You are King of kings
And I will worship You.

la la la la la,
st want to thank You,
la la la la la,
st want to praise You,
la la la la la,
at I can live like this forever.
epeat)

338 Marc James
Copyright © 2000 Vineyard Songs (UK/Eire)/
Adm. by CopyCare

M GIVING YOU MY HEART,
nd all that is within,
ay it all down
or the sake of You, my King.
n giving You my dreams,
n laying down my rights,
n giving up my pride
or the promise of new life.

And I surrender all to You, all to You.
And I surrender all to You, all to You.

n singing You this song,
n waiting at the cross,
nd all the world holds dear,
count it all as loss.
or the sake of knowing You,
e glory of Your name,
know the lasting joy,
en sharing in Your pain.

339 Steve Earl
Copyright © 1998 PDI Worship/
Adm. by CopyCare

M GONNA TRUST IN GOD,
n gonna trust in Jesus
ithout shame and without fear.
n gonna fix my eyes
n the hope of glory,
or His day is drawing near.

How great is the love of God,
How steady is His hand
To guide me through this world.
And though I am weak, in Him I stand,
And you will hear me say today,
In faith, I'm gonna trust in God.

ow when the cares of life
em overwhelming,
nd my heart is sinking down,
n gonna lift my hands
the One who'll help me,
the One who holds my crown.

1340 Johnny Parks
Copyright © 2001 Thankyou Music

I'M GRATEFUL for the way You look at me.
I'm thankful that You don't give up.
You're a friend who's smiled at me a
    thousand times.
When I cause You pain, You bring me love.

I've found a place where I'm free.
I'm dancing now, 'cause You love me.
(You love me, You love me, You love me.)

I love You, You know it's true.
And all I want is to be close to You.

When I've done the worst,
You've seen the best in me.
I was running away,
But You brought some rest to me.
My heart is Yours and I give it all to You.
And when it's tough, I know You'll
Pull me through.

1341 Paul Oakley
Copyright © 1998 Thankyou Music

I'M LEARNING TO LOVE YOU,
To love and to trust You.
I'm learning to give You all that I am.
I'm learning to cling to the words You have
    spoken.
I'm learning to let go my life in Your hands.

For You are faithful in all of Your ways,
In wisdom unsearchable, and full of grace.
Oh, You are beautiful beyond words.
I'm learning to love You.

So teach me to love You,
To love and to trust You,
And teach me to give You all that I am.
And teach me to cling to the words You have
    spoken,
Teach me to let go my life in Your hands.

We are like shadows that change with the
    day;
And like the flowers our beauty will fade.
But Yours is the kingdom and the power;
Forever and ever Your glory will always
    remain.

1342 Matt Redman
Copyright © 2001 Thankyou Music

I'M MAKING MELODY in my heart to You.
I'm making melody in my heart to You.
Pouring out Your praise
With everything within.
I'm making melody in my heart to You.
I'm making melody in my heart to You.
Yours will always be
The song I love to sing.

How can hearts not love Your name?
How can souls not sing Your praise?
Jesus, You put music in my soul.

1343 Dave Bilbrough
Copyright © 2000 Thankyou Music

I'M ON MY KNEES at the cross,
Where Your blood was sacrificed;
So amazed that there is grace
Enough for me.
I don't deserve the love You bring,
But I'm at that place again,
Where I need You
To forgive my foolish heart.

Oh, what mercy,
Oh, what mercy,
Oh, what mercy
Is mine to receive.

1344 Jim Bailey
Copyright © 1994 Thankyou Music

I'M WORKING OUT WHAT IT MEANS to
   follow Jesus,
Adding up what it costs to follow Him;
Counting the times that His love is multiplying,
Realising He took away my sin.
He's always in my memory;
He'll never cancel what He's done for me.
When I add it together I calculate
Jesus is great, Jesus is great!

1345 Reuben Morgan
Copyright © 1999 Reuben Morgan/
Hillsong Publishing/Kingsway Music

IN AWE OF YOU, we worship
And stand amazed at Your great love.
We're changed from glory to glory,
We set our hearts on You, our God.

   Now Your presence fills this place,
   Be exalted in our praise.
   As we worship I believe
   You are near.
   (Repeat)

Blessing and honour
And glory and power
Forever, forever.
(Repeat)

1346 Stuart Townend & Keith Getty
Copyright © 2001 Thankyou Music

IN CHRIST ALONE my hope is found,
He is my light, my strength, my song;
This Cornerstone, this solid Ground,
Firm through the fiercest drought and storm
What heights of love, what depths of peace
When fears are stilled, when strivings cease
My Comforter, my All in All,
Here in the love of Christ I stand.

In Christ alone! – who took on flesh,
Fullness of God in helpless babe!
This gift of love and righteousness,
Scorned by the ones He came to save:
Till on that cross as Jesus died,
The wrath of God was satisfied –
For every sin on Him was laid;
Here in the death of Christ I live.

There in the ground His body lay,
Light of the world by darkness slain:
Then bursting forth in glorious Day
Up from the grave He rose again!
And as He stands in victory
Sin's curse has lost its grip on me,
For I am His and He is mine –
Bought with the precious blood of Christ.

No guilt in life, no fear in death,
This is the power of Christ in me;
From life's first cry to final breath,
Jesus commands my destiny.
No power of hell, no scheme of man,
Can ever pluck me from His hand;
Till He returns or calls me home,
Here in the power of Christ I'll stand!

1347 Paul Oakley & Martin Cooper
Copyright © 2002 Thankyou Music

I NEED YOU like the summer needs the sun
I need You to walk and to run.
I need You like a river needs the rain.
I need You to fill me again.
Without You I run dry;
Without You I won't even survive.

   So wake me, take me with You,
   Chase me where Your river runs,
   Romance me till my heart belongs to You
   Oh, draw me closer to You,
   Lead me in Your ways,
   Enchant me 'cause my life belongs to You

I need You like the stars need the sky.
I need You to help me to shine.
I need You like a singer needs a song.
I need You to carry on.
Without You I run dry,
Without You I won't even survive.

Embrace me, let me feel Your strength,
Hide me in Your shade,
You're my shelter in the rain.

1348 Paul Oakley
Copyright © 1998 Thankyou Music

I NEED YOU NOW,
My King, my Love;
I am more aware this clay
Than all Your power within.
I wait for You,
My Hope, my Love,
Because I've dreamed I'd see
Your kingdom come and I still believe.

So come and breathe on me now,
I am poured out for You.
Come and release Your power.
I'm crying out to You,
I'm crying out to You.

What works have I?
What fruit to show?
I can hardly stand before Your grace,
Yet I, I know
Your love, Your grace
Has lifted me,
But I need You now so I can build
With gold, pure gold.

Your promise alone
Should be enough for me.
Still I'm crying out,
'I need Your touch.'

1349 Kate Simmonds & Stuart Townend
Copyright © 2001 Thankyou Music

IN EVERY DAY THAT DAWNS,
I see the light of Your splendour around me;
And everywhere I turn,
I know the gift of Your favour upon me.
What can I do but give You glory, Lord?
Everything good has come from You.

I'm grateful for the air I breathe,
I'm so thankful for this life I live,
For the mercies that You pour on me,
And the blessings that meet every need.
And the grace that is changing me
From a hopeless case to a child that's free,
Free to give You praise,
For in everything
I know You love me.
I know You love me.

Through all that I have known,
I have been held in the shelter of Your hand;
And as my life unfolds,
You are revealing the wisdom
Of Your sovereign plan.
There are no shadows in Your faithfulness,
There are no limits to Your love.

1350 Polish traditional carol
tr. Edith M.G. Reed (1885–1933)
Copyright Control

INFANT HOLY, Infant lowly,
For His bed a cattle stall;
Oxen lowing, little knowing,
Christ the babe is Lord of all.
Swift are winging angels singing,
Nowells ringing, tidings bringing:
Christ the babe is Lord of all;
Christ the babe is Lord of all.

Flocks were sleeping, shepherds keeping
Vigil till the morning new;
Saw the glory, heard the story,
Tidings of a gospel true.
Thus rejoicing, free from sorrow,
Praises voicing, greet the morrow:
Christ the babe was born for you!
Christ the babe was born for you!

1351 Paul Oakley
Copyright © 1999 Thankyou Music

IN THE SHADOW OF THE CROSS,
Let everything fall into place again.
Jesus Christ, my sacrifice,
How I need to find Your grace again.

And nothing I can do
Could add to all You've done,
So let my soul be satisfied.
As I receive Your favour,
I will overcome.
So in my life be glorified.

Jesus Christ, my perfect Priest,
How You understand my weaknesses.
Thank You for Your gift to me:
Through Your sufferings I now
Possess this peace.

1352

IN THIS PLACE WE GATHER
To worship You together,
To come before You, holy God.
(Repeat)

And as we seek Your face,
Let this be Your dwelling place,
We have come to worship You.
We come to give our all,
It's at Your feet we fall,
We have come to praise You.

We have come to worship,
We have come to worship,
We have come to worship You.

1353

IN THIS STILLNESS I will worship,
Love You, Jesus,
I turn toward to kiss Your face.
I come running, thirsting, longing
For You, Jesus,
In the quiet of this place.
Draw me closer to You, Jesus,
I would be with You.

> *Risen Healer, conquering Saviour,*
> *King of kings and Prince of Peace.*
> *Faithful Father, my Friend forever,*
> *I will live to bring You praise.*

In Your presence I will bow down,
Join with the angels
Singing 'Holy is Your name'.
In this moment heaven's fragrance
Touches earth and
I can feel Your kingdom come.
Draw me closer to You, Jesus,
I would be with You.

1354

IN YOUR ARMS OF LOVE I SING,
Giving glory to my King:
I have come to seek Your face
In this secret, secret place.
And I will bow before Your throne,
For my life is not my own.

And I will praise You,
Every day I'll come before Your throne.
I am holy unto You.
And I will give You
All my hopes, my dreams I lay them
*   down.*
Lord, may I be found in You.

I have taken up my cross,
What was gain I've counted loss.
Father, let Your will be done
For I am broken by this love.
Send Your fire to purify,
Jesus, teach me how to die.

And I will follow You, my Lord,
Forevermore and ever more,
And I will follow You, my Lord,
Forevermore.
(Repeat)

1355

IN YOUR PRESENCE there is fullness of life,
And healing flowing for body, soul and mind
God of miracles, God of the impossible is
    here,
God is here.

> *God is here, let the broken-hearted*
> *   rejoice.*
> *God is here, let the sick say 'I am well.'*
> *God is here, let the weak say 'I am strong.*
> *God is here, His wonders to perform.*

In Your presence there is perfect peace;
In the stillness I behold Your deity.
God of wonder, God of power is here,
God is here.

Oh, His wonders, yes, His wonders,
His wonders to perform.
Oh, His wonders, yes, His wonders,
His wonders to perform.
(Repeat)

1356

IN YOUR PRESENCE THERE IS JOY,
In Your presence there is freedom,
But the greatest joy of all
Is to know we've made You smile.
In Your presence there is life,
In Your presence there is healing,
But the greatest joy of all
Is to know we've reached Your heart.

God of glory, we give You praise,
Lift You up in this holy place;
Our hearts are ready, our lives made new,
It's all we long to do.
God of glory, we give You praise,
We lift You up in this holy place;
Our hearts are ready, our lives made new,
God of glory, we worship You.

 1357 Graham Kendrick
Copyright © 2002 Make Way Music

IN YOU WE LIVE, Jesus,
In You we move.
In You we breathe, Jesus,
In You we love.
And we are Your body here,
We are Your body here.

Your touch – our hands,
Your words – our voice,
Your way – our feet,
Your tears in our eyes,
Your Spirit is here.

You give – we share,
You lead – we go,
You send – we serve,
You build and we grow.
Your Spirit is here.

Across the world, You're moving;
The sound of prayer is growing stronger,
From every tribe and nation
Joining in one salvation song.

You are the light that's dawning,
You are the hope transforming all things;
Freeing the whole creation
To join in one salvation song,
One song.

1358 Judy Bailey
Copyright © 1993 Daybreak Music Ltd

I REACH UP HIGH, *I touch the ground,*
I stomp my feet and turn around.
I've to (woo woo) praise the Lord.
I jump and dance with all my might,
I might look funny, but that's all right,
I've got to (woo woo) praise the Lord.

I'll do anything just for my God
'Cause He's done everything for me.
It doesn't matter who is looking on,
Jesus is the person that I want to please.

May my whole life be a song of praise,
To worship God in every way.
In this song the actions praise His name,
I want my actions every day to do the same.

 1359 Paul Oakley
Copyright © 1999 Thankyou Music

I SEE THE LORD,
And He is high and lifted up,
And His train fills the temple.
I see You, Lord,
And You are high and lifted up,
And Your train fills the temple.

And I cry holy, holy is the Lord,
Holy is the Lord most high.
And I cry holy, holy is the Lord,
Holy, is the Lord most high.

I see Your holiness,
And light surrounds Your throne;
Who am I to come before You?
But now my guilt is gone,
My sins are washed away,
Through Your blood I come.

Who am I that I should gain the Father's love?
Now my eyes have seen the King.
Touch my lips that I may tell of all You've done:
Fill my heart I cry,
Be glorified!

 1360 Michael Sandeman
Copyright © 2001 Thankyou Music

I SEE YOU HANGING THERE,
Nailed to a splintered wooden beam,
Drinking pain and sorrows,
Breathing agony.
And in those dark, dark hours,
As life drained from Your flesh and bones,
I know my life had its beginning at Your cross.
And I thank You, thank You:

For the cross, where You bled,
For the cross, where You died,
For the cross,
Where You've broken Satan's back.
For the cross, where You won,
For the cross of victory,
For the cross,
Where You paid the price for me.

You were my substitute
In laying down Your life for mine,
Being cursed and bearing
The wrath of God for me.
You were crushed by sin,
Your punishment has brought me peace,
And by the wounds You suffered
I'm alive and healed.
And I thank You, thank You:

Two days in the grave,
Then You rose up from the dead –
Now You reign in glory,
Rule in righteousness.
And I was raised with You,
Free at last from all my sin,
Safe forever in the shelter of my King.
And I thank You, thank You:

1361 Ken Riley
Copyright © 1999 Thankyou Music

I THANK YOU FOR THE CROSS
Where all my shame was laid,
Broken by Your power,
Banished to the grave.
You gave Yourself for me,
A sinner for a King,
Offering Your death
And suffering my sin.

And I will give my life
To You, Lord,
For with grace You came
To pay the ransom for my soul.
And I will live my life
For You, Lord.
You brought me back from death,
Into Your mercy on the cross.

1362 Dan Adler
Copyright © 1999 Heart of the City Music/
Word Music Inc./Adm. by CopyCare

IT IS GOOD, it is good,
It is good to give thanks to the Lord on
high,
To sing of Your faithfulness
And loving kindness both day and night;
To play on our instruments
Sweet songs of praise for the things You
do:
It is good, it is good,
It is good to give thanks to You.

For though the wicked
Spring up like the grass and are everywhere,
Soon they will perish;
But all those planted in Your house
Will grow without end.
Sing it again!

For though we struggle
And trials and troubles still come our way,
You won't forsake us;
Your word has told us
Your promises will never end.
Sing it again!

(Leader – All)
Why give Him praise? (Because He is
worthy.)
Why should we sing? (He loves you and me.)
Why give Him thanks? (Because He forgave
us.)
Why celebrate? (Because we are free.)
And when should we thank Him? (In mornin
and evening.)
In what circumstance? (The good and the bad
Is it always easy? (No, it's not so easy.)
But is it good? (Yes, it's good, it is good, it is
good.)

1363 Duke Kerr
Copyright © 1995 Remission Music UK/
Adm. by Sovereign Music UK

IT IS TO YOU I give the glory,
It is to You I give the praise.
Because You have done so much for me,
I will magnify Your name.
It is to You, holy Father,
No one else but You,
And I will praise Your name,
Praise Your name,
And I will praise Your name forevermore.

1364 Rohn Bailey
Copyright © 1999 Thankyou Music

I TREMBLE IN YOUR PRESENCE,
I am humbled that You came,
Yet I know it's all because I choose to praise
You.
I recognise Your fragrance,
As Your glory fills this place;
All I'd planned to say means nothing now.

Oh, how I long for You.
Oh, how I long for You.
Oh, how I long for You, oh.

I shiver in Your presence,
I am frozen by my shame.
My heart is breaking more than I can stand it
Your radiance is blinding,
Yet You hug me like a friend,
I am overcome by Your mercy again.

1365 Joy Webb
Copyright © Salvationist Publishing &
Supplies Ltd/Adm. by CopyCare

IT WAS ON A STARRY NIGHT when the hills
were bright,
Earth lay sleeping, sleeping calm and still;
Then in a cattle shed, in a manger bed
A boy was born, King of all the world.

And all the angels sang for Him,
The bells of heaven rang for Him;
For a boy was born, King of all the world.
(Repeat)

Soon the shepherds came that way, where
  the baby lay,
And were kneeling, kneeling by His side.
And their hearts believed again, for the peace
  of men;
For a boy was born, King of all the world.

1366 Tim Beck
Copyright © 1999 Thankyou Music

I'VE COME TO MEET WITH YOU, my God,
To bless Your heart, my King;
To be with You, to know Your love,
To give an offering.

And I will seek Your lovely face,
Through the veil I'll come,
To love You in Your dwelling place,
To gaze upon Your throne.
(Repeat)

Your grace and love have come to me,
You've set this captive free.
This child is Yours, You have redeemed
For life eternally.

I know the punishment You took for me;
Thank You, Saviour, for the cost,
That set me free,
That set me free.

1367 David Gate
Copyright © 2001 Thankyou Music

I'VE FILLED MY DAYS WITH DETAILS
And all the choices of the earth,
Carried the yoke of worry,
And all the burdens that it brings.
And through the midst of all the rushing,
You whisper to our hearts,
And with Your sweet voice
You say to us:

To be still and know You are God,
To be still and know You are God,
Just to rest in Your arms.

So give me peace and wisdom
To know how to fill my time,
Where I can learn to keep You
At the centre of my life.
So through the midst of all the rushing
There is time to spend with You,
And my foundation
Will daily be:

1368 Matt Redman
Copyright © 2000 Thankyou Music

I'VE THROWN IT ALL AWAY
That I might gain a life in You.
I've found all else is loss
Compared to the joys of knowing You.
Your beauty and Your majesty
Are far beyond compare:
You've won my heart,
Now this will be my prayer.

'Take the world but give me Jesus!'
You're the treasure in this life.
'Take the world but give me Jesus!'
Is my cry.
Now I've seen You as the Saviour,
I will leave the rest behind:
'Take the world but give me Jesus!'
Is my cry.

Into the world I'll go
That I might live this life of love.
I won't be overcome,
For You are in me and You are strong.
For time and for eternity
I know I'm in Your care;
You've won my heart,
Now this will be my prayer.

1369 Paul Oakley
Copyright © 2000 Thankyou Music

I WANT TO BE BEFORE YOUR THRONE,
Where Your glory shines.
I want to see, I want to know
The One who saved my life.

I want to know the One who shines,
The One enthroned above the skies,
The One who gave His life,
Was crucified, and lifted up on high.

I want to know as I am known
In this space and time.
Now I am Yours, and in lover's words:
Jesus, You are mine.

In You I live, in You I move
And have my being.
It's You I love,
It's You I choose to believe in.

1370
Robert Critchley
Copyright © 2001 Thankyou Music

I WILL CALL UPON THE NAME OF THE LORD,
For He is worthy to be praised.
I will shout hosanna to Jesus, my Rock.
(First time)
I believe He is the Mighty One who saves.

(Second time)
I believe He is the Mighty One,
The Mighty One who saves.

> *God of the breakthrough,*
> *God of the breakthrough,*
> *All things are possible with You.*
> *(Lord, I believe You are the)*
> *God of the breakthrough,*
> *God of the breakthrough,*
> *Let Your love shine down on me.*

Let Your love shine down on me. *(x4)*

I will call on Your name, O Lord. *(x4)*
Jesus!

Jehovah Elohim, the Lord is God.
Jehovah Nissi, the Lord is my banner.
Jehovah Rophi, He is the Lord who heals me.
Jehovah Jireh, the Lord who provides.
Jehovah Tsidkenu, the Lord, our
    righteousness.
Jehovah Shalom, He is the Lord of peace.
Jehovah Rohi, the Lord is my Shepherd.
Jehovah Shammah, the Lord is here.

1371
Tim Sherrington
Copyright © 2000 Thankyou Music

I WILL COME, come, come to the waters and
    drink;
I will praise, praise, praise Your name again.
I will rest, rest, rest, rest at Your feet,
For You have won my heart once again.

I will thirst, thirst, thirst for all that You give;
And I will fall, fall, fall into Your arms again.
I will call, call, call to You alone each day,
For You have won my heart once again.

> *And You are God,*
> *With fire in Your eyes,*
> *And You are God,*
> *Adorned in radiant light.*
> *You are God*
> *Whose hands were pierced for all:*
> *What choice do I have,*
> *But to give You my very all?*

I shall wait, wait, wait at the cross where we
    meet;
And I will live, live, live, by Your name I speak.
I will run, run, run for Your face to seek,
For You have won my heart once again.

1372
Lara Martin (Abundant Life Ministries,
Bradford, England)
Copyright © 2002 Thankyou Music

I WILL ENTER YOUR HOUSE with
    thanksgiving,
I will sing of Your goodness to me.
For my heart is eternally grateful,
I am blessed abundantly.

You have given me life in all its fullness,
And joy no words can describe.
But I know it's for more than me,
It's for those, those You sent me to reach.

> *I am blessed, blessed to be a blessing,*
> *I am blessed, I live under an open heaven,*
> *Blessed, that all may see*
> *It's Christ, Christ in me.*
> *(Repeat)*

1373
Matt & Beth Redman
Copyright © 1998 Thankyou Music

I WILL LOVE YOU FOR THE CROSS,
And I will love You for the cost:
Man of sufferings,
Bringer of my peace.
You came into a world of shame,
And paid the price we could not pay:
Death that brought me life,
Blood that brought me home.
Death that brought me life,
Blood that brought me home.

> *And I love You for the cross,*
> *I'm overwhelmed by the mystery.*
> *I love You for the cost,*
> *That Jesus, You would do this for me.*
> *When You were broken, You were beaten,*
> *You were punished, I go free.*
> *When You were wounded and rejected,*
> *In Your mercy, I am healed.*

Jesus Christ, the sinner's friend;
Does this kindness know no bounds?
With Your precious blood
You have purchased me.
O the mystery of the cross,
You were punished, You were crushed;
But that punishment
Has become my peace.
Yes, that punishment
Has become my peace.

1374 Ian Hannah

I WILL NEVER BE THE SAME
Now my eyes are open wide.
I have been forever changed
Through the power of His blood.

I will triumph in the cross
That my Saviour bore for me.
I will stand with confidence
Because of Jesus.
I no longer fear the grave,
I'm a child of His grace.
I no longer feel ashamed,
Because of Jesus.

1375 Paul Oakley & J.K. Jamieson

I WILL NEVER BE THE SAME,
Now that I have seen the cross;
And how You took upon Yourself
The fullness of the wrath of God.
And I may never understand
Just what You suffered in my place;
Jesus, You who knew no sin,
How You were made sin for us.

And oh, how fierce the Father's anger.
And though You were pierced,
All the pain could not compare;
So dark was the hour,
When all heaven turned its face away,
Turned its face away from You.
But how sweet is Your mercy
As it finds its way to me.

1376 Jennifer Atkinson & Robin Mark

JESUS, ALL FOR JESUS;
All I am and have and ever hope to be.
Jesus, all for Jesus;
All I am and have and ever hope to be.

All of my ambitions, hopes and plans,
I surrender these into Your hands.
All of my ambitions, hopes and plans,
I surrender these into Your hands.

For it's only in Your will that I am free.
For it's only in Your will that I am free.
Jesus, all for Jesus;
All I am and have and ever hope to be.

1377 Michael Frye

JESUS, BE THE CENTRE,
Be my source, be my light,
Jesus.

Jesus, be the Centre,
Be my hope, be my song,
Jesus.

Be the fire in my heart,
Be the wind in these sails;
Be the reason that I live,
Jesus, Jesus.

Jesus, be my vision,
Be my path, be my guide,
Jesus.

1378 Noel Richards

JESUS CHRIST,
You came into this world to rescue me.
On the cross,
My sin was laid on You, what agony.
There Your precious life-blood flowed so free.
Every drop that fell still cleanses me.

All Your love (×4)
Pouring out for me like a flood.

I am safe
Upon the ocean of Your mercy.
I am loved
With all the passion of eternity.
It is deeper than the deepest sea;
Like a tidal wave it carries me.

All Your love (×4)
Sweeping over me like a flood.

So I stand
Upon Your promise of eternal grace.
I believe
That I will one day see You face to face.
I will worship You forevermore
In ways I never have before.

All my love (×4)
Flowing out to You like a flood.

1379 Martyn Layzell
Copyright © 2001 Thankyou Music

JESUS CHRIST, EMMANUEL,

The Saviour of the world;
Creator of the universe,
The true and living Word.
Let every tongue confess Your name,
And bow the knee before Your hand of grace,
Giving You the highest praise.

> You are, You are the everlasting Prince of
>   Peace,
> The First, the Last in whom all things were
>   made.
> You reign with love, Counsellor, Almighty
>   God.
> Jesus, You're the Name by which we're
>   saved,
> Jesus, You're the Name above all names.

Holy One upon the throne,
To You the angels sing.
And here we join their heavenly song,
Proclaiming You as King.
Let every tongue confess Your name,
We bow the knee before Your hand of grace,
Giving You the highest praise.

1380 Nathan Fellingham
Copyright © 2002 Thankyou Music

JESUS CHRIST, HOLY ONE,

The lifter of our heads,
Through You I come, conquering Son,
To my Father in heaven.
And I'm confident that I belong to You,
As the Spirit testifies.
I shall not fear, fear has no hold,
So I cry 'Abba Father!'

> What mercies You have poured on me,
> With thankfulness I'll sing;
> I choose to fix my mind
> On all the blessings You have given me.
> For You've revealed to me Your grace,
> The wonder of the cross;
> You've breathed new life to me,
> And in Your victory I now stand today.

1381 John L. Bell & Graham Maule
Copyright © 1998 WGRG, Iona Community

JESUS CHRIST IS WAITING, waiting in the
streets;

No one is His neighbour, all alone He eats.
Listen, Lord Jesus, I am lonely too:
Make me, friend or stranger, fit to wait on
  You.

Jesus Christ is raging, raging in the streets,
Where injustice spirals and real hope retreats.
Listen, Lord Jesus, I am angry too:
In the kingdom's causes, let me rage with
  You.

Jesus Christ is healing, healing in the streets
Curing those who suffer, touching those He
  greets.
Listen, Lord Jesus, I have pity too:
Let my care be active, healing just like You.

Jesus Christ is dancing, dancing in the
  streets,
Where each sign of hatred He, with love,
  defeats.
Listen, Lord Jesus, I should triumph too:
Where good conquers evil, let me dance with
  You.

Jesus Christ is calling, calling in the streets:
'Who will join My journey? I will guide their
  feet.'
Listen, Lord Jesus, let my fears be few:
Walk one step before me; I will follow You.

1382 Margaret Becker & Keith Getty
Copyright © 2001 Modern M. Music/
Adm. by CopyCare/& Thankyou Music

JESUS, DRAW ME EVER NEARER,

As I labour through the storm.
You have called me to this passage,
And I'll follow, though I'm worn.

> May this journey bring a blessing,
> May I rise on wings of faith:
> And at the end of my heart's testing,
> With Your likeness let me wake.

Jesus, guide me through the tempest,
Keep my spirit staid and sure.
When the midnight meets the morning,
Let me love You even more.

Let the treasures of the trial
Form within me as I go.
And at the end of this long passage,
Let me leave them at Your throne.

1383 Geoff Bullock
Copyright © 1995 Word Music Inc./
Maranatha! Music/Adm. by CopyCare

JESUS, GOD'S RIGHTEOUSNESS
REVEALED,

The Son of Man, the Son of God, His
  kingdom comes.
Jesus, redemption's sacrifice,
Now glorified, now justified, His kingdom
  comes.

And His kingdom will know no end,
And its glory shall know no bounds,
For the majesty and power
Of this kingdom's King has come.
And this kingdom's reign,
And this kingdom's rule,
And this kingdom's power and authority,
Jesus, God's righteousness revealed.

Jesus, the expression of God's love,
The grace of God, the Word of God, revealed
   to us;
Jesus, God's holiness displayed,
Now glorified, now justified, His kingdom
   comes.

1384   Philip Lawson Johnston
        Copyright © 1997 Thankyou Music

JESUS, HIGH KING OF HEAVEN,
We bring our high praise to You.
Jesus, high King of heaven,
To whom all high praise is due.

Who can be compared to You, O Holy One?
None in heaven or earth is Your equal.
You will not share Your glory with another;
Honour to Your name.

O Lord God Almighty, who is like You?
Yesterday, today and forever,
Power, mercy, faithfulness surround You;
Eternal is Your name.

You are the image, the radiance of God's
   glory.
Through You the universe was made.
You are the Alpha, Omega, the First and Last,
You are the Beginning and the End

1385   Brian Doerksen
        Copyright © 2002 Integrity's Hosanna! Music/
        Sovereign Music UK

JESUS, HOPE OF THE NATIONS;
Jesus, comfort for all who mourn,
You are the source
Of heaven's hope on earth.

Jesus, light in the darkness,
Jesus, truth in each circumstance,
You are the source
Of heaven's light on earth.

In history, You lived and died,
You broke the chains, You rose to life.

You are the Hope, living in us,
You are the Rock, in whom we trust.
You are the Light,
Shining for all the world to see.
You rose from the dead, conquering fear,
Our Prince of Peace, drawing us near.
Jesus, our Hope,
Living for all who will receive,
Lord, we believe.

1386   Alan Rose
        Copyright © 1999 Thankyou Music

JESUS IS EXALTED to the highest place,
Seated at the right hand of our God.
He reigns in power and glory,
He is God's appointed heir,
He is righteous, He is holy, He is Lord!

   Hallelujah! He is King of kings.
   Hallelujah! He is the Lord.
   Hallelujah! He is Jesus Christ,
   Reigning forevermore, ever more.

The throne of God will last for all eternity,
We will reign with Him as those He has
   redeemed.
For we are a chosen people,
We will be the bride of Christ,
He has chosen us to ever be with Him!

The day is coming when He will appear,
His glory shining like the sun;
And every nation then will see and fear
The mighty and exalted One.

So let us throw aside all that would hinder us,
And run as those who run to win the prize.
For we will see His glory,
We will see Him face to face,
We will join Him as His glory fills the skies!

1387   Stuart Townend & Keith Getty
        Copyright © 2003 Thankyou Music

'JESUS IS LORD' – the cry that echoes
   through creation;
Resplendent power, eternal Word, our Rock.
The Son of God, the King whose glory fills
   the heavens,
Yet bids us come to taste this living Bread.

Jesus is Lord – whose voice sustains the stars
   and planets,
Yet in His wisdom laid aside His crown.
Jesus the Man, who washed our feet, who
   bore our suffering,
Became a curse to bring salvation's plan.

Jesus is Lord – the tomb is gloriously empty!
Not even death could crush this King of love!
The price is paid, the chains are loosed, and
we're forgiven,
And we can run into the arms of God.

'Jesus is Lord' – a shout of joy, a cry of
anguish,
As He returns, and every knee bows low.
Then every eye and every heart will see His
glory,
The Judge of all will take His children home.

1388 David Fellingham
Copyright © 1998 Thankyou Music

JESUS, JESUS, HEALER, SAVIOUR,
Strong Deliverer,
How I love You,
How I love You.

1389 Dave Bilbrough
Copyright © 2000 Thankyou Music

JESUS, JESUS, JESUS,
How I love Your name.

The sweetest name on earth
Will never be enough
To tell the wonder of Your love.
Come hide me in Your arms
And calm my restless heart;
I hunger, Lord, for more of You.

1390 David Lyle Morris & Faith Forster
Copyright © 2000 Thankyou Music

JESUS, KING OF THE AGES,
*Pleading our cause before the throne of
God.*
Jesus, the living Word of God,
Our Prophet, Priest and King,
Our Prophet, Priest and King.

From the start You were there, Word of God,
Ancient promises You came to fulfil;
You came revealing the Father's heart,
His favour, His purpose, His will:
Sharing His good news with the poor,
Declaring God's kingdom is here.

At the cross You poured out costly blood,
Perfect sacrifice, atoning for sin,
So we may enter the holy place
To meet You, our faithful High Priest;
As we come to the mercy seat
We find grace in our time of need.

Jesus shall reign at the Father's hand
Till all of His enemies cease:
Hell and destruction, disease and death
Are under His glorious feet.

We will reign with Christ, *(echo)*
We will reign with Christ, *(echo)*
We will reign with Christ *(echo)*
Forever.

1391 Mike Sandeman
Copyright © 1999 Thankyou Music

JESUS LOVES THE CHURCH,
He gave Himself for His bride.
He knows what we will be,
A conquering army,
An unblemished people.
We're accepted, we're forgiven,
We're united with Him;
Not rejected, not forgotten,
Not abandoned in sin.

> *Can you hear Him singing,*
> *'I love you, I love you'?*
> *Can you hear Him calling,*
> *'I want you, I have chosen you to be*
> *Mine'?*

Jesus loves the church,
His passion through the ages.
Hell will not prevail.
He builds us together,
A living temple.
We're accepted, we're forgiven,
We're united with Him;
Not rejected, not forgotten,
Not abandoned in sin.

1392 Caroline Bonnett & Steve Bassett
Copyright © 2001 Thankyou Music

JESUS, MELT MY COLD HEART,
Break my stony emotions.
'Cause I've been playing with the waves
When I should be swimming in the ocean.

> *Take me deeper,*
> *Show me more.*
> *It's all or nothing;*
> *I give You everything, my Lord.*

Jesus, show Your mercy,
I'm so sorry for waiting;
I should be running to Your heart,
But I know I've been hesitating.

393 Martyn Layzell
Copyright © 2001 Thankyou Music

JESUS, MY DESIRE,
Turn towards Your ways.
Hungry for Your truth,
I'm here to seek Your face.

But in my weakness I cry out to You, only
You,
To be my strength when I am weak,
And do as You do.

With You, it all seems so right.
If the sun don't shine,
There's light in Your eyes.
With You, when mountains fall,
I stand on the Rock
And I am safe in Your arms
When I'm with You,
When I'm with You.
(Last time)
Just to be with You.

How can I stay pure?
Oh, how can I stay true?
By living out Your word
And dwelling in Your truth.

394 Vicky Beeching
Copyright © 2001 Vineyard Songs (UK/Eire)/
Adm. by CopyCare

JESUS, MY PASSION in life is to know You.
May all other goals bow down to
This journey of loving You more.
Jesus, You've showered Your goodness on
me,
Given Your gifts so freely,
But there's one thing I'm longing for.
Hear my heart's cry,
And my prayer for this life.

Above all else, above all else,
Above all else, give me Yourself.

395 Owen Hurter
Copyright © 2000 Thankyou Music

JESUS, NAME ABOVE ALL NAMES,
My soul cries Jesus,
It's the sweetest song.
Jesus, echoing throughout
All of the heavens,
Angelic hosts proclaim.

Morning Star, Rising Sun,
Lily of the Valley,
Rose of Sharon,
Son of God.
Lifted up, glorified,
Praised through all the ages;
The First and Last,
Beginning and End.

1396 Tim Hughes
Copyright © 2001 Thankyou Music

JESUS, REDEEMER,
Friend and King to me.
My refuge, my comfort,
You're everything to me.
And this heart is on fire for You,
Yes, this heart is on fire for You.

For You alone are wonderful,
You alone are Counsellor,
Everlasting Father,
Mighty in the heavens.
Never to forget the love
You displayed upon a cross,
Son of God, I thank You,
Prince of Peace, I love Your name.

Saviour, Healer,
Just and true are You.
Now reigning in glory,
Most high and living God.
And this heart is in awe of You,
Yes, this heart is in awe of You.

1397 James Gregory
Copyright © 2000 Thankyou Music

JESUS TAUGHT US HOW TO PRAY:
Father, hallowed be Your name.
Would You give us what we need,
And forgive our foolish ways?

I know Jesus only prayed,
Father, what You had ordained.

Let Your kingdom come on earth, Lord, as we
pray.
Let Your will be done to glorify Your name.
Let the kingdom that we live for
Be revealed in us today.
Can I see heaven, can I see heaven
Here on earth today?

1398 Tim Hughes
Copyright © 1999 Thankyou Music

JESUS, YOU ALONE shall be
My first love, my first love.
The secret place and highest praise
Shall be Yours, shall be Yours.

To Your throne I'll bring devotion,
May it be the sweetest sound:
Lord, this heart is reaching for You now.

So I'll set my sights upon You,
Set my life upon Your praise;
Never looking to another way.
(Second time)
You alone will be my passion,
Jesus, You will be my song:
You will find me longing after You.

Day and night I lift my eyes
To seek You, to seek You,
Hungry for a glimpse of You
In glory, in glory.

1399 Nathan Fellingham
Copyright © 1999 Thankyou Music

JESUS, YOU ARE SO PRECIOUS to me;
To behold You is all I desire.
Seated in glory, now and forever,
My Jesus, my Saviour, my Lord.

I worship You,
I worship You,
Lord, I worship You,
Yes, I worship You.

Jesus, You are so precious to me;
Your beauty has captured my gaze.
Now I will come and bow down before You,
And pour sweet perfume on Your feet.

1400 Sue Rinaldi & Caroline Bonnett
Copyright © 1998 Thankyou Music

JESUS, YOUR BEAUTY is filling this temple.
Jesus, Your fragrance is drawing me closer,
And with every step I take
You lead me into this holy place,
And it washes me clean,
For my eyes have seen
Messiah.

And I will jump into the holy river,
I will lose myself to my Deliverer.
I will jump into the holy river,
I will lose myself to my Deliverer.
In this holy place I can see Your face,
Messiah.

Jesus, Your passion is filling this temple.
Jesus, Your mercy is drawing me closer,
And with every step I take
You lead me into a world that aches,
And I cannot rest till all eyes have seen
Messiah.

1401 Darlene Zschech
Copyright © 1997 Darlene Zschech/
Hillsong Publishing/Kingsway Music

JESUS, YOU'RE ALL I NEED,
You're all I need.
Now I give my life to You alone,
You are all I need.
Jesus, You're all I need,
You're all I need.
Lord, You gave Yourself so I could live,
You are all I need.

Oh, You purchased my salvation,
And wiped away my tears;
Now I drink Your living water,
And I'll never thirst again.
For You alone are holy,
I'll worship at Your throne;
And You will reign forever,
Holy is the Lord.

1402 Martyn Layzell
Copyright © 2000 Thankyou Music

KING JESUS, I BELIEVE
The words of life You breathe,
Your spoken promises,
A guiding light for our feet.
We fall down to our knees
And weep with those who weep:
Let justice flow upon this earth,
A never failing stream.

I'm thirsty, longing just to see Your
kingdom come,
Praying that today Your love is shown.
I'm hungry for the will of God to be made
known,
Praying for the day of Your return.

You have anointed us
To bind the broken heart:
Proclaim deliverance
For those enslaved in the dark.
You pour the oil of joy
All over my despair.
O Spirit of the Sovereign Lord,
Empower us once again.

We pray, we pray,
We pray for the kingdom.
We pray, we pray.
(Repeat)

1403 David Gate
Copyright © 2001 Thankyou Music

KING OF HISTORY, God of eternity,
You beckon me into Your arms,
Where You reveal Your forgiving love
That You lavish on my broken heart.

Such amazing grace that You pour on me,
And You freely give every day I live.
And I'll never know the depth of love
That You gave to me upon the cross.

So I thank You for Your saving love,
So I thank You for Your saving love.

1404 Jarrod Cooper
Copyright © 1996 Sovereign Lifestyle Music

KING OF KINGS, MAJESTY,
God of heaven living in me.
Gentle Saviour, closest Friend,
Strong Deliverer, Beginning and End:
All within me falls at Your throne.

Your majesty, I can but bow;
I lay my all before You now.
In royal robes I don't deserve,
I live to serve Your majesty.

Earth and heaven worship You,
Love eternal, faithful and true,
Who bought the nations, ransomed souls,
Brought this sinner near to Your throne:
All within me cries out in praise.

1405 Doug Horley
Copyright © 1999 Thankyou Music

KING OF LOVE, *praise You,*
King of love, worship You,
King of love, thank You,
I'm treasure in Your eyes.

I know my heart will love You forever,
I know Your word, I'll always be Your child.
I know my soul is safe for eternity
'Cause You hold me close in Your arms.

Gonna give You all the praise I can,
Gonna give You all the thanks I can.
In Your arms I will be, King of love, holding
  me.
Gonna give You all the love I can,
Gonna give You all the praise I can.
King of love, King of love, I worship You.

1406 David Lyle Morris & Nick Wynne-Jones
Copyright © 2001 Thankyou Music

KING OF OUR LIVES, Your favour rests
On all who know their need of God,
And You will comfort those who mourn.
The humble meek possess the earth,
Your mighty word turns upside down
All that this world considers great.

Jesus, King of our lives, as once they came
To hear Your life-sustaining words,
We gather now with hungry hearts
Your living truth alone can fill.

King of our lives, the pure in heart
Will know the joy of seeing God,
So purify us deep within:
Our thoughts, our words, the things we do,
Your searching word turns inside out –
So touch our hearts and make us clean.

Jesus, we come, sit at Your feet,
Yield You our lives that we may be
Salt of the earth, light of the world.
All of our cares we give to You,
All that we need our Father gives,
So we will put Your kingdom first.

(Final chorus)
King of our lives, as once they came
To hear Your life-transforming word,
We ask You now to rule our hearts
With living words, to do Your will.

King of our lives, Teacher.
Rule in our hearts, Saviour.
King of our lives, Messiah.
Rule in our hearts, Master,
Healer and Friend.

1407 Stuart Townend & Keith Getty
Copyright © 2002 Thankyou Music

KING OF THE AGES, *Almighty God,*
Perfect love, ever just and true.
Who will not fear You and bring You praise?
All the nations will come to You.

Your ways of love have won my heart,
And brought me joy unending.
Your saving power at work in me,
Bringing peace and the hope of glory.

Your arms of love are reaching out
To every soul that seeks You.
Your light will shine in all the earth,
Bringing grace and a great salvation.

The day will come when You appear,
And every eye shall see You.
Then we shall rise with hearts ablaze,
With a song we will sing forever.

1408 Terry Virgo & Stuart Townend
Copyright © 2001 Thankyou Music

KNOWING YOUR GRACE
Has set me free, Lord.
I'm seeking Your face;
I feel Your pleasure,
Your joy in the ones
You have chosen by name.
You've lifted my burdens
And cast off my shame.

Feeling Your touch
Gives me such peace, Lord.
I love You so much,
I know You'll lead me.
Wherever I go I'll be under Your wing,
For I am a child of the King.

You will finish the work You've begun in me,
I'm adopted, a son in Your family!
You've drawn me with kindness and love
Into this holy place.

What can I say?
Your lavish mercy
Turned night into day –
My guilt has gone now.
Forever I'll stand in Your presence and sing,
For I am a child of the King.

1409 Taizé, music: Jacques Berthier (1923–94)
Copyright © Ateliers et Presses de Taizé

KYRIE, KYRIE ELEISON.
Kyrie, Kyrie eleison.

Lord, Lord, have compassion.
Lord, Lord, have compassion.

1410 Darlene Zschech
Copyright © 1999 Darlene Zschech/
Hillsong Publishing/Kingsway Music

LAMP UNTO MY FEET,
Light unto my path,
It is You, Jesus, it is You.
This treasure that I hold,
More than finest gold,
It is You, Jesus, it is You.

With all my heart, with all my soul,
I live to worship You
And praise forevermore,
Praise forevermore.
Lord, every day I need You more,
On wings of heaven I will soar
With You.

You take my brokenness,
Call me to Yourself.
There You stand,
Healing in Your hands.

1411 David Fellingham
Copyright © 2000 Thankyou Music

LAYING ASIDE EVERYTHING
That would hinder us from coming
Into the presence of our
Great and awesome King;
Lifting up holy hands in faith,
We long to see You face to face,
Freely we come, freely we come.

And we're looking to Jesus,
The One who has saved us.
We're looking to Jesus,
The One who can heal us.
To the Author and the Finisher
Of all that we believe,
Freely we come,
Freely we come.

1412 James Edmeston (1791–1867)
In this version Copyright © Jubilate Hymns Ltd

LEAD US, HEAVENLY FATHER, lead us
Through this world's tempestuous sea;
Guard us, guide us, keep us, feed us –
You our only help and plea;
Here possessing every blessing
If our God our Father be.

Saviour, by Your grace restore us,
All our weaknesses are plain;
You have lived on earth before us,
You have felt our grief and pain:
Tempted, taunted, yet undaunted,
From the depths You rose again.

Spirit of our God, descending,
Fill our hearts with holy peace;
Love with every passion blending,
Pleasure that can never cease:
Thus provided, pardoned, guided,
Ever shall our joys increase.

413 Liturgy of St James, c.4th cent.
Tr. Gerard Moultrie (1829–85)

LET ALL MORTAL FLESH keep silence
And with fear and trembling stand;
Ponder nothing earthly minded,
For with blessing in His hand
Christ our God to earth descendeth,
Our full homage to demand.

King of kings, yet born of Mary,
As of old on earth He stood,
Lord of lords, in human vesture,
In the body and the blood:
He will give to all the faithful
His own self for heavenly food.

Rank on rank the host of heaven
Spreads its vanguard on the way,
As the Light of light descendeth
From the realms of endless day,
That the powers of hell may vanish
As the darkness clears away.

At His feet the six-winged seraph;
Cherubim with sleepless eye,
Veil their faces to the Presence,
As with ceaseless voice they cry,
Alleluia, alleluia,
Alleluia, Lord most high!

414 Darrell Patton Evans
Copyright © 1995 Mercy/Vineyard Publishing/
Adm. by CopyCare

LET THE POOR MAN SAY, I AM RICH IN HIM;
Let the lost man say I am found in Him:
Let the river flow.
Let the blind man say, I can see again;
Let that dead man say, I am born again:
Let the river flow.

Let the river flow,
Let the river flow,
Let the river flow.
Holy Spirit, come;
Move in power.
Let the river flow.
(Let the river flow)

415 Bruce Napier
Copyright © 1998 Bruce Napier

LET THERE BE JOY, let there be peace,
Let there be power, let there be praise.
Let there be joy, joy in the Holy Ghost.
It was for freedom that we were set free,
Let every mountain be cast to the sea.
Let there be joy, joy in the Holy Ghost.

We will declare it to the heavens,
The righteousness of God in which we stand.
We will proclaim it to the nations;
Every eye shall see, every ear shall hear,
Every heart will understand.

1416 Reuben Morgan
Copyright © 1998 Reuben Morgan/
Hillsong Publishing/Kingsway Music

LET THE WEAK SAY I AM STRONG,
Let the poor say I am rich,
Let the blind say I can see,
It's what the Lord has done in me.
(Repeat)

> *Hosanna, hosanna*
> *To the Lamb that was slain;*
> *Hosanna, hosanna,*
> *Jesus died and rose again.*

Into the river I will wade,
There my sins are washed away;
From the heavens mercy streams
Of the Saviour's love for me.

I will rise from waters deep
Into the saving arms of God;
I will sing salvation songs:
Jesus Christ has set me free.

1417 David Lyle Morris
Copyright © 2000 Thankyou Music

LET US RUN WITH PERSEVERANCE
The race set out before us;
Let us fix our eyes on Jesus,
The Author and Perfecter of our faith.

In the beginning
The Word was with God,
Through Him all of us were made;
He began a work in us,
A good work to perfect
Until He returns again.

Since we are surrounded
By heaven's cheering crowd,
Let us throw off every chain:
For all that opposes us,
Look to Jesus who endured
So we'll not lose heart again.

For the joy before Him,
He suffered the cross,
He defeated death and shame;
Now He reigns in glory
At the right hand of God –
He is calling us by name.

1418

LIFT HIGH THE CROSS, *the love of Christ*
  proclaim
  Till all the world adore His sacred name!

Come, brethren, follow where our Captain
  trod,
Our King victorious, Christ the Son of God.

Each new-born soldier of the Crucified
Bears on his brow the seal of Him who died.

This is the sign which Satan's legions fear
And angels veil their faces to revere.

Saved by this cross whereon their Lord was
  slain,
The sons of Adam their lost home regain.

From north and south, from east and west
  they raise
In growing unison their song of praise.

O Lord, once lifted on the glorious tree,
As Thou hast promised, draw men unto
  Thee.

Let every race and every language tell
Of Him who saves our souls from death and
  hell.

Set up Thy throne, that earth's despair may
  cease
Beneath the shadow of its healing peace.

1419

LIGHT OF THE WORLD,
You stepped down into darkness,
Opened my eyes, let me see
Beauty that made this heart adore You,
Hope of a life spent with You.

  So here I am to worship,
  Here I am to bow down,
  Here I am to say that You're my God;
  And You're altogether lovely,
  Altogether worthy,
  Altogether wonderful to me.

King of all days,
Oh so highly exalted,
Glorious in heaven above;
Humbly You came
To the earth You created,
All for love's sake became poor.

And I'll never know how much it cost
To see my sin upon that cross.
(Repeat)

1420

LIKE A FRAGRANT OIL,
Like costly perfume poured out,
Let my worship be to You.
Like a fervent prayer,
Like incense rising to Your throne,
In spirit and in truth.

  Jesus,
  You alone are worthy of my praise,
  I owe my life to You.
  Jesus,
  You alone can make me holy,
  So I bow before You.

Like a wedding vow,
'All I am I give to You',
Let my sacrifice be pure.
Like the sweetest sound,
Like a lover's whisper in Your ear,
I've set my heart on You.

1421

LIKE THE SUNSHINE after rainfall,
Like the gentle breeze;
Like the stillness of the morning,
Like the radiant trees:
These things I knew before,
But never have they spoken such life to me;
Oh, the wonder of a Maker
Whose heart delights in me.

Like the nurture of a baby
At its mother's breast;
Like the closeness of a lover,
Like two souls at rest:
These things I knew before,
But never have they spoken such peace to
  me;
Oh, the wonder of Maker
Whose heart delights in me.

The heavens declare His magnificence,
The earth resounds with His praise;
Be still my soul, and be satisfied
To worship Him,
To worship Him.

Like the vastness of a desert,
Like the ocean's roar;
Like the greatness of the mountains,
Where the eagles soar:
These things I knew before,
But never have they spoken such power to
    me;
Oh, the wonder of a Maker
Whose heart delights in me.

1422 Graham Kendrick
Copyright © 1984 Thankyou Music

LOOK TO THE SKIES, there's a celebration,
Lift up your heads, join the angel song,
For our Creator becomes our Saviour,
As a baby born!
Angels, amazed, bow in adoration:
'Glory to God in the highest heaven!'
Send the good news out to every nation
For our hope has come.

> Worship the King – come, see His
>   brightness;
> Worship the King, His wonders tell:
> Jesus our King is born today;
> We welcome You, Emmanuel!

Wonderful Counsellor, Mighty God,
Father forever, the Prince of Peace:
There'll be no end to Your rule of justice,
For it shall increase.
Light of Your face, come to pierce our
    darkness;
Joy of Your heart come to chase our gloom;
Star of the morning, a new day dawning,
Make our hearts Your home.

Quietly He came as a helpless baby –
One day in power He will come again;
Swift through the skies He will burst with
    splendour
On the earth to reign.
Jesus, I bow at Your manger lowly:
Now in my life let Your will be done;
Live in my flesh by Your Spirit holy
Till Your kingdom comes.

1423 Matt Redman
Copyright © 1998 Thankyou Music

LORD, HEAR THE MUSIC OF MY HEART;
Hear all the pourings of my soul.
Songs telling of a life of love:
Jesus, this is all for You.
You've become the ruler of my heart;
You've become the lover of my soul.
You've become the Saviour of this life:
You are everything to me.

(Oh now,) Jesus, Jesus,
I will pour my praise on You.
Worship, worship,
Demonstrates my love for You.
May I come to
Be a blessing to Your heart.
Jesus, Jesus,
Who can tell how wonderful You are,
How wonderful You are!

O, how wonderful You are.

1424 Matt Redman
Copyright © 1998 Thankyou Music

LORD, I AM NOT MY OWN,
No longer my own,
Living now for You,
And everything I think,
All I say and do
Is for You, my Lord.

Now taking up the cross,
Walking on Your paths,
Holding out Your truth,
Running in this race,
Bowing every day,
All for You, my Lord.

> And what I have vowed
> I will make good.
> Every promise made
> Will be fulfilled,
> Till the day I die,
> Every day I live
> Is for You, is for You, is for You,
> Is for You, is for You, is for You.

Earth has nothing I desire
That lives outside of You,
I'm consumed with You.
Treasures have no hold,
Nothing else will do,
Only You, my Lord.

1425 Geraldine Latty
Copyright © 2000 Thankyou Music

LORD, I COME, longing to know You,
Lord, I come, drawn by Your love;
Lord, I come, longing to see Your face,
For You called me to come
Into the holiest place.

> What did I do to deserve Your favour?
> What did I do to deserve Your grace?
> Called by my name into Your presence,
> Undeserved, holy God.

Lord, I come, because of Jesus,
Lord, I come, because He came;
Lord, I bow, as You reveal Your face,
You have called me to come
Into the holiest place.

1426 Colse Leung
Copyright © 2001 Thankyou Music

LORD, I COME TO YOU,
Broken and lost,
Jesus, be the highest part.
Here I am again,
Longing for more,
Waiting for Your presence, here,
Your presence here.

And how can I do anything but praise You?
How can I not worship You,
And how can I live my life
Without You, God?
Lord, You amaze me with Your favour,
Lord, You astound me with Your love,
And how can I live my life
Without You, God?

1427 Stuart Townend & Fred Heumann
Copyright © 2002 Thankyou Music

LORD, I'M GRATEFUL,
Amazed at what You've done.
My finest efforts are filthy rags;
But I'm made righteous
By trusting in the Son:
I have God's riches at Christ's expense!

> *'Cause it's grace!*
> *There's nothing I can do*
> *To make You love me more,*
> *To make You love me less than You do.*
> *And by faith*
> *I'm standing on this Stone*
> *Of Christ and Christ alone,*
> *Your righteousness is all that I need,*
> *'Cause it's grace!*

Called and chosen when I was far away,
You brought me into Your family.
Free, forgiven, my guilt is washed away;
Your loving kindness is life to me.

Grace loves the sinner,
Loves all I am and all I'll ever be;
Makes me a winner
Whatever lies the devil throws at me.

Freely given, but bought with priceless blood,
My life was ransomed at Calvary.
There my Jesus gave everything He could
That I might live for eternity.

1428 Marilyn Baker
Copyright © 1998 Marilyn Baker Music/
Kingsway Music

LORD, I WANT TO TELL YOU
How much I love You;
Your tenderness and mercy
Have overwhelmed my heart.
Let my whole life be
An overflow of worship:
All I have and all I am
I give back, Lord, to You.

Lord, I want to tell You
My heart's desire,
The love You've put within me
Will burn with holy fire.
Let my actions spring
From an overflow of worship:
All I have and all I am
I gladly give back to You.

1429 Philip Lawson Johnston
Copyright © 1997 Thankyou Music

LORD JESUS, ROBED IN SPLENDOUR,
Clothed in glory high over all.
Lord Jesus, King Messiah,
Mighty Saviour, high over all.

Lord Jesus, all resplendent,
Adorned in beauty, who can compare?
Lord Jesus, You are mighty,
Your kingdom rules high over all.

> *Yours is the name by which we are saved,*
> *The Name high over all.*
> *Yours is the name which we will proclaim*
> *For You are Lord of all.*
> *Jesus, Lord, high over,*
> *Jesus, Lord, high over all!*

The heavens declare the glory of God;
The skies proclaim the work of His hands.
The earth will be filled
With the knowledge of His glory
As the waters cover the sea.

1430 Matt Redman
Copyright © 1998 Thankyou Music

LORD, LET YOUR GLORY FALL
As on that ancient day;
Songs of enduring love,
And then Your glory came.
And as a sign to You
That we would love the same,
Our hearts will sing that song:
God, let Your glory come.

You are good, You are good,
And Your love endures.
You are good, You are good,
And Your love endures.
You are good, You are good,
And Your love endures today.

Voices in unison,
Giving You thanks and praise,
Joined by the instruments,
And then Your glory came.
Your presence like a cloud
Upon that ancient day;
The priests were overwhelmed
Because Your glory came.

A sacrifice was made,
And then Your fire came;
They knelt upon the ground,
And with one voice they praised.
(Repeat)

 1431 Mark Baldry
Copyright © 1999 Thankyou Music

LORD, MY REQUEST,
Lord, my desire
Is to touch Your very heart
Through the way I live my life.
Jesus, all I seek,
Saviour, all I want
Is a passion for Your ways
And a heart that longs for You,
Yes, a heart that longs for You.

It's the way You walk with me,
It's the way You talk with me,
And You sacrificed Your all to give me life.
It's the way You took that cross
With Your arms held out in love,
Yes, You sacrificed Your all to give me life.

You gave Your all to give me life. *(×4)*

 1432 Stuart Townend
Copyright © 2001 Thankyou Music

LORD OF EVERY HEART,
I'm coming back to You.
I'm standing in the shallows
Of what Your love can do;
Remembering the joy
Of laughter in the rain,
I'm calling from the desert,
Won't You fill me again?

Fill me again, won't You fill me again?
I'm tired and I'm thirsty
And I've come to the end.
Come cleanse me with fire,
Refresh me with rain.
O Breath of the Spirit, come closer.

Lord of every deed,
Your promise is enough;
You're unreserved in mercy,
And unrestrained in love.
I'm casting down these crowns
Of all that I can do;
I'm trading my ambitions
For a touch of You.

 1433 Timothy Dudley-Smith
Copyright © Timothy Dudley-Smith

LORD OF THE CHURCH,
We pray for our renewing:
Christ over all, our undivided aim;
Fire of the Spirit, burn for our enduing,
Wind of the Spirit, fan the living flame!
We turn to Christ amid our fear and failing,
The will that lacks the courage to be free,
The weary labours, all but unavailing,
To bring us nearer what a church should be.

Lord of the church, we seek a Father's
blessing,
A true repentance and a faith restored,
A swift obedience and a new possessing,
Filled with the Holy Spirit of the Lord!
We turn to Christ from all our restless striving,
Unnumbered voices with a single prayer:
The living water for our souls' reviving,
In Christ to live, and love and serve and care.

Lord of the church, we long for our uniting,
True to one calling, by one vision stirred;
One cross proclaiming and one creed
reciting,
One in the truth of Jesus and His word!
So lead us on; till toil and trouble ended,
One church triumphant one new song shall
sing,
To praise His glory, risen and ascended,
Christ over all, the everlasting King!

1434 David Lyle Morris & Nick Wynne-Jones
Copyright © 2001 Thankyou Music

LORD OF THE CHURCH,
You hold us in Your hand,
And know us through and through.
You speak to us
Of love and faith and strength,
And of our weakness too.

From love grown cold,
Faint faith that seems alive,
From lukewarm lives and pride.
We turn to You,
That we may be revived,
On fire with love renewed.

Your Spirit is speaking,
Your church is listening
To hear, and to obey.

From compromise,
With all that is not true,
With all that is not pure,
We turn to You.
That we may be full of faith,
Holy in all we do.

Lord of the Church,
Your Spirit speaks in love,
To call us back to You.
We ask You, Lord,
To share Your life with us,
And fill Your church with power.

Your Spirit is speaking,
Your church is listening;
We'll hear, and we'll obey,
Lord of the Church.

1435 Shaun & Mel Griffiths
Copyright © 1998 Parachute Music New Zealand/
Adm. by Kingsway Music

LORD OF THE HEAVENS,
I bow my knee and worship You;
I stand before You,
And I am amazed.
I see Your beauty
Displayed in everything You do.

For You are my Saviour, Lord and King,
You are the only One for me;
You are the only One that I adore.
In Your Son atonement, sacrifice:
Through His death redemption gives new life,
And I reach out, receive Your endless love.

1436 James & Hayley Gregory
Copyright © 2000 Thankyou Music

LORD, TO LOVE YOU MORE is all I want,
To hear You speaking to my heart,
To be consumed by You again.
Fix my eyes on You and draw me near,
Let all distractions disappear,
I need You even more today.

For Jesus, I am overwhelmed
By all Your love has done,
And all I want to say is that I adore You, Lord
I'm humbled by the grace of God,
You met my every need,
And Jesus, You will be always my greatest
    love.

I adore You. *(×4)*

1437 Martin E. Leckebusch
Copyright © 1999 Kevin Mayhew Ltd

LORD, WE THANK YOU FOR THE PROMISE
Seen in every human birth;
You have planned each new beginning:
Who could hope for greater worth?
Hear our prayer for those we cherish,
Claim our children as Your own:
In the fertile ground of childhood
May eternal seed be sown.

Lord, we thank You for the vigour
Burning in the years of youth:
Strength to face tomorrow's challenge,
Zest for life and zeal for truth.
In the choice of friends and partners,
When ideas and values form,
May the message of Your kingdom
Be the guide, the goal, the norm.

Lord, we thank You for the harvest
Of the settled, middle years:
Times when work and home can prosper,
When life's richest fruit appears;
But when illness, stress and hardship
Fill so many days with dread,
May Your love renew the vision
Of a clearer road ahead.

Lord, we thank You for the beauty
Of a heart at last mature:
Crowned with peace and rich in wisdom,
Well-respected and secure;
But to those who face the twilight
Frail, bewildered, lacking friends,
Lord, confirm Your gracious offer:
Perfect life which never ends.

1438 Ken Riley
Copyright © 2001 Thankyou Music

LORD, WHEN I THINK OF YOU,
And what I put You through,
I'll never understand Your endless mercy.
To think You chose to come,
Embodied in Your Son
To fall into the hands of Your created.
Oh, feel my heart explode with praise, yeah.

*I give You all my love, I give You
  everything.
You are God of heaven, and head over
  heels with me!
I know You burn with passion, when I call
  on Your name,
Your love runs as a river, washing my
  shame away,
Restoring my faith again, yeah.*

How did You look upon
The sight of Your own blood?
You even took the sin of those who nailed
  You!
For grace and justice meet
In Him who's chosen me
To walk a path that takes me on to heaven.
Oh, feel my heart explode with praise, yeah.

1439 Andrew Rogers
Copyright © 2001 Thankyou Music

LORD, YOU ARE MY RIGHTEOUSNESS,
The One who sanctifies my life,
My Shepherd and my guide.
Banner of deliverance,
Warrior and my defence,
In Your secret place I hide.
Every other throne must fall
And proclaim You Lord of all
At the mention of Your name;
My salvation and my light,
In Your presence I abide
And Your righteousness I claim.

  *Jesus, Jesus,
  Jesus, Jesus.*

Though You are the King of kings,
Yet You are my next of kin,
And my nearest friend.
Laying down Your life for me,
Your amazing grace I see,
And Your love without an end.
How can I keep silent, Lord?
Even stones obey Your word
And they give to You their praise.
You're the Lord of everything,
All creation's voices sing
Of the glory of Your name.

1440 John Hartley & Gary Sadler
Copyright © 2000 worshiptogether.com songs/
Adm. by Kingsway Music/& Integrity's Hosanna!
Music/Sovereign Music UK

LORD, YOU SEE ME through Your mercy:
I am guilty, still You love me.
In Your kindness there is justice;
Through Your goodness
You have brought me

*Here, where truth and mercy meet,
You triumph over me,
Your love has won my heart again.
And still I am so amazed,
My guilt is washed away
Before Your cross of peace,
Where truth and mercy meet.*

King of glory, Lord of mercy,
Risen Saviour, Perfect Wonder.
Through Your kindness
You have drawn me,
By Your suffering
You have saved me.

1441 Graham Kendrick
Copyright © 2001 Make Way Music

LORD, YOU'VE BEEN GOOD TO ME
All my life, all my life;
Your loving kindness never fails.
I will remember all You have done,
Bring from my heart thanksgiving songs.

  *New every morning is Your love,
  Filled with compassion from above.
  Grace and forgiveness full and free,
  Lord, You've been good to me.*

So, may each breath I take
Be for You, Lord, only You,
Giving You back the life I owe.
Love so amazing, mercy so free.
Lord, You've been good,
So good to me.

1442 Stuart Townend
Copyright © 2000 Thankyou Music

LOVE IS PATIENT, love is kind,
It does not envy or speak in pride.
It does not seek its own reward:
Oh, that's how You love me, Lord.

It always hopes and perseveres,
It covers over a wealth of sins,
It shuns all evil, delights in truth:
Oh, I want to be like You.

  *I'm in love with a King,
  I'm in love with a Friend,
  And whatever I do
  This love never ends.
  He's for me, He pleads for me,
  Pours out His life for me;
  What more do I need?
  Amazing love!*

There are tongues now, but they will cease;
There is knowledge – it's incomplete.
For what we know now, we know in part,
But what endures is a loving heart.

1443 David Lyle Morris
Copyright © 2000 Thankyou Music

LOVE, JOY, PEACE and patience,
Kindness, goodness, faithfulness,
Gentleness and self-control:
This is the fruit of the Spirit.
We want the fruit of the Spirit.
Love, joy, peace and patience,
Kindness, goodness, faithfulness,
Gentleness and self-control:
We will reap what we sow,
We will reap what we sow.

We want joy in the Spirit,
We will rejoice in the Spirit of God.
There is peace in the Spirit,
We want to rest in the Spirit of God.

We want life in the Spirit,
We want to live by the Spirit of God.
Keep in step with the Spirit,
We will be led by the Spirit of God.

Walking with the Spirit of Jesus.
Living by the Spirit of Jesus.
Rejoicing in the Spirit of Jesus.
Resting in the Spirit of Jesus.

1444 Steve Bassett & Sue Rinaldi
Copyright © 2002 Thankyou Music

LOVE LIKE A JEWEL has come down,
Most precious gem
In heaven's crown.
Love like a jewel has come down,
The greatest treasure
That I have found.

> And I will seek after You,
> Forsake everything that is distracting me
> From this searching,
> And run to the place
> Where my heart only hears the beat
> Of Your love for this world.

Love like a jewel has come down,
You walk with the hurting,
You're a friend to the poor.
Love like a jewel has come down,
Our greatest treasure,
Where hope can be found.

1445 Taizé, music: Jacques Berthier (1923–94)
Copyright © Ateliers et Presses de Taizé

MAGNIFICAT, magnificat,
Magnificat anima mea Dominum.
Magnificat, magnificat,
Magnificat anima mea!

Sing out, my soul; sing out, my soul.
Sing out and glorify the Lord who sets us
    free.
Sing out, my soul; sing out, my soul.
Sing out and glorify the Lord God!

1446 Matt Redman
Copyright © 1997 Thankyou Music

MANY ARE THE WORDS WE SPEAK,
Many are the songs we sing;
Many kinds of offerings,
But now to live the life.
(Repeat)

> Help us live the life,
> Help us live the life.
> All we want to do
> Is bring You something real,
> Bring You something true.

(We hope that)
Precious are the words we speak,
(We pray that)
Precious are the songs we sing;
Precious all these offerings,
But now to live the life.

Now to go the extra mile,
Now to turn the other cheek,
And to serve You with a life.
Let us share Your fellowship,
Even of Your sufferings;
Never let the passion die.

> Now to live the life. (×6)

1447 Doug Horley
Copyright © 1999 Thankyou Music

MAY MY EYES SEE MORE OF YOU, Lord;
May my heart just beat with Yours.
May my hope be in Your goodness,
May my life be pure.
And every day my cry is just the same:
Make me like Jesus, Lord, I pray.

Because You've captured my heart,
You have captured my heart.
King of love, and King of glory,
Author of creation's story,
I delight in You, and now and forever.
You have captured my heart,
You have captured my heart.
I delight in You, You've captured my heart.

Because You've captured my heart,
You have captured my heart.
In Your throne room there will be
No hiding place in purity,
A life laid bare for all to see,
O God, make me holy.
You have captured my heart,
You have captured my heart.
I delight in You, You've captured my heart.

For this is what I'm glad to do,
It's time to live a life of love
That pleases You.
And I will give my all to You,
Surrender everything I have and follow
    You,
I'll follow You.

Lord, will You be my vision,
Lord, will You be my guide:
Be my hope, be my light, and the way?
And I'll look not for riches,
Nor praises on earth,
Only You'll be the first of my heart.

I will follow, I will follow You. (×4)

1450   S. Monteiro, English: Word & Music
Copyright © S. Monteiro / Copyright Control
English words © 1995 Word & Music/
Jubilate Hymns Ltd

MERCIFUL LORD, in Your lovingkindness
Hear our prayer, listen to our intercession.
Merciful Lord, in Your lovingkindness
Hear our prayer, listen to our intercession.

Ouve Senhor, eu estou clamando,
Tem piedade de mim e me responde.
Ouve Senhor, eu estou clamando,
Tem piedade de mim e me responde.

1448   Kate B. Wilkinson (1859–1928)

MAY THE MIND OF CHRIST MY SAVIOUR
Live in me from day to day,
By His love and power controlling
All I do and say.

May the word of God dwell richly
In my heart from hour to hour,
So that all may see I triumph
Only through His power.

May the peace of God my Father
Rule my life in everything,
That I may be calm to comfort
Sick and sorrowing.

May the love of Jesus fill me,
As the waters fill the sea;
Him exalting, self abasing,
This is victory.

May I run the race before me,
Strong and brave to face the foe,
Looking only unto Jesus,
As I onward go.

1451   Lynn DeShazo & Gary Sadler
Copyright © 1997 Integrity's Hosanna! Music/
Sovereign Music UK

MERCY, *mercy, Lord,*
Your mercy is how we are restored;
Mercy, O mercy, Lord,
Help us to show Your mercy, Lord.

You have been patient with our offences,
You have forgiven all of our sins;
We were deserving only Your judgement,
But Your great mercy triumphed again.

Lord, You have taught us, 'Love one another,'
As You have loved us so we must love;
Always forbearing, always forgiving,
Showing to others the mercy we've known.

1449   Tim Hughes & Rob Hill
Copyright © 2000 Thankyou Music

MAY THE WORDS OF MY MOUTH,
And the thoughts of my heart
Bless Your name, bless Your name, Jesus:
And the deeds of the day,
And the truth in my ways,
Speak of You, speak of You, Jesus.

1452 Reuben Morgan
Copyright © 1999 Reuben Morgan/
Hillsong Publishing/Kingsway Music

MORE THAN I COULD HOPE OR DREAM OF,
You have poured Your favour on me.
One day in the house of God is
Better than a thousand days in the world.
So blessed, I can't contain it,
So much I've got to give it away.
Your love has taught me to live, now,
You are more than enough for me.

1453 James Taylor
Copyright © 1997 Thankyou Music

MY FRIEND AND KING,
Love sweeter than a rose;
You meet me where I am.
What can I do
But bow down on my knees?
Your beauty blows my mind.

Lord, I will call only to You,
For You deserve the highest praise.
And I will live only for You,
For You deserve the highest praise.

To be with You
Is all that I desire;
Lord, may You shine in me.
You gave me life
And sacrificed Your own;
Who else would die for me?

1454 Kate Simmonds & Mark Edwards
Copyright © 2002 Thankyou Music

MY GOD IS A ROCK! My feet are planted
And I'm not gonna stop praising.
This love is alive!
Goodness and mercy all the days of my life.

My God is a Rock who can't be shaken,
No, I won't ever stop praising.
This love is alive
With every promise written over my life.

And in Him I live, for He lives in me.
And in Him I move, and I have my being.
I'm held forever in Your hand
(Rock solid, rock solid).
And now this ground on which I stand
(Is rock solid, it's rock solid).

My God is a Rock and my salvation,
That's why I'll never stop praising.
This love is alive!
My strength and shelter all the days of my
   life.

My God is a Rock who never changes,
How can I ever stop praising?
This love is alive!
Night and day He's watching over my life.

1455 Author unknown
Copyright control

MY GOD IS SO BIG, so strong and so might
There's nothing that He cannot do.
My God is so big, so strong and so mighty,
There's nothing that He cannot do.
The rivers are His, the mountains are His,
The stars are His handiwork too.
My God is so big, so strong and so mighty,
There's nothing that He cannot do.

My God is so big, so strong and so mighty,
There's nothing that He cannot do.
My God is so big, so strong and so mighty,
There's nothing that He cannot do.
He's called you to live for Him every day,
In all that you say and you do.
My God is so big, so strong and so mighty,
There's nothing that He cannot do.

1456 Lara Martin (Abundant Life Ministries,
Bradford, England)
Copyright © 2002 Thankyou Music

MY HEART IS CAPTIVATED, LORD, by You
   alone;
Captured by the awesomeness of You alone
Melted by the grace and mercy You have
   shown,
I stand in wonder.
I reach to You,
The One who makes the blind eyes see,
Who breaks the chains of sickness with authorit
Restoring what was broken,
So it may fly again.

I live to worship You;
I breathe to worship You.
All of my days Your face I will seek.
For as I worship You,
You lead me to that place,
To that place of divine exchange.

1457 Robin Mark
Copyright © 2000 Thankyou Music

MY HOPE IS IN THE LORD
Who has renewed my strength,
When everything seems senseless,
My hope is still in Him
Who has made heaven and earth
And things seen and unseen;
Whatever shade of passing day,
My hope is still in Him.

My hope is in You, Lord.
My hope is in You, Lord.
My hope is in You, Lord.
My hope is in You, Lord.

For I know that my eyes shall see You,
In the latter days to come.
When You stand on the earth,
With my lips, I will confess
That the hope of my heart is come,
That the hope of my heart is come.

 1458 Keith Getty & Richard Creighton
Copyright © 2001 Thankyou Music

MY HOPE RESTS FIRM on Jesus Christ,
He is my only plea:
Though all the world should point and scorn,
His ransom leaves me free,
His ransom leaves me free.

My hope sustains me as I strive
And strain towards the goal;
Though I still stumble into sin,
His death paid for it all,
His death paid for it all.

My hope provides me with a spur
To help me run this race:
I know my tears will turn to joy
The day I see His face,
The day I see His face.

My hope is to be with my Lord,
To know as I am known:
To serve Him gladly all my days
In praise before His throne,
In praise before His throne.

 1459 Robert Critchley
Copyright © 2001 Thankyou Music

MY TROUBLED SOUL, why so weighed
down?
You were not made to bear this heavy load.
Cast all Your burdens upon the Lord;
Jesus cares, He cares for you.

Jesus cares, He cares for you.
And all your worrying
Won't help you make it through.
Cast all your burdens upon the Lord.
And trust again in the promise of His love.

I will praise the mighty name of Jesus,
Praise the Lord, the lifter of my head.
Praise the Rock of my salvation,
All my days are in His faithful hands.

My anxious heart, why so upset?
When trials come, how you so easily forget
To cast your burdens upon the Lord;
Jesus cares, He cares for you.

 1460 Neil Bennetts
Copyright © 2000 Daybreak Music Ltd

NAME ABOVE ALL NAMES,
The Saviour for sinners slain.
You suffered for my sake
To bring me back home again.
When I was lost,
You poured Your life out for me.
Name above all names,
Jesus, I love You.

Giver of mercy,
The fountain of life for me.
My spirit is lifted
To soar on the eagle's wings.
What love is this
That fills my heart with treasure?
Name above all names,
Jesus, I love You.

High King eternal,
The one true and faithful God.
The beautiful Saviour,
Still reigning in power and love.
With all my heart
I'll worship You forever:
Name above all names,
Jesus, I love You.

1461 Matt Redman
Copyright © 1993 Thankyou Music

NO LONGER JUST SERVANTS in the house
of the King,
The banquet is ready and You draw us in.
You call us to eat with You and to be
Your friends, those who love You,
Your friends, those who know You.

Oh, how can it be that I have become
A friend of the King after all that I've done?
A sinner in rags, now a child in Your care,
You showed me the cross and I met You
there.
Your friend, one who loves You,
Your friend, one who knows You.

A servant is trusted with some secret things,
And so, how much more for the friend of a
King.
No eye has yet seen, and no ear has heard
What You've prepared for those who love You,
What You've prepared for those who love You.

And I'll sing a song for the One that I love,
You captured my heart when I met with Your
Son.
And so I will live a life full of praise
For You, Lord and Shepherd,
For You, Friend and King.

1462 Geraldine Latty
Copyright © 2002 Thankyou Music

NONE OTHER is more worthy,
None other is more deserving of our praise.
None other is so holy,
Sovereign God we come to You,
We give the glory due Your name.

1463 Graham Kendrick
Copyright © 1997 Make Way Music

NO SCENES OF STATELY MAJESTY for the
King of kings.
No nights aglow with candle flame for the
King of love.
No flags of empire hung in shame for
Calvary.
No flowers perfumed the lonely way that led
Him to
A borrowed tomb for Easter Day.

No wreaths upon the ground were laid for
the King of kings.
Only a crown of thorns remained where He
gave His love.
A message scrawled in irony – 'King of the
Jews' –
Lay trampled where they turned away, and
no one knew
That it was the first Easter Day.

Yet nature's finest colours blaze for the King
of kings.
And stars in jewelled clusters say, 'Worship
heaven's King.'
Two thousand springtimes more have
bloomed – is that enough?
Oh, how can I be satisfied until He hears
The whole world sing of Easter love?

My prayers shall be a fragrance sweet for the
King of kings.
My love the flowers at His feet for the King of
love.
My vigil is to watch and pray until He comes;
My highest tribute to obey and live to know
The power of that first Easter Day.

I long for scenes of majesty for the risen
King.
Or nights aglow with candle flame for the
King of love.
A nation hushed upon its knees at Calvary,
Where all our sins and griefs were nailed
And hope was born of everlasting Easter Da

1464 Martyn Layzell
Copyright © 1999 Thankyou Music

NOT BY WORDS AND NOT BY DEEDS,
But by grace we have been saved;
And it is the gift of God, the faith we need.
Not by strength and not by might,
But with power from on high,
So that we can only boast, boast in You.

For once I was dead, now I'm alive,
For freedom I'm set free;
And in Your great love, life do I find.
You opened up my eyes.

Not with eloquence or fame,
But in weakness and in shame,
For the power of Your strength is then
revealed.
And the message of Your cross,
Seemed such foolishness to some,
But the mercy of Your grace is hidden there.

1465 Tim Hughes
Copyright © 1998 Thankyou Music

NOTHING IN THIS WORLD,
No treasure man could buy,
Could take the place of drawing near to You
There's nothing I want more
Than to spend my days with You,
Dwelling in Your secret place of praise.

And oh, how I need You.
Jesus, I need You.
You are the One that satisfies,
You are the One that satisfies.

So place within my heart
A fire that burns for You,
That waters cannot quench
Nor wash away.
And let that fire blaze
Through all eternity,
Where one day I shall see You face to face.

466 Matt Redman & Mike Pilavachi
Copyright © 2000 Thankyou Music

)THING IS TOO MUCH TO ASK
ow that I have said I'm Yours,
sus, take the whole of me
reservedly.

sus, take me deeper now
at I might go further too,
e received so much from You
deservedly.

was made to love You, Lord,
was saved to worship You.
u will be the focus
all eternity.

467 Mark Stevens (Abundant Life Ministries,
Bradford, England)
Copyright © 2002 Thankyou Music

)W HAS COME SALVATION,
w has come Your strength,
d the kingdom of my God,
d the power of His Christ,
sus, holy One,
sus, holy One.

You are the One that I love, my Lord,
You are the One all of heaven adores.
You are the One who is high
Over all the earth.
Jesus, my risen Saviour,
Jesus, my risen Saviour.

w has come Your mercy,
w has come Your peace,
d the glory of Your presence,
d the greatness of Your name,
sus, holy One,
sus, holy One.

w has come forgiveness,
w has come Your grace,
d the precious Holy Spirit,
d the freedom that You gave
Jesus, holy One,
sus, holy One.

468 Graham Kendrick
Copyright © 1993 Make Way Music

)W, IN REVERENCE AND AWE
e gather round Your word;
wonder we draw near
mysteries that angels strain to hear,
at prophets dimly saw:
let Your Spirit
ine upon the page and...

Teach me,
Open my eyes with truth to free me,
Light to chase the lies.
Lord Jesus, let me meet You in Your word;
Lord Jesus, let me meet You in Your word.

Lord, Your truth cannot be chained,
It searches everything –
My secrets, my desires.
Your word is like a hammer and a fire,
It breaks, it purifies:
So let Your Spirit
Shine into my heart and...

1469 Timothy Dudley-Smith
Copyright © Timothy Dudley-Smith

O CHANGELESS CHRIST, forever new,
Who walked our earthly ways,
Still draw our hearts as once You drew
The hearts of other days.

As once You spoke by plain and hill
Or taught by shore and sea,
So be today our teacher still,
O Christ of Galilee.

As wind and storm their Master heard
And His command fulfilled,
May troubled hearts receive Your word,
The tempest-tossed be stilled.

And as of old to all who prayed
Your healing hand was shown,
So be Your touch upon us laid,
Unseen but not unknown.

In broken bread, in wine outpoured,
Your new and living way
Proclaim to us, O risen Lord,
O Christ of this our day.

O changeless Christ, till life is past
Your blessing still be given;
Then bring us home, to taste at last
The timeless joys of heaven.

1470 Marty Sampson
Copyright © 1999 Marty Sampson/
Hillsong Publishing/Kingsway Music

O DEAR GOD, WE ASK FOR YOUR FAVOUR,
Come and sweep through this place.
Oh, we desire You.
I just want to be with You, be where You are,
Dwell in Your presence, O God.
Oh, I want to walk with You.

And I will climb this mountain,
And I step off the shore;
And I have chosen to follow,
And be by Your side forevermore.

Tell me what You want me to do, Lord God,
Tell me what You want for my life.
It's Yours, O God, it's Yours.
Do Your will, have Your way,
Be Lord God in this place.
Oh, I want Your will to be done.

1471 William Cowper (1731–1800), adapt. Keith Getty
Copyright © 2001 Thankyou Music

O FOR A CLOSER WALK WITH GOD,
A calm and heavenly frame.
A light that shines upon the road,
Leading to the Lamb.

Where is the blessèdness I knew
When I once saw the Lord?
Where is the soul refreshing view
Living in His word?

A light to be my guide,
The Father's presence at my side.
In Your will my rest I find.
O for a closer walk with God,
Leading to the Lamb.

So shall my walk be close with God
With all the hopes made new.
So purer light shall mark the road
Leading to the Lamb.

1472 Louise & Nathan Fellingham
Copyright © 2000 Thankyou Music

O GOD OF LOVE, I come to You again,
Knowing I'll find mercy.
I can't explain all the things I see,
But I'll trust in You.
In every moment You are there,
Watching over, You hear my prayer.
You go before me, You're behind me,
Nothing's hidden from You.

How good it is to be loved by You,
How good it is.
(Repeat)

O God of strength,
Your hand is on my life,
Bringing peace to me.
You know my frame,
You know how I am made,
You planned all my days.
Hand of mercy, hand of love,
Giving power to overcome.
If all beneath me falls away,
I know that You are God.

Who can stand against us?
In my weakness You are strong.
Your word is everlasting,
I will praise You, faithful One.

1473 James Gregory
Copyright © 2000 Thankyou Music

OH FALLEN ONE, covered now in shame,
He is your hope, He is your life.
Though He should judge,
His anger turns away;
Rise from the dust, beautiful one.

Don't be afraid,
For you're not left alone;
His heart of love is broken for you.
Your Father cares
For all your children now,
Arise in His name, beautiful one.

Arise and shine, your glory has come,
Arise and shine, your glory has come,
Arise and shine,
He is calling you by name;
Though your walls have fallen down,
He'll build you up again.

Lift up your eyes,
Many come to see
The splendour your God has given to you.
Could each of your saints
Become a thousand saints?
Rise up and praise, beautiful one.

So let Your salvation come,
For Your glory, Lord.
Set the captives free, we pray;
These souls are Your reward.

1474 Brenton Brown
Copyright © 1999 Vineyard Songs (UK/Eire)/
Adm. by CopyCare

OH KNEEL ME DOWN AGAIN,
Here at Your feet;
Show me how much You love humility.
Oh Spirit, be the star that leads me to
The humble heart of love I see in You.

You are the God of the broken,
The friend of the weak;
You wash the feet of the weary,
Embrace the ones in need.
I want to be like You, Jesus,
To have this heart in me.
You are the God of the humble,
You are the humble King.

1475 Doug Horley
Copyright © 1997 Thankyou Music

OI, OI, WE ARE GONNA PRAISE THE LORD.

Oi, oi, we are gonna praise the Lord.
Oi, oi, we are gonna praise the Lord.
He's an exciting, powerising, c-colossal,
Humungous-mungous God!

But it's sometimes hard to understand
That the God who made the earth and man
Would point a finger down from heaven and
   shout:
Hey you! I love you.
Hey you! I love you.
Hey you, you!
I love you', but it's true!

1476 Matt Redman
Copyright © 1999 Thankyou Music

O JESUS, SON OF GOD,

So full of grace and truth,
The Father's saving Word:
So wonderful are You.
The angels longed to see,
And prophets searched to find
The glory we have seen revealed.

You shone upon the earth,
But who will understand?
You came unto Your own,
But who will recognise?
Your birth was prophesied,
For You were the Messiah,
Who came and walked upon the earth.
Your glory we have seen,
The one and only King,
And now You're living in our hearts.

Light of the world, Light of the world,
Light of the world, You shine upon us.
Light of the world, Light of the world,
Light of the world, You shine upon us.

In You all things were made,
And nothing without You;
In heaven and on earth,
All things are held in You.
And yet You became flesh,
Living as one of us,
Under the shadow of the cross,
Where through the blood You shed,
You have made peace again,
Peace for the world that God so loves.

1477 Martyn Layzell
Copyright © 1998 Thankyou Music

O LORD, I AM DEVOTED TO YOU,

All that I am I give You,
Nothing do I withhold.
I am nothing without You,
All my hope is upon You,
Simply telling You I am Yours,
I am Yours.

Jesus, may my devotion be pleasing,
Expressed through this song I am singing,
Pouring my heart out to You, only You.
You are the reason for living, I'm
   breathing:
My refuge, my strength and my healing,
So I give my heart unto You,
Only You.

Every earthly distraction
Fades away to the background,
I'm content just to be with You.
Jesus, You satisfy my longing,
To You do I cry, I'm coming,
Kneeling before Your throne,
At Your throne.

1478 Andrew & Shirley Rogers
Copyright © 2000 Thankyou Music

O LORD, OUR LORD, Your name is great

And greatly to be praised.
In heaven and the universe,
Your glory is displayed.
Every knee must bow to You
And every tongue confess:
You are Lord, the Son of God,
Risen from the dead.

You're Jesus, Ruler of the universe.
Majestic is Your name in all the earth.
Kingdoms rise, kingdoms fall,
You are still the Lord of all.
Majestic is Your name
Here on earth.

When I see the moon and stars
Created by Your breath;
Why did You consider me
Worthy of Your death?
When I was the guilty one
You took away my shame:
When I called, You hid me in
The refuge of Your name.

1479 Brian Houston
Copyright © 2000 Thankyou Music

O LORD, WHEN I WAKE UP in the morning,
Let my mouth be filled with praise for You.
O Lord, when I go out in the evening,
Let my mouth be filled with praise for You.
That all might know, yeah,
And many might see, yeah,
That You're my Lord.

Fill me with a spirit of boldness, O my God,
And come and take all of my shame;
That I might see temptation
Melt before my eyes
And watch the demons flee in Jesus' name,
As we lift high the name.

Lift high the name of the Lord.
Lift high the name of the Lord.
That many might know,
That many might see my Lord.

O Lord, when I'm stressed and feeling tired,
Let my mouth be filled with praise to You.
O Lord, when I'm pressed on every side,
Let my mouth be filled with praise to You.
That all might know, yeah,
And many might see, yeah,
That You are Lord.

1480 Jonathan James (Abundant Life Ministries,
Bradford, England)
Copyright © 2002 Thankyou Music

O LORD, YOU ARE FIRST IN MY LIFE;
For You I live as a sacrifice,
Holy in Your sight, pleasing to Your heart,
As I put my trust in You.

Precious Jesus, You paid such a cost,
That I may know Your love,
Your grace, Your touch;
With everything I am,
I want to know You more,
My heart is open to You.

As I seek You, Lord,
You draw me nearer.

I am Yours, Lord, I am Yours,
Completely abandoned to You.
I am Yours, Lord, I am Yours,
Wholly devoted to You.

1481 Stuart Townend
Copyright © 1999 Thankyou Music

**O MY SOUL, ARISE AND BLESS YOUR
MAKER,**
For He is your Master and your Friend.
Slow to wrath but rich and tender mercy:
Worship the Saviour, Jesus.

King of grace, His love is overwhelming;
Bread of Life, He's all I'll ever need,
For His blood has purchased me forever:
Bought at the cross of Jesus.

And I will sing for all my days
Of heaven's love come down.
Each breath I take will speak His praise
Until He calls me home.

When I wake, I know that He is with me;
When I'm weak, I know that He is strong.
Though I fall, His arm is there to lean on:
Safe on the Rock of Jesus.

Stir in me the songs that You are singing;
Fill my gaze with things as yet unseen.
Give me faith to move in works of power,
Making me more like Jesus.

Then one day I'll see Him as He sees me,
Face to face, the Lover and the loved;
No more words, the longing will be over:
There with my precious Jesus.

1482 Kristyn Lennox & Keith Getty
Copyright © 2002 Thankyou Music

ONCE I WAS FAR AWAY,
But now my life is found in You.
Once I was without hope,
But now I have a vision of heaven.

Fallen from grace;
By faith lifted up;
Now I believe

No height, no depth can keep us
From the love of Christ.
No life, no death, no trial
Can tear us from
The love of God in Christ.

ow wonderful the love
ur Father God has given us,
hat we could still be called
hildren of God.

483 Sydney Carter
Copyright © 1971 Stainer & Bell Ltd

NE MORE STEP ALONG THE WORLD I GO,
ne more step along the world I go,
rom the old things to the new,
eep me travelling along with You.

And it's from the old I travel to the new,
Keep me travelling along with You.

ound the corners of the world I turn,
lore and more about the world I learn.
ll the new things that I see,
ou'll be looking at along with me.

s I travel through the bad and good,
eep me travelling the way I should.
Vhere I see no way to go,
ou'll be telling me the way, I know.

ive me courage when the world is rough,
eep me loving when the world is tough.
eap and sing in all I do,
eep me travelling along with You.

ou are older than the world can be,
ou are younger than the life in me.
ver old and ever new,
eep me travelling along with You.

484 James Gregory
Copyright © 2000 Thankyou Music

NE SACRIFICE AND I AM FREE,
he cross of Christ my victory,
nd on this grace I do believe, yes I believe.
esus, in death You set me free,
aking the punishment for me,
is Your blood that covers me, yes I believe.

nd because of what this love has done
ly heart is filled with praise.

And so I lift my voice to You,
Pouring out all this love on You.
What can I give for all You've done for
me?
I know the Saviour lives today,
Heaven and earth may pass away,
But I know Your love will never fail.

nd every day I live, I vow to follow You.

1485 Paul Oakley
Copyright © 2000 Thankyou Music

ONE THING I ASK, one thing I seek,
To see Your face, to gaze upon Your beauty,
To search behind the eyes of love.

To spend my days within the veil,
Where the purity and light pour over me,
And I am changed.

I gaze on the One who so desired
Friendship with one as low as me.
You left behind Your throne
So I'll sing of Your love (sing of Your love).

All I held close I now let go.
All else is loss compared to knowing You,
And I am changed.

The King who became the sacrifice,
Broken and cursed upon the tree,
The Saviour of my soul,
Hallelujah, hallelujah.

1486 Evan Rogers
Copyright © 2000 Thankyou Music

ONE THING I HAVE BEEN ASKING,
One thing I am looking for:
To see Your glory and beauty,
To know Your presence, Lord.

You're the desire of my heart,
And You are all that I want;
You're the desire of my heart,
And You are all that I want.

You have all my attention,
You are the One I'm living for;
In You I find satisfaction,
You are mine and I am Yours.

I am wanting You,
I am needing You much more, Lord.
You have won my heart,
You've given me all that You've got,
Your love was demonstrated on the cross.
Thank You, Lord!

1487 Dave Bilbrough
Copyright © 1999 Thankyou Music

ONE VOICE, one mind, one will to see
The heart of God revealed in power.
Let every nation, tribe and tongue
Come seek the Lord and His great love.

Send a revival, send a revival,
Send a revival, we pray.
Send a revival, send a revival,
Send a revival, we pray.

We will not cease, we will not rest
Until the Prince of Peace is seen.
As God with us, Emmanuel,
The hope of all humanity.

A vision burns within my soul
That all the world will come to know
The healing found at Calvary,
That place where truth and mercy meet.

I hear a sound across the earth;
It tells me that the time is near.
An anthem lifting up His name:
Make straight a path – prepare the way.

1488

ONLY YOU can replace
Rags for riches pure as gold,
And Your mercy saved my soul,
There's none like You.

At Your name demons flee,
Mountains tremble in Your sight,
But You love me like a friend,
There's none like You.

> *Nothing compares to You,*
> *You're the One we love.*
> *Send down Your holy fire*
> *Over all the earth.*
> (Repeat)

You have paid such a cost,
So much more than can be won:
God, You gave Your only Son,
There's none like You.

So we'll bow to the cross
Where the tears of heaven fall.
You have heard the sinner's call:
There's none like You.

1489

OPENING OUR HEARTS TO YOU,
Focusing our eyes on You,
Lifting up our hands to You,
Singing out this song for You.
Praises that will fill the skies,
Raising You over our lives,
Lifting up the Saviour high.

We give You the highest praise,
We give You the highest praise,
We give You the highest praise,
We give You the highest praise.

You are so amazing, Lord,
A beautiful and mighty God,
Compassionate and merciful,
Glorious and powerful.
King over the universe,
Wonderfully in love with us,
Passionate about the earth.

All glory, honour, worship, praise,
With hands held high and voices raised,
We offer up our hearts again to You.
(Repeat)

1490

OPEN THE EYES OF MY HEART, Lord,
Open the eyes of my heart.
I want to see You,
I want to see You.
(Repeat)

To see You high and lifted up,
Shining in the light of Your glory.
Pour out Your power and love,
As we sing holy, holy, holy.

Holy, holy, holy,
Holy, holy,holy,
Holy holy holy,
I want to see You.

1491

OPEN UP THE GATES OF HEAVEN.
Open up the gates of heaven.
Open up the gates of heaven.
Open up the gates of heaven,

And let Your river flow,
And let new mercies fall like rain;
Oh, let me know Your presence.
You are all I need;
Let all earthly passion fade away,

> *('Cause) all I want is to know You more.*
> *All I want is to meet with You in this plac*
> *All I want is to be with You,*
> *To feel Your embrace.*

1492 Chris Tomlin, Louie Giglio & Jesse Reeves
Copyright © 2000 worshiptogether.com songs/
Six Steps Music/Adm. by Kingsway Music

OPEN UP THE SKIES of mercy,
Rain down the cleansing flood;
Healing waters rise around us;
Hear our cries, Lord, let 'em rise.

It's Your kindness, Lord, that leads us to
repentance;
Your favour, Lord, is our desire.
It's Your beauty, Lord, that makes us stand
in silence,
And Your love, Your love is better than
life.

We can feel Your mercy falling;
You are turning our hearts back again.
Hear our praises rise to heaven;
Draw us near, Lord, meet us here.

1493 Matt Redman
Copyright © 1999 Thankyou Music

O SACRED KING, O holy King,
How can I honour You rightly,
Honour that's right for Your name?
O sacred Friend, O holy Friend,
I don't take what You give lightly,
Friendship instead of disgrace.

For it's the mystery of the universe,
You're the God of holiness,
Yet You welcome souls like me.
And with the blessing of Your Father's heart,
You discipline the ones You love,
There's kindness in Your majesty.
Jesus, those who recognise Your power,
Know just how wonderful You are,
That You draw near.

1494 Dave Bilbrough
Copyright © 1999 Thankyou Music

O TASTE AND SEE that the Lord is good.
O taste and see that the Lord is good.

He is a mighty God,
His ways are higher than ours;
There's nothing impossible for Him.
The future is in His hands.
We're a part of His perfect plan,
And we can do all things
Through the power of His love.

1495 D.R. Edwards. adapt. by Graham Kendrick
Words in this version Copyright © 2001 Make
Way Music

O, THE LOVE OF GOD IS BOUNDLESS,
Perfect, causeless, full and free!
Doubts have vanished, fears are groundless,
Now I know that love to me.
Love, the source of all my blessing,
Love that set itself on me.
Love that gave the sinless Victim,
Love told out at Calvary.

O, the cross of Christ is wondrous!
There I learn God's heart to me;
'Midst the silent, deepening darkness
'God is light' I also see.
Holy claims of justice finding
Full expression in that scene;
Light and love alike are telling
What His woe and suffering means.

O, the sight of heaven is glorious!
Man in righteousness is there.
Once the victim, now victorious,
Jesus lives in glory fair!
Him, who met the claims of glory
And the need of ruined man
On the cross, O wondrous story!
God has set at His right hand.

O, what rest of soul in seeing
Jesus on His Father's throne!
Yes, what peace forever flowing
From God's rest in His own Son!
Gazing upward into heaven,
Reading glory in His face,
Knowing that 'tis He, once given
On the cross to take my place.

1496 Stuart Townend & Gary Sadler
Copyright © 2000 Integrity's Hosanna! Music/
Sovereign Music UK & Thankyou Music

OUR GOD IS STRONG AND MIGHTY,
He's lifting up a shout.
It's rolling down like thunder:
Can you feel it shake the ground?
And every stronghold trembles
As we hear the Lion roar!

He's breaking out.
(The Lord our God is breaking out.)
The Lord our God is breaking out.
(The Lord our God)
He's breaking out!

He's rising in this nation,
He's coming into view;
Go tell it in the city
What Jesus' power can do.
We're losing our religion –
He's even greater than we thought!

O God of mercy, God of love,
Come show us the glory of Your name.
We're touched by the passion of Your heart,
And nothing will ever be the same,
Nothing will ever be the same,
Don't let me ever be the same.

Come do a work within me,
Let me see You as You are;
And make the cause of heaven
The obsession of my heart,
Till every tribe and nation
Bows in worship to the King.

 1497 Viola Grafstrom
Copyright © 1998 Thankyou Music

OUR MASTER, OUR SAVIOUR,
You are Lord, our King.
Our Master, our Saviour,
We give our praise to our King,
To our King.

You're the everlasting Father,
The beginning and the end.
There is no one that can take Your place,
There is no other name.

1498 Brenton Brown
Copyright © 1998 Vineyard Songs (UK/Eire)/
Adm. by CopyCare

OVER ALL THE EARTH,
You reign on high,
Every mountain stream,
Every sunset sky.
But my one request,
Lord, my only aim
Is that You'd reign in me again.

Lord, reign in me,
Reign in Your power;
Over all my dreams,
In my darkest hour.
You are the Lord of all I am,
So won't You reign in me again?

Over every thought,
Over every word,
May my life reflect the beauty of my Lord;
'Cause You mean more to me
Than any earthly thing,
So won't You reign in me again?

 1499 Noel Robinson
Copyright © 2000 Thankyou Music

OVER, OVER,
The joy of the Lord is running over.
Over, over,
The joy of the Lord is running over.

Let me tell you of the supernatural joy
That You can find in Him,
The man called Jesus.
He'll take away the sorrow of this life
That brings so much sadness,
Give you overflowing joy
That no man can ever, ever touch, yeah.

Weeping may endure;
Joy comes in the morning.
Weeping may endure;
Joy comes!

1500 Kevin Mayhew
Copyright © 1976 Kevin Mayhew Ltd

PEACE, PERFECT PEACE
Is the gift of Christ our Lord.
Peace, perfect peace,
Is the gift of Christ our Lord.
Thus, says the Lord,
Will the world know My friends.
Peace, perfect peace,
Is the gift of Christ our Lord.

Love, perfect love…

Faith, perfect faith…

Hope, perfect hope…

Joy, perfect joy…

 1501 Russell Fragar
Copyright © 1998 Russell Fragar/
Hillsong Publishing/Kingsway Music

PRAISE HIM, YOU HEAVENS
And all that's above.
Praise Him, you angels
And heavenly hosts.
Let the whole earth praise Him.
Praise Him, the sun, moon
And bright shining stars.
Praise Him, you heavens
And waters and skies.
Let the whole earth praise Him.

Great in power, great in glory,
Great in mercy, King of heaven.
Great in battle, great in wonder,
Great in Zion, King over all the earth.

1502 David Gate
Copyright © 1999 Thankyou Music

RAISES,
For all that You've done I'll sing praises,
For sending Your Son who would save me,
Pouring out grace at the cross
Where You died for me.
Mercies,
Through all of my life I've seen mercies,
Through hardship and strife You are with me,
By my side, You are good,
So good to me.

Through Your death You brought me life,
Took my shame, clothed me in white.

Lord, here I am, amazed again,
That You would die to save a friend.
You clear my sin and pay the cost,
So on my knees I'll stay,
At the foot of the cross.

Worship,
Day after day I will worship,
For glory and grace, and for goodness,
With all of my life I will be Your living praise.
And Jesus,
I'll always look unto Jesus,
For guidance and strength and my focus,
Trying to live how You want Your child to be.

1503 Martin E. Leckebusch /
Chorus words: Graham Kendrick
Copyright © 2000 Kevin Mayhew Ltd
Chorus words Copyright © 2002 Make Way Music

PRAISE TO CHRIST, THE LORD INCARNATE,
Gift of God by human birth:
He it is who came among us,
Shared our life and showed our worth;
Ours the turmoil He encountered,
Ours the fight He made His own;
Now within our hearts His Spirit
Makes His way of freedom known.

Praise to Christ our Saviour and our King.
Praise to Christ our King.

Praise to Christ, the Man of Sorrows,
Tasting death for our release:
His the cup of bitter anguish,
Ours the pardon, ours the peace;
His the blood that seals forgiveness,
Ours the weight of guilt He bore –
So by death and resurrection
Christ has opened heaven's door.

Praise to Christ, the Priest eternal:
Still for us He intercedes;
Still He sees our pains and problems –
How He understands our needs!
Yesterday, today, forever,
Always He remains the same:
Pledged to bring us to the Father,
Strong in grace and free from blame.

1504 Paul Crouch & David Mudie
Copyright © 1991 Daybreak Music Ltd

PRAYER IS LIKE A TELEPHONE
For us to talk to Jesus.
Prayer is like a telephone
For us to talk to God.
Prayer is like a telephone
For us to talk to Jesus.
Pick it up and use it every day.

We can shout out loud,
We can whisper softly,
We can make no noise at all.
But He'll always hear our call.

1505 Dave Bilbrough
Copyright © 2000 Thankyou Music

PREPARE THE WAY of the Lord,
Prepare the way of the Lord.
Prepare the way of the Lord,
Prepare the way of the Lord.

Majestic in holiness,
Awesome in glory,
Doing wonders, this is our God.
We will not be silenced
From speaking His word.
We cry to the nations:

All authority is invested
In the name of Jesus,
And at the sounding of that name,
At the sounding of that name
He will arise.

1506 Evelyn Tarner
Copyright © 1967 Sacred Songs/Word Music/
Adm. by CopyCare

REJOICE IN THE LORD ALWAYS
And again I say rejoice.
Rejoice in the Lord always
And again I say rejoice.

Rejoice, rejoice, and again I say rejoice.
Rejoice, rejoice, and again I say rejoice.

1507
Augustus M. Toplady (1740–78)
adapt. by Graham Kendrick
Words in this version Copyright © 2001 Make
Way Music

ROCK OF AGES, cleft for me,
Let me hide myself in Thee.
Let the water and the blood
From Your wounded side which flowed,
Be of sin the double cure,
Cleanse me from its guilt and power.

My Rock (my Rock),
My Jesus, my Rock.
My Rock (my Rock),
My Jesus, my Rock.

Not the labours of my hands
Can fulfil Your law's demands.
Could my zeal no respite know,
Could my tears forever flow,
All for sin could not atone.
You must save and You alone.

Nothing in my hand I bring,
Simply to Your cross I cling.
Naked, come to You for dress,
Helpless, look to You for grace.
Foul, I to the fountain fly:
Wash me, Saviour, or I die.

While I draw this fleeting breath,
When my eyelids close in death,
When I soar to worlds unknown,
See You on Your judgement throne,
Rock of Ages, cleft for me,
Let me hide myself in Thee.

1508
Sue Rinaldi, Caroline Bonnett & Steve Bassett
Copyright © 2001 Thankyou Music

SACRED, holy, pure,
Lord of space and time,
Dwells in perfect light,
Radiance sublime.
Sacred holy songs
Rise on wings of praise;
All creation rings
With echoes of Your grace.

And oh, my grateful heart rejoices at Your
name.
And oh, my grateful heart rejoices at Your
name.

Sacred, risen Son,
Peerless Lamb of God;
Mercy, grace and peace
Rolling like a flood.
Promise forged in pain,
Forgiveness bought by blood;
Sealed with sacred words
From the mouth of God.

1509
Charlie Hall
Copyright © 1997 worshiptogether.com songs/
Six Steps Music/Adm. by Kingsway Music

SALVATION, SPRING UP from the ground,
Lord, rend the heavens and come down.
Seek the lost and heal the lame;
Jesus, bring glory to Your name.
Let all the prodigals run home,
All of creation waits and groans.
Lord, we've heard of Your great fame;
Father, cause all to shout Your name.

Stir up our hearts, O God;
Open our spirits to awe who You are.
Put a cry in us
So deep inside,
That we cannot find
The words we need,
We just weep and cry out to You.

1510
Tim Sherrington
Copyright © 1998 Thankyou Music

SEARCH MY SOUL, and pierce my heart
With a fire that burns from Your eyes.
And drive me on to the reason for living,
That is just for You,
That is just for You.

How long must I wait for Your coming?
Come quickly, Lord,
'Cause You're the only answer.
And drive me on to the reason for living,
That is just for You,
That is just for You.

Let Your kingdom come,
Let Your will be done,
Let Your rain pour out on my life.
Let Your kingdom come,
Let Your will be done,
Let Your rain drench my life and do Your
will.

Come and break the chains
That hold me back, Lord,
From dancing in Your light
And being a fool for You.
And I'm running back to the reason for living
That is just for You,
That is just for You.

1511 Robert Critchley
Copyright © 1996 Thankyou Music

SEE HOW THE FATHER opens the heavens
To honour His Son.
See how the Spirit descends like a dove
Upon His belovèd One.
This the Lamb of God
Who takes away the sins of the world.
Grace has appeared to heal the nations,
Christ has been given to set us free,
To Him be the glory forevermore.

To Jesus be glory forevermore.
To Jesus be glory forevermore.

See how the Father opens the heavens,
Revealing His Son.
Angels and elders and saints without number
Worship the risen One.
And with a shout they proclaim,
'Worthy is the Lamb who was slain;
To Him be all power and riches and wisdom,
To Him be all the honour, dominion and
    praise,
To Him be the glory forevermore.'

Can you hear the Father saying,
'I am so pleased, just look at My Son,
Just look at My Son'?

1512 Dave Bilbrough
Copyright © 2002 Thankyou Music

SEND YOUR SPIRIT, *(×3)*
O Lord, we pray.

Light our darkness, *(×3)*
O Lord, we pray.

Move in power, *(×3)*
O Lord, we pray.

For the honour of Your name, *(×6)*
O Lord.

1513 Marc James & Tré Sheppard
Copyright © 2001 Vineyard Songs (UK/Eire)/
Adm. by CopyCare

SHINE YOUR LIGHT ON US
That all may see Your goodness.
Shine Your face on us
That all may see Your glory.

Answer me when I call.
You are my only prayer.
When darkness is all around
I know You will be there.

Many are asking,
Who can show us something real?
Longing for hope
Beyond the pain of what they feel.
So I will go down on my knees and say:

I wanna be close to You,
That my life would tell Your story.
I wanna be one with You,
Changed by the light of Your glory.

1514 Taizé, music: Jacques Berthier (1923–94)
Copyright © 1982 Ateliers et Presses de Taizé

SING, PRAISE AND BLESS THE LORD.
Sing, praise and bless the Lord.
Peoples! Nations! Alleluia!

Laudate Dominum,
Laudate Dominum,
Omnes gentes, alleluia!

1515 Jacques Berthier (1923–94)
Copyright © Ateliers et Presses de Taizé

SING PRAISES, ALL YOU PEOPLES,
Sing praises to the Lord.
Sing praises, all you peoples,
Sing praises to the Lord.

Laudate omnes gentes,
Laudate Dominum.
Laudate omnes gentes,
Laudate Dominum.

1516 David Lyle Morris
Copyright © 2001 Thankyou Music

SING PRAISES TO OUR GOD, *sing*
    praises.
Sing praises to the King, sing praises.
(Repeat)

For God is King of all the earth,
Sing to Him a psalm of praise.
God reigns over the nations,
All our worship we will raise.
He's King of all the earth,
Bring to Him a joyful song.
He's Lord of all creation,
Seated on His holy throne.

Clap your hands, all you nations,
Shout to God with cries of joy,
How awesome is the Lord most high.
Clap your hands, all creation,
Cry to God who made us all,
The great King over all the world.

1517 Robert Johnson, altd Lex Loizides
Copyright © 1998 Thankyou Music

SOLDIERS OF OUR GOD, ARISE!
The day is drawing nearer;
Shake the slumber from your eyes,
The light is growing clearer.
Sit no longer idly by
While the heedless millions die.
O, lift the blood-stained banner high,
And take the field for Jesus.

Save the lost! Save the lost!
Spend your might for them;
Give your life for them.
Save the lost! Save the lost!
Don't back down on it;
Win your crown in it,
Soldiers of our God,
Soldiers of our God.

See the brazen hosts of hell
Their art and power employing,
More than human tongue can tell
The blood-bought souls destroying.
See on ruin's hell-bound road
Victims groan beneath their load;
Go forward, O you sons of God,
And dare or die for Jesus.

Warriors of the risen King,
Great army of salvation,
Spread His fame, His praises sing
And conquer every nation.
Raise the glorious standard higher,
Work for victory, never tire;
O, forward march with blood and fire,
And win the world for Jesus.

1518 Martyn Layzell
Copyright © 2002 Thankyou Music

SOVEREIGN LORD, over all,
You are reigning forever.
Worship flows from our lips,
We have come for just one glimpse.

And we sing hallelujah,
Hallelujah, hallelujah.

Majesty, reign in me,
Your right hand enfolding me.
Earth applaud, heavens sing
At the sight of Christ the King.

Lord of lords, now enthroned,
Who can stand in Your presence?
Fire of love, holy One,
You burn brighter than the sun.

1519 Tim Sherrington
Copyright © 2001 Thankyou Music

SPIRIT, MOVE ON THIS LAND,
Take Your people in Your hands.
We're waiting for the day,
The day You come again.
Your Spirit is coming to give to the poor;
So Father, take our lives and shine.

Revival in our land,
Won't rest until we see
Revival in our land.
(Repeat)

1520 Ian White
Copyright © 1997 Thankyou Music

SPIRIT OF THE LORD, come down among us
now;
Minister new life to bones grown dry.
Something in our heart cries out to be made
whole:
The touch of healing love.

Give us just a glimpse of God, of Jesus' heart,
Open ears to hear the voice say, 'Come':
Look up, look up, look up and see
The light of healing love.

1521 Paul Oakley & Martin Cooper
Copyright © 2001 Thankyou Music

STANDING ON HOLY GROUND,
Mercy and grace I've found.
I'm here before Your throne now,
By a new and living way.
Jesus, I come to You.
I lift up my eyes to You.
How You've comforted me,
And now I long to see Your face.

You are my strength, my song;
You are my shield, my Redeemer.
You are my hope, my salvation,
And my God.
(First time)
I'll always bring my praise to You,
O God.

(Second time)
So I will sing to You,
Beautiful things You have done.
Great is Your name in Zion,
Holy One.
I'll always bring my praise to You,
I'll always bring my praise to You,
I'll always bring my praise to You,
O God.

1522
Taizé, music: Jacques Berthier (1923–94)
Copyright © 1980 Ateliers et Presses de Taizé

STAY WITH ME,
Remain here with me,
Watch and pray;
Watch and pray.

1523
David Lyle Morris & Liz Morris
Copyright © 2000 Thankyou Music

SURELY OUR GOD *is the God of gods,*
And the Lord of kings,
The revealer of mysteries.
(Repeat)

He changes the times and the seasons,
He gives rhythm to the tides;
He knows what is hidden
In the darkest of places,
Brings the shadows into His light.

I'll praise You always, my Father,
You are Lord of heaven and earth.
You hide Your secrets
From the 'wise' and the learnèd,
And reveal them to this, Your child.

Thank You for sending Your only Son,
We may know the mystery of God;
He opens the treasures
Of wisdom and knowledge
To the humble, not to the proud.

1524
Noel & Tricia Richards
Copyright © 2000 Thankyou Music

TAKE ME TO YOUR SACRED PLACE,
How I long to see Your face.
I'll be lost in Your embrace
And be loved, and be loved by You.

Take me where Your glory shines,
Where Your holy fire burns.
Purify this heart of mine,
I surrender my life to You.

Draw me, draw me
To Your sacred place.
Draw me, draw me
Till I see Your face.

1525
Robin Mark
Copyright © 1998 Thankyou Music

TAKE US TO THE RIVER,
Take us there in unity to sing
A song of Your salvation
To win this generation for our King.
A song of Your forgiveness,
For it is with grace that river flows;
Take us to the river
In the city of our God.

Take us to Your throne room,
Give us ears to hear the cry of heaven;
For that cry is mercy,
Mercy to the fallen sons of man:
For mercy it has triumphed,
Triumphed over judgement by Your blood;
Take us to the throne room
In the city of our God.

For the Spirit of the Sovereign Lord is
upon us:
This is the year of the Lord.
The Spirit of the Sovereign Lord is upon
us,
This is the year of the Lord.

Take us to the mountain,
Lift us in the shadow of Your hands;
Is this Your mighty angel,
Who stands astride the ocean and the land?
For in his hand Your mercy
Showers on a dry and barren place;
Take us to the mountain
In the city of our God.

1526
David Gate
Copyright © 2001 Thankyou Music

TEACH ME OF YOUR WAYS,
To honour You with all I have,
And that I learn to say:
'Not my will, but Yours, my Lord.'

O Jesus, be glorified
In all of my life.
It's all about You,
And the worship You're due.
So help me to change,
Mould me like clay;
Lord, have Your way,
Lord, have Your way with me.

Lord, I long to be
A faithful child who honours You.
So Jesus, be in me,
Let Your light shine through me now.

1527 Dave Bilbrough
Copyright © 1998 Thankyou Music

TELL THE WORLD *that Jesus is risen,*
Let His praise encircle the globe;
Make it known among all the nations
That Jesus is alive!

From the cradle to the grave,
From a stable to a cross,
His life was offered up in sacrifice for us.
He came from heaven's throne
To seek and save the lost;
To reconcile us back to God.

No eye has seen, no ear has heard what He's
   prepared;
His resurrection means His life is ours to
   share.
The greatest miracle of all has taken place;
Christ is risen, He is Lord!

1528 Darlene Zschech
Copyright © 2000 Darlene Zschech/
Hillsong Publishing/Kingsway Music

THANK YOU FOR THE CROSS, LORD,
Thank You for the price You paid.
Bearing all my sin and shame,
In love You came
And gave amazing grace.

Thank You for this love, Lord,
Thank You for the nail-pierced hands.
Washed me in Your cleansing flow,
Now all I know:
Your forgiveness and embrace.

   Worthy is the Lamb
   Seated on the throne,
   Crown You now with many crowns.
   You reign victorious,
   High and lifted up,
   Jesus, Son of God,
   The darling of heaven crucified.
   Worthy is the Lamb.
   Worthy is the Lamb.

1529 Paul Booth
Copyright © 1999 Thankyou Music

THANK YOU, LORD, FOR YOUR LOVE TO ME.
By Your truth You have set me free.
Through the cross I can enter in.
What seemed impossible till I let You
Wash away my sin,
Take away all shame
By the life-giving blood
Of Jesus, my Redeemer.

Holy, I stand before You,
Truly, I am blameless in Your sight.
Righteous, a royal robe I don't deserve,
Yet You choose to clothe me still,
Precious mercy.

Such mercy, such grace,
Such kindness to save
Even a sinner like me.
I'll love You, I'll serve You,
I'll praise You forever,
Thank You, Lord, for Your love to me.

1530 Paul Oakley & Megamix Kids
Copyright © 2001 Thankyou Music

THANK YOU, LORD, YOU LOVE US,
Thank You, Lord, You care.
Thank You, Lord, You made us,
Thank You, Lord, You're there.
Thank You for forgiveness,
Your gift of life to me.
Thank You for Your faithfulness,
You're always, always, always, always
Good to me.

So we really want to say,
'We love You,'
We really want to shout,
'You're the best!'
We're gonna bring our praise to You,
King of kings and my best friend.
(Repeat)
Oh yeah!

1531 Matt Redman
Copyright © 1999 Thankyou Music

THANK YOU, THANK YOU FOR THE BLOOD
   that You shed,
Standing in its blessing we sing these
   freedom songs.
Thank You, thank You for the battle You won,
Standing in Your victory we sing salvation
   songs,
We sing salvation's song.

You have opened the way to the Father,
When before we could never have come.
Jesus, count us as Yours now forever,
As we sing these freedom songs.

We sing of all You've done,
We sing of all You've done,
We sing of all You've done for us,
Won for us, paid for us.
(Repeat)

1532 Stuart Townend
Copyright © 2000 Thankyou Music

THE BIRDS DON'T WORRY,
The flowers don't fret,
The trees don't hurry
For the food they get;
For God looks after
The things He's made:
They can depend on Him.

> *So don't you worry 'bout the things you*
> *need,*
> *For clothes to wear or for food to eat;*
> *But seek His kingdom and the rest will*
> *come:*
> *You can depend on Him.*

The hills don't grumble,
The stars don't cry,
The sun doesn't tumble
From the big, blue sky;
For God has set everything in place:
They can depend on Him.

> *You can't live longer by worrying more,*
> *You can't get taller than you were before;*
> *So seek His kingdom and the rest will*
> *come:*
> *You can depend on Him.*

1533 Chris Tomlin & Jesse Reeves
Copyright © 2002 worshiptogether.com songs/
Six Steps Music/Adm. by Kingsway Music

THE CROSS BEFORE ME, the world behind;
No turning back, raise the banner high:
It's not for me, it's all for You.
Let the heavens shake and split the sky,
Let the people clap their hands and cry:
It's not for us, it's all for You.

> *Not to us,*
> *But to Your name be the glory.*
> *(Repeat)*

Our hearts unfold before Your throne,
The only place for those who know:
It's not for us, it's all for You.
Send Your holy fire on this offering,
Let our worship burn for the world to see:
It's not for us, it's all for You.

The earth is shaking, the mountains shouting:
It's all for You.
The waves are crashing, the sun is raging:
It's all for You.

The universe spinning and singing:
It's all for You.
Your children dancing, dancing, dancing:
It's all for You, it's all for You.
My all for You, my all for You.

1534 Mark Pendergrass
Copyright © Garden Valley Music/Birdwing Music/
BMG Songs Inc./EMI Christian Music Publishing/
Adm. by CopyCare

THE GREATEST THING IN ALL MY LIFE is
knowing You;
The greatest thing in all my life is knowing
You;
I want to know You more;
I want to know You more.
The greatest thing in all my life is knowing
You.

The greatest thing in all my life is loving You;
The greatest thing in all my life is loving You;
I want to love You more;
I want to love You more.
The greatest thing in all my life is loving You.

The greatest thing in all my life is serving
You;
The greatest thing in all my life is serving
You;
I want to serve You more;
I want to serve You more.
The greatest thing in all my life is serving
You.

1535 David Ruis
Copyright © 2001 Vineyard Songs (Canada)/
Adm. by CopyCare

THE NARROW PATHWAY
Through the needle's eye,
I'm stepping forward
To the place I die.
For I know that You are faithful,
As we walk these fields of white.
To the waiting and the humble
Your kingdom comes.

The way of mercy
Takes me to the least,
Down the road of suffering
To the wedding feast.
For I know that You are faithful,
As we walk these fields of white.
To the weary and the hurting
Your kingdom comes.

1536 David Lyle Morris & Jussi Miettinen
Copyright © 2000 Thankyou Music

THE PEOPLE WHO WALK IN DARKNESS
Will see a great light,
For those who live in the land
Of the shadow of death,
The light will shine.

You will enlarge the nation,
And increase their joy,
So they delight in Your presence
As they will rejoice
At harvest time.

For to us a Child is born,
To us a Son is given,
And the government
Will be upon His shoulders.
Of His government and peace
There will always be increase;
There is no end to His kingdom.

He will be called Wonderful,
Counsellor, Mighty God,
Everlasting Father, Prince of Peace.
(Repeat)
The Prince of Peace.

For to us a Child is born,
To us a Son is given,
And the government
Will be upon Your shoulders.
Come to break our yoke of grief,
The bar across our shoulders;
Lord, smash the rod of our oppressors.

You will be called…

1537 Ed Pask
Copyright © 2001 Thankyou Music

THE PLACE WHERE YOU DWELL
Is where I want to be,
It's where angels in splendour
Worship the King.
And to Jesus in glory
Each voice raised in song:
Holy, holy, holy is the Lord.

In the light of Your presence
I find perfect peace,
And my heart shall adore You
And in You rejoice.
And to Jesus victorious
I lift up my song:
Worthy, worthy, worthy is the Lamb.

It's all for You, Jesus,
Only You, Jesus.
You are my song and my reason to sing;
You have set this heart free
To rise on the wings of Your praise.

1538 Gary Sadler
Copyright © 1998 Integrity's Hosanna! Music/
Sovereign Music UK

THE POWER OF YOUR LOVE is changing me
Changing me, changing me.
O Lord, change me by the power of Your love
(Repeat)

You've drawn me to Your side,
And what else can I do?
My heart is open wide,
My hands reach out to You.
I'm calling out for more;
I'm asking in Your name,
That by Your Spirit, Lord,
I will never be the same.

I'm singing out my praise,
I'm pouring out my thanks,
For the power of Your love is changing me.
I'm lifting up my voice,
I'm dancing in the joy,
For the power of Your love is changing me.

1539 Nathan Fellingham
Copyright © 2001 Thankyou Music

THERE IS A DAY
That all creation's waiting for,
A day of freedom and liberation for the earth.
And on that day
The Lord will come to meet His bride,
And when we see Him
In an instant we'll be changed.

The trumpet sounds
And the dead will then be raised
By His power,
Never to perish again.
Once only flesh,
Now clothed with immortality;
Death has now been
Swallowed up in victory.

We will meet Him in the air
And then we will be like Him,
For we will see Him, as He is,
Oh yeah!
Then all hurt and pain will cease,
And we'll be with Him forever,
And in His glory we will live,
Oh yeah, oh yeah!

So lift your eyes
To the things as yet unseen,
That will remain now
For all eternity.
Though trouble's hard
It's only momentary,
And it's achieving
Our future glory.

1540 James Taylor
Copyright © 1999 Thankyou Music

THERE IS A DEEPER LOVE TO KNOW,
There is a higher place where we can go.
There is a freedom at the cross,
There is a light that shines for all the world.

And I can't hold this joy inside,
I'm jumping in Your arms of mercy.

Everybody sing, everybody shout,
For the joy of the Lord
Is our strength forever.
Hey, everybody sing, everybody shout,
For the joy of the Lord is our strength.

There is a brighter day to come,
When all the world will bow down to Your
    Son.
And all the broken will rejoice,
Even the kings will say, 'You are the Lord'.

And we can't hold this joy inside,
We're dancing in Your arms of mercy.

1541 Kristyn Lennox & Keith Getty
Copyright © 2002 Thankyou Music

THERE IS A HIGHER THRONE
Than all this world has known,
Where faithful ones from every tongue
Will one day come.
Before the Son we'll stand,
Made faultless through the Lamb;
Believing hearts find promised grace:
Salvation comes.

Hear heaven's voices sing,
Their thunderous anthem rings
Through emerald courts and sapphire
    skies,
Their praises rise.
All glory, wisdom, power,
Strength, thanks and honour are
To God, our King who reigns on high
Forever more.

And there we'll find our home,
Our life before the throne;
We'll honour Him in perfect song
Where we belong.
He'll wipe each tear-stained eye,
As thirst and hunger die;
The Lamb becomes our Shepherd King:
We'll reign with Him.

1542 Graham Kendrick
Copyright © 2002 Make Way Music

THERE IS A HOPE SO SURE,
A promise so secure:
The mystery of God at last made known.
Treasures so vast appear,
All wisdom, knowledge here:
It's Christ in us, the hope of glory!

And the life that I now live,
No longer is my own,
Jesus lives in me, the hope of glory.
And each day I live,
No longer is my own,
Jesus lives in me, the hope of glory.

There is a life so true,
A life of love so pure,
For all our sin a perfect sacrifice.
And when that life was nailed,
On cruel cross impaled,
Our sinful flesh with Him was crucified.

There is a life so strong
That a whole world of wrong
And all the powers of hell could not defeat.
For Jesus rose again,
And if we died with Him,
With Him we'll rise to share His endless life.

1543 Nathan Fellingham
Copyright © 2001 Thankyou Music

THERE IS A NAME that's high over all.
There is a King seated on the throne.
And He's interceding for me,
So that I will be made holy,
And I know that in His love
I will stay.

What a Saviour is my Jesus,
He came down
So that I may go free.

There is a Man who walked on the earth,
The Word of God made known to us.
He's the image of the Father,
The Firstborn over creation,
Yet He suffered at the hands of those He saves.

What a Saviour is my Jesus,
He came down
So that I may go free.
How I love You, oh my Jesus,
You came down
So that I may go free.

1544 David Fellingham & Kim Morgan
Copyright © 2001 Thankyou Music

THERE IS A PASSION deep in my heart
To know You, Jesus.
There is a hunger deep in my soul
Only You can satisfy.
I hear You calling, drawing me closer,
I can't resist Your grace.
Almighty power and love so free,
Draw me to Your side.

And I'm lifted into Your presence,
Lifted into Your arms of love.
Lifted into Your presence,
Now has my soul found rest,
Now has my soul found rest.

I see Your face,
I feel Your touch;
Receive Your love,
I worship You.
(Repeat)

1545 Paul Oakley
Copyright © 1998 Thankyou Music

THERE IS A VOICE THAT MUST BE HEARD,
There is a song that must be sung;
There is a name that must be lifted high.
There is a treasure more than gold,
There is a King upon the throne;
There is One whose praise will fill the skies.

His name is Jesus, Friend of sinners,
Jesus, Jesus, Friend of mine.

There is a peace that calms our fears,
There is a love stronger than death;
There is a hope that goes beyond the grave.
There is a Friend who won't let go,
There is a heart that beats for you;
There is one name by which we are saved.

When I was captive to my fears,
You were the One who came to me,
You set me free.

1546 Robin Mark
Copyright © 1999 Integrity's Hosanna! Music/
Sovereign Music UK

THERE IS NO OTHER NAME
By which men can be saved,
There is no other name under heaven.
There is rest for my soul
And the wounded made whole,
And the captives set free and forgiven.

Such love as I had never known,
I've found in the grace that flowed to me
In my unrighteousness;
This is why my heart and soul and tongue
  confess.

1547 Tim Hughes
Copyright © 2002 Thankyou Music

THERE MUST BE MORE than this:
O Breath of God, come breathe within.
There must be more than this:
Spirit of God, we wait for You.
Fill us anew, we pray;
Fill us anew, we pray.

Consuming fire, fan into flame
A passion for Your name.
Spirit of God, fall in this place.
Lord, have Your way,
Lord, have Your way with us.

Come like a rushing wind,
Clothe us with power from on high.
Now set the captives free;
Leave us abandoned to Your praise.
Lord, let Your glory fall;
Lord, let Your glory fall.

1548 Stuart Townend
Copyright © 2001 Thankyou Music

THERE'S A CALL to the people of Zion,
To arise and possess the land;
Every town has its heirs to the promise,
Every nation its sons of light.
We have stayed long enough on this mountain
Now we're called to new realms of faith;
We are more than a temple of worship,
We're an army of praise!

We will go to every place,
Sharing mercy and preaching grace,
For the fields are white for harvest,
And labourers are few.
No place too dark, no soul too lost
For the power of the cross;
For His light will shine in darkness,
And many will believe,
So we will go.

We have drunk of the wine of His presence,
We have feasted upon His word;
Now we're hungry for works of power,
Now we're thirsty to share His love.
He will give us the ground that we walk on,
For the battle belongs to God;
Do not fear, for His grace is sufficient,
When we're weak, He is strong!

 1549 Ken Riley
Copyright © 1999 Thankyou Music

THERE'S A CALLING TO THE NATIONS
To make ready in Your name,
To take up the yoke of Jesus
And proclaim the coming day.
There's a pouring of Your Spirit
As our old men dream Your dreams;
Prophesy through sons and daughters,
Come envision us again.

You're the Word and the Word is Truth,
You're the Promise that was born in You,
And a wave of expectation fills my soul!

> *All over the world we're singing,*
> *All over the world there's praise*
> *To the King of our salvation,*
> *And the Author of our faith.*
> *All over the world we're dancing,*
> *All over the world there's joy,*
> *We've called upon Your name*
> *And we are saved.*

Can it be this generation
That will hear revival's song,
As Your Spirit of creation
Comes awakening the lost?
Let the four winds blow Your justice,
Come and harvest of the earth;
Turn our mourning into dancing
As we herald Your return.

1550 Johnny Parks
Copyright © 2001 Thankyou Music

THERE'S A NEW SONG UPON MY LIPS,
A song I always knew.
Thank You for all that You do.
There is fire burning in my heart,
A fire of faith in You.
I believe all the things we can do.

> *You're the God of great things,*
> *You're the God of great things.*
> *I won't hold back my thanks to You.*
> *Thank You, thank You,*
> *Hey, Jesus, I adore You.*
> *Thank You, thank You,*
> *Hey, Jesus, I live for You.*

There's a beat pounding through my feet,
A new dance of thanks to You.
I'm tasting the joy found in You.
There is courage building in my heart;
A strength that comes from You.
I'm going to live my life for You.

 1551 David Fellingham
Copyright © 1999 Thankyou Music

THERE'S A PAGEANT OF TRIUMPH IN GLORY,
As Jesus the King takes His throne.
The shame of the cross is exchanged for a crown,
And heaven applauds the King.
The Son has the Father's approval,
He perfectly followed the plan
To suffer and die for the sins of the world,
He poured out His love for our shame.

> *Let God arise with shouts of joy,*
> *With songs of praise and trumpet sound;*
> *Let music play and hearts be free,*
> *Let God arise!*

Death could not keep Him in prison,
He burst through the shackles of hell;
He settled the score with the evil one,
And heaven applauds the King.
The fullness of Christ is my treasure,
I've cast off the past with its shame.
The power of the Father has raised me to life,
I'm a son, I'm forgiven and free.

1552 Terry Virgo & Stuart Townend
Copyright © 2000 Thankyou Music

THERE'S A PEOPLE
God has chosen from the nations,
He has ransomed from the prisons
For His joy, for His delight.
He has known them
From before He made the heavens,
And His love has spanned the ages,
How He longs to bring them home!

> *Oh, that we might see Your glory, Lord.*
>   *(Men)*
> *Oh, that we might see Your face. (Women)*
> *Oh, that we might be with You forever.*
>   *(Men)*
> *Oh, that we might be with You. (Women)*
> *Knowing You as You have known us, (All)*
> *Faith eclipsed by what we see:*
> *One with You for all eternity!*

We're that people
You have rescued from our blindness,
You have come to live within us,
To share Your peace, to share Your joy.
Come and fill us,
Flood our spirits with Your fullness,
Let us taste the wine of heaven,
Only You can satisfy.

1553 James Taylor
Copyright © 2000 Thankyou Music

THERE'S NO LOVE GREATER THAN YOUR LOVE,
There's no love greater than You.
There's no love greater than Your love,
There's no love greater than You.

I want to hear it sung around the world
That Jesus, You are Lord of all.
And our praises ring that You are King
Of all the heavens and the earth.
And at Your name we bow,
You've turned our mourning into dancing.

Want to see the day when all will know
That Jesus, You are Lord of all.
And we'll hear the songs of freedom sound
Upon the lips of young and old.
And every knee shall bow,
Let all the earth rejoice with gladness.

You came with love brighter than the day.
Who can deny the wonder of Your name?
Don't let me fall,
I was born to be with You:
There's no love like You.

1554 Vicky Beeching & Steve Mitchinson
Copyright © 1999 Vineyard Songs (UK/Eire)/
Adm. by CopyCare

THERE'S NO ONE LIKE OUR GOD,
No one at all.
He gave His Son for us,
Jesus the Lord.
And who can love us like He does?
No one at all.
Oh, how we love You, Lord.

You are high above all nations,
Your glory shines above the heavens;
Humbled Yourself to love and save us:
Be praised through endless generations.

You lift the needy from the ashes,
And seat them high up with the princes.
You give the barren woman healing;
She'll dance for joy like the mother of children.

1555 Damian Lundy
Copyright © 1978 Kevin Mayhew Ltd

THE SPIRIT LIVES TO SET US FREE,
Walk, walk in the light;
He binds us all in unity,
Walk, walk in the light.

> *Walk in the light,*
> *Walk in the light,*
> *Walk in the light,*
> *Walk in the light of the Lord.*

Jesus promised life to all,
Walk, walk in the light;
The dead were wakened by His call,
Walk, walk in the light.

He died in pain on Calvary,
Walk, walk in the light;
To save the lost like you and me,
Walk, walk in the light.

We know His death was not the end,
Walk, walk in the light;
He gave His Spirit to be our friend,
Walk, walk in the light.

By Jesus' love our wounds are healed,
Walk, walk in the light;
The Father's kindness is revealed,
Walk, walk in the light.

The Spirit lives in you and me,
Walk, walk in the light;
His light will shine for all to see,
Walk, walk in the light.

1556 Dave Bilbrough
Copyright © 2000 Thankyou Music

THE VOICE OF GOD is calling
With words that roar and rage;
The passion of the Father's heart
Resounds through every age.
Multitudes are waiting
For this gospel we proclaim;
Christ Jesus came among us
That all men might be saved.

> *Show Your glory, show Your glory,*
> *Show Your glory over all the earth.*
> *Show Your glory, show Your glory,*
> *Show Your glory over all the earth.*

This is our commission,
To fill the air with praise
And to tell the people of this world
The glory of His name.
With thousands upon thousands
From every tribe and tongue
We cry, 'Worthy is the Lamb once slain,
For He has overcome!'

With tears of intercession,
Through the prayers of all the saints,
We long to reach the nations
With humility and grace.
Come touch this generation
And use us, Lord, we pray;
Fill our hearts with boldness
To do the things You say.

THE WONDER OF FORGIVENESS,
The comfort of Your love,
The all-surpassing pleasure
To be a friend of God.
Your thoughts to me are endless,
This joy will never end.

All I want to say is 'I love You',
All I want to give is my heart.
All I want to do is be near You,
And to walk in Your ways.
Resting in the peace of Your promise,
Trusting in the cross that You bore,
Looking for the day when I see You,
Lord, I thank You for Your faithfulness to
me.

I'm laying down my treasures
To claim the perfect prize.
I'm pulling back the curtain
To look into Your eyes.
You know my inhibitions,
But You can meet me here.

THE WONDER OF YOUR MERCY, Lord,
The beauty of Your grace,
That You would even pardon me
And bring me to this place.
I stand before Your holiness,
I can only stand amazed:
The sinless Saviour died to make
A covenant of grace.

I only want to serve You,
Bring honour to Your name,
And though I've often failed You,
Your faithfulness remains.
I'll glory in my weakness,
That I might know Your strength.
I will live my life at the cross of Christ,
And raise a banner to proclaim:

You welcome us before You,
Into this holy place;
The brilliance of Your glory
Demands our endless praise.
The One, the only Saviour
Has opened heaven's doors;
We can enter in, free from all our sin,
By Your cleansing sacrifice.

THIS CHILD, secretly comes in the night,
O this Child, hiding a heavenly light,
O this Child, coming to us like a stranger,
This heavenly Child.

This Child, heaven come down now
To be with us here,
Heavenly love and mercy appear,
Softly in awe and wonder come near—
To this heavenly Child.

This Child, rising on us like the sun,
O this Child, given to light everyone,
O this Child, guiding our feet on the pathway
To peace on earth.

This Child, raising the humble and poor,
O this Child, making the proud ones to fall;
O this Child, filling the hungry with good
  things,
This heavenly Child.

THIS IS LOVE, not that we loved Him,
But that He first loved us.
Left behind glories of heaven;
Took on the shame of the cross.
But in the place where love was poured
Death could not hold our risen Lord.

On Christ our solid ground,
Our hope for life is found;
The joy of our salvation.
On Christ our solid ground,
Our hope for life is found.
There is no condemnation.
There is no condemnation.

This is peace, not as the world gives,
But the true peace of Christ.
You have claimed our hearts for heaven;
Living by faith, not by sight.
Strengthen our faith in You alone
Until we stand before Your throne.

1561 Reuben Morgan
Copyright © 1995 Reuben Morgan/
Hillsong Publishing/Kingsway Music

THIS IS MY DESIRE, to honour You:
Lord, with all my heart I worship You.
All I have within me, I give You praise:
All that I adore is in You.

Lord, I give You my heart,
I give You my soul;
I live for You alone.
Every breath that I take,
Every moment I'm awake,
Lord, have Your way in me.

1562 Marie Barnett
Copyright © 1995 Mercy/Vineyard Publishing/
Adm. by CopyCare

THIS IS THE AIR I BREATHE,
This is the air I breathe:
Your holy presence living in me.
This is my daily bread,
This is my daily bread:
Your very word spoken to me.

And I, I'm desperate for You.
And I, I'm lost without You.

1563 Ian White
Copyright © 1997 Thankyou Music

THIS IS THE BEST PLACE,
This is the right place,
And we have confidence now to enter:
Let us draw near now,
With hearts sincere now,
In full assurance,
To worship Jesus.

We're worshipping the living God! (×4)

Let us consider,
For one another,
The way to love more,
As the day approaches.
Let us draw near now,
With hearts sincere now;
Let's meet together
To worship Jesus.

1564 Matt Redman
Copyright © 1995 Thankyou Music

THIS MEANS I LOVE YOU,
Singing this song;
Lord, I don't have the words,
But I do have the will.
And this means I love You,
That I take up the cross,
I will sing as I walk out this love.

Jesus, this life is for You,
Everything, Lord, that I do;
Deeds that are pleasing
And ways that are pure,
Lord, may my life bear this fruit.

For these are the plans of my heart,
Yet often I'm missing the mark;
See my desire to live in Your truth,
This surely means I love You.

1565 Graham Kendrick
Copyright © 2001 Make Way Music

THOUGH TRIALS WILL COME,
Don't fear, don't run.
Lift up your eyes,
Hold fast, be strong.
Have faith, keep on believing.
Lift up your eyes
For God is at work in us,
Moulding and shaping us
Out of His love for us,
Making us more like Jesus.

Consider it joy, pure joy
When troubles come.
Many trials will make you strong.
Consider it joy, pure joy
And stand your ground,
Then at last you'll wear a crown.

Though trials will come,
Won't fear, won't run.
We'll lift up our eyes,
Hold fast, be strong.
Have faith, keep on believing.
We'll lift up our eyes
For God is at work in us,
Moulding and shaping us
Out of His love for us,
Making us more like Jesus.

Joy, pure joy,
Consider it joy, pure joy.
Joy, pure joy,
Consider it joy, pure joy.

Patiently trusting Him,
Ready for anything,
Till we're complete in Him,
In everything more like Jesus.

1566 N. Tate (1652–1715) & N. Brady (1659–1726)
New Version, 1696 based on Psalm 34

THROUGH ALL THE CHANGING SCENES OF LIFE,
In trouble and in joy,
The praises of my God shall still
My heart and tongue employ.

Of His deliverance I will boast,
Till all that are distressed
From my example comfort take,
And charm their griefs to rest.

O magnify the Lord with me,
With me exalt His name;
When in distress to Him I called,
He to my rescue came.

The hosts of God encamp around
The dwellings of the just;
Deliverance He affords to all
Who on His succour trust.

O make but trial of His love;
Experience will decide
How blest are they, and only they,
Who in His truth confide.

Fear Him, ye saints, and you will then
Have nothing else to fear;
Make you His service your delight;
Your wants shall be His care.

1567 Graham Kendrick
Copyright © 1998 Make Way Music

THROUGH DAYS OF RAGE AND WONDER
We pursue the end of time,
To seize the day eternal,
The reign of love divine.

Fixing our eyes on Jesus,
We will press on day by day.
This world's vain passing pleasures
Are not our destiny.

*Our ancient rites of passage
Still are the bread and wine:
Our hope a cross that towers
Over the wrecks of time.*

Through days of rage and wonder,
By the awesome power of prayer
God will shake every nation,
Secrets will be laid bare.
And if His light increasing
Casts deeper shadows here,
Safe in His holy presence,
Love will cast out our fear.

Through days of rage and wonder,
You will give us strength to stand
And seek a heavenly city
Not built by human hands.
Now is the only moment
Within our power to change:
To give back in obedience
While life and breath remain.

1568 Matt Redman
Copyright © 2000 Thankyou Music

TIME IS TOO SHORT to say it's okay,
To think I can live this way
For just another day.
So I'll search through the night
For the One my heart loves,
Won't stop till I've found You,
For Lord, I need to hold You close.

*Be the King of this heart again,
Be the Lord of this life.
In my soul there's a cry today:
Be the King of this heart,
Be the King of this heart.*

I've stood in the desert and thirsted for You,
I've run through the city, now I won't let go:
I'm throwing myself on Your mercy, O God,
You say: 'It's all or nothing.'
I'm saying: 'Jesus have it all.'

Be the light for my eyes,
Be the strength for my feet,
Be the love of my soul,
Be my everything.
Be my day and my night,
When I wake, when I sleep,
Undivided my heart will be.

1569 James E. Seddon (1915–83)
Copyright © Mrs M. Seddon/Jubilate Hymns Ltd

TO HIM WE COME –
Jesus Christ our Lord,
God's own living Word,
His dear Son:
In Him there is no east and west,
In Him all nations shall be blest;
To all He offers peace and rest –
Loving Lord!

In Him we live –
Christ our strength and stay,
Life and Truth and Way,
Friend divine:
His power can break the chains of sin,
Still all life's storms without, within,
Help us the daily fight to win –
Living Lord!

For Him we go –
Soldiers of the cross,
Counting all things loss,
Him to know;
Going to every land and race,
Preaching to all redeeming grace,
Building His church in every place –
Conquering Lord!

With Him we serve –
His the work we share
With saints everywhere,
Near and far;
One in the task that faith requires,
One in the zeal that never tires,
One in the hope His love inspires –
Coming Lord!

Onward we go –
Faithful, bold and true,
Called His will to do
Day by day
Till, at the last, with joy we'll see
Jesus in glorious majesty;
Live with Him through eternity –
Reigning Lord!

1570 Matthew Bridle
Copyright © 1998 Thankyou Music

TO WALK WITH YOU, to know You near me,
To know Your voice, to hear You call me;
This is all I ask of You.
To be Your son, to feel You hold me,
To know Your grace, to know You love me;
This is all I ask of You,
This is all I ask of You.

To be Your joy, to give You glory;
To live with You, forever with me.
To love You, Lord, as You have loved me,
Is all I ask of You,
All I ask of You.

To love Your ways, to see Your beauty,
To seek Your face with all that's in me;
This is all I ask of You.
To worship You, to be Yours only,
To cry Your name, my Lord Almighty;
This is all I ask of You,
This is all I ask of You.

To live Your life, to serve You justly,
To tell Your word, to show Your mercy;
This is all I ask of You.
To bring Your light to those who know me,
To be like You, as You are holy;
This is all I ask of You,
This is all I ask of You.

1571 Nathan Fellingham
Copyright © 2002 Thankyou Music

TO YOU, KING JESUS, we sing our song,
The First and the Last, the living One.
With eyes like fire, and feet like bronze,
Your face shines brighter than the sun,
All creation speaks Your name.

Jesus, Son of God,
You stand in all authority,
And at Your name darkness flees.
Oh, Jesus, living Word,
Reigning at the Father's right hand,
And You're clothed with majesty and
power.

To You, King Jesus, we give our hearts,
For You have come to us with Your great
love.
You suffered death, went to the grave,
But now You're crowned with glory.
All Your people speak Your name.

And we now stand at Your side,
A people chosen as Your bride.
You've filled us with the Spirit's power,
This is the hour.
So in Your strength I'll run this race,
Covered by Your daily grace,
Pressing on to win the prize,
Till the day that You return,
And every tribe and every tongue will sing:

1572 Graham Kendrick
Copyright © 1997 Make Way Music

TO YOU, O LORD, I lift up my soul,
In You I trust, O my God.
Do not let me be put to shame,
Nor let my enemies triumph over me.

No one whose hope is in You
Will ever be put to shame;
That's why my eyes are on You, O Lord.
Surround me, defend me,
O, how I need You.
To You I lift up my soul,
To You I lift up my soul.

Show me Your ways and teach me Your
    paths,
Guide me in truth, lead me on;
For You're my God, You are my Saviour,
My hope is in You each moment of the day.

Remember, Lord, Your mercy and love
That ever flow from of old.
Remember not the sins of my youth
Or my rebellious ways.
According to Your love, remember me,
According to Your love,
For You are good, O Lord.

1573
Taizé, music: Jacques Berthier (1923–94)
Copyright © 1980 Ateliers et Presses de Taizé

UBI CARITAS et amor,
Ubi caritas Deus ibi est.

*Living charity and steadfast love,
Living charity shows the heart of God.*

1574
Latin, 15th Century
Tr. Percy Dearmer (1867–1936)
Copyright © Oxford University Press

UNTO US A BOY IS BORN!
King of all creation,
Came He to a world forlorn,
The Lord of every nation,
The Lord of every nation.

Cradled in a stall was He
With sleepy cows and asses;
But the very beasts could see
That He all men surpasses,
That He all men surpasses.

Herod then with fear was filled:
'A Prince,' he said, 'in Jewry!'
All the little boys he killed
At Bethlem in his fury,
At Bethlem in his fury.

Now may Mary's Son who came
So long ago to love us,
Lead us all with hearts aflame
Unto the joys above us,
Unto the joys above us.

Alpha and Omega He!
Let the organ thunder,
While the choir with peals of glee
Doth rend the air asunder,
Doth rend the air asunder!

1575
Jacques Berthier (1923–94)
Copyright © Ateliers et Presses de Taizé

WAIT FOR THE LORD, whose day is near.
Wait for the Lord: keep watch, take heart.

1576
Brian Houston
Copyright © 1999 Thankyou Music

WE ARE CALLED TO BE PROPHETS TO THIS
    NATION,
To be the word of God in every situation;
Change my heart, change my heart today.
Who'll be the salt if the salt should lose its
    flavour?
Who'll be the salt if the salt should lose its
    flavour?
Change my heart, change my heart today.

Lord, loose the chains of oppression;
Lord, set the captives free.
Lord, fill my heart with compassion:
Shine Your light, shine Your light,
Shine Your light through me.

*Work a miracle in my heart,
Work a miracle in my heart,
Work a miracle in my heart,
O Lord, today.*

Lord, take all of my lies and take all of my
    greed;
Let me be a sacrifice for those who are in need.
Change my heart, change my heart today.
Lord, without Your power it's all just good
    intentions;
Lord, without Your grace who could find
    redemption?
Change my heart, change my heart today.

1577
Stuart Townend
Copyright © 2002 Thankyou Music

WE ARE HEIRS OF GOD ALMIGHTY,
Apple of the Father's eye;
Free, forgiven, loved, accepted,
Clothed in righteousness divine.
Chosen to be pure and blameless
From before the world began;
Grace for every situation,
Sheltered in the Father's hand.

We have Christ at work within us,
Shaping us to be like Him;
Resurrection power sustaining
Freedom from the snares of sin.
Saying no to flesh desires,
Saying yes to righteous ways;
Filled with passion and with power,
Lights that burn in darkened days.

We've the Spirit without measure,
Helper, Comforter and Guide;
One who brings the gifts of heaven,
One who comes to walk beside.
Taste of heaven's endless pleasure,
Guarantee of what's to come;
Causing fruit to grow in action,
Bringing glory to the Son.

 1578 Lara Martin (Abundant Life Ministries, Bradford, England)
Copyright © 2002 Thankyou Music

WE ARE JOINED BY ANGELS,
Our purpose the same:
To worship the one and only God,
A little piece of heaven is in this place.

> *And we cry together: Holy, holy*
> *For there is no other like You, Lord.*
> *We declare together: You are awesome,*
> *You are to be feared, honoured and revered,*
> *For You are the Lord.*

We are joined by angels,
With one voice we sing,
As we lift our hands to honour You,
In worship, the angels extend their wings.

1579 Charlie Hall
Copyright © 2000 worshiptogether.com songs/
Six Steps Music/Adm. by Kingsway Music

WE BOW OUR HEARTS,
We bend our knees;
O Spirit, come make us humble.
We turn our eyes from evil things;
O Lord, we cast down our idols.

Give us clean hands,
Give us pure hearts;
Let us not lift our souls to another.
(Repeat)

> *O God, let us be*
> *A generation that seeks,*
> *That seeks Your face,*
> *O God of Jacob.*
> (Repeat)

1580 Kate Simmonds & Mark Edwards
Copyright © 2002 Thankyou Music

WE COME IN YOUR NAME,
For all things You have made,
And by Your word all things You sustain.
The Lamb that was slain
For our sins lives to reign,
The Lord of all, Name above all names.

We have been saved by faith
Into Your glorious name,
And this is a gift of God, freely given us.
Now all our sins are gone,
Defeated at the cross,
And we now live in You,
Raised with You by the power of God.

> *You have been lifted to the highest place*
> *And You now live and rule forever.*
> *We come to bring You the highest praise*
> *For You are King of kings forever:*
> *Son of God, Jesus!*

Holy is the Lamb,
Worthy of glory, worthy of honour.
High and lifted up,
And seated in majesty,
Your throne will last forever (more).
(Repeat)

1581 Matt Redman
Copyright © 2002 Thankyou Music

WE COULD WATCH YOU FROM AFAR,
And forever be amazed
At how glorious You are.
Yet You've drawn us close to You,
Where the wonder's greater still,
And You overwhelm us, God.

> *And we rejoice with trembling in our*
>   *hearts,*
> *Bring You a song of reverence and love.*
> *Jesus, how good, how great You are,*
> *And we rejoice with trembling*
> *Before Your throne.*

Who could fully voice the praise
Of the God of endless days,
Tell a fraction of Your worth?
For we only sing in part
Of the grace of who You are;
Just an echo, just a glimpse.

 1582 Chris Tomlin
Copyright © 1998 worshiptogether.com songs/
Adm. by Kingsway Music

WE FALL DOWN, we lay our crowns
At the feet of Jesus.
The greatness of mercy and love,
At the feet of Jesus.

And we cry holy, holy, holy.
And we cry holy, holy, holy.
And we cry holy, holy, holy
Is the Lamb.

1583 Edward J. Burns
Copyright © Edward J. Burns

WE HAVE A GOSPEL TO PROCLAIM,
Good news for all throughout the earth;
The gospel of a Saviour's name:
We sing His glory, tell His worth.

Tell of His birth at Bethlehem,
Not in a royal house or hall
But in a stable dark and dim:
The Word made flesh, a light for all.

Tell of His death at Calvary,
Hated by those He came to save;
In lonely suffering on the cross
For all He loved His life He gave.

Tell of that glorious Easter morn:
Empty the tomb, for He was free.
He broke the power of death and hell
That we might share His victory.

Tell of His reign at God's right hand,
By all creation glorified;
He sends His Spirit on His Church
To live for Him, the Lamb who died.

Now we rejoice to name Him King:
Jesus is Lord of all the earth.
This gospel message we proclaim:
We sing His glory, tell His worth.

1584 Doug Horley
Copyright © 1999 Thankyou Music

**WE HAVE THIS TREASURE IN JARS OF
    CLAY.**
For all our frailty, You have entrusted us
To shine Your goodness
And life throughout the nations.
We may be pressed hard from every side,
But we will not be crushed,
Your hope will strengthen us.
And when the hard times squeeze so tight,
May they release more
Of the fragrance of Jesus.

And let Your glory shine,
O let Your glory shine.
O let Your glory shine
Through our lives, by Your grace,
May we overflow with Jesus.

May we shine like, may we shine like,
May we shine like stars in the darkness.
May we shine like, may we shine like,
May we shine like stars.

1585 Ken Riley
Copyright © 2001 Thankyou Music

WELL, I CALL UPON MY FATHER
In the name of Christ Your Son,
Let the streams of Your forgiveness
Come upon me as a flood.

I give my love to my Creator,
Reveal my heart unto my God.
I bring my life before the Healer,
For I know in You my shame
Will be thrown down.

For with sin there's separation,
Yet by grace through faith I'm saved;
Can You hear my spirit crying,
'Come and wash my sin away'?

You're washing me down,
You're washing me down.
(Repeat)

Well, I call upon my Father
In the name of Christ Your Son,
Now I've tasted Your forgiveness,
My redemption through Your blood.

1586 Alan Rose
Copyright © 2000 Thankyou Music

WE LOOK TO YOU, ALMIGHTY GOD,
You are high and lifted up,
You are sovereign over all
That You have made.
Over kingdoms and their kings,
You are Lord of everything,
Over things on earth
And things that are unseen.

And we rejoice in You,
We put our trust in You,
And with one voice we give You praise.
Singing, let Your kingdom come,
And let Your will be done,
And through Your people
Make Your glory known.

Lord, we come to seek Your face,
Let Your glory fill this place,
We are hungry for Your
Presence in this hour.
To behold You as You are,
Heaven's bright and morning Star,
Let our hearts be changed,
And let Your kingdom come!

1587 Matt Redman
Copyright © 1998 Thankyou Music

WE'RE GONNA SING LIKE THE SAVED.
We're gonna sing like the saved.
We're gonna sing like the saved.
We're gonna sing like the saved.

It is our duty and our joy,
In every time and every place,
Your gates we'll enter to give thanks,
Your courts we'll run into with praise.

> *A joyful noise we will make* (×4)
>
> *You put Your joy in our hearts* (×4)
>
> *We're gonna dance like the saved* (×4)

1588 Stuart Townend
Copyright © 1998 Thankyou Music

WE'RE LONGING FOR YOUR PRESENCE,
(Men – women echo)
We're waiting on Your promise,
That You will flood the nation
With mercy and with justice.
We've tasted of Your goodness,
We've waded in Your river,
Yet still the streets are deserts,
And men cry out in hunger.
Let sinners find forgiveness,
The lonely find a family;
Cause lips that mock and curse You
To sing of Your salvation.

> (All)
> *Open the heavens and come down.*
> *Come in Your glory and Your power.*
> *Send Your revival rain:*
> *Replenish this land again!*
> *Open the heavens and come down,*
> *Come down!*

We want a way of living *(Men – women echo)*
That ushers in Your kingdom:
Faith, purity and passion,
And love without condition.
Come shake the ground on which we stand,
Till all we need is found in You;
Then pour the fire into our hearts
To do the work that You would do.

> (All)
> *Open the heavens and come down.*
> *Come in Your glory and Your power.*
> *Send Your revival rain:*
> *Replenish this heart again!*
> *Open the heavens and come down,*
> *Come down!*

1589 American Folk Hymn

WERE YOU THERE when they crucified my Lord?
Were you there when they crucified my Lord?
Oh, sometimes it causes me to tremble,
tremble, tremble.
Were you there when they crucified my Lord?

Were you there when they nailed Him to the
tree?
Were you there when they nailed Him to the
tree?
Oh, sometimes it causes me to tremble,
tremble, tremble.
Were you there when they nailed Him to the
tree?

Were you there when they laid Him in the
tomb?
Were you there when they laid Him in the
tomb?
Oh, sometimes it causes me to tremble,
tremble, tremble.
Were you there when they laid Him in the
tomb?

Were you there when God raised Him from
the dead?
Were you there when God raised Him from
the dead?
Oh, sometimes it causes me to tremble,
tremble, tremble.
Were you there when God raised Him from
the dead?

1590 Robin Mark
Copyright © 2000 Integrity's Hosanna! Music/
Sovereign Music UK

WE SEE THE LORD,
And He is high upon the throne,
And His glory fills the heavens and the earth.
One like a Lamb
Who was slain is on the throne,
And so I cast my crown before You
And bow down to praise.

For everything cries holy.
Oh, everything cries holy.
Oh, everything cries holy to You, Lord.
(Repeat)

591 Kate Simmonds & Stuart Townend
Copyright © 2001 Thankyou Music

WE'VE COME TO PRAISE YOU,
'Cause You're worthy.
Nobody like You in Your glory.
We love to praise You,
'Cause You're holy, awesome,
Wonderful, mighty God.

And everything that You do
Comes from a heart of love
And a hand of mercy;
For You are faithful and true,
Working all things for good
For those who love You.

For if God in love did not spare His Son,
But He gave Him up for His chosen ones,
How much more will He freely give to us
Who call upon His Name? *(×4)*

592 Reuben Morgan
Copyright © 1997 Reuben Morgan/
Hillsong Publishing/Kingsway Music

WE WILL SEEK YOUR FACE, Almighty God,
Turn and pray for You to heal our land.
Father, let revival start in us,
Then every heart will know Your kingdom
come.

Lifting up the name of the Lord
In power and in unity,
We will see the nations turn,
Touching heaven, changing earth,
Touching heaven, changing earth.

Never looking back, we'll run the race;
Giving You our lives, we'll gain the prize.
We will take the harvest given us,
Though we sow in tears, we'll reap in joy.

Send revival, send revival,
Send revival to us.
(Repeat)

593 Lara Martin (Abundant Life Ministries,
Bradford, England)
Copyright © 2002 Thankyou Music

WHAT A DAY TO BE ALIVE,
What a time to live my life,
To have a destiny and call,
And see it day by day unfold.
What a day to know You, Lord,
To live and walk within Your love,
To see the wondrous things You've done,
And know there's greater things to come.

And we sense the wonder of it all,
We feel the urgency;
There's not a day to be wasted.
God, help Your church, help us to see.

This is our time, this is our day;
Now's not the time to hold back or delay.
Dreams can live again,
Faith and hope restored.
Taste and see that the Lord is good;
This is the day of salvation,
A time to break free from containment.
People need, people need the Lord.

1594 Neil Bennetts
Copyright © 2001 Thankyou Music

WHAT CAN I SAY but 'I love You'?
What can I say but 'I praise You'?
As the train of Your robe fills this temple,
As the sound of Your voice fills this place.
What can I do but to bow down?
What can I do but to worship?
Only You are the One who is worthy,
Only You are the One who is Lord.

Great is the Lord, so great is the Lord,
Righteous and true God, holy and pure.
I fall on my knees confessing my need
For more of Your presence, Lord.

1595 William Chatterton Dix (1837–98)

WHAT CHILD IS THIS, who, laid to rest
On Mary's lap is sleeping:
Whom angels greet with anthems sweet,
While shepherds watch are keeping?
This, this is Christ the King,
Whom shepherds guard and angels sing:
Haste, haste, to bring Him praise,
The babe, the Son of Mary.

Why lies He in such mean estate,
Where ox and ass are feeding?
Good Christians, fear, for sinners here
The silent Word is pleading.
Nails, spear shall pierce Him through,
The cross be borne for me, for you.
Hail, hail the Word made flesh,
The babe, the Son of Mary.

So bring Him incense, gold and myrrh,
Come, peasant, king, to own Him;
The King of kings salvation brings,
Let loving hearts enthrone Him.
Raise, raise a song on high,
The virgin sings her lullaby.
Joy, joy for Christ is born,
The babe, the Son of Mary.

1596

Dave Bilbrough
Copyright © 1999 Thankyou Music

WHAT LOVE IS THIS,
That took my place?
Instead of wrath,
You poured Your grace on me.
What can I do
But simply come
And worship You?

I surrender, I surrender,
I surrender all to You.

What love is this
That comes to save?
Upon the cross
You bore my guilt and shame.
To You alone
I give my heart
And worship You.

A greater love
No man has seen;
It breaks sin's power
And sets the prisoner free.
With all I have
And all I am,
I worship You.

1597

Doug Horley & Steve Whitehouse
Copyright © 2001 Thankyou Music

WHAT LOVE IS THIS? The love of Jesus,
That gave its all, that cost His life.
Flesh torn by nails, life cruelly taken,
The Father's Son, love's sacrifice.

And I thank You, Lord, for loving me,
And I lift my hands so gratefully.
And I thank You, Lord, that I can be
A child of Yours eternally.

You are my King, You are my Saviour,
You'll always be a friend to me.
Safe in Your arms now and forever
Your love shines bright, my morning star.

Now let Your power rain down upon me;
Such peace and joy cascading down.
May Your love touch all those around me;
I'll shine for You, I'll shine for You.

1598

Joel Houston
Copyright © 1999 Joel Houston/
Hillsong Publishing/Kingsway Music

WHAT TO SAY, LORD?
It's You who gave me life,
And I can't explain just how much You mean
to me
Now that You have saved me, Lord.
I give all that I am to You,
That every day I can be a light that shines
Your name.

Every day, Lord,
I'll learn to stand upon Your word,
And I pray that I,
That I may come to know You more,
That You would guide me
In every single step I take,
That every day I can be Your light unto the
world.

Every day, it's You I'll live for,
Every day, I'll follow after You.
Every day, I'll walk with You, my Lord.

It's You I live for every day,
It's You I live for every day,
It's You I live for every day.

1599

Bob Kauflin
Copyright © 2000 PDI Praise/Adm. by CopyCar

WHAT WISDOM ONCE DEVISED THE PLAN
Where all our sin and pride
Was placed upon the perfect Lamb
Who suffered, bled and died?
The wisdom of a sovereign God
Whose greatness will be shown,
When those who crucified Your Son
Rejoice around Your throne.

And oh, the glory of the cross,
That You would send Your Son for us.
I gladly count my life as loss
That I might come to know
The glory of, the glory of the cross.

What righteousness was there revealed
That sets the guilty free,
That justifies ungodly men
And calls the filthy clean?
A righteousness that proved to all
Your justice has been met,
And holy wrath is satisfied
Through one atoning death.

What mercy now has been proclaimed
for those who would believe?
A love incomprehensible,
Our minds could not conceive.
A mercy that forgives my sin
And makes me like Your Son.
And now I'm loved forevermore,
Because of what You've done.

1600   Stuart Townend
Copyright © 2002 Thankyou Music

WHAT WONDER OF GRACE is this,
What story of passion divine,
Where judgement and mercy kiss,
Where power and love are entwined?
No tongue can speak this glory,
No words express the joy You bring
As I enter the courts of the King.

> *My desire is to come to this place,*
> *My desire is to look on Your face,*
> *Perfect in beauty, in truth and love,*
> *Your glory shines over all the earth;*
> *The King who lavishes grace on us is here.*

Your will is my daily bread,
Enough for my plenty and need;
I'll live by the words You've said,
And follow wherever You lead.
And though my flesh may fail me,
You prove Your grace in all I do,
Lord, my heart is devoted to You.

1601   Jan Struther (1901–53)
Copyright © Oxford University Press

WHEN A KNIGHT WON HIS SPURS in the
stories of old,
He was gentle and brave, he was gallant and
bold;
With a shield on his arm and a lance in his
hand,
For God and for valour he rode through the
land.

No charger have I, and no sword by my side,
Yet still to adventure and battle I ride,
Though back into storyland giants have fled,
And the knights are no more and the dragons
are dead.

Let faith be my shield and let joy be my steed
'Gainst the dragons of anger, the ogres of
greed;
And let me set free, with the sword of my
youth,
From the castle of darkness, the power of the
truth.

1602   Paul Oakley
Copyright © 1998 Thankyou Music

WHEN DEEP CALLS TO DEEP
There's a stirring inside of me,
A feeling that words won't describe;
Like I'm hearing Your song
Touching my spirit,
Calling me deeper with You.

And the thirst in my soul
Just to meet with You, God,
I'm feeling the pull of Your love;
Like the crash of Your waves,
Like the roar or Your waterfalls,
Drawing me on into You.

And all I know is it's You.
And I cry out to You.

> *Give me oil for my wounds,*
> *Give me wine for my heart,*
> *Give me strength for today,*
> *And I will stand.*
> *Give me salve for my eyes,*
> *Give me truth for the lies,*
> *Give me love in my life*
> *And I will run with You.*

1603   Drew Land
Copyright © 2000 Thankyou Music

WHEN I COME FACE TO FACE
With the One the angels praise,
I'm in awe, I'm amazed
With a God full of grace.
It's the love You have shown
That allows me at Your throne
To adore, and how I do:
Father, I'm in love with You.

Here I am with lifted hands,
I give You praise
And I exalt Your holy name
With all I have,
With all the strength that I can raise.
And here I am once again,
I lift my voice
With all the angels 'round Your throne.
I adore and I worship You alone.

I am in love,
I am in love with all my heart,
With all my soul, and all my mind
With all the strength I've ever known.
I am in love,
I am in love with the King
And with His Son, the One who loved
With His life and with His blood.

1604 Sydney Carter
Copyright © 1965 Stainer & Bell Ltd

WHEN I NEEDED A NEIGHBOUR,
Were you there, were you there?
When I needed a neighbour, were you there?

And the creed and the colour
And the name won't matter,
Were you there?

I was hungry and thirsty,
Were you there, were you there?
I was hungry and thirsty, were you there?

I was cold, I was naked,
Were you there, were you there?
I was cold, I was naked, were you there?

When I needed a shelter,
Were you there, were you there?
When I needed a shelter, were you there?

When I needed a healer,
Were you there, were you there?
When I needed a healer, were you there?

Wherever you travel,
I'll be there, I'll be there.
Wherever you travel, I'll be there.

And the creed and the colour
And the name won't matter,
I'll be there.

1605 Noel & Tricia Richards
Copyright © 1999 Thankyou Music

WHEN I SING MY PRAISE to You,
I am lifted up to higher ground.
Something happens in my soul
When I lift my voice to worship You.
Feels like sunshine on my face,
A cool breeze in a desert place.

When I worship You,
Heaven comes to me,
Heaven comes to me.
When I worship You,
Heaven comes to me,
Heaven comes to me.

Heaven is where I belong,
Where the angels sing before Your throne.
I am caught up in their sound,
When I lift my voice to worship You.
From beyond where eyes can see,
Love is pouring over me.

I will worship You,
Heaven come to me,
Heaven come to me.
I will worship You,
Heaven come to me,
Heaven come to me.

 1606 Isaac Watts (1674–1748)
Refrain lyrics: Chris Tomlin & J.D. Walt
Copyright © 2000 worshiptogether.com songs/
Six Steps Music/Adm. by Kingsway Music

WHEN I SURVEY the wondrous cross
On which the Prince of Glory died,
My richest gain I count but loss,
And pour contempt on all my pride.

See from His head, His hands, His feet,
Sorrow and love flow mingled down;
Did e'er such love and sorrow meet
Or thorns compose so rich a crown?

Oh, the wonderful cross,
Oh, the wonderful cross
Bids me come and die and find
That I may truly live.
Oh, the wonderful cross,
Oh, the wonderful cross,
All who gather here by grace
Draw near and bless Your name.

Were the whole realm of nature mine,
That were an offering far too small.
Love so amazing, so divine
Demands my soul, my life, my all.

1607 Kate & Miles Simmonds
Copyright © 2001 Thankyou Music

WHEN I WAS LOST, You came and rescued
me;
Reached down into the pit and lifted me.
O Lord, such love,
I was as far from You as I could be.
You know all the things I've ever done,
But Jesus' blood has cancelled every one.
O Lord, such grace
To qualify me as Your own.

There is a new song in my mouth,
There is a deep cry in my heart,
A hymn of praise to Almighty God –
hallelujah!
And now I stand firm on this Rock,
My life is hidden now with Christ in God.
The old has gone and the new has come
hallelujah!
Your love has lifted me.

ow I have come into Your family,
or the Son of God has died for me.
  Lord, such peace,
am as loved by You as I could be.
 the full assurance of Your love,
ow with every confidence we come.
  Lord, such joy
o know that You delight in us.

any are the wonders You have done,
nd many are the things that You have planned.
ow beautiful the grace that gives to us
ll that we don't deserve,
ll that we cannot earn,
ut is a gift of love.

608 Stuart Townend
Copyright © 2001 Thankyou Music

HEN LOVE CAME DOWN to earth
nd made His home with men,
he hopeless found a hope,
he sinner found a friend.
ot to the powerful
ut to the poor He came,
nd humble, hungry hearts
/ere satisfied again.

What joy, what peace has come to us!
What hope, what help, what love!

/hen every unclean thought,
nd every sinful deed
/as scourged upon His back
nd hammered through His feet.
he Innocent is cursed,
he guilty are released;
he punishment of God
n God has brought me peace.

ome lay your heavy load
own at the Master's feet;
our shame will be removed,
our joy will be complete.
ome crucify your pride,
nd enter as a child;
or those who bow down low
e'll lift up to His side.

609 Alan Rose
Copyright © 2000 Thankyou Music

HEN MY HEART IS FAINT within me,
nd my troubles multiply,
will lift my head to see You
eated at the Father's side.
ou have triumphed over Satan,
ou're the firstborn from the grave.
ou are always interceding,
ou are able now to save.

You are Jesus Christ, faithful One,
Risen King, Champion.
You deserve the highest praise,
The Lamb of God,
Who once was slain for our sin.

In my heart I am persuaded
As the Spirit testifies,
And with glory and rejoicing
'Abba, Father' is my cry.
You have raised me up with Jesus
And in Him I am Your son,
So I glory in Your goodness,
In the things that You have done.

1610 Matt Redman
Copyright © 2001 Thankyou Music

WHEN MY HEART RUNS DRY
And there's no song to sing,
No holy melody,
No words of love within,
I recall the height from which
This fragile heart has slipped.

And I'll remember You,
I will turn back and do
The things I used to do
For the love of You.
Lord, I'll remember You,
I will turn back and do
The things I need to do
For the love You.

You are my soul's desire,
You are the hope within,
You bring my heart to life,
You make my spirit sing.
I recall the height from which
This fragile heart has slipped.

1611 Reuben Morgan
Copyright © 1998 Reuben Morgan/
Hillsong Publishing/Kingsway Music

WHEN THE DARKNESS FILLS MY SENSES,
When my blindness keeps me from Your
  touch,
Jesus come.
When my burden keeps me doubting,
When my memories take the place of You,
Jesus come.

And I'll follow You there,
To the place where we meet,
And I'll lay down my pride
As You search me again.
Your unfailing love, Your unfailing love,
Your unfailing love over me again.

1612

WHEN THE ROAD IS ROUGH AND STEEP,
Fix your eyes upon Jesus.
He alone has power to keep,
Fix your eyes upon Him.
Jesus is a gracious friend,
One on whom you can depend,
He is faithful to the end,
Fix your eyes upon Him.

1613

WHEN WE TURN OUR HEARTS TO HEAVEN
And bow down,
We'll see fathers and the children reconciled.
We'll be the dreamers of Your dreams.
We'll be the dreamers of Your dreams.

When Your fire falls from heaven,
We will rend our hearts to You.
We will tell it to our children,
All the wonders You have done.
And in every generation
We will sing of Your great love.
When Your fire falls from heaven
We'll return to You again!
We'll be the dreamers of Your dreams.
We'll be the dreamers of Your dreams.

1614

WHEN WORDS ARE NOT ENOUGH
To tell of all You've done,
I bow the knee, let silence speak,
And gaze upon Your majesty.

These songs could not convey
A picture of Your love;
And knowing this, my life I give
To You, an offering of praise.

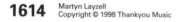

And I surrender all,
And I surrender all;
Unveil my heart to see
The wonder of Your worth,
As I surrender all,
As I surrender all.

The worship You require
Is brokenness of heart;
So here I stand with open hands,
Surrendered to Your love and power.

1615

WHEN YOU PRAYED BENEATH THE TREES,
It was for me, O Lord;
When You cried upon Your knees,
How could it be, O Lord?
When in blood and sweat and tears
You dismissed Your final fears,
When You faced the soldiers' spears,
You stood for me, O Lord.

When their triumph looked complete,
It was for me, O Lord;
When it seemed like Your defeat,
They could not see, O Lord!
When You faced the mob alone
You were silent as a stone,
And a tree became Your throne;
You came for me, O Lord.

When You stumbled up the road,
You walked for me, O Lord,
When You took Your deadly load,
That heavy tree, O Lord;
When they lifted You on high,
And they nailed You up to die,
And when darkness filled the sky,
It was for me, O Lord.

When You spoke with kingly power,
It was for me, O Lord,
In that dread and destined hour,
You made me free, O Lord;
Earth and heaven heard You shout,
Death and hell were put to rout,
For the grave could not hold out;
You are for me, O Lord.

1616

WHERE CAN I GO without You, Lord?
What can I do, how can I stand?
You are my comfort and my strength.
You are my shield and my right hand.

And You pour out healing on me,
Pour out healing.
And You make my spirit soar,
And You make my burden light,
And You soothe me in the storm,
And You go before me in the fight.

1617

Robin Mark
Copyright © 2000 Thankyou Music

WHERE COULD I FIND SOMEONE LIKE YOU?
Unbounded love in all You do.
So I seek to know You more,
I'll press into Your word again,
And drawing on Your Spirit's power,
And drinking from that well again.

For heaven and earth are in Your hands,
This universe within Your plans.
Dust of life no eye can see,
They only stir when You command.
Some divine permission given,
Empowered by Your mighty hand.

And You knew me in the secret place
As my being formed, You beheld my days.
And You know me now, You know all my
*   ways,*
Nothing's hid from You,
I'm with You always.

My weakest means, my poorest words
To tell this world of Your redeeming love.
By Your Holy Spirit's power
Is articulation given,
Message to the poor in heart,
That Jesus Christ is risen again.

And You knew me in the secret place
As my being formed, You decreed my
*   days.*
And You know me now, You know all my
*   ways,*
Nothing's hid from You,
I'm with You always.

1618
Gareth Robinson
Copyright © 2001 Thankyou Music

WHO CAN COMPARE with You, my Father;
Loving and kind, faithful and true?
When You forgive my heart that is broken,
I gratefully sing my love to You.

I worship You,
I love You:
All that I am
Sings this song of praise.

Here I will dwell in the arms of my Father,
Knowing Your grace, hearing Your voice;
Trusting Your word, feeling Your peace,
Resting in You and in Your love.

And I abide in You,
   abide with You.

1619
Geraldine Latty & Carey Luce
Copyright © 2002 Thankyou Music

WHO CAN STAND BEFORE THE LORD
In His holy place?
Who can walk upon the hill of the Lord?
Only he whose hands are clean,
Only he whose heart is pure
Can stand before the Lord.

I will stand, I will come
Before the presence of the King:
For His blood washes me from sin,
I enter in.

There is One who stands for me
In the holy place,
And He walked the lonely hill to the cross.
And I know His hands are clean,
And I know His heart is pure,
He is Jesus Christ the Lamb.

1620
Evan Rogers
Copyright © 1998 Thankyou Music

WHO COULD OFFER US ABUNDANT LIFE?
Who could be the only way?
Who could be the purest sacrifice?
Who could have the power
To rise from the grave?

Who could be our only righteousness?
Who could be the One who saves?
Who could be the God who became flesh?
Who could have the Name above every
   name?

(It's) only Jesus
Shines like the sun.
Only Jesus,
The King of kings, the Holy One.
(It's) only Jesus,
The Son of God, the Son of Man.
Only Jesus,
The Prince of Peace, the great I Am.

Who could give us living water?
Who could be the Bread of Life?
Who could overcome the darkness?
Who could be the Truth, our shining light?

Now only I can offer up my life;
There's nothing less that I could give
To Him who gave up all His heavenly rights
So that I might live.

1621 Joannah Oyeniran
Copyright © 2002 Thankyou Music

WHO IS LIKE YOU, Lord Almighty?
Crowned in splendour, robed in majesty,
Holy is Your name.
God of justice, rich in mercy.
Grace that flows from awesome glory,
The wonder of Your ways.
Mighty in power, perfect in sovereignty,
The revelation, You laid it aside for me
And bore human frame in Jesus.

So I exalt You, God of glory,
And I will worship the Lord of eternity.
King of the nations, my wonderful Saviour,
God our Creator, my heavenly Father.
I worship only You.

1622 Neil Bennetts
Copyright © 2002 Thankyou Music

WHO IS THERE LIKE THE LORD OUR GOD,
Faithful beyond all compare?
Glorious in such holiness
With power to heal and to save.

You shall be called the Saviour eternal,
There is grace in Your heart, and Your name.
And You shall be known through all
generations
As the hope for the life that receives.

Let heaven rejoice, You are wonderful;
Creation sings out to Your praise.
You are the Lord, You are beautiful;
Each work of Your hand shall proclaim.

A love beyond reason, this gift of life;
The mercy of God in Your sacrifice.
The fountain of truth that can satisfy,
And it's found in You, Jesus,
And it's found in You, Jesus,
And it's found in You, Jesus.

1623 David Ruis
Copyright © 1996 Mercy/Vineyard Publishing/
Adm. by CopyCare

WHOM HAVE I BUT YOU?
Whom have I but You?

Though the mountains fall,
They fall into the sea.

Though the coloured dawn
May turn to shades of grey.

Though the questions asked
May never be resolved.

1624 J.A.P. Booth
Copyright © Paul Booth/Adm. by CopyCare

WHO PUT THE COLOURS IN THE RAINBOW
Who put the salt into the sea?
Who put the cold into the snowflake?
Who made you and me?
Who put the hump upon the camel?
Who put the neck on the giraffe?
Who put the tail upon the monkey?
Who made hyenas laugh?
Who made whales and snails and quails?
Who made hogs and dogs and frogs?
Who made bats and rats and cats?
Who made everything?

Who put the gold into the sunshine?
Who put the sparkle in the stars?
Who put the silver in the moonlight?
Who made Earth and Mars?
Who put the scent into the roses?
Who taught the honey bee to dance?
Who put the tree inside the acorn?
It surely can't be chance!
Who made seas and leaves and trees?
Who made snow and winds that blow?
Who made streams and rivers flow?
God made all of these!

1625 Annie Spiers
Copyright © 1992 Annie Spiers

WHO'S THE KING OF THE JUNGLE?
Who's the king of the sea?
Who's the king of the universe
And who's the king of me?
I'll tell you J-E-S-U-S is,
He's the King of me,
He's the King of the universe,
The jungle and the sea.

1626 Scott Underwood
Copyright © 1999 Mercy/Vineyard Publishing/
Adm. by CopyCare

WHO'S THE ONLY LIGHT that shines and
never fades?
The Light of the world, Jesus.
Who's the only light that drives the dark
away?
The Light of the world, Jesus.

It's all about Jesus, Jesus,
It's all about Jesus, Jesus.

Who's the only Word that made all things?
The Word was God, Jesus.
He's the only truth, the fullness of the Lord,
The Son of God, Jesus.

You're the Way, the Truth and the Life.
You're the Way, the Truth and the Life.

WITH A PRAYER You fed the hungry,
With a cry You stilled the storm;
With a look You had compassion
On the desperate and forlorn.
With a touch You healed the leper,
With a shout You raised the dead;
With a word expelled the demons,
With a blessing broke the bread.

Love incarnate, love divine,
Captivate this heart of mine
Till all I do speaks of You.

As a sheep before the shearer
You were silent in Your pain;
You endured humiliation
At the hands of those You'd made.
And as hell unleashed its fury
You were lifted on a tree,
Crying 'Father God, forgive them,
Place their punishment on Me.'

I will feed the poor and hungry,
I will stand up for the truth;
I will take my cross and follow
To the corners of the earth.
And I ask that You so fill me
With Your peace, Your power, Your breath,
That I never love my life so much
To shrink from facing death.

WITH HIS HANDS HE MADE ME,
Breathed His life within me;
With His heart He loved me,
Yet I turned away.
In His love He sought me,
Came to earth to save me;
Punished my rebellion
With His sacrifice.

I'll come to the Giver of life,
I'll drink from His well of delights:
I'll yield to His tender embrace,
I'll be to Him an offering of praise.

Here I stand before You,
Needing Your forgiveness,
Thirsting for Your Spirit,
Longing for Your touch.
Let the flame within me
Grow into a fire,
Banish all my darkness
With Your piercing light.

I'll come to the Giver of life,
I'll drink from His well of delights:
I'll yield to His tender embrace,
I'll be to Him an offering.
I'll rest in the shade of His wings,
I'll feast on the pleasure He brings,
I'll seek Him for all of my days,
I'll be to Him an offering of praise.

WITH THE CHOIR OF ANGELS SINGING,
And the realm of heavenly hosts;
As those elders humbly bow,
I'd love to come to Your throne
With a simple song.

With the living creatures speaking
Praise and praise and praise again;
With the company of heaven,
I'd love to come to Your throne
With a song of love.

Hallelujah, Jesus,
Hallelujah, hallelu.
Hallelujah, Jesus,
Pouring out my heart to You.

I would bring this praise like incense
Rising to Your throne above,
Fill the air with heart-filled songs
In harmony and melody
To the One I love.

And who can tell the adoration
That will rise up to Your throne?
Every knee that day shall bow
To the King of kings,
The Holy One, the only One.
We'll all be singing...

WONDERFUL GRACE,
That gives what I don't deserve,
Pays me what Christ has earned,
Then lets me go free.
Wonderful grace,
That gives me the time to change,
Washes away the stains
That once covered me.

And all that I have
I lay at the feet
Of the wonderful Saviour
Who loves me.

Wonderful love,
That held in the face of death,
Breathed in its latest breath
Forgiveness for me.
Wonderful love,
Whose power can break every chain,
Giving us life again,
Setting us free.

1631 Ashton Gardner
Copyright © 2001 Thankyou Music

WONDERFUL REDEEMER all my life,
Thank You for the grace You have shown to me.
Nothing can compare to Your heart of love,
I have Your eyes.

Sing to the Lord our God,
Lift up His name and exalt Him.
Your holiness is immense,
And we Your people will worship
Your name forever.

Righteous and majestic King of truth,
All mankind will one day bow the knee to
    You.
May our lives reflect the heart of You, O Lord,
We will live for You.

1632 Tim Hughes
Copyright © 2002 Thankyou Music

WONDERFUL, SO WONDERFUL
Is Your unfailing love;
Your cross has spoken mercy over me.
No eye has seen, no ear has heard,
No heart could fully know
How glorious, how beautiful You are.

Beautiful One, I love You,
Beautiful One, I adore,
Beautiful One, my soul must sing.

Powerful, so powerful,
Your glory fills the skies,
Your mighty works displayed for all to see.
The beauty of Your majesty
Awakes my heart to sing
How marvellous, how wonderful You are.

You opened my eyes to Your wonders anew,
You captured my heart with this love,
'Cause nothing on earth
Is as beautiful as You.
(Repeat)

My soul, my soul must sing,
My soul, my soul must sing,
My soul, my soul must sing,
Beautiful One.

1633 Louise Fellingham
Copyright © 1999 Thankyou Music

WORSHIP THE LORD,
See the splendour of His holiness.
Give to the Lord all the glory due His name.
Come and adore,
Come and lay your hearts before Him.
With thankfulness and love,
Come and shout aloud your praise.

Declare His glory among all the nations.
Declare His majesty,
His splendour and power.
Proclaim salvation,
His goodness and mercy;
For great is the Lord and most worthy,
Worthy of praise.

We are His people, belonging to our Father,
Set apart for truth, we are chosen by God.
With confidence we come,
We are free and we're forgiven.
Blessed are the ones
Who put their hope in God.

Please come upon us now,
We want to see Your face, Lord.
Soften our hearts, take us deeper into You.
Spirit, fill our minds
With the knowledge of Your wisdom.
Come and touch our mouths,
Help us tell of all You've done.

1634 Matt Redman
Copyright © 1999 Thankyou Music

WORTHY, YOU ARE WORTHY,
Much more worthy than I've known;
I cannot imagine
Just how glorious You are.
I cannot begin to tell
How deep a love You bring;
Lord, my ears have heard of You,
But now my eyes have seen.

You're worthy, You're worthy, You're worthy,
You're worthy to be praised,
Forever and a day.
(Repeat)

Glory, I give glory
To the One who saved my soul.
You found me and You freed me
From the shame that was my own.
I cannot begin to tell
How merciful You've been;
Lord, my ears have heard of You,
Now my eyes have seen.

You're worthy...

Your glory, Your glory, Your glory,
Your glory reaches high,
So high above the heavens.

1635
Stuart Townend
Copyright © 1997 Thankyou Music

WOVEN TOGETHER within the womb,
Fearfully, wonderfully made;
You know me better than I know myself,
And still You look on with pleasure.
Where can I go from Your Spirit, Lord?
Where can I hide from Your gaze?
Ocean to ocean and shore to shore,
Your hand reaches out to guide me.

> *It's all too wonderful*
> *For me to know;*
> *It's all too marvellous*
> *For me to attain.*
> *The care You show to those*
> *Who love Your name;*
> *It's all too wonderful,*
> *It's all too wonderful for me.*

Lord, You have searched me, You know me
well,
For nothing is hidden from You;
And even before there's a word on my tongue,
You know it completely, Lord.
How precious to me are Your thoughts, O God,
How great is the depth of Your love;
I know that You've numbered the sum of my
days,
I'll rest in Your perfect wisdom.

1636
Kevin Simpson
Copyright © 2000 Thankyou Music

YES, I THANK YOU, O Lord.
Yes, I thank You, O Lord.
Looking back in my life I see
Many things You have done for me.
I thank You, O Lord.

Yes, I love You...

Yes, I praise You...

Hallelujah, hallelujah, glory to Your name.
Hallelujah, hallelujah, glory to Your name.

Oui, je te remercie, Seigneur.
Oui, je te remercie, Seigneur.
En arrière dans ma vie je vois
Toutes choses que tu as fait pour moi.
Je te remercie, Seigneur.

1637
Marilyn Baker
Copyright © 1998 Marilyn Baker Music/
Kingsway Music

YESTERDAY, TODAY AND FOREVER
You're the same,
All the promises of God
Find their 'yes' in You.
Demons flee, strongholds fall,
They must bow before Your name,
No authority, no power is higher than You.

> *Let's sing our praise to the Lord,*
> *Thank You for the great things You have*
> *done.*
> *Let's sing with all of our hearts,*
> *There's no Father like You.*
> *Let's dance for joy to the Lord,*
> *For You have washed our sins away.*
> *We're more than conquerors,*
> *With You close by our side.*

Yesterday, today and forever
You're the same,
We need never fear
To put all our trust in You.
For Your word is a rock
And a light to show the way,
And a sword that will pierce
Through the darkness each day.

1638
Geraldine Latty
Copyright © 2001 Thankyou Music

YET WILL I PRAISE HIM,
I will lift my hands to my Creator.
Yet will I praise Him,
My Saviour and my God.
Yet will I praise Him,
I will put my trust in my Provider.
Yet will I praise Him,
Lord Jehovah, Sovereign God.

Though the fig tree doesn't blossom
And no ripened grapes appear,
Though the harvest fails
And fields provide no food;
I'll be joyful in my Saviour,
The Lord who is my strength;
He will keep my ways
And lead me in His truth.

When the night is overwhelming
And the day is far from clear,
When my heart is restless
For the peace of God;
Let Your song, Lord, through the ages,
Through the prophets You have given,
Lift my mind and heart
To gaze upon You, Lord.

Be the strength, Lord, in my weakness,
Let Your song be in my night;
Be my rock when all around is sinking sand.
Be the light, Lord, in my darkness,
Be the vision of my eyes:
In my passing days
You are the great 'I Am'.

Lord, I will praise You,
I will lift my hands to my Creator.
Lord, I will praise You,
My Saviour and my God.
Lord, I will praise You,
I will put my trust in my Provider.
Yes, I will praise You,
Lord Jehovah, Sovereign God.

1639 Gareth Robinson
Copyright © 2001 Thankyou Music

YOU ARE ALL I WANT,
You're all I need to be set free.
Your cross of death gives life to me,
Your sacrifice brings liberty.
No one else could take my place but You,
The perfect One, the holy God,
Revealed as man in Jesus Christ.
Only You could take my sin, so...

I love You, yeah, I love You, Jesus.
I love You, yeah, I love You, Jesus.

I will give to You my everything,
Abandon all my selfish dreams
To live for You and do Your will every day.
You have touched my heart
And made me whole,
You've made me clean, so I will give
My offering of love to You,
All my life lived just for You, 'cause...

1640 Reuben Morgan
Copyright © 2001 Reuben Morgan/
Hillsong Publishing/Kingsway Music

YOU ARE FOREVER IN MY LIFE,
You see me through the seasons;
Cover me with Your hand,
And lead me in Your righteousness.
And I look to You,
And I wait on You.

I'll sing to You, Lord, a hymn of love
For Your faithfulness to me.
I'm carried in everlasting arms;
You'll never let me go,
Through it all.

Hallelujah, hallelujah,
Hallelujah, hallelujah.
(Repeat)

1641 Matt & Beth Redman
Copyright © 2000 Thankyou Music

YOU ARE GOD IN HEAVEN,
And here am I on earth;
So I'll let my words be few:
Jesus, I am so in love with You.

And I'll stand in awe of You,
Yes, I'll stand in awe of You.
And I'll let my words be few:
Jesus, I am so in love with You.

The simplest of all love songs
I want to bring to You;
So I'll let my words be few:
Jesus, I am so in love with You.

1642 Reuben Morgan
Copyright © 1997 Reuben Morgan/
Hillsong Publishing/Kingsway Music

YOU ARE HOLY, holy,
Lord, there is none like You.
You are holy, holy,
Glory to You alone.

I'll sing Your praises forever,
Deeper in love with You.
Here in Your courts
Where I'm close to Your throne,
I've found where I belong.

1643 Tré Sheppard
Copyright © 2002 Thankyou Music

YOU ARE HOLY, You are mercy,
You are wonder, You are love.
You are faithful, You are gracious,
You are lovely, You are God.

I open my eyes so I
See Your loveliness.
I open my life so I
Know Your holiness.

If You are for us who could
Stand against us?
Surely You are with us,
Surely You are with us.

Surely You are with us,
Surely You are with us,
Surely You are with us,
Surely You are with us.

1644
Robin Mark
Copyright © 2000 Thankyou Music

YOU ARE KNOWN AS THE ROCK OF AGES,
And the holy Ancient of Days.
Men of old who saw Your face, Lord,
Would not ever be the same.
When You came as God incarnate,
Walked this earth, Your glory veiled,
Those who knew You, and who loved You
Would not ever be the same.

For I have seen You, Rock of Ages,
And I will never be the same.
Oh, I love You, Rock of Ages,
And I will always love Your name.

Will You hide me, Rock of Ages,
In Your secret place of peace?
Can I feel Your burning glory?
Can I hear You when You speak?
Will You chasten me and mould me?
Will You hold me in Your will?
Oh to know You, love and serve You
And Your purposes fulfil.

1645
Neil Bennetts
Copyright © 2002 Thankyou Music

YOU ARE LORD, YOU ARE LORD,
And Your glory fills this temple.
You are Lord, You are Lord,
And Your glory fills this place.
In Your presence I will honour,
As I bring my praise to You.
You are Lord, You are Lord,
And Your glory fills this place.

1646
Stuart Townend
Copyright © 2001 Thankyou Music

YOU ARE MY ANCHOR,
My light and my salvation.
You are my refuge,
My heart will not fear.
Though my foes surround me on every hand,
They will stumble and fall
While in grace I stand.
In my day of trouble
You hide me and set me above
To sing this song of love.

One thing I will ask of You, this will I pray:
To dwell in Your house, O Lord, every day,
To gaze upon Your lovely face,
And rest in the Father's embrace.

Teach me Your way, Lord,
Make straight the path before me.
Do not forsake me, my hope is in You.
As I walk through life, I am confident
I will see Your goodness with every step,
And my heart directs me to seek You
In all that I do,
So I will wait for You.

1647
Mark Stevens (Abundant Life Ministries,
Bradford, England)
Copyright © 2002 Thankyou Music

YOU ARE MY FOUNDATION,
You are my salvation,
A very present help in times of need.
You are my protection,
You are my resurrection,
A higher place is where You're taking me.

I get lifted up on eagles' wings,
You lift me up and so I sing:

Hallelujah, hallelujah,
Hallelujah to the King.
(Repeat)

You are my Redeemer,
You are my Healer,
A promise given, one of liberty.
You are my Restorer,
You are my strong tower,
The joy of the Lord will be my strength.

1648
Mark Stevens (Abundant Life Ministries,
Bradford, England)
Copyright © 2002 Thankyou Music

YOU ARE MY KING, I live to know You.
Oh, to walk in the fullness of Your Spirit.
I'll abide in You and You in me,
I'll see Your desire fulfilled within me.

I am changed by You
Into Your image.
I am changed by You,
I become the same.
I am changed by You,
Like my Father God,
King of heaven.
King of heaven.

You placed in me a fire when I met You,
And the flame, it just burns brighter and
   brighter.
I'm coming after You with all that's in me,
I need You more and more each time I wake.

Glory to glory to glory, Lord,
We will never be the same.
Glory to glory to glory, Lord,
Oh, we will never, never be the same.

1649 Scott Underwood
Copyright © 1997 Mercy/Vineyard Publishing/
Adm. by CopyCare

YOU ARE MY SHEPHERD, I have no needs.
You lead me by peaceful streams,
And You refresh my life.
You hold my hand and You guide my steps,
I could walk through the valley of death,
And I won't be afraid.

Because You are in control.
You are in control.
You are in control.
You are in control.

You cause everything to work together,
You truly have a sovereign plan,
And You know who I am,
And You made who I am,
And You love who I am.

1650 Brian Houston
Copyright © 2001 Thankyou Music

YOU ARE MYSTICAL and deep.
You take Your rest, but never sleep.
You watch me like a mother does,
Every scar and every tear and fall.
You suffer long, but Your patience waits,
Your judgement always hesitates.
Your anger stays a moment,
Yet Your favour lasts a whole life long.

And I cannot stand silently
When faced with so much grace.
My chest is pounding with the need
To celebrate You, God,
And the miracle of Your love.

For You're everywhere, in every place,
In every time, in every space,
And every breath that I take You lend.
You're the only One who satisfies,
The only One who makes my life make
sense.

You are generous and kind,
So intimate and close at times,
Yet You reveal Your beauty in the twilight
And the summer evening rain.
You're in the rainbow and the dawn,
You steal my breath and then You're gone,
Yet when the morning sun breaks through,
I look for You and You are here again.

1651 Darren Clarke
Copyright © 1998 Mercy/Vineyard Publishing/
Adm. by CopyCare

YOU ARE THE FOUNTAIN OF MY LIFE
And in Your light I find my reason,
'Cause Your love reaches to the stars,
Even the great deep.
And Your love reaches to this heart
And it makes me sing.

Your love reaches me:
It's what I need, it's what I need.
Your love reaches me:
It's what I need, it's what I need.

O Lord, how priceless
Is Your unending love.
Both high and low
Find refuge in Your shadow.
(Repeat)

1652 Liz Fitzgibbon
Copyright © 2001 Moortown Music/
Kingsway Music

YOU ARE THE KING OF GLORY,
You dwell in holiness.
Your sceptre reaches for me
And I approach Your throne:

To make my prayers known to You;
Your heart of love is for me.
With boldness I draw near
To Your throne, O God,
To Your throne.

You show Your favour to me,
My faith just grows and grows.
Nothing's too hard for my God,
No prayer too hard for You.

I will make my prayers known…

1653 Chris Tomlin & Jesse Reeves
Copyright © 2002 worshiptogether.com songs/
Six Steps Music/Adm. by Kingsway Music

YOU ARE THE LORD,
The famous One, famous One;
Great is Your name in all the earth.
The heavens declare
You're glorious, glorious;
Great is Your fame beyond the earth.

And for all You've done and yet to do,
With every breath, I'm praising You.
Desire of nations and every heart,
You alone are God,
You alone are God.

The Morning Star is shining through,
And every eye is watching You.
Revealed by nature and miracles,
You are beautiful, You are beautiful.

1654 Eoghan Heaslip & Mick Goss
Copyright © 2002 Integrity's Hosanna! Music/
Sovereign Music UK/& Daybreak Music Ltd

YOU ARE THE LORD, the King of heaven
And all the earth, You'll reign forever.
First and the last, You are glorious.

Before Your throne the elders fall,
And angels sing: 'Almighty God.'
Bright Morning Star,
You are glorious, You are glorious.

To You, the nations will come,
Every tribe, every tongue
And worship before You,
The Ancient of Days,
The Name above all names,
Who is worthy of all our praise.
You are glorious.
Yeah, You are glorious.

1655 Sue Rinaldi & Caroline Bonnett
Copyright © 2001 Thankyou Music

YOU ARE THE ONE I LOVE,
You are the One that I adore.
(Repeat)

For You've called me by name,
Drawn me close to Your heart,
Washed away all my shame with Your tears.
For the rest of my days,
I will offer my life
In thanksgiving and praise to my King.

Now with You I will stay,
For Your word is my light,
And Your peace can allay all my fears;
And my victory song
Is the song of the cross,
You have won me love so divine.

Such precious, precious love.

1656 Lara Martin (Abundant Life Ministries,
Bradford, England)
Copyright © 2002 Thankyou Music

YOU ARE THE SONG THAT I SING,
A precious melody.
You are the theme of my heart.
You are my inspiration.

You are the light of my life,
How I love Your word.
It leads me closer to You.

You are my inspiration, You cause me to
sing.
You are my inspiration, the reason I live.
You are my inspiration, I'm glad I'm alive.
You are my inspiration.

Your greatness creation displays,
Such wonders to behold.
In awe I, I live my days.

How then can I be silent,
When my heart is so full?
In You I have discovered
The secret of true love,
And I want the world to know that…

1657 Brian Doerksen
Copyright © 1999 Vineyard Songs (UK/Eire)/
Adm. by CopyCare

YOU ARE THE SOVEREIGN 'I AM',
Your name is holy.
You are the pure, spotless Lamb,
Your name is holy.
You are the Almighty One,
Your name is holy.
You are the Christ, God's own Son,
Your name is holy.

In Your name
There is mercy for sin,
There is safety within,
In Your holy name.
In Your name
There is strength to remain,
To stand, in spite of pain,
In Your holy name.

1658 Tim Hughes
Copyright © 2001 Thankyou Music

YOU CALL US FIRST to love Your name,
To worship You.
To please Your heart our one desire,
O Lord.

If there's one thing we are called to do,
It's to love You, to adore You.
We will bring our all and worship You,
Bow before You, as we love You.

Your honour, Lord, Your name's renown
We long to see.
So let the glory of Your name
Be praised.

I will celebrate this love,
Jesus, You are everything to me.
For what more, Lord, can I do?
I will give this heart, this life to You.

1659 Tim Hughes
Copyright © 1999 Thankyou Music

YOU CAME INTO MY LIFE,
A Saviour to my soul;
You set a hope within this heart of mine.
You said that I am Yours,
That You will never leave me.
Now I surrender all I am to You.

I will never know why You chose me, God,
But You did.
I will never know why You took that cross,
But You did, yes, You did.

*While today is still today
I'll live just for Your praise,
A living sacrifice;
Holding out to be
Faithful unto You,
So in my life be glorified,
I pray.*

In You, O Lord, I trust,
In You, O Lord, I live;
Do not let me stray from Your commands.
Guide me in Your way,
Protect me in Your truth,
Teach me what it means to follow You.

1660 James Taylor
Copyright © 2001 Thankyou Music

YOU CAN HAVE MY WHOLE LIFE,
You can come and have it all:
I don't want to go my own way now,
I love to feel Your presence
And I know Your saving grace.
I am nothing when You are second place.

I've been born to give You praise,
Not to yearn and strive for worldly things.
I've been born to love Your ways,
Take my pride and let me always say:
I want to go Your way now.

1661 Martyn Layzell
Copyright © 2002 Thankyou Music

YOU CHOSE THE CROSS with every breath,
The perfect life, the perfect death:
You chose the cross.
A crown of thorns You wore for us,
And crowned us with eternal life:
You chose the cross.
And though Your soul was overwhelmed with
pain,
Obedient to death You overcame.

*I'm lost in wonder,
I'm lost in love,
I'm lost in praise forevermore.
Because of Jesus' unfailing love
I am forgiven, I am restored.*

You loosed the cords of sinfulness
And broke the chains of my disgrace:
You chose the cross.
Up from the grave victorious,
You rose again so glorious:
You chose the cross.
The sorrow that surrounded You was mine,
'Yet not My will but Yours be done!' You
cried.

1662 Matt Redman
Copyright © 1996 Thankyou Music

YOU CONFIDE IN THOSE WHO FEAR YOU,
Share the secrets of Your heart,
Friendship give to those who seek to
Honour You with every part.
Though I'm one of unclean lips, Lord,
I am crying 'Woe is me!'
Trying now to rid myself of
All the things that hinder me from...

*Knowing You, hearing You speak,
Seeing You move mysteriously.
Your whisperings in my soul's ear:
I want the friendship and the fear
Of knowing You.*

There is one thing You have spoken,
There are two things I have found:
You, O Lord, are ever loving,
You, O Lord, are always strong.
I am longing to discover
Both the closeness and the awe,
Feel the nearness of Your whisper,
Hear the glory of Your roar, just...

1663 Martyn Layzell
Copyright © 2002 Thankyou Music

YOU GAVE YOUR ONLY SON,
Came down from heaven above,
Endured the cross, so I might know
This love that reached for me,
A love that sets me free,
Your sacrifice has saved my soul.

Today I'm reminded of Your grace;
Always living now to sing Your praise,
Your praise.

> *Praise You, Jesus, I praise You,*
> *I lift my hands and sing.*
> *Embrace You, I will embrace You,*
> *My Saviour and my King, my King.*

I could not earn this love,
Such undeserved love;
Jesus, I know You are the way.
You paid the price for me,
Your blood was shed for me,
And in Your mercy took my place.

1664 Nathan & David Fellingham
Copyright © 1998 Thankyou Music

YOU HAVE GIVEN ME NEW LIFE;
Now my heart is satisfied.
I'm tasting the power of the age to come,
I'm living in the glory
Of the resurrected Son.
I'm walking in the light
And all that I now do is for You.

> *Pouring over me,*
> *Everlasting love and mercy,*
> *Over me in a flood of power.*
> *Pouring over me, abounding grace so*
> *free,*
> *Over me Your unending love.*

I've never had a friend like You;
All that You've promised You will do.
I'm drinking from the fountain
That will never run dry,
I'm living in the joy of a heart that's purified.
I'm walking now with You,
And all I have is Yours,
Take my life.

1665 Noel Richards
Copyright © 1999 Thankyou Music

YOU HAVE LAID YOUR HAND ON ME,
I am changed forever;
There is nothing that compares
With knowing You.
You have spoken words of love
That lift my Spirit higher;
Jesus Christ, my dearest friend,
I'm never letting go.

> *How can I live, how can I live,*
> *How can I live without Your love?*
> *How can I live, how can I live,*
> *How can I live without Your love?*

Help me never to forget
What I used to be,
Though the past that I regret
Is over now.
I will never be ashamed
Of calling You my friend.
I no longer hide from You,
I'm running to Your side.

All the riches I possess
Are meaningless to me;
Your love is the greatest gift,
The very air I breathe.

1666 Matt Redman
Copyright © 1999 Thankyou Music

YOU LED ME TO THE CROSS,
And I saw Your face of mercy
In that place of love.
You opened up my eyes
To believe Your sweet salvation,
Where I'd been so blind.
Now that I'm living in Your all-forgiving love,
My every road leads to the cross.

> *Jesus, keep me near the cross,*
> *I won't forget the love You've shown.*
> *Saviour, teach me of the cross,*
> *I won't forget the love,*
> *I won't forget the love You've shown.*

And there's an empty tomb,
That tells me of Your resurrection
And my life in You.
The stone lies rolled away,
Nothing but those folded grave clothes
Where Your body lay.
Now that I'm living as a risen child of God,
My every road leads to the cross.

1667 Gareth Robinson & Joannah Oyeniran
Copyright © 2001 Thankyou Music

YOU POUR OUT GRACE on the broken-
hearted,
And You lift the hope of the weary soul,
And You stretch out Your hand
With Your loving mercy.
You saw this heart that was lost and broken,
And You felt the pain of my loneliness,
And You befriended me
And restored my dignity.

> *You alone revealed the love of God to me,*
> *And You alone have given everything for*
> *me;*
> *And You alone deserve the highest praise,*
> *Jesus.*

You demonstrated the life of love to me,
And how it was that You wanted me to live:
Heart of compassion and hands of healing.
I need Your Spirit to help accomplish this:
Abundant grace and Your strength in
weakness,
And the steady hand of the Father holding
me.

And You have given me great salvation,
And You have given me hope eternal,
And every day I will look to give You
All the glory that's due Your name.

1668 Johnny Parks
Copyright © 2001 Thankyou Music

YOU'RE THE ONE WHO GAVE HIS SON,
Who will freely give us all things,
And nothing can be against us
If God is still for us.
And all things work for good
For those who love the Lord,
And nothing can be against us
When You are still for us.

And we're convinced
That neither death nor life,
Angels or demons,
Height nor depths, nor what's to come
Can cut us off from the love of God.

> *God is still for us, God is still for us,*
> *God is still for us, turn around.*
> *He is still for us, God is still for us,*
> *God is still for us, turn around.*

When hardship or danger comes,
We know that God gave His only Son.
So as a body we are assured
That God is still for us.
We look to You, Lord,
We stand on Your word;
We're holding on
To the promise You've made –
That nothing can be against us
When You are still for us.

1669 Stuart Townend & Keith Getty
Copyright © 2002 Thankyou Music

YOU'RE THE WORD OF GOD THE FATHER,
From before the world began;
Every star and every planet
Has been fashioned by Your hand.
All creation holds together
By the power of Your voice:
Let the skies declare Your glory,
Let the land and seas rejoice!

> *You're the Author of creation,*
> *You're the Lord of every man;*
> *And Your cry of love rings out*
> *Across the lands.*

Yet You left the gaze of angels,
Came to seek and save the lost,
And exchanged the joy of heaven
For the anguish of a cross.
With a prayer You fed the hungry,
With a word You stilled the sea;
Yet how silently You suffered
That the guilty may go free.

With a shout You rose victorious,
Wresting victory from the grave,
And ascended into heaven
Leading captives in Your wake.
Now You stand before the Father
Interceding for Your own.
From each tribe and tongue and nation
You are leading sinners home.

1670 E.H. Plumptre (1821–91) adapt. Keith Getty
Copyright © 2001 Thankyou Music

YOUR HAND, O GOD, HAS GUIDED
Your church from age to age,
The tale of love is written
For us on every page.
Our fathers knew Your goodness,
And we Your works record,
And each of these bear witness:
One church, one faith, one Lord.

One church, one faith, one Lord of life,
One Father, one Spirit, one Christ.
One church, one faith, one Lord of life,
One heavenly King, Lord of all.

Your mercy never fails us,
Or leaves Your work undone;
With Your right hand to help us,
The victory shall be won.
And then with heaven's angels
Your name shall be adored,
And they shall praise You, singing:
One church, one faith, one Lord.

1671 James Gregory
Copyright © 2002 Thankyou Music

YOUR KINDNESS overwhelmed me,
The love that captured me.
You helped me to believe
That You delight in me.
You led me to the Father,
And introduced us there,
The Spirit poured out grace,
And filled me with Your praise.

> *You are wonderful, beautiful,*
> *Merciful, and all my life*
> *And my heart belongs to You.*
> (Repeat)

Your plans for me are greater
Than I had ever thought,
You're daily changing me,
Revealing more to me.
My love for You is growing,
And as I reach for You,
Your Spirit pours out grace
And fills me with Your praise.

1672 Darlene Zschech & David Moyse
Copyright © 2000 Darlene Zschech & David Moyse/
Hillsong Publishing/Kingsway Music

YOUR KINGDOM GENERATION
Declares Your majesty,
And our lives are resounding with Your
   praise.
We see Your Spirit moving,
We burn with holy fire.
Your glory is seen through all the earth.
You set eternity in my heart,
So I'll live for You, for You.

Hallelujah, hallelujah,
Honour and praise forever.
We'll shout a victory cry from here
To eternity.
Hallelujah, hallelujah,
We'll take our place in history.
We'll shout Your awesome love from here
To eternity.

1673 Reuben Morgan
Copyright © 1998 Reuben Morgan/
Hillsong Publishing/Kingsway Music

YOUR LIGHT broke through my night,
Restored exceeding joy.
Your grace fell like the rain,
And made this desert live.

> *You have turned*
> *My mourning into dancing.*
> *You have turned*
> *My sorrow into joy.*

Your hand lifted me up,
I stand on higher ground.
Your praise rose in my heart,
And made this valley sing.

This is how we overcome. *(x6)*

> *You turned...*

1674 Stuart Townend
Copyright © 1999 Thankyou Music

YOUR LOVE, shining like the sun,
Pouring like the rain,
Raging like the storm,
Refreshing me again.
I receive Your love.

Your grace frees me from the past,
It purges every sin,
It purifies my heart
And heals me from within.
I receive Your grace.

> *Pour over me,*
> *Pour over me,*
> *Let Your rain flood this thirsty soul.*
> *Pour over me Your waves of love,*
> *Pour over me.*

I come and lay my burden down
Gladly at Your feet,
I'm opening up my heart;
Come make this joy complete.
I receive Your peace.

1675

Chris Tomlin, Jesse Reeves & Louie Giglio
Copyright © 1999 worshiptogether.com songs/
Adm. by Kingsway Music

YOUR LOVE HAS CAPTURED ME,
Your grace has set me free;
Your life, the air I breathe:
Be glorified in me.

You set my feet to dancing,
You set my heart on fire,
In the presence of a thousand kings
You are my one desire.
And I stand before You now
With trembling hands lifted high,
Be glorified.

1676

Brenton Brown & Brian Doerksen
Copyright © 2000 Vineyard Songs (UK/Eire)/
Adm. by CopyCare

YOUR LOVE IS AMAZING,
Steady and unchanging;
Your love is a mountain,
Firm beneath my feet.
Your love is a mystery,
How You gently lift me;
When I am surrounded,
Your love carries me.

> *Hallelujah, hallelujah,*
> *Hallelujah, Your love makes me sing.*
> *Hallelujah, hallelujah,*
> *Hallelujah, Your love makes me sing.*

Your love is surprising,
I can feel it rising,
All the joy that's growing
Deep inside of me.
Every time I see You,
All Your goodness shines through,
And I can feel this God song
Rising up in me.

1677

Robert Critchley
Copyright © 2000 Thankyou Music

YOUR LOVE IS BETTER THAN WINE,
Your name like sweetest perfume;
Oh, that You would kiss me
With the kisses of Your mouth
And draw me, draw me after You.
I hear You whisper my name,
And like a moth to the flame
I fly into the fire of Your intimate love
As You draw me, draw me after You.

> *Draw me after You,* (×3)
> *And let us run together.*
> (Repeat)

Jesus You're the One, (×3)
That I will love forever.
Jesus You're the One, (×3)
That I will love forevermore.

So amazing, so divine,
I am Yours and You are mine.
For such love there are no words,
'Cause loving You is heaven on earth.

1678

Greg Shepherd
Copyright © 2000 Thankyou Music

YOUR NAME IS LOVE,
The love that went to the cross.
Your name is peace,
You've taken my sins away,
And how I love all that You are,
Your name is Jesus.

Your name is truth,
The truth that sets me free.
Your name is hope,
Hope for eternity,
And how I love all that You are,
Your name is Jesus.

> *Jesus, Name above all names,*
> *I will ever more proclaim:*
> *'Worthy is the Lamb*
> *To receive all power,*
> *To receive all praise.'*

Your name is Lord,
I gladly bow the knee.
You are a friend,
A friend of sinners like me,
And how I love all that You are,
Your name is Jesus.

1679

Dave Bilbrough
Copyright © 2002 Thankyou Music

YOURS IS THE KINGDOM,
The power and the glory,
Forever and ever,
Forever and ever, Amen!
(Repeat)

A trumpet blast will herald
The day of Your return:
Your glory and Your splendour
Will be seen in all the earth!

And oh, what a day,
Oh, what a day that will be,
When the earth joins with heaven
In worship and praise to Jesus!

The time is drawing nearer,
I believe it's coming soon,
When we will rise to greet You
As a bride to meet her groom.

 1680 Vicky Beeching
Copyright © 2001 Vineyard Songs (UK/Eire)/
Adm. by CopyCare

YOUR VOICE is the voice that
Commanded the universe to be.
Your voice is the voice that
Is speaking words of love to me:
How can it be?

> *Awesome God, holy God,*
> *I worship You in wonder.*
> *Awesome God, holy God,*
> *As You draw near I'm humbled*
> *By Your majesty, and the mystery*
> *Of Your great love for me.*

Your arms are the arms that
Hung shining stars in deepest space.
Your arms are the arms that
Surround me in a warm embrace:
Amazing grace.

1681 Brian Houston
Copyright © 2000 Thankyou Music

YOUR WHISPER TO MY SOUL
When I was like a child,
Lifted off the yoke,
Planted fields of hope
In this heart of mine.
You took me as I am,
You knew what I had done,
Still You took my shame,
And You called my name,
I was overcome.

When You broke the bonds
Of how I used to be,
You rolled away the stone,
You set the captive free.

> *I wanna thank You,*
> *You're the God of mercy;*
> *I wanna thank You, Lord,*
> *For giving me peace.*
> *I wanna thank You,*
> *You're the God who loved me;*
> *I wanna thank You,*
> *You're the God who rescued me.*

You covered all my sin,
Restored to me my youth again.
And I am satisfied,
For You have healed me
And redeemed me,
Crowned my head with endless beauty,
Endless beauty.

 1682 Reuben Morgan
Copyright © 1998 Reuben Morgan/
Hillsong Publishing/Kingsway Music

YOU SAID:
'Ask and you will receive
Whatever you need.'
You said:
'Pray, and I'll hear from heaven,
And I'll heal your land.'

You said
Your glory will fill the earth,
Like water the sea.
You said:
'Lift up your eyes,
The harvest is here,
The kingdom is here.'

> *You said:*
> *'Ask, and I'll give the nations to you.'*
> *O Lord, that's the cry of my heart.*
> *Distant shores and the islands will see*
> *Your light as it rises on us.*

O Lord, I ask for the nations.

 1683 Paul Ewing
Copyright © 2000 Paul Ewing/
Hillsong Publishing/Kingsway Music

YOU SET ME APART,
Gave me a new heart,
Filled with compassion
To share Your great love.
Show me Your ways,
I want to know You.
Guide me in truth,
My hope is in You.

> *That I may dwell in Your house forever,*
> *Lifting up Your name;*
> *Dwell in Your house forevermore.*
> *(Repeat)*

I'll hold on to You,
My strength and my refuge.
Whom shall I fear?
I know You are near.
All of my days
I live for You, Lord.
Establish my path,
There's one thing I ask.

Holy Spirit, have Your way.
Sweet anointing, teach our hearts,
Our lives, we pray.

1684 Tim Hughes
Copyright © 2001 Thankyou Music

YOU SHAPED THE HEAVENS and the earth,
Revealed Your splendour.
You spoke Your life into our hearts,
So we belong to You.

You are the Maker of all things,
First and the Last;
Creation sings praise to You, God.
You're reigning in glory,
Ancient of Days;
Your people sing praise to You, God.

Creator God, in You all things
Now hold together,
Working Your wonders day by day,
You'll reign forever.

And earth joins with heaven
Declaring Your glory;
Proclaiming the works of Your hands.
(Repeat)

1685 Matt Redman & Chris Tomlin
Copyright © 2002 worshiptogether.com songs/
Six Steps Music/Thankyou Music/
Adm. by Kingsway Music

YOU SPREAD OUT THE SKIES
Over empty space,
Said 'Let there be light' –
To a dark and formless world
Your light was born.

You spread out Your arms
Over empty hearts,
Said 'Let there be light' –
To a dark and hopeless world
Your Son was born.

You made the world and saw that it was
good,
You sent Your only Son, for You are good.

What a wonderful Maker,
What a wonderful Saviour.
How majestic Your whispers,
And how humble Your love.
With a strength like no other,
And the heart of a Father,
How majestic Your whispers,
What a wonderful God.

No eye has fully seen
How beautiful the cross,
And we have only heard
The faintest whisper of
How great You are.

1686 Dave Bilbrough
Copyright © 2000 Thankyou Music

YOU TAKE ME BY THE HAND,
And though there are times I don't
understand,
Your love will never fail
And my heart belongs to You.
Even when the rain clouds break
And the cold wind blows all around me,
I will not be put to shame;
Lord, my hope is in Your name.
You will carry me on Your shoulders
And lead me home.

Carry me over troubled waters,
Carry me over stormy seas.
When the skies are dark and heavy,
By Your grace You'll carry me.
Though the way can seem uncertain
Because the time of change has come,
You will carry me on Your shoulders
And lead me home.

1687 Stuart Townend
Copyright © 1999 Thankyou Music

YOU'VE PLACED A HUNGER IN MY HEART
To see Your glory,
You've caused a thirst that I cannot ignore;
You've stirred a passion that will
Drive me to Your presence,
And I won't rest until
You've heard me cry for more.

Come as a mighty torrent,
Come as a raging fire,
Come as a hurricane that drives
The heat of my desire.
Come in the smallest whisper,
Come as the quiet dew:
We don't care how You come,
As long as You come to us.

Though people mock the church
And curse the One who made them,
Your kingdom is advancing every day;
Like living stones we're being
Built into a temple,
We've seen the glory
And we cannot turn away.

Is this the summer that will
See a mighty harvest?
A sense of expectation fills the air;
Though sin abounds,
Your love is streaming to the nations,
Let mercy triumph
Over judgement everywhere.

Come to the politician,
Come to the refugee,
Come to the victim of respectable society;
Come to the mighty fallen,
Come to the poor oppressed:
We don't care how You come,
As long as You come to them.

 1688   Lara Martin (Abundant Life Ministries,
Bradford, England)
Copyright © 2002 Thankyou Music

YOU'VE PLACED A SONG WITHIN MY
HEART,
And this song will bless You,
Your praise is always on my lips.
Whatever life may bring,
I know that You are God;
So I can trust in You and sing.

Immanuel, God with us,
Immanuel, You are near.
Immanuel, my God is for me,
My God is for me.
So...

I will bless the Lord at all times,
I will bless the Lord at all times.
In every situation I will give You praise,
I will rejoice in You always.
(Repeat)

1689   Matt Redman
Copyright © 2000 Thankyou Music

YOU'VE PUT A NEW SONG IN MY
MOUTH;
It is a hymn of praise to You.
Justice and mercy are its theme,
And I will live it back to You.

The kind of fast You've chosen, Lord,
It must reach out
To broken lives and to the poor:
So change me, Lord.

I know You are the orphan's hope,
I know You are the widow's song;
You're Father where no father lives,
And to the lonely You're a friend.
O Lord, You're showing me what's on Your
heart.

Lord, I won't bring an empty song;
It's meaningless
Without compassion in my life,
And holiness.

1690   Neil Bennetts
Copyright © 2002 Thankyou Music

YOU'VE TOUCHED MY HEART
With words of Your mercy
And thoughts of Your beauty.
Your presence, God,
Has captured me now
With the hope of Your glory.
You've opened my eyes to see
You're all that this heart can need.

For what is worthy of the King of kings,
But a heart that is satisfied in loving You?
Yours is the song,
Yours is the praise I'll bring,
With a passion for the wonder
Of seeing Your glory here.

This song I'll bring
Is my song of love from
A heart that's been broken.
It's what You've done,
For I've been set free by
The life that You've given.
Faithful and holy One,
Forever I live to sing.

Addresses for Copyright and Information

Company names are under first name or word. Individuals' names are listed under surname.

Ambushed Ltd, 5–9 Surrey Street, Croydon, CR0 1RG, UK.
email: info@follysend.org
website: www.follysend.org

Ateliers et Presses de Taizé, F-71250 Taizé-Communauté, France.
email: community@taize.fr

Barrie, Karen, 511 Maple Ave., Wilmette, Illinois 60091, USA.

Barthow, Mary R., 15 Aunceston Rise, Alfriston, South Auckland, New Zealand.

Behrns, Gary, 2406 Colonial Hills Road, Jefferson City, MO 65109, USA.

Bucks Music Ltd, Onward House, 11 Uxbridge Street, London, W8 7TQ, UK. *(Rights administered in the UK & Republic of Ireland.)*

Central Board of Finance of the Church of England (The), Church House, Great Smith Street, London, SW1P 3NZ, UK.
email: copyright@c-of-e.org.uk

Chance, Kay, Dr. H.-Jasper-Str. 20, D-37581 Bad Gandersheim, Germany.

CopyCare, P.O. Box 77, Hailsham, East Sussex, BN27 3EF, UK.
email: music@copycare.com

Curious? Music UK, P.O. Box 40, Arundel, BN18 0UQ, UK.
email: info@furiousrecords.co.uk

Daniel L. Schutte & New Dawn Music, 5536 North East Hassalo, Portland, OR 97213, USA.

David Higham Associates Ltd, 5–8 Lower John Street, Golden Square, London, W1R 3PE, UK.

Daybreak Music Ltd, P.O. Box 2848, Eastbourne, BN20 7XP, UK.
email: info@daybreakmusic.co.uk

Dudley-Smith, Timothy, 9 Ashlands, Ford, Salisbury, SP4 6DY, UK. *(For Europe, incl. UK & Ireland, and in all territories not controlled by Hope Publishing Company.)*

GIA Publications Inc., 7404 South Mason Avenue, Chicago, IL 60638, USA.
website: www.giamusic.com

Gabriel Music Inc., P.O. Box 840999, Houston, Texas 77284-0999, USA.

Gordon V. Thompson, a division of Warner Chappell Music Canada Ltd, 40 Sheppard Avenue West, Suite 800, Toronto, Ontario, M2N 6K9, Canada.

Grace! Music, 11610 Grandview Road, Kansas City, MO 64137, USA.

Heart of David Music, 14815 Pineview Drive, Grandview, MO 64030, USA.

High-Fye Music Ltd, 8–9 Frith Street, London, W1D 3JB, UK. *(Used by permission of Music Sales Ltd.)*

IQ Music Ltd, Commercial House, 52 Perrymount Road, Haywards Heath, West Sussex, RH16 3DT, UK. *(For the world.)*
email: iq.music@virgin.net

ICG, P.O. Box 24149, Nashville, TN 37202, USA.

Josef Weinberger Ltd, 12–14 Mortimer Street, London, W1N 7RD, UK.

Jubilate Hymns Ltd, Southwick House, 4 Thorne Park Road, Chelston, Torquay, TQ2 6RX, UK.
email: jubilatemw@aol.com

King, Mary Lou, 7013 E. Keynote, Longbeach, CA 90808, USA.

Kingdom Faith Ministries, Foundry Lane, Horsham, West Sussex, RH13 5PX, UK.

Kingsway Music, P.O. Box 75, Eastbourne, East Sussex, BN23 6NW, UK.
email: tym@kingsway.co.uk

Lea, Melva, Larry Lea Ministries, P.O. Box 1102, Sherman, TX75091-1102, USA.

Len Magee Music, P.O. Box 6327, South Tweed Heads, NSW 2486, Australia.

MCA Music Publishing, 2440 Sepulveda Blvd Suite 100, Los Angeles, CA 90064-1712, USA. *(Used by permission of Music Sales Ltd.)*

Make Way Music, P.O. Box 263, Croydon, Surrey, CR9 5AP, UK.
email: info@makewaymusic.com

McIntosh, Mike & Claire, P.O. Box 24000, Federal Way, WA 98093, USA.

OCP Publications, 5536 N.E. Hassalo, Portland, OR 97213, USA.

OMF International, Station Approach, Borough Green, Sevenoaks, TN15 8BG, UK.

Oxford University Press, Great Clarendon Street, Oxford, OX2 6DP, UK.

PolyGram Music Publishing Ltd, 47 British Grove, London W4, UK. *(Used by permission of Music Sales Ltd.)*

Signalgrade Ltd, 48 Chatsworth Avenue, London, SW20 8JZ, UK.

Simmonds, Clive, 22 St Michaels Road, Bedford, MK40 2LT, UK.

Smail, Mary, 151 Elm Park, London, SW2 2EE, UK.

Sound III, Elisnore House, 77 Fulham Palace Road, London, W6 8JA, UK. *(Used by permission of Music Sales Ltd.)*

Sovereign Lifestyle Music, P.O. Box 356, Leighton Buzzard, LU7 3WP, UK.
email: sovereignm@aol.com

Sovereign Music UK, P.O. Box 356, Leighton Buzzard, LU7 3WP, UK.
email: sovereignm@aol.com

Stassen, Linda, 175 Heggie Lane, Erin, TN 37061, USA.

TKO Publishing, P.O. Box 130, Hove, East Sussex, BN3 6QU, UK.

Thankyou Music *(Adm. by worshiptogether.com songs excl. UK & Europe, adm. by Kingsway Music.)* See Kingsway Music.

WGRG (Wild Goose Resource Group), Iona Community, Fourth Floor, Savoy House, 140 Sauchiehall Street, Glasgow, G2 3DH.

World Wide Worship, Buxhall, Stowmarket, Suffolk, IP14 3BW, UK. *(For the UK & European territory only.)*

Index of titles and first lines

(Titles where different from first lines are shown in *italics*)